PMP: Project Management Professional Exam Study Guide, 4th Edition

PMP: Project Management Professional Exam

OBJECTIVE	CHAPTER
INITIATING THE PROJECT	
Conduct Project Selection Methods	2
Define Scope	2
Document Project Risks, Assumptions, and Constraints	2
Identify and Perform Stakeholder Analysis	2
Develop Project Charter	2
Obtain Project Charter Approval	2
PLANNING THE PROJECT	
Define and Record Requirements, Constraints, and Assumptions	3
Identify Project Team and Define Roles and Responsibilities	6
Create the WBS	4
Develop Change Management Plan	3
Identify Risks and Define Risk Strategies	5
Obtain Plan Approval	7
Conduct Kick-off Meeting	2
EXECUTING THE PROJECT	
Execute Tasks Defined in Project Plan	8
Ensure Common Understanding and Set Expectations	8, 9
Implement the Procurement of Project Resources	8
Manage Resource Allocation	8
Implement Quality Management Plan	9
Implement Approved Changes	9
Implement Approved Actions and Workarounds	9
Improve Team Performance	8

Sybex®
An Imprint of

WILEY

OBJECTIVE	CHAPTER
MONITORING AND CONTROLLING THE PROJECT	
Measure Project Performance	10
Verify and Manage Changes to the Project	10
Ensure Project Deliverables Conform to Quality Standards	11
Monitor All Risks	10
CLOSING THE PROJECT	
Obtain Final Acceptance for the Project	11
Obtain Financial, Legal, and Administrative Closure	11
Release Project Resources	11
Identify, Document, and Communicate Lessons Learned	11
Create and Distribute Final Project Report	11
Archive and Retain Project Records	11
Measure Customer Satisfaction	11
PROFESSIONAL AND SOCIAL RESPONSIBILITY	
Ensure Individual Integrity	12
Contribute to the Project Management Knowledge Base	12
Enhance Personal Professional Competence	12
Promote Interaction Among Stakeholders	12

Sybex®
An Imprint of
WILEY

PMP®
Project Management Professional Exam
Study Guide
Fourth Edition

PMP®
Project Management Professional Exam
Study Guide
Fourth Edition

Kim Heldman

BICENTENNIAL
1807
WILEY
2007
BICENTENNIAL

Wiley Publishing, Inc.

Acquisitions Editor: Jeff Kellum
Development Editor: Mary Ellen Schutz
Technical Editor: Jodi Grossman
Production Editors: Sarah Groff-Palermo, Rachel Gunn
Copy Editor: Kim Wimpsett
Production Manager: Tim Tate
Vice President and Executive Group Publisher: Richard Swadley
Vice President and Executive Publisher: Joseph B. Wikert
Vice President and Publisher: Neil Edde
Media Project Supervisor: Laura Atkinson
Media Development Specialist: Angie Denny
Media Quality Assurance: Kit Malone
Book Designers: Bill Gibson, Judy Fung
Compositor: Laurie Stewart, Happenstance Type-O-Rama
Proofreader: Jen Larsen
Indexer: Ted Laux
Anniversary Logo Design: Richard Pacifico
Cover Designer: Ryan Sneed

Sybex®
An Imprint of
WILEY

To Our Valued Readers:

Thank you for looking to Sybex for your PMP exam prep needs. Since publishing the first edition of our *PMP: Project Management Professional Exam Study Guide* in April 2002, Sybex has earned the respect of tens of thousands of PMP candidates for providing accurate and accessible instruction on the skills and knowledge demanded by companies worldwide. Now with the update to the *PMBOK* (Project Management Body of Knowledge) in early 2005 and the recent revision to the PMP exam, the Project Management Institute has raised the standard by which project managers will be assessed in an increasingly competitive marketplace.

The authors and editors have worked hard to ensure that the new edition you hold in your hands is comprehensive, in-depth, and pedagogically sound. We're confident that this book will exceed the demanding standards of the certification marketplace and help you, the PMP certification candidate, succeed in your endeavors.

As always, your feedback is important to us. If you believe you've identified an error in the book, please visit sybex.custhelp.com. And if you have general comments or suggestions, feel free to drop me a line directly at nedde@wiley.com. At Sybex we're continually striving to meet the needs of individuals preparing for certification exams.

Good luck in pursuit of your PMP certification!

Neil Edde
Vice President & Publisher
Sybex, an Imprint of Wiley

To BB, my forever love
—Kimmie

Acknowledgments

Thank you to the thousands of readers who have read previous editions of *PMP: Project Management Professional Study Guide* and recommended it to their friends and co-workers. Because of your success using the book in passing the PMP exam, we are able to continue to upgrade and refresh the study guide with tips and hints from readers and with the changes made by PMI. Thank you also to all of the PMI chapters and instructors who use this book in their classes.

As always, a very special thank you to Neil Edde, vice president and publisher, for taking a chance on the first edition of this book and for giving me the opportunity to write it. Thank you again for the opportunity to revise and update it.

This book clearly fits the definition of a project, and the team at Sybex is the best project team on Earth to work with. I appreciate all the hard work and dedication everyone on the team put into producing this book. First, a special thanks to Jeff Kellum, acquisitions editor, for recommending this updated edition and for overseeing the project. It's always a pleasure to work with Jeff.

Next I'd like to thank Mary Ellen Schutz, development editor, for her encouragement and many kind words about this book. She made some great recommendations for clarification and additions to the text that will improve the reader's understanding of the concepts. She was a delight to work with, and I hope to work with her again on a future project.

Thank you also to Jodi Grossman who was the technical editor for this edition. She was instrumental in catching some statements that needed clarification and tactfully pointed out my blunders. She went over the text with a fine-toothed comb, and I appreciate her keen eye.

Kim Wimpsett was the copyeditor and made certain that what you're reading is grammatically correct. And Sarah Groff-Palermo and Rachel Gunn kept the files coming and made certain we all stayed on track according to schedule. Thanks, Kim, Sarah, and Rachel. Thanks also to the behind-the-scenes team members including proofreader Jen Larsen and compositor Laurie Stewart.

None of this would have been possible without the continued support and encouragement from my best friend in the whole world, BB. I love you, and there's no one else I'd rather spend the rest of my life with. Thank you to Bob and Jean, Owen and Sue, and Dick and Nancy for your prayers and support—they're always coveted. Thanks to my sister, Jill, and her hubby, John, and to Sam, Promise, and Destiny for their cheerleading behind the scenes. Thank you, Mom and Dad, for giving me the love of reading; some of my best memories are of story time. Thanks also to Jason and Leah, Noelle, and Amanda and Steve for your understanding of my time constraints and for your support. And I can't forget the two best grandchildren anywhere in the universe, Kate and Juliette.

About the Author

Kim Heldman, PMP, is the chief information officer for the Colorado Department of Transportation and is responsible for managing projects with IT components ranging from small in scope and budget to multi-million dollar, multi-year, multi-vendor projects. She has over 17 years experience in Information Technology project management. Kim has served in a senior leadership role for the past 9 years and is regarded as a strategic visionary with an innate ability to collaborate with diverse groups and organizations, instill hope and improve morale, and lead her teams in achieving goals they never thought possible.

Kim has extensive experience in the government sector managing projects of various size and scope. Prior to her work at the Department of Transportation, Kim was the CIO for the Colorado Department of Natural Resources where they successfully underwent a long and extensive project to consolidate five disparate networks into one. In addition to her project management work, Kim also has experience managing application development teams, web development teams, network operations teams, and customer service teams. Kim worked for the Department of Revenue as the director of the Project Management Office. She built the PMO from the ground up, establishing policies, procedures, and best-practice approaches for managing the Department of Revenue's multitude of projects. She was also responsible for the ongoing support of Colorado's income tax, sales tax, and delinquency tax system, and a host of smaller taxation systems.

Kim wrote the first edition of the *PMP Project Management Professional Study Guide* published by Sybex in 2002. Since then, thousands of people worldwide have used the Study Guide in preparation for the PMP® Exam. Kim is also the author of *Project Management JumpStart 2nd Edition, Project Manager's Spotlight on Risk Management*, and co-author of *Excel 2007 for Project Manager*.

Most of the Real World Scenarios in the *PMP Study Guide* and the example stories in the other books are based on Kim's real life experiences. The names and circumstances were changed.

Kim continues to write new material based on project management best-practices and speaks frequently at conferences and events. You can contact Kim at `Kim.Heldman@comcast.net`.

Contents at a Glance

Introduction   *xxiii*

Assessment Test   *xxxii*

Chapter   1   **What Is a Project?**   **1**

Chapter   2   **Creating the Project Charter and Preliminary
                   Scope Statement**   **51**

Chapter   3   **Developing the Project Scope Statement**   **91**

Chapter   4   **Creating the WBS and Communicating the Plan**   **133**

Chapter   5   **Risk Planning**   **177**

Chapter   6   **Resource Planning**   **229**

Chapter   7   **Creating the Project Schedule and Budget**   **271**

Chapter   8   **Developing the Project Team**   **325**

Chapter   9   **Measuring and Controlling Project Performance**   **371**

Chapter 10   **Monitoring and Controlling Change**   **417**

Chapter 11   **Controlling Work Results and Closing Out
                   the Project**   **457**

Chapter 12   **Applying Professional Responsibility**   **497**

Appendix   **Process Inputs and Outputs**   **525**

Glossary   **551**

Index   *581*

Contents

Introduction   *xxiii*

Assessment Test   *xxxii*

Chapter   1   What Is a Project?   1

Is It a Project?   2
  Projects versus Operations   3
  Stakeholders   3
  Project Characteristics   5
What Is Project Management?   6
  Programs   7
  Portfolios   7
  Project Management Offices   8
Defining Skills Every Good Project Manager Needs   9
  Communication Skills   10
  Organizational and Planning Skills   10
  Budgeting Skills   11
  Conflict Management Skills   11
  Negotiation and Influencing Skills   11
  Leadership Skills   12
  Team-Building and Motivating Skills   12
Understanding Organizational Structures   13
  Functional Organizations   14
  Projectized Organizations   17
  Matrix Organizations   19
Understanding Project Life Cycles and Project
  Management Processes   22
  Project Phases and Project Life Cycles   23
  Project Management Process Groups   24
Exploring the Project Management Knowledge Areas   31
  Project Integration Management   32
  Project Scope Management   33
  Project Time Management   34
  Project Cost Management   35
  Project Quality Management   36
  Project Human Resource Management   36
  Project Communications Management   37
  Project Risk Management   38
  Project Procurement Management   39
Understanding How This Applies to Your Next Project   40
Summary   41

	Exam Essentials	41
	Key Terms	42
	Review Questions	44
	Answers to Review Questions	49

Chapter 2   Creating the Project Charter and Preliminary Scope Statement   51

Understanding How Projects Come About   52
    Needs and Demands   53
    Feasibility Studies   54
Kicking Off the Project Charter   56
    Project Statement of Work   57
    Enterprise Environmental Factors   58
    Organizational Process Assets   59
Using Tools and Techniques for Charter Development   60
    Selecting and Prioritizing Projects   60
    Using Project Selection Methods   61
    Project Management Methodology and
        Information Systems   69
    Expert Judgment   69
Formalizing and Publishing the Project Charter   70
    Key Stakeholders   70
    Pulling the Project Charter Together   72
    Project Charter Sign-Off   73
Developing a Preliminary Project Scope Statement   74
    Preliminary Scope Statement Inputs and Techniques   74
    The Preliminary Scope Statement Document   75
Introducing the Kitchen Heaven Project Case Study   76
Understanding How This Applies to Your Next Project   80
Summary   81
Exam Essentials   82
Key Terms   83
Review Questions   84
Answers to Review Questions   89

Chapter 3   Developing the Project Scope Statement   91

Developing the Project Management Plan   92
    Developing Inputs   93
    Documenting the Project Management Plan   94
Scoping Out the Project   98
    Understanding the Scope Planning Inputs   98
    Using Scope Planning Tools and Techniques   99
    Documenting the Scope Management Plan   100

Formulating Scope Definition   100
  Product Analysis   101
  Alternatives Identification   102
  Stakeholder Analysis   102
Writing the Project Scope Statement   105
  Understanding the Scope Statement Components   106
  Approving and Publishing the Project Scope Statement   116
  Updating the Project Scope Management Plan   116
Understanding How This Applies to Your Next Project   120
Summary   121
Exam Essentials   122
Key Terms   123
Review Questions   124
Answers to Review Questions   130

Chapter   4   Creating the WBS and Communicating the Plan   133

Creating the Work Breakdown Structure   134
  Gathering the WBS Inputs   135
  Decomposing the Deliverables   135
  Constructing the WBS   137
  Creating WBS Process Outputs   144
Communicating the Plan   146
  Communications Planning Inputs   147
  Tools and Techniques for Communications Planning   147
  Communications Management Plan   150
Identifying Quality Standards   152
  Quality Inputs   152
  Tools and Techniques for Quality Planning   153
  Quality Planning Outputs   159
Understanding How This Applies to Your Next Project   164
Summary   165
Exam Essentials   166
Key Terms   167
Review Questions   169
Answers to Review Questions   174

Chapter   5   Risk Planning   177

Planning for Risks   178
Planning Your Risk Management   179
  Risk Management Planning Inputs   179
  Tools and Techniques for Risk Management Planning   180
  Creating the Risk Management Plan   182
Identifying Potential Risk   186
  Risk Identification Inputs   187

Tools and Techniques for Risk Identification   188
Risk Identification Outputs   193
Analyzing Risks Using Qualitative Techniques   194
Qualitative Risk Analysis Inputs   195
Tools and Techniques for Qualitative Risk Analysis   195
Ranking Risks in the Risk Register   202
Quantifying Risk   202
Tools and Techniques for Quantitative Risk Analysis   203
Quantitative Risk Analysis Outputs   207
Developing a Risk Response Plan   208
Tools and Techniques for Risk Response Planning   209
Risk Response Planning Outputs   212
Understanding How This Applies to Your Next Project   217
Summary   218
Exam Essentials   218
Key Terms   219
Review Questions   221
Answers to Review Questions   226

Chapter   6   Resource Planning   229

Understanding Purchases and Acquisitions   230
Plan Purchases and Acquisitions Inputs   231
Tools and Techniques for Plan Purchases and Acquisitions 233
Plan Purchases and Acquisitions Outputs   236
Plan Contracting   238
Plan Contracting Outputs   239
Human Resource Planning   241
Human Resource Planning Inputs   242
Human Resource Planning Tools and Techniques   244
Human Resource Planning Outputs   246
Defining Activities   248
Activity Definition Process Inputs   249
Tools and Techniques for Defining Activities   249
Activity Definition Outputs   250
Understanding the Activity Sequencing Process   251
Activity Sequencing Tools and Techniques   251
Activity Sequencing Outputs   255
Understanding How This Applies to Your Next Project   258
Summary   259
Exam Essentials   260
Key Terms   261
Review Questions   263
Answers to Review Questions   268

Chapter   7   Creating the Project Schedule and Budget   271

Estimating Activity Resources   272
    Activity Resource Estimating Inputs   273
    Estimating Activities Tools and Techniques   273
    Activity Resource Estimating Outputs   274
Estimating Activity Durations   275
    Activity Duration Estimating Inputs   276
    Activity Duration Estimating Tools and Techniques   276
    Activity Duration Estimating Outputs   279
Developing the Project Schedule   279
    Schedule Development Inputs   280
    Schedule Development Tools and Techniques   281
    Schedule Development Process Outputs   294
Estimating Costs   298
    Cost Estimating Inputs   299
    Cost Estimating Tools and Techniques   299
    Cost Estimating Process Outputs   300
Establishing the Cost Budget Baseline   302
    Cost Budgeting Inputs   302
    Cost Budgeting Tools and Techniques   303
    Cost Budgeting Process Outputs   303
Bringing It All Together   306
Understanding How This Applies to Your Next Project   312
Summary   313
Exam Essentials   314
Key Terms   315
Review Questions   317
Answers to Review Questions   323

Chapter   8   Developing the Project Team   325

Executing the Project Plan   326
    Executing Inputs   328
    Tools and Techniques of Direct and Manage
        Project Execution   329
    Outputs of Direct and Manage Project Execution   330
Acquiring the Project Team   333
    Tools and Techniques of Acquire Project Team   334
    Outputs of Acquire Project Team   335
Developing the Project Team   336
    Tools and Techniques of Develop Project Team   337
    Outputs of Develop Project Team   349
Distributing Project Information   349
    Tools and Techniques of Information Distribution   350
    Outputs of Information Distribution   356

Understanding How This Applies to Your Next Project   359
Summary   360
Exam Essentials   361
Key Terms   362
Review Questions   363
Answers to Review Questions   368

Chapter   9   Measuring and Controlling Project Performance   371

Requesting Seller Responses   372
    Requesting Seller Responses Tools and Techniques   373
    Request Seller Responses Outputs   374
Selecting Sellers   374
Evaluation Criteria   375
Tools and Techniques of Select Sellers   376
    Weighting Systems   376
    Independent Estimates   377
    Screening Systems   377
    Contract Negotiation   377
    Seller Rating Systems   377
    Expert Judgment   378
    Proposal Evaluation Techniques   378
Select Sellers Outputs   380
    Elements of a Contract   380
    Contract Life Cycles   380
    Contract Management Plan   382
Laying Out Quality Assurance Procedures   382
    Inputs to Perform Quality Assurance   382
    Perform Quality Assurance Tools and Techniques   383
    Perform Quality Assurance Outputs   384
Monitoring and Controlling Project Work   385
    Monitor and Control Project Work Inputs   386
    Tools and Techniques of Monitor
      and Control Project Work   386
    Monitor and Control Project Work Outputs   386
Administering the Contract   387
    Contracting Inputs   388
    Administering Contracts Tools and Techniques   389
    Managing Contract Outputs   392
Managing Project Teams   394
    Tools and Techniques for Managing Teams   395
    Managing Project Team Outputs   397
Managing Stakeholders   397
Establishing Performance Measurements   398
    Performance Reporting Inputs   398

	Performance Reporting Tools and Techniques	399
	Performance Reporting Outputs	401
	Understanding How This Applies to Your Next Project	403
	Summary	404
	Exam Essentials	405
	Key Terms	406
	Review Questions	408
	Answers to Review Questions	414

Chapter 10   Monitoring and Controlling Change   417

	Managing Integrated Change Control	418
	How Change Occurs	419
	Change Control Concerns	420
	Configuration Management	421
	Change Control System	421
	Integrated Change Control Inputs	424
	Integrated Change Control Tools and Techniques	425
	Integrated Change Control Outputs	425
	Managing Cost Changes	426
	Cost Control Inputs	426
	Cost Control Tools and Techniques	426
	Cost Control Outputs	435
	Monitoring and Controlling Schedule Changes	437
	Schedule Control Inputs	437
	Schedule and Control Tools and Techniques	437
	Schedule Control Outputs	439
	Monitoring and Controlling Risk	440
	Risk Monitoring and Control Inputs	441
	Risk Monitoring and Control Tools and Techniques	441
	Risk Monitoring and Control Outputs	442
	Understanding How This Applies to Your Next Project	446
	Summary	447
	Exam Essentials	448
	Key Terms	449
	Review Questions	450
	Answers to Review Questions	454

Chapter 11   Controlling Work Results and Closing Out the Project   457

	Utilizing Perform Quality Control Techniques	458
	Perform Quality Control Inputs	459
	Perform Quality Control Tools and Techniques	459
	Perform Quality Control Outputs	466

Verifying Project Scope   468
Controlling Scope Changes   469
    Scope Control Inputs   469
    Scope Control Tools and Techniques   470
    Scope Control Outputs   470
Formulating Project Closeout   471
    Characteristics of Closing   472
    Project Endings   472
Closing Out the Project   475
    Close Project Inputs   476
    Close Project Tools and Techniques   476
    Close Project Outputs   477
Closing Out the Contract   480
    Contract Closure Inputs   481
    Contract Closure Tools and Techniques   481
    Contract Closure Outputs   482
Releasing Project Team Members   483
Celebrate!   485
Understanding How This Applies to Your Next Project   486
Summary   487
Exam Essentials   488
Key Terms   489
Review Questions   490
Answers to Review Questions   495

Chapter 12   Applying Professional Responsibility   497

Ensuring Integrity   498
    Personal Integrity   499
    Conflict of Interest   499
    Professional Demeanor   501
Applying Professional Knowledge   503
    Project Management Knowledge   503
    Truthful Reporting   505
    Laws and Regulations Compliance   506
    Confidential Information   506
Balancing Stakeholders' Interests   508
    Competing Needs   508
    Dealing with Issues and Problems   508
    Balancing Constraints   509
Respecting Differences in Diverse Cultures   510
    Global Competition   511
    Culture Shock   511
    Respecting Your Neighbors   512

Training 512
Perceiving Experiences 512
Understanding How This Applies to Your Next Project 514
Summary 515
Exam Essentials 516
Key Terms 516
Review Questions 517
Answers to Review Questions 523

Appendix **Process Inputs and Outputs** **525**

Initiating Processes 526
Planning Processes 527
Executing Processes 538
Monitoring and Controlling Processes 541
Closing Processes 549

Glossary **551**

Index *581*

PMP®
Project Management Professional Exam
Study Guide
Fourth Edition

Introduction

This book was designed for anyone thinking of taking the Project Management Professional (PMP) exam sponsored by the Project Management Institute (PMI). This certification is growing in popularity and demand in all areas of business. PMI has experienced explosive growth in membership over the last few years, and more and more organizations are recognizing the importance of project management certification.

 Although this book is written primarily for those of you taking the PMP exam, you can also use this book to study for the Certified Associate in Project Management (CAPM) exam. The exams are similar in style, and the information covered in this book will help you with either exam.

This book has been updated to reflect the latest edition of *A Guide to the Project Management Body of Knowledge (PMBOK Guide), Third Edition*. It assumes you have knowledge of general project management practices, although not necessarily specific to the *PMBOK Guide*. It's written so that you can skim through areas you are already familiar with, picking up the specific *PMBOK Guide* terminology where needed to pass the exam. You'll find that the project management processes and techniques discussed in this book are defined in such a way that you'll recognize tasks you've always done and be able to identify them with the *PMBOK Guide* process names or methodologies.

PMI offers the most recognized certification in the field of project management, and this book deals exclusively with its procedures and methods. Project management consists of many methods, each with its own terminology, tools, and procedures. If you're familiar with another organized project management methodology, don't assume you already know the *PMBOK Guide* processes. I strongly recommend that you learn all of the processes—their key inputs, tools and techniques, and outputs. Take the time to memorize the key terms found at the end of every chapter as well. Sometimes just understanding the definition of a term will help you answer a question. It might be that you've always done that particular task or used the methodology described but called it by another name. Know the name of each process and its primary purpose.

What Is the PMP Certification?

The PMI is the leader and the most widely recognized organization in terms of promoting project management best practices. The PMI strives to maintain and endorse standards and ethics in this field and offers publications, training, seminars, chapters, special interest groups, and colleges to further the project management discipline.

The PMI was founded in 1969 and first started offering the PMP certification exam in 1984. PMI is accredited as an American National Standards Institute (ANSI) standards developer and also has the distinction of being the first organization to have its certification program attain International Organization for Standardization (ISO) 9001 recognition.

The PMI boasts a worldwide membership of more than 150,000, with members from 150 different countries. Local PMI chapters meet regularly and allow project managers to exchange information and learn about new tools and techniques of project management or new ways to use established techniques. I encourage you to join a local chapter and get to know other professionals in your field.

Why Become PMP Certified?

The following benefits are associated with becoming PMP certified:

- It demonstrates proof of professional achievement.
- It increases your marketability.
- It provides greater opportunity for advancement in your field.
- It raises customer confidence in you and in your company's services.

Demonstrates Proof of Professional Achievement

PMP certification is a rigorous process that documents your achievements in the field of project management. The exam tests your knowledge of the disciplined approaches, methodologies, and project management practices as described in the *PMBOK Guide*.

You are required to have several years of experience in project management before sitting for the exam, as well as 35 hours of formal project management education. Your certification assures employers and customers that you are well grounded in project management practices and disciplines. It shows that you have the hands-on experience and a mastery of the processes and disciplines to manage projects effectively and motivate teams to produce successful results.

Increases Your Marketability

Many industries are realizing the importance of project management and its role in the organization. They are also seeing that simply proclaiming a head technician to be a "project manager" does not make it so. Project management, just like engineering, information technology, and a host of other trades, has its own specific qualifications and skills. Certification tells potential employers that you have the skills, experience, and knowledge to drive successful projects and ultimately improve the company's bottom line.

A certification will always make you stand out above the competition. If you're certified and you're competing against a project manager without certification, chances are you'll come out as the top pick. As a hiring manager, all other things being equal, I will usually opt for the candidate who has certification over the candidate who doesn't have it. Certification tells potential employers you have gone the extra mile. You've spent time studying techniques and methods as well as employing them in practice. It shows dedication to your own professional growth and enhancement and to adhering to and advancing professional standards.

Provides Opportunity for Advancement

PMP certification displays your willingness to pursue growth in your professional career and shows that you're not afraid of a little hard work to get what you want. Potential employers will interpret your pursuit of this certification as a high-energy, success-driven, can-do attitude on your part. They'll see that you're likely to display these same characteristics on the job, which will help make the company successful. Your certification displays a success-oriented, motivated attitude that will open up opportunities for future career advancements in your current field as well as in new areas you might want to explore.

Raises Customer Confidence

Just as the PMP certification assures employers that you've got the background and experience to handle project management, it assures customers that they have a competent, experienced project manager at the helm. Certification will help your organization sell customers on your ability to manage their projects. Customers, like potential employers, want the reassurance that those working for them have the knowledge and skills necessary to carry out the duties of the position and that professionalism and personal integrity are of utmost importance. Individuals who hold these ideals will translate their ethics and professionalism to their work. This enhances the trust customers will have in you, which in turn will give you the ability to influence them on important project issues.

How to Become PMP Certified

You need to fulfill several requirements in order to sit for the PMP exam. The PMI has detailed the certification process quite extensively at its website. Go to www.pmi.org, and click the Professional Development and Careers tab to reveal the Certifications selection and get the latest information on certification procedures and requirements.

As of this writing, you are required to fill out an application to sit for the PMP exam. You can submit this application online at the PMI's website. You also need to document 35 hours of formal project management education. This might include college classes, seminars, workshops, and training sessions. Be prepared to list the class titles, location, date, and content.

In addition to filling out the application and documenting your formal project management training, there is one additional set of criteria you'll need to meet to sit for the exam. These criteria fall into two categories. You need to meet the requirements for only one of these categories:

- Category 1 is for those who have a baccalaureate degree. You'll need to provide proof, via transcripts, of your degree with your application. In addition, you'll need to complete verification forms—found at the PMI website—that show 4,500 hours of project management experience that spans a minimum of three years and no more than six years.

- Category 2 is for those who do not have a baccalaureate degree but do hold a high school diploma or equivalent. You'll need to complete verification forms documenting 7,500 hours of project management experience that spans a minimum of five years and no more than eight years.

The exam fee at the time this book is being published is $405 for PMI members in good standing and $555 for non-PMI members. Testing is conducted at Thomson Prometric centers. You can find a center near you on the PMI website. You have six months from the time PMI receives and approves your completed application to take the exam. You'll need to bring a form of identification such as a driver's license with you to the Thomson Prometric center on the test day. You will not be allowed to take anything with you into the testing center. You will be given a calculator, pencils, and scrap paper. You will turn in all scrap paper, including the notes and squiggles you've jotted during the test, to the center upon completion of the exam.

The exam is scored immediately, so you will know whether you've passed at the conclusion of the test. You're given four hours to complete the exam, which consists of 200 randomly generated questions. Only 175 of the 200 questions are scored. A passing score requires you to answer 141 of the 175 questions correctly. Twenty-five of the 200 questions are "pretest" questions that will appear randomly throughout the exam. These 25 questions are used by PMI to determine statistical information and to determine whether they can or should be used on future exams. The questions on the exam cover the following process groups and areas:

- Initiating
- Planning
- Executing
- Monitoring and Controlling
- Closing
- Professional Responsibility

All unanswered questions are scored as wrong answers, so it benefits you to guess at an answer if you're stumped on a question.

After you've received your certification, you'll be required to earn 60 professional development units (PDUs) every three years to maintain certification. Approximately one hour of structured learning translates to one PDU. The PMI website details what activities constitute a PDU, how many PDUs each activity earns, and how to register your PDUs with PMI to maintain your certification. As an example, attendance at a local chapter meeting earns one PDU.

How to Become CAPM Certified

If you find you don't have quite enough experience or education to sit for the PMP exam, you should consider sitting for the Certified Associate in Project Management (CAPM) exam. The CAPM exam is structured like the PMP exam only the requirements are not as strict as they are for the PMP. CAPM candidates typically work in a supporting role with a project manager or as a subproject manager. Like the PMP, CAPM has two categories of requirements; each category requires 23 hours of project management education:

- Category 1 is for those who have a baccalaureate degree. You'll need to provide proof, via transcripts, of your degree with your application. In addition, you'll need to complete verification forms that show 1,500 hours of project management experience that spans a minimum of two years and no more than three years.

- Category 2 is for those who do not have a baccalaureate degree but do have a high school diploma or equivalent. You'll need to complete verification forms documenting 2,500 hours of project management experience that spans a minimum of two years and no more than three years.

The CAPM exam fee at the time of this publication is $225 for PMI members in good standing and $300 for non-PMI members.

Included on the CD with this book is a sample CAPM exam. If you're sitting for the CAPM exam, I encourage you to answer all of the end-of-chapter questions and take the bonus exams in addition to the sample CAPM exam. You'll get a much broader sense of the types of questions and the topics you'll encounter on the actual exam by using all of the sample questions provided in this book and on the CD.

Who Should Buy This Book?

If you are serious about passing the PMP exam (or the CAPM exam for that matter), you should buy this book and use it to study for the exam. This book is unique in that it walks you through the project processes from beginning to end, just as projects are performed in practice. When you read this book, you will benefit by learning specific *Guide to the PMBOK* processes and techniques coupled with real-life scenarios that describe how project managers in different situations handle problems and the various issues all project managers are bound to encounter during their career. This study guide describes in detail the exam objective topics in each chapter and has attempted to cover all of the important project management concepts.

How to Use This Book and CD

We've included several testing features, both in the book and on the companion CD. Following this introduction is an assessment test that you can use to check your readiness for the actual exam. Take this test before you start reading the book. It will help you identify the areas you may need to brush up on. The answers to the assessment test appear after the last question of the test. Each answer includes an explanation and a note telling you in which chapter this material appears.

An "Exam Essentials" section appears at the end of every chapter to highlight the topics you'll most likely find on the exam and help you focus on the most important material covered in the chapter so that you'll have a solid understanding of those concepts. However, it isn't possible to predict what questions will be covered on your particular exam, so be sure to study everything in the chapter.

Like the exam itself, this study guide is organized in terms of process groups and the natural sequence of events a project goes through in its life cycle. By contrast, in other study guides, material is organized by Knowledge Area—Human Resource Management, Communications Management, and so on—and it can be confusing when studying for the exam to map the processes in each Knowledge Area to process groups.

Review Questions are also provided at the end of every chapter. You can use these to gauge your understanding of the subject matter before reading the chapter and to point out the areas in which you need to concentrate your study time. As you finish each chapter, answer the Review Questions and then check to see whether your answers are right—the correct answers appear on the pages following the last question. You can go back to reread the section that deals with each question you got wrong to ensure that you answer the question correctly the next time you are tested on the material. If you can answer at least 80 percent of the review questions correctly, you can probably feel comfortable moving on to the next chapter. If you can't answer that many correctly, reread the chapter, or the section that seems to be giving you trouble, and try the questions again. You'll also find more than 200 flashcard questions on the CD for on-the-go review. Download them right onto your Palm PocketPC device for quick and convenient reviewing.

 Don't rely on studying the Review Questions exclusively as your study method. The questions you'll see on the exam will be different from the questions presented in the book. There are 200 randomly generated questions on the PMP exam and 150 on the CAPM, so it isn't possible to cover every potential exam question in the "Review Questions" section of each chapter. Make sure you understand the concepts behind the material presented in each chapter and memorize all the formulas as well.

In addition to the assessment test and the review questions, you'll find bonus exams on the CD. Take these practice exams just as if you were actually taking the exam (that is, without any reference material). When you have finished the first exam, move on to the next exam to solidify your test-taking skills. If you get more than 85 percent of the answers correct, you're ready to take the real exam.

 If you purchased the Standard Edition of this book, there are a total of two bonus PMP exams and two additional CAPM exams. If you purchased the Deluxe Edition, there are a total of eight bonus PMP exams and two additional CAPM exams.

The CD also contains an audio file that you can download to your favorite MP3 player to hear a recap of the key elements covered in each chapter.

Finally, you will notice various "Real-World Scenario" sidebars throughout each chapter. These are designed to give you insight into how the various processes and topic areas apply to real-world situations.

Additionally, if you are going to travel but still need to study for the PMP exam and you have a laptop with a CD drive, you can take this entire book with you just by taking the CD. This book is available in PDF (Adobe Acrobat), so it can be easily read on any computer.

Also on the CD in PDF is the appendix, "Process Inputs and Outputs."

For those of you who purchased the Deluxe Edition, you'll find a series of scenarios and exercises that map to each chapter. These workbook exercises are designed to help you put the theories you've learned in each chapter into practice.

The Exam Objectives

Behind every certification exam, you can be sure to find exam objectives—the broad topics in which the exam developers want to ensure your competency. The official PMP exam objectives are listed in the following sections.

Exam objectives are subject to change at any time without prior notice and at PMI's sole discretion. Please visit the Certification page of the PMI's website, www.pmi.org, for the most current listing of exam objectives.

Domain 1.0: Initiating the Project

The objectives for the Initiating the Project domain are as follows:

1. Conduct Project Selection Methods
2. Define Scope
3. Document Project Risks, Assumptions, and Constraints
4. Identify and Perform Stakeholder Analysis
5. Develop Project Charter
6. Obtain Project Charter Approval

Domain 2.0: Planning the Project

The objectives of the Planning the Project domain are as follows:

1. Define and Record Requirements, Constraints, and Assumptions
2. Identify Project Team and Define Roles and Responsibilities
3. Create the WBS

4. Develop Change Management Plan
5. Identify Risks and Define Risk Strategies
6. Obtain Plan Approval
7. Conduct Kick-off Meeting

Domain 3.0: Executing the Project

The objectives of the Executing the Project domain are as follows:

1. Execute Tasks Defined in Project Plan
2. Ensure Common Understanding and Set Expectations
3. Implement the Procurement of Project Resources
4. Manage Resource Allocation
5. Implement Quality Management Plan
6. Implement Approved Changes
7. Implement Approved Actions and Workarounds
8. Improve Team Performance

Domain 4.0: Monitoring and Controlling the Project

The objectives of the Monitoring and Controlling the Project domain are as follows:

1. Measure Project Performance
2. Verify and Manage Changes to the Project
3. Ensure Project Deliverables Conform to Quality Standards
4. Monitor all Risks

Domain 5.0: Closing the Project

The objectives of the Closing the Project domain are as follows:

1. Obtain Final Acceptance for the Project
2. Obtain Financial, Legal, and Administrative Closure
3. Release Project Resources
4. Identify, Document, and Communicate Lessons Learned
5. Create and Distribute Final Project Report
6. Archive and Retain Project Records
7. Measure Customer Satisfaction

Domain 6.0: Professional and Social Responsibility

The objectives for the Professional and Social Responsibility domain are as follows:

1. Ensure Individual Integrity

2. Contribute to the Project Management Knowledge Base

3. Enhance Professional Competence

4. Promote Interaction Among Stakeholders

Tips for Taking the PMP Exam

Here are some general tips for taking your exam successfully:

- Get to the exam center early so that you can relax and review your study materials.

- Read the exam questions very carefully. Make sure you know exactly what each question is asking, and don't be tempted to answer too quickly.

- Unanswered questions score as wrong answers. It's better to guess than to leave a question unanswered.

- If you're not sure of an answer, use a process of elimination to identify the obvious incorrect answers first. Narrow the remaining choices down by referring back to the question, looking for key words that might tip you off to the correct answer.

- You'll be given scratch paper to take with you to the exam station. As soon as you get to your place, write down all the formulas and any other memory aids you used while studying before starting the exam. That way, you can relax a little because you won't have to remember the formulas when you get to those questions on the exam—you can simply look at your scratch paper.

- Visit the PMI website at www.pmi.org for the latest information regarding certification and to find a testing site near you.

Assessment Test

1. What is one of the most important skills a project manager can have?

    A. Negotiation skills

    B. Influencing skills

    C. Communication skills

    D. Problem-solving skills

2. Project managers have the highest level of authority and the most power in which type of organizational structure?

    A. Projectized

    B. Strong matrix

    C. Functional

    D. Balanced matrix

3. The Project Management Knowledge Areas _____.

    A. include Initiation, Planning, Executing, Monitoring and Controlling, and Closing

    B. consist of nine areas that bring together processes that have things in common

    C. consist of five processes that bring together phases of projects that have things in common

    D. include Planning, Executing, and Monitoring and Controlling processes because these three processes are commonly interlinked

4. The project sponsor has approached you with a dilemma. The CEO announced at the annual stockholders meeting that the project you're managing will be completed by the end of this year. The problem is that this is six months prior to the scheduled completion date. It's too late to go back and correct her mistake, and stockholders are expecting implementation by the announced date. You must speed up the delivery date of this project. Your primary constraint before this occurred was the budget. What actions can you take to help speed up the project?

    A. Hire more resources to get the work completed faster.

    B. Ask for more money so that you can contract out one of the phases you had planned to do with in-house resources.

    C. Utilize negotiation and influencing skills to convince the project sponsor to speak with the CEO and make a correction to her announcement.

    D. Examine the project plan to see whether there are any phases that can be fast tracked, and then revise the project plan to reflect the compression of the schedule.

5. Which of the following describes the Executing process group?

    A. Project plans are put into action.

    B. Project performance measurements are taken and analyzed.

    C. Project plans are developed.

    D. Project plans are published.

6. You have been assigned to a project that will allow job seekers to fill out applications and submit them via the company website. You report to the VP of human resources. You are also responsible for screening applications for the information technology division and setting up interviews. The project coordinator has asked for the latest version of your changes to the online application page for his review. Which organizational structure do you work in?

   A. Functional organization

   B. Weak matrix organization

   C. Projectized organization

   D. Balanced matrix organization

7. According to the *PMBOK Guide*, the project manager is identified and assigned during which process?

   A. Prior to beginning the Develop Project Charter process

   B. At the conclusion of the Develop Project Charter process

   C. Prior to beginning the Planning processes

   D. Prior to beginning the Preliminary Scope Statement process

8. You are refining the product description for your company's new line of ski boots. Which of the following statements is true?

   A. You are in the Initiating processes of your project and know that the product description will contain more detail in this stage and that a decreasing amount of detail will be added to it as the project progresses.

   B. You are in the Planning processes of your project and know that the product description will contain less detail in this stage and greater detail as the project progresses.

   C. You are in the Planning processes of your project and know that the product description should contain the most detail possible at this stage, because this is critical information for the Planning process.

   D. You are in the Initiating process of your project and know that the product description will contain less detail in this stage and greater detail as the project progresses.

9. The business needs, strategic plan, and product scope description all describe elements of which of the following?

   A. Organizational process assets

   B. Tools and techniques of the Initiating processes

   C. The project statement of work

   D. The project charter

10. You are a project manager for Waterways Houseboats, Inc. You've been asked to perform a cost-benefit analysis for two proposed projects. Project A costs $2.4 million, with potential benefits of $12 million and future operating costs of $3 million. Project B costs $2.8 million, with potential benefits of $14 million and future operating costs of $2 million. Which project should you recommend?

   A. Project A, because the cost to implement is cheaper than Project B.

   B. Project A, because the potential benefits plus the future operating costs are less in value than the same calculation for Project B.

   C. Project B, because the potential benefits minus the implementation and future operating costs are greater in value than the same calculation for Project A.

   D. Project B, because the potential benefits minus the costs to implement are greater in value than the same calculation for Project A.

11. What is the purpose of the project charter?

   A. To recognize and acknowledge the project sponsor

   B. To recognize and acknowledge the existence of the project and commit organizational resources to the project

   C. To acknowledge the existence of the project team, project manager, and project sponsor

   D. To describe the selection methods used to choose this project over its competitors

12. Which of the following are tools and techniques of the Preliminary Scope Statement process?

   A. Project management methodology, project management information system, and expert judgment

   B. Project selection methods and expert judgment

   C. Constraints, assumptions, and expert judgment

   D. Project charter, project management information system, and project selection methods

13. You are a project manager for the Swirling Seas Cruises food division. You're considering two different projects regarding food services on the cruise lines. The initial cost of Project Fish'n for Chips will be $800,000, with expected cash inflows of $300,000 per quarter. Project Picnic's payback period is six months. Which project should you recommend?

   A. Project Fish'n for Chips, because its payback period is two months shorter than Project Picnic's.

   B. Project Fish'n for Chips, because the costs on Project Picnic are unknown.

   C. Project Picnic, because Project Fish'n for Chips' payback period is four months longer than Project Picnic's.

   D. Project Picnic, because Project Fish'n for Chips' payback period is two months longer than Project Picnic's.

14. What are decision models?

    A. Project selection criteria

    B. Project selection methods

    C. Project selection committees

    D. Project resource and budget selection methods

15. You've been assigned as a project manager on a research and development project for a new dental procedure. You're working in the Scope Planning process. What is the purpose of the project scope management plan?

    A. The project scope management plan describes and documents a scope baseline to help make future project decisions.

    B. The project scope management plan decomposes project deliverables into smaller units of work.

    C. The project scope management plan describes how project scope will be developed and how changes will be managed.

    D. The project scope management plan describes how cost and time estimates will be developed for project scope changes.

16. You are the project manager for Lucky Stars Candies. You've identified the deliverables and requirements and documented them where?

    A. In the project scope statement, which will be used as an input to the Create WBS process

    B. In the project scope management document, which is used as an input to the Scope Definition process

    C. In the product requirements document, which is an output of the Scope Definition process

    D. In the project specifications document, which is an output of the Scope Planning process

17. Each of the following statements describes an element of the Develop Project Management Plan process except for which one?

    A. Project management methodology

    B. Project specifications

    C. Configuration management system

    D. Expert judgment

18. What are the Scope Definition process tools and techniques?

    A. Cost benefit analysis, templates, and expert judgment

    B. Product analysis, cost benefit analysis, alternatives identification, and expert judgment

    C. Product analysis, alternatives identification, expert judgment, and stakeholder analysis

    D. Alternatives identification, stakeholder analysis, and expert judgment

19. Which of the following statements is true regarding constraints and assumptions?

   A. Constraints restrict the actions of the project team, and assumptions are considered true for planning purposes.

   B. Constraints are considered true for planning purposes, and assumptions limit the options of the project team.

   C. Constraints consider vendor availability and resource availability to be true for planning purposes. Assumptions limit the project team to work within predefined budgets or timelines.

   D. Constraints and assumptions are inputs to the Initiation process. They should be documented, because they will be used throughout the project Planning process.

20. You've just completed the WBS. Which of the following statements is true?

   A. The WBS breaks the project deliverables down to a level where alternatives identification can be used to determine how level-two assignments should be made.

   B. The WBS breaks the project deliverables down to a level where project constraints and assumptions can be easily identified.

   C. The WBS breaks the project deliverables down to the work package level, where product analysis can be documented.

   D. The WBS breaks the project deliverables down to the work package level, where cost and time estimates can be easily determined.

21. You are the project manger for Xylophone Phonics. It produces children's software programs that teach basic reading and math skills. You are performing the Quality Planning process and are identifying nonproductive activities. Part of this involves capturing information such as process boundaries, process configurations, and process metrics. Which of the following does this describe?

   A. The process improvement plan

   B. The quality management plan

   C. The quality metrics

   D. The cost of quality

22. Failure costs are also known as which of the following?

   A. Internal costs

   B. Cost of poor quality

   C. Cost of keeping defects out of the hands of customers

   D. Prevention costs

23. All of the following statements are true regarding Ishikawa diagrams in the Risk Identification process except which one?

   A. Ishikawa diagrams are also called *cause-and-effect diagrams*.

   B. Ishikawa diagrams are also called *fishbone diagrams*.

   C. Ishikawa diagrams are a tool and technique of this process.

   D. Ishikawa diagrams show the steps needed to identify the risk.

24. All of the following statements are true regarding risk events except which one? Choose the least correct answer.

  A. Project risks are uncertain events.

  B. If risks occur, they can have a positive or negative effect on project objectives.

  C. Unknown risks are threats to the project objectives, and nothing can be done to plan for them.

  D. Risks that have more perceived rewards to the organization than the consequences of the risk should be accepted.

25. You are a project manager working on a software development project. You've developed the risk management plan, identified risks, and determined risk responses for the risks. One of the risks you identified occurs, and you implement the response for that risk. Then, another risk occurs as a result of the response you implemented. What type of risk is this called?

  A. Trigger risk

  B. Residual risk

  C. Secondary risk

  D. Mitigated risk

26. Your team is developing the risk management plan. Which tool and technique of this process is used to develop risk cost elements and schedule activities that will be included in the project budget and schedule?

  A. Planning meetings and analysis

  B. Strategies for both threats and opportunities

  C. Information gathering techniques

  D. Risk data quality assessment

27. Monte Carlo analysis can help predict the impact of risks on project deliverables. This is an element of one of the tools and techniques of which of the following processes?

  A. Risk Response Planning

  B. Quantitative Risk Analysis

  C. Risk Identification

  D. Qualitative Risk Analysis

28. All of the following statements are true regarding risks except for which one? Choose the least correct answer.

  A. Risks might be threats to the objectives of the project.

  B. Risks are certain events that may be threats or opportunities to the objectives of the project.

  C. Risks might be opportunities to the objectives of the project.

  D. Risks have causes and consequences.

29. Which of the following contracts should you use for projects that have a degree of uncertainty and require a large investment early in the project life cycle?

   A. Fixed price

   B. Cost reimbursable

   C. Lump sum

   D. T&M

30. All of the following statements are true regarding the ADM method except which one?

   A. The ADM method is a tool and technique of Activity Sequencing.

   B. The ADM method uses one time estimate to determine durations.

   C. The ADA method is also called AOA.

   D. The ADA method is rarely used today.

31. You are the project manger for Xylophone Phonics. This company produces children's software programs that teach basic reading and math skills. You are ready to assign project roles, responsibilities, and reporting relationships. Which project Planning process are you working on?

   A. Resource Planning

   B. Human Resource Planning

   C. Acquire Staff

   D. Human Resource Acquisition

32. Which of the following compression techniques increases risk?

   A. Crashing

   B. Resource leveling

   C. Fast tracking

   D. Lead and lag

33. You are the project manager for Heartthrobs by the Numbers Dating Services. You're working on an updated Internet site that will display pictures as well as short bios of prospective heartbreakers. You have your activity list and resource requirements in hand and are planning to use parametric estimates and reserve analysis to determine activity durations. Which of the following statements is true?

   A. You are using inputs of the Activity Duration Estimating process.

   B. You are using tools and techniques of the Cost Estimating process.

   C. You are using tools and techniques of the Activity Duration Estimating process.

   D. You are using inputs of the Cost Estimating process.

34. You are working on a project that will upgrade the phone system in your customer service center. You have used bottom-up estimating techniques to assign costs to the project activities and have determined the cost baseline. Which of the following statements is true?

    A. You have completed the Cost Estimating process and now need to complete the Cost Budgeting process to determine the project's baseline.

    B. You have completed the Cost Estimating process and established a project baseline to measure future project performance against.

    C. You have completed the Cost Budgeting process and now need to complete the Schedule Development process to establish a project baseline to measure future project performance against.

    D. You have completed the Cost Budgeting process, and the cost baseline will be used to measure future project performance.

35. You are the project manger for Xylophone Phonics. It produces children's software programs that teach basic reading and math skills. You're performing cost estimates for your project and don't have a lot of details yet. Which of the following techniques should you use?

    A. Analogous estimating techniques, because this is a form of expert judgment that uses historical information from similar projects

    B. Bottom-up estimating techniques, because this is a form of expert judgment that uses historical information from similar projects

    C. Monte Carlo analysis, because this is a modeling technique that uses simulation to determine estimates

    D. Parametric modeling, because this is a form of simulation used to determine estimates

36. You are a project manager who has recently held a project team kickoff meeting where all the team members were formally introduced to each other. Some of the team members know each other from other projects and have been working with you for the past three weeks during the Planning processes. Which of the following statements is true?

    A. Team building begins once all the members of the team are identified and introduced to each other. This team is in the storming stage of team development.

    B. Team building begins in the Planning process group. This team is in the storming stage of team development.

    C. Team building begins once all the members of the team are identified and introduced to each other. This team is in the forming stage of team development.

    D. Team building begins in the Planning process group. This team is in the forming stage of team development.

37. Project managers spend what percentage of their time communicating?

    A. 90

    B. 85

    C. 75

    D. 50

38. People are motivated by the need for achievement, power, or affiliation according to which theory?

   A. Expectancy Theory

   B. Achievement Theory

   C. Contingency Theory

   D. Theory X

39. During your project meeting, a problem was discussed, and a resolution to the problem was reached. During the meeting, the participants started wondering why they thought the problem was such a big issue. Sometime after the meeting, you received an email from one of the meeting participants saying they've changed their mind about the solution reached in the meeting and need to resurface the problem. The solution reached during the initial project meeting is a result of which of the following conflict resolution techniques?

   A. Confrontation

   B. Forcing

   C. Smoothing

   D. Storming

40. You are the project manager for Heartthrobs by the Numbers Dating Services. You're working on an updated Internet site that will display pictures as well as short bios of prospective heartbreakers. You've just completed your project staff assignments and published the project team directory. Which process are you in?

   A. Human Resource Planning

   B. Direct and Manage Project Execution

   C. Develop Project Team

   D. Acquire Project Team

41. You need to convey some very complex, detailed information to the project stakeholders. What is the best method for communicating this kind of information?

   A. Verbal

   B. Vertical

   C. Horizontal

   D. Written

42. This process applies evaluation criteria to the bids and proposals received from potential vendors.

   A. Request Seller Responses

   B. Contract Administration

   C. Select Sellers

   D. Quality Assurance

43. The project manager has the greatest influence over quality during which process?

   A. Quality Planning

   B. Quality Assurance

   C. Quality Control

   D. Quality Change Control

44. There are likely to be team loyalty issues in a matrixed environment. All of the following are true regarding this situation as it pertains to the Manage Project Team process except for which one?

   A. Two of the tools and techniques you might use to manage these relationships effectively are communications methods and issue logs.

   B. In this type of structure, team members report to both a functional manager and a project manager.

   C. The project manager is generally responsible for managing this relationship.

   D. The effective management of these reporting relationships is often a critical success factor for the project.

45. The inputs of the Performance Reporting process include all of the following except for which one?

   A. Work performance information

   B. Performance measurements

   C. Forecasted completion

   D. Performance reviews

46. As a result of a face-to-face meeting you recently had to discuss the items in your issues log, you have resolved issues and come away with an approved corrective action and an update to the project management plan. Which process does this describe?

   A. Manage Stakeholders

   B. Performance Reporting

   C. Information Distribution

   D. Manage Project Team

47. Which performance measurement tells you how much more of the budget is required to finish the project?

   A. ETC

   B. EV

   C. AC

   D. EAC

48. All of the following statements are true regarding configuration management except which one?

   A. Configuration management requires acceptance decisions for all change requests to be made through the CCB.

   B. Change control systems are a subset of the configuration management system.

   C. Configuration management describes the physical characteristics of the product of the project.

   D. Configuration management controls changes to the product of the project.

49. Which performance measurement tells you what the projected total cost of the project will be at completion?

   A. ETC

   B. CPI

   C. SPI

   D. EAC

50. You know that PV = 470, AC = 430, EV = 480, EAC = 500, and BAC = 525. What is VAC?

   A. 70

   B. 20

   C. 25

   D. 30

51. All of the following are outputs of the Integrated Change Control process except for which one?

   A. Approved corrective actions

   B. Validated defect repair

   C. Requested changes

   D. Project scope statement updates

52. Every status meeting should have time allotted for Risk Monitoring and Control. Which of the following sentences is not true?

   A. Risk identification and monitoring should occur throughout the life of the project.

   B. Risk audits should occur throughout the life of the project and are specifically interested in measuring the team's performance in the Risk Identification and Risk Monitoring and Control processes.

   C. Risks should be monitored for their status and to determine whether the impacts to the objectives have changed.

   D. Technical performance measurement variances may indicate that a risk is looming and should be reviewed at status meetings.

53. These diagrams rank-order factors for corrective action by frequency of occurrence. They are also a type of histogram.

    A. Control charts

    B. Process flowcharts

    C. Scatter diagrams

    D. Pareto charts

54. The primary function of the Closing processes is to perform which of the following?

    A. Formalize lessons learned and distribute this information to project participants.

    B. Perform audits to verify the project results against the project requirements.

    C. Formalize project completion and disseminate this information to project participants.

    D. Perform post-implementation audits to document project successes and failures.

55. You are the project manager for a construction company that is building a new city and county office building in your city. You recently looked over the construction site to determine whether the work to date was conforming to the requirements and quality standards. Which tool and technique of the Perform Quality Control process are you using?

    A. Defect repair review

    B. Inspection

    C. Sampling

    D. Quality audit

56. Which of the following statements is true regarding Close Project?

    A. Close Project occurs at the end of a project phase and at the end of the project.

    B. Close Project occurs at the end of the project phase only.

    C. Close Project occurs at the end of the project only.

    D. Close Project is performed after Contract Closure.

57. What type of organization experiences the least amount of stress during project closeout?

    A. Projectized

    B. Functional

    C. Weak matrix

    D. Strong matrix

58. All of the following statements are true of the project Closing processes except for which one?

    A. Probability for success is greatest in the project Closing processes.

    B. The project manager's influence is greatest in the project Closing processes.

    C. The stakeholders' influence is least in the project Closing processes.

    D. Risk is greatest in the project Closing processes.

59. You are the project manager for a construction company that is building a new city and county office building in your city. Your CCB recently approved a scope change. You know that scope change might come about as a result of all of the following except which one?

   A. Schedule revisions

   B. Product scope change

   C. Changes to the agreed-upon WBS

   D. Changes to the project requirements

60. Inspections are also called each of the following except for which one?

   A. Reviews

   B. Assessment

   C. Walk-throughs

   D. Audits

61. You are a project manager working in a foreign country. You observe that some of your project team members are having a difficult time adjusting to the new culture. You provided them with training on cultural differences and the customs of this country before arriving, but they still seem uncomfortable and disoriented. Which of the following statements is true?

   A. This is the result of working with teams of people from two different countries.

   B. This condition is known as *culture shock*.

   C. This is the result of jet lag and travel fatigue.

   D. This condition is known as *global culturalism*.

62. Your project involves the research and development of a new food additive. You're ready to release the product to your customer when you discover that a minor reaction might occur in people with certain conditions. The reactions to date have been very minor, and no known long-lasting side effects have been noted. As project manager, what should you do?

   A. Do nothing because the reactions are so minor that very few people will be affected.

   B. Inform the customer that you've discovered this condition and tell them you'll research it further to determine its impacts.

   C. Inform your customer that there is no problem with the additive except for an extremely small percentage of the population and release the product to them.

   D. Tell the customer you'll correct the reaction problems in the next batch, but you'll release the first batch of product to them now to begin using.

63. You have just prepared an RFP for release. Your project involves a substantial amount of contract work detailed in the RFP. Your favorite vendor drops by and offers to give you and your spouse the use of their company condo for your upcoming vacation. It's located in a beautiful resort community that happens to be one of your favorite places to go for a getaway. What is the most appropriate response?

   A. Thank the vendor, but decline the offer because you know this could be considered a conflict of interest.

   B. Thank the vendor, and accept. This vendor is always offering you incentives like this, so this offer does not likely have anything to do with the recent RFP release.

   C. Thank the vendor, accept the offer, and immediately tell your project sponsor so they're aware of what you're doing.

   D. Thank the vendor, but decline the offer because you've already made another arrangement for this vacation. Ask them whether you can take a rain check and arrange another time to use the condo.

64. As a PMP, one of your responsibilities is to ensure integrity on the project. When your personal interests are put above the interests of the project or when you use your influence to cause others to make decisions in your favor without regard for the project outcome, this is considered which of the following?

   A. Conflict of interest

   B. Using professional knowledge inappropriately

   C. Culturally unacceptable

   D. Personal conflict issue

65. Name the ethical code you'll be required to adhere to as a PMP.

   A. *Project Management Policy and Ethics Guide*

   B. *Project Management Professional Standards and Ethics*

   C. *Project Management Code of Professional Ethics*

   D. *Project Management Professional Code of Professional Conduct*

Answers to Assessment Test

1. C. Negotiation, influencing, and problem-solving skills are all important for a project manager to possess. However, good communication skills are the most important skills a project manager can have. For more information, please see Chapter 1.

2. A. Project managers have the highest level of power and authority in a projectized organization. They also have high levels of power and authority in a strong matrix. However, a matrix organization is a blend of functional and projectized organizations. Therefore, the project manager does not have quite the same level of authority as they would in a projectized organization. For more information, please see Chapter 1.

3. B. The project management Knowledge Areas bring processes together that have commonalities. For example, the Project Quality Management Knowledge Area includes the Quality Planning, Perform Quality Assurance, and Perform Quality Control processes. For more information, please see Chapter 1.

4. D. Fast tracking is the best answer in this scenario. Budget was the original constraint on this project, so it's highly unlikely the project manager would get more resources to assist with the project. The next best thing is to compress phases to shorten the project duration. For more information, please see Chapter 1 and Chapter 7.

5. A. The Executing process group takes published project plans and turns them into actions to accomplish the goals of the project. For more information, please see Chapter 1.

6. B. Functional managers who have lots of authority and power working with project coordinators who have minimal authority and power characterizes a weak matrix organization. Project managers in weak matrix organizations are sometimes called *project coordinators*, *project leaders*, or *project expeditors*. For more information, please see Chapter 1.

7. C. According to the *PMBOK Guide*, the project manager should be identified prior to beginning the Planning processes and is named and authorized in the project charter. For more information, please see Chapter 2.

8. D. Product descriptions are used during the Initiating process group and contain less detail now and more detail as the project progresses. For more information, please see Chapter 2.

9. C. These elements are part of the project statement of work used as an input to both of the Initiating processes. For more information, please see Chapter 2.

10. C. Project B's cost-benefit analysis is a $9.2 million benefit to the company, compared to $6.6 million for Project A. Cost-benefit analysis takes into consideration the initial costs to implement and future operating costs. For more information, please see Chapter 2.

11. B. The purpose of a project charter is to recognize and acknowledge the existence of a project and commit resources to the project. The charter names the project manager and project sponsor, but that's not its primary purpose. For more information, please see Chapter 2.

12. A. Preliminary Scope Statement has three tools and techniques: project management methodology, project management information system, and expert judgment. For more information, please see Chapter 2.

13. D. The payback period for Project Fish'n for Chips is eight months. This project will receive $300,000 every three months, or $100,000 per month. The $800,000 will be paid back in eight months. For more information, please see Chapter 2.

14. B. Decision models are project selection methods used as tools and techniques in the Develop Project Charter process. Decision models include benefit measurement methods and mathematical models. For more information, please see Chapter 2.

15. C. The scope management plan outlines how project scope will be managed and how changes will be incorporated into the project. For more information, please see Chapter 3.

16. A. The project scope statement contains an exhaustive list of the project deliverables, their requirements, and the measurable criteria used to determine project completion. The scope statement is an output of the Scope Definition process and is used as an input to the Create WBS process. For more information, please see Chapter 3.

17. B. The tools and techniques of the Develop Project Management Plan include the following: project management methodology, project management information system of which the configuration management system is a component, and expert judgment. Project specifications are an element of the project scope statement. For more information, please see Chapter 3.

18. C. The tools and techniques of the Scope Definition process include product analysis, alternatives identification, expert judgment, and stakeholder analysis. For more information, please see Chapter 3.

19. A. Constraints limit the options of the project team by restricting action or dictating action. Scope, time, and cost are the three most common constraints, and each of these has an effect on quality. Assumptions are presumed to be true for planning purposes. Always validate your assumptions. For more information, please see Chapter 3.

20. D. The work package level is the lowest level in the work breakdown structure. Schedule and cost estimates are easily determined at this level. For more information, please see Chapter 4.

21. A. This describes the process improvement plan, which is a subsidiary of the project management plan and an output of the Quality Planning process. For more information, please see Chapter 4.

22. B. Failure costs are associated with the cost of quality and are also known as cost of poor quality. For more information, please see Chapter 4.

23. D. Cause-and-effect diagrams—also called *Ishikawa* or *fishbone diagrams*—show the relationship between the effects of problems and their causes. Kaoru Ishikawa developed cause-and-effect diagrams. For more information, please see Chapter 5.

24. C. Unknown risks might be threats or opportunities to the project, and the project manager should set aside contingency reserves to deal with them. For more information, please see Chapter 5.

25. C. Secondary risks occur as a result of the implementation of a response to another risk. For more information, please see Chapter 5.

26. A. Planning meetings and analysis is the only tool and technique of the Risk Management Planning Process. For more information, please see Chapter 5.

27. B. Monte Carlo analysis is a modeling and simulation technique that is a tool and technique of the Quantitative Risk Analysis process. For more information, please see Chapter 5.

28. B. Risks are uncertain events that may be threats or opportunities to the objectives of the project. For more information, please see Chapter 5.

29. B. Cost-reimbursable contracts are used when the degree of uncertainty is high and when the project requires a large investment prior to completion of the project. For more information, please see Chapter 6.

30. B. The arrow diagramming method (ADM)—also called activity on arrow (AOA)—uses more than one time estimate to determine project duration. For more information, please see Chapter 6.

31. B. The Human Resource Planning process identifies project resources, documents roles and responsibilities of project team members, and documents reporting relationships. For more information, please see Chapter 6.

32. C. Fast tracking is a compression technique that increases risk and potentially causes rework. Fast tracking is starting two activities previously scheduled to start one after the other at the same time. For more information, please see Chapter 7.

33. C. Parametric estimates and reserve analysis are two of the tools and techniques of the Activity Duration Estimating process. The other tools are expert judgment and analogous estimating. For more information, please see Chapter 7.

34. D. The Cost Budgeting process establishes the cost baseline, which is used to measure and track the project throughout the remaining process groups. For more information, please see Chapter 7.

35. A. Analogous estimating—also called *top-down estimating*—is a form of expert judgment. Analogous estimating can be used to estimate cost or time and considers historical information from previous, similar projects. For more information, please see Chapter 7.

36. D. Team building begins in the Planning processes of your project. In this question, the team members have just been formally introduced to each other, so they are still in the forming stage of Develop Project Team. For more information, please see Chapter 8.

37. A. Project managers spend about 90 percent of their time communicating through status meetings, team meetings, email, verbal communications, and so on. For more information, please see Chapter 8.

38. B. Achievement Theory conjectures that people are motivated by the need for achievement, power, or affiliation. For more information, please see Chapter 8.

39. C. The smoothing technique does not usually result in a permanent solution. The problem is downplayed to make it seem less important than it is, which makes the problem tend to resurface later. For more information, please see Chapter 8.

40. D.   The Acquire Project Team outputs include the project staff assignments, and the project team directory is part of this output. For more information, please see Chapter 8.

41. D.   Information that is complex and detailed is best conveyed in writing. A verbal follow-up would be good to answer questions and clarify information. Vertical and horizontal are ways of communicating within the organization. For more information, please see Chapter 8.

42. C.   The Select Sellers process is where bids and proposals are received from potential vendors and evaluation criteria are applied to them to make a selection. For more information, please see Chapter 9.

43. B.   Quality Assurance is the process where project managers have the greatest amount of influence over quality. For more information, please see Chapter 9.

44. A.   Communications methods are a tool and technique of the Manage Stakeholders process. The tools and techniques of the Manage Project Team process are observation and conversation, project performance appraisals, conflict management, and issue log. For more information, please see Chapter 9.

45. D.   Performance reviews are not an input of the Performance Reporting process. The remaining inputs of this process are quality control measurements, project management plan, approved change requests, and deliverables. For more information, please see Chapter 9.

46. A.   The two clues in this question are the face-to-face meetings (a communication method) and the resolved issues, which is an output of the Manage Stakeholders process. For more information, please see Chapter 9.

47. A.   Estimate to completion (ETC) calculates how much more of the budget is needed to complete the project if everything continues at the current level of performance. For more information, please see Chapter 10.

48. A.   Change control systems are a subset of the configuration management system. Change requests should be approved by the CCB, but in the case of an emergency, change requests may be approved by the project manager in accordance with the process outlined in the configuration management system. The project team might have discretion to approve changes within certain parameters without CCB approval. Configuration management also describes the physical characteristics of the product, controls changes to the product, and tracks the changes requests and their status. For more information, please see Chapter 10.

49. D.   Estimate at completion (EAC) estimates the total cost of the project at completion based on the performance of the project to date. For more information, please see Chapter 10.

50. C.   VAC is calculated this way: VAC = BAC − EAC. Therefore, 525 − 500 = 25. For more information, please see Chapter 10.

51. C.   Approved change requests are an output of this process, not requested change requests. The other tools and techniques of this process are rejected change requests, project management plan updates, approved preventive actions, approved defect repair, and deliverables. For more information, please see Chapter 10.

52. B.   Risk audits should be performed throughout the life of the project and are specifically interested in looking at the implementation and effectiveness of risk strategies. For more information, please see Chapter 10.

53. D.   Pareto charts rank-order important factors for corrective action by frequency of occurrence. For more information, please see Chapter 11.

54. C.   The primary function of the Closing processes is to formalize project completion and disseminate this information to the project participants. For more information, please see Chapter 11.

55. B.   Inspection involves physically looking at, measuring, or testing results to determine whether they conform to your quality standards. For more information, please see Chapter 11.

56. A.   Close Project occurs at the end of the project phase and at the end of the project itself. Close Project is performed after Contract Closure. It is the last process performed on your project. For more information, please see Chapter 11.

57. C.   Weak matrix organizational structures tend to experience the least amount of stress during the project closeout processes. For more information, please see Chapter 11.

58. D.   Risk is lowest during the Closing processes because you've completed the work of the project at this point. For more information, please see Chapter 11.

59. A.   Scope changes will cause schedule revisions, but schedule revisions do not change the project scope. Project requirements are part of the project scope statement, and therefore D is one of the correct responses. For more information, please see Chapter 11.

60. B.   Inspections are also called reviews, peer reviews, walk-throughs, and audits. For more information, please see Chapter 11.

61. B.   When people work in unfamiliar environments, culture shock can occur. Training and researching information about the country you'll be working in can help counteract this. For more information, please see Chapter 12.

62. B.   Honesty and truthful reporting are required of PMPs. In this situation, you would inform the customer of everything you know regarding the problem and work to find alternative solutions. For more information, please see Chapter 12.

63. A.   The best response is to decline the offer. This is a conflict of interest, and accepting the offer puts your own integrity and the contract award process in jeopardy. For more information, please see Chapter 12.

64. A.   A conflict of interest is any situation that compromises the outcome of the project or ignores the impact to the project to benefit yourself or others. For more information, please see Chapter 12.

65. D.   The *Project Management Professional Code of Professional Conduct* is published by PMI, and all PMPs are expected to adhere to its standards. For more information, please see Chapter 12.

Chapter 1

What Is a Project?

Congratulations on your decision to study for and take the Project Management Institute (PMI) Project Management Professional (PMP) certification exam. This book was written with you in mind. The focus and content of this book revolve heavily around the information contained in *A Guide to the Project Management Body of Knowledge (PMBOK Guide), Third Edition*, published by PMI. I will refer to this guide throughout this book and elaborate on those areas that appear on the test. Keep in mind that the test covers all the project management processes, so don't skip anything in your study time.

When possible, I'll pass on hints and study tips that I collected while studying for the exam. My first tip is to familiarize yourself with the terminology used in *PMBOK Guide*. Volunteers from differing industries worked together to come up with the standards and terms used in the guide. These folks worked hard to develop and define standard project management terms, and these terms are used interchangeably among industries. For example, *resource planning* means the same thing to someone working in construction, information technology, or tele-communications. You'll find the *PMBOK Guide* terms explained throughout this book. Even if you are an experienced project manager, you might find you use specific terms for processes or actions you regularly perform but *PMBOK Guide* calls them by another name. So, the first step is to get familiar with the terminology.

This chapter lays the foundation for building and managing your project. I'll address project and project management definitions as well as organizational structures. Good luck!

Is It a Project?

Consider the following scenario: The VP of marketing approaches you with a fabulous idea—"fabulous" because he's the big boss and because he thought it up. He wants to set up kiosks in local grocery stores as mini-offices. "These offices will offer customers the ability to sign up for new wireless phone services, make their wireless phone bill payments, and purchase equipment and accessories. He believes that the exposure in grocery stores will increase awareness of the company's offerings. After all, everyone has to eat, right? He told you that the board of directors has already cleared the project, and he'll dedicate as many resources to this as he can. He wants the new kiosks in place in 12 stores by the end of next year. The best news is he has assigned you to head up this project.

Your first question should be "Is it a project?" This might seem elementary, but confusing projects with ongoing operations happens often. Projects are temporary in nature; have definite start and end dates; produce a unique product, service, or result; and are completed when their goals and objectives have been met and signed off by the stakeholders.

When considering whether you have a project on your hands, you need to keep some issues in mind. First, is it a project or an ongoing operation? Next, if it is a project, who are the stakeholders? And third, what characteristics distinguish this endeavor as a project? We'll look at each of these next.

Projects versus Operations

Projects are temporary in nature and have definitive start dates and definitive end dates. The project is completed when its goals and objectives are accomplished. Sometimes projects end when it's determined that the goals and objectives cannot be accomplished or when the product, service, or result of the project is no longer needed and the project is canceled. Projects exist to bring about a product, service, or result that didn't exist before. This might include tangible products, services such as consulting or project management, and business functions that support the organization. Projects might also produce a result or an outcome, such as a document that details the findings of a research study. In this sense, a project is unique. However, don't get confused by the term *unique*. For example, Ford Motor Company is in the business of designing and assembling cars. Each model that Ford designs and produces can be considered a project. The models differ from each other in their features and are marketed to people with various needs. An SUV serves a different purpose and clientele than a luxury model. The design and marketing of these two models are unique projects. However, the actual assembly of the cars is considered an operation—a repetitive process that is followed for most makes and models.

Determining the characteristics and features of the different car models is carried out through what *PMBOK Guide* terms *progressive elaboration*. This means the characteristics of the product, service, or result of the project (the SUV, for example) are determined incrementally and are continually refined and worked out in detail as the project progresses. This concept goes along with the temporary and unique aspects of a project because when you first start the project, you don't know all the minute details of the end product. Product characteristics typically start out broad-based at the beginning of the project and are progressively elaborated into more and more detail over time until they are complete and finalized. Keep in mind that product characteristics are progressively elaborated, but the work of the project itself stays constant.

Operations are ongoing and repetitive. They involve work that is continuous without an ending date, and you often repeat the same processes and produce the same results. The purpose of operations is to keep the organization functioning, while the purpose of a project is to meet its goals and to conclude. Therefore, operations are ongoing, and projects are unique and temporary.

Stakeholders

A project is successful when it achieves its objectives and meets or exceeds the expectations of the stakeholders. *Stakeholders* are those folks (or organizations) with a vested interest in your project. They are the people who are actively involved with the work of the project or have something to either gain or lose as a result of the project.

Real World Scenario

The New Website Project

You've just been charged with creating a new intranet site for your organization. At the beginning of the project, you don't know a lot of detail other than the high-level purpose of the project. One of the next steps is to discover the elements that should be included on the website. For example, you might need to make available human resources policies and procedures, travel request forms, expense reimbursement forms, and so on. At this point, you are progressively elaborating the scope of the project. Each of these elements will need its own progressive elaboration process to further define its requirements. For example, as you interview stakeholders, you discover that travel request forms require two electronic signatures, one from the employee's supervisor and one from the section manager. Progressive elaboration continues through the Planning processes until the scope and requirements have been discovered and agreed upon by the stakeholders.

Exam Spotlight

Progressive elaboration is most often used when creating project scope, determining requirements, and defining risks and their mitigation plans.

Key stakeholders can make or break the success of a project. Even if all the deliverables are met and the objectives are satisfied, if your key stakeholders aren't happy, nobody is happy.

The *project sponsor*, generally an executive in the organization with the authority to assign resources and enforce decisions regarding the project, is a stakeholder. The customer is a stakeholder, as are contractors and suppliers. The project manager, the project team members, and the managers from other departments in the organization are stakeholders as well. It's important to identify all the stakeholders in your project up front. If you leave out an important stakeholder or their department's function and don't discover the error until well into the project, it could be a project killer.

Figure 1.1 shows a sample listing of the kinds of stakeholders involved on a typical project.

Many times, stakeholders have conflicting interests. It's the project manager's responsibility to understand these conflicts and try to resolve them. It's also the project manager's responsibility to manage stakeholder expectations. Be certain to identify and meet with all key stakeholders early in the project to understand all their needs and constraints. And when in doubt, stakeholder conflicts should always be resolved in favor of the customer.

FIGURE 1.1   Project stakeholders

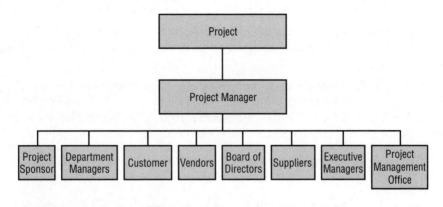

     I'll talk more about stakeholders and their needs in Chapter 3, "Developing the Project Scope Statement."

Project Characteristics

You've just learned that a project has several characteristics:

- Projects are unique.

- Projects are temporary in nature and have a definite beginning and ending date.

- Projects are completed when the project goals are achieved or it's determined the project is no longer viable.

- A successful project is one that meets or exceeds the expectations of your stakeholders.

Using these criteria, let's examine the assignment from the VP of marketing to determine whether it is a project:

Is it unique?   Yes, because the kiosks don't exist in the local grocery stores. This is a new way of offering the company's services to its customer base. Although the service the company is offering isn't new, the way it is presenting its services is.

Does the project have a limited time frame?   Yes, the start date of this project is today, and the end date is the end of next year. It is a temporary endeavor.

Is there a way to determine when the project is completed?   Yes, the kiosks will be installed, and services will be offered from them. Once all the kiosks are intact and operating, the project will come to a close.

Is there a way to determine stakeholder satisfaction?   Yes, the expectations of the stakeholders will be documented in the form of requirements during the planning processes. These requirements will be compared to the finished product to determine whether it meets the expectations of the stakeholder.

Houston, we have a project.

What Is Project Management?

You've determined that you indeed have a project. What now? The notes you scratched on the back of a napkin during your coffee break might get you started, but that's not exactly good project management practice.

We have all witnessed this scenario—an assignment is made, and the project team members jump directly into the project, busying themselves with building the product, service, or result requested. Often, careful thought is not given to the project-planning process. I'm sure you've heard co-workers toss around statements like "That would be a waste of valuable time" or "Why plan when you can just start building?" Project progress is rarely measured against the customer requirements. In the end, the delivered product, service, or result doesn't meet the expectations of the customer! This is a frustrating experience for all those involved. Unfortunately, many projects follow this poorly constructed path.

Project management brings together a set of tools and techniques—performed by people—to describe, organize, and monitor the work of project activities. *Project managers* are the people responsible for managing the project processes and applying the tools and techniques used to carry out the project activities. All projects are composed of processes, even if they employ a haphazard approach. There are many advantages to organizing projects and teams around the project management processes endorsed by PMI. We'll be examining those processes and their advantages in depth throughout the remainder of this book.

Project management involves applying knowledge, skills, and techniques during the course of the project to accomplish the project requirements. It is the responsibility of the project manager to ensure that project management techniques are applied and followed.

Exam Spotlight

For the exam, remember that *project management* is a set of tools and techniques that are used to organize the work of the project to help bring about a successful project.

Project management is a process that includes planning, putting the project plan into action, and measuring progress and performance. It involves identifying the project requirements, establishing project objectives, balancing constraints, and taking the needs and expectations of the key stakeholders into consideration. Planning is one of the most important functions you'll perform during the course of a project. It sets the standard for the rest of the project's life and is used to track future project performance. Before we begin the planning process, let's look at some of the ways the work of project management is organized.

Programs

Programs are groups of related projects that are managed using the same techniques in a coordinated fashion. When projects are managed collectively as programs, they capitalize on benefits that wouldn't be achievable if the projects were managed separately. This would be the case where a very large program exists with many subprojects under it—for example, building a new shopping mall. Many subprojects exist underneath this program, such as excavation, construction, interior design, store placement, marketing, facilities management, and so on. Each of the subprojects is really a project unto itself. Each subproject has its own project manager, who reports to a project manager with responsibility over several of the areas, who in turn reports to the head project manager over the entire program. All the projects are related and are managed together so that collective benefits are realized and controls are implemented and managed in a coordinated fashion. Sometimes programs involve aspects of ongoing operations as well. After the shopping mall in our example is built, the management of the facility becomes the ongoing operations part of this program. The management of this collection of projects is called *program management*. *Program management* involves centrally managing and coordinating groups of related projects to meet the objectives of the program.

Portfolios

Portfolios are collections of programs and projects that meet a specific business goal or objective. Let's say our company is in the construction business. Our organization has several business units: retail, single-family residential, and multifamily residential. All projects and programs associated with the retail business unit belong to the retail portfolio. The program I talked about in the preceding section (the collection of projects associated with building the new shopping mall) is one of the programs that belongs to the retail portfolio. Other programs and projects could be within this portfolio as well. The objective of any program or project in this portfolio is to meet the strategic objectives of the portfolio, which in turn should meet the objectives of the department and ultimately the corporation. *Portfolio management* encompasses managing the collections of programs and projects in the portfolio. This includes weighing the value of each project, or potential project, against the portfolio's strategic objectives. It also concerns monitoring active projects for adherence to objectives, balancing the portfolio among the other investments of the organization, and assuring the efficient use of resources. Portfolio management is generally performed by a senior manager in the organization.

Exam Spotlight

Many project managers find they manage more than one project at time. For example, a project manager in the human resources department might be working on a time-tracking project, a new website, and a new employee training class all at the same time. You could make the argument that this is portfolio management. However, for the exam, remember that portfolio management means the collection of programs and projects as they pertain to the strategic objectives of the portfolio.

Project Management Offices

The concept of a *project management office*, sometimes referred to as the PMO, has been around for several years. You'll find that many organizations are establishing PMOs in many different forms. PMOs might also be called *project offices* or *program management offices*. The PMO is usually a centralized organizational unit that oversees the management of projects and programs throughout the organization. The most common reason a company starts a project management office is to establish and maintain procedures and standards for project management methodologies. In some organizations, project managers and team members might report directly to the PMO and are assigned to projects as they are initiated. In other organizations, the PMO provides support functions only for projects and trains others in project management procedures and techniques. Still others, depending on their size and function, have experts available that assist project managers in project planning, estimating, and business assumption verification tasks. They serve as mentors to junior-level project managers and act as consultants to the senior project managers.

A PMO can exist in all organizational structures—functional, matrix, or projectized. It might have full authority to oversee projects, including the authority to cancel projects, or it might serve only in an advisory role.

The PMO usually has responsibility for maintaining and archiving project documentation for future reference. This office compares project goals with project progress and gives feedback to the project teams. It also measures the project performance of active projects and suggests corrective actions. The PMO evaluates completed projects for their adherence to the project plan and asks questions like "Did the project meet the time frames established?" and "Did it stay within budget?" and "Was the quality acceptable?"

Project management offices are becoming more common in organizations today, if for no other reason than to serve as a collection point for project documentation. Some PMOs are fairly sophisticated and prescribe the standards and methodologies to be used in all project phases across the enterprise. Still others provide all these functions and also offer project management consulting services. However, the establishment of a PMO is not required in order for you to apply good project management practices to your next project.

There Ought to Be a Law

The importance of practicing sound project management techniques has grown significantly over the past several years. The State of Colorado recently passed legislation requiring project managers on large projects conducted by state employees or vendors working on behalf of the state to be certified in project management best practices. This was an attempt to increase the probability of project success and reduce risk. We all know that certified project managers are not a guarantee of project success. But the State of Colorado will likely see more projects delivered on time, on budget, and within scope because of the application of best practices in this area and because their project managers are highly trained and have a great deal of experience at managing projects.

Defining Skills Every Good Project Manager Needs

Many times, organizations will knight their technical experts as project managers. The skill and expertise that made them stars in their technical fields are mistakenly thought to translate into project management skills. This is not necessarily so.

Project managers are generalists with many skills in their repertoires. They are also problem solvers who wear many hats. Project managers might indeed possess technical skills, but technical skills are not a prerequisite for sound project management skills. Your project team should include a few technical experts, and these are the people whom the project manager will rely on for technical details. Understanding and applying good project management techniques, along with a solid understanding of general management skills, are career builders for all aspiring project managers.

Project managers have been likened to small-business owners. They need to know a little bit about every aspect of management. General management skills include every area of management, from accounting to strategic planning, supervision, personnel administration, and more. General management skills are called into play on every project. But some projects require specific skills in certain application areas. Application areas consist of categories of projects that have common elements. These elements, or application areas, can be defined several ways: by industry group (automotive, pharmaceutical), by department (accounting, marketing), and by technical (software development, engineering) or management (procurement, research and development) specialties. These application areas are usually concerned with disciplines, regulations, and the specific needs of the project, the customer, or the industry. For example, most governments have specific procurement rules that apply to their projects that wouldn't be applicable in the construction industry. The pharmaceutical industry is acutely interested in regulations set forth by the Food and Drug Administration, whereas the automotive industry has little or no concern for either of these types of regulations. Having experience in the application area you're working in will give you a leg up when it comes to project management. Although you can call in the experts who have application area knowledge, it doesn't hurt for you to understand the specific aspects of the application areas of your project.

The general management skills listed in this section are the foundation of good project management practices. Your mastery of them (or lack thereof) will likely affect project outcomes. The various skills of a project manager can be broken out in a more or less declining scale of importance. We'll look at an overview of these skills now, and I'll discuss each in more detail in subsequent chapters.

Communication Skills

One of the single most important characteristics of a first-rate project manager is excellent communication skills. Written and oral communications are the backbone of all successful projects. Many forms of communication will exist during the life of your project. As the creator or manager of most of the project communication (project documents, meeting updates, status reports, and so on), it's your job to ensure that the information is explicit, clear, and complete so that your audience will have no trouble understanding what has been communicated. Once the information has been distributed, it is the responsibility of the person receiving the information to make sure they understand it.

 Many forms of communication and communication styles exist. I'll discuss them more in depth in Chapter 8, "Developing the Project Team."

Organizational and Planning Skills

Organizational and planning skills are closely related and probably the most important, after communication skills, a project manager can possess. Organization takes on many forms. As project manager, you'll have project documentation, requirements information, memos, project reports, personnel records, vendor quotes, contracts, and much more, to track and be able to locate at a moment's notice. You will also have to organize meetings, put together teams, and perhaps manage and organize media release schedules, depending on your project.

Time management skills are closely related to organizational skills. It's difficult to stay organized without an understanding of how you're managing your time. I recommend you attend a time management class if you've never been to one. They have some great tips and techniques to help you prioritize problems and interruptions, prioritize your day, and manage your time.

I discuss planning extensively throughout the course of this book. There isn't any aspect of project management that doesn't first involve planning. Planning skills go hand in hand with organizational skills. Combining these two with excellent communication skills is almost a sure guarantee of your success in the project management field.

Budgeting Skills

Project managers establish and manage budgets and therefore need some knowledge of finance and accounting principles. Especially important in this skill area is the ability to perform cost estimates for project budgeting. Different methods are available to determine the project costs. They range from estimating individual activities and rolling the estimates up to estimating the project's cost in one big chunk. I'll discuss these methods more fully in later chapters.

After a budget is determined, you can start spending. This sounds more exciting than it actually is. Reading and understanding vendor quotes, preparing or overseeing purchase orders, and reconciling invoices are budgeting skills that the project manager will use on most projects. These costs will be linked back to project activities and expense items in the project's budget.

Conflict Management Skills

Show me a project, and I'll show you problems. All projects have some problems, as does, in fact, much of everyday life. Isn't that what they say builds character? But I digress.

Conflict management involves solving problems. Problem solving is really a twofold process. First, you must define the problem by separating the causes from the symptoms. Often when defining problems, you end up just describing the symptoms instead of really getting to the heart of what's causing the problem. To avoid that, ask yourself questions like "Is it an internal or external problem?" and "Is it a technical problem?" and "Are there interpersonal problems between team members?" and "Is it managerial?" and "What are the potential impacts or consequences?" These kinds of questions will help you get to the cause of the problem.

Next, after you have defined the problem, you have some decisions to make. It will take a little time to examine and analyze the problem, the situation causing it, and the alternatives available. After this analysis, the project manager will determine the best course of action to take and implement the decision. The timing of the decision is often as important as the decision itself. If you make a good decision but implement it too late, it might turn into a bad decision.

Negotiation and Influencing Skills

Effective problem solving requires negotiation and influencing skills. We all utilize negotiation skills in one form or another every day. For example, on a nightly basis I am asked, "Honey, what do you want for dinner?" Then the negotiations begin, and the fried chicken versus swordfish discussion commences. Simply put, negotiating is working with others to come to an agreement.

Negotiation on projects is necessary in almost every area of the project, from scope definition to budgets, contracts, resource assignments, and more. This might involve one-on-one negotiation or with teams of people, and it can occur many times throughout the project.

Influencing is convincing the other party that swordfish is a better choice than fried chicken, even if fried chicken is what they want. It's also the ability to get things done through others. Influencing requires an understanding of the formal and informal structure of all the organizations involved in the project.

Power and politics are techniques used to influence people to perform. *Power* is the ability to get people to do things they wouldn't do otherwise. It's also the ability to change minds and the course of events and to influence outcomes.

I'll discuss power further in Chapter 8.

Politics involve getting groups of people with different interests to cooperate creatively even in the midst of conflict and disorder.

These skills will be utilized in all areas of project management. Start practicing now because, guaranteed, you'll need these skills on your next project.

Leadership Skills

Leaders and *managers* are not synonymous terms. Leaders impart vision, gain consensus for strategic goals, establish direction, and inspire and motivate others. Managers focus on results and are concerned with getting the job done according to the requirements. Even though leaders and managers are not the same, project managers must exhibit the characteristics of both during different times on the project. Understanding when to switch from leadership to management and then back again is a finely tuned and necessary talent.

Team-Building and Motivating Skills

Project managers will rely heavily on team-building and motivational skills. Teams are often formed with people from different parts of the organization. These people might or might not have worked together before, so some component of team-building groundwork might involve the project manager. The project manager will set the tone for the project team and will help the team members work through the various stages of team development to become fully functional. Motivating the team, especially during long projects or when experiencing a lot of bumps along the way, is another important role the project manager fulfills during the course of the project.

An interesting caveat to the team-building role is that project managers many times are responsible for motivating team members who are not their direct reports. This has its own set of challenges and dilemmas. One way to help this situation is to ask the functional manager to allow you to participate in your project team members' performance reviews. Use the negotiation and influencing skills I talked about earlier to make sure you're part of this process.

Now that you've been properly introduced to some of the skills you need in your tool kit, you'll know to be prepared to communicate, solve problems, lead, and negotiate your way through your next project.

A Mile Wide and an Inch Deep

Project managers are an interesting bunch. They know a little bit about a lot of topics and are excellent communicators. Or, as one person said, they're "a mile wide and an inch deep." They have the ability to motivate people, even those who have no reason to be loyal to the project, and they can make the hard-line calls when necessary. Project managers can get caught in sticky situations that occasionally require making decisions that are good for the company (or the customer) but aren't good for certain stakeholders. These offended stakeholders will then drag their feet, and the project manager has to play the heavy in order to motivate and gain their cooperation again. Some organizations hire contract project managers to run their large, company-altering projects, just because they don't want to burn out a key employee in this role. Fortunately, that doesn't happen often.

Understanding Organizational Structures

Just as projects are unique, so are the organizations in which they're carried out. Organizations have their own styles and cultures that influence how project work is performed. One of the keys to determining the type of organization you work in is measuring how much authority senior management is willing to delegate to project managers. Although uniqueness abounds in business cultures, all organizations are structured in one of three ways: functional, projectized, or matrix. Variations and combinations exist among these three structures, such as a projectized structure within a functional organization and weak matrix, balanced matrix, and strong matrix organizations.

It pays to know and understand the organizational structure and the culture of the entity in which you're working. Companies with aggressive cultures that are comfortable in a leading-edge position within their industries are highly likely to take on risky projects. Project managers who are willing to suggest new ideas and projects that have never been undertaken before are likely to receive a warm reception in this kind of environment. Conversely, organizational cultures that are risk averse and prefer the follow-the-leader position within their industries are highly unlikely to take on risky endeavors. Project managers with risk-seeking, aggressive styles are likely to receive a cool reception in a culture like this.

The level of authority the project manager enjoys is denoted by the organizational structure. For example, a project manager within a functional organization has little to no formal authority. And their title might not be project manager; instead, they might be called a *project leader*, a *project coordinator*, or perhaps a *project expeditor*.

We'll now take a look at each of these types of organizations individually to better understand how the project management role works in each one.

Functional Organizations

One common type of organization is the *functional organization.* Chances are you have worked in this type of organization. This is probably the oldest style of organization and is therefore known as the traditional approach to organizing businesses.

Functional organizations are centered on specialties and grouped by function, which is why it's called *functional organization.* As an example, the organization might have a human resources department, finance department, marketing department, and so on. The work in these departments is specialized and requires people who have the skill sets and experiences in these specialized functions to perform specific duties for the department. Figure 1.2 shows a typical organizational chart for a functional organization.

You can see that this type of organization is set up to be a hierarchy. Staff personnel report to managers who report to department heads who report to vice presidents who report to the CEO. In other words, each employee reports to only one manager; ultimately, one person at the top is in charge. Many companies today, as well as governmental agencies, are structured in a hierarchical fashion. In organizations like this, be aware of the chain of command. A strict chain of command might exist, and the corporate culture might dictate that you follow it. Roughly translated: *Don't talk to the big boss without first talking to your boss who talks to their boss who talks to the big boss.* Wise project managers should determine whether there is a chain of command, how strictly it's enforced, and how the chain is linked before venturing outside it.

FIGURE 1.2   Functional organizational chart

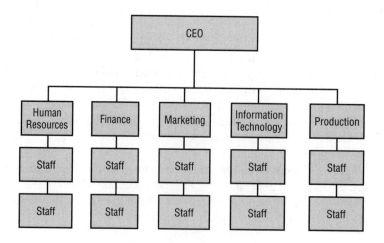

Each department or group in a functional organization is managed independently and has a limited span of control. Marketing doesn't run the finance department or its projects, for example. The marketing department is concerned with its own functions and projects. If it were necessary for the marketing department to get input from the finance department on a project, the marketing team members would follow the chain of command. A marketing manager would speak to a manager in finance to get the needed information and then pass it back down to the project team.

Human Resources in a Functional Organization

Commonalities exist among the personnel assigned to the various departments in a functional organization. In theory, people with similar skills and experiences are easier to manage as a group. Instead of scattering them throughout the organization, it is more efficient to keep them functioning together. Work assignments are easily distributed to those who are best suited for the task when everyone with the same skill works together. Usually, the supervisors and managers of these workers are experienced in the area they supervise and are able to recommend training and career enrichment activities for their employees.

 Workers in functional organizations specialize in an area of expertise—finance or personnel administration, for instance—and then become very good at their specialty.

People in a functional organization can see a clear upward career path. An assistant budget analyst might be promoted to a budget analyst and then eventually to a department manager over many budget analysts.

The Downside of Functional Organizations

Functional organizations have their disadvantages. If this is the kind of organization you work in, you probably have experienced some of them.

One of the greatest disadvantages for the project manager is that they have little to no formal authority. This does not mean project managers in functional organizations are doomed to failure. Many projects are undertaken and successfully completed within this type of organization. Good communication and interpersonal and influencing skills on the part of the project manager are required to bring about a successful project under this structure.

In a functional organization, the vice president or senior department manager is usually the one responsible for projects. The title of project manager denotes authority, and in a functional structure, that authority rests with the VP.

Managing Projects in a Functional Organization

Projects are typically undertaken in a divided approach in a functional organization. For example, the marketing department will work on its portion of the project and then hand it off to the manufacturing department to complete its part, and so on. The work the marketing department does is considered a marketing project, while the work the manufacturing department does is considered a manufacturing project.

Some projects require project team members from different departments to work together at the same time on various aspects of the project. Project team members in this structure will more than likely remain loyal to their functional managers. The functional manager is responsible for their performance reviews, and their career opportunities lie within the functional department—not within the project team. Exhibiting leadership skills by forming a common vision regarding the project and the ability to motivate people to work toward that vision are great skills to exercise in this situation. As previously mentioned, it also doesn't hurt to have the project manager work with the functional manager in contributing to the employee's performance review.

Resource Pressures in a Functional Organization

Competition for resources and project priorities can become fierce when multiple projects are undertaken within a functional organization. For example, in my organization, it's common to have competing project requests from three or more departments all vying for the same resources. Thrown into the heap is the requirement to make, for example, mandated tax law changes, which automatically usurps all other priorities. This sometimes causes frustration and political infighting. One department thinks their project is more important than another and will do anything to get that project pushed ahead of the others. Again, it takes great skill and diplomatic abilities to keep projects on track and functioning smoothly. In a later chapter, I'll discuss the importance of gaining stakeholder buy-in and of prioritization and communication distribution to avert some of these problems.

Project managers have little authority in functional organizations, but with the right skills, they can successfully accomplish many projects. Table 1.1 highlights the advantages and disadvantages of this type of organization.

TABLE 1.1   Functional Organizations

Advantages	Disadvantages
There is an enduring organizational structure.	Project managers have little to no formal authority.
There is a clear career path with separation of functions, allowing specialty skills to flourish.	Multiple projects compete for limited resources and priority.
Employees have one supervisor with a clear chain of command.	Project team members are loyal to the functional manager.

Projectized Organizations

Projectized organizations are nearly the opposite of functional organizations. The focus of this type of organization is the project itself. The idea behind a projectized organization is to develop loyalty to the project, not to a functional manager.

Figure 1.3 shows a typical organizational chart for a projectized organization.

FIGURE 1.3   Projectized organizational chart

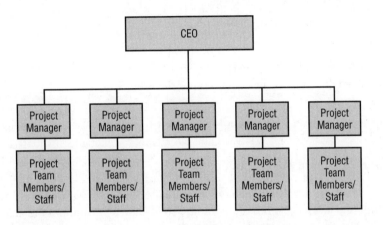

Organizational resources are dedicated to projects and project work in purely projectized organizations. Project managers almost always have ultimate authority over the project in this structure and report directly to the CEO. In a purely projectized organization, supporting functions such as human resources and accounting might report directly to the project manager as well. Project managers are responsible for making decisions regarding the project and acquiring and assigning resources. They have the authority to choose and assign resources from other areas in the organization or to hire them from outside if needed. For example, if there isn't enough money in the budget to hire additional resources, the project manager will have to come up with alternatives to solve this problem. This is known as a *constraint*. Project managers in all organizational structures are limited by the triple constraints commonly known as project scope, schedule, and cost (or budget). Quality is sometimes considered a constraint, and it's generally affected by scope, schedule, and/or cost. We'll talk more about constraints in Chapter 2, "Creating the Project Charter and Preliminary Scope Statement."

Teams are formed and often *co-located*, which means team members physically work at the same location. Project team members report to the project manager, not to a functional or departmental manager. One obvious drawback to a projectized organization is that project team members might find themselves out of work at the end of the project. An example of this might be a consultant who works on a project until completion and then is put on the bench or let go at the end of the project. Some inefficiency exists in this kind of organization when it comes to resource utilization. If you have a situation where you need a highly specialized skill at certain times throughout the project, the resource you're using to perform this function might be idle during other times in the project.

In summary, you can identify projectized organizations in several ways:

- Project managers have ultimate authority over the project.
- The focus of the organization is the project.
- The organization's resources are focused on projects and project work.
- Team members are co-located.
- Loyalties are formed to the project, not to a functional manager.
- Project teams are dissolved at the conclusion of the project.

 Real World Scenario

The Projectized Graphic Artist

You've been appointed project manager for your company's website design and implementation. You're working in a projectized organization, so you have the authority to acquire and assign resources. You put together your team, including programmers, technical writers, testers, and business analysts. Debbie, a highly qualified graphic arts designer, is also part of your team. Debbie's specialized graphic arts skills are needed only at certain times throughout the project. When she has completed the graphic design portion of the screen she's working on, she doesn't have anything else to do until the next page is ready. Depending on how involved the project is and how the work is structured, days or weeks might pass before Debbie's skills are needed. This is where the inefficiency occurs in a purely projectized organization. The project manager will have to find other duties that Debbie can perform during these down times. It's not practical to let her go and then hire her back when she's needed again.

In this situation, you might assign Debbie to other project duties when she's not working on graphic design. Perhaps she can edit the text for the web pages or assist with the design of the upcoming marketing campaign. You might also share Debbie's time with another project manager in the organization.

During the planning process, you will discover the skills and abilities of all your team members so that you can plan their schedules accordingly and eliminate idle time.

Matrix Organizations

Matrix organizations came about to minimize the differences between, and take advantage of, the strengths and weaknesses of functional and projectized organizations. The idea at play here is that the best of both organizational structures can be realized by combining them into one. The project objectives are fulfilled and good project management techniques are utilized while still maintaining a hierarchical structure in the organization.

Employees in a matrix organization report to one functional manager and to at least one project manager. It's possible that employees could report to multiple project managers if they are working on multiple projects at one time. Functional managers pick up the administrative portion of the duties and assign employees to projects. They also monitor the work of their employees on the various projects. Project managers are responsible for executing the project and giving out work assignments based on project activities. Project managers and functional managers share the responsibility of performance reviews for the employee.

In a nutshell, functional managers assign employees to projects, while project managers assign tasks associated with the project in a matrix organization.

Matrix organizations have unique characteristics. We'll look at how projects are conducted and managed and how project and functional managers share the work in this organizational structure next.

Project Focus in a Matrix Organization

Matrix organizations allow project managers to focus on the project and project work just as in a projectized organization. The project team is free to focus on the project objectives with minimal distractions from the functional department.

Project managers should take care when working up activity and project estimates for the project in a matrix organization. The estimates should be given to the functional managers for input before publishing. The functional manager is the one in charge of assigning or freeing up resources to work on projects. If the project manager is counting on a certain employee to work on the project at a certain time, the project manager should determine their availability up front with the functional manager. Project estimates might have to be modified if it's discovered that the employee they were counting on is not available when needed.

Balance of Power in a Matrix Organization

As we've discussed, a lot of communication and negotiation takes place between the project manager and the functional manager. This calls for a balance of power between the two, or one will dominate the other.

In a strong matrix organization, the balance of power rests with the project manager. They have the ability to strong-arm the functional managers into giving up their best resources for projects. Sometimes, more resources than necessary are assembled for the project, and then project managers negotiate these resources among themselves, cutting out the functional manager altogether, as you can see in Figure 1.4.

On the other end of the spectrum is the weak matrix (see Figure 1.5). As you would suspect, the functional managers have all the power in this structure. Project managers are really project coordinators or expeditors with part-time responsibilities on projects in a weak matrix organization. Project managers have little to no authority, just as in the functional organization. On the other hand, the functional managers have a lot of authority and make all the work assignments. The project manager simply expedites the project.

FIGURE 1.4   Strong matrix organizational chart

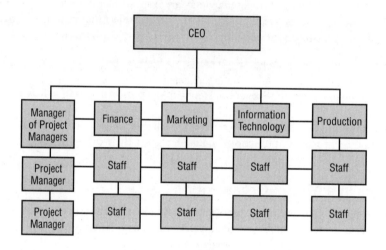

FIGURE 1.5   Weak matrix organizational chart

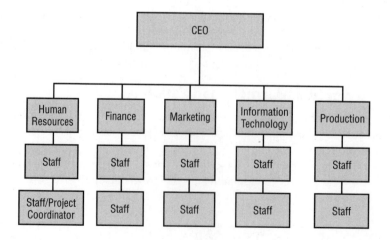

FIGURE 1.6 Balanced matrix organizational chart

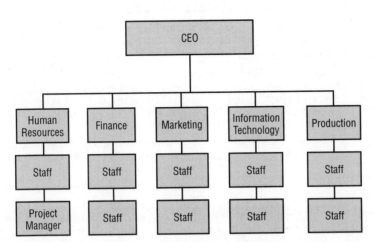

In between the weak matrix and the strong matrix is an organizational structure called the *balanced matrix* (see Figure 1.6). The features of the balanced matrix are what I've been discussing throughout this section. The power is balanced between project managers and functional managers. Each manager has responsibility for their parts of the project or organization, and employees get assigned to projects based on the needs of the project, not the strength or weakness of the manager's position.

Matrix organizations have subtle differences, and it's important to understand their differences for the PMP exam. The easiest way to remember them is that the weak matrix has many of the same characteristics as the functional organization, while the strong matrix has many of the same characteristics as the projectized organization. The balanced matrix is exactly that—a balance between weak and strong, where the project manager shares authority and responsibility with the functional manager. Table 1.2 compares all three structures.

TABLE 1.2 Comparing Matrix Structures

	Weak Matrix	**Balanced Matrix**	**Strong Matrix**
Project Manager's Title:	Project coordinator, project leader, or project expeditor	Project manager	Project manager
Project Manager's Focus:	Split focus between project and functional responsibilities	Projects and project work	Projects and project work
Project Manager's Power:	Minimal authority and power	Balance of authority and power	Significant authority and power

TABLE 1.2   Comparing Matrix Structures *(continued)*

	Weak Matrix	Balanced Matrix	Strong Matrix
Project Manager's Time:	Part-time on projects	Full-time on projects	Full-time on projects
Organization Style:	Most like functional organization	Blend of both weak and strong matrix	Most like a projectized organization
Project Manager Reports To:	Functional manager	A functional manager, but shares authority and power	Manager of project managers

Most organizations today use some combination of the organizational structures described here. They're a composite of functional, projectized, and matrix structures. It's rare that an organization would be purely functional or purely projectized. For example, projectized structures can coexist within functional organizations.

In the case of a high-profile, critical project, the functional organization might appoint a special project team to work only on that project. The team is structured outside the bounds of the functional organization, and the project manager has ultimate authority for the project. This is a workable project management approach and ensures open communication between the project manager and team members. At the end of the project, the project team is dissolved, and the project members return to their functional areas to resume their usual duties.

Exam Spotlight

Understand the characteristics of each organizational structure and their strengths and weaknesses for the exam.

Organizations are unique, as are the projects they undertake. Understanding the organizational structure will help you, as a project manager, with the cultural influences and communication avenues that exist in the organization to gain cooperation and successfully bring your projects to a close.

Understanding Project Life Cycles and Project Management Processes

Project life cycles are similar to the life cycle that parents experience raising their children to adulthood. Children start out as infants and generate lots of excitement wherever they go.

However, not much is known about them at first. So, you study them as they grow, and you assess their needs. Over time, they mature and grow (and cost a lot of money in the process), until one day the parents' job is done.

Projects start out just like this and progress along a similar path. Someone comes up with a great idea for a project and actively solicits support for it. The project, after being approved, progresses through the intermediate phases to the ending phase, where it is completed and closed out.

Project Phases and Project Life Cycles

All projects are divided into phases, and all projects, large or small, have a similar life cycle structure. At a minimum, a project will have a beginning or initiation phase, an intermediate phase or phases, and an ending phase. The number of phases depends on the project complexity and the industry. For example, information technology projects might progress through phases such as requirements, design, program, test, and implement. All the collective phases the project progresses through in concert are called the *project life cycle*.

The end of each phase allows the project manager, stakeholders, and project sponsor the opportunity to determine whether the project should continue to the next phase. In order to progress to the next phase, the deliverable from the phase before it must be reviewed for accuracy and approved. As each phase is completed, it's handed off to the next phase. You'll look at handoffs and progressions through these phases next.

Handoffs

Project phases evolve through the life cycle in a series of phase sequences called *handoffs*, or technical transfers. The end of one phase sequence typically marks the beginning of the next. However, the completion of one phase does not automatically signal the beginning of the next phase. For example, in the construction industry, feasibility studies often take place in the beginning phase of a project.

The purpose of the *feasibility study* is to determine whether the project is worth undertaking and whether the project will be profitable to the organization. A feasibility study is a preliminary assessment of the viability of the project; the viability or perhaps marketability of the product, service, or result of the project; and the project's value to the organization. It might also determine whether the product, service, or result of the project is safe and meets industry or governmental standards and regulations. The completion and approval of the feasibility study triggers the beginning of the requirements phase, where requirements are documented and then handed off to the design phase, where blueprints are produced. The feasibility might also show that the project is not worth pursuing and the project is then terminated; thus, the next phase never begins.

Phase Completion

You will recognize phase completion because each phase has a specific *deliverable*, or multiple deliverables, that marks the end of the phase. A *deliverable* is an output that must be produced, reviewed, and approved to bring the phase or project to completion. Deliverables are tangible and can be measured and easily proved. For instance, a hypothetical deliverable produced in the beginning phase of a construction industry project would be the feasibility study.

Deliverables might also include things such as design documents, project budgets, blueprints, project schedules, prototypes, and so on. This analysis allows those involved with the opportunity to determine whether the project should continue to the next phase. The feasibility study might show that environmental impacts of an enormous nature would result if the construction project were undertaken at the proposed location. Based on this information, a go or no-go decision can be made at the end of this phase. The end of a phase gives the project manager the ability to discover, address, and take corrective action against errors discovered during the phase.

The *PMBOK Guide* states that phase-ending reviews are also known by a few other names: *phase exits, phase gates,* or *kill points.*

Sometimes phases are overlapped to shorten or compress the project schedule. This is called *fast tracking.* Fast tracking means that a later phase is started prior to completing and approving the phase, or phases, that come before it. This technique is used to shorten the overall duration of the project.

Most projects follow phase sequences within a project life cycle and, as a result, have the following characteristics in common: In the beginning phase, which is where the project is initiated, costs are low, and few team members are assigned to the project. As the project progresses, costs and staffing increase and then taper off at the closing phase. The potential that the project will come to a successful ending is lowest at the beginning of the project; its chance for success increases as the project progresses through its phases and life cycle stages. Risk is highest at the beginning of the project and gradually decreases the closer the project comes to completion. Stakeholders have the greatest chance of influencing the project and the characteristics of the product, service, or result of the project in the beginning phases and have less and less influence as the project progresses. This same phenomenon exists within the project management processes as well. We'll look at those next.

Project Management Process Groups

Project management processes organize and describe the work of the project. The *PMBOK Guide* describes five process groups used to accomplish this end. These processes are performed by people and, much like project phases, are interrelated and dependent on one another.

These are the five project management process groups that the *PMBOK Guide* documents:

- Initiating
- Planning
- Executing
- Monitoring and Controlling
- Closing

All these process groups have individual processes that collectively make up the group. For example, the Initiating process group has two processes called Develop Project Charter and

Develop Preliminary Project Scope Statement. Collectively, these process groups—including all their individual processes—make up the project management process. Projects start with the Initiating process and progress through all the processes in the Planning process group, the Executing process group, and so on, until the project is successfully completed or it's canceled. All projects must complete the Closing processes, even if the project is killed. Phase handoffs (the design phase handoff to manufacturing, for example) also occur within these life cycles.

Don't confuse project phases and life cycles with the project management process groups. *PMBOK Guide* makes a strong point of this. Project phases and life cycles describe how the work associated with the product of the project will be completed. For example, a construction project might have phases such as feasibility study, design, build, inspection, and turnover. The five project management process groups (Initiating, Planning, Executing, Monitoring and Controlling, and Closing) organize and describe how the project activities will be conducted in order to meet the project requirements. These processes are generally performed for each phase of a large project. The five process groups are the heart of the *PMBOK Guide* and the exam. As you progress through this book, be certain you understand each of these processes as they're described in the *PMBOK Guide*.

Let's start with a high-level overview of each process group. The remainder of this book will cover each of these processes in detail. If you want to peek ahead, Appendix A on the CD lists each of the process groups, the individual processes that make up each process group, and the Knowledge Areas in which they belong. (I'll introduce Knowledge Areas in the "The Project Management *Knowledge Areas*" section later in this chapter.)

Initiating

The *Initiating* process group, as its name implies, occurs at the beginning of the project and at the beginning of each project phase for large projects. Initiating acknowledges that a project, or the next project phase, should begin. This process group grants the approval to commit the organization's resources to working on the project or phase and authorizes the project manager to begin working on the project. The outputs of the Initiating process group, including the project charter and preliminary project scope statement, become inputs into the Planning process group.

Planning

The *Planning* process is the process group of formulating and revising project goals and objectives and creating the project management plan that will be used to achieve the goals the project was undertaken to address. The Planning process group also involves determining alternative courses of action and selecting from among the best of those to produce the project's goals. This process group is where the project requirements are fleshed out and stakeholders are identified. Planning has more processes than any of the other project management process groups. In order to carry out their functions, the Executing, Monitoring and Controlling, and Closing process groups all rely on the Planning processes and the documentation produced during the Planning processes. Project managers will perform frequent iterations of the Planning processes prior to project completion. Projects are unique and, as such, have never been done before. Therefore, Planning must encompass all areas of project management and consider budgets, activity definition, scope planning, schedule development, risk identification, staff acquisition, procurement planning, and more. The greatest conflicts a project manager will encounter in this process group are project prioritization issues.

Executing

The *Executing* process group involves putting the project management plan into action. It's here that the project manager will coordinate and direct project resources to meet the objectives of the project plan. The Executing process keeps the project plan on track and ensures that future execution of project plans stays in line with project objectives. This process group is typically where approved changes are implemented. The Executing process group will utilize the most project time and resources, and as a result, costs are usually highest during the Executing process. Project managers will experience the greatest conflicts over schedules in this cycle.

Monitoring and Controlling

The *Monitoring and Controlling* process group is where project performance measurements are taken and analyzed to determine whether the project is staying true to the project plan. The idea is to identify problems as soon as possible and apply corrective action to control the work of the project and assure successful outcomes. For example, if you discover that variances exist, you'll apply corrective action to get the project activities realigned with the project plan. This might require additional passes through the Planning processes to adjust project activities, resources, schedules, budgets, and so on.

 Monitoring and Controlling is used to track the progress of work being performed and identify problems and variances within a process group as well as the project as a whole.

Closing

The *Closing* process group is probably the most often skipped process group in project management. Closing brings a formal, orderly end to the activities of a project phase or to the project itself. Once the project objectives have been met, most of us are ready to move on to the next project. However, Closing is important because all the project information is gathered and stored for future reference. The documentation collected during the Closing process group can be reviewed and utilized to avert potential problems on future projects. Contract closeout occurs here, and formal acceptance and approval are obtained from project stakeholders.

> **Exam Spotlight**
>
> The project manager and project team are responsible for determining which processes within each process group are appropriate for the project on which you're working. This is called *tailoring*. You should consider the size and complexity of the project and the various inputs and outputs of each of the processes when determining which processes to implement and perform. Small independent projects might not require the rigor of each of the processes within a process group, but every process should be addressed and its level of implementation determined. Use your judgment when deciding which processes to follow, particularly for small projects.

Characteristics of the Process Groups

The progression through the project management process groups exhibits the same characteristics as progression through the project phases. That is, costs are lowest during the Initiating processes, and few team members are involved. Costs and staffing increase in the Executing process group and then decrease as you approach the Closing process group. The chances for success are lowest during Initiating and highest during Closing. The chances for risks occurring are higher during Initiating, Planning, and Executing, but the impacts of risks are greater during the later processes. Stakeholders have the greatest influence during the Initiating and Planning processes and less and less influence as you progress through Executing, Monitoring and Controlling, and Closing. To give you a better idea of when certain characteristics influence a project, refer to Table 1.3.

TABLE 1.3   Characteristics of the Project Process Groups

	Initiating	Planning	Executing	Monitoring and Controlling	Closing
Costs	Low	Low	Highest	Lower	Lowest
Staffing Levels	Low	Lower	High	High	Low
Chance for Successful Completion	Lowest	Low	Medium	High	Highest
Stakeholder Influence	Highest	High	Medium	Low	Lowest
Risk Probability	Lowest	Low	High	High	Lower

The Process Flow

You should not think of the five process groups as one-time processes that are performed as discrete elements. Rather, these processes interact and overlap with each other. They are *iterative* and might be revisited and revised throughout the project's life several times as the project is refined. The *PMBOK Guide* calls this process of going back through the process groups an *iterative process*. The conclusion of each process group allows the project manager and stakeholders to reexamine the business needs of the project and determine whether the project is satisfying those needs. And it is another opportunity to make a go or no-go decision.

Figure 1.7 shows the five process groups in a typical project. Keep in mind that during phases of a project, the Closing process group can provide input to the Initiating process group. For example, once the feasibility study discussed earlier is accepted or closed, it becomes input to the Initiating process group of the design phase.

FIGURE 1.7   Project management process groups

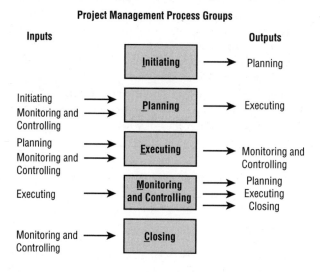

It's important to understand the flow of these processes for the exam. If you remember the processes and their inputs and outputs, it will help you when you're trying to decipher an exam question. The outputs of one process group become the inputs into the next process group (or the outputs might be a deliverable of the project). Sometimes just understanding which process the question is asking about will help you determine the answer. One trick you can use to memorize these processes is to remember syrup of ipecac. You probably have some of this poison antidote in your medicine cabinet at home. If you think of the Monitoring and Controlling process group as simply "Controlling," when you sound out the first initial of each of the processes, it sounds like "ipecac"—IPECC (Initiating, Planning, Executing, *Monitoring and* Controlling, and Closing).

As I stated earlier, individual processes make up each of the process groups. For example, the Closing life cycle process group consists of two processes: Close Project and Contract Closure. Each process takes inputs and uses them in conjunction with various tools and techniques to produce outputs.

 It's outside the scope of this book to explain all the inputs, tools and techniques, and outputs for each process in each process group (although each is listed in Appendix A). You'll find all the inputs, tools and techniques, and outputs detailed in the *PMBOK Guide*, and I highly recommend you get familiar with them.

Exam Spotlight

Understand each project management process group and all the processes that make up these groups. Appendix A on the CD contains a table of all the process, their inputs, their tools and techniques, their outputs, and the Knowledge Area in which they each belong. (I'll introduce Knowledge Areas in the "The Project Management *Knowledge Areas*" section later in this chapter.)

You'll see test questions regarding inputs, tools and techniques, and outputs of many of the processes within each process group. One way to keep them all straight is to remember that tools and techniques usually require action of some sort, be it measuring, applying some skill or technique, planning, or using expert judgment. Outputs are usually in the form of a deliverable. Remember that a deliverable is characterized with results or outcomes that can be measured, are tangible, and are provable. Last but not least, outputs from one process sometimes serve as inputs to another process.

Process Interactions

We've covered a lot of material, but I'll explain one more concept before the next section. As stated earlier, project managers must determine the processes that are appropriate for effectively managing a project based on the complexity and scope of the project, available resources, budget, and so on. As the project progresses, the project management processes might be revisited and revised to update the project management plan as more information becomes known. Underlying the concept that process groups are iterative is a cycle the *PMBOK Guide* describes as the Plan-Do-Check-Act cycle that was originally defined by Walter Shewhart and later modified by Edward Deming. The idea behind this concept is that each element in the cycle is results oriented. The results from the Plan cycle become inputs into the Do cycle, and so on, much like the way the project management process groups interact. The cycle interactions can be mapped to work in conjunction with the five project management process groups. For example, the Plan cycle maps to the Planning process group. Before going any further, here's a brief refresher:

- Project phases describe how the work required to produce the product of the project will be completed.

- Project management process groups organize and describe how the project activities will be completed in order to meet the goals of the project.

- The Plan-Do-Check-Act cycle is an underlying concept that shows the integrative nature of the process groups.

Figure 1.8 shows the relationships and interactions of the concepts you've learned so far. Please bear in mind that a simple figure can't get across all the interactions and iterative nature of these interactions; however, I think you'll see that the figure ties the basic elements of these concepts together.

FIGURE 1.8   Project management process groups

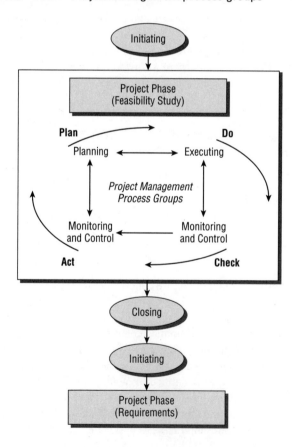

Exploring the Project Management Knowledge Areas

You can classify the processes from each project management process group in one more way. The *PMBOK Guide* groups these processes into nine categories that it calls the *Project Management Knowledge Areas*. These groupings, or Knowledge Areas, bring together processes that have characteristics in common. For example, the Project Cost Management Knowledge Area involves all aspects of the budgeting process, as you would suspect. Therefore, processes such as Cost Estimating, Cost Budgeting, and Cost Control belong to this Knowledge Area. Here's the tricky part—these processes don't belong to the same project management process groups (Cost Estimating and Cost Budgeting are part of the Planning process group, and Cost Control is part of the Monitoring and Controlling process group). Think of it this way: Knowledge Areas bring together processes by commonalities, whereas project management process groups are more or less the order you perform the project management processes (although remember you can come back through these processes more than once). The nine Knowledge Areas are as follows:

- Project Integration Management
- Project Scope Management
- Project Time Management
- Project Cost Management
- Project Quality Management
- Project Human Resource Management
- Project Communications Management
- Project Risk Management
- Project Procurement Management

Let's take a closer look at each Knowledge Area so you understand how they relate to the process groups. Included in each of the following sections are tables that illustrate the processes that make up that Knowledge Area and the project management process group to which each process belongs. This will help you see the big picture in terms of process groups compared to Knowledge Areas. I'll discuss each of the processes in the various Knowledge Areas throughout the book, but for now, you'll take a high-level look at each of them.

Exam Spotlight

The PMP exam will most likely have a question or two regarding the processes that make up a Knowledge Area. Remember that Knowledge Areas bring together processes by commonalities, so thinking about the knowledge area itself should tip you off to the processes that belong to it. Projects are executed in process group order, but the Knowledge Areas allow a project manager to think about groups of processes that require specific skills. This makes the job of assigning resources easier because team members with specific skills might be able to work on and complete several processes at once. To broaden your understanding of the Knowledge Areas, cross-reference the purposes and the processes that make up each Knowledge Area with the *PMBOK Guide*.

Project Integration Management

The Project Integration Management Knowledge Area comprises seven processes, as shown in Table 1.4.

TABLE 1.4   Project Integration Management

Process Name	Project Management Process Group
Develop Project Charter	Initiating
Develop Preliminary Project Scope Statement	Initiating
Develop Project Management Plan	Planning
Direct and Manage Project Execution	Executing
Monitor and Control Project Work	Monitoring and Controlling
Integrated Change Control	Monitoring and Controlling
Close Project	Closing

The Project Integration Management Knowledge Area is concerned with coordinating all aspects of the project plan and is highly interactive. This Knowledge Area involves identifying and defining the work of the project and combining, unifying, and integrating the appropriate processes. This Knowledge Area also takes into account satisfactorily meeting the requirements of the customer and stakeholder and managing their expectations.

Project planning, project execution, project work monitoring, and change control occur throughout the project and are repeated continuously while working on the project. Project planning and execution involve weighing the objectives of the project against the alternatives to bring the project to a successful completion. This includes making choices about how to effectively use resources and coordinating the work of the project on a continuous basis. Monitoring the work of the project involves anticipating potential problems and issues and dealing with them before they reach the critical point. Change control impacts the project plan, which in turn impacts the work of the project, which in turn can impact the project management plan, so you can see that these processes are tightly linked. The processes in this area, as with all the Knowledge Areas, also interact with other processes in the remaining Knowledge Areas. For example, the Close Project process uses outputs from the Contract Administration process and produces inputs to the Contract Closure process.

The Project Integration Management knowledge area has two tools for assisting with process integration: Earned Value Management (EVM) and project management software. EVM is a project-integrating methodology used in this knowledge area to integrate the processes and measure project performance through a project's life cycle. I'll further define EVM and talk more about project management software tools in Chapter 7, "Creating the Project Schedule and Budget."

Project Scope Management

The Project Scope Management Knowledge Area has five processes, as shown in Table 1.5.

TABLE 1.5   Project Scope Management

Process Name	Project Management Process Group
Scope Planning	Planning
Scope Definition	Planning
Create WBS	Planning
Scope Verification	Monitoring and Controlling
Scope Control	Monitoring and Controlling

Project Scope Management is concerned with defining all the work of the project and only the work needed to successfully meet the project goals. These processes are highly interactive. They define and control what is and what is not part of the project. Each process occurs at least once—and often many times—throughout the project's life.

Project Scope Management encompasses both product scope and project scope. *Product scope* concerns the characteristics of the product, service, or result of the project. It's measured against the product requirements to determine successful completion or fulfillment. The application area usually dictates the process tools and techniques you'll use to define and manage product scope. *Project scope* involves managing the work of the project and only the work of the project. Project scope is measured against the project management plan, the project scope statement, the work breakdown structure (WBS), and the WBS dictionary.

 To ensure a successful project, both product and project scope must be well integrated. This implies that Project Scope Management is well integrated with the other Knowledge Area processes.

Scope Planning, Scope Definition, Create WBS, Scope Verification, and Scope Control involve the following:

- Detailing the requirements of the product of the project
- Verifying those details using measurement techniques
- Creating a project scope management plan
- Creating a WBS
- Controlling changes to these processes

Project Time Management

The *Project Time Management* Knowledge Area has six processes, as shown in Table 1.6.

TABLE 1.6   Project Time Management

Process Name	Project Management Process Group
Activity Definition	Planning
Activity Sequencing	Planning
Activity Resource Estimating	Planning
Activity Duration Estimating	Planning
Schedule Development	Planning
Schedule Control	Monitoring and Controlling

This Knowledge Area is concerned with estimating the duration of the project plan activities, devising a project schedule, and monitoring and controlling deviations from the schedule. Collectively, this Knowledge Area deals with completing the project in a timely manner. Time management is an important aspect of project management because it concerns keeping the project activities on track and monitoring those activities against the project plan to ensure that the project is completed on time.

Although each process in this Knowledge Area occurs at least once in every project (and sometimes more), in many cases, particularly on small projects, Activity Sequencing, Activity Duration Estimating, and Schedule Development are completed as one activity. Only one person is needed to complete these processes for small projects, and they're all worked on at the same time.

Project Cost Management

As its name implies, the *Project Cost Management* Knowledge Area centers around costs and budgets. Table 1.7 shows the processes that make up this Knowledge Area.

TABLE 1.7   Project Cost Management

Process Name	Project Management Process Group
Cost Estimating	Planning
Cost Budgeting	Planning
Cost Control	Monitoring and Controlling

The activities in the Project Cost Management Knowledge Area establish cost estimates for resources, establish budgets, and keep watch over those costs to ensure that the project stays within the approved budget. This Knowledge Area is primarily concerned with the costs of resources, but you should think about other costs as well. For example, make certain to examine ongoing maintenance and support costs for software you're considering for the project.

Depending on the complexity of the project, these processes might need the involvement of more than one person. For example, the finance person might not have expertise about the resources documented in the staffing management plan so the project manager will need to bring in a staff member with those skills to assist with the activities in this process.

Two techniques are used in this Knowledge Area to decide among alternatives and improve the project process: life cycle costing and value engineering. The *life cycle costing* technique considers a group of costs collectively (such as acquisition, operations, disposal, and so on) when deciding among or comparing alternatives. The *value engineering* technique helps improve project schedules, profits, quality, and resource usage and optimizes life cycle costs, among others. These techniques can improve decision making, reduce costs, reduce activity durations, and improve the quality of the deliverables. Some application areas require additional financial analysis to help predict project performance. Techniques such as payback analysis, return on investment, and discounted cash flows are a few of the tools used to accomplish this.

I'll discuss these techniques and others in further detail in Chapter 2.

Project Quality Management

The *Project Quality Management* Knowledge Area is composed of three processes, as shown in Table 1.8.

TABLE 1.8   Project Quality Management

Process Name	Project Management Process Group
Quality Planning	Planning
Perform Quality Assurance	Executing
Perform Quality Control	Monitoring and Controlling

The *Project Quality Management* Knowledge Area assures that the project meets the requirements that it was undertaken to produce. This Knowledge Area focuses on product quality as well as on the quality of the project management process used during the project. These processes measure overall performance and monitor project results and compare them to the quality standards set out in the project-planning process to assure the customers will receive the product, service, or result they commissioned.

Project Human Resource Management

The *Project Human Resource Management* Knowledge Area consists of four processes, as shown in Table 1.9.

TABLE 1.9   Project Human Resource Management

Process Name	Project Management Process Group
Human Resource Planning	Planning
Acquire Project Team	Executing
Develop Project Team	Executing
Manage Project Team	Monitoring and Controlling

Project Human Resource Management involves all aspects of people management and personal interaction, including leading, coaching, dealing with conflict, conducting performance appraisals, and more. These processes ensure that the human resources assigned to the project are used in the most effective way possible. Some of the project participants whom you'll get to practice these skills on include stakeholders, team members, and customers. Each requires the use of different communication styles, leadership skills, and team-building skills. A good project manager knows when to enact certain skills and communication styles based on the situation.

Projects are unique and temporary and so usually are project teams. Teams are put together based on the skills and resources needed to complete the activities of the project, and many times project team members might not know one another. Because the makeup of each team is different and the stakeholders involved in the various stages of the project might change, you'll use different techniques at different times throughout the project to manage the processes in this Knowledge Area.

Project Communications Management

Four processes make up the *Project Communications Management* Knowledge Area, as shown in Table 1.10.

The processes in the Project Communications Management Knowledge Area are related to general communication skills, but they encompass much more than an exchange of information. Communication skills are considered general management skills that the project manager utilizes on a daily basis. The processes in the Process Communications Management Knowledge Area seek to ensure that all project information—including project plans, risk assessments, meeting notes, and more—is collected, documented, archived, and disposed of at the proper time. These processes also ensure that information is distributed and shared with stakeholders, management, and project members at appropriate times. When the project is closed, the information is archived and used as a reference for future projects. This is referred to as *historical information* in several project processes.

Everyone on the project has some involvement with this Knowledge Area because all project members will send and/or receive project communication throughout the life of the project. It is important that all team members and stakeholders understand how communication affects the project.

TABLE 1.10   Project Communication Management

Process Name	Project Management Process Group
Communications Planning	Planning
Information Distribution	Executing
Performance Reporting	Monitoring and Controlling
Manage Stakeholders	Monitoring and Controlling

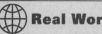 **Real World Scenario**

Time to Communicate

Communication management is probably the most important Knowledge Area on any project. And most project managers understand the importance of good communication skills and making sure stakeholders are informed of project status. I know a project manager who had difficulties getting time with the project sponsor. The project sponsor had agreed to meet with the project manager, had even set up the meetings himself, and then had canceled or simply hadn't shown up. The poor project manager was at wits end about how to communicate with the sponsor and get some answers to the questions she had. Her desk was not far outside the project sponsor's office. One day as she peeked around the corner of her cube, she decided if the sponsor wouldn't come to her, she would go to him. From then on, every time the sponsor left his office, she would jump up from her chair and ride with him on the elevator. He was a captive audience. She was able to get some easy questions answered and finally convince him, after the fourth or fifth elevator ride, that they needed regular face-to-face meetings. She understood the importance of communication and went to great lengths to make certain the sponsor did too.

Project Risk Management

Project Risk Management, as shown in Table 1.11, contains six processes.

TABLE 1.11   Project Risk Management

Process Name	Project Management Process Group
Risk Management Planning	Planning
Risk Identification	Planning
Qualitative Risk Analysis	Planning
Quantitative Risk Analysis	Planning
Risk Response Planning	Planning
Risk Monitoring and Control	Monitoring and Controlling

Risks include both threats to and opportunities within the project. The processes in this Knowledge Area are concerned with identifying, analyzing, and planning for potential risks, both positive and negative, that might impact the project. This means minimizing the probability and impact of negative risks while maximizing the probability and impact of positive risks. These processes are also used to identify the positive consequences of risk and exploit them to improve project objectives or discover efficiencies that might improve project performance.

Organizations will often combine several of these processes into one step. For example, Risk Identification, Qualitative Risk Analysis, and Quantitative Risk Analysis might be performed at the same time. The important factor of the Project Risk Management Knowledge Area is that you should strive to identify all the risks and develop responses for those with the greatest consequences to the project objectives.

Project Procurement Management

Six processes are in the *Project Procurement Management* Knowledge Area, as shown in Table 1.12.

The Project Procurement Management Knowledge Area includes the processes involved with purchasing goods or services from vendors, contractors, suppliers, and others outside the project team. When discussing the Project Procurement Management processes, it's assumed that the discussion is taking place from your perspective as a buyer, while sellers are external to the project team. Interestingly, the seller might manage their work as a project, particularly when the work is performed on contract, and you as the buyer become a key stakeholder in their project.

The remainder of this book will deal with processes and process groups as they occur in order (that is, Initiating, Planning, Executing, Monitoring and Controlling, and Closing), because this is the way you will encounter and manage them during a project.

TABLE 1.12   Project Procurement Management

Process Name	Project Management Process Group
Plan Purchases and Acquisitions	Planning
Plan Contracting	Planning
Request Seller Reponses	Executing
Select Sellers	Executing
Contract Administration	Monitoring and Controlling
Contract Closure	Closing

Understanding How This Applies to Your Next Project

As you can tell from this first chapter, managing projects is not for the faint of heart. You must master multiple skills and techniques in order to complete projects successfully. In your day-to-day work environment, it probably doesn't matter much if you're working in a functional or strong matrix organization. More important are your communication, conflict management, and negotiation and influencing skills. And good communications are the hallmark of successful projects. (We'll talk more about communication and give you some communication tips in the coming chapters.)

In any organizational structure, you'll find leaders, and you'll find people who have the title of leader. Again, the organizational structure itself probably isn't as important as knowing who the real leaders and influencers are in the organization. These are the people you'll lean on to help with difficult project decisions and hurdles.

I talked about the definition of a project in this chapter. You'd be surprised how many people think ongoing operations are projects. Here's a tip to help you explain the definition to your stakeholders: projects involve the five project process groups (Initiating through Closing). Ongoing operations typically involve the Planning, Executing, and Monitoring and Controlling processes. But here's the differentiator: ongoing operations don't include Initiating or Closing process groups because ongoing operations don't have a beginning or an end.

Most projects I've ever worked on involved more than one stakeholder. And stakeholders often have conflicting interests. On your next project, make certain to find out what those stakeholder interests are. It's easier to resolve conflicts at the beginning of the project than it is at the end. Resolving conflicts will likely involve negotiating and influencing skills.

I've made the mistake of thinking the project process groups are overkill for a small project. My team once embarked on a small project and thought that within a matter of weeks we'd have it wrapped up and delivered. We neglected to get signatures from the project requestor on the agreed upon scope, and you guessed it, the scope grew and grew and changed several times before we were able to get the project back under control. If you're reading between the lines here, you can also tell we didn't have adequate change control in place. As you progress through the book, I'll highlight the important processes you'll want to include on all projects, large and small, so you don't get caught in this trap.

Summary

Phew! I covered a lot of ground in this chapter. You learned that projects exist to bring about a unique product, service, or result. Projects are temporary in nature and have definite beginning and ending dates.

Stakeholders are those people or organizations that have a vested interest in the outcome of the project. Stakeholders include people such as the project sponsor, the customer, key management personnel, the project manager, contractors, suppliers, and more. Projects are considered complete when the project meets or exceeds the expectations of the stakeholders.

Project management is a discipline that brings together a set of tools and techniques to describe, organize, and monitor the work of project activities. Project managers are the ones responsible for carrying out these activities. Projects might be organized into programs or portfolios and might be managed centrally by a PMO.

Project managers have a wide variety of skills. Not only should they be versed in the field they're working in but in general management skills as well. Communication is the most important skill a project manager will use in the course of a project.

Organizational structures come in variations of three forms: functional, projectized, and matrix organizations. Functional organizations are traditional with hierarchical reporting structures. Project managers have little to no authority in this organization. Projectized organizations are structured around project work, and staff personnel report to project managers. Project managers have full authority in this organizational structure. Matrix organizations are a combination of the functional and projectized. A project manager's authority varies depending on the structure of the matrix, be it a weak matrix, a balanced matrix, or a strong matrix.

Projects progress through phases along a life cycle path to complete the product of the project. The project management process groups are performed throughout the project's life cycle. The process groups described in the *PMBOK Guide* are Initiating, Planning, Executing, Monitoring and Controlling, and Closing. Additionally, nine Knowledge Areas bring together processes that have characteristics in common.

Exam Essentials

Be able to describe the difference between projects and operations.   A project is temporary in nature with a definite beginning and ending date. Projects produce unique products, services, or results. Operations are ongoing and use repetitive processes that typically produce the same result over and over.

Be able to denote some of the skills every good project manager should possess.   Communication, budgeting, organizational, problem solving, negotiation and influencing, leading, and team building are skills a project manager should possess.

Be able to differentiate the different organizational structures and the project manager's authority in each.   Organizations are usually structured in some combination of the following: functional, projectized, and matrix (including weak matrix, balanced matrix, and strong matrix). Project managers have the most authority in a projectized organization and the least amount of authority in a functional organization.

Be able to name the five project management processes.   The five project management processes are Initiating, Planning, Executing, Monitoring and Controlling, and Closing.

Be able to name the nine Project Management Knowledge Areas.   The nine Project Management Knowledge Areas are Project Integration Management, Project Scope Management, Project Time Management, Project Cost Management, Project Quality Management, Project Human Resource Management, Project Communications Management, Project Risk Management, and Project Procurement Management.

Key Terms

I've introduced the processes you'll use while managing projects. You need to understand each of these processes to be an effective project manager and know them by the names used in the *PMBOK* to be successful on the exam. I will discuss each in greater detail in the chapters to come.

Closing	Project Integration Management
Executing	Project Management Knowledge Areas
Initiating	Project Procurement Management
Monitoring and Controlling	Project Quality Management
Planning	Project Risk Management
Project Communications Management	Project Scope Management
Project Cost Management	Project Time Management
Project Human Resource Management	

You've learned a lot of new key words in this chapter. PMI has worked hard to develop and define standard project management terms that apply across industries. Here is a list of some of the terms you came across in this chapter:

balanced matrix	power
co-located	product scope
deliverable	program management
fast tracking	programs
feasibility study	progressive elaboration
functional organization	project life cycle
handoffs	project management
historical information	project management office
iterative	project managers
leaders	project scope
managers	project sponsor
matrix organizations	projectized organizations
operations	projects
politics	stakeholders
portfolio management	tailoring
portfolios	

Review Questions

1. Which organization has set the de facto standards for project management techniques?

    A. PMBOK

    B. PMO

    C. PMI

    D. PMA

2. The VP of marketing approaches you and requests that you change the visitor logon screen on the company's website to include a username with at least six characters. This is considered

    A. project initiation

    B. ongoing operations

    C. a project

    D. project execution

3. Your company manufactures small kitchen appliances. It is introducing a new product line of appliances in designer colors with distinctive features for kitchens in small spaces. These new products will be offered indefinitely starting with the spring catalog release. Which of the following is true?

    A. This is a project because this new product line has never been manufactured and sold by this company before.

    B. This is an ongoing operation because the company is in the business of manufacturing kitchen appliances. Introducing designer colors and features is simply a new twist on an existing process.

    C. This is an ongoing operation because the new product line will be sold indefinitely. It's not temporary.

    D. This is not a project or an ongoing operation. This is a new product introduction not affecting ongoing operations.

4. Your company manufactures small kitchen appliances. It is introducing a new product line of appliances in designer colors with distinctive features for kitchens in small spaces. These new products will be offered indefinitely starting with the spring catalog release. To determine the characteristics and features of the new product line, you will have to perform which of the following?

    A. Fast tracking

    B. Consulting with the stakeholders

    C. Planning the project life cycle

    D. Progressive elaboration

5. A project is considered successful when

    A. the product of the project has been manufactured

    B. the project sponsor announces the completion of the project

    C. the product of the project is turned over to the operations area to handle the ongoing aspects of the project

    D. the project meets or exceeds the expectations of the stakeholders

6. The VP of customer service has expressed concern over a project in which you're involved. His specific concern is that if the project is implemented as planned, he'll have to purchase additional equipment to staff his customer service center. The cost is substantial and was not taken into consideration in the project budget. The project sponsor insists that the project must go forward as originally planned or the customer will suffer. Which of the following is true?

    A. The VP of customer service is correct. Since the cost was not taken into account at the beginning of the project, the project should not go forward as planned. Project initiation should be revisited to examine the project plan and determine how changes can be made to accommodate customer service.

    B. The conflict should be resolved in favor of the customer.

    C. The conflict should be resolved in favor of the project sponsor.

    D. The conflict should be resolved in favor of the VP of customer service.

7. Which of the following brings together a set of tools and techniques used to describe, organize, and monitor the work of project activities?

    A. Project managers

    B. The *PMBOK Guide*

    C. Project management

    D. Stakeholders

8. The Project Integration Management Knowledge Area consists of some of the following processes. Which of these belong to Project Integration Management?

    A. Scope Definition, Close Project, and Integrated Change Control

    B. Develop Project Management Plan, Direct and Manage Project Execution, and Integrated Change Control

    C. Preliminary Scope Statement, Direct and Manage Project Execution, and Manage Stakeholders

    D. Preliminary Scope Statement, Scope Planning, and Close Project

9. You are the project manager for Fun Days Vacation Resorts. Your new project assignment is to head up the Fun Days resort opening in Austin, Texas. You are estimating the duration of the project plan activities, devising the project schedule, and monitoring and controlling deviations from the schedule. Which of the Project Management Knowledge Areas are you working in?

    A. Project Scope Management

    B. Project Quality Management

    C. Project Integration Management

    D. Project Time Management

10. You are the project manager for a large construction project. The project objective is to construct a set of outbuildings to house the Olympic support team that will be arriving in your city 18 months from the project start date. Resources are not readily available because they are currently assigned to other projects. Jack, an expert crane operator, is needed for this project two months from today. Which of the following skills will you use to get Jack assigned to your project?

   A. Negotiation and influencing skills

   B. Communication and organizational skills

   C. Communication skills

   D. Problem-solving skills

11. You've decided to try your hand at project management in the entertainment industry. You're working on a movie production, and the team has just completed the storyboard phase of the project. Which of the following is true?

   A. The storyboard is a deliverable that marks the end of the phase. The deliverable must be approved before the next phase begins.

   B. The storyboard phase marks the end of the Initiating process group, and the next phase of the project should begin.

   C. All the phases of this project together make up a program.

   D. The division of phases and determining which processes to use in each phase is called *tailoring.*

12. You are managing a project to install a new postage software system that will automatically print labels and administer postage for certified mailings, overnight packages, and other special mailing needs. You've attempted to gain the cooperation of the business analyst working on this project, and you need some answers. She is elusive and tells you that this project is not her top priority. What should you do to avoid situations like this in the future?

   A. Establish the business analyst's duties well ahead of due dates, and tell her you'll be reporting on her performance to her functional manager.

   B. Establish the business analyst's duties well ahead of due dates, and tell her you are expecting her to meet these expectations because the customer is counting on the project meeting due dates to save significant costs on their annual mailings.

   C. Negotiate with the business analyst's functional manager during the planning process to establish expectations and request to participate in the business analyst's annual performance review.

   D. Negotiate with the business analyst's functional manager during the planning process to establish expectations, and inform the functional manager of the requirements of the project. Agreement from the functional manager will assure the cooperation of the business analyst.

13. The amount of authority a project manager possesses can be related to

    A. the project manager's communication skills

    B. the organizational structure

    C. the amount of authority the manager of the project manager possesses

    D. the key stakeholder's influence on the project

14. What is one of the advantages of a functional organization?

    A. All employees report to one manager and have a clear chain of command.

    B. All employees report to two or more managers, but project team members show loyalty to functional managers.

    C. The organization is focused on projects and project work.

    D. Teams are co-located.

15. You have been assigned to a project in which the objectives are to direct customer calls to an interactive voice response system before being connected to a live agent. You are in charge of the media communications for this project. You report to the project manager in charge of this project and the VP of marketing, who share responsibility for this project. Which organizational structure do you work in?

    A. Functional organization

    B. Weak matrix organization

    C. Projectized organization

    D. Balanced matrix organization

16. You have been assigned to a project in which the objectives are to expand three miles of the north-to-south highway through your city by two lanes in each direction. You are in charge of the demolition phase of this project, and you report to the project manager in charge of this project. You have been hired on contract and will be released at the completion of the demolition phase. What type of organizational structure does this represent?

    A. Functional organization

    B. Weak matrix organization

    C. Projectized organization

    D. Balanced matrix organization

17. What are the five project management process groups, in order?

    A. Initiating, Executing, Planning, Monitoring and Controlling, and Closing

    B. Initiating, Monitoring and Controlling, Planning, Executing, and Closing

    C. Initiating, Planning, Monitoring and Controlling, Executing, and Closing

    D. Initiating, Planning, Executing, Monitoring and Controlling, and Closing

18. You have been assigned to a project in which the objectives are to expand three miles of the north-to-south highway through your city by two lanes in each direction. You are interested in implementing a new project process called Design-Build in order to speed up the project schedule. The idea is that the construction team will work on the first mile of the highway reconstruction at the same time the design team is coming up with plans for the third mile of the reconstruction rather than completing all design before any construction begins. This is an example of

    A. managing the projects as a program

    B. fast tracking

    C. progressive elaboration

    D. co-location

19. During which project management process are risk and stakeholder's ability to influence project outcomes the highest at the beginning of the process?

    A. Planning

    B. Executing

    C. Initiating

    D. Monitoring and Controlling

20. You are a project manager working on gathering requirements and establishing estimates for the project. Which process group are you in?

    A. Planning

    B. Executing

    C. Initiating

    D. Monitoring and Controlling

Answers to Review Questions

1. C. The Project Management Institute (PMI) is the industry-recognized standard for project management practices.

2. B. Projects exist to create a unique product, service, or result. The logon screen in this question is not a unique product. A minor change has been requested, indicating this is an ongoing operation function. Some of the criteria for projects are that they are unique, temporary with definitive start and end dates, and considered complete when the project goals are achieved.

3. A. This is a project. The product line is new, which implies that this is a unique product—it hasn't been done before. You can discern a definite start and end date by the fact that the new appliances must be ready by the spring catalog release.

4. D. Progressive elaboration is the process of determining the characteristics and features of the product of the project. Progressive elaboration is carried out via steps in detailed fashion.

5. D. A project is considered successful when stakeholder needs and expectations are met or exceeded.

6. B. Conflicts between stakeholders should always be resolved in favor of the customer. This question emphasizes the importance of identifying your stakeholders and their needs as early as possible in the project.

7. C. Project management brings together a set of tools and techniques to organize project activities. Project managers are the ones responsible for managing the project processes.

8. B. The Project Integration Management Knowledge Area consists of the following processes: Develop Project Charter, Develop Preliminary Scope Statement, Develop Project Management Plan, Direct and Manage Project Execution, Monitor and Control Project Work, Integrated Change Control, and Close Project.

9. D. Project Time Management involves the following processes: Activity Definition, Activity Sequencing, Activity Duration Estimating, Schedule Development, and Schedule Control.

10. A. Negotiation and influencing skills are needed to convince Jack's boss and come to agreement concerning his assignment.

11. A. The storyboard is a deliverable. Phase endings are characterized by the completion, review, and approval of the deliverable. The next phase should not begin until the deliverable is approved.

12. C. The best answer to this question according to the *PMBOK Guide* standard is to negotiate with the functional manager to participate in the business analyst's annual performance review. D is an appropriate response but doesn't include the *PMBOK Guide's* direction that the project manager should participate in the performance review.

13. B. The level of authority the project manager has is determined by the organizational structure. For instance, in a functional organization, the project manager has little to no authority, but in a projectized structure, the project manager has full authority.

14. A. Advantages for employees in a functional organization are that they have only one supervisor and a clear chain of command exists.

15. D. Employees in a balanced matrix often report to two or more managers. Functional managers and project managers share authority and responsibility for projects. There is a balance of power between the functional managers and project managers.

16. C. Projectized organizations are focused on the project itself. One issue with this type of structure is determining what to do with project team members when they are not actively involved on the project. One alternative is to release them when they are no longer needed.

17. D. Remember the acronym that sounds like syrup of ipecac: IPECC (Initiating, Planning, Executing, *Monitoring and* Controlling, and Closing).

18. B. Fast tracking is starting a new phase before the phase you're working on is completed. This compresses the project schedule, and as a result, the project is completed sooner.

19. C. The Initiating process is where stakeholders have the greatest ability to influence outcomes of the project. Risk is highest during this stage because of the high degree of unknown factors.

20. A. The Planning process is where requirements are fleshed out, stakeholders are identified, and estimates on project costs and time are made.

Chapter

2

Creating the Project Charter and Preliminary Scope Statement

THE PMP EXAM CONTENT FROM THE INITIATING THE PROJECT PERFORMANCE DOMAIN COVERED IN THIS CHAPTER INCLUDES THE FOLLOWING:

- ✓ Conduct Project Selection Methods
- ✓ Define Scope
- ✓ Document Project Risks, Assumptions, and Constraints
- ✓ Identify and Perform Stakeholder Analysis
- ✓ Develop Project Charter
- ✓ Obtain Project Charter Approval

THE PMP EXAM CONTENT FROM THE PLANNING THE PROJECT PERFORMANCE DOMAIN COVERED IN THIS CHAPTER INCLUDES THE FOLLOWING:

- ✓ Conduct Kick-off Meeting

Now that you're fully armed with a detailed overview of project management, you can easily determine whether your next assignment really is a project or an ongoing operation. You've also learned some of the basics of good project management techniques and the Knowledge Areas where you might need specific expertise. You'll now start putting those techniques into practice during the Initiating process group, which is where all projects start. And, as you've probably already guessed, you'll be using some of the general management skills outlined in Chapter 1, "What Is a Project?"

One of the first skills you will put to use will be your communication skills. Are you surprised? Of course you're not. It all starts with communication. You can't start defining the project until you've first talked to the project sponsor, key stakeholders, and management personnel. All good project managers have honed their communication skills to a nice sharp edge.

You'll remember from Chapter 1 that *Initiating* is the first process group in the five project management process groups. You can think of it as the official project kickoff. Initiating acknowledges that the project, or the next phase in an active project, should begin. This process group culminates in the publication of a project charter and a preliminary project scope statement. I'll cover each in this chapter.

At the end of this chapter, I'll introduce a case study that will illustrate the main points of the chapter. I'll expand on this case study from chapter to chapter, and you'll begin building a project using each of the skills you learn.

Understanding How Projects Come About

Your company's quarterly meeting is scheduled for today. You take your seat, and each of the department heads gets up and gives their usual "We can do it" rah-rah speech, one after the other. You sit up a little straighter when the CEO takes the stage. He starts his part of the program pretty much the same way the other department heads did, and before long, you find yourself drifting off. You are mentally reviewing the status of your current project when suddenly your daydreaming trance is shattered. You perk up as you hear the CEO say, "And the new phone system will be installed by Thanksgiving."

Wait a minute. You work in the telecom department and haven't heard a word about this project until today. You also have a funny feeling that you've been elected to manage this project. It's amazing how good communication skills are so important for project managers but not for, well, we won't go there.

Project *initiation* is the formal recognition that a project, or the next phase in an existing project, should begin, and resources should be committed to the project. Unfortunately, many projects are initiated the way the CEO did in this example. Each of us, at one time or another, has experienced being handed a project with little to no information and told to "make it happen." The new phone system scenario is an excellent example of how *not* to initiate a project.

Taking one step back leads you to ask, "How do projects come about in the first place? Do CEOs just make them up like in this example?" Even though your CEO announced this new project at the company meeting with no forewarning, no doubt it came about as a result of a legitimate need. Believe it or not, CEOs don't just dream up projects just to give you something to do. They're concerned about the future of the company and the needs of the business and its customers.

The business might drive the need for a project, customers might demand changes to products, or legal requirements might create the need for a new project. According to the *PMBOK Guide*, projects come about as a result of one of six needs or demands. Once those needs and demands are identified, the next logical step might include performing a feasibility study to determine the viability of the project. I'll cover these topics next.

Needs and Demands

Organizations exist to generate profits or serve the public. To stay competitive, organizations are always examining new ways of creating business, new ways of gaining efficiencies, or new ways of serving their customers. Sometimes laws are passed to force organizations to make their products safer or to make them less harmful to the environment. Projects might result from any of these needs as well as from business requirements, opportunities, or problems. Most projects will fit one of the six needs and demands described next. Let's take a closer look at each of these areas:

Market demand   The demands of the marketplace can drive the need for a project. For example, a bank initiates a project to offer customers the ability to apply for mortgage loans over the Internet because of a drop in interest rates and an increase in demand for refinancing and new home loans.

Business need   The new phone system talked about earlier that was announced at the quarterly meeting came about as a result of a business need. The CEO, on advice from his staff, was advised that call volumes were maxed on the existing system. Without a new system, customer service response times would suffer, and that would eventually affect the bottom line.

Customer request   Customer requests run the gamut. Generally speaking, most companies have customers, and their requests can drive new projects. Customers can be internal or external to the organization. Government agencies don't have external customers per se (we're captive customers at any rate), but there are internal customers within departments and across agencies.

Perhaps you work for a company that sells remittance-processing equipment and you've just landed a contract with a local utility company. This project is driven by the need of the utility company to automate its process or upgrade its existing process. The utility company's request to purchase your equipment and consulting services is the project driver.

Technological advance   Do you happen to own one of those electronic personal digital assistants? They keep names and addresses handy and usually come with a calendar and a to-do list of some kind. I couldn't live without mine. However, a newer, better version is always coming to market. The introduction of satellite communications now allows these little devices to connect to the Web or get e-mail almost anywhere in the world. The introduction of satellite communications is an example of a technological advance. Because of this introduction, electronics manufacturers revamped their products to take advantage of this new technology.

Legal requirement   Private industry and government agencies both generate new projects as a result of laws passed during every legislative season. For example, new sales tax laws might require new programming to the existing sales tax system. The requirement that food labels appear on every package describing the ingredients and the recommended daily allowances is another example of a project driven by legal requirements.

Social need   The last need is a result of social demands. For example, perhaps a developing country is experiencing a fast-spreading disease that's infecting large portions of the population. Medical supplies and facilities are needed to vaccinate and cure those infected with the disease. Another example might include manufacturing or processing plants that voluntarily remove their waste products from water prior to putting the water back into a local river or stream to prevent contamination.

Exam Spotlight

Understand the needs and demands that bring about a project for the exam.

All of these needs and demands represent opportunities, business requirements, or problems that need to be solved. Management must decide how to respond to these needs and demands, which will more often than not initiate new projects.

Feasibility Studies

After the opportunity for a project becomes evident, the next step might be to initiate it, which means you're ready to jump right into creating a project charter for the project. But before you take that plunge, you should know that some organizations will require a feasibility study prior to making a final decision about starting the project.

Feasibility studies are undertaken for several reasons. One is to determine whether the project is a viable project. A second reason is to determine the probability of the project succeeding. Feasibility studies can also examine the viability of the product, service, or result of

Real World Scenario

Project Initiation

Corey is an information technology manager who works for the National Park Service. One warm spring Sunday morning he was leafing through the newspaper and came across an article about new services being offered at some of the national parks. He really perked up when he saw his boss's name describing the changing nature of technology and how it impacted the types of services the public would like to see at the parks. Corey knew that the public had been asking when wireless Internet services would be available in some of the larger parks. He had also been involved in the discussions about the resources needed to make this happen. But the project never seemed to get off the ground. A higher-priority project always took precedence. However, all that changed when Corey saw the next sentence in the paper, which was his boss promising wireless access in two of the largest parks in their region by July 4. It looks like the customer requests finally won out, and Corey just learned he has a new project on his hands.

the project. For example, the study might ask, "Will the new lemon-flavored soda be a hit? Or is it marketable?" The study might also look at the technical issues related to the project and determine whether the technology proposed is feasible, reliable, and easily assimilated into the organization's existing technology structure.

Feasibility studies might be conducted as separate projects, as subprojects, or as the first life cycle phase of the project. When you don't know the outcome of the study, it's best to treat it as a separate project. The group of people conducting the feasibility study should not be the same people who will work on the project. Project team members might have built-in biases toward the project and will tend to influence the feasibility outcome toward those biases.

 Real World Scenario

The Interactive Voice Response (IVR) Tax-Filing System

Jason, Sam, and Kate are web programmers working for the Department of Revenue in the State of Bliss. Ron, their manager, approaches them one day with an idea.

"Team, business unit managers are thinking it would be a great idea to offer taxpayers the ability to file their income tax returns over the telephone. We already offer them the ability to file on the Internet, thanks to all your efforts on that project last year. It has been a fabulous success. No other state has had the success that Bliss has had with our Internet system.

"Kate, I know you've had previous experience with IVR technology, but I'm not sure about you guys, so this is new territory for us. I'd like to hear what each of you thinks about this project."

Jason speaks up first. "I think it's a great idea. You know me, I'm always up for learning new things, especially when it comes to programming. When can we start?"

Sam echoes Jason's comments.

"This technology is pretty sophisticated," Kate says. "Jason and Sam are excellent coders and could work on the programming side of things, but I would have to pick up the telephony piece on my own. After we're up and running, we could go over the telephony portions step by step, so Jason and Sam could help me support it going forward. I'd really like to take on this project. It would be good for the team and good for the department."

Ron thinks for a minute. "Let's not jump right into this. I know you're anxious to get started, but I think a feasibility study is in order. The senior director of the tax business unit doesn't know whether this project is cost justified and has some concerns about its life span. A feasibility study will tell us the answers to those questions. It should also help us determine whether we're using the right technology to accomplish our goals, and it will outline alternative ways of performing the project that we haven't considered. I don't want Kate going it alone without first examining all the issues and potential impacts to the organization."

Kicking Off the Project Charter

Your first stop in the Initiating group is a process called Develop the Project Charter. As the name of the process suggests, your purpose is to create a project charter. As I talked about in Chapter 1, the purpose for the Initiating group is to authorize a project, or the next phase of a project, to begin. It also gives the project manager the authority to apply resources to the project. These are also the purposes of a project charter: formally authorizing the project to begin and committing resources.

    The charter contains several elements that I'll discuss in the section "Formal-
NOTE   izing and Publishing the Project Charter" later in this chapter.

Exam Spotlight

The *project charter* (which is an output of the Develop the Project Charter process) is the written acknowledgment that the project exists. The project charter names the project manager and gives that person the authority to assign organizational resources to the project.

As you'll discover, every process has inputs, tools and techniques, and outputs, and this one is no exception. You'll start with the inputs. Let's get to it.

Inputs to the project processes are typically informational in nature, or they are outputs from previously completed processes. Inputs are used in combination with the tools and techniques to produce the outputs of each process. Process outputs are usually tangible, such as a report or an update or a list, for example. To get to the output, you have to start with the inputs. Let's take a look at the *Develop Project Charter* process inputs:

- Contract (where applicable)
- Project statement of work
- Enterprise environmental factors
- Organizational process assets

The first input, a contract, is applicable only when the organization you are working for is performing a project for a customer external to the organization. The contract is used as an input to this process because it typically documents the conditions under which the project will be executed, the time frame, and a description of the work.

Project Statement of Work

The *project statement of work (SOW)* describes the product, service, or result the project was undertaken to complete. This is usually a document written by either the project sponsor or the initiator of the project. When the project is external to the organization, the buyer typically writes the SOW. For example, suppose you work for a consulting firm and have been assigned as the project manager for a project your company is performing on contract. The customer, the organization you'll be performing the project for, is the one who writes the SOW.

According to the *PMBOK Guide*, a project SOW should contain or consider all the following elements:

Business need   The business need for the project here relates to the needs of the organization itself. The need might be based on training, governmental standards, technological advances, market demands, or a legal requirement.

Product scope description   The product scope description describes the characteristics of the product, service, or result of the project. The product scope description should be documented and should also include a description of the relationship between the business need or demand that's driving the project and the products being created.

Product descriptions contain less detail in the early phases of a project and more detail as the project progresses. Product scope descriptions, like the work of the project, are progressively elaborated. They will contain the greatest amount of detail in the project Executing processes.

When a project is performed under contract, typically the buyer of the product or service will provide the product description to the vendor or contractor. The product description can serve as a statement of work when the project is contracted to a vendor. A statement of work describes the product, service, or result in enough detail so that the vendor can accurately price the contract and satisfactorily fulfill the requirements of the project.

Strategic plan   Part of the responsibility of a project manager during the Initiating processes is to take into consideration the company's strategic plan. Perhaps the strategic plan states that one of the company goals is to build 15 new stores by the end of the next fiscal year. If your project entails installing a new human resources software system, it makes sense to write the requirements for your project with the 15 new stores in mind. Your management team will refer to the strategic plan when choosing which new projects to initiate and which ones to drop, depending on their relationship to the strategic vision of the company.

Enterprise Environmental Factors

The enterprise environmental factors input shows up as an input to many of the other processes we'll discuss throughout the book. This input refers to the factors outside the project that have (or might have) significant influence on the success of the project. According to the *PMBOK Guide*, the environmental factors include the following:

Organizational or company culture and structure   I talked about organizational structures and their influence on the organization in Chapter 1.

Governmental or industry standards   These include elements such as regulatory standards and regulations (for instance, doctors must be licensed to practice medicine on people or pets), quality standards (International Standards Organization standards, for example), product standards, and workmanship standards.

Infrastructure   This refers to the organization's facilities and capital equipment. I'll also include information technology in this category, even though PMI doesn't mention it.

Human resources   This refers to the existing staff's skills and knowledge.

Personnel administration   These are guidelines for hiring and firing, training, and employee performance reviews.

Organization's work authorization system   This defines how the work of the project is authorized.

Marketplace conditions   The old supply-and-demand theory applies here along with economic and financial factors.

Stakeholder risk tolerance   This is the level of risk stakeholders are willing to take on. I'll talk more about this in Chapter 5, "Risk Planning."

Commercial databases   These refer to industry-specific information, risk databases, and so on.

Project management information systems   This is typically a software product that allows you to schedule project activities and resources and collect and distribute project information.

These factors can influence the way you manage the project and, in some cases, the outcomes of the project. For example, perhaps the folks assigned to your project are junior level and don't have the skills, experience, or knowledge needed to complete the work of the project. It's up to the project manager to understand the organization's environmental factors and account for and consider how they can influence the management and outcomes of the project.

Organizational Process Assets

Organizational process assets are the organization's policies, guidelines, procedures, plans, approaches, or standards for conducting work, including project work. This includes a wide range of elements that might affect several aspects of the project, such as project management policies, safety policies, performance measurement criteria, templates, financial controls, communication requirements, issue and defect management procedures, change control procedures, risk control procedures, and the procedures used for authorizing work.

Organizational process assets also include the information the organization has learned on previous projects (including how to store and retrieve that information). For example, previous project risks, performance measurements, earned value data, and schedules for past projects are valuable resources of knowledge for the current project. This information is also known as *historical information*. If you don't capture and store this information, however, it won't be available when starting a new project. You'll want to capture and store information such as project financial data (budgets, costs, overruns), historical information, lessons learned, project files, issues and defects, process measurements, and configuration management knowledge.

 Several elements are included in the organizational process assets title, and I'll cover each of them in later chapters of the book.

Organizational process assets and historical information should be reviewed and examined when starting a new project. Historical information can be very useful to project managers and to stakeholders. When you're evaluating new projects, historical information about previous projects of a similar nature can be handy in determining whether the new project should be accepted and initiated. Historical information gathered and documented during an active project is used to assist in determining whether the project should proceed to the next phase. Historical information will help you with the project charter, preliminary project scope statement, project scope statement, development of the project management plan, the process of defining and estimating activities, and more, during the project-planning processes.

Understanding previous projects of a similar nature—their problems, successes, issues, and outcomes—will help you avoid repeating mistakes while reusing successful techniques to accomplish the goals of this project to the satisfaction of the stakeholders. Many of the processes in the project management process groups have organizational process assets as an input, implying that you should review the pertinent organizational assets that apply for the process you're about to start. For example, when performing the Cost Estimating process, you might find it helpful to review the activity estimates and budgets on past projects of similar size and scope before estimating the costs for the activities on the new project.

Exam Spotlight

Remember that organizational process assets encompass many elements including policies, guidelines, standards, and so on. It also includes historical information about previous projects. Make certain you understand what the organizational process assets entail for the exam and that you can differentiate them from the enterprise environmental factors input.

Using Tools and Techniques for Charter Development

The Develop Project Charter process has four tools and techniques you can use to help you produce the project charter. They are project selection methods, project management methodology, project management information system, and expert judgment. You'll look at each one next.

Selecting and Prioritizing Projects

Most organizations don't have the luxury of performing every project that's proposed. Even consulting organizations that sell their project management services must pick and choose the projects on which they want to work. Selection methods help organizations decide among alternative projects. The project selection methods tool and technique calculates measurable differences between projects and determines the tangible benefits to the company of choosing or not choosing the project.

Project selection methods will vary depending on the company, the people serving on the selection committee, the criteria used, and the project. Sometimes selection methods will be purely financial, sometimes purely marketing, and sometimes they'll be based on public perception or political perception. In most cases, the decision is based on a combination of all these and more.

Most organizations have a formal, or at least semiformal, process for selecting and prioritizing projects. In my organization, a steering committee is responsible for project review, selection, and prioritization. A *steering committee* is a group of folks comprising senior managers and sometimes midlevel managers who represent each of the functional areas in the organization.

Here's how our process works: The steering committee requests project ideas from the business staff prior to the beginning of the fiscal year. These project ideas are submitted in writing and contain a high-level overview of the project goals, a description of the deliverables, the business justification for the project, a desired implementation date, what the organization stands to gain from implementing the project, a list of the functional business areas affected by the project, and (if applicable) a cost-benefit analysis (I'll talk about that in a bit).

A meeting is called to review the projects, and a determination is made on each project about whether it will be included on the upcoming list of projects for the new year. Once the no-go projects have been weeded out, the remaining projects are prioritized according to their importance and benefit to the organization. The projects are documented on an official project list, and progress is reported on the active projects at the regular monthly steering committee meetings.

In theory, it's a great idea. In practice, it works only moderately well. Priorities can and do change throughout the year. New projects come up that weren't originally submitted during the call for projects, and they must be added to the list. Reprioritization begins anew, and resource alignment and assignments are shuffled. But again, I'm getting ahead of myself. Just be aware that organizations usually have a process to recognize and screen project requests, accept or reject those requests based on some selection criteria, and prioritize the projects based on some criteria.

The project selection methods I'll talk about next are ones you should know and understand for the exam. However, keep in mind they are only one aspect of project selection in the real world. The individual opinion, and power, of selection committee members also plays a part in the projects the organization chooses to perform. Don't underestimate the importance of the authority, political standing, and individual aspirations of selection committee members. Those committee members who happen to carry a lot of weight in company circles, so to speak, are likely to get their projects approved just because they are who they are. This is sometimes how project selection works in my organization. How about yours?

Using Project Selection Methods

Project selection methods are concerned with the advantages or merits of the product of the project. In other words, selection methods measure the value of what the product, service, or result of the project will produce and how it will benefit the organization. Selection methods involve the types of concerns executive managers are typically thinking about. This includes factors such as market share, financial benefits, return on investment, customer retention and loyalty, and public perceptions. Most of these are reflected in the organization's strategic goals. Projects, whether large or small, should always be weighed against the strategic plan. If the project doesn't help the organization reach its goals (increased market share, for example), then the project probably shouldn't be undertaken.

According to the *PMBOK Guide*, there are two categories of selection methods: *mathematical models* (also known as *calculation methods*) and *benefit measurement methods* (also known as *decision models*). Decision models examine different criteria used in making decisions regarding project selection, while calculation methods provide a way to calculate the value of the project, which is then used in project selection decision making.

Mathematical Models

For the exam, all you need to understand about mathematical models is that they use linear, dynamic, integer, nonlinear, and/or multi-objective programming in the form of algorithms—or in other words, a specific set of steps to solve a particular problem. These are complicated mathematical formulas and algorithms that are beyond the scope of this book and require an engineering, statistical, or mathematical background to fully understand. Organizations considering undertaking projects of enormous complexity might use mathematical modeling techniques to make decisions regarding these projects. Mathematical models are also known as *constrained optimization methods*. The vast majority of project selection techniques will use the benefit measurement methods to make project selection decisions.

Exam Spotlight

Project selection methods are also used to evaluate and choose between alternative ways of performing the project.

Benefit Measurement Methods

Benefit measurement methods employ various forms of analysis and comparative approaches to make project decisions. These methods include comparative approaches such as cost-benefit analysis, scoring models, and benefit contribution methods that include various cash flow techniques and economic models. You'll examine several of these methods, starting with cost-benefit.

Cost-Benefit Analysis

One common benefit measurement method is the *cost-benefit* analysis. The name of this method implies what it does—it compares the cost to produce the product, service, or result of the project to the benefit (usually financial in the form of savings or revenue generation) that the organization will receive as a result of executing the project. Obviously, a sound project choice is one where the costs to implement or produce the product of the project are less than the financial benefits. How much less is the organization's decision. Some companies are comfortable with a small margin, while others are comfortable with a much larger margin between the two figures.

 Cost-benefit analysis is also known as *benefit/cost analysis*. The techniques are the same. *Benefit/cost* has a more positive connotation because it shows the benefit, or the good stuff, before the cost, which is the not-so-good stuff.

When examining costs for a cost-benefit analysis, include the costs to produce the product or service, the costs to take the product to market, and the ongoing operational support costs. For example, let's say your company is considering writing and marketing a database software product that will allow banks to dissect their customer base, determine which types of customers buy which types of products, and then market more effectively to those customers. You will take into account some of the following costs:

- The costs to develop the software, such as programmer costs, hardware costs, testing, and testing costs

- Marketing costs such as advertising, traveling costs to perform demos at potential customer sites, and so on
- Ongoing costs such as having a customer support staff available during business hours to assist customers with product questions and problems

Let's say the cost to produce this software plus the ongoing support costs total $5 million. Initial projections look like the demand for this product is high. Over a three-year period, which is the potential life of the software in its proposed form, projected revenues are $12 million. Taking only the financial information into account, the benefits outweigh the costs of this project. This project should receive a go recommendation.

 Projects of significant cost or complexity usually involve more than one benefit measurement method when go or no-go decisions are being made or one project is being chosen over another. Keep in mind that selection methods can take subjective considerations into account as well—the project is a go because it's the new CEO's pet project; nothing else needs to be said.

Scoring Models

Another project selection technique in the benefit measurement category is a *scoring model*, or *weighted scoring model*. My organization uses weighted scoring models not only to choose between projects but also as a method to choose between competing bids on outsourced projects.

Weighted scoring models are quite simple. The project selection committee decides on the criteria that will be used on the scoring model—for example, profit potential, marketability of the product or service, ability of the company to quickly and easily produce the product or service, and so on. Each of these criteria is assigned a weight depending on its importance to the project committee. More important criteria should carry a higher weight than less important criteria.

Then each project is rated on a scale from 1 to 5 (or some such assignment), with the higher number being the more desirable outcome to the company and the lower number having the opposite effect. This rating is then multiplied by the weight of the criteria factor and added to other weighted criteria scores for a total weighted score. Table 2.1 shows an example that brings this together.

TABLE 2.1 Weighted Scoring Model

Criteria	Weight	Project A Score*	Project A Totals	Project B Score*	Project B Totals	Project C Score*	Project C Totals
Profit potential	5	5	25	5	25	3	15
Marketability	3	4	12	3	9	4	12

TABLE 2.1   Weighted Scoring Model *(continued)*

Criteria	Weight	Project A Score*	Project A Totals	Project B Score*	Project B Totals	Project C Score*	Project C Totals
Ease to produce/ support	1	4	4	3	3	2	2
Weighted score	—	—	41	—	37	—	29

*5 = highest

In this example, Project A is the obvious choice.

Cash Flow Analysis Techniques

The remaining benefit measurement methods involve a variety of cash flow analysis techniques, including payback period, discounted cash flows, net present value, and internal rate of return. We'll look at each of these techniques individually, and I'll provide you with a crash course on their meanings and calculations.

PAYBACK PERIOD

The *payback period* is the length of time it takes the company to recoup the initial costs of producing the product, service, or result of the project. This method compares the initial investment to the cash inflows expected over the life of the product, service, or result. For example, say the initial investment on a project is $200,000, with expected cash inflows of $25,000 per quarter every quarter for the first two years and $50,000 per quarter from then on. The payback period is two years and can be calculated as follows:

Initial investment = $200,000

Cash inflows = $25,000 × 4 (quarters in a year) = $100,000/year total inflow

Initial investment ($200,000) – year 1 inflows ($100,000) = $100,000 remaining balance

Year 1 inflows remaining balance – year 2 inflows = $0

Total cash flow year 1 and year 2 = $200,000

The payback is reached in two years.

The fact that inflows are $50,000 per quarter starting in year 3 makes no difference because payback is reached in two years.

The payback period is the least precise of all the cash flow calculations. That's because the payback period does not consider the value of the cash inflows made in later years, commonly called the *time value of money*. For example, if you have a project with a five-year payback period, the cash inflows in year 5 are worth less than they are if you received them today. The next section will explain this idea more fully.

DISCOUNTED CASH FLOWS

As I just stated, money received in the future is worth less than money received today. The reason for that is the time value of money. If I borrowed $2,000 from you today and promised to pay it back in three years, you would expect me to pay interest in addition to the original amount borrowed. OK, if you were a family member or a really close friend, maybe you wouldn't, but ordinarily this is the way it works. You would have had the use of the $2,000 had you not lent it to me. If you had invested the money (does this bring back memories of your mom telling you to save your money?), you'd receive a return on it. Therefore, the future value of the $2,000 you lent me today is $2,315.25 in three years from now at 5 percent interest per year. Here's the formula for future value calculations:

$$FV = PV(1 + i)n$$

In English, this formula says the future value (FV) of the investment equals the present value (PV) times (1 plus the interest rate) raised to the value of the number of time periods (n) the interest is paid. Let's plug in the numbers:

$$FV = 2,000(1.05)^3$$

$$FV = 2,000(1.157625)$$

$$FV = \$2,315.25$$

The *discounted cash flow* technique compares the value of the future cash flows of the project to today's dollars. In order to calculate discounted cash flows, you need to know the value of the investment in today's terms, or the PV. PV is calculated as follows:

$$PV = FV / (1 + i)n$$

This is the reverse of the FV formula talked about earlier. So, if you ask the question, "What is $2,315.25 in three years from now worth today given a 5 percent interest rate?" you'd use the preceding formula. Let's try it:

$$PV = \$2,315.25 / (1 + .05)^3$$

$$PV = \$2,315.25 / 1.157625$$

$$PV = 2,000$$

$2,315.25 in three years from now is worth $2,000 today.

Discounted cash flow is calculated just like this for the projects you're comparing for selection purposes or when considering alternative ways of doing the project. Apply the PV formula to the projects you're considering, and then compare the discounted cash flows of all the projects against each other to make a selection. Here is an example comparison of two projects using this technique:

Project A is expected to make $100,000 in two years.

Project B is expected to make $120,000 in three years.

If the cost of capital is 12 percent, which project should you choose?
Using the PV formula used previously, calculate each project's worth:

The PV of Project A = $79,719.

The PV of Project B = $85,414.

Project B is the project that will return the highest investment to the company and should be chosen over Project A.

NET PRESENT VALUE

Projects might begin with a company investing some amount of money into the project to complete and accomplish its goals. In return, the company expects to receive revenues, or cash inflows, from the resulting project. *Net present value (NPV)* allows you to calculate an accurate value for the project in today's dollars. The mathematical formula for NPV is complicated, and you do not need to memorize it in that form for the test. However, you do need to know how to calculate NPV for the exam, so I've given you some examples of a less complicated way to perform this calculation in Table 2.2 and Table 2.3 using the formulas you've already seen.

TABLE 2.2   Project A

Year	Inflows	PV
1	10,000	8,929
2	15,000	11,958
3	5,000	3,559
Total	30,000	24,446
Less investment	—	24,000
NPV	—	**446**

TABLE 2.3   Project B

Year	Inflows	PV
1	7,000	6,250
2	13,000	10,364
3	10,000	7,118
Total	30,000	23,732
Less investment	—	24,000
NPV	—	**<268>**

Net present value works like discounted cash flows in that you bring the value of future monies received into today's dollars. With NPV, you evaluate the cash inflows using the discounted cash flow technique applied to each period the inflows are expected instead of in one sum. The total present value of the cash flows is then deducted from your initial investment to determine NPV. NPV assumes that cash inflows are reinvested at the cost of capital.

Here's the rule: If the NPV calculation is greater than zero, accept the project. If the NPV calculation is less than zero, reject the project.

Look at the two project examples in Tables 2.2 and 2.3. Project A and Project B have total cash inflows that are the same at the end of the project, but the amount of inflows at each period differs for each project. We'll stick with a 12 percent cost of capital. Note that the PV calculations were rounded to two decimal places.

Project A has an NPV greater than zero and should be accepted. Project B has an NPV less than zero and should be rejected. When you get a positive value for NPV, it means that the project will earn a return at least equal to or greater than the cost of capital.

Another note on NPV calculations: projects with high returns early in the project are better projects than projects with lower returns early in the project. In the preceding examples, Project A fits this criterion also.

INTERNAL RATE OF RETURN

The *internal rate of return (IRR)* is the most difficult equation to calculate all the cash flow techniques we've discussed. It is a complicated formula and should be performed on a financial calculator or computer. IRR can be figured manually, but it's a trial-and-error approach to get to the answer.

Technically speaking, IRR is the discount rate when the present value of the cash inflows equals the original investment. When choosing between projects or when choosing alternative methods of doing the project, projects with higher IRR values are generally considered better than projects with low IRR values.

Exam Spotlight

For the exam, you need to know three facts concerning IRR:

- IRR is the discount rate when NPV equals zero.

- IRR assumes that cash inflows are reinvested at the IRR value.

- You should choose projects with the highest IRR value.

Exam Spotlight

Although the *PMBOK Guide* doesn't specifically address these cash flow techniques, you'll likely see exam questions on these topics. They are inferred in the *PMBOK Guide* under the heading "Benefit Measurement Methods."

Applying Project Selection Methods

Now that we've discussed some of the techniques used in the project selection methods tool and technique, let's look at how to apply them when choosing projects or project alternatives. You can use one, two, or several of the benefit measurement methods alone or in combination to come up with a selection decision. Remember that payback period is the least precise of all the cash flow techniques, NPV is the most conservative cash flow technique, and NPV and IRR will generally bring you to the same accept/reject conclusion.

You can use project selection methods, and particularly the benefit measurement methods, to evaluate multiple projects or a single project. You might be weighing one project against another or simply considering whether the project you're proposing is worth doing. Remember that project selection methods are a tool and technique of the Develop Project Charter process, and this tool and technique covers two broad categories called *mathematical methods* (also known as *constrained optimization methods*) and *benefit measurement methods*. Both of these together are often called *decision models*.

 Real World Scenario

Fun Days Vacation Resorts

Jerry is a project manager for Fun Days Vacation Resorts. He is working on three different project proposals to present to the executive steering committee for review. As part of the information-gathering process, Jerry visits the various resorts pretending to be a guest. This gives him a feel for what Fun Days guests experience on their vacations, and it better prepares him to present project particulars and alternatives.

Jerry has prepared the project overviews for three projects and called upon the experts in marketing to help him out with the projected revenue figures. He works up the numbers and finds the following:

- Project A: payback period = 5 years; IRR = 8 percent

- Project B: payback period = 3.5 years; IRR = 3 percent

- Project C: payback period = 2 years; IRR = 3 percent

Funding exists for only one of the projects. Jerry recommends Project A and predicts this is the project the steering committee will choose since the projects are mutually exclusive.

Jerry's turn to present comes up at the steering committee. Let's listen in on the action:

"And, on top of all the benefits I've just described, Project A provides an IRR of 8 percent, a full 5 percent higher than the other two projects we discussed. I recommend the committee choose Project A."

"Thank you Jerry," Colleen says. "Good presentation." Colleen is the executive chairperson of the steering committee and has the authority to break ties or make final decisions when the committee can't seem to agree.

"However, here at Fun Days we like to have our fun sooner rather than later." Chuckles ensue from the steering committee. They've all heard this before. "I do agree that an 8 percent IRR is a terrific return, but the payback is just too far out into the future. There are too many risks and unknowns for us to take on a project with a payback period this long. As you know, our industry is directly impacted by the health of the economy. Anything can happen in five years' time. I think we're much better off going with Project C. I recommend we accept Project C. Committee members, do you have anything to add?"

Project Management Methodology and Information Systems

The two techniques of project management methodology and information systems are similar, so I've put them together under the same heading. The project management methodology tool and technique refers to a methodology for managing projects much like the *PMBOK Guide* process groups and all the processes contained within each of them. A project management methodology might be a formal, recognized project management standard like the one outlined in this book or an informal technique. Whether formal or informal, the methodology should help the project manager develop the project charter.

Project management information system (PMIS) is listed in this process as a tool and technique. Notice that this is also listed as one of the enterprise environmental factors. A PMIS is a set of automated tools (generally a software program) that allows you to schedule project activities and resources and collect and distribute project information. As a tool and technique of the Develop Project Charter process, the PMIS facilitates the creation of the project charter, provides a way to capture feedback and changes to the charter, and publishes the finalized, approved charter.

Expert Judgment

Expert judgment is the last tool and technique in this process. The concept behind expert judgment is to rely on individuals, or groups of people, who have training, specialized knowledge, or skills in the areas you're assessing. These folks might be stakeholders, consultants, other experts in the organization, or technical or professional organizations. Expert judgment is a tool and technique used in other planning processes as well.

In the case of developing a project charter, expert judgment would be helpful in assessing the inputs of this process, the environmental factors, and organizational assets—that is, the project statement of work, product descriptions, strategic plan, project selection methods, and historical information. For example, as the project manager, you might rely on the expertise of your executive committee to help you understand how the proposed project gels with the strategic plan. Or you might rely on team members who have participated on similar projects in the past to make recommendations regarding the proposed project.

Formalizing and Publishing the Project Charter

The *project charter* is the official, written acknowledgment and recognition that a project exists. It ties the work of the project with the ongoing operations of the organization. It's usually issued by senior management and gives the project manager the authority to assign organizational resources to the project.

The charter documents the business need or demand that the project was initiated to address and the project justification, and it includes a description of the product, service, or result of the project. It is usually the first official document of the project once acceptance of the project has been granted. Project charters are often used as a means to introduce a project to the organization. Since this document outlines the high-level project description, the business opportunity or need, and the project's purpose, executive managers can get a "first-glance" look at the benefits of the project. Good project charters that are well documented will address many of the questions your stakeholders are likely to have up front.

Let's take a brief look at the key stakeholders who might be involved with the project charter and the role they'll play in its development and on the project in the future.

Key Stakeholders

The *PMBOK Guide* states that the project sponsor or initiator is the one who provides the information for the project charter. It also says a manager who is external to the project should publish the charter. However, the *PMBOK Guide* and common project management practices don't always match up. In practice, my experience has been that the project charter is published under the name of the project sponsor. It also involves the input of key stakeholders. Often, the project sponsor or initiator won't have all the information needed to complete the charter and you'll be charged with digging out all the facts needed to create this document as well as the preliminary project scope statement. But remember, you're studying to pass the exam, so you should know that the *PMBOK Guide* states that the author of the project charter should be a manager external to the project and input comes from the initiator or sponsor.

Project Manager

The project manager is the person who assumes responsibility for the success of the project. The project charter identifies the project manager and describes the authority the project manager has in carrying out the project. The project manager's primary responsibilities are project planning and then executing and managing the work of the project. By overseeing the project charter and the project planning documents created later in the project, the project manager is assured that everyone knows and understands what's expected of them and what constitutes a successful project.

Project managers are responsible for setting the standards and policies for the projects on which they work. As a project manager, it is your job to establish and communicate the project procedures to the project team and stakeholders.

Project managers will identify activities and tasks, resource requirements, project costs, project requirements, performance measures, and more. Communication and documentation must become the project manager's best friends. Keeping stakeholders, the project sponsor, the project team, and all other interested parties informed is "job one," as the famous car manufacturer's ads say.

Project Sponsor

Have you ever attended a conference or event that was put on by a sponsor? In the information technology field, software development companies often sponsor conferences and seminars. The sponsor pays for the event, the facilities, and the goodies and provides an opportunity for vendors to display their wares. In return, the sponsor comes out looking like a winner. Because it is footing the bill for all this fun, the sponsor gets to call the shots on conference content, and it gets the prime spots for discussing its particular solutions. And last but not least, it usually provides the keynote speaker and gets to present its information to a captive audience.

Project sponsors are similar to this in that they rally support from stakeholders and the executive management team for the project. The project sponsor is usually an executive in the organization who has the power and authority to make decisions and settle disputes or conflicts regarding the project. The sponsor takes the project into the limelight, so to speak, and gets to call the shots regarding project outcomes. The project sponsor is also the one with the big bucks who provides funds for your project. The project sponsor should be named in the project charter and identified as the final authority and decision maker for project issues.

Sponsors are actively involved in the Initiating and Planning phases of the project and tend to have less involvement during the Execution and Monitoring and Controlling phases. It's up to the project manager to keep the project sponsor informed of all project activities, project progress, and any conflicts or issues that arise. The sponsor is the one with the authority to resolve conflicts and set priorities when these things can't be dealt with any other way.

Project Champion

The project champion is another strong project supporter. Unlike the sponsor, the project champion doesn't necessarily have a lot of authority or executive powers. The champion helps focus attention on the project from a technical perspective. The project champion is usually someone with a great deal of technical expertise or industry knowledge regarding the project. They can lend credibility to the viability of the project and to the skills and abilities of the key project team members to carry out project activities. Sometimes, the project manager might act as project champion.

The project champion isn't necessarily identified in the project charter. But as a project manager, you'll want to know who this person is because the person is a strong project advocate and because you might need them later to help rally support for project decisions.

Functional Managers

I covered functional managers briefly in Chapter 1. Project managers must work with and gain the support of functional managers in order to complete the project. Functional managers fulfill the administrative duties of the organization, provide and assign staff members to projects, and conduct performance reviews for their staff. It's a good idea to identify the functional managers who will be working on project tasks or assigned project responsibilities in the charter.

It's also a good idea to identify the key project stakeholders in the project charter. Although this isn't explicitly stated as part of this process, you'll see in the next section that stakeholder influences make up one of the components of the project charter. To identify stakeholder influences, it's also necessary to identify the stakeholders and describe their roles in high-level terms as I've done here.

Pulling the Project Charter Together

According to the *PMBOK Guide*, to create a useful and well-documented project charter, you should include at least these elements:

- Purpose or justification for the project
- Business need for the project
- Business case justification for the project, including return on investment analysis
- High-level project description or product requirements
- Requirements that must be completed satisfactorily according to stakeholder, sponsor, and customer expectations
- Stakeholder influences
- Involvement of other departments (in the functional organization) and the level of participation needed
- Constraints
- Assumptions
- Summary milestone schedule (preliminary)
- Summary budget (preliminary)
- Name of the project manager and their authority levels

I've already discussed some of these elements, and I covered the purpose of the project, business need, and business justification in earlier sections of this chapter. In the previous section, I talked some about stakeholders and their roles. I'll cover this topic more thoroughly in the next chapter. The roles or involvement of other departments and their level of participation is a matter of defining the level of involvement and the types of actions required from the other departments to fulfill the purpose and requirements of the project.

A constraint is anything that restricts the actions of the project team. Perhaps the project has a hard end date. The date cannot move because of circumstances outside the control of the project. Or perhaps the project has a set budget. Both of these issues are examples of constraints. Assumptions are events or actions believed to be true. Both constraints and assumptions should be documented in the project charter. However, many of these elements are included in the processes related to creating a scope statement and become further refined as you get into the Planning process, so I'll talk more about these topics in Chapter 3, "Developing the Scope Statement."

The important factors to remember for the exam about the project charter are that it authorizes the project to begin, it authorizes the project manager to assign resources to the project, it documents the business need and justification, it describes the customer's requirements, and it ties the project to the ongoing work of the organization.

Exam Spotlight

In some organizations, the project manager might write the project charter. However, if you (as the project manager) are asked to write the charter, remember that your name should not appear as the author of the project charter document. Since the project charter authorizes the project and authorizes you as the project manager, it doesn't make sense for you to write a document authorizing yourself to manage the project. The author of the charter should be an executive manager in your organization (external to the project) with the power and authority to assign resources to this project. Remember for the exam that the charter is authorized external to the project organization.

Project Charter Sign-Off

The project charter isn't complete until you've received sign-off from the project sponsor, senior management, and key stakeholders. Sign-off indicates that the document has been read by those signing it (let's hope so, anyway) and that they agree with its contents and are on board with the project. It also involves the major stakeholders right from the beginning and should win their continued participation in the project going forward. If someone has a problem with any of the elements in the charter, now is the time to raise the red flag.

Prior to publishing the charter, I like to hold a kickoff meeting with the key stakeholders to discuss the charter and then obtain their sign-off. Although the *PMBOK Guide* doesn't bring stakeholders into the picture until the Planning processes, I think it's imperative you identify your key stakeholders as soon as possible and involve them in the creation of the project charter and preliminary scope statement. Remember for the exam, however, that the initiator or sponsor provides the input for the charter and preliminary scope statement.

I'll talk more about key stakeholder roles in Chapter 3.

Signing the project charter document is the equivalent of agreeing to and endorsing the project. This doesn't mean the project charter is set in stone, however. Project charters will change throughout the course of the project. As more details are uncovered and outlined and as the Planning processes begin, more project issues will come to light. This is part of the iterative process of project management and is to be expected. The charter will occasionally be revised to reflect these new details, project plans will be revised, and project execution will change to incorporate the new information or direction.

The last step in this process is publishing the charter. Publishing, in this case, simply means distributing a copy of the project charter to the key stakeholders, the customer, the management team, and others who might be involved with the project. Publication can take several forms, including printed format or electronic format distributed via the company email system or on the company's intranet.

Next, I'll further describe the work of the project in a preliminary project scope statement.

Developing a Preliminary Project Scope Statement

The *preliminary scope statement* is the first blush, so to speak, of what the project entails. This preliminary document is a high-level look at the project objectives and deliverables. It serves the purpose of capturing the intended outcome of the project and its deliverables. It provides a brief background of the project and describes the business opportunity from which the company is attempting to benefit. It also describes the business objectives the project should meet.

The preliminary scope statement is based on information provided by the project sponsor or initiator and lays the groundwork for future consensus on deliverables and project expectations; it will be further elaborated in the Scope Definition process that I'll talk about in Chapter 3.

Preliminary Scope Statement Inputs and Techniques

The inputs for this process are as follows:

- Project charter
- Project SOW
- Enterprise environmental factors
- Organizational process assets

You've seen all these previously in this chapter. Remember that many times, outputs from one process become inputs into the next process. That's the case here, where you'll examine the project charter, meet with the project sponsor or initiator, and develop the preliminary project scope statement. Before getting to what the scope statement contains, you'll look at the tools and techniques of this process. These will look familiar too.

The tools and techniques for the *Develop Preliminary Scope Statement* process include project management methodology, project management information system, and expert judgment.

The Preliminary Scope Statement Document

The preliminary scope statement document contains several elements, most of which are repeated in the final scope statement created during the Planning process group. Creating a preliminary scope statement is good for very large projects or projects with multiple phases. On large projects, each phase has its own preliminary scope statement document that can be reexamined, revised, and elaborated as the new phase begins. Small- to medium-sized projects probably will not need a preliminary scope statement. You could skip straight to the Planning processes from here, but I urge you, don't turn the page. You do need to know about this process for the exam even if you'll use it only a few times in the course of your project work. And remember, it's up to the project manager (that's you) to determine which processes should be completed for the project. My guess is the majority of the time you'll skip this one.

Exam Spotlight

For the exam, understand the purpose of the preliminary scope document, which is to describe the characteristics of the product of the project; what is and what is *not* included in project scope (The *PMBOK Guide* calls these *boundaries*); how the final product, service, or result of the project will be accepted; and how scope will be controlled.

According to the *PMBOK Guide*, the preliminary scope statement should contain these elements:

- Project objectives
- Characteristics of the product, service, or result of the project (that is, a product description)
- Product objectives
- Project deliverables
- Requirements (both product and project)
- Exclusions from scope (project boundaries)
- Constraints
- Assumptions
- High-level risk list and definition
- Milestones
- Initial WBS
- Cost estimate (order of magnitude)
- Configuration management requirements
- Project acceptance criteria

I know you're dying to know more about some of these elements! I don't mean to keep you in suspense, but it makes a lot more sense to cover these elements when talking about the scope statement in Chapter 3. You will *always* create a scope statement for your project, no matter how large or small. (You do this, right?) Besides, I've covered a lot of material in these first two chapters and you probably need a little breather to absorb what you've learned. Kick back, run through the case study and the review questions, and then you'll be ready to jump into these topics.

Introducing the Kitchen Heaven Project Case Study

This chapter introduces a case study that we'll follow throughout the remainder of the book. You'll find an updated case study closing out every chapter. They're designed to show you how a project manager might apply the material covered in the chapter to a real-life project. As happens in real life, not every detail of every process is followed during all projects. Remember that the processes from the *PMBOK Guide* that I'll cover in the remaining chapters are project management guidelines. You will often combine processes during your projects, which will allow you to perform several steps at once. The case studies will present situations or processes that you might find during your projects and describe how one project manager resolves them.

 Real World Scenario

Project Case Study: New Kitchen Heaven Retail Store

You are a project manager for Kitchen Heaven, a chain of retail stores specializing in kitchen utensils, cookware, dishes, small appliances, and some gourmet foodstuffs such as bottled sauces and spices. You're fairly new to the position, having been hired to replace a project manager who recently retired.

Kitchen Heaven currently owns 49 stores in 34 states and Canada. The world headquarters for Kitchen Heaven is in Denver, Colorado. Counting full-time and part-time employees, the company employs 1,500 people, 200 of whom work at headquarters.

The company's mission statement reads: "Great gadgets for people interested in great food."

Recently, the vice president of marketing paid you a visit. Dirk Perrier is a very nice, well-dressed man with the formal air you would expect a person in his capacity might have. He shakes your hand and gives you a broad, friendly smile.

"We've decided to go forward with our 50th store opening! Sales are up, and our new line of ceramic cookware is a hot seller, no pun intended. I don't know if you're familiar with our store philosophy, so let me take a moment to explain it. We like to place our stores in neighborhoods that are somewhat affluent. The plain fact is that most of our shoppers have incomes of more than $150,000 a year. So, we make an effort to place our stores in areas where those folks usually shop.

"We're interested in targeting the nongourmet customer, one who is interested in cooking but won't be making Peking duck. So, the stores are upbeat and convey a little bit of a laid-back feel, if you will.

"Our next store is going to be right here in our home area—Colorado Springs. We have a store in Boulder and one in Denver, but none down south. Because this is going to be our 50th store, we plan on having a 50th grand-opening celebration, with the kind of surprises and activities you might expect for such a notable opening.

"Our stores generally occupy from 2,000 to 4,000 square feet of retail space, and we typically use local contractors for the build-out. A store build-out usually takes 120 days from the date the property has been procured until the doors open to the public. I can give you our last opening's project plan so you have a feel for what happens. Your job will be to procure the property, negotiate the lease, procure the shelving and associated store furnishings, get a contractor on the job, and prepare the 50th store festivities. My marketing folks will assist you with that last part.

"You have six months to complete the project. Any questions?"

You take in a deep breath and collect your thoughts. Dirk has just given you a lot of information with hardly a pause in between thoughts. A few initial ideas drift through your head while you're reaching for your notebook.

You work in a functional organization with a separate projectized department responsible for carrying out projects of this nature. You've been with the company long enough to know that Dirk is high up there in the executive ranks and carries the authority and power to make things happen. Therefore, Dirk is the perfect candidate for project sponsor.

You grab your notebook and start documenting some of the things Dirk talked about, clarifying with him as you write:

- The project objective is to open a new store in Colorado Springs six months from today.

- The store should be located in an affluent area.

- The store will carry the full line of products from utensils to gourmet food items.

- The grand opening will be accompanied by lots of fanfare because this is the 50th store opening.

You have a question or two for Dirk.

"Is there a special reason we have to open, let's see, six months from now, which is February 1?"

He responds, "Yes, we want the store open the first week in February. Early February is when the Garden and Home Show conference hits the Springs area. We'll have a trade show booth there. We know from experience in other areas that our stores generally see a surge in sales during this month as a result of the trade show. It's a great way to get a lot of advertising out there and let folks know where we're located."

"Another question, Dirk. Is there a budget set for this project yet?"

"We haven't set a hard figure," Dirk replies. "But again, from past experience we know it takes anywhere from $1.5 to $2 million to open a new store. And we don't want to forget the big bash for the grand opening."

"Thanks, Dirk. I'll get started writing the project charter right away. I'll be putting your name on the document since you're the project sponsor."

Dirk concludes with, "Feel free to come to me with questions or concerns at any time."

One week later.

You review your notes and reread the project charter you've prepared for the Kitchen Heaven retail store one last time before looking for Dirk. You finally run across Dirk in a hallway near the executive washroom.

"Dirk, I'm glad I caught you. I'd like to go over the project charter with you before the kickoff meeting tomorrow. Do you have a few minutes?"

"Sure," Dirk says to you. "Let's have it."

"The project charter states the purpose of the project, which of course is to open the 50th Kitchen Heaven store in Colorado Springs. I also documented some of the high-level requirements, many of which we talked about last time we met. I documented the assumptions and constraints you gave me with the understanding that we'll define these much more closely when I create the scope statement. I've included a section that outlines a preliminary milestone schedule, and I've included some preliminary return on investment calculations. Using your estimate of $2 million as our initial budget request and based on the projected inflows you gave me last week, I've calculated a payback period of 16 months, with an IRR of 22 percent."

"That's impressive," replies Dirk. "That's even better than our Phoenix store. If I recall, the payback period there was just over two years. Let's hope those numbers hold true."

"I think they're reliable figures," you say. "I researched our data based on recent store openings in similar-sized cities and factored in the economic conditions of the Colorado Springs area. Since they're on a growth pattern, we think the timing is perfect.

"As you know, the project kickoff is scheduled for tomorrow. What I'll need then is for you to talk about the project and the goals, talk about the commitment you'll need from the management team to support this project, and introduce me as the project manager. I've already forwarded a copy of the project charter to the meeting attendees so that they can review it before the meeting. And I included a list of the assumptions we've made so far as an appendix to the charter. Lastly, I'll need you to ask everyone present to sign a copy of the project charter."

"Sounds like you've covered everything," Dirk says. "I don't anticipate any problems tomorrow, because everyone is looking forward to this store opening."

Project Case Study Checklist

Project objective: To open a new store in Colorado Springs six months from today.

Business need or demand for project: Company data concludes that the Kitchen Heaven consumers have incomes of more than $150,000 a year. The Colorado Springs area is home to a large number of people with that income. Currently, there is not a Kitchen Heaven there, but there appears to be a demand for one.

Project sponsor: Dirk Perrier, VP of marketing.

Organizational structure: Functional organization with a separate projectized department.

Project selection methods: Payback period calculated at 16 months and IRR calculated at 22 percent.

Created project charter: Project charter contains the following:

- High-level overview of project

- List of requirements that will satisfy sponsor expectations

- Business case and justification for the project

- High-level milestone schedule with initial completion date of February 1

- Initial budget of $2 million

- Definition of roles of project sponsor and project manager

Next steps: Kickoff meeting set up to discuss charter and obtain sign-off.

Understanding How This Applies to Your Next Project

There are as many ways to select and prioritize projects as there are organizations. You might be profit driven, so money will be king. You might have a stakeholder committee that weighs the pros and cons, or you might have an executive director who determines which project is up next. Scoring models and cash flow analysis techniques are useful on the job. Whether you use these methods or others, you'll need an organized, consistent way to select and prioritize projects. I know I could work the next 100 years straight and probably still not get all the projects completed my organization would like to see implemented. What I've found is that the selection method must be fair and reasonable. If you have an arbitrary method—say you like Tara better than Joe, so Tara's projects always end up on the "yes" list—it won't be long before your stakeholders demand that you devise a way to select projects that everyone can understand. Whatever method you're using, stick to it consistently.

If you're like me, when I'm faced with a new project, I want to get right to the heart of the matter and understand the purpose of the project. Projects come about for many reasons. Most of the time, understanding the reason it came about will give you some insight into its purpose. For example, if a new law is passed that requires anyone applying for a driver's license to show two forms of identification but the existing system has the space to record verification of only one document, you immediately have a firm grasp on the purpose of the project—you'll have to update the system to include additional space for recording the second document.

It has been my experience in working with project teams that when the team understands the reason or the need that brought about the project and it understands the goal of the project, the project is more successful. Now I don't have any scientific evidence for this, but when the teams have a clear understanding of what they're working on and why, they tend to stay more focused, and fewer unplanned changes make their way into the project. Don't assume everyone on the project team understands the goal of the project. It's good practice to review the project goal early in the project and again once the work of the project is underway. Reminding the team of the goal helps keep the work on track.

I usually write a project charter for all but the smallest of projects. I believe the most important sections of the charter are the goals of the project, the business justification, and the constraints. The goal of the project tells you what it is you're producing or providing, the justification tells you why you should take the project on, and the constraints tell you how many hurdles have already been put in your path. I don't mean for that to sound negative. Understanding the constraints of the project will help you the most in the planning stage. And always make sure you know whether there are time or budget constraints. It's embarrassing to present the project sponsor with a project schedule hot off the press that shows a six-month timeframe when the sponsor was expecting four months.

If the project is so small that a charter seems like too much, I'll write a statement of work. It's important that the goal of the project is written down, no matter how small the project is, so that the team and the stakeholders know what they're working toward.

I have to admit, I've never used a preliminary scope statement. I'm a "do-it-once-and-do-it-right" kind of person, so the idea of writing a charter, writing a preliminary scope statement, and then writing the scope statement is a little overkill for me. (I'll talk about scope statements in the next chapter.) And as it is, writing the charter usually follows an exercise in writing the business justification (which can be copied into the charter) and/or a feasibility study. In practice, it's easy enough to incorporate the elements of the preliminary scope statement into the charter if you know that level of information early on. But as you progressively elaborate the scope of the project, you'll learn more about the deliverables and requirements themselves. That information is captured in the scope statement.

Always, and I mean *always*, get approval and signatures on the project charter. You will use this document as your basis for project planning, so you want to make certain both you and the sponsor understand the goals of the project the same way.

And one last point: the project sponsor should write the project charter (but remember for the exam a manager external to the project should write it). This will help reduce the risk of an incomplete or inaccurate goal statement. And it helps hold them accountable, to some degree at least, for communicating their vision for the project.

Summary

This chapter started with a discussion of how projects are initiated. Projects come about as a result of one of six needs or demands: market demand, business need, customer requests, technological advances, legal requirements, and social needs.

Then I talked about the Develop the Project Charter process. The project statement of work is an input to this process that describes the product, service, or result the project was undertaken to complete. The SOW should include the business needs of the organization and a product scope description and should map to the organization's strategic plan.

Enterprise environmental factors are factors outside the project that might have significant influence on the success of the project. Organizational process assets refer to policies, guidelines, and procedures for conducting the project work.

Project selection methods are a tool and technique of the Develop Project Charter process. Selection methods include decision models in the form of benefit measurement methods and mathematical models (also called *constrained optimization methods*). The mathematical methods utilize mathematical models. Benefit measurement methods come in the form of cost-benefit analyses, scoring models, and economic analyses. These are primarily comparative approaches. Besides cost-benefit analysis, the most commonly used form of benefit measurement methods is cash flow analysis.

Analysis of cash flows includes payback period, discounted cash flows, net present value (NPV), and internal rate of return (IRR). These last three methods are concerned with the time value of money—or in other words, converting future dollars into today's value. Generally, projects with a shorter payback period are desired over those with longer payback periods. Projects that have an NPV greater than zero should be accepted. Projects with the highest IRR value are considered a better benefit to the organization than projects with low IRR values.

Expert judgment is another tool and technique of this process. Experts usually have specialized knowledge or skills and can include staff from other departments in the company, external or internal consultants, and members of professional and technical associations or industry groups.

The output of this process is the project charter, which is the formal recognition that a project, or the next project phase, should begin. The charter authorizes the project to begin, it authorizes the project manager to assign resources to the project, it documents the business need and justification, it describes the customer's requirements, and it ties the project to the ongoing work of the organization.

The preliminary project scope statement is a high-level definition of what the project entails, including the project objectives and deliverables. It describes the business opportunity the company is attempting to benefit from and the business objectives the project intends to meet. Many of the elements included in the preliminary scope statement are also part of the project scope statement.

Exam Essentials

Be able to distinguish between the six needs or demands that bring about project creation. The six needs or demands that bring about project creation are market demand, business need, customer requests, technological advances, legal requirements, and social needs.

Be able to denote the Develop the Project Charter inputs. The inputs for Develop the Project Charter are contract (where applicable), project statement of work, enterprise environmental factors, and organizational process assets.

Be able to define decision models. Decision models are project selection methods that are a tool and technique of the Develop Project Charter process. Decision models include benefit measurement methods and mathematical models.

Be able to describe and calculate payback period. Payback period is the amount of time it will take the company to recoup its initial investment in the product of the project. It's calculated by adding up the expected cash inflows and comparing them to the initial investment to determine how many periods it takes for the cash inflows to equal the initial investment.

Be able to denote the decision criteria for NPV and IRR. Projects with an NPV greater than zero should be accepted, and those with an NPV less than zero should be rejected. Projects with high IRR values should be accepted over projects with lower IRR values. IRR is the discount rate when NPV is equal to zero, and IRR assumes reinvestment at the IRR rate.

Be able to describe the importance of the project charter. The project charter is the document that officially recognizes and acknowledges that a project exists. The charter authorizes the project to begin, it authorizes the project manager to assign resources to the project, it documents the business need and justification, it describes the customer's requirements, and it ties the project to the ongoing work of the organization.

Key Terms

You've learned just how important a charter is to every project. Be sure you understand the elements essential to the document and the processes used to ensure that your charter is complete. Skimping on the planning steps is almost certain to spell disaster down the road. Know these processes, and know them by the names used in the PMBOK:

Develop Project Charter

Develop Preliminary Scope Statement

Initiating

You've also learned a lot of new key words in this chapter. PMI has worked hard to develop and define standard project management terms that apply across industries. Here is a list of some of the terms you came across in this chapter:

benefit measurement methods	mathematical models
calculation methods	net present value (NPV)
constrained optimization methods	payback period
cost-benefit	preliminary scope statement
decision models	project charter
discounted cash flow	project statement of work (SOW)
expert judgment	scoring model
initiation	steering committee
internal rate of return (IRR)	weighted scoring model

Review Questions

1. When a project is being performed under contract, the SOW is provided by which of the following?

    A. The buyer

    B. The project sponsor

    C. The project manager

    D. The contractor

2. You've been hired as a manager for the adjustments department of a nationwide bank based in your city. The adjustments department is responsible for making corrections to customer accounts. This is a large department, with several smaller sections that deal with specific accounts, such as personal checking or commercial checking. You've received your first set of management reports and can't make heads or tails of the information. Each section appears to use a different methodology to audit their work and record the data for the management report. You request a project manager from the PMO to come down and get started right away on a project to streamline this process and make the data and reports consistent. This project came about as a result of which of the following?

    A. Technological advance

    B. Business need

    C. Customer request

    D. Legal requirement

3. What are the inputs to the Develop Project Charter process?

    A. Contract, project SOW, enterprise environmental factors, and organizational process assets

    B. Project SOW, project selection methods, and organizational process assets

    C. Contract, project selection methods, enterprise environmental factors, and organizational process assets

    D. Project SOW, project selection methods, and enterprise environmental factors

4. You work for a large manufacturing plant. Your firm is thinking of initiating a new project to release an overseas product line. This is the company's first experience in the overseas market, and it wants to make a big splash with the introduction of this product. The project entails producing your product in a concentrated formula and packaging it in smaller containers than the U.S. product uses. A new machine is needed in order to mix the first set of ingredients in the concentrated formula. Which of the following actions should the project manager take?

   A. The project manager should document the project's objectives and business justification in a project charter document and recommend that the project should proceed.

   B. The project manager knows the project is a go and should document the project's objectives and known deliverables in a preliminary scope statement document.

   C. The project manager should document the business need for the project and recommend that a feasibility study be performed to determine viability of the project.

   D. The project manager should document the high-level product requirements and stakeholder expectations in a preliminary scope statement.

5. Which of the following lists the inputs and the tools and techniques that the two processes within the Initiating process group share?

   A. Project SOW, enterprise environment factors, organizational process assets, project selection methods, and expert judgment

   B. Enterprise environment factors, organizational process assets, PMIS, and expert judgment

   C. Project SOW, enterprise environment factors, organizational process assets, project management methodology, PMIS, and expert judgment

   D. Project SOW, enterprise environment factors, and organizational process assets

6. According to the *PMBOK Guide*, the project statement of work should contain or reference all the following elements except for which one?

   A. Strategic plan, product scope description, stakeholder influences, and business need

   B. Business need, strategic plan, product scope description

   C. Project purpose, business case, stakeholder influences, product scope description

   D. Requirements, business need, stakeholder expectations

7. Your nonprofit organization is preparing to host its first annual 5K run/walk in City Park. You worked on a similar project for the organization two years ago when it cohosted the 10K run through Overland Pass. Which of the organizational process assets might be helpful to you on your new project?

   A. The strategic plan, because you'll want to make sure the project reflects the overall strategic direction of the organization

   B. Historical information on the 10K run project

   C. The project SOW, which describes the high-level details of the run/walk program

   D. The organization's PMIS system

8. Which of the following is true regarding product scope descriptions?

    A. The product scope description is a component of the output of the Develop Project Charter process. It describes the characteristics of the product, service, or result and contains a good deal of detail in the later phases of the project.

    B. The product description is a component of the output of the Preliminary Scope Statement process. It describes the characteristics of the product, service, or result and contains less detail in the early phases of the project.

    C. The product description is a component of an input of the Preliminary Scope Statement process. It describes the characteristics of the product, service, or result and contains a good deal of detail in the early phases of the project.

    D. The product description is a component of an input of the Develop Project Charter process. It describes the characteristics of the product, service, or result and contains less detail in the early phases of the project.

9. Comparative methods, scoring methods, and economic and cash flow analysis are all part of which of the following?

    A. Benefit measurement methods, which are a component of a tool and technique in the Develop Project Charter process

    B. Constrained optimization methods, which are a component of a tool and technique in the Preliminary Scope Statement process

    C. Benefit measurement methods, which are a component of an input to the Develop Project Charter process

    D. Mathematical modes, which are a component of an input to the Preliminary Scope Statement process

10. You are the project manager for the Late Night Smooth Jazz Club chain, with stores in 12 states. Smooth Jazz is considering opening a new club in Arizona or Nevada. You have derived the following information:

    Project Arizona: The payback period is 18 months, and the NPV is <250>.

    Project Nevada: The payback period is 24 months, and the NPV is 300.

    Which project would you recommend to the selection committee?

    A. Project Arizona, because the payback period is shorter than the payback period for Project Nevada

    B. Project Nevada, because its NPV is a positive number

    C. Project Arizona because its NPV is a negative number

    D. Project Nevada, because its NPV is a higher number than Project Arizona's NPV

11. You are the project manager for the Late Night Smooth Jazz Club chain, with stores in 12 states. Smooth Jazz is considering opening a new club in Kansas City or Spokane. You have derived the following information:

    Project Kansas City: The payback period is 27 months, and the IRR is 35 percent.

    Project Spokane: The payback period is 25 months, and the IRR is 32 percent.

Which project should you recommend to the selection committee?

A. Project Spokane, because the payback period is the shortest

B. Project Kansas City, because the IRR is the highest

C. Project Spokane, because the IRR is the lowest

D. Project Kansas City, because the payback period is the longest

12. Which of the following is true regarding NPV?

A. NPV assumes reinvestment at the cost of capital.

B. NPV decisions should be made based on the highest value for all the selections.

C. NPV assumes reinvestment at the prevailing rate.

D. NPV assumes reinvestment at the NPV rate.

13. You are the project manager for Insomniacs International. Since you don't sleep much, you get a lot of project work done. You're considering recommending a project that costs $575,000; expected inflows are $25,000 per quarter for the first two years and then $75,000 per quarter thereafter. What is the payback period?

A. 40 months

B. 38 months

C. 39 months

D. 41 months

14. Which of the following is true regarding IRR?

A. IRR assumes reinvestment at the cost of capital.

B. IRR is the discount rate when NPV is greater than zero.

C. IRR is a constrained optimization method.

D. IRR is the discount rate when NPV is equal to zero.

15. Mathematical models using linear, dynamic, integer, or algorithm models are considered

A. Project selection criteria

B. A form of expert judgment

C. Project selection methods

D. A form of historical information

16. Your project selection committee used a weighted scoring model and found that Project B, with a score of 54, should be chosen over the other competing projects. Which of the following is true?

A. Weighted scoring models are benefit measurement methods, which are used as a tool and technique during the Develop Project Charter process.

B. Weighted scoring models are constrained optimization methods, which are used as a tool and technique in both Initiating process group processes.

C. Weighted scoring models are benefit measurement methods and are the least efficient method of project selection.

D. Weighted scoring models are a type of mathematical model that can be used both for project selection and vendor selection.

17. Your selection committee is debating between two projects. Project A has a payback period of 18 months. Project B has a cost of $125,000, with expected cash inflows of $50,000 the first year and $25,000 per quarter after that. Which project should you recommend?

    A. Either Project A or Project B, because the payback periods are equal

    B. Project A, because Project B's payback period is 21 months

    C. Project A, because Project B's payback period is 24 months

    D. Project A, because Project B's payback period is 20 months

18. Which of the following is true?

    A. Discounted cash flow analysis is the least precise of the cash flow techniques, because it does not consider the time value of money.

    B. NPV is the least precise of the cash flow analysis techniques, because it assumes reinvestment at the discount rate.

    C. Payback period is the least precise of the cash flow analysis techniques, because it does not consider the time value of money.

    D. IRR is the least precise of the cash flow analysis techniques, because it assumes reinvestment at the cost of capital.

19. You are a project manager for Zippy Tees. Your selection committee has just chosen a project you recommended for implementation. Your project is to manufacture a line of miniature stuffed bears that will be attached to your company's trendy T-shirts. The bears will be wearing the same T-shirt design as the shirt to which they're attached. Your project sponsor thinks you've really impressed the big boss and wants you to skip to the manufacturing process right away. What is your response?

    A. Agree with the project sponsor because that person is your boss and has a lot of authority and power in the company.

    B. Require that a preliminary budget be established and a resource list be put together to alert other managers of the requirements of this project. This should be published and signed by the other managers who are impacted by this project.

    C. Require a project charter be written and signed off on by all stakeholders before proceeding.

    D. Suggest that a preliminary scope statement be written because this will outline the objectives of the project and greatly assist in the development of the scope statement in the Planning processes.

20. Which of the following is true regarding the project charter?

    A. The project charter should be published under the name of a manager external to the project.

    B. The project charter should be published under the project sponsor's name.

    C. The project charter should be published under the name of the project manager.

    D. The project charter should be published under the name of the project champion.

Answers to Review Questions

1. A. The buyer provides SOW when projects are performed under contract.

2. B. This came about because of a business need. Staff members were spending unproductive hours producing information for the management report that wasn't consistent or meaningful.

3. A. Develop Project Charter has four inputs, and they are contract, project SOW, enterprise environmental factors, and organizational process assets.

4. C. The most correct answer is to perform a feasibility study. Since this project is taking the company into a new, unknown market, there's lots of potential for error and failure. A feasibility study would help the stakeholders determine whether the project is viable and cost effective and whether it has a high potential for success.

5. C. The Develop Project Charter and Preliminary Scope Statement processes both have the following as inputs: project SOW, enterprise environment factors, and organizational process assets. Both processes share the following tools and techniques: project management methodology, PMIS, and expert judgment.

6. B. The project SOW should contain the business need for the project and the product scope description and should support the organization's strategic plan.

7. B. Historical information on projects of a similar nature can be helpful when initiating new projects. They can help in formulating project deliverables and identifying constraints and assumptions and will be helpful later in the project Planning processes as well.

8. D. The product description is a component of the project SOW, which is an input of both the Develop Project Charter and Preliminary Scope Statement processes. It describes the characteristics of the product, service, or result and contains less detail in the early phases of the project and more detail as the project progresses.

9. A. Benefit measurement methods include comparative methods, scoring models, and cash flow analysis, which are all part of the project selection method tools and techniques in the Develop Project Charter process.

10. B. Projects with NPV greater than zero should be given an accept recommendation.

11. B. Projects with the highest IRR value are favored over projects with lower IRR values.

12. A. Net present value (NPV) assumes reinvestment is made at the cost of capital.

13. C. Year 1 and 2 inflows are each $100,000 for a total of $200,000. Year 3 inflows are an additional $300,000. Add one more quarter to this total, and the $575,000 is reached in three years and three months, or 39 months.

14. D. IRR assumes reinvestment at the IRR rate and is the discount rate when NPV is equal to zero.

15. C. Mathematical models are one of the methods described in the project selection methods tool and technique of the Develop Project Charter process.

16. A. Benefit measurement methods include comparative methods and scoring models, among others, to make project selections during the Develop Project Charter process.

17. B. Project B has a payback period of 21 months; $50,000 is received in the first 12 months, with another $75,000 coming in over each of the next three quarters, or nine months.

18. C. Payback period does not consider the time value of money and is therefore the least precise of all the cash flow analysis techniques.

19. C. The project should be kicked off with a project charter that authorizes the project to begin, assigns the project manager, and describes the project objectives and business need for the project. This ensures that everyone is working with the same purposes in mind.

20. A. According to the *PMBOK Guide*, the project charter should be published by a manager external to the project but with sufficient power and authority to carry it off.

Chapter

3

Developing the Project Scope Statement

THE PMP EXAM CONTENT FROM THE PLANNING THE PROJECT PERFORMANCE DOMAIN COVERED IN THIS CHAPTER INCLUDES THE FOLLOWING:

✓ Define and Record Requirements, Constraints, and Assumptions

✓ Develop Change Management Plan

Great job! You've successfully completed the project Initiating processes and published the project charter and the preliminary scope statement. The project is officially underway. Stakeholders have been informed, you have management buy-in on the project, the project manager has been assigned, and the project objectives and description have been identified. A solid foundation for the Planning process is in place.

In this chapter, we will begin the Planning processes for the project. In fact, I will continue discussing the Planning processes through Chapter 7, "Creating the Project Schedule and Budget." Planning is a significant activity in any project and, if done correctly, will go a long way toward ensuring project success.

This chapter begins with the Develop Project Management Plan process. This process will describe the overall approach you'll use to manage the project. The result of this process is the project management plan document that describes how you'll execute, monitor, and control the project outcomes as the project progresses and how you'll close out the project once it concludes.

Then you'll move on to the Scope Planning process. You'll use the project charter and preliminary scope statement you created in the previous chapter—plus some other inputs—and then apply the tools and techniques of this process to come up with the project scope management plan. From there, you're off to the Scope Definition process, where you'll further elaborate the project objectives and deliverables. I'll talk in depth about project objectives, requirements, constraints, assumptions, and other elements of writing the project scope statement, which is an output of this process.

Developing the Project Management Plan

The first process in the Planning process group is the *Develop Project Management Plan* process. It's first for good reason. This process is part of the Integration Management Knowledge Area and is concerned with defining, coordinating, and integrating all the various ancillary project plans.

This process involves defining and documenting the processes you're going to use to manage this project. For example, let's say you and the project team have determined you will use project management processes involving costs, human resources, risks, and a project schedule. (Warning: this is a demonstration only—don't try this at home. In reality, professionals perform many more processes than this on a typical project.) Each particular process might have a management plan that describes it. For instance, a cost management plan would describe how costs will be managed and controlled and how changes to costs will be approved and managed throughout the project. The Develop Project Management Plan process brings all these subsidiary plans together, along with the outputs of the Planning group processes, into one document called the *project management plan*.

In Chapter 1 ("What Is a Project?"), I talked about *tailoring*—determining which processes within each process group are appropriate for the project on which you're working. Tailoring is used in the Develop Project Management Plan process because it's here you'll determine what processes to use to best manage the project.

To create and document the plan, you need to gather some inputs and build on the information you've already collected.

Developing Inputs

The Develop Project Management Plan has four inputs:

- Preliminary project scope statement
- Project management processes
- Enterprise environmental factors
- Organizational process assets

Organizational process assets here are the same ones you considered when developing the project charter in Chapter 2, "Creating the Project Charter and Preliminary Scope Statement." You should note some important elements in the remaining inputs:

Preliminary project scope statement   You'll recall that the preliminary project scope statement describes the objectives of the project and the high-level requirements needed to satisfy stakeholder expectations. The reason it's an input into this process is because the content of the preliminary project scope statement—including objectives, product requirements, schedule milestones, and so on—will help you and the team determine exactly which project management processes to use on the project.

Remember, you're studying for the exam, so the correct input into this process is the preliminary project scope statement. However, if you skipped that process and produced only a project charter, you could use it as an input to this process.

Project management processes   The project management processes include all the individual processes that make up the process groups we're talking about throughout this book. The Initiating group, for example, has two processes, Planning has a zillion (OK, not that many, but it seems like it), and so on. Each of the processes you determine to use on the project will be documented in the project management plan.

Enterprise environmental factors   You've seen enterprise environmental factors before. Some of the key elements of the environmental factors you should consider when choosing the processes to perform for this project include standards and regulations (both industry and governmental), company culture, skills and knowledge of existing personnel, risk tolerances of stakeholders, and the project management information system (PMIS).

As I talked about in Chapter 1, the processes you choose to perform for the project will be based on the complexity of the project, the project scope, and the type of industry in which you work. Your organization's standards, guidelines, and policies (a component of organizational process assets) or the project management office (PMO) might also dictate the types of processes you'll use for the project. You should also consider whether your organization has existing change control processes in place, templates that you're required to use, or financial controls and processes. Don't forget to look for historical information and then use it to help you decide which processes to use for this project.

The tools and techniques for this process are also familiar. They include project management methodology, expert judgment, and PMIS. We covered expert judgment and project management methodology in Chapter 2, if you need a refresher.

Exam Spotlight

Be aware that the *PMBOK Guide* lists the PMIS as a tool and technique of some processes *and* as an input (it's part of the enterprise environmental factors) of others. The PMIS in the Develop Project Management Plan process includes a subsystem called the *configuration management system* (I'll cover this in Chapter 9, "Measuring and Controlling Project Performance") and the change control system, which is a subsystem of the configuration management system.

The PMIS in this case is an automated system used to document the subsidiary plans and the project management plan, facilitate the feedback process, and revise the documents. It incorporates the configuration management system and the change control system, both of which I'll cover in Chapter 9. Later in the project, the PMIS can be used to control changes to any of the plans. When you're thinking about the PMIS as an input (that is, as part of the enterprise environmental factors), think of it as a collection and distribution point for information as well as an easy way to revise and update documents. When you're thinking about the PMIS as a tool and technique, think of it just that way—as a tool to facilitate the automation of data collection and distribution and to automate and monitor processes such as scheduling, resource leveling, budgeting, and web interfaces.

Documenting the Project Management Plan

The purpose of most processes is, of course, to produce an output. Outputs are usually a report or document of some type or a deliverable. In this case, you end up with a document—the project management plan—that describes, integrates, and coordinates subsidiary plans for the processes you've determined to use for the project. The project management plan can be detailed or a high-level summary based on the needs of the project.

According to the *PMBOK Guide*, the project management plan defines how the project is executed, how it's monitored and controlled, and how it's closed. It also documents the outputs of the Planning group processes, which I'll cover over the next several chapters. The project management plan should include or discuss the following elements:

- Processes you'll use to perform the project
- Degrees of execution of each of the processes selected for the project
- Tools and techniques to use for each process
- Essential inputs and outputs from each of the processes and how they'll be used to manage the project
- Dependencies and interactions of the processes used to manage the project
- Methods for executing the work of the project to fulfill the objectives
- Methods for monitoring and controlling changes
- Methods to perform configuration management
- Methods for determining and maintaining the validity of performance baselines
- Communication needs of the stakeholders and techniques to fulfill those needs
- Project life cycle
- Project phases for multiphased projects
- Management reviews of issues and pending decisions

In addition to the elements just listed, the subsidiary plans that are associated with the processes you'll be using for this project should be documented in the project management plan. Each of these subsidiary management plans might contain the same elements as the overall project management plan does, but they're specifically related to the topic at hand. For example, the cost management plan should define how changes to cost estimates will be reflected in the project budget and how changes or variances with a significant impact should be communicated to the project sponsor and stakeholders. The schedule management plan describes how changes to the schedule will be managed, and so on.

The subsidiary plans might be detailed or simply a synopsis, depending on the needs of the project. I've listed the subsidiary plans along with a brief description next. I will cover each of these plans in more detail throughout the remainder of this book. According to the *PMBOK Guide*, the subsidiary plans are as follows:

Project scope management plan   Describes the process for determining project scope, facilitates creating the work breakdown structure (WBS), describes how the product or service of the project is verified and accepted, and documents how changes to scope will be handled.

Schedule management plan   Describes how the project schedule will be developed and controlled and how changes will be incorporated into the project schedule.

Cost management plan   Describes how costs will be managed and controlled and how changes to costs will be approved and managed.

Quality management plan   Describes how the organization's quality policy will be implemented. It must address and describe quality control procedures and measures, quality assurance procedures and measures, and continuous process improvement.

Process improvement plan   Describes how processes will be analyzed for the value they bring to the performance of project management. This analysis focuses on excluding or eliminating inefficiencies and waste.

Staffing management plan   Describes how human resource requirements for the project will be met, including how staff acquisition will occur and the time frames in which resources are needed.

Communications management plan   Describes the communication needs of the stakeholders, including timing, frequency, and methods of communications.

Risk management plan   Describes how risks will be managed and controlled during the project. This should include risk management methodology; roles and responsibilities; definitions of probability and impact; when project management will be performed; and the categories of risk, risk tolerances, and reporting and tracking formats.

Procurement management plan   Describes how the procurement processes will be managed throughout the project. This might include elements such as type of contract, procurement documents, and lead times for purchases.

The project management plan is not limited to the subsidiary plans listed here. You might include other plans and documentation that help describe how the project will be executed or monitored and controlled. Perhaps you're working on a project that requires precise calculations and exact adherence to requirements. You could include a plan that describes these calculations, how they'll be monitored and measured, and the processes you'll use to make changes or corrections.

This output has one more piece to it. Each of the processes associated with the subsidiary plans has components that you should consider when developing the plans. The components that the *PMBOK Guide* recommends you consider are as follows:

- Milestone list
- Resource calendar
- Schedule baseline
- Cost baseline
- Quality baseline
- Risk register

I'll talk about each of these in the remaining chapters as well.

WARNING

Be aware that I'm about to get on my soapbox. If you don't want to indulge me, skip the next few sentences and go to the next paragraph. I find it a little disconcerting that the 2004 version of the *PMBOK Guide* presents information that the reader has no knowledge of in advance of learning the process. It's almost as if you need to be well versed in all the processes before you read the book! You're going to see several places throughout the remainder of this book where I introduce topics, as in the previous list, that you don't know anything about yet. Rest assured, I will cover these topics in their proper places. If I began to tell you now about the risk management plan and risk register, for example, I'd first have to explain what risks are, the processes involved, and how the risk register is produced. I think it will make much more sense for you to see these elements in context of the processes in which they're produced. Thanks, I feel better now.

Exam Spotlight

Understand that the purpose of the project management plan is to define how the project is executed, monitored and controlled, and closed, as well as to document the outputs of the Planning group processes you'll use during the project.

As the project progresses and more and more processes are performed, the subsidiary plans and the project management plan itself might change. These changes should be reviewed, and the project management plan should be updated to reflect the approved changes. Depending on the nature of the changes, the project manager, stakeholders, or sponsor (or some combination) should review and approve the changes.

Exam Spotlight

In practice, you'll find that you'll prepare the project management plan after you've progressed through several of the other Planning processes. It's difficult to create some of these subsidiary plans without performing the process they're associated with first. However, for the exam, remember that Develop Project Management Plan is the first process in the Planning group, and it should be performed first.

Scoping Out the Project

Scope Planning is the first process in the Project Scope Management Knowledge Area and the second process in the Planning process group. You might recall from Chapter 1 that the purpose of the Project Scope Management Knowledge Area is to describe and control what is and what is *not* work of the project. *Scope* is collectively the product, service, or result of the project and the deliverables the project intends to produce.

The primary purpose of Scope Planning is to document the scope management plan. This is a planning tool that documents how the project team will go about defining project scope, how the work breakdown structure will be developed, how changes to scope will be controlled, and how project scope will be verified.

 I'll talk more about this in the section "Documenting the Scope Management Plan" later in this chapter.

For now you'll concentrate on the inputs to this process, which will help you get started documenting the decisions about the Scope Planning process for your project.

Understanding the Scope Planning Inputs

You've seen the inputs to the Scope Planning process before. They are as follows:

- Enterprise environmental factors
- Organizational process assets
- Project charter
- Preliminary project scope statement
- Project management plan

Even though I've talked about these before, you'll want to look at specific elements of some of these inputs closely. Defining project scope, and managing to that scope as you progress through the project, has a direct relationship to the success of the project. It's difficult to document how you'll define project scope if you don't first understand the purpose behind the project; the product, service, or result you're trying to produce; and the environmental factors and organizational process assets under which you're working. The process of how you'll go about defining and managing scope is what the scope management plan (which is what you're ultimately getting to with this process) is about.

One of the environmental factors that might influence the way scope is managed is the human resources involved on the project. Their skills, knowledge, and abilities to communicate and escalate issues appropriately might influence the way project scope is managed. Personnel policies governing those resources might also have an effect. For example, you might have a team member who has a close relationship with one of the stakeholders. Let's say the stakeholder wants a change to the project. The stakeholder and team member grab a cup of coffee together at the corner deli, and the next thing you know, the team member is incorporating the change into the project. Scope can't be managed efficiently when it's being changed without the knowledge of the project manager or project team.

Other environmental factors that might affect scope management are the organization's culture, economic conditions, and physical and technological infrastructure.

 Real World Scenario

Scope Management Plan Requirements

Phil Reid is a gifted engineer. He works as an accident reconstructionist and has a 90 percent success rate at assisting his clients (who are attorneys) at winning court cases. Phil can intuitively and scientifically determine whether the scene of an accident is real or is insurance fraud. Most cases Phil works on are managed as projects because each accident is unique, the cause of each accident is unique, and each investigation has a definite beginning and ending. The attorneys that Phil's organization works with want the final results of the investigation delivered in different formats. Although Phil is exceptionally good at determining the forensic evidence needed to prove or disprove how the accident occurred, he is not at all gifted in oral communication skills. As a result, the scope management plan requires the client to define how the outcome of the investigation should be presented and whether the engineer might be required to testify regarding the results of the investigation. That way, Phil's organization can plan in advance how to use his talents on the project and assign a resource to work with him who has the communication skills and ability to testify whether that's required.

Organizational process assets typically include policies and procedures, whether formal or informal. Your organization's policies or the policies and guidelines of your industry might have an effect on scope management, so make certain you're familiar with them. And don't forget historical information. You can review the scope management plan from previous projects of similar size and scope to help you craft the one for this project.

The project charter and preliminary scope statement describe the purpose and high-level requirements of the project. Analyzing the information in these documents will help you determine the appropriate tools and methodologies to use (as well as which processes to perform) for the project. The idea here is that you want to understand the size and complexity of the project so that you don't spend more time documenting how you're going to go about defining and managing scope than what's needed.

Using Scope Planning Tools and Techniques

Scope Planning consists of two tools and techniques:

Expert judgment You'll rely on the expert judgment of people or groups with specific skills, knowledge, or training to help assess the process inputs. One expert you can count on in this process is the executive manager who wrote or contributed to the project charter. This person can clarify questions you might have about the project objectives as well as the product description. Stakeholders or other project managers with previous experience on projects similar to yours can help you determine how scope management should work for this project.

Templates, forms, and standards   Your PMO might have scope management templates, forms, and standards that you can use to help define the scope management plan. Work breakdown structure templates and scope change control forms might also help because they outline how to break down the work of the project and what elements are needed to describe changes.

Documenting the Scope Management Plan

The only output of the Scope Planning process is the *project scope management plan*. This plan describes how the project team will go about defining project scope, verifying the work of the project, and managing and controlling scope. According to the *PMBOK Guide*, the project scope management plan should contain the following:

- The process you'll use to prepare the project scope statement. The project scope statement (which I'll define later in this chapter) contains a detailed description of what the deliverables and requirements of the project are and is based on the information contained in the preliminary scope.

- A process for creating the WBS. The WBS (I'll cover that in the next chapter) further defines the work of the project (as defined in the project scope statement) by breaking down the deliverables into smaller pieces of work.

- A definition of how the deliverables will be verified for accuracy and the process used for accepting deliverables.

- A description of the process for controlling scope change requests, including the procedure for requesting changes and how to obtain a change request form.

Exam Spotlight

The project scope management plan is a planning tool that documents how the project team will go about defining project scope, how the work breakdown structure will be developed, how changes to scope will be controlled, and how the work of the project will be verified and accepted. And don't forget, the scope management plan is a component of (or a subsidiary of) the project management plan.

Formulating Scope Definition

Now you're getting to the meat of the project Planning process group. The high-level objectives and deliverables and the initial constraints and assumptions of the project were defined in the preliminary scope statement. When you prepared the preliminary scope statement, it was, well, preliminary. Now you're ready to further define these in the *Scope Definition* process and prepare a detailed project scope statement because more information is known. The project scope statement (which you'll get to shortly) is what you'll use to further define the deliverables of the project and the work needed to produce them.

Exam Spotlight

You'll want to pay particular attention to the accuracy and completeness of this process. Defining project scope is critical to the success of the project since it spells out exactly what the product or service of the project looks like. Conversely, poor scope definition might lead to cost increases, rework, schedule delays, and poor morale.

First you'll examine the inputs and tools and techniques of this process.

The inputs to the Scope Definition process are as follows:

- Organizational process assets
- Project charter
- Preliminary project scope statement
- Project scope management plan
- Approved change requests

Some of the important information you'll want to key in on from these inputs are historical information; the product description; and the project objectives, assumptions, and constraints. (I'll cover each of these in the section "Writing the Project Scope Statement" later in this chapter.)

The approved change requests input will obviously impact the project scope. They might also impact quality, estimated costs, or the project schedule. As changes are approved, you'll have to modify the project scope statement (and other planning documents) to reflect them.

You'll see some new tools and techniques in this process:

- Product analysis
- Alternatives identification
- Expert judgment
- Stakeholder analysis

I've covered expert judgment before. I'll cover product analysis, alternatives identification, and stakeholders in the following sections.

Product Analysis

Product analysis goes hand in hand with the product scope description. Product analysis is a method for converting the product description and project objectives into deliverables and requirements. According to the *PMBOK Guide*, product analysis might include performing value analysis, functional analysis, systems-engineering techniques, systems analysis, or value-engineering techniques to further define the product or service.

Exam Spotlight

In practice, you'll often find that you'll skip over the preliminary scope statement process and begin writing the project scope statement after the charter is documented. However, you're studying for the exam, so remember that the project scope statement is further elaborated based on the information contained in the preliminary scope statement. Most of the information found in the preliminary scope statement is also found in the project scope statement.

Also note that if either the project charter or the preliminary project scope statement is missing or was not developed, you should use the product scope description as an input to this process.

Exam Spotlight

It's beyond the scope of this book to go into the various analysis techniques used in product analysis. For exam purposes, remember that product analysis is a tool and technique of the Scope Definition process, and memorize the list of analysis techniques that might be performed in this process.

Alternatives Identification

Alternatives identification is a technique used for discovering different methods or ways of accomplishing the project. For example, brainstorming might be used to discover alternative ways of achieving one of the project objectives. Perhaps the project's budget doesn't allow for a portion of the project that the stakeholders really think needs to be included. Brainstorming might uncover an alternative that would allow the needed portion to be accomplished.

Lateral thinking is a form of alternatives identification that can be used to help define scope. Edward de Bono created this term and has done extensive research and writing on the topic of lateral thinking. The simplest definition is that it's thinking outside the box. Lateral thinking is a process of separating the problem—or in our case the components of project scope (the deliverables and requirements)—looking at them from angles other than their obvious presentation and encouraging team members to come up with ways to solve problems or look at scope that are not apparently obvious.

Stakeholder Analysis

During stakeholder analysis, you'll want to identify the influences stakeholders have in regard to the project and understand their expectations, needs, and desires. From there, you'll derive more specifics regarding the project goals and deliverables. Be warned that stakeholders are mostly concerned about their own interests and what they (or their organizations) have to gain

---

Outside the Box

Lateral thinking is a way of reasoning and thinking about problems from perspectives other than the obvious. It challenges our perceptions and assumptions. Consider these two examples of lateral thinking that I crafted based on some puzzles I found at this website: www.folj.com/ lateral/. Use your favorite search engine and run a query on "lateral thinking puzzles" to find many more examples.

Question: How could your pet Yorkie fall from the window of an 18-story building and live?

Answer: The question asks how your pet could fall from an 18-story building and live; however, the question doesn't state your pet fell from the 18th floor. So, your pet Yorkie fell from the basement-level window.

Question: Eight chocolates are arranged in an antique candy dish. Eight people each take one chocolate. There is one chocolate remaining in the dish. How can that be?

Answer: If there are eight chocolates in an antique dish, how can the last person take the last chocolate but yet one remains in the dish? Well, the last person to take a chocolate took the dish as well—therefore the last chocolate remained in the dish.

Remember these examples the next time you're defining scope or looking for alternative answers to a problem.

---

or lose from the project. In all fairness, we all fall into the stakeholder category, so we're all guilty of focusing on those issues that impact us most.

The *PMBOK Guide* doesn't heavily reference stakeholders prior to this process. You'll recall they state that the information for the project charter and preliminary scope statement comes from the project requestor or sponsor. In practice, you'll want to bring your stakeholders into the project as early in the process as you can, preferably when the project charter or preliminary scope statement is being written. Your objective at this point is to begin defining exactly what the stakeholders' expectations are of project outcomes. This should include information such as the project's objectives and how you'll recognize when the project is successfully completed. At the end of this identification and analysis process, you'll be able to describe and prioritize their expectations in terms of project requirements. But I'm getting ahead of myself. I'll define objectives and requirements shortly. Let's discover who those stakeholders are first.

Identifying Stakeholders

Think of stakeholders and project participants as a highly polished orchestra. Each participant has a part to play. Some play more parts than others, and alas, some don't play their parts as well as others. An integral part of project management is getting to know your stakeholders and the parts they play. You'll remember from Chapter 1 that stakeholders are those people or organizations who have a vested interest in the outcome of the project. They have something to either gain or lose as a result of the project, and they have the ability to influence project results. Stakeholders are officially identified in the Planning process. In practice, key stakeholders will have to be contacted early on to get their input for the project goals and deliverables.

Identifying key stakeholders seems like it should be fairly easy, but once you get beyond the obvious stakeholders, the process can get difficult. Sometimes stakeholders, even key stakeholders, will change throughout the project's life. The key stakeholders on a project might include the project sponsor, the customer (who might also be the project sponsor), the project manager, project team members, management personnel, contractors, suppliers, and so on. Stakeholders can be internal or external to the organization. One way to uncover stakeholders whom you might not have thought about at the start is to ask known stakeholders if they're aware of anyone else who might be impacted by this project. Ask team members whether they're aware of stakeholders who haven't been identified. Stakeholders might also come to the forefront once you start uncovering some of the goals and deliverables of the project.

Don't forget important stakeholders. That could be a project killer. Leaving out an important stakeholder, or one whose business processes weren't considered during the Initiating and Planning processes, could spell disaster for your project.

Understanding Stakeholder Roles

It's important for the project manager to understand each stakeholder's role in the project and their role in the organization. Get to know them and their interests. Determine the relationship structure among the various stakeholders. Start cultivating partnerships with these stakeholders now, because it's going to get pretty cozy during the course of your project. If you establish good working relationships up front and learn a little about their business concerns and needs, it might be easier to negotiate or motivate them later when you have a pressing issue that needs action. Knowing which stakeholders work well together and which don't can also help you in the future. One stakeholder might have the authority or influence to twist the arm of another, figuratively speaking, of course. Or conversely, you might know of two stakeholders who are like oil and water when put into the same room together. This can be valuable information to keep under your hat for future reference.

Stakeholders might have a significant amount of influence over the project and its outcomes. Understanding the organizational structure, and where the stakeholders fit in that structure, should be your first step in determining the level of influence they have. For example, if Melanie in accounting wields a significant amount of power and influence over the organization, when you need input or decisions from her regarding costs or budgets for the project, you better believe that those decisions are not likely going to get overridden. Conversely, if stakeholders with little influence provide direction that you don't verify, that input could be overridden at a later date by a more powerful stakeholder, causing changes to the project.

Communicating with Stakeholders

Now those finely honed communication skills are going to come in handy. You're just about ready to start documenting the deliverables and requirements of the project. To determine the specifics of your project, you'll want to meet with each of the key stakeholders and document their needs, wants, and expectations. You might want to ask them what business process the project will likely change, enhance, or replace. Perhaps the existing business processes, and the systems that support them, are so old that little documentation exists for them. Determine whether there is a critical business need for this project or whether it's a "nice to have," as we say around our office. What will be the result of this project? Will customer service be improved or sales increased? Find out what prevents the stakeholders today from achieving the results they hope the project will accomplish. Ask about the deliverables and how they can be verified and measured. And always ask the stakeholders how they will know that the project was completed successfully.

One way to help identify project objectives (which I'll talk about in the next section) is to talk about what is not included in a project. For example, let's say you're working on a highway project to create a new on-ramp from a downtown city street. The goal of this project is to have a new on-ramp constructed and ready for traffic in 18 months from the project start date. Specifically excluded from this project is the demolition of a deteriorating bridge adjacent to the new on-ramp. Make sure you state this in the project scope statement.

Remember that the definition of a successful project is one that accomplishes the goals of the project and meets or exceeds stakeholders' expectations. Understand and document those expectations, and you're off to a good start.

Writing the Project Scope Statement

The purpose of the *project scope statement* is to document the project objectives, deliverables, and requirements so that they can be used to direct the project team's work and as a basis for future project decisions. The scope statement is an agreement between the project and the project customer that states precisely what the work of the project will produce. Simply put, the scope statement tells everyone concerned with the project exactly what they're going to get when the work is finished.

Since the scope statement serves as a baseline for the project, if questions arise or changes are proposed later in the project, they can be compared to what's documented in the scope statement. Making change decisions is easier when the original deliverables and requirements are well documented. You'll also know what is out of scope for the project simply because the work isn't documented here (or conversely, deliverables or elements are documented and noted as being specifically out of scope). The criteria outlined in the scope statement will also be used to determine whether the project was completed successfully. I hope you're already seeing the importance of documenting project scope.

Understanding the Scope Statement Components

According to the *PMBOK Guide*, the project scope statement should include all of the following:

- Project objectives
- Product scope description
- Project deliverables
- Project requirements
- Project boundaries
- Product acceptance criteria
- Project constraints
- Project assumptions
- Initial project organization
- Initial defined risks
- Schedule milestones
- Fund limitations
- Cost estimates
- Project configuration management requirements
- Project specifications
- Approval requirements

If the details surrounding these are spelled out in other documents, you don't have to reenter all the information in the scope statement. Simply reference the other document in the scope statement so that readers know where to find it.

Are we there yet? Remember in Chapter 2 that I promised you I would get to the details of the preliminary scope statement when you got to this point? You're there! All the elements in the preceding list are part of the preliminary scope statement as well as the project scope statement, and I'll discuss each of them. The explanations given here apply to these elements as they pertain to the preliminary *and* the project scope statements. The difference is that at this point in the project you know more than you did earlier, so there'll be more detail here than in the preliminary scope statement.

NOTE   Several terms are tossed around when we start talking about project scope, and sometimes they're used interchangeably. They are words such as *goals*, *objectives*, *requirements*, and *deliverables* (I'll get to these last two later in this section). I've referenced the term *objectives* several times throughout this chapter. Goals and objectives are the purpose for undertaking the project. These are the "what" you're trying to accomplish. They describe the final result of the project. "Increase warehouse space by 17 percent to house the new product line for distribution" and "Improve turnaround times by 25 percent on loan application services" are both examples of objectives. They state the purpose for the project and the desired end result. In practice, some project managers use the term *goals* to describe what the *PMBOK Guide* terms *objectives*. The *PMBOK Guide* doesn't use the word *goals*, and you won't find it in its glossary. Be that as it might, I'll stick with the term it uses, *objective*. Just keep in mind that you can think of goals and objectives as being interchangeable.

Project Objectives

Objectives are quantifiable criteria used to measure project success. They describe the "what" you're trying to do, accomplish, or produce. Quantifiable criteria should at least include schedule, cost, and quality measures. You might use business measures or quality targets as well. In the case of project objectives, these elements are used as measurements to determine project satisfaction and successful completion. Costs are typically stated in monetary units (U.S. dollars, euros, and so on) and should be specific. Schedules are typically stated in time measurements, and I recommend sticking with a consistent measurement throughout your project. If you use hours, state all schedule-related topics in hours.

You've probably seen the acronym SMART regarding goals and objectives a dozen times, but it's worth repeating. If you follow these principles, you'll be certain that your objectives meet the "quantifiable criteria" needed to measure success. Objectives should follow the SMART rule:

S—Specific   Objectives should be specific and written in clear, concise, and understandable terms.

M—Measurable   Objectives should be measurable.

A—Accurate   Objectives should be accurate and should describe precisely what's required.

R—Realistic and tangible   Objectives that are impossible to accomplish are not realistic and not attainable. Objectives must be centered in reality. For example, it's not likely you and I will be sending up rocket ships full of chocolate candies to sell to tourists visiting the moon anytime soon.

T—Time bound   Objectives should have a time frame with an end date assigned to them.

Let's look at some examples of the tangible terms, or quantifiable criteria, we talked about earlier. If your objective is to increase warehouse space, it is better to say the objective is to build four new warehouses. Describing the number of new warehouses to be built is specific and tangible. For that reason, you'll know the project is completed when this objective is met.

The objective of offering faster loan approvals might be better stated that the company will provide loan applications over the Internet to increase the speed of the application process by 25 percent by the end of the calendar year. In other words, the purpose for the project is to do something or accomplish something—an objective.

Let's say your company is going to produce a run of holiday beer. Your objective statement might be stated this way: "Beer Buddies, Inc., will produce two million cases of holiday beer to be shipped to our distributors by October 30 at a cost of $1.5 million or less." The objective criteria in this statement are clearly stated, and fulfillment of the project objective can be easily measured. Stakeholders will know the objective is met when the two million cases are produced and shipped by the due date within the budget stated.

Product Scope Description

The *product scope description* describes the characteristics of the product, service, or result of the project. I talked about this in Chapter 2. If the product scope description is contained in the project charter, you can reference the project charter in the project scope statement. Chances are very good you'll be using a word processing system of some sort to write these documents. An even better idea is to copy and paste the information from the project charter into the scope statement. It won't hurt anything to have it in both places and will make reading the scope statement easier.

Project Deliverables

Deliverables are measurable outcomes, measurable results, or specific items that must be produced to consider the project or project phase completed. Deliverables, like objectives, must be specific and verifiable. For example, one of your deliverables might include widgets with a three-inch diameter that will in turn be assembled into the final product. This deliverable, a three-inch-diameter widget, is specific and measurable. However, if the deliverable was not documented or not communicated to the manager or vendor responsible for manufacturing the widgets, there could be a disaster waiting to happen. If they deliver two-inch widgets instead of the required three-inch version, it would throw the entire project off schedule or perhaps cause the project to fail. This could be a career-limiting move for the project manager, because it's the project manager's responsibility to document deliverables and monitor the progress of those deliverables throughout the project. Most projects have multiple deliverables. As in this example, if you are assembling a new product with many parts, each of the parts might be considered independent deliverables.

The *PMBOK Guide* describes a project deliverable as either a unique and verifiable product or result or a service that's performed. The product or service must be produced or performed in order to consider the project complete. The deliverables might also include supplementary outcomes such as documentation or project management reports.

The bottom line is this: no matter how well you apply your project skills, if the wrong deliverables are produced or the project is managed to the wrong objectives, you will have an unsuccessful project on your hands.

Critical Success Factors

Deliverables and objectives are sometimes referred to as *critical success factors*. Critical success factors are those elements that must be completed in order for the project to be considered complete. For example, if you're building a bridge, one of the deliverables might be to produce a specific number of trusses that will be used to help support the bridge. Without the trusses, the bridge can't be completed; in fact, the bridge might not stand without them. The trusses, in this case, are a critical success factor. Not all deliverables are necessarily critical success factors, but many of them will fall into this category and should be documented as such.

Project Requirements

After all the deliverables are identified, the project manager needs to discover and document all the requirements of the project. *Requirements* describe the characteristics of the deliverables. They might also describe functionality that the deliverable must have or specific conditions the deliverable must meet in order to satisfy the objective of the project. According to the *PMBOK Guide*, requirements are conditions that must be met or criteria that the product or service of the project must possess in order to satisfy the project documents, a contract, a standard, or a specification. Requirements quantify and prioritize the wants, needs, and expectations of the project sponsor and stakeholders.

Requirements might include elements such as dimensions, ease of use, color, specific ingredients, and so on. If you return to the holiday beer example, you'll recall that the project objective was to produce a new bottle of beer for the holidays. One of the major deliverables is the cartons to hold the bottles. The requirements for that deliverable might include carton design, photographs that will appear on the carton, color choices, and so on.

Again, the project manager needs to pull those communications skills out of her tool bag and use them to interview stakeholders, customers, project team members, and business process owners about the project requirements. Although the project manager is responsible for making certain the requirements are documented, it doesn't mean this task must be performed by the project manager. The project manager can enlist the help of stakeholders, business analysts, requirements analysts, business process owners, and other team members to conduct the interviews and document the requirements. The project manager then reviews the requirements and incorporates them into the project documentation and project plan.

Business process owners are those people who are experts in their particular area of the business. They are invaluable resources to the project manager. They are usually the midlevel managers and line managers who still have their fingers in the day-to-day portion of the business. For example, it takes many experts in various areas to produce and market a great bottle of beer. Machinists regulate and keep the stainless steel and copper drums in top working order. Chemists check and adjust the secret formulas brewing in the vats daily. Graphic artists must develop colorful and interesting labels and cartons to attract the attention of those thirsty patrons. And of course, those great TV commercials advertising the tasty brew are produced by yet another set of business experts. These are the kinds of people you'll interview and ask to assist you in identifying requirements.

Documenting *All* the Deliverables and Requirements

One of the project manager's primary functions is to accurately document the deliverables and requirements of the project and then manage the project so that they are produced according to the agreed-upon criteria. Deliverables describe the components of the goals and objectives in a quantifiable way. Requirements are the specifications of the deliverables.

The project manager should use the project charter and preliminary scope statement as a starting point for identifying and progressively elaborating project deliverables, but it's possible that only some of the deliverables will be documented there. Remember that the charter was written by a manager external to the project, and it was the first take at defining the project objectives and deliverables. As the project manager, it's your job to make certain *all* the deliverables are identified and documented in the project scope statement. That's because the scope statement (not the project charter) serves as the agreement among stakeholders—including the customer of the project—regarding what project objectives and deliverables will be produced in order to meet and satisfy the requirements of the project.

Interview the stakeholders, other project managers, project team members, customers, management staff, industry experts, and any other experts who can help you identify all the deliverables of the project. Depending on the size of the project, you might be able to accomplish this in a group setting using simple brainstorming techniques, but large complex projects might have scope statements for each deliverable of the project. Remember that the project scope statement is progressively elaborated into finer detail and is used later to help decompose the work of the project into smaller tasks and activities.

You can use the same techniques to determine requirements as you did to determine deliverables. I discuss several techniques in Chapter 5, "Risk Planning," that you can use during the Scope Definition process to identify deliverables and requirements.

Getting the business process owners and stakeholders (who could be one and the same, depending on the project) together in a meeting room and brainstorming the requirements can produce terrific results. Depending on the size of the project, this isn't always possible, but the idea holds true. Interview your stakeholders and business experts to get at the requirements and then document them in the project scope statement. Remember that, according to the *PMBOK*

Guide, the stakeholder analysis (a tool and technique of the Scope Definition process—yes, I'm still talking about that process) you performed ultimately turns their needs and expectations into prioritized requirements that are documented in the project scope statement.

Exam Spotlight

Understand the differences between objectives, deliverables, and requirements. These are first defined during the Initiating processes and are fine-tuned in more detail during the Planning processes.

Project Boundaries

Project boundaries define what is and what is not included in the work of the project. In this section of the scope statement, you'll state what is excluded from scope. The following statement might seem obvious, but I'll note it anyway: objectives, deliverables, and requirements not specifically included in the project scope statement are explicitly excluded from the project. Stakeholders cannot become confused later and expect that a specific product or deliverable was going to be included in the project when it's stated here that it will not be produced.

Product Acceptance Criteria

Product *acceptance criteria* includes the process and criteria that will be used to determine whether the deliverables and the final product, service, or result of the project are acceptable and satisfactory. Acceptance criteria might include any number of elements, such as quality criteria, fitness for use, and performance criteria.

Project Constraints

Constraints are anything that either restricts the actions of the project team or dictates the actions of the project team. Constraints put you in a box. (I hope you're not claustrophobic.) As a project manager, you have to manage *to* the project constraints, which sometimes requires creativity.

In my organization, and I'm sure the same is true in yours, we have far more project requests than we have resources to work on them. In this case, resources are a constraint. You'll find that a similar phenomenon occurs on individual projects as well. Almost every project you'll encounter must work within the triple constraint combination of scope, time, and cost. The quality of the project (or the outcomes of the project) is affected by how well these three constraints are managed. Usually one or two triple constraints, and sometimes all three, apply, which restricts the actions of the project team. You might work on projects where you have an almost unlimited budget (don't we wish!) but time is the limitation. For example, if the president mandated that NASA put an astronaut on Mars by the end of 2008, you'd have a time-constrained project on your hands.

Other projects might present the opposite scenario. You have all the time you need to complete the project, but the budget is fixed. Still other projects might incorporate two or three of the constraints. Government agencies are notorious for starting projects that have at least two and sometimes all three constraints. For example, new tax laws are passed that impact the computer programs, requiring new programs to calculate and track the tax changes. Typically, a due date is given when the tax law takes effect, and the organization responsible is required to implement the changes with no additions to budget or staff. In other words, they are told to use existing resources to accomplish the objectives of the project, and the specific requirements, or scope, of the project are such that they cannot be changed to try to meet the time deadline.

As a project manager, one of your biggest jobs is to balance the project constraints while meeting or exceeding the expectations of your stakeholders. In most projects, you will usually have to balance only one or two of the triple constraints. For example, if one of the project objectives is to complete the project by the end of the year, the saying goes, "I can give it to you fast or I can give it to you cheap, but I can't give it to you fast and cheap."

Constraints can take on many forms and aren't limited to time, cost, and scope. Anything that impedes your project team's ability to perform the work of the project or specifically dictates the way the project should be performed is considered a constraint. Governments are a good example here. Let's say in order to fulfill some of the deliverables of your project you'll have to purchase a large amount of materials and equipment. Procurement processes can be so cumbersome that ordering supplies for a project might add months to the project schedule. The procurement process itself becomes a constraint because of the methods and procedures you're required to use to get the materials.

You're likely to encounter the following constraints on your future projects:

Time constraint   As I said, time can be a project constraint. This usually comes in the form of an enforced deadline, commonly known as the "make it happen now" scenario. If you are in charge of the company's holiday bash scheduled for December 10, your project is time constrained. Once the invitations are out and the hall has been rented, you can't move the date. All activities on this project are driven by the due date.

Budget constraints   Budgets are another one of the triple constraints. Budgets limit the project team's ability to obtain resources and might potentially limit the scope of the project. For example, component X cannot be part of this project because the budget doesn't support it.

Quality constraints   Although the *PMBOK Guide* doesn't list quality as a constraint, you'll find in practice that quality can often be a constraint. Quality constraints typically are restricted by the specifications of the product or service. The specifications for those three-inch widgets talked about earlier could be considered a quality constraint. Most of the time, if quality is a constraint, one of the other constraints—time or budget—has to have some give. You can't produce high quality on a restricted budget and within a tightly restricted time schedule. Of course, there are exceptions, but only in the movies.

Schedule constraints   Schedule constraints can cause interesting dilemmas for the project manager. For example, say you're the project manager in charge of building a new football stadium in your city. The construction of the stadium will require the use of cranes—and crane operators—at certain times during the project. If crane operators are not available when your project plan calls for them, you'll have to make schedule adjustments so that the crane operators can come in at the right time.

Technology constraints   Technology is marvelous. In fact, how did humans survive prior to the invention of computers and cell phones? However, it can also be a project constraint. For example, your project might require the use of new technology that is still so new it hasn't been released on a wide-scale basis. One impact might be that the project will take an additional six months because the new technology isn't ready or hasn't been tested yet.

Directive constraints   Directives from management can be constraints as well. Your department might have specific policies that management requires for the type of work you're about to undertake. This might add time to the project, so you must consider those policies when identifying project constraints. And when you're performing work on contract, the provisions of the contract can be constraints.

Constraints, particularly the triple constraints, can be used to help drive out the objectives and requirements of the project. If it's difficult to discern which constraint is the primary constraint, ask the project sponsor something like this, "Ms. Sponsor, if you could have only one of these two alternatives, which would you choose? The project is delivered on the date you've stated, or we don't spend one penny more than the approved budget." If Ms. Sponsor replies with the date response, you know your primary constraint is time. If push comes to shove during the project Planning processes for this project, the budget might have to give because time cannot.

You'll want to understand what the primary constraint is on the project. If you assume the primary constraint is budget when in actuality the primary constraint is time, in the immortal words of two-year-olds worldwide, "Uh-oh." Understanding the constraints and which one carries the most importance will help you later in the project Planning process group with details such as scope planning, scheduling, estimating, and project plan development. That's assuming your project gets to the project Planning processes, which brings me to the next topic: project assumptions.

Project Assumptions

You've probably heard the old saying about the word *assume*, something about what it makes out of "u" and "me." In the case of project management, however, throw this old saying out the window, because it's not true.

Assumptions, for the purposes of project management, are things you believe to be true. For example, if you're working on a large construction project, you might make assumptions about the availability of materials. You might assume that concrete, lumber, drywall, and so on, are widely available and reasonably priced. You might also assume that finding contract labor is either easy or difficult, depending on the economic times and the availability of labor in your locale. Each project will have its own set of assumptions, and the assumptions should be identified, documented, and updated throughout the project.

It's essential to understand and document the assumptions you're making, and the assumptions your stakeholders are making, about the project. It's also important to find out as many of the assumptions as you can up front. Projects can fail, sometimes after lots of progress has been made, because an important assumption was forgotten or the assumption was incorrect. You will have more assumptions at this point in the project than you did when creating the project charter because more is known about the goals and deliverables of the project. Defining new assumptions and refining old ones are other forms of progressive elaboration.

Let's say you make plans to meet your buddy for lunch at 11:30 on Friday at your favorite spot. When Friday rolls around, you assume he's going to show up, barring any catastrophes between the office and the restaurant. Project assumptions work the same way. For planning purposes, you presume the event or thing you've made the assumptions about is true, real, or certain. For example, you might assume that key resources will be available when needed on the project. Document that assumption. If Nancy is the one and only resource who can perform a specific task at a certain point in the project, document your assumption that Nancy will be available and run it by her manager. If Nancy happens to be on a plane for Helsinki at the time you thought she was going to be working on the project, you could have a real problem on your hands.

Other assumptions could be factors such as vendor delivery times, product availability, contractor availability, the accuracy of the project plan, the assumption that key project members will perform adequately, contract signing dates, project start dates, and project phase start dates. This is not an exhaustive list, but it should get you thinking in the right direction. As you interview your stakeholders, ask them about their assumptions, and add them to your list. Use brainstorming exercises with your team and other project participants to come up with additional assumptions.

Think about some of the factors you usually take for granted when you're trying to identify assumptions. Many times they're the elements everyone expects will be available or will behave in a specific way. Think about factors such as key team members' availability, access to information, access to equipment, management support, and vendor reliability.

Try to validate your assumptions whenever possible. When discussing assumptions with vendors, make them put them in writing. In fact, if the services or goods you're expecting to be delivered by your suppliers are critical to the project, include a clause in the contract to assure a contingency plan in case your suppliers fail to perform. For example, if you're expecting 200 computers to be delivered, configured, and installed by a certain date, require the vendor to pay the cost of rental equipment in the event the vendor can't deliver on the promised due date.

Remember, when assumptions are incorrect or not documented, it could cause problems partway through the project and might even be a project killer.

Initial Project Organization

In the initial project organization section, you'll document who the project team members and stakeholders are for the project. I talked about stakeholders earlier in this chapter.

Initial Defined Risks

Risks pose threats and opportunities to the project. This section should list all known risks.

I'll cover risks in much more detail in Chapter 5.

Schedule Milestones

Milestones are typically points in the project where something significant is achieved or completed. List the major milestones that you know about in this section of the project scope statement.

I'll talk more about milestones in Chapter 7.

Fund Limitations

Fund limitations really refer to the cost constraint. If there are fund limitations (and I've never worked on a project where there weren't), document them here. Also document any time frames associated with the funding limitations. For example, I often work on projects where funding runs out at the end of the fiscal year. If you haven't spent the money by then, you'll no longer have access to it.

Cost Estimates

Cost estimates is the section where you list the cost estimates for the project. This should include overall costs for the project and some level of confidence in that estimate.

Project Configuration Management Requirements

Configuration management describes the characteristics of the product of the project and ensures that the description is accurate and complete.

I'll talk more about configuration management in Chapter 9.

Project Specifications

If the project should comply with specification documents—for example, industry specifications or technology specifications—note that in the project specifications section.

Approval Requirements

Approval requirements refer to how the objectives, deliverables, project management documents, and other outcomes and results of the project will be approved. This is different from product acceptance criteria—that element describes how the product itself will be approved, whereas this element describes the requirements that must be met in order to approve the objectives, and so on. An example product acceptance criteria might be "All widgets must measure three inches." A deliverable approval requirement might be that the director of sales must approve a prototype before the project can proceed. This section might also contain the process and approval requirements of the project scope statement.

Approving and Publishing the Project Scope Statement

Just like the project charter, the project scope statement should be approved, agreed upon, published, and distributed to the stakeholders, key management personnel, and project team members. You can accomplish this with a formal sign-off procedure that's documented as part of the approval requirements section of the scope statement. When stakeholders sign off and agree to the scope statement, they're agreeing to the deliverables and requirements of the project. And, as with the project charter, their agreement and endorsement of the project requirements and deliverables will likely sustain their participation and cooperation throughout the rest of the project. That doesn't mean they'll agree to everything as the project progresses, but it does mean the stakeholders are informed and will likely remain active project participants.

Updating the Project Scope Management Plan

Two outputs of the Scope Definition process remain. Those outputs are requested changes and project scope management plan updates. When you're in the midst of defining deliverables and requirements, you'll often find that changes to the original objectives and requirements will occur. These requested changes, once reviewed and approved, will change the scope of the project. If the project scope statement has been approved and published, you'll need to make changes to it and notify stakeholders that changes have been made.

 Real World Scenario

Mountain Streams Services

Maria Sanchez is the CEO of Mountain Streams Services. She recently accepted a prestigious industry award on behalf of the company. Maria knows that without the dedication and support of her employees, Mountain Streams Services wouldn't have achieved this great milestone.

Maria wants to host a reception for the employees and their guests in recognition of all their hard work and contributions to the company. Maria has appointed you to arrange the reception.

The reception is scheduled for April 12, and Maria has given you a budget of $125 per person. The company employs 200 people. The reception should be semiformal.

You've documented the deliverables as follows:

- Location selection

- Food and beverage menu

- Invitations

- Entertainment

- Insurance coverage

- Decorations

- Photographer

- Agenda

In addition to the deliverables, you want to go over the following requirements with Maria to be certain you both are in agreement:

- The location should be somewhere in the downtown area.

- Employees are encouraged to bring one guest but no children.

- There will be an open bar paid for by Maria.

- The agenda will include a speech by Maria, followed by the distribution of bonus checks to every employee. This is to be kept secret until the reception.

- The decorations should include gold-trimmed fountain pens with the company logo at every place setting for the attendees to keep.

Once you've documented all the particulars, you ask to speak with Maria to go over this project scope statement and get her approval before proceeding with the project.

 Real World Scenario

Project Case Study: New Kitchen Heaven Retail Store

The project charter kickoff meeting was held and well attended. You're ready to start writing the project scope statement and have a question or two for Dirk. You knock on his door, and he invites you in.

"Shoot," he says.

"I'm ready to define the deliverables and requirements for this project. I want to make sure I get the right folks involved in the meeting. Who are key stakeholders you recommend I speak with?"

"I can think of a few people right off that you don't want to miss. There's Jake Peterson over in Facilities. He's in charge of store furnishings, shelving, things like that—any supplies for the stores that aren't retail products. He can help out with store build-outs, too. He supervised our last eight stores and did a terrific job."

"Anyone else?" you ask.

"You should also talk to Jill Overstreet, the director in charge of retail products. She can help with the initial store stocking, and once the store is open, her group will take over the ongoing operations. All the district managers report to Jill."

You thank Dirk and tell him you're going to contact Jake and Jill and set up a brainstorming session to determine requirements.

A few days later.

You review your notes and reread the first draft of the project scope statement you've prepared for the Kitchen Heaven retail store before looking for Dirk. After your meetings with the stakeholders, you were better able to refine the project objectives and deliverables.

"Dirk, I'm glad I caught you. I'd like to go over the project scope statement with you before I give it to the stakeholders. Do you have a few minutes?"

"Sure," Dirk says to you. "Let's have it."

"The project objective is to open the 50th Kitchen Heaven store in Colorado Springs by February 1. When I met with Jake, he confirmed it takes 120 days to do the store build-out. That includes having the shelves set up and in place, ready to stock with inventory."

Dirk asks whether Jake told you about his store location idea.

"Yes, Jake gave me a contact name of the leasing agent, and I've left her a voicemail. The sooner we can get that lease signed, the better. It takes Jake 120 days to do the build-out, and Jill said she needs two weeks lead time to order the initial inventory and stock the shelves. That puts us pretty close to our February 1 deadline, counting the time to get the lease papers signed."

"Sounds good so far," Dirk replies. "What else?"

You continue, "I've included an updated description of the products and services the new store will offer, based on the documentation that was written from the last store opening. Jill reviewed the updates to the description, so we should be in the clear there. The store will include some new lines that we've decided to take on—cookware from famous chefs, that kind of thing.

"Jake has already made contact with a general contractor in Colorado Springs, and he is ready to roll once we've signed the lease.

"One more thing, Dirk. Since we're including the big bash at grand opening as part of the deliverables, I talked to some of your folks in marketing to get some ideas. They are thinking we should have some great giveaways as door prizes and that we will want the food catered. They also thought having some live cooking demonstrations with some local chefs would be a good attraction."

"Sounds like you're on the right track. So, what's next?" Dirk asks.

"Once you approve the scope statement, I'd like to send a copy to the stakeholders. My next step is to break down the deliverables and requirements I've documented here into activities so we can get rolling on the work of the project."

Project Case Study Checklist

Stakeholder analysis: Jake Peterson and Jill Overstreet interviewed. Needs, wants, and expectations recorded and requirements prioritized.

Organizational structure: Functional organization with a separate projectized department.

Constraints: February 1 date to coincide with home and garden show.

Assumptions: These are the assumptions:

- A store build-out usually takes 120 days.

- Jill Overstreet will help with the initial store stocking.

- Jake Peterson will provide supplies for the stores that aren't retail products, such as store furnishings, shelving, and so on, and can help with the store build-out as well.

- The budget for the project will be anywhere from $1.5 to $2 million.

The project scope statement includes the following:

Project objectives: Open 50th store by February 1 in Colorado Springs.

Project deliverables: These are the project deliverables:

- Build out storefront, including shelving.

- Retail product line will be delivered two weeks prior to grand opening.

- Have grand-opening party with cooking demos.

Project requirements: These are the project requirements:

- Sign lease within 14 days.

- Offer new line of gourmet food products.

- Have classroom space in back of store for cooking demos and classes.

  Constraints: February 1 date will coincide with home and garden show.

  Fund limitations: Spend no more than $2 million for the project.

  Assumptions: (These are the same as listed earlier.)

 I'll talk more about change control and change request processes in Chapter 9.

Approved changes might also impact the project scope management plan or some of the subsidiary plans that make up this plan. Make certain you update this plan as a result of the changes made during the Scope Definition process.

Understanding How This Applies to Your Next Project

As a manager who prides myself and my team on excellent customer service, I have once or twice gotten my team into precarious situations because I was so focused on helping the customer that I hurt them and our department in the process. If you're wondering how that happened, it's because we didn't take the time to document the scope of the project and the final acceptance criteria. In the interest of getting the project completed quickly because of our customer's own internal deadlines, we decided the project was straightforward enough that we didn't need to document deliverables. The customer promised to work side by side with us as we produced the work of the project. Unfortunately, that wasn't the case, and we didn't meet the expectations of our customer. Further, after we did implement the project (two months behind schedule), we went through another six weeks of "fixes" because of the miscommunication between the customer and the project team on what constituted some of the features of the final product. There's always a great reason for cutting corners—but they almost always come back to haunt you.

Early in this chapter, I talked about creating the scope management plan. If you're working on a long-term, highly complex, risky project, I recommend taking the time to write a scope management plan. If you are experienced at project management, you're likely familiar with how to go about defining scope, how to create the WBS, and so on, so this shouldn't be an insurmountable task, if you decide it's needed. Small- to medium-sized projects don't necessarily need scope management plans—especially if you work on the same kinds of projects consistently because you can reuse the same processes on your current project to define scope. And if your organization has a PMO, it might have processes already outlined that determine how scope should be defined.

One of the topics I briefly touched on in this chapter is understanding stakeholder roles. This is an important factor on any project, and you should give considerable weight to understanding your stakeholder influences within the organization. Some stakeholders are bound to have more pull with the project sponsor than others. If you know your stakeholders well enough, you'll know what angles they might work behind the scenes that could impact your project in terms of resource allocation, budget, schedule, and so on. If you don't know them well, talk to others who do know them and see whether they can give you an indication of how much influence this stakeholder has and how their decisions might influence the project. That way, you can take their unique needs or reactions into account before you begin planning rather than having to revise the plan later, or worse, revising it after the work of the project has started.

I believe the most important idea to take from this chapter is a simple one: always use a scope statement, including the measurable goals and deliverables, and always get it signed.

Summary

This chapter started you on the road to project planning via the Develop Project Management Plan process, the Scope Planning process, and the Scope Definition process.

The output of the Develop Project Management Plan process is the project management plan, which is concerned with defining, coordinating, and integrating all the ancillary project plans. The purpose of this plan is to define how the project is executed, how it's monitored and controlled, and how it's closed.

Scope Planning is where you produce the scope management plan, which is a planning tool that documents how the project team will go about defining project scope, how the work breakdown structure will be developed, how changes to scope will be controlled, and how project scope will be verified.

The scope statement is produced during the Scope Definition process. It describes the project objectives, deliverables, and requirements. The scope statement forms a baseline you'll use to weigh future project decisions, most particularly change requests. The scope statement contains a list of project deliverables that will be used in future Planning processes. Measurement criteria for project objectives are agreed upon by the stakeholders and project manager. These criteria are associated with the deliverables and documented in the scope statement to track project progress.

The deliverables, requirements, and measurement criteria should be spelled out clearly and concisely in the scope statement to avoid any misunderstandings later in the project. Formal acceptance of the scope statement is required by the stakeholders and project manager. Acceptance is usually accompanied by sign-offs on the document indicating that it has been read and that the signing party agrees with the deliverables and requirements of the project.

The project scope statement contains many elements, including objectives, deliverables, requirements, boundary descriptions (exclusions from scope), constraints, assumptions, product acceptance criteria, project organization, initial risks, schedule milestones, fund limitations, configuration management requirements, cost estimates, project specifications, and approval requirements.

Constraints restrict or dictate the actions of the project team. Constraints usually involve time, cost, and scope but can also include schedules, technology, and more.

Assumptions are things believed to be true. You'll want to document project assumptions and validate them as the project progresses.

Exam Essentials

Be able to state the purpose of the Develop Project Management Plan process.   It defines, coordinates, and integrates all subsidiary project plans.

Be able to explain the purpose of the project management plan.   This plan defines how the project is executed, how it's monitored and controlled, and how it's closed and also documents the outputs of the Planning group processes. The size and complexity of the project will determine the level of detail contained in this plan.

Be able to describe the purpose of the scope management plan.   The scope management plan has a direct influence on the project's success and describes the process for determining project scope, facilitates creating the WBS, describes how the product or service of the project is verified and accepted, and documents how changes to scope will be handled. The scope management plan is a subsidiary plan of the project management plan.

Be able to name the Scope Definition tools and techniques and outputs.   The tools and techniques from the Scope Definition process are product analysis, alternatives identification, expert judgment, and stakeholder analysis. The outputs are the project scope statement, requested changes, and project scope management plan updates.

Understand the purpose of the project scope statement.   The scope statement serves as a common understanding of project scope among the stakeholders. The project objectives and deliverables and their quantifiable criteria are documented in the scope statement and are used by the project manager and the stakeholders to determine whether the project was completed successfully. It also serves as a basis for future project decisions.

Be able to define project constraints and assumptions.   Project constraints limit the options of the project team and restrict their actions. Sometimes constraints dictate actions. Time, budget, and quality are the most common constraints. Assumptions are conditions that are presumed to be true or real.

Key Terms

Planning, planning, planning...I can't stress enough how important the planning processes are to a successful project. In this chapter, you learned about the processes involved in developing your project scope statement. Understand these processes well, and know them by the name used in the *PMBOK*:

Develop Project Management Plan

Scope Definition

Scope Planning

Before you take the exam, also be certain you are familiar with the following terms:

acceptance criteria

alternatives identification

approval requirements

assumptions

constraints

critical success factors

deliverables

objectives

product analysis

project boundaries

project management plan

project scope management plan

project scope statement

requirements

scope

Review Questions

1. You are a project manager for Laredo Pioneer's Traveling Rodeo Show. You're heading up a project to promote a new line of souvenirs to be sold at the shows. You are getting ready to write the project management plan and know that all the following are true regarding the PMIS, except for one. Which of the following is true?

   A. The PMIS is a tool and technique of the Scope Planning process.

   B. The configuration management system is a subsystem of the PMIS.

   C. The PMIS includes a change control system.

   D. The PMIS is an automated system.

2. Which of the following is true?

   A. You are a project manager for Laredo Pioneer's Traveling Rodeo Show. You're heading up a project to promote a new line of souvenirs to be sold at the shows. You're ready to document the processes you'll use to perform the project as well as define how the project will be executed, controlled, and closed. You are working on the project scope management plan.

   B. You are a project manager for Laredo Pioneer's Traveling Rodeo Show. You're heading up a project to promote a new line of souvenirs to be sold at the shows. You're ready to document the processes you'll use to perform the project as well as define how the project will be executed, controlled, and closed. You are working on the product scope statement.

   C. You are a project manager for Laredo Pioneer's Traveling Rodeo Show. You're heading up a project to promote a new line of souvenirs to be sold at the shows. You're ready to document the processes you'll use to perform the project as well as define how the project will be executed, controlled, and closed. You are working on the project management plan.

   D. You are a project manager for Laredo Pioneer's Traveling Rodeo Show. You're heading up a project to promote a new line of souvenirs to be sold at the shows. You're ready to document the processes you'll use to perform the project as well as define how the project will be executed, controlled, and closed. You are working on the project scope statement.

3. You are a project manager responsible for the construction of a new office complex. You are taking over for a project manager who recently left the company. The prior project manager completed the scope statement and scope management plan for this project. In your interviews with some key team members, you conclude which of the following?

   A. They understand that the scope statement assesses the stability of the project scope and outlines how scope will be verified and used to control changes.

   B. They understand that the scope management plan describes how project scope will be defined and verified and used to control project scope.

   C. They understand that the scope management plan is deliverables oriented and includes cost estimates and stakeholder needs and expectations.

   D. They understand that the scope statement describes how the high-level deliverables and requirements will be defined and verified.

4. Some of the functions of this process include describing the methods for executing the work of the project to fulfill the project objectives, documenting dependencies and interactions among the processes, determining the validity of and maintaining the performance baselines, and determining key management reviews for pending decisions. Which of the following does this describe? Choose the best answer.

A. This process belongs to the Project Scope Management Knowledge Area.

B. The output of the process is the project scope management plan.

C. The project charter is an input of the process.

D. The project scope management plan and quality management plan are two examples of the subsidiary plans contained in the output of the process.

5. Which of the following is true regarding the project scope statement?

A. The project scope statement includes a change control system that describes how to make changes to the project scope.

B. The project scope further elaborates the Initiating processes and serves as a basis for future project decisions.

C. The project scope statement describes how the team will define and develop the work breakdown structure.

D. The project scope statement assesses the reliability of the project scope and describes the process for verifying and accepting completed deliverables.

6. You are a project manager for an agricultural supply company. You have just completed and obtained sign-off on the project scope statement for your new Natural Bug Busters project. A key stakeholder has informed you that a deliverable is missing from the project scope statement. This deliverable is a critical success factor. Which of the following actions should you take?

A. Inform the stakeholder that work not stated in the scope statement is excluded from the project.

B. Modify the scope statement to reflect the new deliverable.

C. Inform the stakeholder that this deliverable must be included in phase two of this project since sign-off has already been obtained.

D. Modify the scope statement after an approved change request has been received from the stakeholder.

7. Your company has asked you to be the project manager for the product introduction of its new DeskTop Rock media system. You recently published a document that establishes the detailed project deliverables. Which of the following is true?

A. This is the project scope statement, which is an output of the Scope Definition process.

B. This is the scope management plan, which is an output of the Scope Planning process.

C. This is the project scope statement, which is an output of the Scope Planning process.

D. This is the scope management plan, which is an output of the Scope Definition process.

8. Which of the following statements is true regarding brainstorming and lateral thinking?

   A. They are forms of expert judgment used to help define and develop the project scope statement.

   B. They are used to elaborate the product scope description, which is an element of the output of the Scope Planning process.

   C. They are organizational process assets that are used to help define and develop the project management plan.

   D. They are an alternatives identification technique, which is a tool and technique of the Scope Definition process.

9. Your company has asked you to be the project manager for the product introduction of its new DeskTop Rock media system. You recently published the project scope statement. Which of the following is not contained in the project scope statement?

   A. Constraints

   B. Project specifications

   C. Requested changes

   D. Project configuration management requirements

10. You are a project manager for Giraffe Enterprises. You've recently taken over for a project manager who lied about his PMI certification and was subsequently fired. Unfortunately, he did a poor job of scope definition. Which of the following could happen if you don't correct this?

   A. The stakeholders will require overtime from the project team to keep the project on schedule.

   B. The poor scope definition will adversely affect the creation of the work breakdown structure, and costs will increase.

   C. The project management plan's process for verification and acceptance of the deliverables needs to be updated as a result of the poor scope definition.

   D. The project costs could increase, there might be rework, and schedule delays might result.

11. You work for a large manufacturing plant. You're working on a new project for an overseas product release. This is the company's first experience in the overseas market, and it wants to make a big splash with the introduction of this product. The project entails producing your product in a concentrated formula and packaging it in smaller containers than the U.S. product uses. A new machine is needed in order to mix the first set of ingredients in the concentrated formula. Which of the following is true?

   A. The new machine, the concentrated formula, and the smaller package are all project constraints.

   B. The new machine, the concentrated formula, and the smaller package description must be incorporated into the product description document.

   C. The new machine, the concentrated formula, and the smaller package are all project assumptions.

   D. The new machine, the concentrated formula, and the smaller package are all considered deliverables.

12. Objectives can be described as all of the following except for which one? Choose the least correct answer.

   A. The purpose for undertaking the project

   B. The functionality and specific conditions that must be met in order to satisfy the project, contract, standard, or specification

   C. The monetary units used to express the cost criteria for the project

   D. The quantifiable results used to measure project success that should include schedule, cost, and quality criteria

13. You are a project manager working on a new software product your company plans to market to businesses. The project sponsor told you that the project must be completed by September 1. The company plans to demo the new software product at a trade show in late September and therefore needs the project completed in time for the trade show. However, the sponsor has also told you that the budget is fixed at $85,000, and it would take an act of Congress to get it increased. You must complete the project within the given time frame and budget. Which of the following is the primary constraint for this project?

   A. Budget

   B. Scope

   C. Time

   D. Schedule

14. All of the following are true regarding stakeholder analysis except for which one?

   A. It's a tool and technique of the Scope Definition process.

   B. It determines communication needs and methods for updating stakeholders.

   C. It documents the needs, wants, and expectations of the stakeholders.

   D. It prioritizes and quantifies needs and wants to create project requirements.

15. You are in the process of translating project objectives into tangible deliverables and requirements. All the following are techniques used in the product analysis tool and technique of the Scope Definition process, except for which one?

   A. Value engineering and value analysis

   B. Product configuration and specification analysis

   C. Systems analysis and systems engineering

   D. Product breakdown and functional analysis

16. You are a project manager for a documentary film company. In light of a recent regional trag-edy, the company president wants to get a new documentary on the rescue efforts of the heroic rescue teams to air as soon as possible. She's looking to you to make this documentary the best that has ever been produced in the history of this company. She guarantees you free rein to use whatever resources you need to get this project done quickly. However, the best photographer in the company is currently working on another assignment. Which of the following is true?

    A. The primary constraint is time because the president wants the film done quickly. She told you to get it to air as soon as possible.

    B. Resources are the primary constraint. Even though the president has given you free rein on resource use, you assume she didn't mean those actively assigned to projects.

    C. The schedule is the primary constraint. Even though the president has given you free rein on resource use, you assume she didn't mean those actively assigned to projects. The pho-tographer won't be finished for another three weeks on his current assignment, so schedule adjustments will have to be made.

    D. The primary constraint is quality because the president wants this to be the best film ever produced by this company. She's given you free rein to use whatever resources needed to get the job done.

17. Your project depends on a key deliverable from a vendor you've used several times before with great success. You're counting on the delivery to arrive on June 1. This is an example of a/an

    A. constraint

    B. objective

    C. assumption

    D. requirement

18. What limits the options of the project team?

    A. Technology

    B. Constraints

    C. Deliverables

    D. Assumptions

19. Your company provides answering services for several major catalog retailers. The number of calls coming into the service center per month has continued to increase over the past 18 months. The phone system is approaching the maximum load limits and needs to be upgraded. You've been assigned to head up the upgrade project. Based on the company's experience with the ven-dor who worked on the last phone upgrade project, you're confident they'll be able to assist you with this project as well. Which of the following is true?

    A. You've made an assumption about vendor availability and expertise. The project came about because of a business need.

    B. Vendor availability and expertise are constraints. The project came about because of a business need.

    C. You've made an assumption about vendor availability and expertise. The project came about because of a market demand.

    D. Vendor availability and expertise are constraints. The project came about because of a market demand.

20. You are a project manager for Giraffe Enterprises. You've recently taken over for a project manager who lied about his PMI certification and was subsequently fired. Unfortunately, he didn't create a project charter or a preliminary scope statement. You are ready to elaborate the deliverables and requirements of the project and know that you can use one of the following in place of the charter or preliminary scope statement. Which one can you use?

A. Business justification

B. Product scope description

C. Strategic plan

D. Expert judgment

Answers to Review Questions

1. A. The PMIS is a tool and technique of the Develop Project Management Plan process. It's one of the elements of the enterprise environmental factors, which is an input to the Scope Planning process.

2. C. The project management plan describes the processes you'll use to perform the project and describes how the project will be executed, monitored, controlled, and closed.

3. B. The scope management plan describes how project scope will be defined and verified, how the scope statement will be developed, how the WBS will be developed, and how project scope will be controlled.

4. D. The Develop Project Management Plan involves describing the methods for executing the work of the project, documenting dependencies and interactions among the processes, determining the validity of and maintaining the performance baselines, and determining key management reviews for pending decisions, among other elements. The project scope management plan and quality management plans are examples of the subsidiary plans contained within the project management plan, which is the output of this process.

5. B. The scope statement further elaborates the project objectives, deliverables, requirements, and constraints and assumptions defined in the preliminary scope statement. It serves as a basis for future project decisions.

6. D. The project scope statement will change throughout the project as change requests are received and approved. Project managers must be certain to discover all deliverables before publishing the project scope statement to prevent situations like the one described in this question.

7. A. The project scope statement documents the detailed project deliverables and is an output of the Scope Definition process.

8. D. Alternatives identification is a tool and technique of the Scope Definition process that includes brainstorming and lateral thinking techniques.

9. C. Requested changes are an output of the Scope Definition process. They are not part of the project scope statement.

10. D. Option A might seem like a correct answer, but option D is more correct. There isn't enough information to determine whether stakeholders will require overtime. We do know that poor scope definition might lead to cost increases, rework, schedule delays, and poor morale.

11. D. Deliverables are tangible, verifiable outcomes or items that must be produced in order to complete the project or project phase. These items wouldn't be considered objectives, because the objective of the project is to break into the overseas market with a successful product revamped for that audience.

12. B. According to the *PMBOK Guide*, functionality and specific conditions that must be met in order to satisfy the project, contract, standard, or specification describe the criteria for requirements, not objectives.

13. C. The primary constraint is time. Since the trade show demos depend on project completion and the trade show is in late September, the date cannot be moved. The budget is the secondary constraint in this example.

14. B. The best answer to this question is B. Stakeholder analysis is a tool and technique of Scope Definition used to determine and document the needs, wants, and expectations of stakeholders and prioritize and quantify those needs into project requirements.

15. B. Product analysis includes techniques such as value engineering, value analysis, systems analysis, systems engineering, product breakdown, and functional analysis.

16. D. The primary constraint is quality. If you made the assumption as stated in B, you assumed incorrectly. Clarify these assumptions with your stakeholders and project sponsors. This applies to C as well.

17. C. This is an example of an assumption. You've used this vendor before and not had any problems. You're assuming there will be no problems with this delivery based on your past experience.

18. B. Constraints restrict the actions of the project team.

19. A. The project came about because of a business need. The phones have to be answered because that's the core business. Upgrading the system to handle more volume is a business need. An assumption has been made regarding vendor availability. Always validate your assumptions.

20. B. The product scope description can be used as an input to the Scope Definition process when the project charter and/or preliminary project scope statement are missing.

Chapter

4

Creating the WBS and Communicating the Plan

THE PMP EXAM CONTENT FROM THE PLANNING THE PROJECT PERFORMANCE DOMAIN COVERED IN THIS CHAPTER INCLUDES THE FOLLOWING:

✓ Create the WBS

Now that you have the deliverables and requirements well defined, you'll begin the process of breaking down the work of the project via a work breakdown structure. You'll accomplish this task in the Create WBS process. The WBS defines the scope of the project and breaks the work down into components that can be scheduled and estimated, as well as easily monitored and controlled.

Next I'll talk about how project information is documented and communicated. I've talked a lot about documentation so far, and I will discuss it more in this chapter. Documentation is something you will do throughout the remainder of the project, and the Communications Planning process details how to collect information, how to store it, and when and how to distribute it to stakeholders.

I'll end this chapter by defining the quality plan in the Quality Planning process. This process focuses on determining the quality standards that are necessary for the project and documenting how you'll go about meeting them.

Creating the Work Breakdown Structure

Have you ever mapped out a family tree? In the *Create WBS* process, you'll construct something like it called a *work breakdown structure (WBS)*. It maps the deliverables of the project with subdeliverables and other components stemming from each major deliverable in a tree or chart format. The *PMBOK Guide* describes a WBS as "a deliverable-oriented hierarchical decomposition of the work to be executed by the project team, to accomplish the project objectives and create the required deliverables. The WBS defines the total scope of the project." Simply put, a WBS is a deliverable-oriented hierarchy that defines and organizes the work of the project and only the work of the project. Like the scope statement, the WBS serves as a foundational agreement among the stakeholders and project team members regarding project scope.

The WBS will be used throughout many of the remaining Planning processes and is an important part of project planning. As you probably have concluded, everything you've done so far builds on the previous step. The project charter and preliminary scope statement outline the project goals and major deliverables. The project scope statement further refines these deliverables into an exhaustive list and documents the requirements of the deliverables. Now you'll use that comprehensive list of deliverables produced in the project scope statement to build the framework of the WBS.

I can't stress the importance of the work you've done up to this point enough. Your WBS will be only as accurate as your list of deliverables. The deliverables will become the groupings that will form the higher levels of the WBS from which activities will be derived later in the Planning processes.

The WBS should detail the full scope of work needed to complete the project. This breakdown will smooth the way for estimating project cost and time, scheduling resources, and determining quality controls later in the Planning processes. Project progress will be based on the estimates and measurements assigned to the WBS segments. So, again, accuracy and completeness are required when composing your WBS.

Before you begin constructing the WBS, you'll need to gather and review some important project documents. You'll look at those next.

Gathering the WBS Inputs

The inputs to the Create WBS process aren't new. They are as follows:

- Organizational process assets
- Project scope statement
- Project scope management plan
- Approved change requests

The important aspect to note about the inputs to this process is that the approved project scope statement is the document you will use to define and organize the work of the project in the WBS. Make certain you're using the most current version of the scope statement. And note also that the WBS, just like the project scope statement, contains the work of the project and only the work of the project.

Decomposing the Deliverables

The Create WBS process consists of two tools and techniques. The first is the work breakdown structure templates. Many organizations and application areas (industries) have WBS templates they use for their projects. Keep in mind that you might use a WBS from a previous project as a template for your current project also. If you work in the same organization, and in the same department within the organization, you'll often find yourself working on the same types of projects. WBS templates lend themselves well to this situation because even though a project is unique, it might be similar to projects you've worked on in the past and might have similar life cycle phases. Check with your PMO because it might also have WBS templates.

The next tool and technique is called *decomposition*. This technique involves breaking down the deliverables into smaller, more manageable components of work. The idea here is to break down the deliverables to a point where you can easily plan, execute, monitor and control, and close out the project deliverables. Decomposition typically pertains to breaking deliverables down into smaller deliverables, or component deliverables, where each level of the WBS (or each level of decomposition) is a more detailed definition of the level above it.

This breaking-down or decomposing process will accomplish several tasks for you, one of which is improving estimates. It's easier to estimate the costs, time, and resources needed for individual work components than it is to estimate them for a whole body of work or deliverable. Using smaller components also makes it easier to assign performance measures and controls. These give you a baseline to compare against throughout the project or phase. And finally, assigning resources and responsibility for the components of work makes better sense because several resources with different skills might be needed to complete one deliverable. Breaking them down assures that an assignment, and the responsibility for that assignment, goes to the proper parties.

According to the *PMBOK Guide*, decomposition is a five-step process:

1. Identify the deliverables and work. This step involves identifying all the major project deliverables and related work. The *PMBOK Guide* makes a point of noting that you can use the expert judgment technique to analyze the project scope statement and identify the major deliverables.

2. Organize the WBS. This step involves organizing the work of the project and determining the WBS structure.

I'll talk more about this in the next section, "Constructing the WBS."

3. Define the WBS components. This step involves decomposing the WBS levels into lower-level components. WBS components, like the deliverables and requirements, should be defined in tangible, verifiable terms so that performance and successful completion (or delivery) are easily measured and verified. Each component must clearly describe the product, service, or result in verifiable terms, and it must be assigned to a unit in the organization that will take responsibility for completing the work and making certain of its accuracy.

4. Assign identification codes. This step is a process where you assign identification codes or numbers to each of the WBS components.

5. Verify the WBS. This step is a verification step. Examine the decomposition to determine whether all the components are clear and complete. Determine whether each component listed is absolutely necessary to fulfill the requirements of the deliverable, and verify that the decomposition is sufficient to describe the work.

I'll talk more about the process in step 4 in the section "Unique WBS Identifiers" later in this chapter.

You can now plug the components you've identified into the WBS. This all sounds like a lot of work. I won't kid you—it is, but it's essential to project success. If you don't perform the WBS process adequately and accurately, you might end up setting yourself up for a failed project at worst or for lots of project changes, delayed schedules, and increased costs at best, not to mention all those team members who'll throw up their hands when you return to them for the third or fourth time to ask that they redo work they've already completed. I know you won't let this happen, so let's move on to constructing the WBS.

The Create WBS process has several outputs, one of which is the WBS. You'll look at the specifics of how to create the WBS next.

Constructing the WBS

There is no "right" way to construct a WBS. In practice, the chart structure is used quite often. (This structure resembles an organization chart with different levels of detail.) But a WBS could be composed in outline form as well. The choice is yours. You'll look at both ways shortly, along with some figures that depict the different levels of a WBS.

According to the *PMBOK Guide*, you can organize the WBS in several ways:

Major deliverables and subprojects   The major deliverables of the project are used as the first level of decomposition in this structure. If you're opening a new store, for example, the deliverables might include determining location, store build-out, furnishings, product, and so on. I'll talk about subprojects in the next section.

Subproject executed outside the project team   Another way to organize the work is by subprojects. Perhaps you're expanding an existing highway, and several subprojects are involved. Some of your first level of decomposition might include these subprojects: demolition, design, bridgework, and paving. Each of the subproject managers will develop a WBS for their subproject that details the work required for that deliverable. When subproject work is involved, often times the subproject work is contracted out. In this example, if you contracted out the bridgework deliverable, this subproject requires its own WBS, which the seller (the bridgework subcontractor) is responsible for creating as part of the contract and contract work.

Project phases   Many projects are structured or organized by project phases. For example, let's say you work in the construction industry. The project phases used in your industry might include project initiation, planning, design, build, inspection, and turnover. A feasibility study might be a deliverable under the project initiation phase, blueprints might be a deliverable under the planning phase, and so on. Each phase listed here would be the first level of decomposition (that is, the first level of the WBS), their deliverables would be the next level, and so on.

Combination approach   This approach combines some or all of the methods I've discussed. You might use the project phases and major deliverables together as the first level of decomposition. Or you could have subprojects listed with major deliverables. You can use this approach in other levels of the WBS structure as well, not just the first level.

You'll take a look at some example WBS structures next.

Understanding the Various WBS Levels

Although the project manager is free to determine the number of levels in the WBS based on the complexity of the project, all WBS structures start with the project itself. Some WBS structures show the project as level one. Others show the level under the project, or the first level of decomposition, as level one. The *PMBOK Guide* notes that level one is the first level of decomposition, so I'll follow that example here.

The first level of decomposition might be the deliverables, phases, or subprojects, as I talked about earlier. The levels that follow show more and more detail and might include more deliverables, followed by requirements, and so on. Each of these breakouts is called a *level* in the WBS. The lowest level of any WBS is called the *work package level*. (I'll talk more about this in "Defining Work Packages" later in this chapter.) The goal is to construct the WBS to the work package level where you can easily and reliably estimate cost and schedule dates.

Exam Spotlight

Remember that each descending level of the WBS is a more detailed description of the project deliverables than the level above it. Each component of the WBS should be defined clearly and completely and should describe how the work of the project will be performed and controlled.

There is some controversy among project managers over whether activities should be listed on the WBS. The *PMBOK Guide* doesn't have a rule regarding this; it's up to the project manager to determine how far to break the deliverables down and whether to include activities. In practice, I often include activities on my work breakdown structure for small projects because it facilitates other Planning processes later. In this case, the activities are the work package level. However, you should realize that large, complex projects will not likely list activities on the WBS. And for the exam, remember that you will decompose activities during the Activity Definition process that I'll talk about in Chapter 6, "Resource Planning," and that activities are *not* part of the WBS.

The easiest way to describe the steps for creating a WBS is with an example. Let's suppose you work for a software company that publishes children's games. You're the project manager for the new Billy Bob's Bassoon game, which teaches children about music, musical rhythm, and beginning sight reading. The first box on the WBS is the project name; it appears at the top of the WBS, as shown in Figure 4.1.

The next level is the first level of decomposition and should describe the major deliverables for the project. In this example, some of the deliverables might be requirements definition, design specifications, and programming. This isn't an exhaustive list of deliverables; in practice, you would go on to place all of your major deliverables into the WBS as level-one content.

For illustration purposes, just look at a slice of the WBS for this project. Refer to Figure 4.1 to see the WBS with level-one detail added.

Level-two content might be the component deliverables that are further broken out from the major deliverables of level one, or it might be products, results, or activities that contribute to the deliverable. The Billy Bob's Bassoon example shows further deliverables as level-two content. See Figure 4.2 for an illustration of the WBS so far.

The goal here is to eventually break the work out to the point where the responsibility and accountability for each work package can be assigned to an organizational unit or a team of people. I've decomposed this WBS to the activity level because it's a small project. An easy way to differentiate between deliverables and activities in the WBS is to use nouns as the deliverable descriptors and verbs as activity descriptors. Reaching way back to my grade-school English, I recall that a noun is a person, place, or thing. In this example, the deliverables in level one and level two are described using nouns. The activity level, level three in the example in Figure 4.3, is described using verbs, or action words. Some of the verbs used in level three are *define*, *design*, and *determine*. Many more activities would go with these deliverables, but for the sake of illustration, I've listed just a few for each deliverable to give you an idea of how you construct the WBS.

FIGURE 4.1   WBS level one

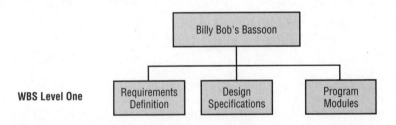

FIGURE 4.2   WBS levels one and two

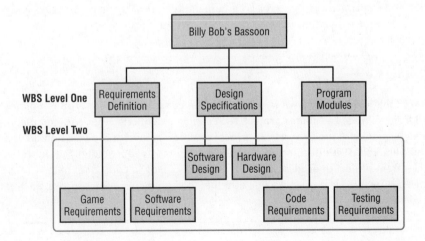

FIGURE 4.3   WBS levels one, two, and three

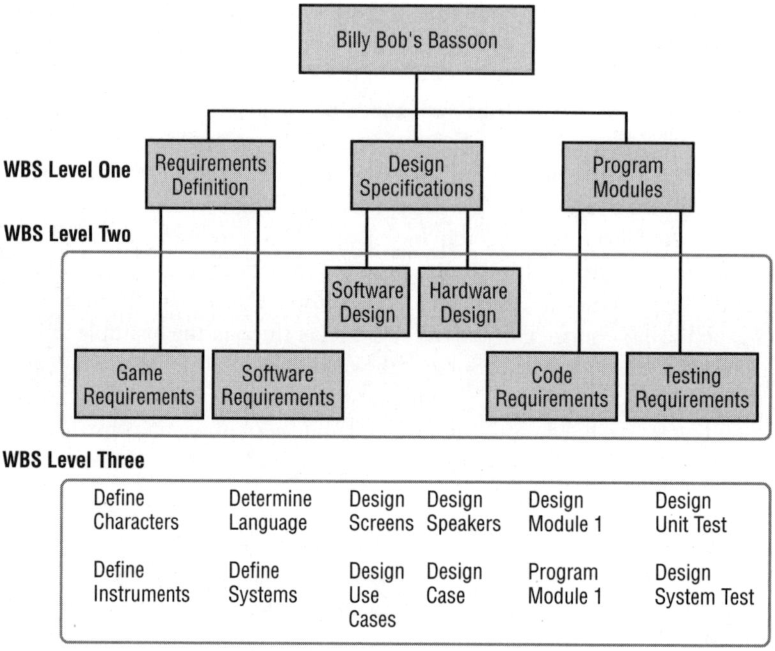

You can see from these illustrations how a poor scope definition or inadequate list of deliverables will lead to a poorly constructed WBS. Not only will this make the WBS look sickly, but the project itself will suffer and might even succumb to the dreaded premature project demise. The final cost of the project will be higher than estimated, and lots of rework (translation: late nights and weekends) will be needed to account for the missing work not listed on the WBS. You can construct a good WBS and maintain a healthy project by taking the time to document all the deliverables during the Scope Definition process.

WBS Templates

Don't forget that work breakdown structures can be constructed using WBS templates or the WBS from a similar completed project. A bit earlier, I mentioned that WBS templates are a tool and technique of the Create WBS process. Although every project is unique, many companies and industries perform the same kind of projects repeatedly. The deliverables are similar from project to project, and they generally follow a consistent path. The WBS templates can be used in a case like this as a tool to simplify the WBS process, saving the project manager time.

Large, complex projects are often composed of several subprojects that collectively make up the main project. The WBS for a project such as this would show the subprojects as level-one detail. These subprojects' major deliverables would then be listed as level-two content, perhaps more deliverables as level three, and so on.

Don't get too carried away when creating a WBS. The object is to define the work of the project so you can easily plan, manage, monitor, and control the work. But, you don't want to take this too far. If you decompose the work to the point that you're showing every minute detail, you've ventured into inefficiency and will find it more difficult to plan and manage. In addition, you're potentially stifling the creativity of the people working on the project because everything is so narrowly defined.

Sometimes, particularly when working on large projects that consist of several subprojects, some of the subprojects might not be scheduled to be worked on until a future date. Obviously, it makes sense to develop the WBS in detail at that future date when the deliverables and subprojects are better known and more details are available. This technique is called *rolling wave planning*. The idea behind this technique is that you elaborate the work of the project to the level of detail you know about at the time. If a subproject or deliverable is scheduled sometime in the future, the only component that might appear on the WBS today is the subproject itself. As you get closer to the subproject, you'll elaborate the details of the subproject and record them on the WBS.

Exam Spotlight

Understand that rolling wave planning is a process of elaborating deliverables, project phases, or subprojects in the WBS to differing levels of decomposition depending on the expected date of the work. Work in the near term is elaborated in more detail than work to be performed in the future.

Understanding the Unique WBS Identifiers

Each element at each level of the WBS is generally assigned a unique identifier according to The *PMBOK Guide*. This unique identifier is typically a number, and it's used to sum and track the costs, schedule, and resources associated with the WBS elements. These numbers are usually associated with the corporation's chart of accounts, which is used to track costs by category. Collectively, these numeric identifiers are known as the *code of accounts*. The unique identifiers for the requirements definition branch of the WBS might look something like this:

10 Requirements Definition

10-1 Game Requirements

  10-1-1 Define Characters

  10-1-2 Define Instruments

10-2 Software Requirements

    10-2-1 Determine Language

    10-2-2 Define Systems

Defining Work Packages

As mentioned earlier, the project manager is free to determine the number of levels in the WBS based on the complexity of the project. You need to include enough levels to accurately estimate project time and costs but not so many levels that it's difficult to distinguish between the components. Regardless of the number of levels in a WBS, the lowest level in a WBS is called the *work package level*.

Work packages are the components that can be easily assigned to one person, or a team of people, with clear accountability and responsibility for completing the assignment. Assignments are easily made at the work package level; however, assignments can be made at any level in the WBS. The work package level is where time estimates, cost estimates, and resource estimates are determined.

Work package levels on large projects can represent subprojects that are further decomposed into their own work breakdown structures. They might also consist of project work that will be completed by a vendor, another organization, or another department in your organization. If you're giving project work to another department in your organization, you'll assign the work packages to individual managers, who will in turn break them down into activities during the Activity Definition process later in the Planning process group.

Work packages might be assigned to vendors or others external to the organization. For example, perhaps one of the deliverables in your project is special packaging and a vendor is responsible for completing this work. The vendor will likely treat this deliverable as a project within its own organization and construct its own WBS with several levels of decomposition. However, for your project, it's a deliverable listed at the work package level of the WBS.

This might seem self-evident, but work elements not shown on the WBS are not included in the project. The same holds true for the project scope statement—if the deliverable isn't noted there, it isn't part of the project.

Understanding Other Breakdown Structures

One point that the *PMBOK Guide* makes that I want you to be aware of is that you should not confuse the WBS with other types of breakdown structures. I'm not sure why you would confuse them, but the team who wrote the guide makes a point of telling you about it, so you

Real World Scenario

The Lincoln Street Office Building

Flagship International has just purchased a new building to house its growing staff. The folks at Flagship consider themselves very lucky to have won the bid on the property located in a prime section of the downtown area. The building is a historic building and is in need of some repairs and upgrades to make it suitable for office space. Constructing the renovations will require special handling and care, as outlined in the *Historical Society Building Revisions Guide*.

Alfredo Martini is the project manager assigned to the renovation project. Alfredo has already determined the deliverables for this project. In so doing, he has discovered that he will not be able to manage all the work himself. He will need several subproject managers working on individual deliverables, all reporting to him. Alfredo calls a meeting with the other project managers to develop the WBS. Let's eavesdrop on the meeting.

"As you all know, we're planning to move into the Lincoln Street building by November 1. There is quite a bit of work to do between now and then, and I'm enlisting each of you to manage a segment of this project. Take a look at this WBS."

A portion of the WBS Alfredo constructed looks like this:

Lincoln Street Building Renovation

> 1.0 Facility Safety
>
> > 1.1 Sprinkler System
> >
> > 1.2 Elevators
> >
> > 1.3 Emergency Evacuation Plans
>
> 2.0 Asbestos Abatement
>
> > 2.1 Inspection and Identification
> >
> > 2.2 Plans for Removal
>
> 3.0 Office Space
>
> > 3.1 Building Floor Plans
> >
> > 3.2 Plans for Office Space Allocation
> >
> > 3.3 Plans for Break Room Facilities
> >
> > 3.4 Plans for Employee Workout Room

Alfredo continues, "I'm going to manage the Facility Safety project. Adrian, I'd like you to take the Asbestos Abatement project, and Orlando, you're responsible for the Office Space project."

"Alfredo," Adrian says. "Asbestos abatement is going to take contractors and specialized equipment. We don't have staff to do these tasks."

"I understand. You'll need to take charge of securing the contractor to handle this. Your responsibility will be to manage the contractor and keep them on schedule," Alfredo answers.

Orlando reminds Alfredo that he has missed a deliverable on the WBS. "Part of the Office Space project needs to include the network communications and telecommunications equipment rooms. I don't see that on here."

"Good point, Orlando," Alfredo says. "The level-two and level-three elements of this WBS are not complete. Each of you has been assigned to the subproject level, level one. Your first assignment is to meet back here in two weeks with a WBS for your subproject. And I'd like to see some ideas about the staff assignments you'd make at the work package level and how long you think these components will take. We'll refine those after we meet next."

should be aware of it for the exam. Here are the other structures they point out that you'll see as you proceed through the remaining project processes:

Organization breakdown structure (OBS)   This is an organization chart that describes the hierarchical nature of the organization, what departments exist, and who reports to whom. It can be used to identify the organizational units responsible for the work package levels of the WBS.

Bill of materials (BOM)   BOMs are typically used in the manufacturing industry and identify the components needed to produce the product.

Risk breakdown structure (RBS)   This is a hierarchical picture of the risks identified on the project arranged by risk category.

Resource breakdown structure (RBS)   This is a hierarchical description of the resources, arranged by type, that will work on the project.

Now you'll move on to the remaining outputs of the Create WBS process.

Creating WBS Process Outputs

The Create WBS process has six outputs:

- Project scope statement updates
- Work breakdown structure
- WBS dictionary
- Scope baseline
- Project scope management plan updates
- Requested changes

I've covered the WBS in detail already. Updates to the scope statement and scope management plan might come about as a result of approved changes that occur when you're creating the WBS. You can see from the examples you've walked through in this chapter how new deliverables or requirements might surface as a result of working on the WBS. These requested changes (the last output here) should be reviewed and either approved or denied using your change control processes. (I'll talk about that in Chapter 9, "Measuring and Controlling Project Performance.") The approved changes should be noted in the project scope statement, and the project management plan should be updated to reflect the new approved project scope statement.

You'll look at the remaining outputs next.

WBS Dictionary

The *WBS dictionary* is where work component descriptions are documented. According to the *PMBOK Guide*, the WBS dictionary should include the following elements for each component of the WBS:

- Code of accounts identifier
- Statement of work, which describes the work of the component
- Organization responsible for completing the component
- List of schedule milestones

Here are some other elements that you might include in the WBS dictionary for each component:

- Contract information
- Quality requirements for the component
- Technical references that assist the responsible party with defining performance of the work

Let's look at an example of what a WBS dictionary entry might look like. You'll use the work package level defined in the sidebar "The Lincoln Street Office Building" earlier called Inspection and Identification. The WBS dictionary entry for this might look like the following:

2.1 Inspection and Identification

Statement of work: Inspect the building for asbestos, and identify all areas where it's found. Update the plan for removal (WBS 2.2) with each location identified.

Responsible organization: Adrian in Facilities will hire and oversee a contractor to perform this work.

Schedule milestones: Inspection and identification to start after contractor is identified and hired (no later than July 1). Work should be completed no later than September 15.

Contract information: Two contractors have been identified as qualified and experienced in this type of work. Contract process should close no later than June 12.

Scope Baseline

Remember how I said that everything you've done so far has built upon itself? This is an important concept you should know for this output. The *scope baseline* for the project is the approved project scope statement, the WBS, and the WBS dictionary. (You'll recall from Chapter 3 that the project scope statement serves as a baseline for future project decisions because it helps the team determine whether requested changes are inside or outside of scope.) In other words, these documents together describe in detail all the work of the project. From these documents, you'll document schedules, assign resources, and monitor and control the work of the project according to what's described here.

Exam Spotlight

The scope baseline is defined as the detailed project scope statement, the WBS, and the WBS dictionary. Understand this concept for the exam.

If the WBS is constructed well, you've given yourself a huge helping hand with the remaining Planning processes. The completion of many of the remaining processes depends on the project scope statement and WBS being accurate and complete. In Chapter 6, for example, you'll use the work packages created here to further elaborate the work into activities. From there, you can estimate costs, develop schedules, and so on. Before we get there, though, you'll take a little breather and look at some of the other Planning processes important to your project. Don't forget about the WBS! You'll return to this in the later planning chapters of this book.

Communicating the Plan

I've talked a good deal about documentation so far, and this topic will continue to come up throughout the remainder of the book. Keeping good documentation should become the motto of all good project managers. "Is that documented?" should be an ever-present question on the mind of the project manager. Documentation can save your bacon, so to speak, later in the project. Documentation is only one side of the equation, though—communication is the other. You and your stakeholders need to know who gets what information and when.

The *Communications Planning* process involves determining the communication needs of the stakeholders by defining the types of information needed, the format for communicating the information, how often it's distributed, and who prepares it. All of this is documented in the communications management plan, which is the only output of this process.

Pop quiz: Do you remember where else the communications management plan belongs? I'll give you the answer later in the section "Communications Management Plan."

Communications Planning Inputs

The inputs to the Communications Planning process will look familiar to you. They are as follows:

- Enterprise environmental factors
- Organizational process assets
- Project scope statement
- Constraints and assumptions elements of the project management plan

The *PMBOK Guide* notes that all the elements described in the enterprise environmental factors and in the organizational process assets are inputs to this process. However, special note is made of the lessons learned and historical information elements of the organizational process assets input. Information you learn as you're progressing through the project is documented as lessons learned. This information is helpful for future projects of similar scope and complexity. Historical information is also useful to review when starting the Communications Planning process. Either of these documents might contain information about communication decisions on past projects and their results. Why reinvent the wheel? If something didn't work well on a past project, you'd want to know that before implementing that procedure on this project, so review past project documentation.

The project scope management plan (I talked about this in Chapter 3) provides a common understanding of project scope among the stakeholders and serves as a basis for future project decisions. (I'm sure you have this definition memorized by now—that's good.) Since you performed stakeholder analysis as part of the Scope Definition process (which produced the project scope statement as an output that became an input to this process), you should review the stakeholder analysis and refresh your memory on their communication needs.

The project management plan defines how the subsidiary plans will be defined and integrated into the overall project management plan. As such, it's rich with constraints and assumptions that you should review as they pertain to stakeholder communication needs.

Tools and Techniques for Communications Planning

The Communications Planning process concerns defining and documenting the types of information you're going to deliver, the format it will take, to whom it will be delivered, and when. The process consists of two tools and techniques to help determine these elements. They are communications requirements analysis and communications technology. You'll look at both of these next.

Communications Requirements Analysis

Communications requirements analysis involves analyzing and determining the communication needs of the project stakeholders. According to the *PMBOK Guide*, there are several sources of information you can examine to help determine these needs, including the following:

- Company and departmental organizational charts
- Stakeholder relationships

- Other departments and business units involved on the project
- The number of resources involved on the project and where they're located in relation to project activities
- External needs that organizations such as the media, government, or industry groups might have that require communication updates
- Communication needs that are internal to the organization
- Stakeholder information (a lot of this was documented during stakeholder analysis)

This tool and technique requires an analysis of the items in the preceding list to make certain you're communicating information that's valuable to the stakeholders. Communicating valuable information doesn't mean you always paint a rosy picture. Communications to stakeholders might consist of either good or bad news—the point is that you don't want to bury stakeholders in too much information, but you want give them enough so that they're informed and can make appropriate decisions.

Project communication will always involve more than one person, even on the tiniest of projects. As such, communication network models have been devised to try to explain the relationships between people and the number or type of interactions needed between project participants. What you need to remember for the exam is that network models consist of nodes with lines connecting the nodes that indicate the number of communication channels, also known as *lines of communication*. Figure 4.4 shows an example of a network communication model with six channels of communication.

FIGURE 4.4 Network communication model

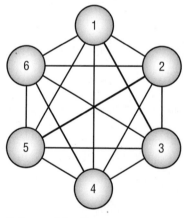

Nodes = participants
Lines = lines of communication between participants

Real World Scenario

Stakeholder Relationships

Bill is an information technology manager working on an enterprise resource planning project. He's one of the key stakeholders on this project. Bill reports to the CIO who in turn reports to the executive vice president, who also happens to be the project sponsor. Bill is close friends with the human resources director but doesn't get along so well with the accounting department director. This project requires heavy involvement from the accounting department and medium-level involvement from the human resources department.

You are the project manager for this project and are new to the organization. You know Bill's relationship with both the accounting and human resource directors. What you don't know is the relationship the two directors have with each other. Since all three stakeholders are key to the success of this project, it's important that all three communicate with you as well as with each other. You set up an interview with each of these stakeholders to determine several pieces of information: other departments that might need to be involved on the project, stakeholder communication needs and timing, external needs, timing of status updates for the company newsletter, and other department members aside from the stakeholders who need to be involved in the project. You also plant a few surreptitious questions that will give you some insight into the relationships the stakeholders have with each other and with the project sponsor.

You discover that the human resources and accounting directors have known each other for several years and worked together at another organization prior to coming to work here. This tells you that if you can get one of them to buy in on project decisions, the other will likely follow suit. They both have the utmost respect for Bill and his technical capabilities, even though the accounting director doesn't care for his abrupt, direct communication style. You also learn that although they both have respect for the position of the executive vice president, they don't believe the person filling that role is competent to do the job. They question his decision-making ability—or lack thereof—and warn you that you need to write down his answers and direction so that he doesn't change his story halfway through the project. Although you won't formally document this valuable piece of information, you'll definitely put it into action right away.

The nodes are the participants, and the lines show the connection between them all. You'll need to know how to calculate the number of communication channels when you take the exam. You could draw them out as in this example and count up the lines, but there's an easier way. The formula for calculating the lines of communication is as follows:

(number of participants × (number of participants less 1)) divided by 2

Here's the calculation in mathematical terms:

$$n(n-1)/2$$

Figure 4.4 shows six participants, so let's plug that into the formula to determine the lines of communication:

$$6(6-1)/2 = 15$$

Exam Spotlight

I recommend you memorize the communications channel formula before taking the exam.

Communications Technology

The second tool and technique of this process is communications technology. This examines the methods (or technology) used to communicate the information to, from, and among the stakeholders. Methods of communicating can take many forms, such as written, spoken, email, formal status reports, meetings, online databases, online schedules, and so on. This tool and technique examines the technology elements that might affect project communications. You should consider several factors before deciding what methods you'll choose to transfer information. The timing of the information exchange or need for updates is the first factor. The availability of the technology you're planning on using to communicate project information is important as well. Do you need to procure new technology or systems, or are there systems already in place that will work? Staff experience with the technology is another factor. Are the project team members and stakeholders experienced at using this technology, or will you need to train them? Finally, consider the duration of the project and the project environment. Will the technology you're choosing work throughout the life of the project, or will it have to be upgraded or updated at some point? And how does the project team function? Are they all located together or spread out across several campuses or locations?

The answers to these questions should be documented in the communications management plan. I'll cover that next.

Communications Management Plan

All projects require sound communication plans, but not all projects will have the same types of communication or the same methods for distributing the information. The *communications management plan*, which is the only output of the Communications Planning process, documents the types of information needs the stakeholders have, when the information should be distributed, and how the information will be delivered. The answer to the earlier pop quiz is the communications management plan, which is a subsidiary plan of the project management plan I talked about in Chapter 3.

The type of information you will typically communicate includes project status, project scope statements and scope statement updates, project baseline information, risks, action items, performance measures, deliverable acceptance, and so on. I'll cover all these topics in greater detail in the remaining chapters of this book. What's important to know now is that the information needs of the stakeholders should be determined as early in the Planning process group as possible so that as you and your team develop project planning documents, you already know who should receive copies of them and how they should be delivered.

According to the *PMBOK Guide*, the communications management plan typically describes the following elements:

- Name of the item to be communicated

- Purpose for communication

- Frequency of communications

- Time frame for distribution, including starting and ending dates

- Format of the communication and method of transmission

- Person responsible for distributing the information

The information that will be shared with stakeholders and the distribution methods are based on the needs of the stakeholders, the project complexity, and the organizational policies. Some communications might be informal—a chat by the coffee maker, for instance—while other communications are written and a copy is filed with the project files.

Exam Spotlight

The communications management plan documents how the communication needs of the stakeholders will be met, including the types of information that will be communicated, who will communicate it, who receives the communication, the methods used to communicate, the timing and frequency, the method for updating this plan as the project progresses, the escalation process, and a glossary of common terms.

You might consider setting up an intranet site for your project and posting the appropriate project documentation there for the stakeholders to access anytime they want. If you use this method, make sure to document it in the communications management plan and notify your stakeholders when updates or new communication is posted.

 Chapter 8, "Developing the Project Team," discusses communication methods in more depth.

Identifying Quality Standards

Quality is affected by the triple constraints (project scope, schedule, and cost), and quality concerns are found in all projects. Quality typically defines whether stakeholder expectations were met. Being on time and on budget is one thing; if you deliver the wrong product or an inferior product, on time and on budget suddenly don't mean much.

The *Quality Planning* process is concerned with targeting quality standards that are relevant to the project at hand and devising a plan to meet and satisfy those standards. The quality management plan is an output of this process that describes how the quality policy will be implemented by the project management team during the course of the project. Another key output of this process is the process improvement plan, which documents the actions for analyzing processes to ultimately increase customer value. Everything discussed in this section, including the inputs and tools and techniques of this process, will be used to help develop these two primary outputs.

Exam Spotlight

Quality Planning is a key process performed during the Planning processes and when developing the project management plan. It should be performed in conjunction with other Planning processes. According to the *PMBOK Guide*, "quality is planned, designed, and built in—not inspected in."

Quality Inputs

The Quality Planning process has several inputs:

- Enterprise environmental factors
- Organizational process assets
- Project scope statement
- Project management plan

The two key elements I'll cover regarding inputs are standards and regulations (which are part of the enterprise environmental factors input) and the quality policy (which is part of the organizational process assets input).

Standards and Regulations

The project manager should consider any standards, regulations, guidelines, or rules that exist concerning the work of the project when writing the quality plan. A *standard* is something that's approved by a recognized body and that employs rules, guidelines, or characteristics that should be followed. For example, the Americans with Disabilities Act (ADA) has established standards for web page designers that outline alternative viewing options of web pages for people with disabilities. PMI guidelines regarding project management are another example of standards.

Standards aren't legally mandatory, but it's a good idea to follow them. Many organizations (or industries) have standards in place that are proven best practice techniques. Disregarding accepted standards can have significant consequences. For example, if you're creating a new software product that ignores standard protocols, your customers won't be able to use it. Standards can be set by the organization, independent bodies or organizations such as the International Organization for Standardization (ISO), and so on.

A *regulation* is mandatory. Regulations are almost always imposed by governments or institutions like the American Medical Association. However, organizations might have their own self-imposed regulations that you should be aware of as well. Regulations require strict adherence, particularly in the case of government-imposed regulations, or stiff penalties and fines could result—maybe even jail time if the offense is serious enough. Hmm, it might be tough to practice project management from behind bars—not a recommended career move.

If possible, it's a good idea to include information from the quality policy (I'll cover this in the next section) and any standards, regulations, or guidelines that affect the project in the quality management plan. If it's not possible to include this information in the quality management plan, then at least make reference to the information and where it can be found. It's the project management team's responsibility to be certain all stakeholders are aware of and understand the policy issues and standards or regulations that might impact the project.

NOTE   Contracts might have certain provisions for quality requirements that you should account for in the quality management plan. These provisions will also be discussed during the Procurement Planning processes. If the quality management plan has already been written by the time these processes are performed, you should update the quality plan to reflect it.

Quality Policy

The quality policy is part of the organizational process assets input. It's a guideline published by executive management that describes what quality policies should be adopted for projects the company undertakes. It's up to the project manager to understand this policy and incorporate any predetermined company guidelines into the quality plan. If a quality policy does not exist, it's up to the project management team to create one for the project.

Tools and Techniques for Quality Planning

The Quality Planning process has five tools and techniques used to help construct the quality management plan:

- Cost-benefit analysis
- Benchmarking
- Design of experiments

- Cost of quality
- Additional quality planning tools

Make sure you understand each of these tools and techniques and its purpose for the exam. You'll take a look at them now.

Cost-Benefit Analysis

You've seen the cost-benefit analysis technique before in the Initiating process group. In the case of quality management, you'll want to consider the trade-offs of the cost of quality. It's cheaper and more efficient to prevent defects in the first place than to spend time and money fixing them later. The benefits of meeting quality requirements are as follows:

- Stakeholder satisfaction is increased.
- Costs are lower.
- Productivity is higher.
- There is less rework.

The *PMBOK Guide* notes that the primary cost of meeting quality requirements for a project is the expense incurred while performing project quality management activities.

Benchmarking

Benchmarking is a process of comparing previous similar activities to the current project activities to provide a standard to measure performance against. This comparison will also help you derive ideas for quality improvements on the current project. For example, if your current printer can produce 8 pages per minute and you're considering a new printer that produces 14 pages per minute, the benchmark is 8 pages per minute.

Design of Experiments

Design of experiments (DOE) is a statistical technique that identifies the elements—or variables—that will have the greatest effect on overall project outcomes. It is used most often concerning the product of the project but can also be applied to project management processes to examine trade-offs. DOE designs and sets up experiments to determine the ideal solution for a problem using a limited number of sample cases. It analyzes several variables at once, allowing you to change all (or some of) the variables at the same time and determine which combination will produce the best result at a reasonable cost.

Exam Spotlight

For the exam, remember that the key to DOE is that it equips you with a statistical framework that allows you to change the variables that have the greatest effect on overall project outcomes at once instead of changing one variable at a time.

Cost of Quality

The *cost of quality (COQ)* is the total cost to produce the product or service of the project according to the quality standards. These costs include all the work necessary to meet the product requirements whether the work was planned or unplanned. It also includes the costs of work performed because of nonconforming quality requirements.

Three costs are associated with the cost of quality:

Prevention costs   Prevention means keeping defects out of the hands of customers. *Prevention costs* are the costs associated with satisfying customer requirements by producing a product without defects. These costs are manifested early in the process and include aspects such as quality planning, training, design review, and contractor and supplier costs.

Appraisal costs   *Appraisal costs* are the costs expended to examine the product or process and make certain the requirements are being met. Appraisal costs might include costs associated with aspects such as inspections and testing. Prevention and appraisal costs are often passed on to the acquiring organization because of the limited duration of the project.

Failure costs   *Failure costs* are what it costs when things don't go according to plan. Failure costs are also known as cost of poor quality. Two types of failure costs exist:

Internal failure costs   These result when customer requirements are not satisfied while the product is still in the control of the organization. Internal failure costs might include corrective action, rework, scrapping, and downtime.

External failure costs   These occur when the product has reached the customer who determines that the requirements have not been met. Costs associated with external failure costs might include inspections at the customer site, returns, and customer service costs.

The cost of quality can be affected by project decisions. Let's say you're producing a new product. Unfortunately, the product scope description or project scope statement was inadequate to describe the functionality of the product. And, the project team produced the product exactly as specified in the project scope statement, WBS, and other planning documents. Once the product hit the store shelves, the organization was bombarded with returns and warranty claims because of the poor quality. Therefore, your project decisions impacted the cost of quality. Recalls of products can also impact the cost of quality.

Cost of quality is a topic you'll likely encounter on the exam. The following sections will discuss some of the pioneers in this field. Quality must be planned into the project, not inspected in after the fact to make certain the product or service meets stakeholders' expectations.

Four people in particular are responsible for the rise of the quality management movement and the theories behind the cost of quality: Philip B. Crosby, Joseph M. Juran, W. Edwards Deming, and Walter Shewhart. Each of these men developed steps or points that led to commonly accepted quality processes that we use today and either developed or were the foundation for the development of quality processes such as Total Quality Management, Six Sigma, Cost of Quality, and Continuous Improvement. I'll also cover a quality technique called the Kaizen approach that originated in Japan.

Philip B. Crosby

Philip B. Crosby devised the *zero defects* practice, which means, basically, do it right the first time. (Didn't your dad use to tell you this?) Crosby says that costs will increase when quality planning isn't performed up front, which means you'll have to engage in rework, thus affecting productivity. Prevention is the key to Crosby's theory. If you prevent the defect from occurring in the first place, costs are lower, conformance to requirements is easily met, and the cost measurement for quality becomes the cost of nonconformance rather than the cost of rework.

Joseph M. Juran

Joseph M. Juran is noted for his *fitness for use* premise. Simply put, this means the stakeholders' and customers' expectations are met or exceeded. This says that conformance to specifications—meaning the product of the project that was produced is what the project set out to produce—is met or exceeded. Fitness for use specifically reflects the customers' or stakeholders' view of quality and answers the following questions:

"Did the product or service produced meet the quality expectation?"

"Did it satisfy a real need?"

"Is it reliable and safe?"

Juran also proposed that there could be grades of quality. However, you should not confuse grade with quality. *Grade* is a category for products or services that are of the same type but have differing technical characteristics. *Quality* describes how well the product or service (or characteristics of the product or service) fulfills the requirements. Low quality is usually not an acceptable condition; however, low grade might be. For example, your new Dad's Dollars Credit Card software tracking system might be of high quality, meaning it has no bugs and the product performs as advertised, but of low grade, meaning it has few features. You'll almost always want to strive for high quality, regardless of the acceptable grade level.

Exam Spotlight

Understand the difference between quality and grade for the exam.

W. Edwards Deming

W. Edwards Deming suggested that as much as 85 percent of the cost of quality is a management problem. Once the quality issue has hit the floor, or the worker level, the workers have little control. For example, if you're constructing a new highway and the management team that bid on the project proposed using inferior-grade asphalt, the workers laying the asphalt have little control over its quality. They're at the mercy of the management team responsible for purchasing the supplies.

Deming also proposed that workers cannot figure out quality on their own and thus cannot perform at their best. He believed that workers need to be shown what acceptable quality is and that they need to be made to understand that quality and continuous improvement are necessary elements of any organization—or project in your case.

Many consider Deming to be the founder (or major contributor) of *Total Quality Management (TQM)*. TQM, like Deming, says that the process is the problem, not people. Every person and all activities the company undertakes are involved with quality. TQM stipulates that quality must be managed in and that quality improvement should be a continuous way of doing business, not a one-time performance of a specific task or process.

Six Sigma is a quality management approach that is similar to TQM and is typically used in manufacturing and service-related industries. Six Sigma is a measurement-based strategy that focuses on process improvement and variation reduction by applying Six Sigma methodologies to the project. There are two Six Sigma methodologies. The first is known as DMADV (define, measure, analyze, design, and verify) and is used to develop new processes or products at the Six Sigma level. The second is called DMAIC (define, measure, analyze, improve, and control) and is used to improve existing processes or products. Another tidbit you should understand about Six Sigma is that it aims to eliminate defects and stipulates that no more than 3.4 defects per million are produced.

Walter Shewhart

Some sources say that Walter Shewhart is considered the grandfather of TQM that was further popularized by Deming. Shewhart developed statistical tools to examine when a corrective action must be applied to a process. He invented control chart techniques (control charts are a tool and technique of the Perform Quality Control process) and was also the inventor of the Plan-Do-Check-Act cycle that I talked about in Chapter 1.

Kaizen Approach

The Kaizen approach is a quality technique from Japan. In fact, *Kaizen* means *continuous improvement* in Japanese. With this technique, all project team members and managers should be constantly watching for quality improvement opportunities. The Kaizen approach states that you should improve the quality of the people first and then the quality of the products or service.

Continuous improvement involves everyone in the organization watching for ways to improve quality, whether incrementally or by incorporating new ideas into the process. This involves taking measurements, improving processes by making them repeatable and systemized, reducing variations in production or performance, reducing defects, and improving cycle times. TQM and Six Sigma are examples of continuous improvement.

Exam Spotlight

Understand each of these men's theories on the cost of quality for the exam. Here's a key to help you remember:

- Crosby = Zero defects and prevention or rework results.

- Juran = Fitness for use, conformance. Quality by design.

- Deming = Quality is a management problem.

- Shewhart = Plan-Do-Check-Act cycle.

- TQM = Quality must be managed in and must be a continuous process.

- Six Sigma = Six Sigma is a measurement-based strategy; no more than 3.4 defects per million.

- Kaizen = Continuous improvement; improve quality of people first.

- Continuous improvement = Watch continuously for ways to improve quality.

Additional Quality Planning Tools

The last tool and technique of the Quality Planning process is additional quality-planning tools. The *PMBOK Guide* lists these additional tools as follows:

- Brainstorming and the Nominal Group Technique (covered in Chapter 5, "Risk Planning")
- Flowcharts (covered in Chapter 10, "Monitoring and Controlling Change.")
- Affinity diagrams
- Force field analysis
- Matrix diagram
- Prioritization matrices

Affinity diagrams are used to group and organize thoughts and facts and can be used in conjunction with brainstorming. After you've gathered all ideas possible with brainstorming, you group similar ideas together on an affinity diagram.

Force field analysis is a method of examining the pros and cons of a decision. You could use the old T-square approach and list all the pros down the left column and all the cons in the right. Determine which of these elements in the list are barriers and which are enablers to the project. Assign a priority or rank to each, and develop strategies for leveraging the strengths of the high-priority enablers while minimizing the highest-ranked barriers.

Matrix diagrams are also used as a decision-making tool, particularly when several options or alternatives are available. Using a spreadsheet format, you list common elements down the rows in the first column and then list each alternative in its own column to the right of this one. Then rank each alternative in the corresponding cell where the common element and the alternative intersect.

Prioritization matrices are useful when you need to prioritize complex issues that have numerous criteria for decision making. They're best used in situations where you can use data or inputs to score the criteria. They work similarly to a weighted scoring model (I talked about those in Chapter 2) in that the most important criteria carries the greatest weight.

You should memorize the names of these additional quality planning tools for the exam, but more important, you should understand both the names and concepts of the other tools and techniques I talked about earlier in this chapter.

Quality Planning Outputs

Quality Planning uses many techniques to determine the areas of quality improvement that can be implemented, controlled, and measured throughout the rest of the project, as you've seen. These are recorded in the primary output of this process, which is called the *quality management plan*. The following list includes other outputs of this process:

- Quality metrics
- Quality checklists
- Process improvement plan
- Quality baseline
- Project management plan updates

Project management plan updates include the quality management plan and process improvement plan and might come about as a result of changes or corrections resulting from the Perform Quality Assurance process. I'll talk about Perform Quality Assurance in Chapter 9. You'll look at the remaining outputs of Quality Planning next.

Quality Management Plan

The *quality management plan* describes how the project management team will enact the quality policy. It should document the resources needed to carry out the quality plan, the responsibilities of the project team in implementing quality, and all the processes and procedures the project team and organization should use to satisfy quality requirements, including quality control, quality assurance techniques, and continuous improvement processes.

The project manager in cooperation with the project staff writes the quality management plan. You can assign quality actions to the activities listed on the WBS based on the quality plan requirements. Isn't that WBS a handy thing? Later in the Perform Quality Control process, measurements will be taken to determine whether the quality to date is on track with the quality standards outlined in the quality management plan.

Exam Spotlight

The Quality Management Knowledge Area, which includes the Quality Planning, Perform Quality Assurance, and Perform Quality Control processes, involves the quality management of the project as well as the quality aspects of the product or service the project was undertaken to produce. I'll discuss Quality Assurance and Quality Control in later chapters.

Quality Metrics

A *quality metric*, also known as *operational definition*, describes what is being measured and how it will be measured by the Perform Quality Control process. For example, let's say you're managing the opening of a new restaurant in July of next year. Perhaps one of the deliverables is the procurement of flatware for 500 place settings. The operational definition in this case might include the date the flatware must be delivered and a counting or inventory process to ensure you received the number of place settings you ordered. Measurements consist of actual values, not "yes" or "no" results. In our example, receiving the flatware is a "yes" or "no" result (you have it or you don't), but the date it was delivered and the number of pieces delivered are actual values. Failure rates are another type of quality metric that is measurable, as are reliability, availability, test coverage, and defect density measurements.

Quality Checklists

If you're like me, you start your day at the office with a big to-do list that has so many items on it you won't be able to finish them all. Nevertheless, you faithfully write the list every day and check off the items that you accomplish throughout the day. *Checklists* are like this in that they provide a means to determine whether the required steps in a process have been followed. As each step is completed, it's checked off the list. Checklists can be activity specific or industry specific and might be very complex or easy to follow. Sometimes, organizations might have standard checklists they use for projects. You might also be able to obtain checklists from professional associations.

Exam Spotlight

Be aware that a checklist shows up as both a process output and a tool and technique. Quality checklists are an output of the Quality Planning process, and checklist analysis is a tool and technique of the Risk Identification process.

Real World Scenario

Candy Works

Juliette Walters is a contract project manager for Candy Works. She is leading a project that will introduce a new line of hard candy drops in various exotic flavors: café latte, hot buttered popcorn, and jalapeño spice, just to name a few.

Juliette is writing the quality management plan for this project. After interviewing stakeholders and key team members, she has found several quality factors of importance to the organization. Quality will be measured by the following criteria:

Candy size   Each piece should measure 3 mm.

Appearance   No visible cracks or breaks should appear in the candy.

Flavor   Flavor must be distinguishable when taste tested.

Number produced   The production target is 9,000 pieces per week. The current machine has been benchmarked at 9,200 candies per week.

Intensity of color   There should be no opaqueness in the darker colors.

Wrappers   Properly fitting wrappers cover the candies, folding over twice in back and twisted on each side. There is a different wrapper for each flavor of candy, and they must match exactly.

The candy is cooked and then pulled into a long cylinder shape roughly 6 feet long and 2 feet in diameter. This cylinder is fed into the machine that molds and cuts the candy into drops. The cylinders vary a little in size, because they're hand-stretched by expert candy makers prior to feeding them into the drop maker machine. As a result, the end of one flavor batch—the café latte flavor—and the beginning of the next batch—the hot buttered popcorn flavor—merge. This means the drops that fall into the collection bins are intermingled during the last run of the first flavor batch. In other words, the last bin of the café latte flavor run has some hot buttered popcorn drops mixed in. And, there isn't a way to separate the drops once they've hit the bin. From here, the drops go on to the candy-wrapping machine, where brightly colored wrappers are matched to the candy flavor. According to the quality plan, hot buttered popcorn drops cannot be wrapped as café latte drops. Juliette ponders what to do.

As she tosses and turns that night thinking about the problem, it occurs to her to present this problem as an opportunity to the company rather than as a problem. To keep production in the 9,000 candies per week category, the machines can't be stopped every time a new batch is introduced. So, Juliette comes up with the idea to wrap candies from the intermixed bins with wrappers that say "Mystery Flavor." This way, production keeps pace with the plan, and the wrapper/flavor quality problem is mitigated.

Process Improvement Plan

The *process improvement plan* focuses on finding inefficiencies in a process or activity and eliminating them. The idea here is that if you're doing activities or performing processes that don't add any value, you'll want to either stop doing what you're doing or modify the process so that you are adding value. You should note that the process improvement plan is a subsidiary plan of the project management plan. Some of the elements you should consider when thinking about process improvement are the process boundaries, which describes the purpose for the process and its expected start and end dates; the process configuration so that you know what processes are performed when and how they interact; the process metrics; and any specific elements you want to target for improvement.

Quality Baseline

Almost everything you've done throughout this process culminates in the quality baseline. The *quality baseline* is the quality objective of the project. It's what you'll use to measure and report quality against as you perform the remaining Quality processes.

One of the results of the Quality Planning process is that your product or process might require adjustments to conform to the quality policy and standards. These changes might result in cost changes and schedule changes. You might also discover that you'll need to perform risk analysis techniques for problems you uncover or when making adjustments as a result of this process.

 Real World Scenario

Project Case Study: New Kitchen Heaven Retail Store

You're just finishing a phone conversation with Jill, and you see Dirk headed toward your office.

Dirk walks in, crosses his arms over his chest, and stands next to your desk with an "I'm here for answers" look.

"I thought I'd drop by and see whether you have signed a lease and gotten Jake started on that build-out yet," says Dirk.

"I just got off the phone with Jill," you reply. "The realtor found a great location, and we've set up a tour at the end of this week."

"What has been the holdup?" Dirk asks. "I thought we'd be ready to start the build-out about now."

"I've been working on the project plans."

"Project plans," Dirk interrupts. "We already have a plan. That scope thing you drew up last week spelled things out pretty clearly."

"The charter was the project kickoff, and the project scope statement listed all the deliverables and requirements. From there I had to break the work of the project down into manageable units of work. So, I've drawn up a work breakdown structure with all the deliverables shown in a tree structure that I'd like to go over with you before showing it to the project team."

"We aren't building trees; we're building a new store. I don't understand why you're wasting all this time planning. We all know what the objectives are."

"Dirk," you reply, "if we put the right amount of effort and time into planning, the actual work of the project should go pretty smoothly. Planning is probably one of the most important things we can do on this project. If we don't plan correctly, we might miss something very important that could delay the store opening. That date is pretty firm, I thought."

"Yes, the date is firm. But I don't see how we could miss anything. You and I have met several times, and I know you've met with Jill and Jake. They're the other key players on this."

"You're right. I have met with Jill and Jake. And that's a perfect example of why we need to plan. When I met with Jill, she told me how all the store's data is communicated via a satellite network connection on a nightly basis. That means we need to involve the IT group."

You glance down at your notes. "Ricardo Ramirez heads up IT. I spoke with him last week about his deliverables, and I've included his group as a subproject on the work breakdown structure."

"Oh," Dirk replies. "I forgot about IT. You're right, that's an important part of the project, and we can't leave them out. Don't tell Ricardo I said this, but I'm not very technical myself and don't really know what you're going to need from him. I do know he also takes care of wiring and installing the point-of-sale terminals, but you'll have to work all that out with him. OK, I'm beginning to see why you're taking planning seriously. Let's have a look at this work break-down structure."

You hand Dirk a copy of the WBS. A partial version is shown here.

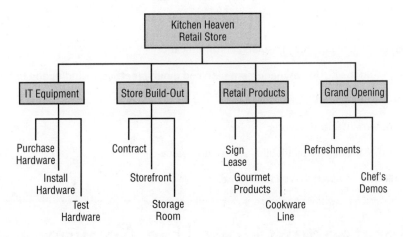

"Looks good to me."

"Great. Two more items, Dirk. After meeting with Jake, Ricardo, and Jill, I've also drafted a communication plan and a quality management plan. The communication plan describes the kind of information they need to receive, when, and how. And the quality management plan—well you know the old saying, 'Do it right the first time.' It describes the plan for implementing our quality policy. I also took the time to write down the specific quality metrics we're looking for, including the lease signing date (this one must start and finish on time) and the IT equipment specifications, and Jill has documented the gourmet products and the cookware line specifications."

Decomposed deliverables into a WBS

The WBS includes the following:

- Level one is subprojects or deliverables.

- Level two is deliverables or activities.

- Remaining levels are activities.

- Last level of WBS is the work package level, where time and cost estimates can be defined in the next process.

Documented the communications management plan, including the following:

- Stakeholder communication needs

- Types of project communication and their format

- Frequency and method of communication

- Person responsible for producing communication

Documented the quality management plan and quality metrics, including the following:

- Lease signing start and end dates

- IT equipment specifications

- Gourmet products—availability rates and defects

- Cookware products—availability rates

Understanding How This Applies to Your Next Project

In this chapter, you dealt with the realities of life on the job. The reality is, many project managers I know are managing several projects at once as opposed to one large project. Although every concept presented in this chapter is a sound one, it's important to note that you have to balance the amount of effort you'll put into project management processes against the size and complexity of the project.

Decomposing the deliverables is the first step toward determining resource requirements and estimates. A WBS is always a good idea, no matter the size of the project. I have to admit I have cheated a time or two on small projects and used the project schedule as both the WBS and the schedule. And in all fairness that's worked out fine when the team is small and there aren't more than three or four people working on the project. If you get many more than four people on the project team, it can be a little cumbersome to track deliverables with a schedule only. The WBS is the perfect tool to use to assign names to work packages, and it's the foundation for determining estimates for the work of the project.

The five-step process outlined by the *PMBOK Guide* works very well. Starting with the 50,000-foot view, the team determines the major deliverables of the project. From there, the deliverables are decomposed into ever smaller units of work. The trick here is to break the work down into measurable units so that you can verify the status of the work and the completion and acceptance of the work when you're finished. If you have "fuzzy" WBS levels or work packages, you won't be able to determine status accurately. In the information technology field, we have a saying about the status of projects: "It's 90 percent complete." The problem is it always seems that the last 10 percent takes twice as long to complete as the first 90 did. If you've taken the time to document a WBS, you'll have a much better idea of what that 90 percent constitutes. The last step is the verification step where you determine whether everything you've identified in the WBS is absolutely necessary to fulfill the work of the project and whether it's decomposed enough to adequately describe the work. It has been my experience that documenting the WBS will save you time later in the Planning processes, particularly developing the project schedule and determining the project budget.

The communication management plan is a must-have for every project. I can't stress enough how often I've seen the root cause of project issues end up being communication problems. Never assume keeping the stakeholders informed is an easy job. Even if you know the stakeholders well, always create a communication plan. Document how you'll communicate status, baseline information, risks, and deliverables acceptance. That way there's no question as to how information will be relayed, who's going to receive it, or when it will be delivered.

The quality baseline is another important element of your project plan. Again, you should take into consideration the final result or product of the project and the complexity of the project. You might not necessarily need a multipage document with detailed specifications. Depending on the project complexity, a few sentences stating the measurements or criteria you'll use to determine the quality objective might be all that's needed.

Summary

A WBS is a deliverable-oriented group of project essentials. The highest levels of the WBS are described using nouns, and the lowest levels are described with verbs. Each element in the WBS has its own set of objectives and deliverables that must be met in order to fulfill the deliverables of the next highest level and ultimately the project itself. In this way, the WBS validates the completeness of the work.

The lowest level of the WBS is known as work packages. This breakdown allows the project manager to determine cost estimates, time estimates, resource assignments, and quality controls.

The purpose of the communications management plan is determining the communication needs of the stakeholders by defining the types of information needed, the format for communicating the information, how often it's distributed, and who prepares it. This plan is a subsidiary plan of the project management plan.

Quality Planning targets the quality standards that are relevant to your project. The quality management plan outlines how the project team will enact the quality policy.

You need to consider the cost of quality when considering stakeholder needs. Four men led to the rise of the cost of quality theories. Crosby is known for his zero defects theory, Juran for the fitness for use theory, Deming for attributing 85 percent of cost of quality to the management team, and Shewhart for the Plan-Do-Check-Act cycle (he's also considered the grandfather of TQM). The Kaizen approach says that the project team should continuously be on the lookout for ways to improve the process and that people should be improved first and then the quality of the products or services. TQM and Six Sigma are examples of continuous improvement techniques.

Cost-benefit analysis considers trade-offs in the Quality Planning process. Benchmarking compares previous similar activities to the current project activities to provide a standard to measure performance against. Design of experiments is an analytical technique that determines what variables have the greatest effect on the project outcomes. This technique equips you with a statistical framework, allowing you to change all the important variables at once instead of changing one variable at a time.

Cost of quality involves three types of costs: prevention, appraisal, and failure costs; the latter is also known as the cost of poor quality. Failure costs include both internal and external costs.

The process improvement plan is a subsidiary plan of the project management plan and targets inefficiencies in a process or activity. The quality baseline is used to document the quality objectives of the project and is used as a basis for future Quality processes.

Exam Essentials

Be able to define a WBS and its components.   The WBS is a deliverable-oriented hierarchy. It uses the deliverables from the project scope statement or similar documents and decomposes them into logical, manageable units of work. Level one is the major deliverable level or subproject level, level two is a further elaboration of the deliverables, and so on. The lowest level of any WBS is called a work package.

Be able to describe the purpose of the communications management plan.   The communications management plan determines the communication needs of the stakeholders. It documents what information will be distributed, how it will be distributed, to whom, and the timing of the distribution.

Be able to identify the benefits of meeting quality requirements.   The benefits of meeting quality requirements include increased stakeholder satisfaction, lower costs, higher productivity, and less rework and are discovered during the Quality Planning process.

Be able to define the cost of quality. The COQ is the total cost to produce the product or service of the project according to the quality standards. These costs include all the work necessary to meet the product requirements for quality. The three costs associated with cost of quality are prevention, appraisal, and failure costs (also known as cost of poor quality).

Be able to name four people associated with COQ and some of the techniques they helped establish. They are Crosby, Juran, Deming, and Shewhart. Some of the techniques they helped to establish are TQM, Six Sigma, cost of quality, and continuous improvement. The Kaizen approach concerns continuous improvement and says people should be improved first.

Be able to name the tools and techniques of the Quality Planning process. The Quality Planning process consists of cost-benefit analysis, benchmarking, design of experiments, cost of quality, additional quality planning tools.

Key Terms

In this chapter, you began to see just how important communication is to every successful project. You learned about planning what work needs to be done, how you will communicate during the project, and how you will judge whether the project is successful. The processes that follow allow you to accomplish those portions of project planning. Understand them well, and know each process by the name used in the *PMBOK*:

Create WBS

Communications Planning

Quality Planning

Before you take the exam, also be certain you are familiar with the following terms:

appraisal costs	fitness for use
benchmarking	Kaizen
checklists	operational definition
code of accounts	prevention costs
communications management plan	process improvement plan
continuous improvement	quality baseline
cost of quality (COQ)	quality management plan
decomposition	quality metric
design of experiments (DOE)	regulation
failure costs	rolling wave planning

scope baseline   WBS dictionary

Six Sigma   work breakdown structure (WBS)

standard   work package

Total Quality Management (TQM)   zero defects

Review Questions

1. Which of the following makes up the project scope baseline?

    A. The project scope statement

    B. The scope management plan and WBS

    C. The WBS, project scope statement, and WBS dictionary

    D. The scope management plan, the WBS, and the WBS dictionary

2. You are working on a project that is similar in scope to a project performed last year by your company. You might consider which of the following?

    A. Using the previous project's alternatives identification as a template

    B. Reusing the previous project's cost-benefit analysis as justification for this project

    C. Using the previous project's WBS as a template

    D. Reusing the previous project's product description when writing the scope statement

3. Your company, Kick That Ball Sports, has appointed you project manager for its new Cricket product line introduction. This is a national effort, and all the retail stores across the country need to have the new products on the shelves before the media advertising blitz begins. The product line involves three new products, two of which will be introduced together and a third one that will follow within two years. You are ready to create the WBS. All of the following are true expect for which one?

    A. Each of the three products should be elaborated to the same number of levels. This is known as rolling wave planning.

    B. The WBS should be elaborated to a level where costs and schedule are easily estimated. This is known as the work package level.

    C. The WBS can be structured using each product as a level-one entry.

    D. Each level of the WBS represents verifiable products or results.

4. Your company, Kick That Ball Sports, has appointed you project manager for its new Cricket product line introduction. This is a national effort, and all the retail stores across the country need to have the new products on the shelves before the media advertising blitz begins. The product line involves three new products, two of which will be introduced together and a third one that will follow within two years. Product number three will be elaborated in more detail closer to the product's release date, while the first two products will be elaborated in great detail now. The scope management plan has just been completed. Which of the following is true? (Choose the best response.)

   A. Only the deliverables associated with the work of the project should be listed on the WBS. Since product number three isn't being released until a later date it should not yet be included on the WBS.

   B. The WBS template from a previous project, a tool and technique of the Create WBS process, was used to create the WBS for this project. The WBS encompasses the major deliverables for the project.

   C. The WBS should be created next, and it encompasses the full scope of work for the project. Only the work of the project is listed on the WBS.

   D. The WBS encompasses the full scope of work for the project and the technique in the question is called rolling wave planning.

5. You work for a large manufacturing plant. You are working on a new project to release an overseas product line. This is the company's first experience in the overseas market, and it want to make a big splash with the introduction of this product. The project entails producing your product in a concentrated formula and packaging it in smaller containers than the U.S. product uses. A new machine is needed in order to mix the ingredients into a concentrated formula. To complete the Create WBS process sufficiently, you decide to do which of the following?

   A. Use the organizational breakdown structure and the WBS together, and present this scope baseline to stakeholders.

   B. Record the code of account identifier, an SOW, responsible organization, and milestone schedule in the WBS dictionary for the components of the WBS.

   C. Elaborate the WBS to the point where the new machine specifications are clear and highly detailed.

   D. Record the approved change requests as one of the outputs of this process.

6. You are the project manager for Lucky Stars nightclubs. They specialize in live country and western band performances. Your newest project is in the Planning process group. You've published the scope statement and scope management plan. The document that describes who will receive copies of this information as well as future project information, how it should be distributed, and who will prepare it is which of the following?

   A. Scope management plan

   B. Communications management plan

   C. Information distribution plan

   D. Project charter

7. You are the project manager for Lucky Stars nightclubs. They specialize in live country and western band performances. Your newest project is in the Planning processes group. You are working on the WBS. The finance manager has given you a numbering system to assign to the WBS. Which of the following is true?

   A. The numbering system is a unique identifier known as the code of accounts, which is used to track the costs of the WBS elements.

   B. The numbering system is a unique identifier known as the WBS dictionary, which is used to track the descriptions of individual work elements.

   C. The numbering system is a unique identifier known as the code of accounts, which is used to track time and resource assignments for individual work elements.

   D. The numbering system is a unique identifier known as the WBS dictionary, which is used to assign quality control codes to the individual work elements.

8. You've constructed the WBS for your recent project. You've requested that the subproject managers report to you in three weeks with each of their individual WBSs constructed. Which statement is not true regarding the subproject managers' WBS?

   A. The work package level facilitates resource assignments.

   B. The work package level is the lowest level in the WBS.

   C. The work package level defines the agreed-upon deliverables.

   D. The work package level facilitates cost and time estimates.

9. Which of the following statements about decomposition is the least true?

   A. Decomposition involves structuring and organizing the WBS so that deliverables are always listed at level one.

   B. Decomposition requires a degree of expert judgment and also requires close analysis of the project scope statement.

   C. Decomposition is a tool and technique used to create a WBS.

   D. Decomposition subdivides the major deliverables into smaller components until the work package level is reached.

10. Which of the following is not a major step of decomposition?

   A. Identify major deliverables.

   B. Identify components.

   C. Determine adequate cost and schedule estimates.

   D. Verify correctness of decomposition.

11. You have eight key stakeholders to communicate with on your project. Which of the following is true?

    A. There are 36 channels of communication, and this should be a consideration when using the communications technology tool and technique.

    B. There are 28 channels of communication, and this should be a consideration when using the communications requirements analysis tool and technique.

    C. There are 28 channels of communication, and this should be a consideration when using the communications technology tool and technique.

    D. There are 36 channels of communication, and this should be a consideration when using the communications requirements analysis tool and technique.

12. All of the following are true regarding Communications Planning except for which one?

    A. It's the only output of the Communications Planning process.

    B. It should be completed as early in the project phases as possible.

    C. It's tightly linked with enterprise environmental factors and organizational influences, and lessons learned and historical information are two inputs that should get a lot of attention during this process.

    D. Communications requirements analysis, communications technology, and PMIS are tools and techniques of this process.

13. All of the following are true regarding the Quality Planning process except for which one?

    A. DOE is a tool and technique of this process that provides statistical analysis for changing product or process elements one at a time to optimize the process.

    B. This is one of the key processes performed during the Planning process group and during the development of the project management plan.

    C. Changes to the product as a result of meeting quality standards might require cost or schedule adjustments.

    D. The tools and techniques of this process are cost-benefit analysis, benchmarking, DOE, COQ, and additional quality planning tools.

14. Four people are responsible for establishing cost of quality theories. Crosby and Juran are two them, and their theories respectively are

    A. grades of quality, fitness for use

    B. fitness for use, zero defects

    C. zero defects, fitness for use

    D. cost of quality, zero defects

15. The theory that 85 percent of the cost of quality is a management problem is attributed to which of the following?

    A. Deming

    B. Shewhart

    C. Juran

    D. Crosby

16. All of the following are benefits of meeting quality requirements except which one?

   A. An increase in stakeholder satisfaction

   B. Less rework

   C. Low turnover

   D. Higher productivity

17. Which of the following describes the cost of quality associated with scrapping, rework, and downtime?

   A. Internal failure costs

   B. External failure costs

   C. Prevention costs

   D. Appraisal costs

18. The quality management plan documents how the project team will implement the quality policy. It must address all of the following except which one?

   A. Quality control

   B. Quality checklists

   C. Quality assurance

   D. Continuous process improvement

19. You work for a furniture manufacturer. Your project is going to design and produce a new office chair. The chair will have the ability to function as a regular chair and also the ability to transform its occupant into an upright, kneeling position. The design team is trying to determine the combination of comfort and ease of transformation to the new position that will give the chair the best characteristics while keeping the costs reasonable. Several different combinations have been tested. This is an example of which of the following tools and techniques of Quality Planning?

   A. Benchmarking

   B. Quality metrics

   C. COQ

   D. DOE

20. Which of the following best characterizes Six Sigma?

   A. Stipulates that quality must be managed in

   B. Focuses on process improvement and variation reduction by using a measurement-based strategy

   C. Asserts that quality must be a continuous way of doing business

   D. Focuses on improving the quality of the people first, then improving the quality of the process or project

Answers to Review Questions

1. C. The scope baseline consists of the project scope statement, the WBS, and the WBS dictionary.

2. C. WBSs from previous projects can be used as templates on projects that are producing similar products, services, or results. Some companies write WBS templates to be used for projects of similar scope.

3. A. Each of the three products might have different amounts of elaboration and levels. The question said the third product would not be introduced until two years after the first two. This WBS entry might contain only one level stating the product name.

4. D. There isn't enough information in the question to know whether B is correct, although it could be. C is not correct because the next process after the scope management plan is created is the Scope Definition process. The WBS details the entire scope of the project and includes all deliverables. It is an output of the Create WBS process and the technique of elaborating some deliverables at a later date is called rolling wave planning.

5. B. The WBS dictionary should be documented with the code of account identifier, an SOW, the responsible organization, and a milestone schedule for the WBS components. C is not correct because the amount of elaboration and detail the question describes would make the WBS inefficient. You need only enough detail to make it easier for the project team to plan, manage, and control the work. Approved change requests are inputs to this process. Requested changes are the output.

6. B. The communications management plan documents what information will be distributed, how it will be distributed, to whom, by whom, and the timing of the distribution.

7. A. Each element in the WBS is assigned a unique identifier. These are collectively known as the *code of accounts*. Typically, these codes are associated with a corporate chart of accounts and are used to track the costs of the individual work elements in the WBS.

8. C. The work package level is the lowest level in the WBS and facilitates resource assignment and cost and time estimates. The agreed-upon deliverables in C would appear in the higher levels in the WBS.

9. A. Decomposition subdivides the major deliverables into smaller components. It is a tool and technique of the Create WBS process, along with WBS templates, and is used to create a WBS. Level two components might be deliverables, phases, subprojects, or some combination.

10. C. The steps of decomposition include identify major deliverables, organize and determine the structure, identify lower-level components, assign identification codes, and verify correctness of decomposition.

11. B. There are 28 channels of communication, which is considered when using the communications requirements analysis tool and technique.

12. D. Communications requirements analysis and communications technology are the tools and techniques of the Communications Planning process.

13. A. Design of experiments is a tool and technique of the Quality Planning process that provides statistical analysis for changing key product or process elements all at once (not one at a time) to optimize the process.

14. C. Philip Crosby devised the zero defects theory, meaning do it right the first time. Proper Quality Planning leads to less rework and higher productivity. Joseph Juran's fitness for use says that stakeholders' and customers' expectations are met or exceeded.

15. A. W. Edwards Deming conjectured that the cost of quality is a management problem 85 percent of the time and that once the problem trickles down to the workers, it is outside their control.

16. C. The benefits of meeting quality requirements are increased stakeholder satisfaction, lower costs, higher productivity, and less rework.

17. A. Internal failure costs are costs associated with not meeting the customer's expectations while you still had control over the product. This results in rework, scrapping, and downtime.

18. B. Quality checklists are an output of the Quality Planning process.

19. D. This is an example of design of experiments.

20. B. Six Sigma is a measurement-based strategy that focuses on process improvement and variation reduction by applying Six Sigma methodologies to the project.

Chapter

5

Risk Planning

THE PMP EXAM CONTENT FROM THE PLANNING THE PROJECT PERFORMANCE DOMAIN COVERED IN THIS CHAPTER INCLUDES THE FOLLOWING:

✓ Identify Risks and Define Risk Strategies

In this chapter, you'll take a breather from defining scope and breaking down the work of the project to look at the potential for threats or opportunities on your project, otherwise known as *risk*. The processes I'll discuss have outputs that become inputs to the Planning processes I'll discuss in the coming chapters.

Risk is evident in everything we do. When it comes to project management, understanding risk and knowing how to minimize its impacts (or take full advantage of its opportunities) on your project are essential for success. This entire chapter is dedicated to project risk. Five of the six risk processes (all contained in the Risk Management Knowledge Area) fall in the Planning process group. I'll cover Risk Management Planning, Risk Identification, Qualitative Risk Analysis, Quantitative Risk Analysis, and Risk Response Planning in this chapter. I'll follow up with the last risk process, Risk Monitoring and Control, in Chapter 9, "Monitoring and Controlling Project Performance."

Hold on to your hats! I'm going to cover a lot of material in this chapter, but it will go fast, I promise.

Planning for Risks

Every one of us takes risks on a daily basis. Just getting out of bed in the morning is a risk. You might stub your toe in the dark on the way to the light switch or trip over the dog and break a leg. These events don't usually happen, but the possibility exists. The same is true for your project. Risk exists on all projects, and the potential that a particular risk will occur depends on the nature of the risk.

Risk, like most of the elements of the other Planning processes, changes as the project progresses and should be monitored throughout the project. As you get close to a risk event, that's the time to reassess your original assumptions about the risk and your plans to deal with the risk and to make any adjustments as required.

Not all risks are bad. Risks can present opportunities as well as threats to a project. All risks have causes, and if the risk event occurs during a project, there are consequences as a result of that risk. Those consequences will likely impact one or more of the project objectives, and you'll need to know whether the consequences have positive or negative impacts.

Risk is, after all, uncertainty. The more you know about risks and their impacts beforehand, the better equipped you are to handle a risk when it occurs. The processes that involve risk, probably more than any other project Planning process, concern balance. You want to find that point where you and the stakeholders are comfortable taking the risk based on the benefits you can potentially gain. In a nutshell, you're balancing the action of taking a risk against avoiding the consequences or impacts of a risk. The rest of this chapter will deal with finding out what risks might occur (and how to deal with those risks that are unknown), determining an organization's tolerance for risk taking, and developing action plans for those risks you've determined have hefty impacts. The first step is performing the Risk Management Planning process. Here, you determine the approach you'll use for risk management activities and document your plans for them in a risk management plan. You'll look at that process now.

Planning Your Risk Management

Risks come about for many reasons. Some are internal to the project, and some are external. The project environment, the planning process, the project management process, inadequate resources, and so on, can all contribute to risk. Some risks you'll know about in advance and plan for during this process; others will occur unannounced during the project. The *Risk Management Planning* process determines how you'll plan for risks on your project.

Exam Spotlight

The *PMBOK Guide* states that the Risk Management Planning process is the foundation for all the Risk processes that follow. The risk management plan assures that the appropriate amount of resources and the appropriate time are dedicated to risk management. "Appropriate" is determined based on the levels, the importance, and the types of risks. The most important function the risk management plan serves is that it's an agreed-upon baseline for evaluating project risk.

To document the risk management plan, you need to gather some inputs that will help you determine your organization's risk policies and tolerance for risk. You'll look at those inputs next.

Risk Management Planning Inputs

Risks associated with a project generally concern the project objectives, which in turn impact time, cost, scope, or quality or any combination of the four. As you might have guessed, the project scope statement is an input to this process since it spells out your project objectives. The inputs of this process are as follows:

- Enterprise environmental factors
- Organizational process assets
- Project scope statement
- Project management plan

One of the key elements of the enterprise environmental factors to consider as in input in this process is the *risk tolerance* levels of the organization and the stakeholders. Risk tolerance is that balance I talked about earlier where stakeholders are comfortable taking a risk because the benefits to be gained outweigh what could be lost—or just the opposite. They will avoid taking a risk because the cost or impact is too great given the amount of benefit that can be derived. Here's an example to describe risk tolerance: Suppose you're a 275-pound brute who's surrounded by three bodyguards of equal proportion everywhere you go. Chances are, walking down a dark alley in the middle of the night doesn't faze you in the least. That means your risk tolerance for this activity is high. However, if you're a petite 90-pounder without benefit of bodyguards or karate lessons, performing this same activity might give you cause for concern. Your risk tolerance is low, meaning you wouldn't likely do this activity. The higher your tolerance for risk, the more you're willing to take on risk and its consequences.

Organizations and stakeholders, as well as individuals, all have different tolerances for risk. One organization might believe that the risk of a potential 7 percent cost overrun is high, while another might think it's low. However, either one of these organizations might decide to accept the risk if it believes the risk in balance with the potential rewards. It's important for the project manager to understand the tolerance level that the organization and the stakeholders have for risk before evaluating and ranking risk.

Remember that organizational process assets include policies and guidelines that might already exist in the organization. Your organization's risk management policies are any policies it might have that you should consider when planning for risks. Defined roles and responsibilities that outline what authority levels the stakeholders and project manager have for making decisions regarding risk planning might exist in these policies. (Do consider that these decisions can affect other planning processes.) Your organization might also have preexisting templates that you can use during this process. These templates should be updated on a regular basis and examined for their appropriateness on this project.

The project scope statement, as mentioned earlier, contains the project objectives and deliverables. This is the first place you'll start looking when identifying risks and should be considered when determining the process you'll use to evaluate risks. The risk management plan (the only output of this process) will become part of the project management plan; therefore, obviously, other project management processes and guidelines should be considered when performing this process so that the risk management plan is in line with the overall direction and management of the project.

Tools and Techniques for Risk Management Planning

The Risk Management Planning process has only one tool and technique: planning meetings and analysis. The purpose of these meetings, which are held with project team members, stakeholders, functional managers, and others who might have involvement in the risk management process, is to contribute to the risk management plan. During these meetings, the fundamental plans for performing risk management activities will be discussed and determined and then documented in the risk management plan.

The key outcomes of performing these planning meetings are as follows:

- Risk cost elements are developed for inclusion in the project budget.

- Schedule activities associated with risk are developed for inclusion in the project schedule.

- Risk responsibilities are assigned.

- Templates for risk categories are defined or modified for this project.

- Definitions of terms (*probability*, *impact*, *risk types*, *risk levels*, and so on) are developed and documented.

- The probability and impact matrix is defined or modified for this project.

I'll discuss risk responsibilities, define the terms in the preceding list, and help you construct your own probability and impact matrix in the remaining sections of this chapter.

Ultimately, your goal for this process concerns documenting the risk management plan (the output of this process). This document is the basis for understanding the remaining risk processes. Since the risk management plan encompasses a wealth of information, I've given this topic its own section. Let's get to it.

 Real World Scenario

Do We Need a Risk Management Plan?

Julia is the project manager for a small project her department is undertaking. The project objective is to give customers the ability to download videos of the properties her organization has listed for lease. Two programmers from the information technology department will be working on the updates to the website, programming the links, and so on. The project sponsor wants to fast track this project. She'd like to skip most of the Planning processes, and she sees no need for a risk management plan. Julia explains to the sponsor that the risk management plan for a project this size might be only a paragraph or two long. She emphasizes the importance of documenting how they'll identify risks, how they'll quantify them, and how they'll monitor the risks as the project progresses. Julia has project management experience on projects of all sizes and knows first-hand that ignoring this step could bring some unexpected surprises to the sponsor later in the project. She explains a bad past experience where this step was ignored and then assures the sponsor they can probably agree to the plan, identify and quantify the risks, and determine response plans in an hour and a half or less. The sponsor now understands the issues and agrees to the meeting.

Creating the Risk Management Plan

The purpose of the Risk Management Planning process is to create a *risk management plan*, which describes how you will define, monitor, and control risks throughout the project. The risk management plan is a subsidiary of the project management plan, and it's the only output of this process.

The risk management plan details how risk management processes (including Risk Identification, Qualitative Risk Analysis, Quantitative Risk Analysis, Risk Response Planning, and Risk Monitoring and Control) will be implemented, monitored, and controlled throughout the life of the project. It details how you will manage risks but does not attempt to define responses to individual risks.

 I'll talk about how to develop those response plans in the section "Developing a Risk Response Plan" later in this chapter.

According to the *PMBOK Guide*, the risk management plan should include the following elements:

- Methodology
- Roles and responsibilities
- Budgeting
- Timing
- Risk categories
- Definitions of risk probability and impact
- Probability and impact matrix
- Revised stakeholder tolerances
- Reporting formats
- Tracking

Exam Spotlight

It's important to spend time developing the risk management plan because it's an input to every other risk-planning process and enhances the probability of risk management success.

You'll take a look at most of these elements next. However, risk categories, probability and impact, and probability and impact matrix are pretty meaty topics, so I'll cover those in their own sections following this one.

Methodology   Methodology is a description of how you'll perform risk management, including elements such as methods, tools, and where you might find risk data that you can use in the later processes.

Roles and responsibilities   Roles and responsibilities describe the people who are responsible for managing the identified risks and their responses and for each type of activity identified in the risk management plan. These risk teams might not be the same as the project team. Risk analysis should be unbiased, which might not be possible when project team members are involved.

Budgeting   The budget for risk management is included in the plan as well. In this section, you'll assign resources and estimate the costs of risk management and its methods. These costs will then be included in the project cost baseline. (I'll talk about that in Chapter 7, "Creating the Project Schedule and Budget.")

Timing   Timing documents the timing of the risk management processes (including when and how often they'll be performed on the project) and includes the activities associated with risk management in the project schedule.

Revised stakeholder tolerances   This is just as it implies. As you proceed through the risk management processes, you might find that risk tolerances will change. Document those new tolerance levels in the risk management plan.

Reporting formats   Reporting formats describe the content of the risk register and the format of this document. (I'll talk more about the risk register later in this chapter.) Reporting formats also detail how risk management information will be maintained, updated, analyzed, and reported to project participants.

Tracking   This includes a description of how you'll document the history of the risk activities for the current project and how the risk processes will be audited. You can reference this information when you're performing risk-planning processes later in the current project or on future projects. This information is also helpful for lessons learned, which I'll cover in Chapter 11, "Controlling Work Results and Closing Out the Project."

Risk Categories

Risk categories are a way to systematically identify risks and provide a foundation for understanding. When determining and identifying risks, the use of risk categories helps improve the process by giving everyone involved a common language or basis for describing risk.

Risk categories should be identified during this process and documented in the risk management plan. You will use these categories during the next process, Risk Identification, to help identify risks. The following list includes some of the categories you might identify during this process (or modify based on previous project information):

- Technical, quality, or performance risks
- Project management risks
- Organizational risks
- External risks

You can go about describing categories of risk in a couple of ways. One way is simply listing them. You could, and should, review prior projects for risk categories and then tailor them for this project.

You could also construct a *risk breakdown structure (RBS)*, which lists the categories and subcategories. Figure 5.1 shows a sample of an RBS.

FIGURE 5.1   Risk breakdown structure

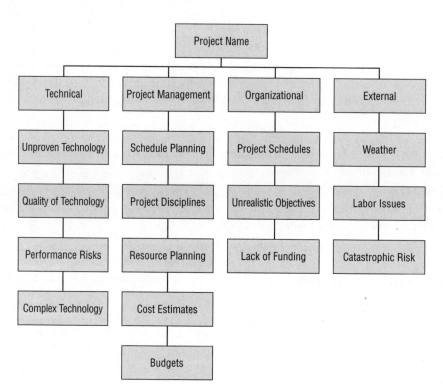

> Remember that the organizational process assets input might include an RBS that you can reference for this project. And don't forget your PMO. They might have templates or an RBS already developed.

Risk categories might reflect the type of industry or application area in which the project exists. For example, information technology projects will likely have many risks that fall into the technical category, whereas construction projects might be more subject to risks that fall into the external risks category. The categories do not have to be industry specific, however. Keep in mind that project management, for example, is a risk on every project in every industry. You can find a description of each of the categories next:

Technical/quality/performance risks   Technical, quality, or performance risks include risks associated with unproven technology, complex technology, or changes to technology anticipated during the course of the project. Performance risks might include unrealistic performance goals. Perhaps one of the project deliverables concerns a component manufactured to specific performance standards that have never been achieved. That's a performance risk.

Project management risks   The project management risk category includes improper schedule and resource planning, poor project planning, and improper or poor project management disciplines or methodologies.

Organizational risks   The organizational risk category can include resource conflicts because of multiple projects occurring at the same time in the organization; scope, time, and cost objectives that are unrealistic given the organization's resources or structure; and lack of funding for the project or diverting funds from this project to other projects.

External risks   The external risk category includes those aspects that are external to the project, such as new laws or regulations, labor issues, weather, changes in ownership, and foreign policy for projects performed in other countries. Catastrophic risks—known as *force majeure*—are usually outside the scope of risk management planning and instead require disaster recovery techniques. Force majeure includes events such as earthquakes, meteorites, volcanoes, floods, civil unrest, terrorism, and so on.

Defining Probability and Impact

When you're writing the risk management plan, you'll want to document how probability and impact will be defined for the project. Probability describes the potential for the risk event occurring, while impact describes the effects or consequences the project will experience if the risk event occurs. This definition can be sophisticated or simple. For example, you might use numeric values to define probability and impact or simply assign a high-medium-low rating to each risk. What's important to note now is that you don't use these probability and impact definitions here. You use these definitions later in the Qualitative Risk Analysis process. (I'll talk in depth about probability and impact in the section "Analyzing Risks Using Qualitative Techniques" later in this chapter.) But you should define and document them here in the risk management plan.

Probability and Impact Matrix

A *probability and impact matrix* defines the combination of probability and impact that helps you determine which risks need detailed risk response plans. For example, a risk with a high probability of occurring and a high impact will likely need a response plan. This matrix is typically defined by the organization, but if you don't have one, you'll need to develop this now—during your planning meeting and analysis (the tool and technique of this process). You'll use this matrix in the Qualitative Risk Analysis process, and I'll talk more in depth in the "Analyzing Risks Using Qualitative Techniques" section later in this chapter. Again, you want to define (or modify) the probability and impact matrix in the risk management plan.

The key point about this process is that you'll define what the probability and impact tools look like now during Risk Management Planning so that the team has an agreed-upon basis for evaluating the identified risks later during the Qualitative Risk Analysis process.

To recap, the steps associated with these last few elements of the risk management plan are as follows:

1. Define the risk categories (to be used in the Risk Identification process).

2. Determine how probability and impact will be defined (to be used in the Qualitative Risk Analysis process).

3. Define or modify the probability and impact matrix (to be used in the Qualitative Risk Analysis process).

Doing all these steps, together with the other elements of the risk management plan, give you and the risk management team a common understanding for evaluating risks throughout the remainder of the project.

Identifying Potential Risk

The *Risk Identification* process involves identifying all the risks that might impact the project, documenting them, and documenting their characteristics. Risk Identification is an iterative process that continually builds on itself. As you progress through the project, more risks might present themselves (those you didn't identify early in the Planning process). Once you've identified or discovered a potential new risk, you should analyze it to determine whether a response plan is needed. You can see that the risk management cycle starts again with Risk Identification and progresses through the remaining risk processes to determine what to do about them.

You can include several groups of folks to help identify risks, including project team members, stakeholders, subject matter experts, users of the final product or service, and anyone else who you think might help in the process. Perhaps in the first round of Risk Identification, you include just the project team and subject matter experts and then bring in the stakeholders or risk management team to further flesh out risks during the second round of identification.

 I'll talk more about the techniques you can use to identify risks in the section "Tools and Techniques Used to Identify Risk."

Risks might or might not adversely affect the project. Some risks have positive consequences, while others have negative consequences. However, you should identify all risk events and their consequences. Here's a partial list to get you thinking about where risk might be found:

-   Budgets/funding
-   Schedules
-   Scope or requirements changes
-   Project plan
-   Project management processes
-   Technical issues
-   Personnel issues

- Hardware
- Contracts
- Political concerns
- Business risk
- Legal risk
- Environmental risk
- Management risk

This is by no means an exhaustive list. Remember that risk is uncertainty, and realize that risk (uncertainty) is lurking almost anywhere on your project. It's your job to discover as many of the potential risks as possible using the tools and techniques of this process and to document these risks.

Risk Identification Inputs

The inputs to the Risk Identification process are as follows:

- Enterprise environmental factors
- Organizational process assets
- Project scope statement
- Risk management plan
- Project management plan

As usual, the enterprise environmental factors input concerns aspects from outside the project that might help you determine or influence project outcomes. Be certain to check for industry information (commercial databases, checklists, benchmarking studies, and so on) or academic research that might exist for your application areas regarding risk information.

As always, don't forget about historical information such as previous project experiences via the project files. Project team knowledge is another form of historical information.

The project scope statement contains a list of project assumptions. Assumptions are issues believed to be true. It's imperative during the risk-planning stages of your project and throughout the work of the project to revisit and revalidate your project assumptions. At the time you recorded an assumption about vendor deliveries, for example, the vendor had a great track record and never missed a date. Months later on the project, that vendor merges with one of its competitors. Now you'll need to reexamine your assumptions about delivery times and determine whether the assumption is still valid or whether you have a risk on your hands.

You should pay particular attention to the roles and responsibilities section of the risk management plan and the budget and schedule for risk activities, and don't forget to examine the categories of risks. This is a great place to start when you get the team together and begin brainstorming your list of risks.

The project management plan contains several other management plans (such as schedule, quality, and cost) that can be helpful sources also when identifying risks.

Although the *PMBOK Guide* doesn't mention it, I've found that other elements of your project are helpful when identifying risk, such as the work breakdown structure (WBS), cost and schedule estimates, the staffing management plan, project staff assignments, and resource availability. You should really examine the outputs of most of the processes.

Tools and Techniques for Risk Identification

The Risk Identification process is undertaken using five tools and techniques:

- Documentation reviews
- Information-gathering techniques
- Checklist analysis
- Assumptions analysis
- Diagramming techniques

You'll learn more about each of these in the following sections.

Documentation Reviews

Documentation reviews involve reviewing project plans, assumptions, and historical information from a total project perspective as well as at the individual deliverables or activities level. This review helps the project team identify risks associated with the project objectives. Pay attention to the quality of the plans (is the content complete, or does it seem to be lacking detail?) and the consistency between plans. An exceptionally documented schedule is great, but if the budget isn't as well documented, you might have some potential risks.

Information Gathering

Information gathering encompasses several techniques, including brainstorming, the Delphi technique, interviewing, root cause identification, and strength and weakness analysis. The goal of these techniques is to end up with a comprehensive list of risks at the end of the meeting. Let's take a quick look at each of these techniques.

Brainstorming

Brainstorming is probably the most often used technique of the Risk Identification process. You've probably used this technique many times for many purposes. Brainstorming involves getting subject matter experts, team members, risk management team members, and anyone else who might benefit the process in a room and asking them to start identifying possible risk events. The trick here is that one person's idea might spawn another idea, and so on, so that by the end of the session you've identified all the possible risks. The facilitator could start the group off by going through the categories of risks to get everyone thinking in the right direction.

Delphi Technique

The *Delphi technique* is a lot like brainstorming, only the people participating in the meeting don't necessarily know each other. In fact, the people participating in this technique don't all have to be located in the same place and can participate anonymously. You can use email to facilitate the Delphi technique easily.

What you do is assemble your experts, from both inside and outside the company, and ask them via a questionnaire to identify potential risks. They in turn send their responses back to you (or to the facilitator of this process). All the responses are organized by content and sent back to the Delphi members for further input, additions, or comments. The participants then send their comments back one more time, and the facilitator compiles a final list of risks.

The Delphi technique is a great tool that allows consensus to be reached quickly. It also helps prevent one person from unduly influencing the others in the group and thus prevents bias in the outcome because the participants are usually anonymous and don't necessarily know how others in the group responded.

Nominal Group Technique

Another technique that is similar to the Delphi technique is the *Nominal Group Technique*. It isn't a named tool and technique of this process, but it is a technique you might find useful and that you might find on the exam.

This technique requires the participants to be together in the same room. Each participant has paper and pencil in front of them, and they are asked to write down what risks they think the project faces. Using sticky-backed notes is a good way to do this. Each piece of paper should contain only one risk. The papers are given to the facilitator, who sticks them up to the wall or a white board. The panel is then asked to review all the risks posted on the board; rank them and prioritize them, in writing; and submit the ranking to the facilitator. Once this is done, you should have a complete list of risks.

Interviewing

Interviews are question-and-answer sessions held with others, including other project managers, subject matter experts, stakeholders, customers, the management team, project team members, and users. These folks provide you with possible risks based on their past experiences with similar projects.

This technique involves interviewing those folks with previous experience on projects similar to yours or those with specialized knowledge or industry expertise. Ask them to tell you about any risks that they've experienced or that they think might happen on your project. Show them the WBS and your list of assumptions to help get them started thinking in the right direction.

Root Cause Identification

Did you ever hear someone say you're looking at the symptoms and not at the problem? That's the idea here. Root cause identification involves digging deeper than the risk itself and looking at what the cause of the risk is. This helps define the risk more clearly, and it also helps you later when it's time to develop the response plan for the risk.

Strengths, Weaknesses, Opportunities, and Threats (SWOT)

Strengths, weaknesses, opportunities, and threats (also known as SWOT analysis) is an analysis technique that examines through each of these viewpoints (SWOT) the project itself, project management processes, resources, the organization, and so on. It also helps broaden your perspective of where to look for risks.

Exam Spotlight

Not all the techniques listed here are detailed in the *PMBOK Guide*. Be aware that there might be questions about any of the techniques I've shown here. Understand the difference between the various information-gathering techniques for the exam.

Checklist Analysis

Checklists used during the Risk Identification process are usually developed based on historical information and previous project team experience. If you typically work on projects that are similar in nature, begin to compile a list of risks. You can then convert this to a checklist that will allow you to identify risks on future projects quickly and easily. You can also use the lowest level of the RBS as a checklist. However, don't rely solely on checklists for Risk Identification because you might miss important risks. It isn't possible for a single checklist to be an exhaustive source for all projects. You can improve your checklists at the end of the project by adding the new risks that were identified.

Assumptions Analysis

Assumptions analysis is a matter of validating the assumptions you identified and documented during the course of the project Planning processes. Assumptions should be accurate, complete, and consistent. Examine all your assumptions for these qualities. Assumptions are also used as a jumping-off point to further identify risks.

The important point to note about the project assumptions is that all assumptions are tested against two factors:

- The strength of the assumption or the validity of the assumption
- The consequences that might impact the project if the assumption turns out to be false

All assumptions that turn out to be false should be evaluated and scored just as risks.

Diagramming Techniques

Three types of diagramming techniques are used in Risk Identification: cause-and-effect, system or process flowcharts, and influence diagrams. *Cause-and-effect diagrams* show the relationship between the effects of problems and their causes. This diagram depicts every potential cause and subcause of a problem and the effect that each proposed solution will have on the problem. This diagram is also called a *fishbone diagram* or *Ishikawa diagram* after its developer, Kaoru Ishikawa. Figure 5.2 shows an example cause-and-effect diagram.

The system or process flowchart shows the logical steps needed to accomplish an objective, how the elements of a system relate to each other, and what actions cause what responses. This flowchart is probably the one with which you're most familiar. It's usually constructed with rectangles and parallelograms that step through a logical sequence and allow for "yes" and "no" branches (or some similar type of decision). Figure 5.3 shows a flowchart to help determine whether risk response plans should be developed for the risk (I'll talk about response plans in the "Developing a Risk Response Plan" section later in this chapter).

Cause-and-effect diagrams and system or process flowcharts are used in the Risk Identification process as well as in the Perform Quality Control process.

A third diagramming technique used during Risk Identification is called *influence diagramming*. According to the *PMBOK Guide*, influence diagrams typically show the casual influences among project variables, the timing or time ordering of events, and the relationships among other project variables and their outcomes. Simply put, they visually depict risks (or decisions), uncertainties or impacts, and how they influence each other. Figure 5.4 shows an influence diagram for a product introduction decision. The weather is a variable that could impact delivery time, and delivery time is a variable that can impact when revenues will occur.

Each of these techniques provides a way for you to help identify project risks. It's important that you identify all the risks early in the process. The better job you do of identifying the project's risks at the Planning stage, the more comprehensive the risk response plan will be. Risk Identification is not an area of project Planning that you should skip.

FIGURE 5.2   Cause-and-effect diagram

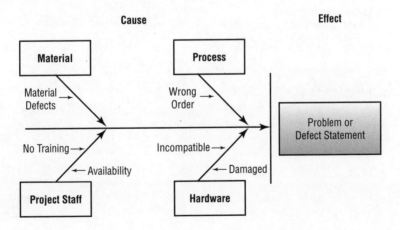

FIGURE 5.3   Flowchart diagram

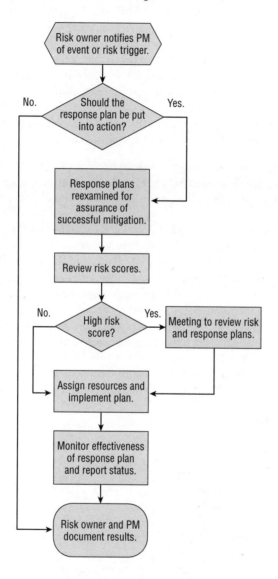

FIGURE 5.4   Influence diagram

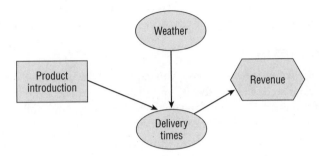

Risk Identification Outputs

The output of the Risk Identification process is the *risk register*. Everything you've done in this process up to this point will get documented here. The risk register contains the following elements:

- List of identified risks
- List of potential responses
- Root causes of risks
- Updated risk categories

   You'll take a look at each one next. Understand that all risks should be documented, tracked, reviewed, and managed throughout the project.

List of Identified Risks

Risks are all the potential events and their subsequent consequences that could occur as identified by you and others during this process. You might want to consider logging your risks in a risk database or tracking system to organize them and keep a close eye on their status. This can easily be done in spreadsheet format or whatever method you choose. List the risks, and assign each risk a tracking number. This gives you a means to track the risks, their occurrence, and the responses implemented.

List of Potential Responses

You might identify potential responses to risk at the same time you're identifying the risks. Sometimes just identifying the risk will tell you the appropriate response. Document those responses here. You'll refer to them again in the Risk Response Planning process a little later in this chapter.

Root Causes of Risk

I talked about this one before. When you're identifying risks, be sure you go further than that and try to identify the cause. Document those causes you've identified here in the risk register.

Updated Risk Categories

As a result of identifying and documenting your risks, you might well discover some categories of risk need to be changed or updated to reflect the risks for the current project. This might also include updating the RBS. It's a good practice to update those categories now, while you're in the midst of the process. Your next project will be all the better for it.

Triggers

If you've ever suffered from a hay fever attack, you can't mistake the itchy, runny nose and scratchy throat that can come on suddenly and send you into a sneezing frenzy. Signals like this are known as *triggers* and work the same way when determining whether a risk event is about to occur. For example, if you're planning an outdoor gathering and rain clouds start rolling in from the north on the morning of the activity, you probably have a risk event waiting to happen. A key team member hinting about job hunting is a warning sign that the person might be thinking of leaving, which in turn can cause schedule delays, increased costs, and so on. This is another example of a trigger.

Triggers are *not* listed as one of the risk register elements, but in practice, this is an appropriate place to list them. You will likely encounter questions on the exam about triggers, so don't say I didn't warn you. Also, throughout the remainder of the project, be on the alert for triggers that might signal that a risk event is about to occur.

Analyzing Risks Using Qualitative Techniques

The *Qualitative Risk Analysis* process involves determining what impact the identified risks will have on the project objectives and the probability they'll occur. It also ranks the risks in priority order according to their effect on the project objectives. This helps the team determine whether Quantitative Risk Analysis should be performed or whether you can skip right to developing response plans. The Qualitative Risk Analysis process also considers risk tolerance levels, especially as they relate to the project constraints (scope, time, cost, and quality) and the time frames of the potential risk events.

The Qualitative Risk Analysis process should be performed throughout the project. This process is the one you'll find you'll use most often when prioritizing project risks because it's fast, relatively easy to perform, and cost effective. The *PMBOK Guide* mentions two techniques you can use during this process to help correct biases that can occur in the data you've gathered: definitions of probability and impact (this is part of the risk management plan I discussed earlier in this chapter) and expert interviewing (I talked about this in the Risk Identification section of this chapter).

Qualitative Risk Analysis Inputs

The Qualitative Risk Analysis process has four inputs:

- Organizational process assets
- Project scope statement
- Risk management plan
- The risk register

As with the Risk Identification process, you should examine historical information and lessons learned from past projects as a guide for prioritizing the risks for this project. As I've discussed before, these are part of the organizational process assets input. The project scope statement describes the deliverables of the project, and from there you should be able to determine whether you're dealing with a high level of uncertainty or a project that's similar in size and scope to one you've performed before. Projects with high levels of uncertainty or that are more complex than what the team has undertaken before require more diligence during the Qualitative Risk Analysis process.

The risk management plan documented the roles and responsibilities of risk team members, budget and schedule factors for risk activities, the stakeholder risk tolerances, the definitions for probability and impact, and the probability and impact matrix, all of which should be utilized when prioritizing risks. You'll examine probability and impact more closely in the next section, "Using the Tools and Techniques of Qualitative Risk Analysis."

The critical element in this process, as with most of the processes you'll find where risk register is an input, is the list of risks.

The real key to this process lies in the tools and techniques you'll use to prioritize risks. Hold on tight because you're going in the deep end.

Tools and Techniques for Qualitative Risk Analysis

The Qualitative Risk Analysis process's tools and techniques are primarily concerned with discovering the probability of a risk event and determining the impact (or consequences) the risk will have if it does occur. The output of this process is a risk register update where you'll document the prioritized risks you've scored using these tools and techniques. All the information you gather regarding risks and probability needs to be as accurate as possible. It's also important that you gather unbiased information so that you don't unintentionally overlook risks with great potential or consequences.

The purpose of this process is to determine risk event probability and risk impact. You'll use the tools and techniques of this process to establish risk scores, which is a way of categorizing the probability and risk impact. The Qualitative Risk Analysis process includes the following tools and techniques:

- Risk probability and impact assessment
- Probability and impact matrix
- Risk data quality assessment

- Risk categorization
- Risk urgency assessment

You'll look at each of these tools and techniques next.

Risk Probability and Impact Assessment

This tool and technique assesses the probability that the risk events you've identified will occur, and it determines the effect their impacts have on the project objectives, including time, scope, quality, and cost. Analyzing risks in this way allows you to determine which risks require the most aggressive management. When determining probabilities and impacts, you'll refer to the risk management plan element called "definitions of risk probability and impact."

Probability

Probability is the likelihood that an event will occur. The classic example is flipping a coin. There is a .50 probability of getting heads and a .50 probability of getting tails on the flip. Note that the probability that an event will occur plus the probability that the event will not occur always equals 1.0. In this coin-flipping example, you have a .50 chance that you'll get heads on the flip. Therefore, you have a .50 chance you will not get heads on the flip. The two responses added together equal 1.0. Probability is expressed as a number from 0.0—which means there is no probability of the event occurring—to 1.0—which means there is 100 percent certainty the risk will occur.

Determining risk probability can be difficult because it's most commonly accomplished using expert judgment. In non-PMP terms, this means you're guessing (or asking other experts to guess) at the probability a risk event will occur. Granted, you're basing your guess on past experiences with similar projects or risk events, but no two risk events (or projects) are ever the same. It's best to fully develop the criteria for determining probability and get as many experts involved as you can. Carefully weigh their responses to come up with the best probability values possible.

Impact

Impact is the amount of pain (or the amount of gain) the risk event poses to the project. The risk *impact scale* can be a relative scale that assigns values such as high-medium-low (or some combination of these) or a numeric scale known as a *cardinal scale*. Cardinal scale values are actual numeric values assigned to the risk impact. Cardinal scales are expressed as values from 0.0 to 1.0 and can be stated in equal (linear) or unequal (nonlinear) increments.

Table 5.1 shows a typical risk impact scale for cost, time, and quality objectives based on a high-high to low-low scale. You'll notice that each of the high-medium-low value combinations on this impact scale have been assigned a cardinal value. I'll use these in the next section when I talk about the probability and impact matrix.

When you're using a high-medium-low scale, it's important that your risk team understands what criteria was used to determine a high score versus a medium or low score and how these should be applied to the project objectives.

TABLE 5.1   Risk Impact Scale

Objectives	Low-Low	Low	Medium	High	High-High
	0.05	0.20	0.40	0.60	0.80
Cost	No significant impact	Less than 6% increase	7–12% increase	13–18% increase	More than 18% increase
Time	No significant impact	Less than 6% increase	7–12% increase	13–18% increase	More than 18% increase
Quality	No significant impact	Few components impacted	Significant impact requiring customer approval to proceed	Unacceptable quality	Product not usable

Assessing Probability and Impact

The idea behind both probability and impact values is to develop predefined measurements that describe what value to place on a risk event.

Exam Spotlight

For the exam, don't forget that you define probability and impact values during the Risk Management Planning process.

If these scales have not yet been determined, develop them as early in the project as possible. You can use any of the techniques I talked about earlier in the section "Tools and Techniques Used to Identify Risk," such as brainstorming or the Delphi technique, to come up with the values for probability and impact.

During the Qualitative Risk Analysis process, you'll determine and assess probability and impact for every risk identified during the Risk Identification process. You could interview or hold meetings with project team members, subject matter experts, stakeholders, or others to help assess these factors. During this process, you should document not only the probability and impact but also the assumptions your team members used to arrive at these determinations. The next technique—probability and impact matrix—takes the probability and impact values one step further by assigning an overall risk score.

Probability and Impact Matrix

The outcome of a probability and impact matrix is an overall risk rating for each of the project's identified risks. The combination of probability and impact results in a classification usually expressed as high, medium, or low. According to the *PMBOK Guide*, high risks are considered a red condition, medium risks are considered a yellow condition, and low risks are considered a green condition. This type of ranking is known as an *ordinal scale* because the values are ordered by rank from high to low. (In practice, ordinal values might also include ranking by position. In other words, the risks are listed in order by rank as the first, the second, the third, and so on.)

Exam Spotlight

The *PMBOK Guide* notes that the probability and impact matrix values are usually set by the organization and are part of the organizational process assets.

Now let's look at an example. You have identified a risk event that could impact project costs, and your experts believe costs could increase by as much as 9 percent. According to the risk impact rating matrix in Table 5.1, this risk carries a medium impact, with a value of 0.40. Hold on to that number because you're going to plug it into the probability impact matrix— along with the probability value—to determine an overall risk value next.

You'll remember from the discussion previously that probability values should be assigned numbers from 0.0 to 1.0. In this example, the team has determined that there is a 0.2 probability of this risk event occurring. The risk impact scale shows a medium or 0.4 impact should the event occur.

Now, to determine whether the combination of the probability and impact of this risk is high, medium, or low, you'll need to check the probability impact matrix. Table 5.2 shows a sample probability and impact matrix.

TABLE 5.2   Sample Probability and Impact Matrix

| | Impact Values* | | | | |
| | Low-Low | Low | Medium | High | High-high |
Probability	.05	.20	.40	.60	.80
.8	.04	.16	*.32*	*.48*	*.64*
.6	.03	.12	**.24**	*.36*	*.48*
.4	.02	**.08**	**.16**	**.24**	*.32*
.2	.01	.04	.08	**.12**	**.16**

*No formatting = low assignment or green condition; **bold** = medium assignment or yellow condition; ***bold italic*** = high assignment or red condition.

First look at the probability column. Your risk event has a probability of .2. Now follow that row across until you find the column that shows the impact score of .40 (it's the Medium column). According to your probability and impact matrix values, this risk carries an overall score of .08 and falls in the low threshold, so this risk is assigned a low (or green condition) value.

The values assigned to the risks determine how Risk Response Planning is carried out for the risks later during the risk-planning processes. Obviously, risks with high probability and high impact are going to need further analysis and formal responses. Remember that the values for this matrix (and the probability and impact scales discussed earlier) are determined prior to the start of this process and documented in the risk management plan. Also keep in mind that probability and impact do not have to be assigned the same values as I've done here. You might use 0.8, 0.6, 0.4, and 0.2 for probability, for example, and assign .05, 0.1, .03, 0.5, and 0.7 for impact scales.

 Real World Scenario

Screen Scrapers, Inc.

Screen Scrapers is a software-manufacturing company that produces a software product that looks at your mainframe screens, commonly called *green screens*, and converts them to browser-based screens. The browser-based screens look like any other Windows-compatible screens with buttons, scroll bars, and drop-down lists.

Screen Scrapers devised this product for companies that use mainframe programs to update and store data because many of the entry-level workers beginning their careers today are not familiar with green screens. They're cumbersome and difficult to learn, and no consistency exists from screen to screen or from program to program. An F5 key in one program might mean go back one page, while an F5 key in another program might mean clear the screen. New users are easily confused, make a lot of mistakes, and have to write tablets full of notes on how to navigate all the screens.

Your company has purchased the Screen Scraper product and has appointed you the project manager over the installation. This project consists of a lot of issues to address, and you've made great headway. You're now at the risk identification and qualitative risk analysis stage. You decide to use the Delphi technique to assist you in identifying risk and assigning probability and impact rankings. Some experts are available in your company to serve on the Delphi panel, as well as some folks in industry organizations you belong to outside the company.

You assemble the group, set up a summary of the project, and send it out via email, requesting responses to your questions about risk. After the first pass, you compile the list of risks as follows (this list is an example and isn't exhaustive because your list will be project specific):

- Vendor viability (will the software company stay in business?)

- Vendor responsiveness with problems after implementation

- Software compatibility risks with existing systems

- Hardware compatibility risk

- Connection to the mainframe risk

- Training IT staff members to maintain the product

You send this list back to the Delphi members and ask them to assign a probability of 0.0–1.0 and an impact of high-high, high, medium, low, or low-low to each risk. The Delphi members assign probability and impact based on a probability scale and an impact scale designed by the risk management team. The values of the impact scale are as follows:

- High-high = 0.8

- High = 0.6

- Medium = 0.4

- Low = 0.2

- Low-low = 0.05

The team sends you the following probability and impact values:

- Vendor viability = .6 probability, high impact

- Vendor responsiveness = .4 probability, medium impact

- Software compatibility = .4 probability, medium impact

- Hardware compatibility = .6 probability, high-high impact

- Mainframe connection = .2 probability, high-high impact

- Training = .2 probability, low-low impact

The probability and impact matrix you used to assign the overall risk scores were derived from the probability and impact matrix shown in Table 5.3.

Based on the probability and impact matrix thresholds, the project risks are assigned the following overall probabilities:

- Vendor viability = high

- Vendor responsiveness = medium

- Software compatibility = medium

- Hardware compatibility = high

- Mainframe connection = medium

- Training = low

TABLE 5.3 PI Matrix for Screen Scrapers, Inc.

Probability	Impact Scores* .05	.20	.40	.60	.80
.8	.04	.16	*.32*	*.48*	*.64*
.6	.03	.12	.24	*.36*	*.48*
.4	.02	.08	.16	.24	*.32*
.2	.01	.04	.08	.12	.16

*No formatting = low assignment or green condition; **bold** = medium assignment or yellow condition; ***bold italic*** = high assignment or red condition.

Risk Data Quality Assessment

The data quality assessment involves determining the usefulness of the data gathered to evaluate risk. Most important, the data must be unbiased and accurate. You will want to examine elements such as the following when performing this tool and technique:

- The quality of the data used
- The availability of data regarding the risks
- How well the risk is understood
- The reliability and integrity of the data
- The accuracy of the data

Low-quality data will render the Qualitative Risk Analysis process's findings almost useless. Spend the time to validate and verify the information you've collected about risks so that your prioritization and analysis is as accurate as it can be. If you find that the quality of the data is questionable, you guessed it—go back and get better data.

Risk Categorizations

This tool and technique is used to determine the effects risk has on the project. You can examine not only the categories of risk determined during the Risk Management Planning process (and described in the RBS) but also the project phase and the WBS to determine the elements of the project that are affected by risk.

Risk Urgency Assessment

Using this tool you'll determine how soon the potential risks might occur and quickly determine responses for those risks that could occur soon. You should consider the risk triggers, the time to develop and implement a response, and the overall risk rating when determining how quickly responses are needed.

Ranking Risks in the Risk Register

The goal of the Qualitative Risk Analysis process is to rank the risks and determine which ones need further analysis and, eventually, risk response plans. The output of this process is risk register updates. As you can probably guess, you'll update the register with the following information:

- Risk ranking (or priority) for the identified risks
- Risks grouped by categories
- List of risks requiring near-term responses
- List of risks for additional analysis and response
- Watch list of low-priority risks
- Trends in Qualitative Risk Analysis results

Each element becomes a new entry in the risk register. For example, risk ranking assigns the risk score or priority you determined using the probability and impact matrix to the list of identified risks previously recorded in the risk register. I discussed the categories and the list of risks requiring near-term responses earlier. Note these in the risk register.

You'll also note those risks that require further analysis (including using the Quantitative Risk Analysis process), you'll create a list of risks that have low risk scores to review periodically, and you should note any trends in qualitative risk analysis that become evident as you perform this process.

Quantifying Risk

The *Quantitative Risk Analysis* process evaluates the impacts of risk prioritized during the Qualitative Risk Analysis process and quantifies risk exposure for the project by assigning numeric probabilities to each risk and their impacts on project objectives. This quantitative approach is accomplished using techniques such as Monte Carlo simulation and decision tree analysis. To paraphrase the *PMBOK Guide*, the purpose of this process is to perform the following:

- Quantify the project's possible outcomes and probabilities.
- Determine the probability of achieving the project objectives.
- Identify risks that need the most attention by quantifying their contribution to overall project risk.
- Identify realistic and achievable schedule, cost, or scope targets.
- Determine the best project management decisions possible when outcomes are uncertain.

Quantitative Risk Analysis—like Qualitative Risk Analysis—examines each risk and its potential impact on the project objectives. You might choose to use both of these processes to assess all risks or only one of them, depending on the complexity of the project and the organizational policy regarding risk planning. The Quantitative Risk Analysis process can follow either the Risk Identification process or the Qualitative Risk Analysis process. If you do use this process, be certain to repeat it every time the Risk Response Planning process is performed and as part of the Risk Monitoring and Control process.

I've already covered many of the inputs to the Quantitative Risk Analysis process in previous sections of this chapter. They are as follows:

- Organizational process assets
- Project scope statement
- Risk management plan
- Risk register
- Project management plan

The elements of the project management plan you'll want to pay close attention to as an input to this process are the project schedule management plan and the project cost management plan.

Tools and Techniques for Quantitative Risk Analysis

The Quantitative Risk Analysis process consists of two sets of tools and techniques: data gathering and representation techniques, and quantitative risk analysis and modeling techniques. Each of these sets of techniques includes three techniques that you'll examine next.

Data Gathering and Representation Techniques

The data gathering techniques include interviewing techniques, probability distributions, and expert judgment.

Interviewing

This technique is like the interviewing technique discussed earlier in the section "Identifying Potential Risk." Project team members, stakeholders, and subject matter experts are prime candidates for risk interviews. Ask them about their experiences on past projects and about working with the types of technology or processes you'll use during this project.

 For the exam, remember that interviewing is a tool and technique of the Quantitative Risk Analysis process. Although you can use this technique in the Risk Identification process, remember that it's part of the data gathering and representation technique and not a named tool and technique.

When using this technique, you should first determine what methods of probability distribution (described next) you'll use to analyze your information. The technique you choose will dictate the type of information you need to gather. For example, you might use a three-point scale that assesses the optimistic, pessimistic, and most likely risk scenarios or take it a step further and use standard deviations calculations. I'll talk more about three-point estimates in Chapter 7.

Make certain you document how the interviewees decided upon the risk ranges, the criteria they used to place risks in certain categories, and the results of the interview. This will help you later in developing risk responses as well.

Exam Spotlight

For the exam, you should know that several types of probability distributions exist that are useful in determining and displaying risk information. The type of distribution you use determines the type of information you should gather during the interviewing process.

Probability Distributions

It's beyond the scope of this book to delve into probability distributions and calculations, so I'll point out a few aspects of them that you should remember for the exam.

Continuous probability distributions (particularly beta and triangular distributions) are commonly used in Quantitative Risk Analysis. According to the *PMBOK Guide*, continuous probability distributions include normal, lognormal, triangular, beta, and uniform distributions. Distributions are graphically displayed and represent both the probability and time or cost elements.

Triangular distributions use estimates based on the three-point estimate (the pessimistic, most likely, and optimistic values). This means that during your interviews, you'll gather these pieces of information from your experts. Then you'll use them to quantify risk for each WBS element.

Normal and lognormal distributions use mean and standard deviations to quantify risk, which also require gathering the optimistic, most likely, and pessimistic estimates.

Expert Judgment

I've talked about this tool and technique before. Experts can come from inside or outside the organization and should have experience that's applicable to your project. For example, if your project involves manufacturing a new product or part, you might want to consider experts such as engineers or statisticians. If you're dealing with sensitive data in an information technology project, consider bringing on a security expert.

Quantitative Risk Analysis and Modeling Techniques

Four techniques are encompassed in this tool and technique: sensitivity analysis, expected monetary value analysis, decision tree analysis, and modeling and simulation. Let's take a brief look at each of them.

Sensitivity Analysis

Sensitivity analysis is a quantitative method of analyzing the potential impact of risk events on the project and determining which risk event (or events) has the greatest potential for impact by examining all the uncertain elements at their baseline values. One of the ways sensitivity analysis data is displayed is a *tornado diagram*. Figure 5.5 shows a sample tornado diagram.

FIGURE 5.5   Tornado diagram

You can see by the arrangement of horizontal bars (each representing a sensitivity variable) how the diagram gets its name. The idea is that each sensitivity bar displays the low and high value possible for that element. (It's beyond the scope of this book to explain how these values are determined. The questions you might encounter on the exam are focused on the context of this type of analysis.) The variables with the greatest effect on the project appear at the top of the graph and decrease in impact as you progress down through the graph. This gives you a quick overview of how much the project can be affected by uncertainty in the various elements. It also allows you to see at a glance which risks might have the biggest impacts on the project and will require carefully crafted, detailed response plans. You can use tornado diagrams to determine sensitivity in cost, time, and quality objectives or for risks you've identified during this process.

Sensitivity analysis can also be used to determine stakeholder risk tolerance levels.

Expected Monetary Value (EMV) Analysis

Expected monetary value (EMV) analysis is a statistical technique that calculates the average, anticipated impact of the decision. EMV is calculated by multiplying the probability of the risk by its impact and then adding them together. EMV is used in conjunction with the decision tree analysis technique, which is covered next. I'll give you an example of the EMV formula in the next section. Positive results generally mean the risks you're assessing pose opportunities to the project, while negative results generally indicate a threat to the project.

Decision Tree Analysis

Unfortunately, this isn't a tree outside your office door that produces "yes" and "no" leaves that you can pick to help you make a decision. *Decision trees* are diagrams that show the sequence of interrelated decisions and the expected results of choosing one alternative over the other. Typically, more than one choice or option is available when you're faced with a decision or, in this case, potential outcomes from a risk event. The available choices are depicted in tree form starting at the left with the risk decision branching out to the right with possible outcomes. Decision trees are usually used for risk events associated with time or cost.

Figure 5.6 shows a sample decision tree using expected monetary value (EMV) as one of its inputs.

FIGURE 5.6   Decision tree

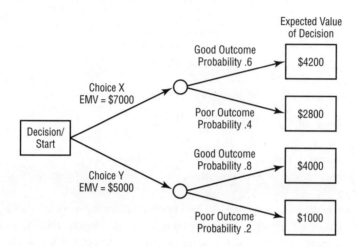

The expected monetary value of the decision is a result of the probability of the risk event multiplied by the impact and then adding their results. The squares in this figure represent decisions to be made, and the circles represent the points where risk events might occur.

The decision with an expected value of $7,000 is the correct decision to make because the resulting outcome has the greatest value.

Modeling and Simulation

Modeling and simulation techniques are often used for schedule risk analysis and cost analysis. For example, modeling allows you to translate the potential risks at specific points in the project into their impacts so you can determine how the project objectives are affected. Simulation techniques compute the project model using various inputs, such as cost or schedule duration, to determine a probability distribution for the variable chosen. (Cost risks typically use either a work breakdown structure or a cost breakdown structure as the input variable. Schedule risks always use the precedence diagramming method as the input variable. I'll cover schedule diagramming methods in Chapter 7.) If you used simulation techniques to determine project cost and use the cost of the project elements as the input variable, a probability distribution for the total cost of the project would be produced after running the simulation numerous times. Modeling and simulation techniques examine the identified risks and their potential impacts to the project objectives from the perspective of the whole project.

Monte Carlo analysis is an example of a simulation technique. Monte Carlo analysis is replicated many times, typically using cost or schedule variables. Every time the analysis is performed, the values for the variable are changed using a probability distribution for each variable. Monte Carlo analysis can also be used during the Schedule Development process.

Exam Spotlight

According to the *PMBOK Guide*, simulation techniques are recommended for predicting schedule or cost risks because they're more powerful than EMV and less likely to be misused. For the exam, remember that simulation techniques are used to predict schedule or cost risks. Schedule simulations are usually performed using the precedence diagramming method, while cost simulation typically uses the WBS as its basis.

Quantitative Risk Analysis Outputs

The output of the Quantitative Risk Analysis process is—I'll bet you can guess—risk register updates. As with the Qualitative Risk Analysis process, you'll record the following new elements in the risk register:

Probabilistic analysis of the project   Probabilistic analysis of the project is the forecasted results of the project schedule and costs as determined by the outcomes of risk analysis. These results include projected completion dates and costs, along with a confidence level associated with each. According to the *PMBOK Guide*, this output is often expressed as a cumulative distribution, and you'll use these results along with stakeholder risk tolerances to quantify the time and cost contingency reserves. (I'll talk about contingency reserves in the section "Developing a Risk Response Plan" later in this chapter.)

Confidence levels can also be used to describe the level of confidence placed on the outcome of the forecasted results. For example, suppose the projected schedule completion date is July 12 and the confidence level is .85. This says you believe the project will finish on or before July 12 and that you have an 85 percent level of confidence that this date is accurate.

Probability of achieving the cost and time objectives   Using the tools and techniques of Quantitative Risk Analysis allows you to assign a probability of achieving the cost and time objectives of the project. This output documents those probabilities and as such requires a thorough understanding of the current project objectives and knowledge of the risks.

Prioritized list of quantified risks   The prioritized list in this process is similar to the list produced during the Qualitative Risk Analysis process. The list of risks includes those that present the greatest risk or threat to the project and their impacts. It also lists those risks that present the greatest opportunities to the project. This list should also indicate which risks are most likely to impact the critical path and those that have the largest cost contingency.

Trends in Quantitative Risk Analysis results   Trends in Quantitative Risk Analysis will likely appear as you repeat the risk analysis processes. This information is useful as you progress, making those risks with the greatest threat to the project more evident, which gives you the opportunity to perform further analysis or go on to develop risk response plans.

Exam Spotlight

Understand the differences between the Qualitative Risk Analysis and Quantitative Risk Analysis processes for the exam.

Developing a Risk Response Plan

The *Risk Response Planning* process is the last process covered in this chapter. (I hear you cheering out there!) Risk Response Planning is a process of deciding what actions to take to reduce threats and take advantage of the opportunities discovered during the risk analysis processes. This process also includes assigning departments or individual staff members the responsibility of carrying out the risk response plans you'll outline in this process. These folks are known as *risk owners*.

> The more effective your risk response plans are, the better your chances for a successful project. Well-developed and well-written risk response plans will decrease overall project risk.

Generally, you'll want to develop risk response plans for those risks with a combination of high probability of occurrence and significant impact to the project, those ranked high (or red) on the probability/impact matrix, or those ranked high as a result of quantitative risk analysis. Developing risk response plans for risks of low severity or insignificant impact is not an efficient or good use of the project team's time. Spend your time planning responses that are appropriate given the impact the risk itself poses (or the opportunity the risk presents), and don't spend more time, money, or energy to produce a response than the risk event itself would produce if it occurred.

Several strategies are used in this process to reduce or control risk. It's important that you choose the right strategy for each risk so that the risk and its impacts are dealt with effectively. After deciding on which strategy to use, you'll develop an action plan to put this strategy into play should the risk event occur. You might also choose to designate a secondary or backup strategy.

Exam Spotlight

The rank of the risk will dictate the level of risk response planning that should be performed. For example, a risk with low severity wouldn't warrant the time it takes to develop a detailed risk response plan. Risk responses should be cost effective—if the cost of the response is more than the consequences of the risk, you might want to examine a different risk response. Risk responses should also be timely, agreed to by all the project stakeholders, and assigned to an individual (risk owner) who is responsible for monitoring and carrying out the risk response plan if needed.

Tools and Techniques for Risk Response Planning

The Risk Response Planning process consists of four tools and techniques, and each one of them involves a strategy. The tools and techniques are as follows:

- Strategies for negative risks or threats
- Strategies for positive risks or opportunities
- Strategies for both threats and opportunities
- Contingent response strategy

You'll take a look at each.

Strategies for Negative Risks or Threats

Three strategies exist to deal with negative risks or threats to the project objectives. They are avoid, transfer, and mitigate.

Avoid

To *avoid* a risk means you'll evade it altogether, eliminate the cause of the risk event, or change the project plan to protect the project objectives from the risk event. Let's say you're going to take a car trip from your home to a point 800 miles away. You know—because your friends who just took the same trip told you—that there is a long stretch of construction on one of the highways you're planning on using. To avoid the risk of delay, you plan the trip around the construction work and use another highway for that stretch of driving. In this way, you change your plans, avoid the risk of getting held up in construction traffic, and arrive at your destination on time.

With risk avoidance, you essentially eradicate the risk by eliminating its cause. Here's another example: suppose your project was kicked off without adequate scope definition and requirements gathering. You run a high probability of experiencing *scope creep*—ever-changing requirements—as the project progresses, thus impacting the project schedule. You can avoid this risk by adequately documenting the project scope and requirements during the Planning processes and taking steps to monitor and control changes to scope so it doesn't get out of hand.

Risks that occur early in the project might easily be avoided by improving communications, refining requirements, assigning additional resources to project activities, refining the project scope to avoid risk events, and so on.

Transfer

The idea behind a risk *transfer* is to transfer the risk and the consequences of that risk to a third party. The risk hasn't gone away, but the responsibility for the management of that risk now rests with another party. Most companies aren't willing to take on someone else's risk without a little cash thrown in for good measure. This strategy will impact the project budget and should be included in the cost estimate exercises if you know you're going to use it.

Transfer of risk can occur in many forms but is most effective when dealing with financial risks. Insurance is one form of risk transfer. You are probably familiar with how insurance works. Car insurance is a good example. You purchase car insurance so that if you come upon an obstacle in the road and there is no way to avoid hitting it, the cost to repair the damage to the car is paid by the insurance company...OK, minus the deductible and all the calculations for the age of the car, the mileage, the color and make of the car, the weather conditions the day you were driving—but I digress.

Another method of risk transfer is contracting. Contracting transfers specific risks to the vendor, depending on the work required by the contract. The vendor accepts the responsibility for the cost of failure. Again, this doesn't come without a price. Contractors charge for their services, and depending on the type of contract you negotiate, the cost might be quite high. For example, in a fixed-price contract, which I'll talk more about in Chapter 6, "Resource Planning," the vendor (or seller) increases the cost of the contract to compensate for the level of risk they're accepting. A cost reimbursable contract, however, leaves the majority of the risk with you, the buyer. This type of contract might reduce costs if there are project changes midway through the project.

Keep in mind that contracting isn't a cure-all. You might just be swapping one risk for another. For example, say you hire a driver to go with you on your road trip, and that person's job is to do all the driving. If the driver becomes ill or in some way can't fulfill their obligation, you aren't going to get to your destination on time. You've placed the risks associated with the trip on the contract driver; however, you've taken on a risk of delay because of nonperformance, which means you've just swapped one risk for another. You'll have to weigh your options in cases like this and determine which side of the risk coin your organization can more readily accept.

Other forms of transference include warranties, guarantees, and performance bonds.

Mitigate

When you *mitigate* a risk, you attempt to reduce the probability of a risk event and its impacts to an acceptable level. This strategy is a lot like defensive driving. You see an obstacle in the road ahead, survey your options, and take the necessary steps to avoid the obstacle and proceed safely on your journey. Seeing the obstacle ahead (identifying risk) allows you to reduce the threat by planning ways around it or planning ways to reduce its impact if the risk does occur (mitigation strategies).

According to the *PMBOK Guide*, the purpose of mitigation is to reduce the probability that a risk will occur and reduce the impact of the risk to a level where you can accept the risk and its outcomes. It's easier to take actions early on that will reduce the probability of a risk or its consequences than it is to fix the damage once it has occurred. Some examples of risk mitigation include performing more tests, using less complicated processes, creating prototypes, and choosing more reliable vendors.

Exam Spotlight

Understand all the strategies and their characteristics in each tool and technique for the exam.

New Convention Center Wing

You work for a small hotel and resort in western Colorado. Your company has taken on a project to expand the convention center by adding another wing. This wing will add six more meeting rooms (four of which can be combined into a large room by folding back the movable walls to accommodate large groups). This is a popular resort, and one of the risks identified with this project was an increase in demand for conference reservations after the construction finishes. The marketing team members decide they'll mitigate this risk by contacting the organizations who've consistently reserved space with them over the past three years and offer them incentives on their next reservation if they book their convention before the construction is completed. That way, their most important customers won't be turned away when the new reservations start pouring in.

Strategies for Positive Risk or Opportunities

Three strategies exist to deal with opportunities or positive risks that might present themselves on the project: exploit, share, and enhance.

Exploit

When you *exploit* a risk event, you're looking for opportunities for positive impacts. This is the strategy of choice when you've identified positive risks that you want to make certain will occur on the project. Examples of exploiting a risk include reducing the amount of time to complete the project by bringing on more qualified resources or by providing even better quality than originally planned.

Share

The *share* strategy is similar to transferring because you'll assign the risk to a third-party owner who is best able to bring about the opportunity the risk event presents. For example, perhaps what your organization does best is investing. However, it isn't so good at marketing. Forming a joint venture with a marketing firm to capitalize on a positive risk will make the most of the opportunities.

Enhance

The *enhance* strategy closely watches the probability or impact of the risk event to assure that the organization realizes the benefits. This entails watching for and emphasizing risk triggers and identifying the root causes of the risk to help enhance impacts or probability.

Strategies for Both Threats and Opportunities

The third tool and technique of the Risk Response Planning process, strategies for both threats and opportunities, is called the *acceptance strategy*. *Acceptance* of a risk event is a strategy that can be used for risks that pose either threats or opportunities to the project. *Passive acceptance* is a strategy that means you won't make any plans to try to avoid or mitigate the risk. You're willing to accept the consequences of the risk should it occur. Acceptance might also mean the project team was unable to come up with an adequate response strategy and must accept the risk and its consequences. *Active acceptance* might include developing contingency reserves to deal with risks should they occur. (You'll look at contingency reserves in the next section.)

Let's revisit the road trip example. You could plan the trip using the original route and just accept the risk of running into construction. If you get to that point and you're delayed, you'll just accept it. This is passive acceptance. You could also go ahead and make plans to take an alternate route but not enact those plans until you actually reach the construction and know for certain that it is going to impede your progress. This is active acceptance and might involve developing a contingency plan.

Contingency Planning

The last tool and technique of the Risk Response Planning process is called the *contingent response strategy*, better known as *contingency planning*. Contingency planning involves planning alternatives to deal with the risks should they occur. This is different from mitigation planning in that mitigation looks to reduce the probability of the risk and its impact, whereas contingency planning doesn't necessarily attempt to reduce the probability of a risk event or its impacts. Contingency planning says the risk might very well occur, and you better have plans in place to deal with it when it does.

Contingency comes into play when the risk event occurs. This implies you need to plan for your contingencies well in advance of the threat occurring. After the risks have been identified and quantified, contingency plans should be developed and kept at the ready.

Contingency allowances or reserves are a common contingency response. *Contingency reserves* include project funds that are held in reserve to offset any unavoidable threats that might occur to project scope, schedule, cost, or quality. It also includes reserving time and resources to account for risks. You should consider stakeholder risk tolerances when determining the amount of contingency reserves.

Fallback plans should be developed for risks with high impact or for risks with identified strategies that might not be the most effective at dealing with the risk.

In practice, you'll find that identifying, prioritizing, quantifying, and developing responses for potential threats might happen simultaneously. In any case, you don't want to be taken by surprise, and that's the point of the risk processes. If you know about potential risks early, you can often mitigate them or prepare appropriate response plans or contingency plans to deal with them.

Risk Response Planning Outputs

As you've no doubt concluded, the purpose of the Risk Response Planning process is to develop risk responses for those risks with the highest threat to or best opportunity for the project objectives. The Risk Response Planning process has three outputs: risk register updates, project management plan updates, and risk-related contractual agreements.

Risk Register Updates

Again, the risk register is updated at the end of this process with the information you've discovered during this process. The response plans are recorded in the risk register. You'll recall that the risk register lists the risk in order of priority (those with the highest potential for threat or opportunity first), so it makes sense that the response plans you have for these risks will be more detailed than the remaining lists. Some risks might not require response plans at all, but you should put them on a watch list and monitor them throughout the project.

Let's take a look at what the risk register should contain at this point. According to the *PMBOK Guide*, after Risk Identification, Qualitative Risk Analysis, and Quantitative Risk Analysis are preformed, the following elements should appear in the risk register:

- List of identified risks, including their descriptions, what WBS element they impact (or area of the project), categories (RBS), root causes, and how the risk impacts the project objectives

- Risk owners and their responsibility

- Risk triggers

- Response plans and strategies, including the steps to take to implement the strategy

- Cost and schedule activities needed to implement risk responses

- Contingency reserves for cost and time

- Contingency plans

- Fallback plans

- List of residual and secondary risks

- Probabilistic analysis of the project and other outputs of the Qualitative and Quantitative Risk Analysis processes

The only elements in the preceding list I haven't talked about so far are residual and secondary risks. A *residual risk* is a leftover risk, so to speak. After you've implemented a risk response strategy—say mitigation, for example—some minor risk might still remain. The contingency reserve is set up to handle situations like this.

Secondary risks are risks that come about as a result of implementing a risk response. The example given previously where you transferred risk by hiring a driver to take you to your destination but the person became ill along the way is an example of a secondary risk. The driver's illness delayed your arrival time, which is a risk directly caused by hiring the driver or implementing a risk response. When planning for risk, identify and plan responses for secondary risks that could occur.

Risk-Related Contractual Agreements

If you're planning on using strategies such as transference or sharing, for example, you might need to purchase services or items from third parties. You can prepare the contracts for those services now and discuss them with the appropriate parties.

Risks exist on all projects, and risk planning is an important part of the project Planning processes. Just the act of identifying risks and planning responses can decrease their impact if they occur. Don't take the "What I don't know won't hurt me" approach to risk planning. This is definitely a case where not knowing something can be devastating. Risks that are easily identified and have planned responses aren't likely to kill projects or your career. Risks that you should have known about but ignored could end up costing the organization thousands or millions of dollars, causing schedule delays, loss of competitive advantage, or ultimately killing the project. There could be a personal cost as well, because cost and schedule overruns due to poor planning on your part are not easily explained.

 Real World Scenario

Project Case Study: New Kitchen Heaven Retail Store

Ricardo knocks on your office door and asks whether you have a few minutes to talk. "Of course," you reply, and he takes a seat on one of the comfy chairs at the conference table. You have a feeling this might take a while.

"I think you should know that I'm concerned about the availability of the T1 line. I've already put in the call to get us on the list because, as I said last week, there's a 30- to 45-day lead time on these orders."

"We're only midway through the Planning processes. Do you need to order the T1 so soon? We don't even know the store location yet," you say.

"Even though they say lead time is 30 to 45 days, I've waited as long as five or six months to get a T1 installed in the past. I know we're really pushing for the early February store opening, so I thought I'd get the ball rolling now. What I need from you is the location address, and I'll need that pretty quick."

"We're narrowing down the choices between a couple of properties, so I should have that for you within the next couple of weeks. Is that soon enough?"

"The sooner, the better," Ricardo replies.

"Great. I'm glad you stopped by, Ricardo. I wanted to talk with you about risk anyway, and you led us right into the discussion. Let me ask you, what probability would you assign to the T1 line installation happening six months from now?"

"I'd say the probability for six months is low. It's more likely that if there is a delay, it would be within a three- to four-month time frame."

"If they didn't get to it for six months, would it be a showstopper? In other words, is there some other way we could transfer Jill's data until the T1 did get installed?"

"Sure, we could use other methods. Jill won't want to do that for very long, but workarounds are available."

"Good. Now, what about the risk for contractor availability and hardware availability and delivery schedules?" you ask.

You and Ricardo go on to discuss the risks associated with the IT tasks. Later, you ask Jill and Jake the same kinds of questions and compile a list of risks. In addition, you review the project information for the Atlanta store opening, because it's similar in size and scope to this store. You add those risks to your list as well. You divide some of the risks into the following categories: IT, Facilities, and Retail. A sample portion of your list appears as follows, with overall assignments made based on Qualitative Risk Analysis and the probability and impact matrix:

Category: IT

- T1 line availability and installation. Risk score: Low

- Contractor availability for Ethernet installation. Risk score: Medium

- POS and server hardware availability. Risk score: Medium

Category: Facilities

- Desirable location in the right price range. Risk score: High

- Contractor availability for build-out. Risk score: Low

- Availability of fixtures and shelving. Risk score: Low

Category: Retail

- Product availability. Risk score: Medium

- Shipment dates for product. Risk score: Medium

After examining the risks, you decide that response plans should be developed for the last two items listed under the IT source, the first item under Facilities, and both of the risks listed under Retail.

Ricardo has already mitigated the T1 connection and installation risk by signing up several months ahead of the date when the installation is needed. The contractor availability can be handled with a contingency plan that specifies a backup contractor should the first choice not be available. For the POS terminals and hardware, you decide to use the transfer strategy. As part of the contract, you'll require these vendors to deliver on time, and if they cannot, they'll be required to provide and pay for rental equipment until they can get your gear delivered.

The Facilities risk and Retail risks will be handled with a combination of acceptance, contingency plans, and mitigation.

You've calculated the expected monetary value for several potential risk events. Two of them are detailed here.

Desirable location has an expected monetary value of $780,000. The probability of choosing an incorrect or less than desirable location is 60 percent. The potential loss in sales is the difference between $2.5 million in sales per year that a high-producing store generates versus $1.2 million in sales per year that an average store generates.

The expected monetary value of the product availability event is $50,000. The probability of the event occurring is 40 percent. The potential loss in sales is $125,000 for not opening the store in conjunction with the Garden and Home Show.

Project Case Study Checklist

> Risk Management Planning
>
> Risk Identification

- Documentation reviews
- Information-gathering techniques

> Qualitative Risk Analysis

- Risk probability and impact
- Probability and impact rating
- List of prioritized risks

> Quantitative Risk Analysis

- Interviewing
- Expected monetary value

> Risk Response Planning

- Avoidance, transference, mitigation, and acceptance strategies
- Risk response plans documented

Understanding How This Applies to Your Next Project

Risk management and all the processes it involves is not a process I recommend you skip on any size of project. This is where the Boy Scouts of America motto "Be Prepared" is wise advice. If you haven't examined what could be lurking around the corner on your project and come up with a plan to deal with it, then you can be assured you're in for some surprises. Then again, if you like living on the edge, never knowing what might occur next, you'll probably find yourself back on the job-hunting scene sooner than you planned (oh, wait, you didn't plan because you're living on the edge).

In all seriousness, as with most of the Planning processes I've discussed so far, risk management should be scaled to match the complexity and size of your project. If you're working on a small project with a handful of team members and a short timeline, it doesn't make sense to spend a lot of time on risk planning. However, it does warrant spending *some* time identifying project risk, determining impact and probability, and documenting a plan to deal with the risk.

My two favorite risk identification techniques are brainstorming and the Nominal Group Technique. Both techniques help you quickly get to the risks with the greatest probability and impact because, more than likely, these are the first risks that come to mind. Risk identification can also help the project team find alternative ways of completing the work of the project. Further digging and the ideas generated from initial identification might reveal opportunities or alternatives you wouldn't have thought about during the regular Planning Process.

After you've identified the risks with the greatest impact to the project, document response plans that are appropriate for the risk. Small projects might have only one or two risks that need a response plan. The plans might consist of only a sentence or two depending on the size of the project. I would question a project where no risks require a response plan. If it seems too good to be true, it probably is.

The avoid, transfer, and mitigate strategies are the most often used strategies to deal with risk, along with contingency planning. Of these, mitigation and contingency planning are probably the most common. Mitigation generally recognizes that the risk will likely occur and attempts to reduce the impact.

I have used brainstorming and the Nominal Group Technique to strategize response plans for risks on small projects. When you're working on a small project, you can typically identify, quantify, and create response plans for risks at one meeting.

Identifying positive risk, in my experience, is fairly rare. Typically, when my teams perform risk identification, it's to determine what can go wrong and how bad the impact will it be if it does. The two most important concepts from this chapter that you should apply to your next project are that you and your team should identify risks and create response plans to deal with the most significant ones.

Summary

Congratulations! You've completed another fun-filled, action-packed chapter and all of it on a single topic—risk. Risk is inherent in all projects, and risks pose both threats and opportunities to the project. Understanding the risks facing the project better equips you to determine the appropriate strategies to deal with those risks and helps you determine the response plans for the risks (and the level of effort you should put into preparing those plans).

The Risk Management Planning process determines how you will plan for risks on your project. Its only output is the risk management plan, which details how you'll define, monitor, and control risks throughout the project. The risk management plan is a subsidiary of the project management plan.

The Risk Identification process seeks to identify and document the project risks using brainstorming, the Delphi technique, interviewing, root cause identification, and SWOT. This list of risks gets recorded in the risk register, the only output of this process.

Qualitative Risk Analysis and Quantitative Risk Analysis involve evaluating risks and assigning probability and impact values to the risks. Many tools and techniques are used during these processes, including risk probability and impact, probability and impact matrix, interviewing, probability distributions, expert judgment, sensitivity analysis, decision tree analysis, and simulation.

A probability and impact matrix uses the probability multiplied by the impact value to determine the risk score. The threshold of risk based on high, medium, and low tolerances is determined by comparing the risk score based on the probability level to the probability and impact matrix.

Monte Carlo simulation is a technique used to quantify schedule or cost risks. Decision trees graphically display decisions and their various choices and outcomes and is typically used in combination with earned monetary value.

The Risk Response Planning process is the last Planning process and culminates with an update to the risk register documenting the risk response plans. The risk response plans detail the strategies you'll use to respond to risk and assign individuals to manage each risk response. Risk response strategies for negative risks include avoidance, mitigation, and transference. Risk strategies for positive risks include exploit, share, and enhance. Acceptance is a strategy for both negative and positive risks.

Contingency planning involves planning alternatives to deal with risk events should they occur. Contingency reserves are set aside to deal with risks associated with cost and time according to the stakeholder tolerance levels.

Exam Essentials

Be able to define the purpose of the risk management plan. The risk management plan describes how you will define, monitor, and control risks throughout the project. It details how risk management processes (including Risk Identification, Qualitative Risk Analysis,

Quantitative Risk Analysis, Risk Response Planning, and Risk Monitoring and Control) will be implemented, monitored, and controlled throughout the life of the project. It describes how you will manage risks but does not attempt to define responses to individual risks. The risk management plan is a subsidiary of the project management plan, and it's the only output of the Risk Management Planning process.

Be able to name the purpose of Risk Identification.   The purpose of the Risk Identification process is to identify all risks that might impact the project, document them, and identify their characteristics.

Be able to define the purpose of Qualitative Risk Analysis.   Qualitative Risk Analysis determines the impact the identified risks will have on the project and the probability they'll occur, and it puts the risks in priority order according to their effects on the project objectives.

Be able to define the purpose of Quantitative Risk Analysis.   Quantitative Risk Analysis evaluates the impacts of risk prioritized during the Qualitative Risk Analysis process and quantifies risk exposure for the project by assigning numeric probabilities to each risk and their impacts on project objectives.

Be able to define the purpose of the Risk Response Planning process.   Risk Response planning is the process where risk response plans are developed using strategies such as avoid, transfer, mitigate, exploit, share, and enhance. The risk response plan describes the actions to take should the identified risks occur. It should include all the identified risks, a description of the risks, how they'll impact the project objectives, and the people assigned to manage the risk responses.

Be able to define the risk register and some of its primary elements.   The risk register is an output of the Risk Identification process, and updates to the risk register occur as an output of every risk process that follows this one. By the end of the Risk Response Planning process, the risk register contains these primary elements: identified list of risks, risk owners, risk triggers, risk strategies, contingency plans, and contingency reserves.

Key Terms

Life is a risky business, but with proper planning, your project doesn't have to be. Using processes I've discussed in this chapter, you'll be prepared for the foreseeable and the not so foreseeable. Understand them well, and know each process by the name used in the *PMBOK*:

Qualitative Risk Analysis	Risk Management Planning
Quantitative Risk Analysis	Risk Response Planning
Risk Identification	

Before you take the exam, also be certain you are familiar with the following terms:

acceptance	Monte Carlo analysis
avoid	Nominal Group Technique
brainstorming	ordinal scale
cardinal scale	passive acceptance
cause-and-effect diagrams	probability
contingency planning	probability and impact matrix
contingency reserves	residual risk
decision trees	risk breakdown structure (RBS)
Delphi technique	risk categories
enhance	risk management plan
expected monetary value (EMV)	risk register
exploit	risk tolerance
force majeure	secondary risks
impact	sensitivity analysis
impact scale	share
influence diagramming	tornado diagram
interviews	transfer
mitigate	triggers

Review Questions

1. You are a project manager for Fountain of Youth Spring Water bottlers. Your project involves installing a new accounting system, and you're performing the risk-planning processes. You have identified several problems along with the causes of those problems. Which of the following diagrams will you use to show the problem and its causes and effects?

   A. Decision tree diagram

   B. Fishbone diagram

   C. Benchmark diagram

   D. Simulation tree diagram

2. The process of assessing the probability and consequences of identified risks to the project objectives, assigning a risk score to each risk, and creating a list of prioritized risks describes which of the following processes?

   A. Quantitative Risk Analysis

   B. Risk Identification

   C. Qualitative Risk Analysis

   D. Risk Management Planning

3. Each of the following statements is true regarding the risk management plan except for which one?

   A. The risk management plan is an output of the Risk Management Planning process.

   B. The risk management plan includes a description of the responses to risks and triggers.

   C. The risk management plan includes thresholds, scoring and interpretation methods, responsible parties, and budgets.

   D. The risk management plan is an input to all the remaining risk-planning processes.

4. You are using the interviewing technique of the Quantitative Risk Analysis process. You intend to use normal and lognormal distributions. All of the following statements are true regarding this question except which one?

   A. Interviewing techniques are used to quantify the probability and impact of the risks on project objectives.

   B. Normal and lognormal distributions use mean and standard deviation to quantify risks.

   C. Distributions graphically display the impacts of risk to the project objectives.

   D. Triangular distributions rely on optimistic, pessimistic, and most likely estimates to quantify risks.

5. The information-gathering techniques used in the Risk Identification process include all of the following except _____.

   A. root cause identification

   B. the Delphi technique

   C. SWOT analysis

   D. checklist analysis

6. Which of the following processes assesses the likelihood of risk occurrences and their consequences using a numerical rating?

   A. Qualitative Risk Analysis

   B. Risk Identification

   C. Quantitative Risk Analysis

   D. Risk Response Planning

7. You are the project manager for a new website for the local zoo. You need to perform Qualitative Risk Analysis. When you've completed this process, you'll produce all of the following as part of the risk register update output except which one?

   A. Priority list of risks

   B. Watch list of low-priority risks

   C. Probability of achieving time and cost estimates

   D. Risks grouped by categories

8. You've identified a risk event on your current project that could save $100,000 in project costs if it occurs. Which of the following is true based on this statement? (Choose the best answer.)

   A. This is a risk event that should be accepted, because the rewards outweigh the threat to the project.

   B. This risk event is an opportunity to the project and should be exploited.

   C. This risk event should be mitigated to take advantage of the savings.

   D. This a risk event that should be shared to take full advantage of the potential savings.

9. You've identified a risk event on your current project that could save $500,000 in project costs if it occurs. Your organization is considering hiring a consulting firm to help establish proper project management techniques in order to assure it realizes these savings. Which of the following is true based on this statement? (Choose the best answer.)

   A. This is a risk event that should be accepted, because the rewards outweigh the threat to the project.

   B. This risk event is an opportunity to the project and should be exploited.

   C. This risk event should be mitigated to take advantage of the savings.

   D. This a risk event that should be shared to take full advantage of the potential savings.

10. Your hardware vendor left you a voicemail saying that a snowstorm in the Midwest might prevent your equipment from arriving on time. She wanted to give you a heads-up and asked that you return the call. Which of the following statements is true? (Choose the best answer.)

   A. This is a trigger.

   B. This is a contingency plan.

   C. This is a residual risk.

   D. This is a secondary risk.

11. You are constructing a probability and impact matrix for your project. Which of the following statements is true?

   A. The probability and impact matrix multiplies the risk's probability by the cost of the impact to determine an expected value of the risk event.

   B. The probability and impact matrix multiplies the risk's probability—which fall from 0.0 to 1.0—and the risk's impact and then adds them together to determine a risk score.

   C. The probability and impact matrix multiplies the risk's probability by the expected value of the risk event to determine a risk score based on a predetermined threshold.

   D. The probability and impact matrix multiplies the risk's probability by the risk impact—which both fall from 0.0 to 1.0—to determine a risk score.

12. Your stakeholders have asked for an analysis of the cost risk. All of the following are true except for which one?

   A. Monte Carlo analysis is the preferred method to use to determine the cost risk.

   B. Monte Carlo analysis is a modeling technique.

   C. A traditional work breakdown structure can be used as an input variable for the cost analysis.

   D. A cost breakdown structure can be used as an input variable for the cost analysis.

13. Your hardware vendor left you a voicemail saying that a snowstorm in the Midwest will prevent your equipment from arriving on time. You identified a risk response strategy for this risk and have arranged for a local company to lease you the needed equipment until yours arrives. This is an example of which risk response strategy?

   A. Transfer

   B. Acceptance

   C. Mitigate

   D. Avoid

14. All of the following are elements of inputs of the Risk Identification process that you should evaluate except for which one?

   A. Assumptions analysis

   B. Historical information

   C. Roles and responsibilities

   D. Industry information

15. You work for a large manufacturing plant. You are working on a new project to release an overseas product line. This is the company's first experience in the overseas market, and it wants to make a big splash with the introduction of this product. The stakeholders are a bit nervous about the project and historically proceed cautiously and take a considerable amount of time to examine information before making a final decision. The project entails producing your product in a concentrated formula and packaging it in smaller containers than the U.S. product uses. A new machine is needed in order to mix the ingredients into a concentrated formula. After speaking with one of your stakeholders, you discover this will be the first machine your organization has purchased from your new supplier. Which of the following statements is true given the information in this question?

A. The question describes risk tolerance levels of the stakeholders, which should be considered as an input to the Risk Management Planning process.

B. This question describes the interviewing tool and technique used during the Risk Identification process.

C. This question describes risk triggers that are derived using interviewing techniques and recorded in the risk register during the Qualitative Risk Analysis process.

D. This question describes a risk that requires a response strategy from the positive risk category.

16. Your project team has identified several potential risks on your current project that could have a significant impact if they occurred. The team examined the impact of the risks by keeping all the uncertain elements at their baseline values. What type of diagram will the team use to display this information?

A. Fishbone diagram

B. Tornado diagram

C. Influence diagram

D. Process flowchart

17. Your project team is in the process of identifying project risks on your current project. The team has the option to use all of the following tools and techniques to diagram some of these potential risks except for which one?

A. Ishikawa diagram

B. Decision tree diagram

C. Process flowchart

D. Influence diagram

18. All of the following statements are true regarding the RBS except for which one?

A. The RBS is contained in the risk management plan.

B. It describes risk categories, which are a systematic way to identify risks and provide a foundation for understanding for everyone involved on the project.

C. The lowest level of the RBS can be used as a checklist, which is a tool and technique of the Risk Identification process.

D. The RBS is similar to the WBS in that the lowest levels of both are easily assigned to a responsible party or owner.

19. Your team has identified the risks on the project and determined their risk score. The team is in the midst of determining what strategies to put in place should the risks occur. After some discussion, the team members have determined that the risk of losing their network administrator is a risk they'll just deal with if and when it occurs. Although they think it's a possibility and the impact would be significant, they've decided to simply deal with it after the fact. Which of the following is true regarding this question?

A. This is a negative response strategy.

B. This is a positive response strategy.

C. This is a response strategy for either positive or negative risk known as *contingency planning*.

D. This is a response strategy for either positive or negative risks known as *passive acceptance*.

20. All of the following are true regarding the Qualitative Risk Analysis process except which one?

A. Probability and impact and expert interview are used to help correct biases that occur in the data you've gathered during this process.

B. The probability and impact matrix is used during this process to assign red, yellow, and green conditions to risks.

C. Qualitative Risk Analysis is an easy method of determining risk probability and impact that usually takes a good deal of time to perform.

D. Risk urgency assessment is a tool and technique of this process used to determine which risks need near-term response plans.

Answers to Review Questions

1. B. The cause-and-effect flowcharts—also called *fishbone diagrams* or *Ishikawa diagrams*—show the relationship between the causes and effects of problems.

2. C. The purpose of Qualitative Risk Analysis is to determine what impact the identified risks will have on the project and the probability they'll occur. It also puts risks in priority order according to their effects on the project objectives and assigns a risk score for the project.

3. B. The risk management plan details how risk management processes will be implemented, monitored, and controlled throughout the life of the project. The risk management plan does not include responses to risks or triggers. Responses to risks are documented in the risk register as part of the Risk Response Planning process.

4. C. Distributions graphically display the probability of risk to the project objectives as well as the time or cost elements.

5. D. The information-gathering techniques in the Risk Identification process are brainstorming, the Delphi technique, interviewing, root cause identification, and SWOT analysis.

6. C. Quantitative Risk Analysis analyzes the probability of risks and their consequences using a numerical rating. Qualitative Risk Analysis might use numeric ratings but can use a high-medium-low scale as well.

7. C. Probability of achieving time and cost estimates is an update that is produced from the Quantitative Risk Analysis process.

8. B. This risk event has the potential to save money on project costs, so it's an opportunity, and the appropriate strategy to use in this case is the exploit strategy.

9. D. This risk event has the potential to save money on project costs. Sharing involves using a third party to help assure that the opportunity take place.

10. A. The best answer is A. Triggers are warning signs of an impending risk.

11. C. The probability and impact matrix multiplies the probability and impact to determine a risk score. A high, medium, or low designation is assigned to the risk based on a predetermined threshold.

12. B. Monte Carlo analysis is a simulation technique.

13. C. Mitigation attempts to reduce the impact of a risk event should it occur. Making plans to arrange for the leased equipment reduces the consequences of the risk.

14. A. Assumptions analysis is a tool and technique of the Risk Identification process.

15. A. This question describes risk tolerance levels of the stakeholders. Risk triggers are recorded in the risk register during the Risk Response Planning process. The risk of buying a machine from a new supplier would pose a threat to the project, not an opportunity. Interviewing might have been used, but this question wasn't describing the Risk Identification process.

16. B. The question describes sensitivity analysis, which is a tool and technique of the Quantitative Risk Analysis process. Tornado diagrams are often used to display sensitivity analysis data.

17. B. Decision tree diagrams are used during the Quantitative Risk Analysis process. All the other options are diagramming techniques of the Risk Identification process.

18. D. The RBS describes risk categories, and the lowest level can be used as a checklist to help identify risks. Risk owners are not assigned from the RBS; they're assigned during the Risk Response Planning process.

19. D. This is a response strategy known as *passive acceptance* because the team has decided to take no action and make no plans for the risk. This is a strategy that can be used for either positive or negative risks.

20. C. Qualitative Risk Analysis is a fast and easy method of determining probability and impact.

Chapter

6

Resource Planning

THE PMP EXAM CONTENT FROM THE PLANNING THE PROJECT PERFORMANCE DOMAIN COVERED IN THIS CHAPTER INCLUDES THE FOLLOWING:

✓ Identify Project Team and Define Roles and Responsibilities

You're closing in on finishing up the Planning group processes. You're at a place where I need to talk about some processes that aren't necessarily related to each other but need to be completed before you can construct the project schedule and budget. So, you'll start out this chapter with two procurement processes—Plan Purchases and Acquisitions and Plan Contracting—and then move on to Human Resource Planning, where you will develop the staffing management plan. This plan will help guide you later on in acquiring your project team members.

Then you'll get back on track with a theme by finishing up the chapter with two processes that will start you off on the right foot toward estimating and scheduling activities. They are the Activity Definition process and the Activity Sequencing process.

All the processes I'll talk about in this chapter are used to develop both the project schedule and the budget, which are two of the most important documents in the project plan (I'll discuss those in the next chapter). Let's get going.

Understanding Purchases and Acquisitions

Plan Purchases and Acquisitions is a process of identifying what goods or services you're going to purchase from outside the organization and which project the project team needs can meet. Part of what you'll accomplish in this process is determining whether you should purchase the goods or services and, if so, how much and when. Keep in mind that I'm discussing the procurement from the buyer's perspective, because this is the approach used in the *PMBOK Guide*.

The Plan Purchases and Acquisitions process can influence the project schedule, and the project schedule can influence this process. For example, the availability of a contractor or special-order materials might have a significant impact on the schedule. And conversely, your organization's business cycle might have an impact on the Plan Purchases and Acquisitions process if the organization is dependent on seasonal activity. The Activity Resource Estimating process, which I'll cover in Chapter 7, also can be influenced by this process, as will make-or-buy decisions (I'll get to those shortly).

You need to perform each process in the Project Procurement Management Knowledge Area (beginning with Plan Purchases and Acquisitions and ending with Contract Closure) for each product or service that you're buying outside the organization. If you're procuring all your resources from within the organization, the only process you'll perform in this Knowledge Area is the Plan Purchases and Acquisitions process.

Sometimes, you'll procure all the materials and resources for your project from a vendor. In cases like these, the vendor will have a project manager assigned to the project. Your organization might choose to have an internal project manager assigned as well to act as the conduit between your company and the vendor and to provide information and monitor your organization's deliverables. When this happens, the vendor or contracting company is responsible for fulfilling all the project management processes as part of the contract. In the case of an outsourced project, the seller—also known as the *vendor*, *supplier*, or *contractor*—manages the project and the buyer becomes the stakeholder. If you're hiring a vendor, don't forget to consider permits or professional licenses that might be required for the type of work you need them to perform.

Several inputs are needed when planning for purchases. You'll look at them next.

Plan Purchases and Acquisitions Inputs

The Plan Purchases and Acquisitions process has six inputs:

- Enterprise environmental factors
- Organizational process assets
- Project scope statement
- Work breakdown structure
- WBS dictionary
- Project management plan

The project management plan can include risk register, risk-related contractual agreements, resource requirements, project schedule, activity cost estimates, and cost baseline.

Marketplace conditions are the key element of enterprise environmental factors you should consider for this process. The organization's guidelines, policies, and organizational policies (including any procurement policies) are the elements of the organizational process assets you should pay attention to here.

Many organizations have procurement departments that are responsible for procuring goods and services and writing and managing contracts. Some organizations also require all contracts be reviewed by their legal department prior to signing. These are organizational process assets that you should consider when you need to procure goods and services.

It's important for the project manager to understand organizational policies because they might impact many of the Planning processes, including the Procurement Planning processes. For example, the organization might have purchasing approval processes that must be followed. Perhaps orders for goods or services that exceed certain dollar amounts need different levels of approval. As the project manager, you need to be aware of policies like this so you're certain you can execute the project smoothly. It's frustrating to find out later that you should have followed a certain process or policy and now, because you didn't, you've got schedule delays or worse. You could consider using the "Sin now, ask forgiveness later" technique in extreme emergencies, but you didn't hear that from me. (By the way, that's not a technique that's authorized by the *PMBOK Guide*.)

The project manager and the project team will be responsible for coordinating all the organizational interfaces for the project, including technical, human resource, purchasing, and finance. It will serve you well to understand the policies and politics involved in each of these areas in your organization.

My organization is steeped in policy. (A government organization steeped in policy? Go figure!) It's so steeped in policy that we have to request the funds for large projects at least two years in advance. There are mounds and mounds of request forms, justification forms, approval forms, routing forms—you get the idea. But my point is if you miss one of the forms or don't fill out the information correctly, you can set your project back by a minimum of a year, if not two. Then once the money is awarded, there are more forms to fill out and policies to follow. Again, if you don't follow the policies correctly, you can jeopardize future project funds. Many organizations have a practice of not giving you all the project money up front in one lump sum. In other words, you must meet major milestones or complete a project phase before they'll fund your next phase. Know what your organizational policies are well ahead of time. Talk to the people who can walk you through the process and ask them to check your work to avoid surprises.

The project scope statement lists the deliverables and the acceptance criteria for the product or service of the project. Obviously, you'll want to consider these when thinking about procuring goods and services. You'll also want to consider the constraints (issues such as availability and timing of funds, availability of resources, delivery dates, and vendor availability) and assumptions (issues such as reliability of the vendor, assuming availability of key resources, and adequate stakeholder involvement). The product scope description is included in the project scope statement as well and might alert you to special considerations (services, technical requirements, and skills) needed to produce the product of the project.

The WBS and WBS dictionary identify the deliverables and describe the work required for each element of the WBS. The project management plan will provide you with guidance for procuring goods and services. For example, the risk-related contractual agreements component of this plan describes the types of services of goods needed for risk management. The transference strategy might require the purchase of insurance. You should review each of these elements when determining which goods and services will be performed within the project and which will be purchased.

Tools and Techniques for Plan Purchases and Acquisitions

The Plan Purchases and Acquisitions process consists of three tools and techniques. They are make-or-buy analysis, expert judgment, and contract types. I've already covered expert judgment, so you'll look at make-or-buy analysis next, and then I'll cover contract types.

Make-or-Buy Analysis

The main decision you're trying to get to in *make-or-buy analysis* is whether it's more cost effective to buy the products and services or more cost effective for the organization to produce the goods and services needed for the project. Costs should include both direct costs—in other words, the actual cost to purchase the product or service—and indirect costs, such as the salary of the manager overseeing the purchase process or ongoing maintenance costs. Costs don't necessarily mean the cost to purchase. In make-or-buy analysis, you might weigh the cost of leasing items versus buying them. For example, perhaps your project requires using a specialized piece of hardware that you know will be outdated by the end of the project. In a case like this, leasing might be a better option so that when the project is ready to be implemented, a newer version of the hardware can be tested and put into production during rollout.

Other considerations in make-or-buy analysis might include elements such as capacity issues, skills, availability, and trade secrets. Strict control might be needed for a certain process, and thus the process cannot be outsourced. Perhaps your organization has the skills in-house to complete the project but your current project list is so backlogged that you can't get to the new project for months, so you need to bring in a vendor.

Make-or-buy analysis is considered a general management technique and concludes with the decision to do one or the other.

Contract Types

A *contract* is a compulsory agreement between two or more parties and is used to acquire products or services from outside the organization. Typically, money is exchanged for the goods or services. Contracts are enforceable by law and require an offer and an acceptance.

There are different types of contracts for different purposes. The *PMBOK Guide* divides contracts into three categories:

- Fixed price or lump sum
- Cost reimbursable
- Time and materials (T&M)

Within the fixed price and cost reimbursable categories are different types of contracts. You'll look at each in the following sections. Keep in mind that several factors will impact the type of contract you should use. The product requirements (or service criteria) might drive the contract type. The market conditions might drive availability and price—remember back in the year 2000 when there wasn't a programmer to be found for less than $200 an hour? And the amount of risk—for the seller, the buyer, and the project itself—will help determine contract type.

Exam Spotlight

There might be an exam question or two regarding contract types, so spend some time getting familiar with them.

Fixed-Price or Lump-Sum Contracts

Fixed-price contracts (also referred to as *lump-sum contracts*) set a specific, firm price for the goods or services rendered. The buyer and seller agree on a well-defined deliverable for a set price. In this kind of contract, the biggest risk is borne by the seller. The seller—or contractor—must take great strides to assure they've covered their costs and will make a comfortable profit on the transaction. The seller assumes the risks of increasing costs, nonperformance, or other problems. However, to counter these unforeseen risks, the seller builds in the cost of the risk to the contract price.

Fixed-price contracts can be disastrous for both the buyer and the seller if the scope of the project is not well defined or the scope changes dramatically. It's important to have accurate, well-defined deliverables when you're using this type of contract. Conversely, fixed-price contracts are relatively safe for both buyer and seller when the original scope is well defined and remains unchanged. They typically reap only small profits for the seller and force the contractor to work productively and efficiently. This type of contract also minimizes cost and quality uncertainty.

Fixed-price plus incentive contracts are another type of fixed-price contract. The difference here is that the contract includes an incentive—or bonus—for early completion or for some other agreed-upon performance criterion that's exceeded according to contract specifications. The criteria for early completion, or other performance enhancements, must be spelled out in the contract so both parties understand the terms and conditions.

Another aspect of fixed-price plus incentive contracts to consider is that some of the risk is borne by the buyer as opposed to the firm fixed-price contract, where most of the risk is borne by the seller. The buyer takes some risk, albeit minimal, by offering the incentive to, for example, get the work done earlier. Suppose the buyer really would like the product delivered 30 days prior to when the seller thinks they can deliver. In this case, the buyer assumes the risk for the early delivery via the incentive.

Cost-Reimbursable Contracts

Cost-reimbursable contracts are as the name implies. The allowable costs—allowable is defined by the contract—associated with producing the goods or services are charged to the buyer. All the costs the seller takes on during the project are charged back to the buyer; thus, the seller is reimbursed.

Cost-reimbursable contracts carry the highest risk to the buyer because the total costs are uncertain. As problems arise, the buyer has to shell out even more money to correct the problems. However, the advantage to the buyer with this type of contract is that scope changes are easy to make and can be made as often as you want—but it will cost you.

Cost-reimbursable contracts have a lot of uncertainty associated with them. The contractor has little incentive to work efficiently or be productive. This type of contract protects the contractor's profit because increasing costs are passed to the buyer rather than taken out of profits, as would be the case with a fixed-price contract. Be certain to audit your statements when using a contract like this so that charges from some other project the vendor is working on don't accidentally end up on your bill.

Cost-reimbursable contracts are used most often when the project scope contains a lot of uncertainty, such as for cutting-edge projects and research and development. They are also used for projects that have large investments early in the project life. I'll now discuss the three kinds of cost-reimbursable contracts:

Cost plus fee (CPF) or cost plus percentage of cost (CPPC)   In the *cost plus fee (CPF)* contract, also called *cost plus percentage of cost (CPPC)*, the seller is reimbursed for allowable costs plus a fee that's calculated as a percentage of the costs. The percentage is agreed upon beforehand and documented in the contract. Since the fee is based on costs, the fee is variable. The lower the costs, the lower the fee, so the seller doesn't have a lot of motivation to keep costs low.

Cost plus fixed fee (CPFF)   *Cost plus fixed fee (CPFF)* contracts charge back all allowable project costs to the seller and include a fixed fee upon completion of the contract. This is how the seller makes money on the deal; the fixed fee portion is the seller's profit. The fee is always firm in this kind of contract, but the costs are variable. The seller doesn't necessarily have a lot of motivation to control costs with this type of contract, as you can imagine. And one of the strongest motivators for completing the project is driven by the fixed fee portion of the contract.

Cost plus incentive fee (CPIF)   The next category of cost reimbursable contract is *cost plus incentive fee (CPIF)*. This is the type of contract in which the buyer reimburses the seller for the seller's allowable costs and includes an incentive for exceeding the performance criteria laid out in the contract. An incentive fee actually encourages better cost performance by the seller, and there is a possibility of shared savings between the seller and buyer if performance criteria are exceeded. The qualification for exceeded performance must be written into the contract and agreed to by both parties, as should the definition of allowable costs; the seller can possibly lose the incentive fee if agreed-upon targets are not reached.

There is moderate risk for the buyer under the cost plus incentive fee contract, and if well-written, it can be more beneficial for both the seller and then buyer than a cost-reimbursable contract.

Time and Materials (T&M) Contracts

Time and materials (T&M) contracts are a cross between fixed-price and cost-reimbursable contracts. The full amount of the material costs is not known at the time the contract is awarded. This resembles a cost-reimbursable contract because the costs will continue to grow during the contract's life and are reimbursable to the contractor. The buyer bears the biggest risk in this type of contract.

T&M contracts can resemble fixed-price contracts when unit rates are used, for example. Unit rates might be used to preset the rates of certain elements or portions of the project. For example, a contracting agency might charge you $135 per hour for a Java programmer, or a leasing company might charge you $2,000 per month for the hardware you're renting during the testing phase of your project. These rates are preset and agreed upon by the buyer and seller ahead of time.

Exam Spotlight

Understand the difference between a fixed-price contract and a cost-reimbursable contract for the exam. Also know when each type of contract should be used, and know which party bears the most risk under each type of contract.

Plan Purchases and Acquisitions Outputs

The Plan Purchases and Acquisitions process consists of four outputs. The first is the *procurement management plan.* You've seen a lot of other outputs whose names end with the words *management plan*, so you're probably already ahead of me on this one. But hold the phone—I'll make sure to touch on the important points. The other outputs are the contract statement of work, make-or-buy decisions, and requested changes.

Procurement Management Plan

The procurement management plan details how the procurement process will be managed. It includes the following information:

- The types of contract to use
- The authority of the project team
- How the procurement process will be integrated with other project processes
- Where to find standard procurement documents (provided your organization uses standard documents)
- How many vendors or contractors are involved and how they'll be managed

- How the procurement process will be coordinated with other project processes, such as performance reporting and scheduling
- How the constraints and assumptions might be impacted by purchasing
- How multiple vendors or contractors will be managed
- The coordination of purchasing lead times with the development of the project schedule
- The schedule dates that are determined in each contract
- Identification of prequalified sellers (if known)

The procurement management plan, like all the other management plans, becomes a subsidiary of the project management plan.

 Real World Scenario

Streamlining Purchases

Russ is a project manager for a real estate development company in Hometown, USA. Recently he transferred to the office headquarters to develop a process for streamlining purchases and purchase requests for the construction teams in the field. His first step was to develop a procurement management plan for the construction managers to use when ordering materials and equipment. Russ decided the procurement management plan could be used as a template for all new projects. That meant the project managers in the field didn't have to write their own procurement management plan when starting a new construction project. They could use the template, which had many of the fields prepopulated with corporate headquarters processes, and then they could fill in the information specific to their project. For example, the Types of Contracts section states that all equipment and materials purchases require fixed-price contracts. When human resources are needed for the project on a contract basis, a T&M contract should be used with the unit rates stated in the contract. A "not to exceed" amount should also be written into the contract so that there are no surprises as to the total amount of dollars the company will be charged for the resources.

Contract Statement of Work

A *contract statement of work (SOW)* contains the details of the procurement item in clear, concise terms. It includes the following elements:

- The project objectives
- A description of the work of the project and any postproject operational support needed
- Concise specifications of the product or services required
- The project schedule, time period of services, and work location

The contract SOW might be prepared by either the buyer or the seller. Buyers might prepare the contract SOW and give it to the sellers, who in turn rewrite it so that they can price the work properly. If the buyer does not know how to prepare a contract SOW or the seller would be better at creating the SOW because of their expertise about the product or service, the seller might prepare it and then give it to the buyer to review. In either case, the contract statement of work is developed from the project scope statement and the WBS and WBS dictionary.

The seller uses the contract SOW to determine whether they are able to produce the goods or services as specified. In addition, it wouldn't hurt to include a copy of the WBS with the contract SOW. Any information the seller can use to properly price the goods or services helps both sides understand what's needed and how it will be provided.

Projects might require some or all of the work of the project to be provided by a vendor. The Plan Purchases and Acquisitions process determines whether goods or services should be produced within the organization or procured from outside, and if goods or services are procured from outside, it describes what will be outsourced and what kind of contract to use and then documents the information in the contract SOW and procurement management plan.

> You prepared a SOW during the Develop Project Charter process. You can use that SOW as the contract SOW during this process if you're contracting out the entire project. Otherwise, you can use just those portions of the SOW that describe the work for which you're contracted.

Make-or-Buy Decisions

The make-or-buy decision is a document that outlines the decisions made during the process regarding which goods and or services will be produced by the organization and which will be purchased. This can include any number of items, including services, products, insurance policies, performance, and performance bonds.

Requested Changes

Like many of the other processes I've discussed so far, requested changes might come about as a result of the Plan Purchases and Acquisitions process. Those changes, like all the others, should be administered through the Integrated Change Control process.

Once you've determined which goods and services you're going to procure and decided on the best type of contract to use for your situation, you can move into the Plan Contracting processes to prepare the information needed for choosing a vendor.

Plan Contracting

The purpose of *Plan Contracting* is to prepare the documents you'll use in the Request Seller Responses and Select Sellers processes. I'll discuss these processes in Chapter 9, "Measuring and Controlling Project Performance." The inputs to this process are the procurement management plan, contract statement of work, make-or-buy decisions, and the project management plan (with special attention to the risk register, risk-related contractual agreements, resource requirements, project schedule, activity cost estimates, and cost baseline, which I will cover in coming chapters).

The tools and techniques of Plan Contracting are standard forms and expert judgment. Standard forms are used to facilitate the procurement process. These are forms that are standardized for your organization and for the types of goods or services typically procured by the organization. Your organization might or might not have standard forms. They are usually found in organizations that write a lot of contracts and procure a significant number of goods and services. They might include standard contract forms, nondisclosure agreements, proposal evaluation criteria, and so on.

Plan Contracting Outputs

The three outputs of the Plan Contracting process are procurement documents, evaluation criteria, and contract statement of work updates. You'll now take a quick look at each.

Procurement Documents

Procurement documents are used to solicit vendors and suppliers to bid on your procurement needs. You're probably familiar with some of the titles of procurement documents. They might be called request for proposal (RFP), request for information (RFI), invitation for bid (IFB), request for quotation (RFQ), and so on.

Procurement documents should clearly state the description of the work requested, they should include the contract SOW, and they should explain how sellers should format and submit their responses. These documents are prepared by the buyer to assure as accurate and complete a response as possible from all potential bidders. Any special provisions or contractual needs should be spelled out as well. For example, many organizations have data concerning their marketing policies, new products introductions planned for the next few years, trade secrets, and so on. The vendor will have access to this private information, and in order to ensure they maintain confidentiality, you should require that they sign a nondisclosure agreement.

A few terms are used during this process—usually interchangeably even though they have distinct definitions—that you should understand. When your decision is going to be made primarily on price, the terms *bid* and *quotation* are used, as in IFB or RFQ. When considerations other than price (such as technology or specific approaches to the project) are the deciding factor, the term *proposal* is used, as in RFP. These terms are used interchangeably in practice, even though they have specific meanings in the *PMBOK Guide*.

 NOTE   In my organization, all solicitation requests are submitted as RFPs, even though our primary decision factor is price.

Procurement documents are posted or advertised according to your organizational policies. This might include ads in newspapers and magazines or ads/posts on the Internet.

Exam Spotlight

Understand the difference between bid and/or quotation and proposal for the exam. Bids or quotations are used when price is the only deciding factor among bidders. Proposals are used when there are considerations other than price.

Evaluation Criteria

Evaluation criteria refers to the method your organization will use to choose a vendor from among the proposals you receive. The criteria might be subjective or objective. In some cases, price might be the only criteria, and that means the vendor that submits the lowest bid will win the contract. You should use purchase price (which should include costs associated with purchase price, such as delivery and setup charges) as the sole criteria only when you have multiple qualified sellers from which to choose.

Other projects might require more extensive criteria than price alone. In this case, you might use scoring models as well as rating models, or you might utilize purely subjective methods of selection. I described an example weighted scoring method in Chapter 2, "Creating the Project Charter and Preliminary Scope Statement." You can use this method to score vendor proposals.

Sometimes, the evaluation criteria are made public in the procurement process so that vendors know exactly what you want in a vendor. This approach has pros and cons. If the organization typically makes known the evaluation criteria, you'll find that almost all the vendors that bid on the project meet every criteria you've outlined (in writing, that is). When it comes time to perform the contract, however, you might encounter some surprises. The vendor might have done a great job of writing the bid based on your criteria, but in reality they don't know how to put the criteria into practice. On the other hand, having all the criteria publicly known beforehand gives ground to great discussion points and discovery later in the procurement processes.

The following list includes some of the criteria you can consider using for evaluating proposals and bids:

- Comprehension and understanding of the needs of the project as documented in the contract SOW

- Technical ability of vendor and their proposed team

- Experience on projects of similar size and scope, including references

- Project management approach

- Management approach

- Financial stability and capacity

- Intellectual and proprietary rights

You could include these in a weighted scoring model and rate each vendor on how well they responded to these issues.

Contract SOW Updates

You might find that changes to the contract statement of work are needed as a result of developing the procurement documents. These updates are usually made at the end of the Plan Contracting process.

I'll switch gears now and explain how you plan for the types of resources you'll need on the project in the Human Resource Planning process.

The Customer Relationship Management System Response

Ryan Hunter is preparing the evaluation criteria for an RFP for a customer relationship management (CRM) software system. After meeting with key stakeholders and other project managers in the company who've had experience working on projects of this size and scope, he devised the first draft of the evaluation criteria. A partial list is as follows:

- Successful bidder's response must detail how business processes (as documented in the RFP page 24) will be addressed with their solution.

- Successful bidder must document their project management approach, which must follow PMI's *PMBOK Guide* project practices. Must provide an example project management plan based on a previous project experience of similar size and scope to the one documented in the RFP.

- Successful bidder must document previous successful implementations, including integration with existing organization's PBX and network operating system, and must provide references.

- Successful bidder must provide financial statements for the previous three years.

Human Resource Planning

All projects require human resources, from the smallest project to the largest. The *Human Resource Planning* process documents the roles and responsibilities of individuals or groups for various project elements and then documents the reporting relationships for each. Reporting relationships can be assigned to groups as well as to individuals, and the groups or individuals might be internal or external to the organization or a combination of both. Communications Planning goes hand in hand with Human Resource Planning, because the organizational structure affects the way communications are carried out among project participants and the project interfaces.

The three outputs of this process include the roles and responsibilities document, the staffing management plan, and the project organization chart.

Human Resource Planning Inputs

Human Resource Planning has three inputs: enterprise environmental factors, organizational process assets, and project management plan (particularly the activity resource requirements). You'll look at the key elements of each of these next.

Key Environmental Factors for Human Resource Planning

Enterprise environmental factors play a key role in determining human resource roles and responsibilities. The type of organization you work in, the reporting relationships, and the technical skills needed to complete the project work are a few of the factors you should consider when developing the staffing management plan. These are the factors the *PMBOK Guide* details:

Organizational factors   Consider what departments or organization units will have a role in the project, the interactions between and among departments, and the level of formality in these working relationships.

Technical factors   Consider the types of specialized skills needed to complete the work of the project (for example, programming languages, engineering skills, knowledge of pharmaceuticals) and any technical considerations during handoff from phase to phase or from project completion to production.

Interpersonal factors   Interpersonal factors have to do with potential project team members. You should consider their experience, skills, current reporting relationships, cultural considerations, and perceptions regarding their levels of trust and respect for co-workers and superiors.

Location and logistics   Consider where the project team is physically located and whether they are all located together or at separate facilities (or cities or countries).

Political factors   Political factors involve your stakeholders. Consider the amount of influence the stakeholders have, their interactions and influence with each other, and the power they can exert over the project.

In addition to these factors, you should also consider project constraints. The topic of constraints seems to come up a lot, so you probably remember that constraints are factors that limit the options available to the project team. These typically involve time, costs, scope, and quality. However, you should know about a few new constraints regarding project teams:

Organizational structures   Organizational structures can be constraints. For example, a strong matrix organization provides the project manager with much more authority and power than the weak matrix organization does. Functional organizations typically do not empower their project managers with the proper authority to carry out a project. If you work in a functional organization as I do, it's important to be aware that you'll likely face power struggles with other managers and, in some cases, a flat-out lack of cooperation. Don't tell them I said this, but functional managers tend to be territorial and aren't likely to give up control easily. The best advice I have for you in this case is as follows:

- Establish open communications early in the project.

- Include all the functional managers with key roles in important decisions.

- Get the support of your project sponsor to empower you (as the project manager) with as much authority as possible. It's important that the sponsor makes it clear to the other managers that their cooperation on project activities is expected.

Collective bargaining agreements   Collective bargaining agreements are actually contractual obligations of the organization with employees. Collective bargaining is typically associated with unions and organized employee associations. Other organized employee associations or groups might require specialized reporting relationships as well—especially if they involve contractual obligations. You will not likely be involved in the negotiations of collective bargaining agreements, but if you have an opportunity to voice opinions regarding employee duties or agreements that would be helpful to your project or future projects, by all means take it.

Economic conditions   These conditions refer to the availability of funds for the project team to perform training, hire staff, and travel. If funds are severely limited and your project requires frequent trips to other locations, you have an economic constraint on your hands.

Exam Spotlight

Understand the key environmental factors and the three constraints that can impact the Human Resource Planning process for the exam.

Organizational Process Assets in Human Resource Planning

You should consider two primary elements of the organizational process assets input during this process. They are templates and checklists.

The term *templates*, in this case, refers to documentation such as project descriptions, organizational charts, performance appraisals, the organization's conflict management process, and so on.

Checklists might include elements such as training requirements, project roles and responsibilities, skills and competency levels, safety issues, and so on.

Exam Spotlight

According to the *PMBOK Guide*, using templates and checklists is one way to ensure that you don't miss any key responsibilities when planning the project and will help reduce the amount of time spent on project planning.

Project Management Plan

You've examined the project management plan as an input to other Planning processes. In the Human Resource Planning process, you'll want to pay particular attention to the activity resource requirements because they outline the types and quantities of resources needed for project activities. (Activity resource requirements are an output of the Activity Resource Estimating process, which I'll talk about in Chapter 7, "Creating the Project Schedule and Budget.")

Human Resource Planning Tools and Techniques

The Human Resource Planning process consists of three tools and techniques. Remember that your goal is to produce the organizational chart, roles and responsibilities document, and staffing management plan outputs at the end of this process. You'll see that the tools and techniques directly contribute to these outputs. They are organization charts and position descriptions, networking, and organizational theory. You'll look at each of these in the following sections.

Organization Charts and Position Descriptions

We've all seen an organization chart. It usually documents your name, your position, your boss, your boss's boss, your boss's boss's boss, and so on. The important point to note about this tool and technique is that this information might be presented in one of three ways: hierarchical (which describes most organization charts), matrix, and text.

Hierarchical Charts

Hierarchical charts, like a WBS, are designed in a top-down format. For example, the organization or department head is at the top, the management employees who report to the organization head are next, and so on, descending down the structure. An *organization breakdown structure (OBS)* is a form of organization chart that shows how the WBS elements relate to the organization's departments, work units, or teams rather than individuals.

A *resource breakdown structure (RBS)* is another type of hierarchical chart that breaks down the work of the project according to the types of resources needed. (RBS also stands for *risk breakdown structure,* as you learned in the previous chapter.) For example, you might have programmers, database analysts, and network analysts as resource types on the RBS. However, they won't all necessarily work on the project team. You might have programmers reporting to the project team, the finance department, and the customer service department, for example. An RBS can help track project costs because it ties to the organization's accounting system. Let's suppose you have programming resources in the RBS at the junior, advanced, and senior levels. Each of these levels of programmer has an average hourly salary recorded in the accounting system that makes it easy for you to track project costs. Ten senior programmers, 14 advanced, and 25 junior-level programmers are easy to calculate and track.

Matrix-Based Charts

Matrix-based charts are used to show the type of resource and the responsibility they have on the project. Many times a project manager will use a *responsibility assignment matrix (RAM)* to graphically display this information. A RAM is usually depicted as a chart with resource names listed in each row (for example, programmers, testers, and trainers) and project phases or WBS elements listed as the columns. (It can also be constructed using team member names.) Indicators in the intersections show where the resources are needed. However, the level of detail is up to you. One RAM might be developed showing only project phases. Another RAM might show level-two WBS elements for a complex project, with more RAMs subsequently produced for the additional WBS levels. Or a RAM might be constructed with level-three elements only.

Exam Spotlight

According to the *PMBOK Guide*, the RAM relates the OBS to the WBS to assure that every component of the work of the project is assigned to an individual.

Table 6.1 shows a sample portion of a type of RAM called a *RACI chart* for a software development team. In this example, the RACI chart shows the level of accountability each of the participants has on the project. The letters in the acronym RACI are the designations shown in the chart:

R = Responsible for performing the work

A = Accountable, the one who is responsible for producing the deliverable or work package and approves or signs off on the work

C = Consult, someone who has input to the work or decisions

I = Inform, someone who must be informed of the decisions or results

TABLE 6.1   Sample RAM

	Karen	Rae	Melinee	JoJo
Design	R	A	C	C
Test	I	R	C	A
Implement	C	I	R	A

R = Responsible, A = Accountable, C = Consult, I = Inform

In this example, Karen is responsible for design, meaning she creates the software programming design document, but Rae is accountable and is the one who must make certain the work of the project is completed and approved. This is a great tool because it shows at a glance not only where a resource is working but what that resource's responsibility level is on the project.

Text-Oriented Formats

Text-oriented formats are used when you have a significant amount of detail to record. These are also called *position descriptions* or *role-responsibility-authority forms*. These forms detail (as the name implies) the role, responsibility, and authority of the resource, and they make great templates to use for future projects.

Don't forget that other subsidiary plans of the project management plan might also describe roles and responsibilities. For example, you'll recall from Chapter 5, "Risk Planning," that the risk register lists the risk owners and their responsibility, so be certain to check these documents when outlining roles and responsibilities as well.

Networking

Networking in this process doesn't refer to the technical kind of networking with servers, switches, and fiber. It means human resource networking; that is, you know someone who knows someone who knows someone. According to the *PMBOK Guide*, several types of networking activities exist: proactive communication, lunch meetings (my personal favorite), informal conversations (ah, the information you learn by hanging out at the espresso machine), and trade conferences (another favorite because they get you out of the office). Networking might help when you have a specific resource need on the project but can't seem to locate someone with that set of skills.

Organizational Theory

Organizational theory refers to all the theories that attempt to explain what makes people, teams, and work units perform the way they do. I'll talk more about motivation techniques (which are a type of organizational theory) in Chapter 8, "Developing the Project Team." Organizational theory improves the probability that planning will be effective and helps shorten the amount of time it takes to produce the Human Resource Planning outputs.

Human Resource Planning Outputs

The Human Resource Planning process has three outputs: roles and responsibilities, project organizational charts, and the staffing management plan. I've already covered organizational charts in detail, so I'll cover the other two outputs now.

Roles and Responsibilities

This output is the list of roles and responsibilities for the project team. It can take the form of the RAM or RACI chart I talked about earlier, or the roles and responsibilities can be recorded in text format. The following are the key elements you should include in the roles and responsibilities documentation:

Roles   Describes what part of the project the individuals or teams are accountable for. This should also include a description of authority levels, responsibilities, and what work is not included as part of the role.

Authority   Describes the amount of authority the resource has to make decisions, dictate direction, and approve the work.

Responsibility   Describes the work required to complete the project activities.

Competency   Describes the skills and ability needed to perform the project activities.

Staffing Management Plan

The staffing management plan documents how and when human resources are introduced to the project and the criteria for releasing them. As with the other management plans I've discussed, the level and amount of detail contained in this plan are up to you. It can be formal or informal, and it can contain lots of detail or only high-level detail.

The staffing management plan is a subsidiary plan to the project management plan and should be updated throughout the project. You should consider several elements for inclusion in the staffing management plan, including the following:

Staff acquisition   This describes how team members are acquired (from inside or outside the organization), where they're located, and the costs for specific skills and expertise. I'll talk more about staff acquisition in Chapter 8.

Timetable   This describes the time frames in which the resources will be needed on the project and when the recruitment process should begin. The resources can be described individually, by teams, or by function (programmers, testers, and so on). Many staffing management plans use a resource histogram. This is usually drawn in chart form, with project time along the horizontal axis and hours needed along the vertical axis. The following example histogram shows the hours needed for an asphalt crew on a construction project:

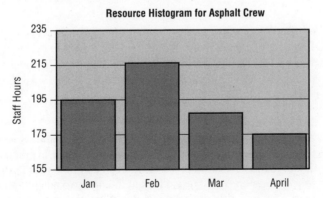

Resource Histogram for Asphalt Crew

Release criteria   Attention should be given to how you'll release project team members at the end of their assignment. You should have reassignment procedures in place to move folks on to other projects or back to assignments they had before the project. This reduces overall project costs because you pay them only for the time they work and then release them. You won't have a tendency to simply keep them busy between assignments or until the end of their scheduled end date if they complete their activities early. Having these procedures in place will also improve morale because everyone will be clear about how reassignment will occur. This should reduce anxiety about their opportunity for employment at the conclusion of the project or their assignment.

Training needs   This describes any training plans needed for team members who don't have the required skills or abilities to perform project tasks.

Recognition and rewards   This describes the systems you'll use to reward and reinforce desired behavior. I'll talk more about recognition and rewards in Chapter 8.

Compliance   If your project involves regulations that must be met or contractual obligations (such as union contracts), the staffing management plan should detail these and any human resource policies the organization has in place that deal with compliance issues.

Safety   Any safety policies and procedures that are applicable to the project or industry you work in should be included in the staffing management plan.

Exam Spotlight

Make certain you understand the roles and responsibilities and the staffing management output and what each of these entails for the exam.

Defining Activities

Now you're off and running toward the development of your project schedule. To develop the schedule, you first need to define the activities, sequence them in the right order, estimate resources, and estimate the time it will take to complete the tasks. I'll cover the Activity Definition here, cover Activity Sequencing processes next, and pick up with the estimating processes in the next chapter.

Activity Definition and Activity Sequencing are separate processes, each with their own inputs, tools and techniques, and outputs. In practice, especially for small- to medium-sized projects, you can combine these processes into one process or step. You'll take a look at the first two activity-related processes now. Chapter 7 describes the remaining Activity-related processes including Activity Resource Estimating, Activity Duration Estimating, and Schedule Development processes.

The *Activity Definition* process is a further breakdown of the work package elements of the WBS. It documents the specific activities needed to fulfill the deliverables detailed on the WBS. This process might be performed by the project manager, or when the WBS is broken down to the subproject level, this process (and all the Activity-related processes that follow) might be assigned to a subproject manager.

Activity Definition Process Inputs

The following are inputs to the Activity Definition process and the key elements that you should consider as inputs to this process:

- Enterprise environmental factors (project management information systems and scheduling software tools)
- Organizational process assets (existing guidelines and policies)
- Project scope statement (deliverables, constraints, and assumptions)
- WBS (this is the primary input to this process)
- WBS dictionary
- Project management plan (schedule management plan)

Tools and Techniques for Defining Activities

The tools and techniques of the Activity Definition process are as follows:

- Decomposition
- Templates
- Rolling-wave planning
- Expert judgment
- Planning component

Decomposition is the process of breaking the work packages into smaller, more manageable units of work called *schedule activities*. These are not deliverables but the individual units of work that must be completed to fulfill the deliverables. Activity lists (which are one of the outputs of this process) from prior projects can be used as templates in this process. Rolling-wave planning involves planning near-term work in more detail than future-term work. Expert judgment, in the form of project team members with prior experience developing project scope statements and WBSs, can help you define activities.

The planning component is a new tool and technique you haven't seen before. Two of the planning components discussed in the *PMBOK Guide* are the control account and the planning package. The idea with this tool and technique is that you might have WBS elements that really can't be broken down much further. In that case, the work package level in those branches of the WBS can be used to develop high-level schedules and plan future work at higher levels of the WBS. You can use a control account within the WBS to assign a management control point anywhere above the work package level to use as a basis for planning when the work package level hasn't been planned. The planning package is any element on the WBS that's below the control account but still above the work package level used for planning purposes.

Exam Spotlight

The purpose of the Activity Definition process is to decompose the work packages into schedule activities where the basis for estimating, scheduling, executing, and monitoring and controlling the work of the project is easily supported and accomplished.

Activity Definition Outputs

Activity Definition has four outputs:

- Activity list
- Activity attributes
- Milestone list
- Requested changes

You'll be happy to know that you aren't going to create an Activity Definition management plan at the end of this process. You've looked at requested changes before. You'll examine the rest of the outputs here.

Activity List

One primary output of the Activity Definition process is an *activity list*. The activity list should contain all the schedule activities that will be performed for the project, with a scope of work description of each activity and an identifier (such as a code or number) so that team members understand what the work is and how it is to be completed. The schedule activities are individual elements of the project schedule, and the activity list is a subsidiary of the project management plan.

In practice, when you're working on a small project or projects that aren't that complex, you might accomplish Activity Definition during the construction of the WBS, and the activities themselves become the work package level. However, for the exam, remember that activities are elements of the project schedule, but they are *not* part of the WBS.

Activity Attributes

Activity attributes describe the characteristics of the activities and are an extension of the activity list. Activity attributes might describe information such as the activity identifier or code, descriptions, constraints and assumptions associated with the activity, activities that come before this activity (predecessor activities) and after this activity (successor activities), resource requirements, the individual responsible for completing the work, and so on. The activity attributes are used in the schedule model tool and technique of the Schedule Development process (I'll talk about this in the next chapter).

Milestone Lists

Milestones are typically major accomplishments of the project and mark the completion of major deliverables or some other key event in the project. For example, approval and sign-off on project deliverables might be considered milestones. Other examples might be the completion of a prototype, system testing, contract approval, and so on. The milestone list records these accomplishments and documents whether the milestone is mandatory or optional. The milestone list is part of the project management plan and is also used to help develop the project schedule.

Understanding the Activity Sequencing Process

Now that you've identified the schedule activities, you need to sequence them in a logical order and find out whether dependencies exist among the activities. The interactivity of logical relationships must be sequenced correctly in order to facilitate the development of a realistic, achievable project schedule in a later process.

Consider a classic example. Let's say you're going to paint your house, but, unfortunately, it's fallen into a little disrepair. The old paint is peeling and chipping and will need to be scraped before a coat of primer can be sprayed on the house. After the primer dries, the painting can commence. In this example, the primer activity depends on the scraping. You can't—OK, *you shouldn't*—prime the house before scraping off the peeling paint. The painting activity depends on the primer activity in the same way. You really shouldn't start painting until the primer has dried.

During *Activity Sequencing*, you will use a host of inputs and tools and techniques to produce the primary output, project schedule network diagrams. You've already seen all the inputs. They are project scope statement, activity list, activity attributes, milestone list, and approved change requests. I discussed them in this and previous chapters. You'll look at several new tools and techniques now.

Activity Sequencing Tools and Techniques

Activity Sequencing has five tools and techniques, all of which are new to you:

- Precedence diagramming method (PDM)
- Arrow diagramming method (ADM)

- Schedule network templates
- Dependency determination
- Applying leads and lags

I'll switch the order of these and cover dependency determination first. In practice, you'll define dependencies either before or while you're using the PDM or ADM methods to draw your network templates, so to make sure you're on the same page with the *PMBOK Guide* terminology regarding dependencies, I'll cover them first and then move on to the other tools and techniques.

Dependency Determination

Dependencies are relationships between the activities in which one activity is dependent on another to complete an action, or perhaps an activity is dependent on another to start an action before it can proceed. Dependency determination is a matter of determining where those dependencies exist. Thinking back to the house-painting example, you couldn't paint until the scraping and priming activities were completed. You'll want to know about three types of dependencies for the exam:

- Mandatory dependencies
- Discretionary dependencies
- External dependencies

As you've probably guessed, the *PMBOK Guide* defines dependencies differently depending on their characteristics:

Mandatory dependencies *Mandatory dependencies*, also known as *hard logic* or *hard dependencies*, are defined by the type of work being performed. The scraping, primer, and painting sequence is an example of mandatory dependencies. The nature of the work itself dictates the order in which the activities should be performed. Activities with physical limitations are a telltale sign that you have a mandatory dependency on your hands.

Discretionary dependencies *Discretionary dependencies* are defined by the project management team. Discretionary dependencies are also known as *preferred logic*, *soft logic*, or *preferential logic*. These are usually process or procedure-driven or "best-practice" techniques based on past experience. For example, both past experience and best practices on house-painting projects have shown that all trim work should be hand-painted while the bulk of the main painting work should be done with a sprayer.

External dependencies *External dependencies* are, well, external to the project. This might seem obvious, but the *PMBOK Guide* points out that even though the dependency is external to the project (and therefore a nonproject activity), it impacts project activities. For example, perhaps your project is researching and marketing a new drug. The FDA must approve the drug before your company can market it. This is not a project activity, but the project cannot move forward until approval occurs. That means FDA approval is an external dependency.

Once you've identified the dependencies and assembled all the other inputs for the Activity Sequencing process, you'll take this information and produce a diagram—or schematic display—of the project activities. The project schedule network diagram shows the dependencies—or logical relationships—that exist among the activities. You can use one of the other tools and techniques of this process to produce this output. You'll now examine each in detail.

Precedence Diagramming Method (PDM)

The *precedence diagramming method (PDM)* is what most project management software programs use to do activity sequencing. Precedence diagrams use boxes or rectangles to represent the activities (called *nodes*). The nodes are connected with arrows showing the dependencies between the activities. This method is also called *activity on node (AON)*.

The minimum information that should be displayed on the node is the activity name, but you might put as much information about the activity on the node as you'd like. Sometimes the nodes are displayed with activity name, activity number, start and stop dates, due dates, slack time, and so on. (I'll cover slack time in Chapter 7. For the exam, remember that the PDM uses only one time estimate to determine duration.)

The following graphic shows a PDM—or AON—of the house-painting example.

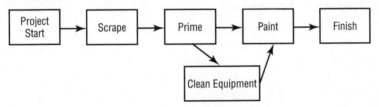

The PDM is further defined by four types of *logical relationships*. The terms *dependencies* and *precedence relationships* also are used to describe these relationships. You might already be familiar with these if you've used Microsoft Project or similar project management software program. The four dependencies, or logical relationships, are as follows:

Finish-to-start (FS)   The finish-to-start relationship is the most frequently used relationship. This relationship says that the predecessor—or *from* activity—must finish before the successor—or *to* activity—can start. In PDM diagrams, this is the most often used logical relationship.

Start-to-finish (SF)   The start-to-finish relationship says that the predecessor activity must start before the successor activity can finish. This logical relationship is seldom used.

Finish-to-finish (FF)   The finish-to-finish relationship says that the predecessor activity must finish before the successor activity finishes.

Start-to-start (SS)   I think you're getting the hang of this. The start-to-start relationship says that the predecessor activity must start before the successive activity can start.

Keep these logical relationships (or dependencies) in mind when constructing your project schedule network diagram. Remember that finish-to-start is the most commonly used dependency in the PDM method.

Arrow Diagramming Method (ADM)

The *arrow diagramming method (ADM)* is visually the opposite of the PDM. The arrow diagramming method places activities on the arrows, which are connected to dependent activities with nodes. This method is also called *activity on arrow (AOA)*. This technique isn't used nearly as often as PDM, but some industries prefer the ADM to the PDM. For the record, note that ADM allows for more than one time estimate to determine duration and uses only the finish-to-start dependency. And there's one more unique note about ADM to tuck away: sometimes dummy activities must be plugged into the diagram to accurately display the dependencies.

The following example shows the ADM method applied to the house-painting example:

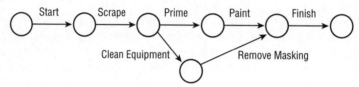

Schedule Network Templates

Schedule network templates are like the templates I've talked about in other processes. Perhaps the project you're working on is similar to a project that has been completed in the past. You can use a previous project schedule network diagram as a template for the current project. Or you might be working on a project with several deliverables that are fairly identical. You can use the first network diagram as a template and then modify it for each of the other deliverables.

Applying Leads and Lags

Leads and lags should be considered when determining dependencies. *Lags* delay *successor activities* (those that follow a predecessor activity) and require time added either to the start date or to the finish date of the activity you're scheduling. *Leads*, conversely, speed up the successor activities and require time to be subtracted from the start date or the finish date of the activity you're scheduling.

Let's revisit the house-painting example to put all this in perspective. In order to paint, you first need to scrape the peeling paint and then prime. However, you can't begin painting until the primer has dried, so you shouldn't schedule priming for Monday and painting for Tuesday if you need the primer to dry on Tuesday. Therefore, the priming activity requires lag time, so you need to add time to the end of this activity to allow for the drying time needed before you can start painting.

Lead time works just the opposite. Suppose, for this example, you could start priming before the scraping is finished. Maybe certain areas on the house don't require scraping, so you don't really need to wait until the scraping activity finishes to begin the priming activity. Priming in this example has lead time subtracted from the beginning of the activity so that this activity begins prior to the previous activity finishing.

I recommend you memorize the following graphic to help you remember the tools and techniques of the Activity Sequencing process and their characteristics for the exam. This might look a little strange, but I think it will work for you now that you understand what each of these diagramming methods is. This is information you need to know for the exam. If this graphic isn't useful for you, come up with your own mnemonic or sample that will help you remember which of these is which. Don't say I didn't warn you.

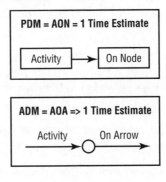

Activity Sequencing Outputs

Here are the outputs of the Activity Sequencing process:

- Project schedule network diagrams
- Activity list updates
- Activity attributes updates
- Requested changes

You've just spent a good deal of time describing the different types of project schedule network diagrams you can construct using PDM or ADM techniques. You can generate project schedule network diagrams on a computer, or you can draw them out by hand. Like the WBS, these diagrams might contain all the project details or might contain only summary-level details, depending on the complexity of the project. Summary-level activities are a collection of related activities also known as *hammocks*. Think of hammocks as a group of related activities rolled up into a summary heading that describes the activities likely to be contained in that grouping.

Keep in mind that the construction of these project schedule network diagrams might bring activities to light that you missed when defining your activity list, or it might make you break an activity down into two activities in places where you thought one activity might work. If this is the case, you will produce both activity list updates based on this new information as well as activity attributes updates.

After the activities are sequenced, the next steps involve estimating the resources and estimating the durations of the activities so that they can be plugged into the project schedule. You'll look at these topics in the next chapter.

Project Case Study: New Kitchen Heaven Retail Store

"Thanks everyone for your timely responses. I'll look over your list of roles and responsibilities, skills needed for the activities, and your activity lists." The meeting adjourns, and you head back to your office to review the documents. You'd like to get the project schedule constructed soon and go over it with Dirk.

Ricardo Ramirez from the IT department has outlined his resource needs and activity list. He reminds you that data is sent from each store over a T1 connection, not over satellite as Jill told you originally. Ricardo's activities are as follows. He has also taken the trouble to write them in sequential order:

1. Procure the T1 connection. This can be done concurrently with the other activities listed here. Ricardo will work on the procurement documents for this activity.

2. Run Ethernet cable throughout the building. This activity depends on the lease being signed and must finish before the build-out can start. Ricardo has one person on staff who can complete this specialized activity. His first available date is October 5.

3. Purchase the router, switch, server, and rack for the equipment room and four point-of-service terminals. Delivery time is two weeks. Ricardo will prepare the procurement documents for these items.

4. Install the router and test the connection. Testing depends on the T1 installation at demarcation. Ricardo's staff will do this activity.

5. Install the switch. Ricardo's staff will do this activity.

6. Install the server and test. The testing depends on the T1 connection installation. Ricardo's staff will do this activity.

7. The web team will add the new store location and phone number to the lookup function on the Internet site. Ricardo will assign his applications programming manager to this activity. This activity depends on the lease being signed.

Jake and Jill give you similar activity lists with human resource needs. You use a project management software tool to create a first draft of the project schedule network diagram. As you're staring at the screen, Dirk walks into your office.

"You look worried," Dirk says.

"Yes, I think we might have a problem. Jill mentioned she needs some lead time to stock shelves and that might interfere with the store build-out activity assigned to Jake's team. I don't have enough information yet to finish this. I need to get some time and cost estimates from everyone before I know for sure whether there's a problem."

"I'd rather know sooner than later if there's a problem, so get right on those estimates."

You toggle over to the calendaring system and see all three stakeholders are free Thursday morning. You set up a meeting time so you can explain to each of them what information you need next.

Project Case Study Checklist

Procurement

- Make-or-buy analysis

- Expert judgment

- Procurement documents prepared

Human Resource Planning

- Roles and responsibilities documented

Activity Definition

- Decomposition

- Expert judgment

- Activity list created

Activity Sequencing

- Dependencies determined

- Leads and lags determined

- Project schedule network diagram drafted

Exam Spotlight

You might find that the Activity Sequencing process gets a lot of coverage on the exam. Be certain you understand its inputs and tools and techniques well. Then again, remember the exam is randomly generated from a pool of questions, so don't ever concentrate all your memorization efforts on only one or two processes.

Understanding How This Applies to Your Next Project

In my organization, the Plan Purchases and Acquisitions process comes right after finalizing project scope because it takes a great deal of time and effort to procure goods and services. That means we have to start procuring resources as early in the project as possible in order to meet the project deadlines.

Many organizations, including mine, have procurement departments. Don't make the mistake of thinking they'll take care of the procurement for you. At a minimum, you will likely be responsible for writing the statement of work, writing the RFP, writing the contract requirements (as they pertain to the work of the project), creating the vendor selection criteria, and determining the schedule dates for contract work.

In all the organizations I've worked in, someone has always been responsible for procurement—whether it was a single person or an entire department. Typically, the procurement department defines many elements of the procurement management plan. Sure, the project team determines how many vendors need to be involved and how they'll be managed along with the schedule dates, but many other elements are predetermined such as the type of contract to use, the authority of the project team regarding the contract, how multiple vendors will be managed, and the identification of prequalified sellers.

The procurement department also determines what type of procurement document you should use depending on the types of resources you're acquiring and the amount of money you're spending. Typically, they'll have a template for you to use with all the legalese sections prepopulated, and you'll work on the sections that describe the work or resources you need for the project, milestones or schedule dates, and evaluation criteria.

Assumptions and constraints are listed as one of the elements of the procurement management plan. On the job, I include assumptions and constraints in the scope statement. Since procurement is an important factor in most every project I undertake, I know the assumptions and constraints (including procurement assumptions and constraints) can have a serious impact on my overall schedule, budget, and scope.

Human Resource Planning is a process you might not need to complete depending on the size and complexity of the project. I typically work with the same team members over and over again, so I know their skills, capabilities, and availability. However, if you're hiring contract resources for the project or you typically work with new team members on each project, I recommend creating a staffing management plan.

You can accomplish Activity Definition and Activity Sequencing on small- to medium-sized projects of minimal complexity in one step. In fact, I often combine these two processes with the Schedule Development process (I'll get to that one in the next chapter) and create the rough draft of a project schedule that shows all the activities and their sequences. I'll use the project schedule (with its listed activities) to obtain activity estimates and determine resource allocation. On large or complex projects, it isn't quite this easy. Defining every activity on a large project probably doesn't make sense because you'll end up with a schedule so long it can circle the earth twice. Large projects require you decompose the work to a point where you can assign it to an individual or team and you can easily measure progress. That doesn't mean every single activity needs to show up on the project schedule. Use your judgment when you're working with the processes leading up to and including Schedule Development. Here's a rule of thumb: if you're spending more time decomposing the work into activities than it takes to complete the activities, you've probably gone too far. On the other hand, if your team is confused about what needs to be accomplished in order to consider the milestone complete, you probably haven't decomposed enough.

Summary

This chapter's focus was on planning for project resources. Several aspects are involved in these planning activities, including procuring goods and services, planning human resource, and defining the activities in which human resources will be involved.

This chapter started with the Plan Purchases and Acquisitions process. This process identifies the goods or services you're going to purchase from outside the organization and determines which project the project team needs can meet. This involves tools and techniques such as make-or-buy decisions, expert judgment, and contract types. The procurement management plan is one of the outputs of this process and describes how procurement services will be managed throughout the project. The contract SOW (another output of this process) describes the work that will be contracted.

Plan Contracting creates the documents you'll use to procure the goods and services needed from outside the organization.

The Human Resource Planning process identifies and assigns roles and responsibilities and reporting relationships. Many times the roles and responsibilities assignments are depicted in a Responsibility Assignment Matrix (RAM) or a RACI chart. The staffing management plan describes how and when project team members will be acquired and is an output of the Human Resource Planning process.

The Activity Definition process involves decomposing the work packages into schedule activities that can be easily assigned and estimated. The output of this process is the activity list, activity attributes, milestone list, and requested changes.

The Activity Sequencing process takes the activities and puts them in a logical, sequential order based on dependencies. Dependencies exist when the current activity relies on some action from a predecessor activity or it impacts a successor activity. Three types of dependencies exist: mandatory, discretionary, and external. PDM (also known as AON) and ADM (also known as AOA) are two methods for displaying project schedule network diagrams. PDM has four logical relationships, or dependencies: finish-to-start, start-to-finish, finish-to-finish, and start-to-start.

Exam Essentials

Be able to name the purpose for the Plan Purchases and Acquisitions process.   The purpose of the Plan Purchases and Acquisitions process is to identify which project needs should be obtained from outside the organization. Make-or-buy analysis is used as a tool and technique to help determine this.

Be able to identify the contract types and their usage.   Contract types are a tool and technique of the Plan Purchases and Acquisitions process and include fixed price and cost reimbursable contracts. Use fixed price contracts for well-defined projects with a high value to the company, and use cost reimbursable contracts for projects with uncertainty and large investments early in the project life. The three types of cost reimbursable contracts are CPF (or CPPC), CPFF, and CPIF. Time and materials contracts are a cross between fixed-price and cost-reimbursable contracts.

Be able to name the outputs of the Plan Contracting process.   The outputs of Plan Contracting are procurement documents, evaluation criteria, and contract statement of work updates.

Be able to name the purpose of the Human Resource Planning process.   Human Resource Planning involves determining roles and responsibilities, reporting relationships for the project, and creating the staffing management plan, which describes how team members are acquired and the criteria for their release.

Be able to name the purpose of the Activity Definition process.   The Activity Definition process decomposes the work packages into schedule activities and creates an activity list, activity attributes, milestone list, and requested changes as its outputs.

Be able to identify the tools and techniques of Activity Sequencing.   The tools and techniques of Activity Sequencing are the precedence diagramming method (PDM), the arrow diagramming method (ADM), schedule network templates, dependency determination, and the application of leads and lags.

Be able to discuss the difference between PDM and ADM.   PDM (also known as AON) displays activity on nodes with connecting arrows showing dependencies. PDM has four logical relationships and uses the finish-to-start relationship most often. ADM (also known as AOA) displays activities on arrows with connecting nodes showing dependencies and uses only the finish-to-start relationship.

Key Terms

You're almost finished with the Planning process. The processes you worked with in this chapter help you make your case for the resources you need to complete project work. To be successful as a project manager, you'll need to thoroughly understand each of these processes. To be successful on the exam, you need to know them by the names used in *A Guide to the PMBOK*:

Activity Definition

Activity Sequencing

Human Resource Planning

Plan Contracting

Plan Purchases and Acquisitions

You've learned a lot of new key words in this chapter. PMI has worked hard to develop and define standard project management terms that apply across industries. Here is a list of some of the terms you came across in this chapter:

activity list	fixed-price contracts
Activity On Arrow (AOA)	fixed-price plus incentive contracts
Activity On Node (AON)	hammocks
Arrow Diagramming Method (ADM)	hard dependencies
contract	hard logic
contract statement of work (SOW)	lags
cost plus fee (CPF)	leads
cost plus fixed fee (CPFF)	logical relationships
cost plus incentive fee (CPIF)	lump-sum contracts
cost plus percentage of cost (CPCC)	make-or-buy analysis
cost-reimbursable contracts	mandatory dependencies
dependencies	milestones
discretionary dependencies	Organization breakdown structure (OBS)
external dependencies	precedence diagramming method (PDM)

precedence relationships

preferential logic

preferred logic

procurement documents

procurement management plan

RACI chart

resource breakdown structure (RBS)

responsibility assignment matrix (RAM)

soft logic

successor activities

Time and materials (T&M) contracts

Review Questions

1. You are the project manager for an upcoming outdoor concert event. You're working on the procurement plan for the computer software program that will control the lighting and screen projections during the concert. You're comparing the cost of purchasing a software product to the cost of your company programmers writing a custom software program. You are engaged in which of the following?

    A. Procurement planning

    B. Using expert judgment

    C. Creating the procurement management plan

    D. Make-or-buy analysis

2. You are the project manager for an outdoor concert event scheduled for one year from today. You're working on the procurement plan for the computer software program that will control the lighting and screen projections during the concert. You've decided to contract with a professional services company that specializes in writing custom software programs. You want to minimize the risk to the organization, so you'll opt for which contract type?

    A. Fixed price plus incentive

    B. Cost plus fixed fee

    C. Fixed price

    D. Cost plus incentive

3. You are the project manager for the Heart of Texas casual clothing company. It's introducing a new line of clothing called Black Sheep Ranch Wear. You will outsource the production of this clothing line to a vendor. The vendor has requested a contract SOW. All of the following statements are true except for which one?

    A. The SOW contains a description of the new clothing line.

    B. As the purchaser, you are required to write the SOW.

    C. The SOW contains the objectives of the project.

    D. The vendor requires a SOW to determine whether it can produce the clothing line given the detailed specifications of this product.

4. You are the project manager for the Heart of Texas casual clothing company. It's introducing a new line of clothing called Black Sheep Ranch Wear. You will outsource the production of this clothing line to a vendor. Your legal department has recommended you use a contract that reimburses the seller's allowable costs and builds in a bonus based on performance criteria they've outlined in their memo. Which of the following contract types will you use?

    A. CPIF

    B. CPFF

    C. CPF

    D. CPPC

5. All of the following statements are true regarding the Human Resource Planning process except for which one?

    A. Human Resource Planning involves determining roles and responsibilities.

    B. One of the Human Resource Planning outputs includes project organization charts that show the project's reporting relationships.

    C. The staffing management plan created in this process describes how and when resources will be acquired and released.

    D. A RAM (or RACI chart) is an output of this process that allows you to see all the people assigned to an activity.

6. Sally is a project manager working on a project that will require a specially engineered machine. Only three manufacturers can make the machine to the specifications Sally needs. The price of this machine is particularly critical to this project. The budget is limited, and there's no chance of securing additional funds if the bids for the machine come in higher than budgeted. She's developing the evaluation criteria for the bidders' responses and knows all of the following are true except for which one?

    A. Sally will use standard contract forms provided by her procurement department to write the contract for this machine.

    B. Sally will review the project management plan, including the risk register, as inputs to this process.

    C. Sally will base the evaluation criteria on price alone since the budget is a constraint.

    D. Sally will update the contract statement of work with any new information.

7. Which of the following are constraints that you might find during the Human Resource Planning process?

    A. Organizational structures, collective bargaining agreements, and economic conditions

    B. Organizational structures, technical interfaces, and interpersonal interfaces

    C. Organizational interfaces, collective bargaining agreements, and economic conditions

    D. Organizational interfaces, technical interfaces, and interpersonal interfaces

8. You are the project manager for a scheduled version release of your company's software tracking product. You have identified resources according to their activities. You might want to display this information in which of the following?

    A. AON

    B. PDM

    C. AOA

    D. RAM

9. All of the following statements describe the activity list except which one?

   A. The activity list is an output of the Activity Definition process.

   B. The activity list includes all activities of the project.

   C. The activity list is an extension of and a component of the WBS.

   D. The activity list includes an identifier and description of the activity.

10. You are the project manager for Design Your Web Site, Inc. Your company is designing the website for a national grocery store chain. You have your activity list in hand and are ready to diagram the activity dependencies using the PDM technique. Which of the following statements is true?

   A. PDM is also the AON diagramming method.

   B. PDM is also the AOA diagramming method.

   C. PDM is also the ADM diagramming method.

   D. PDM is also the AND diagramming method.

11. You are the project manager for Design Your Web Site, Inc. Your company is designing the website for a national grocery store chain. You have your activity list in hand and several alternative time estimates for each activity and are ready to diagram the activity dependencies. You should use which of the following?

   A. PDM techniques

   B. PDM or ADM techniques

   C. AON techniques

   D. ADM techniques

12. You are the project manager for Changing Tides video games. You have produced a project schedule network diagram and have updated the activity list. Which process have you just finished?

   A. The Activity Sequencing process, which identifies all the specific activities of the project

   B. The Activity Sequencing process, which identifies all the activity dependencies

   C. The Activity Definition process, which diagrams project network time estimates

   D. The Activity Definition process, which identifies all the activity attributes

13. You are working on a project that requires resources with expertise in the areas of hospitality management and entertainment. You are preparing your project schedule network diagram and know that you will use only finish-to-start dependencies. Which of the following diagramming methods does this describe?

   A. PDM

   B. ADM

   C. AON

   D. Network template

14. You have been hired as a contract project manager for Grapevine Vineyards. Grapevine wants you to design an Internet wine club for its customers. Customers must register before being allowed to order wine over the Internet so that legal age can be established. You know that the module to verify registration must be written and tested using data from Grapevine's existing database. This new module cannot be tested until the data from the existing system is loaded. This is an example of which of the following?

   A. Preferential logic

   B. Soft logic

   C. Discretionary dependency

   D. Hard logic

15. Which logical relationship does the PDM use most often?

   A. Start-to-finish

   B. Start-to-start

   C. Finish-to-finish

   D. Finish-to-start

16. You have been hired as a contract project manager for Grapevine Vineyards. Grapevine wants you to design an Internet wine club for its customers. Customers must register before being allowed to order wine over the Internet so that legal age can be established. You know that the module to verify registration must be written and tested using data from Grapevine's existing database. This new module cannot be tested until the data from the existing system is loaded. You are going to hire a vendor to perform the programming and testing tasks for this module to help speed up the project schedule. Since they'll have access to your customer list and potentially other trade secrets, you'll asked them to sign a nondisclosure agreement. This is an example of which of the following?

   A. Standard form

   B. Organizational process asset

   C. Fixed cost contract

   D. Procurement documents

17. You are the project manager for BB Tops, a nationwide toy store chain. Your new project involves a creating a prototype display at several stores across the country. You are using a RACI chart to display individuals and activities. What does RACI stand for?

   A. Responsible, accountable, consult, inform

   B. Responsible, assignment, control, inform

   C. Resource, activity, control, identify

   D. Resource, accountable, consult, identify

18. This process can directly influence the project schedule.

    A. Human Resource Planning

    B. Plan Purchases and Acquisitions

    C. Activity Sequencing

    D. Plan Contracting

19. You are the project manager for BB Tops, a nationwide toy store chain. Your new project involves a creating a prototype display at several stores across the country. You are hiring a contractor for portions of the project. The contract stipulates that you'll pay all allowable costs and an 8 percent fee over and above the allowable costs at the end of the contract. All of the following describe this type of contract except for which one?

    A. CPPC

    B. CPIF

    C. CPF

    D. Cost-reimbursable contract

20. This process uses tools like decomposition and rolling-wave planning to produce the activity list and other outputs. Because of the purpose of this process, which of the following is considered its primary input?

    A. WBS

    B. Project management plan

    C. PMIS (as part of enterprise environmental factors)

    D. Constraints and assumptions

Answers to Review Questions

1. D. Make-or-buy analysis is determining whether it's more cost effective to purchase the goods or services needed for the project or more cost effective for the organization to produce them internally.

2. C. Fixed-price contracts have the highest risk to the seller and the least amount of risk to the buyer. However, the price the vendor charges for the product or service will compensate for the amount of risk they're taking on.

3. B. Either the buyer or the seller can write the SOW. Sometimes the buyer will write the SOW and the seller might modify it and send it back to the buyer for verification and approval.

4. A. The cost plus incentive fee contract is one that the buyer reimburses the seller for the seller's allowable costs and includes an incentive or bonus for exceeding the performance criteria laid out in the contract.

5. D. The RAM and RACI charts are tools and techniques of this process.

6. C. Evaluation criteria can be based on price alone when there are many vendors who can readily supply the good or services. The question states that only three vendors make the machine, which means evaluation criteria should be based on more than price.

7. A. Constraints can be anything that limits the option of the project team. Organizational structures, collective bargaining agreements, and economic conditions are all constraints that you might encounter during this process.

8. D. The responsibility assignment matrix (RAM) links project resources with project activities.

9. C. The activity list is a component of the project schedule, not the WBS. The activity list includes all the project activities, an identifier, and a description of the activity. The activity list is an output of the Activity Definition process.

10. A. The precedence diagramming method is also known as the activity on node (AON) diagramming method.

11. D. PDM uses one time estimate to determine duration, while ADM can use more than one time estimate.

12. B. The Activity Sequencing process produces project schedule network diagrams, updates to the activity list, updates to the activity attributes, and requested changes. The purpose of this process is to identify all activity dependencies.

13. B. The arrow diagramming method uses only finish-to-start dependencies.

14. D. This is an example of a mandatory dependency, also known as *hard logic*. Mandatory dependencies are inherent in the nature of the work. Discretionary dependencies, also called *preferred logic*, *preferential logic*, and *soft logic*, are defined by the project management team.

15. D. Finish-to-start (FS) is the most commonly used logical relationship in PDM and most project management software packages.

16. A. Standard forms are a tool and technique of the Plan Contracting process. Standard forms can be nondisclosure agreements, standardized contracts, and so on.

17. A. RACI stands for responsible, accountable, consult, and inform.

18. B. Plan Purchases and Acquisitions can directly influence the project schedule, and the project schedule can directly influence this process.

19. B. This is a cost-reimbursable contract that includes a fee as a percentage of allowable costs. This type of contract is known as a cost plus fee (CPF) or a cost plus percentage of cost (CPPC) contract. A CPIF is a cost plus incentive fee contract that reimburses allowable costs and adds an incentive for exceeding the performance criteria laid out in the contract.

20. A. This question is describing the Activity Definition process. The purpose of this project is to decompose the work package elements of the WBS into activities. The WBS is the primary input of this process.

Chapter

7

Creating the Project Schedule and Budget

THE PMP EXAM CONTENT FROM THE PLANNING THE PROJECT PERFORMANCE DOMAIN COVERED IN THIS CHAPTER INCLUDES THE FOLLOWING:

✓ Obtain Plan Approval

The Planning process group has more processes than any other process group. As a result, a lot of time and effort goes into the Planning processes of any project. You'll find on some projects that you might spend almost as much time planning the project as you do executing and controlling it. This isn't a bad thing. The better planning you do up front, the more likely you'll have a successful project. Speaking of planning, together the Planning, Executing, and Monitoring and Controlling process groups account for almost 70 percent of the PMP exam questions, so *plan* on spending about the same percentage of your study time on these areas.

This is another fun-filled, action-packed chapter. You'll pick up from where you left off in the previous chapter and create estimates for your project activities and then wrap up the remaining Planning processes. I'll spend a good deal of time on showing how to develop the project schedule and discussing the project budget. These two documents are two of your most important planning documents. Everything you've done up to this point will help you create an accurate schedule and budget. You'll use these documents throughout the Executing and Monitoring and Controlling processes (along with several other documents you've created along the way) to help measure the progress of the project.

You'll start the Executing process group in the next chapter. But before you do that, though, here you'll get a good grasp of the project schedule and budget.

Estimating Activity Resources

All projects, from the smallest to the largest, require resources. The term *resources* in this case does not mean just people; it means all the physical resources required to complete the project. The *PMBOK Guide* defines resources as people, equipment, and materials. In reality, this includes people, equipment, supplies, materials, software, hardware—the list goes on depending on the project on which you're working. *Activity Resource Estimating* is concerned with determining the types of resources needed (both human and materials) and in what quantities for each schedule activity within a work package. You might be asking, "Didn't we already do the people part in the Human Resource Planning process?" The answer is no. Remember that Human Activity Resource Estimating determines roles and responsibilities and describes reporting relationships. Activity Resource Estimating determines what types or resources are needed and how many.

Remember, the activity resource output from this process is an input to the Human Activity Resource Estimating process.

The *PMBOK Guide* notes that Activity Resource Estimating should be closely coordinated with the Cost Estimating process (I'll talk about Cost Estimating later in this chapter). That's because resources—whether people or material or both—are typically the largest expense you'll have on any project. Identifying the resources becomes a critical component of the project planning process so estimates—and ultimately the project budget—can be accurately derived. You'll look at the inputs and tools and techniques that will help you document these requirements next.

Activity Resource Estimating Inputs

The Activity Resource Estimating process has several inputs you already know:

- Enterprise environmental factors
- Organizational process assets
- Activity list
- Activity attributes
- Resource availability
- Project management plan

The only one you haven't seen before is resource availability.

Resource availability is an output of the Acquire Project Team and Select Seller processes. The Acquire Project Team process isn't performed until the Executing process group, so this is a little out of order. In practice, you'll likely perform both Human Resource Planning and Acquire Project Team during the Planning stages of the project. For the exam, remember that resource availability isn't determined until the Executing stage and becomes an input to the Activity Resource Estimating process.

The resource availability output describes, believe it or not, the time frames in which resources (both human and material) are available. This will help you estimate the types of resources you might need for the project. For example, if you are working on a project that requires the use of specialized equipment during one of the project phases and the resource availability document shows that this equipment isn't available until sometime after the time frame in which you need it, you know you'll need to either make schedule adjustments or find another supplier who can provide the equipment when you need it. The same is true for human resources.

Estimating Activities Tools and Techniques

Your goal with the Activity Resource Estimating process is to determine the activity resource requirements, including quantity and availability. This process has five tools and techniques to help accomplish this output: expert judgment, alternatives analysis, published estimating data, project management software, and bottom-up estimating. You already know what expert judgment entails, so take a look at the remaining tools:

Alternatives analysis   Alternatives analysis is used when thinking about the methods you might use to accomplish the activities your resources have been assigned. Many times, you can accomplish an activity in more than one way, and alternatives analysis helps decide among the possibilities. For example, a subcompact car drives on the same roads a six-figure sports car travels. The sports car has a lot more features than the subcompact, it's faster, it's probably more comfortable, and it has a visual appeal that the subcompact doesn't. The sports car might be the valid resource choice for the project, but you should consider any alternatives. The same idea applies to human resources in that you might apply senior-level resources versus junior-level resources, or you could add resources to speed up the schedule. You can also consider make-or-buy analysis when determining alternatives.

Published estimating data   Estimating data might include organizational guidelines, industry rates or estimates, production rates, and so on. For example, your organization might have established price agreements with vendors that outline rates by resource type, or there might be industry estimates for production rates for your particular activity.

Project management software   Here you see project management software named as a tool and technique rather than as an enterprise environmental factor input. Project management software can help estimate resource needs and document resource availability. It might also produce an RBS, resource rates, calendars, and availability.

Bottom-up estimating   Bottom-up estimating is a process of estimating individual schedule activities or costs and then adding these together to come up with a total estimate for the work package. Here you estimate every schedule activity individually and then roll up that estimate, or add them all together, to come up with a total. This is an accurate means of estimating provided the estimates at the schedule activity level are accurate. However, it takes a considerable amount of time to perform bottom-up estimating because every activity must be assessed and estimated accurately to be included in the bottom-up calculation. The smaller and more detailed the activity, the greater the accuracy and cost of this technique.

Activity Resource Estimating Outputs

As mentioned, the purpose of the Activity Resource Estimating process is to develop the activity resource requirements output that describes the types of resources and the quantity needed for each schedule activity. Work package estimates are derived from the cumulative total of each schedule activity within the work package. You should also prepare a narrative description for this output that describes how you determined the estimate and the assumptions you made about the resources and their availability.

You'll use the information from this output in the next process (Activity Duration Estimates) to determine the length of time each activity will take to complete. That, of course, depends on the quantity and skill level of the resources assigned, which is the reason you estimate resources before you try to determine duration.

The remaining outputs of this process are activity attribute updates, resource breakdown structure, resource calendar updates, and requested changes. I've covered each of these outputs previously with the exception of resource calendar updates.

Resource calendars look at a particular resource or groups of resources and their skills, abilities, quantity, and availability. Perhaps your project calls for a marketing resource and the person assigned to the marketing activities is on an extended vacation in October. The resource calendar would show this person's vacation schedule. It also shows holidays the company recognizes. Resource calendars also examine the quantity, capability, and availability of equipment and material resources that have a potential to impact the project schedule. For example, suppose your project calls for a hydraulic drill, and your organization owns only one. The resource calendar will tell you whether it's scheduled for another job at the same time it's needed for your project. The updates portion of this output refers to updating the resource calendar with changes to any of the elements you've recorded here.

You can see how these "Activity" processes have built upon each other. First you defined the activities, then you determined dependencies and sequenced them in the correct order, and next you determined what types and quantities of resources are required to complete the activities. Now you're ready to begin estimating the duration of these activities so you can plug them into the project schedule.

Estimating Activity Durations

The *Activity Duration Estimating* process attempts to estimate the work effort, resources, and number of work periods needed to complete each schedule activity. The *activity duration estimates* are the primary output of this process. These are quantifiable estimates expressed as the number of work periods needed to complete a schedule activity. Work periods are usually expressed in hours or days. However, larger projects might express duration in weeks or months. Work periods are the activity duration estimates, and they become inputs to the project schedule in a later process.

When estimating activity duration, make certain to include all the time that will elapse from the beginning of the activity until the work is completed. For example, consider the earlier example of the house-painting project. You estimate that it will take three days, including drying time, to prime the house. Now, let's say priming is scheduled to begin on Saturday, but your crew doesn't work on Sunday. The activity duration in this case is four days, which includes the three days to prime and dry plus the Sunday the crew doesn't work. Most project management software programs will handle this kind of situation automatically.

Progressive elaboration comes into play during this process also. Estimates typically start at a fairly high level, and as more and more details are known about the deliverables and their associated activities, the estimates become more accurate. You should rely on those folks who have the most knowledge of the activities you're trying to estimate to help you with this process.

Activity Duration Estimating Inputs

The inputs to this process include enterprise environmental factors, organization process assets, project scope statement, activity list, activity attributes, activity resource requirements, resource calendars, and the project management plan, including the risk register and activity cost estimates.

A few of the important elements regarding these inputs apply here as you've seen in past processes, including databases, historical information, constraints, and assumptions. The project calendars (considered a part of the organizational process assets) and activity resource requirements are especially useful during this process.

Activity Duration Estimating Tools and Techniques

The Activity Duration Estimating process has several new tools and techniques:

- Expert judgment
- Analogous estimating
- Parametric estimating
- Three-point estimates
- Reserve analysis

You'll take a look at each of these tools and techniques next.

Expert Judgment

The staff members who will perform activities will most accurately estimate them. In this case, team members use expert judgment because of their experience with similar activities in the past. You should be careful with these estimates, though, because they are subject to bias and aren't based on any scientific means. Your experts should consider that resource levels, resource productivity, resource capability, risks, and other factors can impact estimates. It's good practice to combine expert judgment with historical information and use as many experts as you can.

Analogous Estimating (a.k.a. Top-Down Estimating)

Analogous estimating, also called *top-down estimating,* is a form of expert judgment. With this technique, you will use the actual duration of a similar activity completed on a previous project to determine the duration of the current activity—provided the information was documented and stored with the project information on the previous project. This technique is most useful when the previous activities you're comparing are similar to the activity you're estimating and don't just appear to be similar. And you want the folks who are working on the estimate to have experience with these activities so they can provide reasonable estimates. This technique is especially helpful when detailed information about the project is not available, such as in the early phases of the project.

Top-down estimating techniques are also used to estimate total project duration, particularly when you have a limited amount of information about the project. The best way to think about top-down techniques is to look at the estimate as a whole. Think about being on a mountaintop where you can see the whole picture as one rather than all the individual items that make up the picture.

For instance, let's return to the house-painting example. You would compare a previous house-painting project to the current house-painting project, where the houses are of similar size and the paint you're using is the same quality. You can use the first house-painting project to estimate the project duration for the second house-painting project because of the similarities in the project.

Top-down techniques are useful when you're early in the project Planning processes and are only just beginning to flesh out all the details of the project. Sometimes during the project selection process, the selection committee might want an idea of the project's duration. You can derive a project estimate at this stage by using top-down techniques.

Exam Spotlight

The *PMBOK Guide* states that you can also use analogous estimating to determine overall project duration. *However* (this is the key word), calculating overall project duration is performed during the Schedule Development process, not the Activity Duration Estimating process.

Parametric Estimating

Parametric estimating is a quantitatively based estimating method that multiplies the quantity of work by the rate. The best way to describe it with is with an example. Suppose you are working on a companywide network upgrade project. This requires you to run new cable to the switches on every floor in the building. You can use parametric estimates to determine activity duration estimates by taking a known element—in this case, the amount of cable needed—and multiplying it by the amount of time it takes to install a unit of cable to come up with an estimate. In other words, suppose you have 10,000 meters of new cable to run. You know from past experience it takes one hour to install 100 meters. Using this measurement, you can determine an estimate for this activity of 100 hours to run the new cable. Therefore, the cable activity duration estimate is 100 hours.

Three-Point Estimates

Three-point estimates, as you can probably guess, use three estimates that are averaged to come up with a final estimate. The three estimates are the most likely, optimistic, and pessimistic. You'll want to rely on experienced folks to give you these estimates. The most likely estimate assumes there are no disasters and the activity can be completed as planned. The optimistic estimate is the fastest time frame in which your resource can complete the activity. And the pessimistic estimate assumes the worst happens and it takes much longer than planned to get the activity completed. You'd average these three estimates to come up with an overall estimate.

 You'll look more closely at this tool and technique later in this chapter in the section "Schedule Development Tools and Techniques."

Reserve Analysis

Reserve time—also called *buffer* or *contingency time* in the *PMBOK Guide* —means adding a portion of time to the activity to account for schedule risk. You might choose to add a percentage of time or a set number of work periods to the activity or the overall schedule. For example, you know it will take 100 hours to run new cable based on the quantitative estimate you came up with earlier. You also know that sometimes you hit problem areas when running the cable. To make sure you don't impact the project schedule, you build in a reserve time of 10 percent of your original estimate to account for the problems you might encounter. This brings your activity duration estimate to 110 hours for this activity.

 Real World Scenario

Desert State University (DSU)

DSU has hired a contract agency to create its new registration website. The website will allow students in good academic standing to register for classes over the Internet. You have been appointed the project manager for the DSU side of this project. You'll be working with Henry Lu from Websites International to complete this project.

Henry has given you an activity list and asked for time estimates that he can plug into the project plan.

Your first stop is Mike Walter's desk. He's the expert on the mainframe registration system and will be writing the interface programs to accept registration data from the new website. Mike will also create the download that the Internet program will use to verify students' academic standing. Mike has created other programs just like this in the past. His expertise and judgment are very reliable.

The next stop is Kate Langdon. She's the new team leader over the testing group. Kate has been with DSU for only one month. Since she has no experience working with DSU data and staff members, she tells you she'll get back to you within a week with estimates for the testing activities. She plans to read through the project binders of some similar projects and base her estimates against the historical information on similar projects. She'll run the estimates by her lead tester before giving them to you.

You've asked both of your resources to provide you with three-point estimates. Mike Walter's estimates are an example of using the tool and technique of expert judgment to derive activity duration estimates. The estimates expected from Kate Langdon will be derived using historical information (implied by the research she's going to do into past similar projects) and expert judgment because she's involving her lead tester to verify the estimates.

Activity Duration Estimating Outputs

Everything I've discussed to this point has brought you to the primary output of this process: the activity duration estimates. You use the inputs and tools and techniques to establish these estimates. As mentioned earlier, activity duration estimates are an estimate of the required work periods needed to complete the activity. This is a quantitative measure usually expressed in hours, weeks, days, or months.

One factor to note about your final estimates as an output to this process is that they should contain a range of possible results. In the cable-running example, you would state the activity duration estimates as "100 hours ±10 hours" to show that the actual duration will take at least 90 hours and might go as long as 110 hours. Or you could use percentages to express this range.

The other output of Activity Duration Estimating is activity attribute updates. You will update the activity attributes with the duration estimate and the assumptions you used when deriving the estimates.

Now that you have all the activity information in hand, along with a host of other inputs, you're ready to develop the project schedule.

 Real World Scenario

Exam Spotlight

Remember that you perform the "Activity" processes in this order: Activity Definition, Activity Sequencing, Activity Resource Estimating, and Activity Duration Estimating. Schedule Development comes after you've completed these processes.

Developing the Project Schedule

The *Schedule Development* process is the heart of the Planning process group. This is where you lay out the schedule for your project activities, determine their start and finish dates, and finalize activity sequences and durations. Schedule Development, along with Activity Resource Estimating and Activity Duration Estimating, is repeated several times before you actually come up with the project schedule. The project schedule, once it's approved, serves as the *schedule baseline* for the project that you can track against in later processes.

You'll learn later in this section that project management software comes in handy during this process. In fact, it is one of the tools and techniques of this process.

Remember that you cannot perform Schedule Development until you have completed all the following processes of project Planning: Scope Planning, Scope Definition, Create WBS, Risk Identification, Risk Response Planning, Plan Purchases and Acquisitions, Activity Resource Estimating, Activity Definition, Activity Sequencing, and Activity Duration Estimating.

It's interesting to note that there is a schedule management plan but it isn't created during this process, and it isn't an output of this process as other management plans have been. The *PMBOK Guide* notes that the schedule management plan (a subsidiary of the project management plan) is produced as part of the Develop Project Management Plan process and contains the criteria for formatting, developing, and controlling the project schedule.

This process has a lot of material to cover. I'll start with the inputs to the Schedule Development process and then follow up with an in-depth discussion of the tools and techniques of the process. These techniques will help you get to the primary output of this process, which is the project schedule.

Schedule Development Inputs

Schedule Development has nine inputs, seven of which are outputs from other Planning processes. The inputs are as follows:

- Organizational process assets
- Project scope statement
- Activity list
- Activity attributes
- Project schedule network diagrams
- Activity resource requirements
- Resource calendars
- Activity duration estimates
- Project management plan (risk register)

You can see how important it is to perform all the Planning processes accurately because the information you derive from almost every process in the Planning group is used somewhere else in Planning, many of them here. Your project schedule will reflect the information you know at this point in time. If you have incorrectly estimated activity durations or didn't identify the right dependencies, for example, the inputs to this process will be distorted, and your project schedule will not be correct. It's definitely worth the investment of time to correctly plan your project and come up with accurate outputs for each of the Planning processes.

As with several other processes, constraints and assumptions are highlighted as the elements of the project scope statement to pay particular attention to. Constraints are with you throughout the life of the project. The most important constraints to consider in the Schedule Development process are time constraints. According to the *PMBOK Guide*, the time constraints in this process fall into two categories: imposed dates and key events/major milestones.

Imposed dates restrict the start or finish date of activities. The two most common constraints, *start no earlier than* and *finish no later than*, are used by most computerized project management software programs. Let's look once again at the house-painting example. The painting activity cannot start until the primer has dried. If the primer takes 24 hours to dry and is scheduled to be completed on Wednesday, this implies the painting activity can *start no earlier than* Thursday. This is an example of an imposed date.

Key events or milestones refer to the completion of specific deliverables by a specific date. Stakeholders, customers, or management staff might request that certain deliverables be completed or delivered by specific dates. Once you've agreed to those dates (even if the agreement is only verbal), it's often cast in stone and difficult to change. These dates, therefore, become constraints.

Be careful of the delivery dates you commit to your stakeholders or customers. You might think you're simply discussing the matter or throwing out ideas, while the stakeholder might take what you've said as fact. Once the stakeholder believes the deliverable or activity will be completed by a specific date, there's almost no convincing them that the date needs changing.

Schedule Development Tools and Techniques

The primary output of Schedule Development is the project schedule. You can employ several tools and techniques in order to produce this output. The tools and techniques you choose will depend on the complexity of the project. For the exam, however, you'll need to know them all.

Schedule Development has 10 tools and techniques:

- Schedule network analysis
- Critical path method
- Schedule compression
- What-if scenario analysis
- Resource leveling
- Critical chain method
- Project management software
- Applying calendars
- Adjusting leads and lags
- Schedule model

A lot of information is packed into some of these tools and techniques, and you should dedicate study time to each of them for the exam. I discussed a few of these inputs earlier but they have new twists in the Schedule Development process, so you'll take a look at each of them next.

Schedule Network Analysis

Schedule network analysis produces the project schedule. It involves calculating early and late start dates and early and late finish dates for project activities (as does the critical path method).

It uses a schedule model and other analytical techniques such as critical path and critical chain method, what-if analysis, and resource leveling (all of which are other tools and techniques in this process) to help calculate these dates and create the schedule. These calculations are performed without taking resource limitations into consideration, so the dates you end up with are theoretical. What you're attempting to establish at this point is the time periods within which the activities can be scheduled. Resource limitations and other constraints will be taken into consideration when you get to the outputs of this process.

Critical Path Method

Critical path method (CPM) is a schedule network analysis technique. It determines the amount of float, or schedule flexibility, for each of the network paths by calculating the earliest start date, earliest finish date, latest start date, and latest finish date for each activity. This is a schedule network analysis technique that relies on sequential networks (one activity occurs before the next, a series of activities occurring concurrently is completed before the next series of activities, and so on) and on a single duration estimate for each activity. Keep in mind that CPM is a method to determine schedule durations without regard to resource availability.

The *critical path (CP)* is generally the longest full path on the project. Any project activity with a float time that equals zero is considered a critical path task. The critical path can change under a few conditions. When activities with float time use up all their float, they can become critical path tasks. Or you might have a milestone midway through the project with a *finish no later than* constraint that can change the critical path if it isn't met.

Float time is also called *slack time,* and you'll see these terms used interchangeably. There are two types of float: total float and free float. *Total float (TF)* is the amount of time you can delay the earliest start of a task without delaying the ending of the project. *Free float (FF)* is the amount of time you can delay the start of a task without delaying the earliest start of a successor task.

In the following section, you'll calculate the CP for a sample project, and I'll illustrate how you derive all the dates, the CP, and the float times.

Gathering Activity and Dependency Information

Let's say you are the project manager for a new software project. The company you are working for is venturing into the movie rental business over the Web. You need to devise a software system that tracks all the information related to rentals and also supplies the management team with reports that will help them make good business decisions. For purposes of illustration, I'm showing only a limited portion of the tasks that you would have on a project like this.

You'll start this example by plugging information from the processes you've already completed into a table (a complete example is shown later in Table 7.1 in the section "Calculating the Critical Path"). The list of activities comes from the Activity Definition process. The durations for each activity are listed in the Duration column and were derived during the Activity Duration Estimating process. The duration times are listed in days.

The Dependency column lists the activities that require a previous activity to finish before the current activity can start. You're using only finish-to-start relationships. For example, you'll see that activity 2 and activity 4 each depend on activity 1 to finish before they can begin. The dependency information came from the Activity Sequencing process. Now, you'll proceed to calculating the dates.

Calculating the Forward and Backward Pass

Project Deliverables is the first activity and, obviously, where the project starts. This activity begins on April 1. Project Deliverables has a 12-day duration. So, take April 1 and add 12 days to this to come up with an early finish date of April 12. Watch out, because you need to count day one, or April 1, as a full workday. The simplest way to do this calculation is to take the early start date, add the duration, and subtract one. Therefore, the early finish date for the first activity is April 12. By the way, we are ignoring weekends and holidays for this example. Activity 2 depends on activity 1, so it cannot start until activity 1 has finished. Its earliest start date is April 13, because activity 1 finished at the end of the previous day. Add the duration to this date minus one to come up with the finish date.

You'll notice that, since activity 4 depends on activity 1 finishing, its earliest start date is also April 13. Continue to calculate the remaining early start and early finish dates in the same manner. This calculation is called a *forward pass.*

To calculate the latest start and latest finish dates, you begin with the last activity. The latest finish for activity 9 is July 10. Since the duration is only one day, July 10 is also the latest start date. You know that activity 8 must finish before activity 9 can begin, so activity 8's latest finish date, July 9, is one day prior to activity 9's latest start date, July 10. Subtract the duration of activity 8 (three days) from July 9 and add one day to get the latest start date of July 7. You're performing the opposite calculation that you did for the forward pass. This calculation is called a *backward pass,* as you might have guessed. Continue calculating the latest start and latest finish through activity 4.

Activity 3 adds a new twist. Here's how it works: activity 7 cannot begin until activity 3 and activity 6 are completed. No other activity depends on the completion of activity 3. If activity 7's latest start date is June 29, activity 3's latest finish date must be June 28. June 28 minus eight days plus one gives you a latest start date of June 21. Activity 3 depends on activity 2, so activity 2 must be completed prior to beginning activity 3. Calculate these dates just as you did for activities 9 through 4.

Activity 1 still remains. Activity 4 cannot start until activity 1 is completed. If activity 4's latest start date is April 13, the latest finish date for activity 1 must be April 12. Subtract the duration of activity 1, and add one to come up with a latest start date of April 1. Alternatively, you can calculate the forward pass and backward pass by saying the first task starts on day zero and then adding the duration to this. For example, activity number 1's earliest start date is April 1, which is day zero. Add 12 days to day zero, and you come up with an earliest finish date of April 12.

You determine the calculation for float/slack time by subtracting the earliest start date from the latest start date. If the float time equals zero, the activity is on the critical path.

Calculating the Critical Path

To determine the CP duration of the project, add the duration of every activity with zero float. You should come up with 101 days because you're adding the duration for all activities except for activity 2 and activity 3. A critical path task is any task that cannot be changed without impacting the project end date. By definition, these are all tasks with zero float.

Another way to determine the critical path is by looking at the network diagram. If the duration is included with the information on the node or if start and end dates are given, you simply calculate the duration and then add the duration of the longest path in the diagram to determine the CP. However, this method is not as accurate as what's shown in Table 7.1. Figure 7.1 shows the same project in diagram form. The duration is printed in the top-right corner of each node. Add the duration of each path to determine which one is the critical path.

Remember that CP is usually the path with the longest duration. In Figure 7.1, path 1-2-3-7-8-9 equals 34 days. Path 1-4-5-6-7-8-9 equals 101 days; therefore, this path is the critical path.

TABLE 7.1   CPM Calculation

Activity Number	Activity Description	Dependency	Duration	Early Start	Early Finish	Late Start	Late Finish	Float/ Slack
1	Project Deliverables	—	12	4/1	4/12	4/1	4/12	0
2	Procure Hardware	1	2	4/13	4/14	6/19	6/20	67
3	Test Hardware	2	8	4/15	4/22	6/21	6/28	67
4	Procure Software Tools	1	10	4/13	4/22	4/13	4/22	0
5	Write Programs	4	45	4/23	6/6	4/23	6/6	0
6	Test and Debug	5	22	6/7	6/28	6/7	6/28	0
7	Install	3, 6	8	6/29	7/6	6/29	7/6	0
8	Training	7	3	7/7	7/9	7/7	7/9	0
9	Acceptance	8	1	7/10	7/10	7/10	7/10	0

FIGURE 7.1 Critical path diagram

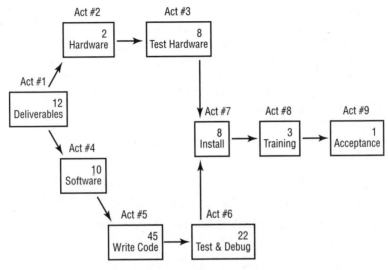

Calculating Expected Value Using PERT

Program Evaluation and Review Technique (PERT) is a method that isn't discussed in the *PMBOK Guide,* but you might encounter it on the exam. The United States Navy developed PERT in the 1950s. The Navy was working on one of the most complex engineering projects in history at the time—the Polaris Missile Program—and needed a way to manage the project and forecast the project schedule with a high degree of reliability. PERT was developed to do just that.

PERT and CPM are similar techniques. The difference is that CPM uses the most likely duration to determine project duration, while PERT uses what's called *expected value* (or the weighted average). *Expected value* is calculated using the three-point estimates for activity duration (I talked about three-point estimates earlier in this chapter) and then finding the weighted average of those estimates (I'll talk about weighted average in the "Calculating Expected Value" section later in this chapter). If you take this one step further and determine the standard deviation of each activity, you can assign a confidence factor to your project estimates. Without getting too heavily involved in the mathematics of probability, understand that for data that fits a bell curve, which is what you're about to calculate with the PERT technique, the following is true:

- Work will finish within plus or minus three standard deviations 99.73 percent of the time.

- Work will finish within plus or minus two standard deviations 95.44 percent of the time.

- Work will finish within plus or minus one standard deviation 68.26 percent of the time.

Calculating Expected Value

The three-point estimates used to calculate expected value are the optimistic estimate, the pessimistic estimate, and the most likely estimate. Going back to the software example, let's find out what these three time estimates might look like for the activity called Write Programs. You get these estimates by asking the lead programmer, or key team member, to estimate the optimistic, pessimistic, and most likely duration for the activity based on past experience. Other historical information could be used to determine these estimates as well. Say in this case that you're given 38 days for the optimistic time, 57 days for the pessimistic, and 45 days for the most likely. (Forty-five days was derived from the Activity Duration Estimating process and is the estimate you used to calculate CPM.)

The formula to calculate expected value is as follows:

(optimistic + pessimistic + (4 × most likely)) ÷ 6

The expected value for the Write Programs activity is as follows:

(38 + 57 + (4 × 45)) 6 = 45.83

The formula for standard deviation, which helps you determine confidence level, is as follows:

(pessimistic – optimistic) ÷ 6

The standard deviation for your activity is as follows:

(57 – 38) ÷ 6 = 3.17

You could say the following given the information you now have:

- There is a 68.26 percent chance that the Write Programs activity will be completed in 42.66 days to 49 days.

- There is a 95.44 percent chance that the Write Programs activity will be completed in 39.49 days to 52.17 days.

You calculated the range of dates for the 68.26 percent chance by adding and subtracting one standard deviation, 3.17, from the expected value, 45.83. You calculated the 95.44 percent chance by multiplying the standard deviation times 2, which equals 6.34, and adding and subtracting that result from the expected value to come up with the least number of days and the most number of days it will take to finish the activity. Generally speaking, two standard deviations, or 95.44 percent, is a close enough estimate for most purposes.

The higher the standard deviation is for an activity, the higher the risk. Since standard deviation measures the difference between the pessimistic and the optimistic times, a greater spread between the two, which results in a higher number, indicates a greater risk. Conversely, a low standard deviation means less risk.

Determining Date Ranges for Project Duration

Let's bring your table of activities back and plug in the expected values and the standard deviation for each (please see Table 7.2).

Now let's look at the total project duration using PERT and the standard deviation to determine a range of dates for project duration. You should add only the tasks that are on the critical path. Remember from the CPM example that activities 2 and 3 are not on the critical path, so their expected value and standard deviation calculations have been left blank in this table. When you add all the remaining tasks, the total expected value duration is 102.99 days, or 103 days rounded to the nearest day.

TABLE 7.2   PERT Calculation

Activity Number	Activity Description	Optimistic	Pessimistic	Most Likely	Expected Value	Standard Deviation	SD Squared
1	Project Deliverables	10	14	12	12.00	0.67	0.45
2	Procure Hardware	—	—	—	—	—	—
3	Test Hardware	—	—	—	—	—	—
4	Procure Software Tools	8	14	10	10.33	1.00	1.0
5	Write Programs	38	57	45	45.83	3.17	10.05
6	Test and Debug	20	30	22	23.00	1.67	2.79
7	Install	5	10	8	7.83	0.83	0.69
8	Training	3	3	3	3.00	0	0
9	Acceptance	1	1	1	1.00	0	0
Totals for CP Tasks					**102.99**		**14.98**

Your next logical conclusion might be to add the Standard Deviation column to get the standard deviation for the project. Unfortunately, you cannot add the standard deviations because you will come out with a number that is much too high. Totaling the standard deviations assumes that all the tasks will run over schedule, and that's not likely. It is likely that a few tasks will run over but not every one of them. So now you're probably wondering how to calculate the magic number.

You might have noticed an extra column at the right called SD Squared. This is the standard deviation squared—or for those of you with math phobias out there, the standard deviation multiplied by itself.

Once you have calculated the standard deviation squared for each activity, add the squares, for a total of 14.98. There's one more step, and you're done. Take the square root of 14.98 (you'll need a calculator) to come up with 3.87. This is the standard deviation you will use to determine your range of projected completion dates. Here's a recap of these last few calculations:

Total expected value = 103.00

Sum of SD Squared = 14.98

Square root of SD Squared = 3.87

You can now make the following predictions regarding your project:

- There is a 68.26 percent chance that the project will be completed in 99.13 days to 106.87 days.

- There is a 95.44 percent chance that the project will be completed in 95.26 days to 110.74 days.

Exam Spotlight

For the exam, I recommend you know that one standard deviation gives you a 68 percent (rounded) probability and two standard deviations gives you a 95 percent (rounded) probability. Also, know how to calculate the range of project duration dates based on the expected value and standard deviation calculation. You probably don't need to memorize how to calculate the standard deviation, because most of the questions give you this information. You should, however, memorize the PERT formula and know how it works. It wouldn't hurt to memorize the standard deviation formula as well—you never know what might show up on the exam.

PERT is not used often today. When it is, it's used for very large, highly complex projects. However, PERT is a useful technique to determine project duration when your activity durations are uncertain. It's also useful for calculating the duration for individual tasks in your schedule that might be complex or risky. You might decide to use PERT for a handful of the activities (those with the highest amount of risk, for example) and use other techniques to determine duration for the remaining activities.

Schedule Compression

Schedule compression is a form of mathematical analysis that's used to shorten the project schedule without changing the project scope. Compression is simply shortening the project schedule to accomplish all the activities sooner than estimated.

Schedule compression might happen when the project end date has been predetermined or if, after performing the CPM or PERT techniques, you discover that the project is going to take longer than the original promised date. In the CPM example, you calculated the end date to be July 10. What if the project was undertaken and a July 2 date was promised? That's when you'll need to employ one or both of the duration compression techniques: crashing and fast tracking.

Crashing

Crashing is a compression technique that looks at cost and schedule trade-offs. One of the things you might do to crash the schedule is add resources—from either inside or outside the organization—to the critical path tasks. It wouldn't help you to add resources to noncritical path tasks, because these tasks don't impact the schedule end date anyway because they have float time. You might also limit or reduce the project requirements. Ask stakeholders whether the features or functions are "nice to have" or necessary. You might also try changing the sequence of tasks. This sometimes shortens the schedule but isn't always possible.

Fast Tracking

I talked about fast tracking in Chapter 1, "What Is a Project?" *Fast tracking* is performing two tasks in parallel that were previously scheduled to start sequentially. Fast tracking can increase project risk and might cause the project team to have to rework tasks. For example, fast tracking is often performed in object-oriented programming. The programmers might begin writing code on several modules at once, out of sequential order and prior to the completion of the design phase.

Be certain to check the critical path when you've used the crashing technique because crashing might have changed the critical path. Also consider that crashing doesn't always come up with a reasonable result. It often increases the costs of the project as well. The idea with crashing is to try to gain the greatest amount of schedule compression with the least amount of cost.

What-If Scenario Analysis

What-if scenario analysis uses different sets of activity assumptions to produce multiple project durations. For example, what would happen if a major deliverable was delayed or the weather prevents you from completing a deliverable on time? What-if analysis weighs these questions and their assumptions and determines the feasibility of the project schedule under these conditions. Simulation techniques such as Monte Carlo analysis use a range of probable activity durations for each activity, and those ranges are then used to calculate a range of probable duration results for the project itself. Monte Carlo runs the possible activity durations and schedule projections many, many times to come up with the schedule projections and their probability, critical path duration estimates, and float time.

Exam Spotlight

For the exam, remember that Monte Carlo is a simulation technique that shows the probability of all the possible project completion dates.

Resource Leveling

Earlier, I said that CPM and PERT do not consider resource availability. Now that you have a schedule of activities and have determined the critical path, it's time to plug in resources for those activities and adjust the schedule according to any resource constraints you discover.

Resource leveling—also called the *resource-based method*—is used when resources are limited or time constrained (especially those assigned to critical path activities) and when specific schedule dates need to be met.

Remember that you identified resources and resource estimates during the Human Resource Planning and Activity Resource Estimating processes. Now during Schedule Development, resources are assigned to specific activities. Usually, you'll find that your initial schedule has periods of time with more activities than you have resources to work on them. You will also find that it isn't always possible to assign 100 percent of your team members' time to tasks. Sometimes your schedule will show a team member who is overallocated, meaning they're assigned to more work than they can physically perform in the given time period. Other times, they might not be assigned enough work to keep them busy during the time period. This problem is easy to fix. You can assign underallocated resources to multiple tasks to keep them busy.

Resource Assignments

Having overallocated resources is a little more difficult problem to resolve. Resource leveling attempts to smooth out the resource assignments to get tasks completed without overloading the individual while trying to keep the project on schedule. This typically takes the form of allocating resources to critical path tasks first.

The project manager can accomplish resource leveling in several ways. You might delay the start of a task to match the availability of a key team member. Or you might adjust the resource assignments so that more tasks are given to team members who are underallocated. You could require the resources to work mandatory overtime—that one always goes over well! Perhaps you can split some tasks so that the team member with the pertinent knowledge or skill performs the critical part of the task and the noncritical part of the task is given to a less-skilled team member. All these methods are forms of resource leveling.

Generally speaking, resource leveling of overallocated team members extends the project end date. If you're under a date constraint, you'll have to rework the schedule after assigning resources to keep the project on track with the committed completion date. This might include moving key resources from noncritical tasks and assigning them to critical path tasks or adjusting assignments as previously mentioned. Reallocating those team members with slack time to critical path tasks to keep them on schedule is another option. Don't forget, fast tracking is an option to keep the project on schedule also.

Reverse Resource Allocation Scheduling

Reverse resource allocation scheduling is a technique used when key resources—like a thermodynamic expert, for example—are required at a specific point in the project and they are the only resource, or resources, available to perform these activities. This technique requires the resources to be scheduled in reverse order (that is, from the end date of the project rather than the beginning) in order to assign this key resource at the correct time.

Exam Spotlight

Resource leveling can cause the original critical path to change.

Critical Chain Method

Critical chain method is a schedule network analysis technique that accounts for limited or restricted resources when modifying the project schedule. This method typically schedules high-risk tasks early in the project so that problems can be identified and addressed right away. It allows for combining several tasks into one task when one resource is assigned to all the tasks.

Critical chain uses both deterministic (step-by-step) and probabilistic approaches. A few steps are involved in the critical chain process:

- Construct the schedule network diagram using activity duration estimates (you'll use nonconservative estimates in this method).
- Define dependencies.
- Define constraints.
- Calculate critical path.
- Enter resource availability into the schedule.

Often, the critical path will change once you've entered the resource availability. That's because the critical chain method adds nonwork activities where needed as duration buffers to help manage the planned activity durations. After the buffers are added, the planned activities are then scheduled at their latest start and finish dates.

Project Management Software

Given the examples you've worked through on Schedule Development and resource leveling, you probably already have concluded how much project management software might help you with these processes. Project management software automates the mathematical calculations (such as forward and backward pass) and performs resource-leveling functions for you.

Exam Spotlight

CPM manages the total float of schedule networks paths, whereas critical chain manages buffer activity durations and resources.

Obviously, you can then print the schedule that has been produced for final approval and ongoing updates. It's common practice to email updated schedules with project notes so that stakeholders know what activities are completed and which ones remain to be done.

It's beyond the scope of this book to go into all the various software programs available to project managers. Suffice it to say that project management software ranges from the simple to the complex. The level of sophistication and the types of project management techniques that you're involved with will determine which software product you should choose. Many project managers that I know have had great success with Microsoft Project software and use it exclusively. It contains a robust set of features and reporting tools that will serve most projects well.

Don't forget that you are the project manager, and your good judgment should never be usurped by the recommendation of a software product. Your finely tuned skills and experience will tell you whether relationship issues between team members might cause bigger problems than what the resource-leveling function indicates. Constraints and stakeholder expectations are difficult for a software package to factor in. Rely on your expertise when in doubt. If you don't have the experience yet to make knowledge-based decisions, seek out another project manager or a senior stakeholder, manager, or team member and ask them to confirm whether you're on the right track. And a word of caution: don't become so involved with the software that you're managing the software instead of managing the project. Project management software is a wonderful tool, but it is not a substitute for sound project management practices or experience.

 Real World Scenario

Sunny Surgeons, Inc.

Kate Newman is a project manager for Sunny Surgeons, Inc. Sunny Surgeons, Inc., is a software company that produces software for handheld display devices for the medical profession. The software allows surgeons to keep notes regarding patients, upcoming surgeries, and ideas about new medicines and techniques to research. Kate's latest project is to write an enhanced version of the patient-tracking program with system integration capabilities to a well-known desktop software product used by the medical industry.

The programming department has had some recent turnover. Fortunately, Stephen, the senior programmer who led the development effort on the original version of the patient tracker, still works for Sunny. His expertise with handheld technologies, as well as his knowledge of the desktop software product, makes him an invaluable resource for this project.

Kate discovered a problem during the development of the project schedule. Stephen is overallocated for three key activities. Kate decides to see what his take is on the situation before deciding what to do.

Stephen, the eternal optimist programmer who loves his job and does all but sleep in his office at night, says he can easily complete all the activities and that Kate shouldn't give it a second thought. He also suggests to Kate that Karen Wong, a junior programmer on his team who worked on the last project with him, might be able to handle the noncritical path task on her own, with a little direction from Stephen.

Kate thinks better of the idea of overallocating her key project resource, even if he does think he can do the entire thing single-handed. She decides to try some resource leveling to see what that turns up.

Kate discovers that rearranging the order of activities, along with assigning Karen to handle the noncritical path activity, might be a possible solution. However, this scenario lengthens the project by a total of eight days. Since Kate knows the primary constraint on this project is quality, she's fairly sure she can get buy-off from the project sponsor and stakeholders on the later schedule date. She can also sell the resource-leveled schedule as a low-risk option as opposed to assigning Stephen to all the activities and keeping the project end date the same. Overallocating resources can cause burnout and stress-related illnesses, which will ultimately have a negative impact on the project schedule.

Applying Calendars

Calendars are divided into two types: project calendars and resource calendars. *Project calendars* concern all the resources involved in the project and specify the working periods for those resources. For example, if your project work will be completed during normal working hours, the project calendar shows work periods from Monday through Friday between the hours of 8 A.M. and 5 P.M. Project calendars are also a part of the organizational process input for this process.

Resource calendars look at a particular resource or groups of resources and their availability, which I discussed earlier in this chapter. Perhaps your project calls for a marketing resource, but the person assigned to the marketing activities is on an extended vacation in October. The resource calendar would show this person's vacation schedule and their lack of availability during the time period in October.

Exam Spotlight

Know the difference between project calendars and resource calendars for the exam.

Adjusting Leads and Lags

I talked about leads and lags in Chapter 6. You'll recall that lags delay successor activities and require time added either to the start date or to the finish date of the activity you're scheduling. Leads require time to be subtracted from the start date or the finish date of the activity. Keep in mind that as you go about creating your project schedule, you might need to adjust lead and lag time to come up with a workable schedule.

Schedule Model

Schedule model is a tool that you use to create your project schedule. You can think of this as a template. After you've determined activities, estimates, durations, dependencies, and resources, you use the schedule model in combination with your project management software to create the schedule.

Schedule Development Process Outputs

The Schedule Development process has eight outputs:

- Project schedule
- Schedule model data
- Schedule baseline
- Resource requirement updates
- Activity attributes updates
- Project calendar updates
- Requested changes
- Project management plan updates (updates to the schedule management plan)

You'll take a look at the first three outputs of this process. I've covered all the other outputs previously. Take note that the two primary outputs from this process that will carry forward throughout the rest of the project are the project schedule and the schedule baseline.

Project Schedule

The purpose of the Schedule Development process is to determine the start and finish dates for each of the project activities. One of the primary outputs of this process is the *project schedule,* which details this information as well as the resource assignments. However, depending on the size and complexity of your project or your organization's culture, the resource assignments and start and finish dates might not be completed yet. If that's the case, the project schedule is considered preliminary until the resources are assigned to the activities.

In the *PMBOK Guide* terms, the project schedule is considered preliminary until resources are assigned. In reality, beware that once you've published the project schedule (even though it's in a preliminary state), some stakeholders might regard this as the actual schedule and expect you to manage to the dates shown. Use caution when publishing a schedule in its preliminary form.

The project schedule should be approved and signed off by stakeholders and functional managers. This assures you that they have read the schedule, understand the dates and resource commitments, and will likely cooperate. You'll also need to obtain confirmation that resources will be available as outlined in the schedule when you're working in a functional organization. The schedule cannot be finalized until you receive approval and commitment for the resource assignments outlined in it.

Once the schedule is approved, it will become your baseline for the remainder of the project. Project progress and task completion will be monitored and tracked against the project schedule to determine whether the project is on course as planned.

You can create the schedule in a variety of ways, some of which are variations on what you've already seen. Project schedule network diagrams, like the ones discussed in Chapter 6, will work as schedule diagrams when you add the start and finish dates to each activity. These diagrams usually show the activity dependencies and critical path. Figure 7.2 shows a sample portion of a project schedule network diagram highlighting the programming activities.

FIGURE 7.2   Project schedule network diagram with activity dates

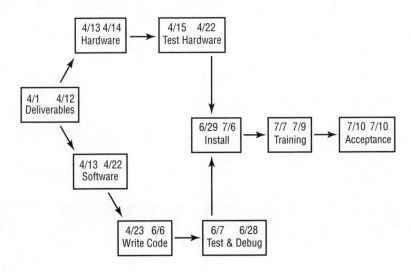

Gantt charts are easy to read and commonly used to display schedule activities. Depending on the software you're using to produce the Gantt chart, it might also show activity sequences, activity start and end dates, resource assignments, activity dependencies, and the critical path. Figure 7.3 is a simple example that plots various activities against time. These activities do not relate to the activities in the tables or other figures shown so far. Gantt charts are also known as *bar charts*.

FIGURE 7.3   Gantt chart

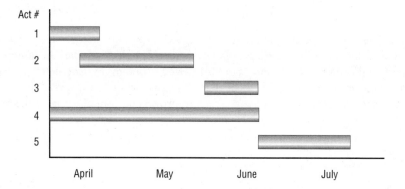

Milestone charts are another way to depict schedule information. Milestones mark the completion of major deliverables or some other key event in the project. For example, approval and sign-off on project deliverables might be considered a milestone. Other examples might be completion of a prototype, system testing, contract approval, and so on.

Milestone charts might show the key events and their start or completion dates in a bar chart form similar to a Gantt chart. Or they can be written in a simple table format with milestones listed in the rows and expected schedule dates in one column and actual completion dates in another, as in the following example. As the milestones are met, the Actual Date column is filled in. This information can be included with the project status reports.

Milestone	Scheduled Date	Actual Date
Sign-off on deliverables	4/12	4/12
Sign-off on hardware test	4/22	4/25
Programming completed	6/06	
Testing completed	6/28	
Acceptance and sign-off	7/10	
Project closeout	7/10	

Schedule Model Data

The schedule model data refers to documenting the supporting data for the schedule. The minimum amount of information in this output includes the milestones, schedule activities and activity attributes, and the assumptions and constraints regarding the schedule. You should document any other information that doesn't necessarily fit into the other categories. Always err on the side of too much documentation rather than not enough.

You will have to be the judge of what other information to include here, because it will depend on the nature of the project. The *PMBOK Guide* suggests that you might include resource histograms. Chapter 6 contains an example resource histogram if you need to review. Resource histograms typically display hours needed on one axis and period of time (days, weeks, months, years) on the other axis. You might also include alternative schedules or contingency schedule reserves in this section.

Schedule Baseline

I think of the schedule baseline as the final, approved version of the project schedule with baseline start and baseline finish dates and resource assignments. The *PMBOK Guide* notes that you derive this baseline from a schedule network analysis of the schedule model.

As I've noted during discussions of some of the other Planning processes, project planning and project management are iterative processes. Rarely is anything cast in cement. You will continue to revisit processes throughout the project to refine and adjust. Eventually, processes do get put to bed. You wouldn't want to return to the Planning process at the conclusion of the project, for example, but keep in mind that the Planning, Executing, and Monitoring and Controlling process groups are iterative, and it's not unusual to have to revise processes within these process groups as you progress on the project.

In practice, for small- to medium-sized projects, you can easily complete Activity Definition, Activity Sequencing, Activity Resource Estimating, Activity Duration Estimating, and Schedule Development at the same time with the aid of good project management software. You can easily produce Gantt charts, critical path, resource allocation, activity dependencies, what-if analysis, and various reports after plugging your scheduling information in to most project management software tools. Regardless of your methods, be certain to obtain sign-off of the project schedule and provide your stakeholders and project sponsor with regular updates. And keep your schedule handy—there will likely be changes and modifications as you go. While you're at it, make certain to save a schedule baseline for comparative purposes. Once you get into the Executing and Monitoring and Controlling processes, you'll be able to compare what you planned to do against what actually happened.

Now you're ready to prepare your last planning document, the project budget. First you'll look at some cost estimating techniques, and then you'll plug those estimates into the project budget.

Estimating Costs

You now have an exhaustive breakdown of project activities, and you have some pretty good duration estimates. Now the question that's forever on the mind of the executive management staff: how much is it going to cost? The purpose of the Cost Estimating process is to answer that question.

Every project has a budget, and part of completing a project successfully is completing it within the approved budget. Sometimes project managers are not responsible for the budget portion of the project. This function is assigned instead to a functional manager who is responsible for tracking and reporting all the project costs. I believe project mangers will have more and more responsibility in this area as the project management discipline evolves. Keep in mind that if you, as the project manager, don't have responsibility for the project budget, your performance evaluation for the project should not include budget or cost measurements.

Before diving into the Cost Estimating and Cost Budgeting process particulars, you should know that these processes are governed by a cost management plan that is created when you perform the Develop Project Management Plan process. You should know a couple of facts about this plan for the exam. Like all the other management plans, it's a subsidiary of the project management plan. According to the *PMBOK Guide*, some of the elements of this plan include, but aren't limited to, the following:

- Precision levels, or the rounding you'll use for project costs (hundreds, thousands, and so on)
- Units of measure for resources such has hours for staff resources and hourly rates for contractor staff
- Control account links so that cost estimates for WBS elements can be linked directly to the accounting system
- Variance thresholds for costs
- Earned value rules (covered in the "Cost Estimating Tools and Techniques" section)
- Reporting formats
- Process descriptions

As with time estimates, the work breakdown structure (WBS) is the key to determining accurate cost estimates. The *Cost Estimating* process develops a cost estimate for the resources (human and material) required for each schedule activity. This includes weighing alternative options and examining trade-offs.

Let's look at an example. Many times software development projects take on a life of their own. The requested project completion dates are unrealistic; however, the project team commits to completing the project on time and on budget anyway. How do they do this? They do this by cutting things such as design, analysis, and documentation. In the end, the project might get completed on time and on budget, but was it really? The costs associated with the extended support period because of a lack of design and documentation and the hours needed by the software programmers to fix the reported bugs aren't included in the original cost of the project (but they should have been). Therefore, the costs actually exceed what was budgeted. You should examine trade-offs such as these when determining cost estimates.

When you are determining cost estimates, be certain to include all the costs of the project over its entire life cycle. As in the preceding example, software projects often have warranty periods that guarantee bug fixes or problem resolution within a certain time frame. This is a legitimate cost that should be included in your estimates.

 Don't confuse pricing with Cost Estimating. If you are working for a company that performs consulting services on contract, for example, the price you will charge for your services is not the same as the costs to perform the project. The costs are centered on the resources needed to produce the product or service of the project. The price your company might charge for the service includes not only these costs but a profit margin as well.

Cost Estimating Inputs

You are already familiar with all the Cost Estimating inputs. They are as follows:

- Enterprise environmental factors
- Organizational process assets
- Project scope statement
- WBS
- WBS dictionary
- Project management plan (including the schedule management plan, staffing management plan, and risk register)

As with several other processes I've covered, keep in mind organizational policies (such as cost estimating policies or templates), historical information, previous project files, constraints, and assumptions when deriving your cost estimates.

Cost Estimating Tools and Techniques

Cost Estimating has eight tools and techniques used to derive estimates:

- Analogous estimating
- Determine resource cost rates
- Bottom-up estimating
- Parametric estimating
- Project management software
- Vendor bid analysis
- Reserve analysis
- Cost of quality

I covered analogous, parametric estimating, and reserve analysis techniques in the Activity Duration Estimating section. All of that information applies here as well, except you're using the tools and techniques to derive cost estimates. And, in the case of reserve analysis, you're adding cost reserves (or contingencies) during this process, not schedule reserves. You could aggregate these cost contingencies and assign them to a schedule activity or work package level. The project management software is a tool that can help you establish project cost estimates and can help you quickly determine estimates given different variables and alternatives. I talked about cost of quality way back in Chapter 4. You'll look at the remaining techniques next.

Determine Resource Rates

You can determine resource rates a number of ways. Your organization might have a vendor list with published rates that you'll use. These are usually updated once or twice a year. You could request quotes from vendors or do some Internet searching to find rates. Don't forget to include the resource rates of the folks who work within the organization as well. These rates apply to both human resources and materials.

Bottom-Up Estimating

I discussed this technique in the Activity Resource Estimating process. This technique estimates costs associated with every activity individually and then rolls them up to derive a total project estimate. You wouldn't choose this technique to provide a cost estimate for the project during Initiating if one were requested because you don't have enough information at that stage to use the bottom-up technique. Instead, use the top-down estimation technique (analogous estimating) when a project cost estimate is needed early in the project selection stage.

Vendor Bid Analysis

As the name implies, this is a process of gathering information from vendors to help you establish cost estimates. You can accomplish this by requesting bids or quotes or working with some of your trusted vendor sources for estimates. You should compare vendor bids when using this tool and technique and not rely solely on one vendor to provide you with estimates.

Exam Spotlight

For the exam, make sure you're familiar with all the cost estimating tools and techniques, their benefits, and under what conditions you use them.

Cost Estimating Process Outputs

Obviously, one of the outputs of the Cost Estimating process is the activity cost estimates. These are quantitative amounts—usually stated in monetary units—that reflect the cost of the resources needed to complete the project activities. The tools and techniques I just described help you derive these estimates. Resources in this case include human resources, material, equipment, information technology needs, and so on, as well as any contingency reserve amounts and inflation factors (if you're using them).

Activity Cost Estimating supporting detail, requested changes, and cost management plan updates are the remaining Cost Estimating outputs. Supporting detail is just as you've seen in other processes. You also need to document any information that supports how the estimates were developed, what assumptions were made during the Cost Estimating process, and any other details you think are needed. According to the *PMBOK Guide*, the supporting detail should include the following:

- A description of the work that was estimated.

- A description of how the estimate was developed or the basis for the estimate.

- A description of the assumptions made about the estimates or the method used to determine them.

- A description of the constraints.

- A range of possible results. Like the time estimates, you should state the cost estimates within ranges such as $500 ± $75.

 Real World Scenario

This Older House

Janie is an accomplished project manager. She and her husband recently purchased an 80-year-old home in need of several repairs and modern updates. She decided to put her project management skills to work on the house project. First, they hired a general contractor to oversee all the individual projects needed to bring the house up-to-date. Janie worked with the general contractor to construct a WBS, and she ended up with 23 work packages. With each work package (or multiple work packages in some cases) assigned to a subcontractor, it was easy to track who was responsible for completing the work and for determining duration estimates. Janie and the general contractor worked together to determine schedule dependencies and make certain the work was performed in the correct order and that each subcontractor knew when their activity was to begin and end.

Some of the cost estimates for certain work packages were easy to determine using the parametric estimating method. Others required expert judgment and the experience of the general contractor (analogous techniques) to determine a cost estimate. Resource rates for laborers for some of the work packages were agreed to when the subcontractors bid on the work. Once Janie had all the cost estimates, she used the bottom-up estimating technique to come up with an overall cost estimate for the project. She added a contingency reserve in addition to the overall estimate for unforeseen risk events.

Cost variances will occur and estimates will be refined as you get further into your project. As a result, you'll update cost estimates and ultimately the project budget to reflect these changes.

Cost Estimating uses several techniques to make an accurate assessment of the project costs. In practice, using a combination of techniques is your best bet to come up with the most reliable cost estimates. The activity cost estimates will become an input to the Cost Budgeting process, which allows you to establish a baseline for project costs to track against.

Establishing the Cost Budget Baseline

The next process concerns determining the cost baseline, which is the primary output of the Cost Budgeting process. The *Cost Budgeting* process aggregates the cost estimates of activities and establishes a cost baseline for the project that is used to measure performance of the project throughout the remaining process groups. Only the costs associated with the project become part of the project budget. For example, future period operating costs are not project costs and therefore aren't included in the project budget.

The *cost baseline* is the expected cost for the project. Remember that costs are tied to the financial system through the chart of accounts—or code of accounts—and are assigned to project activities at the work package level of the WBS.

The budget will be used as a plan for allocating costs to project activities.

Cost Budgeting Inputs

The Schedule Development and Cost Estimating processes must be completed prior to working on Cost Budgeting because some of their outputs become the inputs to this process. The inputs for Cost Budgeting are as follows:

- Project scope statement
- Work breakdown structure
- WBS dictionary
- Activity cost estimates
- Activity cost estimate supporting detail
- Project schedule
- Resource calendars
- Contract
- Cost management plan

I've covered all these inputs before. As usual, don't forget to look at project constraints, particularly funding limitations in this case.

Cost Budgeting Tools and Techniques

The Cost Budgeting process has four tools and techniques, including two you haven't seen before:

- Cost aggregation
- Reserve analysis
- Parametric estimating
- Funding limit reconciliation

I've covered reserve analysis and parametric estimating already. Note that reserve analysis in this process also takes into consideration management contingency reserves for unplanned changes to project scope and project costs.

Cost aggregation   Cost aggregation is the process of tallying the schedule activity cost estimates at the work package level and then totaling the work package levels to higher-level WBS component levels (such as the control accounts).

Funding limit reconciliation   Funding limit reconciliation involves reconciling the amount of funds spent with the amount of funds budgeted for the project. The organization or the customer sets these limits. Reconciling the project expenses will require adjusting the schedule so that the expenses can be smoothed. You do this by placing imposed date constraints (I talked about these in the Schedule Development process) on work packages or other WBS components in the project schedule.

Cost Budgeting Process Outputs

The goal of Cost Budgeting is to develop a cost baseline (an output of this process) for the project that you can use in the Executing and Monitoring and Controlling processes to measure performance. You now have all the information you need to create the cost baseline. In addition, you'll establish the project funding requirements.

The following are all the outputs of the Cost Budgeting process:

- Cost baseline
- Project funding requirements
- Cost management plan updates
- Requested changes

I've already covered the cost management plan updates and requested changes outputs. You'll look at the cost baseline in the following section.

Documenting the Cost Baseline

You develop the cost baseline, the first output of Cost Budgeting, by adding the costs of the WBS elements (remember, these costs were aggregated with the cost aggregation tool and technique) according to time periods. This is also known as the project's *time-phased budget*. Most projects span some length of time, and most organizations time the funding with the project. In other words, you won't get all the funds for the project at the beginning of the project; they'll likely be disbursed over time. The cost baseline provides the basis for measurement, over time, of the expected cash flows (or funding disbursements) against the requirements.

Cost baselines can be displayed graphically, with time increments on one axis and dollars expended on the other axis, as shown in Figure 7.4. The costs shown on this graph are cumulative costs, meaning that what you spent this period is added to what was spent last period and then charted. Many variations of this graph exist showing dollars budgeted against dollars expended to date and so on. Cost budgets can be displayed using this type of graph as well, by plotting the sum of the estimated costs excepted per period.

FIGURE 7.4   Cost baseline

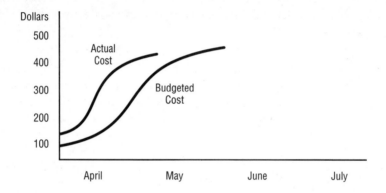

The cost baseline should contain the costs for all of the expected work on the project. You would have identified most of these costs in the Cost Estimating process. You'll find most projects' largest expense is resource costs (as in labor costs). In the case of projects where you're purchasing the final product, the purchase price is the largest cost.

Schedule Development might have uncovered additional activities that need to be added to the budget as well, so don't forget to add them to your budget.

Exam Spotlight

For the exam, remember that cost baselines are displayed as an S curve. The reason for this is that project spending starts out slowly, gradually increases over the project's life until it reaches a peak, and then tapers off again as the project wraps up. Large projects are difficult to graph in this manner because the timescale isn't wide enough to accurately show fluctuations in spending. There are other methods that more accurately graph costs that you'll look at in the Cost Control process.

Large projects might have more than one cost baseline. For example, you might be required to track human resource costs, material costs, and contractor costs separately.

The cost baseline should also contain appropriations for risk response. I covered several categories and tools of Risk Response Planning in Chapter 5, "Risk Planning," including avoidance, mitigation, insurance, and contingency plans. Some of the budget should be allocated to each of the techniques you identified in your risk management plan. Additionally, you'll want to set aside money for contingency reserves. This is for the unforeseen, unplanned risks that might occur. Even with all the time and effort you spend on planning, unexpected issues do crop up. It's better to have the money set aside and not need it than to need it and not have it.

You'll revisit the cost baseline when you learn about the Cost Control process and examine different ways to measure costs.

Gathering the Project Funding Requirements

Project funding requirements are the total amount of money spent on the project. They are determined from the cost baseline and might include a management contingency reserve that's used to manage cost overruns, particularly early in the project. As I said earlier, spending usually starts out slowly on the project and picks up speed as you progress. Sometimes, the expected cash flows don't match the pace of spending. Project funding requirements accounts for this by using a management reserve contingency (usually a margin or percentage of the cost baseline) that's released in increments with the project budget. Figure 7.5 shows the cost baseline, the funding requirements, and the expected cash flows plotted on the S curve. This example shows a negative amount of management reserve because the difference between the funding requirements and the cost baseline at the end of project is the management reserve.

FIGURE 7.5   Cost baseline, funding requirements, and cash flow

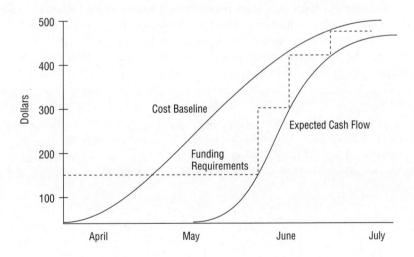

Bringing It All Together

Believe it or not, you have officially completed the Planning process group. Along the way, I've mentioned gaining approvals for portions of the project plan such as the schedule and budget.

The *project plan* is the approved, formal, documented plan that's used to guide you through-out the project Executing process group. The plan consists of all the outputs of the Planning process groups, including the project management plan. It's the map that tells you where you're going and how to perform the activities of the project plan during the Project Plan Execution process. It serves several purposes, the most important of which is tracking and measuring project performance through the Executing and Monitoring and Controlling processes and making future project decisions. The project plan is critical in all communications you'll have from here forward with the stakeholders, management, and customers. The project plan also documents all project planning assumptions, all project planning decisions, and important management reviews needed.

The project plan encompasses everything I've talked about up to now and is represented in a formal document, or collection of documents. This document contains the project scope statement, deliverables, assumptions, risks, WBS, milestones, project schedule, resources, and more. It becomes the baseline you'll use to measure and track progress against. It's also used to help you control the components that tend to stray from the original plan so you can get them back in line.

The project plan is used as a communication and information tool for stakeholders, team members, and the management team. They will use the project plan to review and gauge progress as well.

Exam Spotlight

Performance measurement baselines are management controls that should change only infrequently. Examples of the performance measurement baselines you've looked at so far are Cost Budgeting, quality, and schedule baselines. However, the project plan itself also becomes a baseline. If changes in scope or schedule do occur after Planning is complete, you should go through a formalized process (which I'll cover in Chapter 10, "Monitoring and Controlling Change") to implement the changes.

Don't forget that sign-off is an important part of this process. Your last step in the Planning process group is obtaining sign-off of the project plan from stakeholders, the sponsor, and the management team. If they've been an integral part of the Planning processes all along (and I know you know how important this is), obtaining sign-off of the project plan should simply be a formality.

Note that you use all the management plans I discussed during the Planning processes—the project management plan and its subsidiary plans, including the scope management plan, the schedule management plan and so on, plus the cost budgeting baseline and the schedule baseline—throughout the Executing process group to manage the project and keep the performance of the project on track with the project objectives. If you don't have a project plan, you'll have no way of managing the process. You'll find that even with a project plan, project scope has a way of changing. Stakeholders and others tend to sneak in a few of the "Oh, I didn't understand that before" statements and hope that they slide right by you. With that signed, approved project plan in your files, you are allowed to gently remind them that they read and agreed to the project plan and you're sticking to it.

Project Case Study: New Kitchen Heaven Retail Store

Performance measurement baselines are management controls that should change only infrequently. Examples of the performance measurement baselines you've looked at so far are Cost Budgeting, quality, and schedule baselines. However, the project plan itself also becomes a baseline. If changes in scope or schedule do occur after Planning is complete, you should go through a formalized process (which I'll cover in Chapter 10, "Monitoring and Controlling Change") to implement the changes.

The stakeholders provided you with an activity list the last time you met. After creating a complete activity list and the first draft of the project schedule network diagram, you went back to each of them to ask for time and cost estimates for each of the activities. Ricardo's estimates are shown here with the activities he gave you last time:

1. Procure the T1 connection. This takes 30 to 45 days and will have ongoing costs of $300 per month. This can be done concurrently with the other activities listed here. Ricardo will handle this activity.

2. Run Ethernet cable throughout the building. This activity depends on the lease being signed and must finish before the build-out can start. The estimated time to complete is 16 hours, which was figured using parametric estimating techniques. Ricardo has one person on staff who can complete this specialized activity. His first available date is October 5.

3. Purchase the router, switch, server, and rack for the equipment room and four point-of-service terminals. The estimated costs are $17,000. Delivery time is two weeks. Ricardo will do this activity.

4. Install the router and test the connection. Testing depends on the T1 installation at demarcation. The time estimate to install is eight hours. Ricardo's staff will do this activity.

5. Install the switch. Based on past experience, the time estimate to install is two hours. Ricardo's staff will do this activity.

6. Install the server and test. The testing depends on the T1 connection installation. Based on past experience, the time estimate to install is six hours. Ricardo's staff will do this activity.

7. The web team will add the new store location and phone number to the lookup function on the Internet site. The time estimate is eight hours. Ricardo will assign his applications programming manager to this activity. This activity depends on the lease being signed.

Jake and Jill have each written similar lists with estimates and resource assignments. You begin to align all the activities in sequential order and discover a problem. Jill needs 14 days to hire personnel and stock shelves, meaning that the build-out must be finished by January 16. Build-out takes approximately 120 days and can't start before September 20 because of the contractor's availability. This is a problem because Ricardo's Ethernet cable expert isn't available until October 5, and he needs 2 days to complete the cabling. This pushes out the build-out start date by almost 2 weeks, which means the project completion date, or store-opening date, is delayed by 2 weeks.

After gathering more information from Ricardo, you head to Dirk's office.

"So, Dirk," you conclude after filling him in on all the details, "we have two options. Hire a contractor to perform the cable run since Ricardo's person isn't available or push the store opening out by two weeks."

Dirk asks, "How much will the contractor charge to run the cable, and are they available within the time frame you need?"

"Yes, they are available, and I've already requested Ricardo book the week of September 18 to hold this option open for us. They've quoted a price of $10,000."

"OK, let's bring in the contractor. At this point, $10,000 isn't going to break the budget. How is that planning coming anyway? Signed a lease yet?"

"Yes, we've signed the lease. Jake has been meeting with Gomez construction on the build-out. We've used Gomez on three out of the last five new stores and have had good luck with them."

You spend the next couple of days working on the project schedule in Microsoft Project, clarifying tasks and activities with Jake, Ricardo, and Jill. You decide that a Gantt chart will work excellently for reporting status for this project. A portion of your first draft of the Gantt chart shows the following at the end of the project:

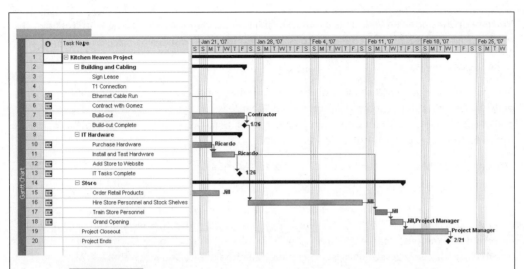

		Task Name	Duration	Start	Finish	Predecessors	Resource Names
1		⊟ Kitchen Heaven Project	172.38 days	Mon 8/21/06	Wed 2/21/07		
2		⊟ Building and Cabling	148.13 days	Mon 8/21/06	Fri 1/26/07		
3		Sign Lease	1 day	Mon 8/21/06	Mon 8/21/06		Jill,Project Manager
4		T1 Connection	45 days	Mon 8/21/06	Fri 10/6/06		Ricardo
5	▦	Ethernet Cable Run	2 days	Mon 9/18/06	Tue 9/19/06	3	Ricardo
6	▦	Contract with Gomez	2 days	Mon 9/11/06	Tue 9/12/06	3	Jake,Project Manage
7	▦	Build-out	120 days	Wed 9/20/06	Fri 1/26/07	5,6	Contractor
8		Build-out Complete	0 days	Fri 1/26/07	Fri 1/26/07	7	
9		⊟ IT Hardware	18 days	Mon 1/8/07	Fri 1/26/07		
10	▦	Purchase Hardware	14 days	Mon 1/8/07	Mon 1/22/07		Ricardo
11		Install and Test Hardware	3 days	Mon 1/22/07	Thu 1/25/07	5,10	Ricardo
12	▦	Add Store to Website	1 day	Tue 1/9/07	Tue 1/9/07		Ricardo
13	▦	IT Tasks Complete	0 days	Fri 1/26/07	Fri 1/26/07	11	
14		⊟ Store	38 days	Mon 1/8/07	Thu 2/15/07		
15	▦	Order Retail Products	15 days	Mon 1/8/07	Tue 1/23/07		Jill
16	▦	Hire Store Personnel and Stock Shelves	14 days	Sat 1/27/07	Sat 2/10/07	8	Jill
17	▦	Train Store Personnel	2 days	Mon 2/12/07	Tue 2/13/07	11,16	Jill
18	▦	Grand Opening	2 days	Wed 2/14/07	Thu 2/15/07	17	Jill,Project Manager
19		Project Closeout	5 days	Thu 2/15/07	Wed 2/21/07	18	Project Manager
20		Project Ends	0 days	Wed 2/21/07	Wed 2/21/07	19	

You stare intensely at the problem you see on the screen. The Grand Opening task (number 18) is scheduled to occur 13 days later than when you need it! Grand opening must happen February 1 and 2, not February 14 and 15 as the schedule shows. You trace the problem back and see that Grand Opening task depends on Train Store Personnel, which itself depends on several other tasks, including Hire Store Personnel and Install and Test Hardware. Digging deeper, build-out can't begin until the Ethernet cable is run throughout the building. Ricardo already set up the time with the contractor to run the cable September 18. This date cannot move, which means build-out cannot start any sooner than September 20, which works with Gomez's availability.

You pick up the phone and dial Jake's number. "Jake," you say into the receiver, "I'm working on the project schedule, and I have some issues with the Gomez activity."

"Shoot," Jake says.

"Gomez Construction can't start work until the Ethernet cable is run. I've already confirmed with Ricardo that there is no negotiation on this. Ricardo is hiring a contractor for this activity, and the earliest they can start is September 18. It takes them two days to run the cable, which puts the start date for build-out at September 20."

"What's the problem with the September 20 date?" Jake asks.

"Jill wants to have the build-out finished prior to hiring the store personnel. During the last store opening, those activities overlapped, and she said it was unmanageable. She wants to hire folks and have them stock the shelves in preparation for store opening but doesn't want contractors in there while they're doing it. A September 20 start date for Gomez puts us at a finish date of January 26, which is too late to give Jill time to hire and stock shelves. My question is this, is 120 days to finish a build-out a firm estimate?"

"Always—I've got this down to a science. Gomez has worked with me on enough of these build-outs that we can come within just a couple of days of this estimate either way," Jake says.

You pick up your schedule detail and continue, "I've scheduled Gomez's resource calendar as you told me originally. Gomez doesn't work Sundays, and neither do we. Their holidays are Labor Day, a couple of days at Thanksgiving, Christmas, and New Year's, but this puts us too far out on the schedule. We must have our February 1 opening coincide with the Garden and Home Show dates."

"I can't change the 120 days. Sounds like you have a problem."

"I need to crash the schedule," you say. "What would the chances be of Gomez agreeing to split the build-out tasks? We could hire a second contractor to come in and work alongside Gomez's crew to speed up this task. That would shorten the duration to 100 days, which means we could meet the February 1 date."

"Won't happen. I know Gomez. They're a big outfit and have all their own crews. We typically work with them exclusively. If I brought another contractor into the picture, I might have a hard time negotiating any kind of favors with them later if we get into a bind."

"All right," you say. "How about this? I'm making some changes to the resource calendar while we're talking. What if we authorize Gomez's crew to work six 10-hour days, which still leaves them with Sundays off, and we ask them to work Labor Day and take only one day at Thanksgiving instead of two?"

The detail showing these changes is as follows:

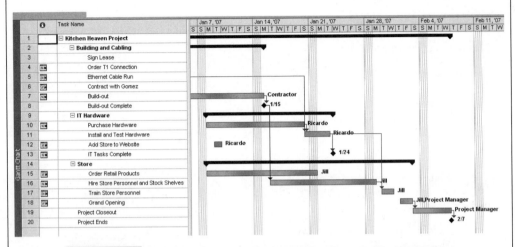

	ⓘ	Task Name	Duration	Start	Finish	Predecessors	Resource Names
1		⊟ Kitchen Heaven Project	178.25 days	Mon 8/21/06	Wed 2/7/07		
2		⊟ Building and Cabling	152.5 days	Mon 8/21/06	Mon 1/15/07		
3		Sign Lease	1 day	Mon 8/21/06	Mon 8/21/06		Jill,Project Manager
4	🔲	Order T1 Connection	45 days	Mon 8/21/06	Mon 10/2/06		Ricardo
5	🔲	Ethernet Cable Run	2 days	Mon 9/18/06	Tue 9/19/06	3	Ricardo
6	🔲	Contract with Gomez	2 days	Mon 9/11/06	Tue 9/12/06	3	Jake,Project Manage
7	🔲	Build-out	120 days	Wed 9/20/06	Mon 1/15/07		Contractor
8		Build-out Complete	0 days	Mon 1/15/07	Mon 1/15/07	7	
9		⊟ IT Hardware	17.5 days	Mon 1/8/07	Wed 1/24/07		
10	🔲	Purchase Hardware	14 days	Mon 1/8/07	Sat 1/20/07		Ricardo
11		Install and Test Hardware	3 days	Sat 1/20/07	Tue 1/23/07	5,10	Ricardo
12	🔲	Add Store to Website	1 day	Tue 1/9/07	Tue 1/9/07	11	Ricardo
13	🔲	IT Tasks Complete	0 days	Wed 1/24/07	Wed 1/24/07	11	
14		⊟ Store	28.5 days	Mon 1/8/07	Fri 2/2/07		
15	🔲	Order Retail Products	15 days	Mon 1/8/07	Mon 1/22/07		Jill
16	🔲	Hire Store Personnel and Stock Shelves	14 days	Tue 1/16/07	Mon 1/29/07	8	Jill
17	🔲	Train Store Personnel	2 days	Tue 1/30/07	Wed 1/31/07	11,16	Jill
18	🔲	Grand Opening	2 days	Thu 2/1/07	Fri 2/2/07		Jill,Project Manager
19		Project Closeout	5 days	Fri 2/2/07	Wed 2/7/07	18	Project Manager
20		Project Ends	0 days	Wed 2/7/07	Wed 2/7/07	19	

"I think Gomez would go for that. You realize it's going to cost you?"

"Project management is all about trade-offs. We can't move the start date, so chances are the budget might take a hit to accommodate schedule changes or risk. Fortunately, I'm just now wrapping up the final funding requirements, or the cost budget, so if you can get me the increased cost from Gomez soon, I'd appreciate it. This change will keep us on track and resolve Jill's issues too."

"I don't think Gomez's crew will mind the overtime during the holiday season. Everyone can use a little extra cash at that time of year, it seems. I'll have the figures for you in a day or two."

Project Case Study Checklist

Activity Duration Estimating

Activity Resource Estimating

Developing project schedule

- Calendars

- Lead and lag time

- Critical path

Duration compression

- Crashing

- Fast tracking

Utilizing project management software

Producing project schedule

- Milestones

- Gantt chart

- Resource leveling

Cost estimates

Cost baseline

Finalized project plan

Understanding How This Applies to Your Next Project

Activity Definition and Activity Sequencing are the first two processes in the "Activity" sequence you'll complete on the road to Schedule Development. (I covered those two processes in the previous chapter.) You perform Activity Resource Estimating to determine the resource requirements and quantity of resources needed for each schedule activity. I've found for small- to medium-sized projects, you can perform this process at the same time as the Activity Duration Estimating process. And, if you work in an organization where the same resource pool is used for project after project, you already know the people's skills sets and availability, so you can perform this process at the same time you're creating the project schedule. The same logic holds for projects where the material resources are similar for every project you conduct. If you don't have the need to perform this process, I do recommend that you create a resource calendar at a minimum so that you can note whether team members have extended vacations or family issues that could impact the project schedule. Needless to say, if you're working on a large project or your project teams are new for every project, you should perform the Activity Resource Estimating process. It will come in handy later when you're ready to plug names into the activities listed on the project schedule.

Activity Duration Estimating is a process you'll perform for most project you work on. For larger projects, I'm a big fan of PERT estimates. PERT gives you estimates with a high degree of reliability, which is needed for projects that are critical to the organization, projects that haven't been undertaken before, or projects that involve complex processes or scope, Three-point estimates work well for small- to medium-sized projects and is the technique I use more often than any other. It's easy to create a spreadsheet template to automatically calculate these estimates for you. List your schedule activities (or work packages) in each row, and in the individual columns to the right, record the most likely, pessimistic, and optimistic estimates. The final column can hold the calculation to average these three estimates, and you can transfer the estimates to your schedule. You can easily add columns to calculate PERT and standard deviation as well.

In theory, if you've performed all the "Activity" processes, the schedule should almost be a no-brainer. You can plug the activity list, resources, estimates, and successor and predecessor tasks into the schedule. From there, you will want to take the next step and determine the critical path. The critical path is, well, critical to your project's success. If you don't know which activities are on the critical path, you won't know what the impacts of delays or risk events will have on the project. No matter how big or small the project, be sure you know and understand the critical-path activities.

Cost estimating is something I have to do rather early in the project because of a long procurement cycle. I rely on vendors as well as my own project team to help me with this. If the project is large enough that it has to go out for bid, I have a well-defined scope and some idea of schedule dates, but I won't complete the schedule until after the contract is awarded. In an ideal world, I would prefer to create the schedule prior to determining cost estimates and budgets…but we don't live in an ideal world, and that's what this section is all about.

Summary

Great job, you've made it through the entire Planning process group. I covered several processes in this chapter, including Activity Resource Estimating, Activity Duration Estimating, Schedule Development, Cost Estimating, and Cost Budgeting.

The Activity Resource Estimating process considers all the resources needed and the quantity of resources needed to perform project activities. This information is determined for each schedule activity and is documented in the activity resource requirements output.

Duration estimates are produced as a result of the Activity Duration Estimating process. Activity duration estimates document the number of work periods needed for each activity, including their elapsed time. Analogous estimating—also called *top-down estimating*—is one way to determine activity duration estimates. You can also use top-down techniques to estimate project durations and total project costs. Parametric estimating techniques multiply a known element—such as the quantity of materials needed—by the time it takes to install or complete one unit of materials. The result is a total estimate for the activity. Three-point estimates average the most likely estimate, a pessimistic estimate, and an optimistic estimate. Reserve analysis takes schedule risk into consideration by adding a percentage of time or another work period to the estimate just in case you run into trouble.

Schedule Development is the process in which you assign beginning and ending dates to activities and determine their duration. You might use CPM to accomplish this. CPM calculates early start, early finish, late start, and late finish dates. It also determines float time. All tasks with zero float are critical path tasks. The critical path is the longest path of tasks in the project.

PERT calculates a weighted average estimate for each activity by using the optimistic, pessimistic, and most likely times. It then determines variances, or standard deviations, to come up with a total project duration within a given confidence range. Work will finish within plus or minus one standard deviation 68.26 percent of the time. Work will finish within plus or minus two standard deviations 95.44 percent of the time.

Schedules sometimes need to be compressed to meet promised dates or to shorten the schedule times. Crashing looks at cost and schedule trade-offs. Adding resources to critical path tasks and limiting or reducing the project requirements or scope are ways to crash the schedule. Fast tracking involves performing tasks in parallel that were originally scheduled to start one after the other. Fast tracking usually increases project risk. You can use Monte Carlo analysis in the Schedule Development process to determine multiple, probable project durations.

Resource leveling attempts to smooth out the schedule and properly allocate resources to critical path tasks. This might require updates to the resource management plan.

The project schedule details the activities in graphical form through the use of project schedule network diagrams with dates, Gantt charts, milestone charts, or project schedule network diagrams.

The Cost Estimating process determines how much the project resources will cost, and these costs are usually stated in monetary amounts. Analogous estimating is one technique that you can use to determine cost estimates. Another technique is parametric estimating. You can use bottom-up estimating for project cost estimates. This involves estimating the cost of each schedule activity and then rolling these up to come up with a total work package cost.

You'll use the Cost Budgeting baseline throughout the project to measure project expenditures, variance, and project performance. The cost baseline is graphically displayed as an S curve.

Exam Essentials

Be able to name the purpose of the Activity Resource Estimating process.   The purpose of Activity Resource Estimating is to determine the types of resources needed (human, equipment, and materials) and in what quantities for each schedule activity within a work package.

Be able to name the tools and techniques of Activity Duration Estimating.   The tools and techniques of Activity Duration Estimating are expert judgment, analogous estimating, parametric estimating, three-point estimates, and reserve analysis.

Be able to define the difference between analogous estimating and bottom-up estimating. Analogous estimating is a top-down technique that uses expert judgment and historical information. Bottom-up estimating performs estimates for each work item and rolls them up to a total.

Be able to calculate the critical path.   The critical path includes the activities whose durations add up to the longest path of the project schedule network diagram. Critical path is calculated using the forward pass, backward pass, and float calculations.

Be able to define a critical path task.   A critical path task is a project activity with zero float.

Be able to describe and calculate PERT duration estimates.   This is a weighted average technique that uses three estimates: optimistic, pessimistic, and most likely. The formula is as follows: (optimistic + pessimistic + (4 × most likely)) ÷ 6.

Be able to name the duration compression techniques.   The duration compression techniques are crashing and fast tracking.

Be able to identify and describe the primary output of the Cost Estimating process.   The primary output of Cost Estimating is activity cost estimates. These estimates are quantitative amounts—usually stated in monetary units—that reflect the cost of the resources needed to complete the project activities.

Be able to describe the cost baseline.   The cost baseline is the expected cost of the project and is used to measure performance. It's displayed as an S curve.

Key Terms

Accurately planning a project budget and schedule is one of the most difficult tasks you'll face as a project manager. Know the processes I've discussed and the terms used to identify them in the *PMBOK*. Here's a list of the budget and schedule planning processes you'll need to be successful.

Activity Duration Estimating

Activity Resource Estimating

Cost Budgeting

Cost Estimating

Schedule Development

You've also learned a lot of new key words in this chapter. PMI has worked hard to develop and define standard project management terms that apply across industries. Here is a list of some of the terms you came across in this chapter:

activity duration estimates	Program Evaluation and Review Technique (PERT)
analogous estimating	project calendars
backward pass	project plan
bar charts	project schedule
buffer	reserve time
contingency time	resource calendars
cost baseline	resource leveling
crashing	resource-based method
critical chain method	resources
critical path (CP)	reverse resource allocation scheduling
critical path method (CPM)	schedule baseline
fast tracking	schedule compression
float time	schedule network analysis
forward pass	slack time
Gantt charts	three-point estimates
milestone charts	top-down estimating
parametric estimating	

Review Questions

1. You are the project manager for Changing Tides video games. You have gathered the inputs for the Activity Duration Estimating process. Which of the following tools and techniques will you employ to produce the outputs for this process?

    A. Activity list, expert judgment, alternatives analysis, project management software, and bottom-up estimating

    B. Activity list, expert judgment, published estimating data, and project management software

    C. Expert judgment, alternatives analysis, published estimating data, project management software, and bottom-up estimating

    D. Expert judgment, alternatives analysis, published estimating data, and bottom-up estimating

2. Your project sponsor has requested a cost estimate for the project on which you're working. This project is similar in scope to a project you worked on last year. She would like to get the cost estimates as soon as possible. Accuracy is not her primary concern right now. She needs a ballpark figure by tomorrow. You decide to use _____.

    A. analogous estimating techniques

    B. bottom-up estimating techniques

    C. parametric modeling techniques

    D. computerized modeling techniques

3. Your project's primary constraint is quality. To make certain the project team members don't feel too pressed for time and to avoid schedule risk, you decide to use which of the following activity estimating tools?

    A. Expert judgment

    B. Quantitatively based durations

    C. Reserve analysis

    D. Analogous estimating

4. You have been hired as a contract project manger for Grapevine Vineyards. Grapevine wants you to design an Internet wine club for its customers. One of the activities for this project is the installation and testing of several new servers. You know from past experience it takes about 16 hours per server to accomplish this task. Since you're installing 10 new servers, you estimate this activity to take 160 hours. Which of the estimating techniques have you used?

    A. Analogous estimating

    B. Bottom-up estimating

    C. Parametric estimating

    D. Reserve analysis

5. Your project sponsor has requested a cost estimate for the project. She would like the cost estimate to be as accurate as possible because this might be her one and only chance to secure the budget for this project because of recent cuts in special projects. You decide to use _____.

    A. analogous estimating techniques

    B. bottom-up estimating techniques

    C. top-down estimating techniques

    D. expert judgment techniques

6. The project schedule is used to determine all of the following except which one?

    A. Cost estimates

    B. Activity start dates

    C. Float times

    D. Activity end dates

7. You are a project manager for Picture Shades, Inc. It manufactures window shades that have replicas of Renaissance-era paintings on the inside for hotel chains. Picture Shades is taking its product to the home market, and you're managing the new project. It will offer its products at retail stores as well as on its website. You're developing the project schedule for this undertaking and have determined the critical path. Which of the following statements is true?

    A. You calculated the most likely start date and most likely finish dates, float time, and weighted average estimates.

    B. You calculated the activity dependency and the optimistic and pessimistic activity duration estimates.

    C. You calculated the early and late start dates, the early and late finish dates, and float times for all activities.

    D. You calculated the optimistic, pessimistic, and most likely duration times and the float times for all activities.

8. You are a project manager for Picture Shades, Inc. It manufactures window shades that have replicas of Renaissance-era paintings on the inside for hotel chains. Picture Shades is taking its product to the home market, and you're managing the new project. It will offer its products at retail stores as well as on its website. You're developing the project schedule for this undertaking. Looking at the following graph, which path is the critical path?

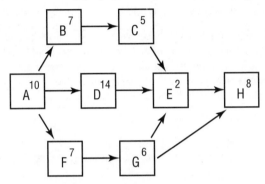

A. A-B-C-E-H

B. A-D-E-H

C. A-F-G-H

D. A-F-G-E-H

9. Use the following graphic to answer this question. If the duration of activity B was changed to 10 days and the duration of activity G was changed to 9 days, which path is the critical path?

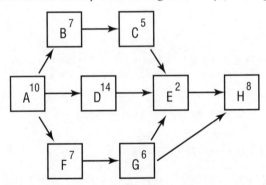

A. A-B-C-E-H

B. A-D-E-H

C. A-F-G-H

D. A-F-G-E-H

10. Which of the following statements is true regarding the critical path?

   A. It should never be compressed.

   B. It allows for looping and branching.

   C. The critical path technique is the same as PERT.

   D. It's the duration of all tasks with zero float.

11. You are a project manager for Move It Now trucking company. Your company specializes in moving household goods across the city or across the country. Your project involves upgrading the nationwide computer network for the company. Your lead engineer has given you the following estimates for a critical path activity: 60 days most likely, 72 days pessimistic, 48 days optimistic. What is the weighted average or expected value?

   A. 54

   B. 66

   C. 60

   D. 30

12. You are a project manager for Move It Now trucking company. Your company specializes in moving household goods across the city or across the country. Your project involves upgrading the nationwide computer network for the company. Your lead engineer has given you the following estimates for a critical path activity: 60 days most likely, 72 days pessimistic, 48 days optimistic. What is the standard deviation?

   A. 22

   B. 20

   C. 2

   D. 4

13. If you know expected value is 500 and the standard deviation is 12, you can say with approximately a 95 percent confidence rating which of the following?

   A. The activity will take from 488 to 512 days.

   B. The activity will take from 464 to 536 days.

   C. The activity will take from 494 to 506 days.

   D. The activity will take from 476 to 524 days.

14. If your expected value is 110 and the standard deviation is 12, which of the following is true?

   A. There is approximately a 99 percent chance of completing this activity in 86 to 134 days.

   B. There is approximately a 68 percent chance of completing this activity in 98 to 122 days.

   C. There is approximately a 95 percent chance of completing this activity in 98 to 122 days.

   D. There is approximately a 75 percent chance of completing this activity in 86 to 134 days.

15. You are the project manager working on a research project for a new drug treatment. Your preliminary project schedule runs past the due date for a federal grant application. The manager of the R&D department has agreed to release two resources to work on your project in order to meet the federal grant application date. This is an example of _____.

    A. crashing

    B. fast tracking

    C. resource leveling

    D. adjusting the resource calendar

16. You are the project manager for Rivera Gourmet Adventure Vacations. Rivera combines the wonderful tastes of great gourmet food with outdoor adventure activities. Your project involves installing a new human resources software system. Jason, the database analyst working on this project, is overallocated. Which of the following statements is true?

    A. You should use resource requirements updates to determine availability and smooth out resource overallocation.

    B. You should use crashing to resource level the critical path tasks.

    C. You should use resource leveling to smooth out resource assignments.

    D. You should use fast tracking to resource level the critical path tasks.

17. What is one of the problems with project management software?

    A. The project manager manages the software instead of the project.

    B. Project duration calculations are sometimes approximate.

    C. You cannot override the project management software decisions regarding schedules.

    D. It's expensive and difficult to use.

18. Obtaining formal project plan approval and sign-off is important for all of the following reasons except which one?

    A. Stakeholders are able to recommend a project Planning methodology to follow throughout the remaining process groups.

    B. Stakeholders are aware of the project details, which makes them more likely to participate in future project decisions.

    C. Stakeholders will be more likely to cooperate.

    D. Stakeholders are aware of the specific details regarding project schedules, budgets, and risks.

19. You are the project manager for a custom home-building construction company. You are working on the model home project for the upcoming Show Homes Tour. The model home includes Internet connections in every room and talking appliances. You are working on the cost budget for this project. All of the following statements are true except which one?

A. This process assigns cost estimates to project activities, including risks and contingency plans.

B. The cost baseline will be used to measure variances and future project performance.

C. This process assigns cost estimates for expected future period operating costs.

D. The cost baseline is the expected cost for the project.

20. Which of the following is displayed as an S curve?

A. Gantt

B. Cost baseline

C. Critical path

D. Schedule baseline

Answers to Review Questions

1. C. The tools and techniques for Activity Duration Estimating are expert judgment, alternatives analysis, published estimating data, project management software, and bottom-up estimating.

2. A. Analogous—or top-down—estimating techniques are a form of expert judgment. Since this project is similar to another recent project, you can use the cost estimates from the previous project to help you quickly determine estimates for the current project.

3. C. Reserve analysis takes schedule risk into consideration and adds a percentage of time or additional work periods to the estimate to prevent schedule delays.

4. C. Parametric estimating multiplies a known element—such as the quantity of materials needed—by the time it takes to install or complete one unit of materials. The result is a total estimate for the activity. In this case, 10 servers multiplied by 16 hours per server gives you a 160-hour total duration estimate.

5. B. Bottom-up techniques are the most time-consuming and the most accurate estimates you can use. With bottom-up estimating, each work item is estimated and rolled up to a project total.

6. A. The project schedule determines the start and ending dates of activities, determines float times, generally shows resource assignments, and details the activity sequences and durations.

7. C. The CPM calculates a single early and late start date and a single early and late finish date for each activity. Once these dates are known, float time is calculated for each activity to determine the critical path. The other answers contain elements of PERT calculations.

8. B. The only information you have for this example is activity duration; therefore, the critical path is the path with the longest duration. Path A-D-E-H with a duration of 34 days is the critical path.

9. D. The only information you have for this example is activity duration, so you must calculate the critical path based on the durations given. The duration of A-B-C-E-H increased by 3 days for a total of 35 days. The duration of A-F-G-H and A-F-G-E-H each increased by 3 days. A-F-G-E-H totals 36 days and becomes the new critical path.

10. D. You calculate the critical path by adding together the durations of all the tasks with zero float. The critical path can be compressed using crashing techniques.

11. C. The calculation for PERT is the sum of optimistic time plus pessimistic time plus four times the most likely time divided by 6. The calculation for this example is as follows: $(48 + 72 + (4 \times 60)) \div 6 = 60$.

12. D. You calculate the standard deviation by subtracting the optimistic time from the pessimistic time and dividing the result by 6. The calculation for this example is as follows: $(72 - 48) \div 6 = 4$.

13. D. There is a 95 percent probability that the work will finish within plus or minus two standard deviations. The expected value is 500, and the standard deviation times 2 is 24, so the activity will take from 476 to 524 days.

14. B. A 68 percent probability is calculated using plus or minus one standard deviation, a 95 percent probability uses plus or minus two standard deviations, and a 99 percent probability uses plus or minus three standard deviations.

15. A. Crashing the schedule includes tasks such as adding resources to the critical path tasks or limiting project requirements.

16. C. Resource leveling attempts to smooth out resource assignments by splitting tasks, assigning underallocated team members to more tasks, or delaying the start of tasks to match team members' availability.

17. A. Project management software is a useful tool for the project manager, and it automates project scheduling, allowing for what-if analysis and easy changes. But if you focus too much on the tool and ignore the project, the tool becomes a hindrance.

18. A. Stakeholders ordinarily will not have much say in the project Planning methodology used by the project manager. The organization, the project office, or the project manager usually determines the methodology employed.

19. C. Future period operating costs are considered ongoing costs and are not part of project costs.

20. B. The cost baseline is displayed as an S curve because of the way project spending occurs. Spending begins slowly, picks up speed until the spending peak is reached, and then tapers off as the project winds down.

Chapter

8

Developing the Project Team

THE PMP EXAM CONTENT FROM THE EXECUTING THE PROJECT PERFORMANCE DOMAIN COVERED IN THIS CHAPTER INCLUDES THE FOLLOWING:

- ✓ Execute Tasks Defined in Project Plan
- ✓ Ensure Common Understanding and Set Expectations
- ✓ Implement the Procurement of Project Resources
- ✓ Manage Resource Allocation
- ✓ Improve Team Performance

This chapter begins the project Executing process group. I'll cover four of the processes in this chapter: Direct and Manage Project Execution, Acquire Project Team, Develop Project Team, and Distributing Information. I'll jump around a bit in this chapter, as you can tell from the processes I'll cover. Many of these processes are extensions, so to speak, of the Planning processes leading up to them. I'll cover the remaining Executing processes in the next chapter.

Direct and Manage Project Execution is the action process. This is where you'll put the plans into action and begin working on the project activities. Execution also involves keeping the project in line with the original project plan and bringing wayward activities back into alignment.

Several things happen during the Executing processes. The majority of the project budget will be spent during this process group, and often the majority of the project time is expended here as well. The greatest conflicts you'll see during the project Executing processes are schedule conflicts. In addition, the product description will be finalized here and contain more detail than it did in the Planning processes.

Hang with me during this chapter, because I make several references to the next process—the Monitoring and Controlling process group—that are inputs to the Executing process group. These are the only two process groups that serve as inputs to each other. Since I can't discuss both of them at the same time, I'll tell you when there's something specific from the Monitoring and Controlling process group that I'll discuss in a later chapter.

There might be several exam questions from every process within the Executing process group. You'll find the majority of questions are about the Direct and Manage Project Execution, Acquire Project Team, and Develop Project Team processes. Don't skip studying the other processes, however, because roughly a quarter of the exam questions concern the entire Executing process group. Are you ready to dive into Executing? Let's go.

Executing the Project Plan

The purpose of the *Direct and Manage Project Execution* process is to carry out the project plan. This is where your project comes to life and the work of the project happens. The work is authorized to begin and activities are performed. Resources are committed and carry out their assigned activities to create the product, result, or service of the project. Funds are spent to accomplish project objectives. Performing project activities, training, selecting sellers, collecting project data, utilizing resources, and so on, are all integrated with or are part of this process.

Direct and Manage Project Execution is where the rubber meets the road. If you've done a good job planning the project, things should go relatively smoothly for you during this process. The deliverables and requirements are agreed to, the resources have been identified and are ready to go, and the stakeholders know exactly where you're headed because you had them review, agree to, and approve the project plan.

Some project managers think this is the time for them to kick back and put their feet up. After all, the project plan is done, everyone knows what to do and what's expected of them, and the work of the project should almost carry itself out because your project plan is a work of genius, right? Wrong! You must stay involved. Your job now is a matter of overseeing the actual work, staying on top of issues and problems, and keeping the work lined up with the project plan.

Exam Spotlight

The project plan serves as the project baseline. During the Executing processes, you should continually compare and monitor project performance against the baseline so that corrective actions can be taken and implemented at the right time to prevent disaster. This information will also be fed into the Monitoring and Controlling processes for further analysis.

One of the most difficult aspects of this process is coordinating and integrating all the elements of the project. Although you do have the project plan as your guide, you still have a lot of balls in the air. You'll find yourself coordinating and monitoring many project elements—occasionally all at the same time—during the course of the Direct and Manage Project Execution process. You might be negotiating for team members at the same time you're negotiating with vendors at the same time you're working with another manager to get a project component completed so your deliverables stay on schedule. You should monitor risks and risk triggers closely. The Plan Purchases and Acquisitions process might need intervention or cause you delays. The organizational, technical, and interpersonal interfaces might require intense coordination and oversight. And of course, you should always be concerned about the pulse of your stakeholders. Are they actively involved in the project? Are they throwing up roadblocks now that the work has started?

According to the *PMBOK Guide*, this process also requires implementing corrective actions to bring the work of the project back into alignment with the project plan, preventive actions to reduce the probability of negative consequences, and defect repairs to correct product defects discovered during the quality processes.

As you can see, your work as project manager is not done yet. Many elements of the project require your attention, so let's get to work.

 Later in this chapter I'll also talk about Develop Project Team because this is an integral part of the Direct and Manage Project Execution process as well. You'll want to monitor the team's performance, the status of their work, and their interactions with you and other team members as you execute the project plan.

Executing Inputs

Direct and Manage Project Execution has seven inputs:

- Project management plan
- Approved corrective actions
- Approved preventive actions
- Approved change requests
- Approved defect repair
- Validated defect repair
- Administrative closure procedure

The project management plan documents the collection of outputs of the Planning processes and describes and defines how the project should be executed, monitored, controlled, and closed. You'll take a brief look at each of the other inputs next.

Approved Corrective Actions

In my organization, a corrective action means an employee has big trouble coming. Fortunately, this isn't what's meant here. *Corrective actions* are taken to get the anticipated future project outcomes to align with the project plan. Maybe you've discovered that one of your programmers is adding an unplanned feature to the software project because he's friends with the user. You'll have to redirect him to the activities assigned to him originally to avoid schedule delays. Perhaps your vendor isn't able to deliver the laboratory equipment needed for the next project phase. You'll want to exercise your contract options (let's hope there's a clause in the contract that says the vendor must provide rental equipment until they can deliver your order), put your contingency plan into place, and get the lab the equipment that's needed to keep the project on schedule.

Corrective actions are outputs of processes in the Monitoring and Controlling process group, but they serve as inputs to the Direct and Manage Project Execution process. I'll talk more about corrective actions in Chapter 10, "Monitoring and Controlling Change."

Approved Preventive Action

Preventive action involves anything that will reduce the potential impacts of risk events should they occur. Contingency plans and risk responses are examples of preventive action. I described these and other risk responses while talking about the Risk Response Planning process in Chapter 5, "Risk Planning." You should be aware of contingency plans and risk responses so that you're ready to implement them at the first sign of trouble. Approved preventive actions are an output of processes in the Monitoring and Controlling process group.

Approved Change Requests

Approved change requests, another output of the Monitoring and Controlling process group, are changes that either expand or reduce project scope. Approved changes might also cause revisions to project budgets, schedules, procedures, project management plans, and so on. Change requests can be internal or external to the project or organization. For example, a new law that's passed that affects your project might require changes.

Approved Defect Repairs

OK, it's your turn to figure it out: defect repairs are an output of what process? Approved defect repairs authorize corrections to product defects that are discovered during the Perform Quality Assurance process (primarily during product inspection or during quality audits). Approved defect repairs are an output of the Integrated Change Control process.

Validated Defect Repair

The difference between a validated defect repair and a defect repair is that the validated defect repair is the result of a reinspection of the original defect repair. In other words, you found a problem with the product during the Quality processes, you corrected the problem (defect repair), and now you're reinspecting that repair (validated defect repair) to make certain the fix is accurate, correct, and fixed the problem.

Administrative Closure Procedure

The *administrative closure procedure* is a document that outlines how administrative closure will occur on the project, the activities needed to perform this procedure, and the essential roles and responsibilities.

Exam Spotlight

For the exam, remember that the outputs of the Executing and Monitoring and Controlling process groups are also inputs to each other.

Tools and Techniques of Direct and Manage Project Execution

The tools and techniques of the Direct and Manage Project Execution process are project management methodology and project management information system. You've looked at both of these before. Remember that in the Executing processes, you'll be actively using both of these tools (employing the methodology you've developed in Planning and referring to the PMIS to update and track progress).

A curious thing happens here. Although the *PMBOK Guide* no longer lists work authorization systems as a tool and technique of the Direct and Manage Project Execution process, it's still listed in its glossary as a tool. It's also a subsystem of the project management system. Even though this isn't listed in the *PMBOK Guide*, I recommend that you understand what a work authorization system is for the exam and how you use it. And for the record, you'll use these during the Executing processes.

Work authorization systems clarify and initiate the work of each work package or activity. This is a formal procedure that authorizes work to begin in the correct sequence and at the right time. Work authorization systems are usually written procedures defined by the organization. They might include email, intranet-based, or paper-based systems. Verbal instructions might work well with small projects. You should understand the complexity of the project and balance the cost of instituting a work authorization system against the benefit you'll receive from it. This might be overkill on small projects, and as stated earlier, verbal instructions might work just as well.

Work is usually authorized using a form that describes the task, the responsible party, anticipated start and end dates, special instructions, and whatever else is particular to the activity or project. Depending on the organizational structure, the work is assigned and authorized by either the project manager or the functional manager.

Some of the outputs of this process are going to look familiar. You'll examine them next.

Outputs of Direct and Manage Project Execution

The Direct and Manage Project Execution process utilizes most of the outputs of the Planning process group and some of the outputs of the Monitoring and Controlling process group. The outputs of the Direct and Manage Project Execution process are as follows:

- Deliverables
- Requested changes
- Implemented change requests
- Implemented corrective actions
- Implemented preventive actions
- Implemented defect repairs
- Work performance information

The two primary outputs are deliverables, meaning actually accomplishing the activities leading to the completion of the product, result, or service you set out to produce, and work performance information. Without having completed the prior processes, you wouldn't know what the work of the project should look like.

The outputs starting with *implemented* were covered in the tools and techniques section. The only difference between the tools and techniques and the output is that during the output, the action or request is implemented. Because I haven't mentioned it in a while, now is a good time for a documentation reminder—it's not a bad idea to record all the approved and implemented actions for future reference. You'll now look at the other three outputs.

Deliverables

During Direct and Manage Project Execution, you'll gather and record information regarding the outcomes of the work, including activity completion dates, milestone completions, the status of the deliverables, the quality of the deliverables, costs, schedule progress and updates, and so on. Deliverables aren't always tangible. For example, perhaps your team members require training on a piece of specialized equipment. Completion of the training is recorded as a work result. Capabilities required to perform a service that's described in the project management plan are also considered a deliverable. All of this information gets used during the Performance Reporting process, which I'll discuss during the Monitoring and Controlling processes.

Executing and Monitoring and Controlling are two process groups that work hand in hand. As you gather the information from work results, you'll measure the outputs and take corrective actions where necessary. This means you'll loop back through the Executing processes to put the corrections into place. The *PMBOK Guide* breaks these processes up for ease of explanation, but in practice, you'll work through several of the Executing and Monitoring and Controlling processes together.

Requested Changes

As a result of working through activities and producing your product, service, or result, you will inevitably come upon things that need to be changed. Changes can also come about from stakeholder requests, external sources, technological advances, and so on. These change requests might encompass schedule, scope, requirement, or resource changes. The list really could go on. Your job as project manager, if you choose to accept it, is to collect the change requests and make determinations about their impact to the project.

I'll discuss change requests in the coming chapters. Requested changes are an output of several process, including the Direct and Manage Project Execution process and the Performance Reporting process in the Monitoring and Controlling process group. Remember that Executing and Monitoring and Controlling outputs feed each other as inputs.

Exam Spotlight

Direct and Manage Project Execution is where the work of the project is performed and the project plan is put into action and carried out. In this process, the project manager is like an orchestra conductor signaling the instruments to begin their activities, monitoring what should be winding down, and keeping that smile going to remind everyone that they should be enjoying themselves. I recommend that you know the outputs of the Direct and Manage Project Execution process for the exam.

Real World Scenario

We All Scream for Ice Cream

Heather is a pharmaceutical sales person who is fed up with the rat race. She ran the numbers, decided to quit her day job, and bought an ice cream shop in a quaint tourist town. Having been involved in a few research and development projects, she understands the value of project management planning and using that plan as her guide to perform the work of the project.

Heather documented the deliverables needed to prepare for opening day in her scope statement. Some of those deliverables are as follows: remodel, develop staffing plan, procure equipment, and procure materials. Confident in her planning, Heather hired a contractor and began remodeling the shop. And then real life happened. The contractors discovered a water problem in the storage room. They installed a sump pump, which took care of the water, but discovered an even bigger problem when they moved the storage shelves. There was mold growing up the drywall. The drywall had to be removed, as did the insulation behind it, and the mold remaining on permanent fixtures had to be eliminated. Then new insulation and drywall had to be installed. The drywall had to be primed and painted, and Heather decided since that portion of the storage room was getting a fresh coat of paint, the contractors might as well paint the entire room.

All of these actions required another pass through the Planning processes. The schedule didn't require much modification because other work could be started at the same time the water problem was being addressed, but the budget needed to be modified as a result of the additional work. To avoid more surprises, Heather requested that the contractor perform a through inspection of the property and determine whether there were any other hidden issues. Armed with the inspection report, Heather could knowledgeably plan corrective action for other items that needed to be addressed.

Work Performance Information

Work performance information concerns gathering, documenting, and recording the status of project activities. According to the *PMBOK Guide*, these are the types of information you might gather during this process:

- Schedule status and progress
- Status of deliverable completion
- Progress and status of schedule activities
- Adherence to quality standards
- Status of costs (those authorized and costs incurred to date)
- Schedule activity completion estimates for those activities started

- Schedule activities percent complete
- Lessons learned
- Resource consumption and utilization

Work performance information becomes an input to a few of the Monitoring and Controlling processes where you'll perform further analysis on the data. It's important that you document this information so that when you get to the Monitoring and Controlling processes, you don't have to backtrack.

I'm going to switch topics now. I told you the Executing process group is about performing the work of the project, and in order to do that, you need resources. You'll look at two processes, Acquire the Project Team and Develop the Project Team, in the next few sections.

Acquiring the Project Team

The *Acquire Project Team* process involves attaining and assigning human resources to the project. Project staff might come from inside the company or from outside the company in the form of employees hired specifically for the project or as contract help. In any case, it's your job as the project manager to ensure that resources are available and skilled in the project activities to which they're assigned. However, in practice, you might find that you don't always have control over the selection of team members. Someone else, the big boss for example, might hand-pick the folks they want working on the project, and it's up to you to assess their skills and decide where they best fit on the project.

The Acquire Project Team process inputs are as follows: enterprise environmental factors, organizational process assets, roles and responsibilities, project organization charts, and staffing management plan.

Some project activities might require special skills or knowledge in order to be completed. The enterprise environmental factors input involves taking this information into account as well as considering personal interests, characteristics, and availability of potential team members before making assignments. For example, consider the previous experience of the staff member you're thinking of assigning to a specific activity. Have they performed this function before? Do they have the experience necessary for the level of complexity this project activity calls for? Are they competent and proficient at these skills?

Personal interests and personal characteristics play a big role as well. If the person you're thinking of just isn't interested in the project, they aren't likely to perform at their best. If you can, think about assigning someone else in a case like this. Unfortunately, some people just don't play well with others. When you're assigning staff, if at all possible, don't put the only two people in the whole company who can't get along together on the same project. If the staff member you need has a skill no one else has or they can perform a function like no one else can, you might not have a choice. In this case, you'll have to employ other techniques to keep the team cohesive and working well together despite the not-so-friendly characteristics of the vital team member.

One final consideration: check on the availability of key team members. If the team member you must have for the activity scheduled in February is on their honeymoon, you probably aren't going to win the toss.

Exam Spotlight

Even though the availability, experience levels, interests, cost, and abilities of your resources are considered part of the enterprise environmental factors input, you should understand these inputs and their importance to the Acquire Project Team process for the exam.

Recruitment practices are an example of the organizational process assets to watch for in this process. This is a matter of making certain you consult any organizational procedures or policies currently in place when hiring and assigning staff. Organizational policies that dictate recruitment practices are constraints.

You've looked at the other inputs in previous processes, so you'll move on to the tools and techniques of this process.

Tools and Techniques of Acquire Project Team

Preassignment, negotiation, acquisitions, and virtual teams are tools and techniques of the Acquire Project Team process. As the project manager, you will use the negotiation technique a lot. You'll have to negotiate with functional managers and other organizational department managers—and sometimes with the vendor to get some of their best people—for resources for your project and for the timing of those resources.

Preassignment can happen when the project is put out for bid and specific team members are promised as part of the proposal or when internal project team members are promised and assigned as a condition of the project. When staff members are promised as part of the project proposal—particularly on internal projects—they should be identified in the project charter.

Availability is one part of the negotiating equation. You'll have to work with the functional manager or other project managers to ensure that the staff member you're requesting is available when the schedule says they're needed.

The second part of the equation is the competency level of the staff member they're assigning to your project. I remember hearing someone say once that availability is not a skill set. Be wary of functional managers who are willing to offer up certain individuals "anytime" while others are "never available." Be certain your negotiations include discussions about the skills and personal characteristics of the team members you want on your project.

Acquisition is another tool and technique of the Acquire Project Team process. It involves hiring individuals or teams of people for certain project activities, either as employees or as contract help during the course of the project or project phase or for specific project activities. Procurement is usually required when the organization does not have employees with the required skills and competencies available to work on the project.

Chapter 6, "Resource Planning," covers the Plan Purchases and Acquisitions process in more detail.

Virtual teams are teams that don't necessarily work in the same location but all share the goals of the project and have a role on the project. This type of team allows you to include folks from different geographic locations, those who work different hours or shifts than the other team members, those with mobility limitations, and so on. According to the *PMBOK Guide*, "Virtual teams can be defined as groups of people with a shared goal, who fulfill their roles with little or no time spent meeting face to face." In today's wonderful world of technology, team members can use the Internet, email, videoconferencing, and teleconferencing to meet and communicate on a regular basis. This of course brings to light the importance of communication. Make certain all team members are aware of the protocols for communicating in a virtual team environment, understand the expectations, and are clear regarding decision making processes. It's vital in this type of team structure that you as the project manager give credit to the appropriate team members for their performance and actions on the project. You might be the only one who fully understands the contributions individual team members have made. When teams are co-located, members have the opportunity to see for themselves the extraordinary efforts others are making on the project. Virtual team members don't necessarily know what their teammates have contributed to the project (or the level of effort they've exerted), so it's up to you to let everyone know about outstanding performance.

Outputs of Acquire Project Team

The resulting outputs of the Acquire Project Team process are project staff assignment, resource availability, and staffing management plan updates.

Your ability to influence the selection of resources (using the negotiating technique) will impact the project staff assignment output. After determining elements such as the roles and responsibilities, reviewing recruitment practices, and negotiating for staff, you assign project team members to project activities. Along with this output, a project team directory is published listing the names of all project team members and stakeholders. Don't forget to also include team member names in project organization charts, RAM charts, and other planning documents if their assignments or names weren't known when you created those documents.

 Real World Scenario

The Only Candidate

"Hey, did you hear?" your friend Story asks. "Roger has been assigned to the project team."

"Over my dead body," you reply, pushing away from your computer screen. You head straight for the project manager's office and don't wait for a response from Story.

Ann seats the phone into the cradle just as you walk through the door. Fortunately for you, Ann's door is always open, and she welcomes drop-ins.

"Seems like something is on your mind," Ann says. "What can I help with?"

"Story just told me that Roger has been assigned to the project team. I can't work with Roger. He's arrogant and doesn't respect anyone's work but his own. He belittles me in front of others, and I don't deserve that. I write good code copy, and I don't need Roger looking over my shoulder. I want to be on this team, but not if Roger is part of it."

Ann thinks for a minute and replies, "I want you to work on this project; it's a great opportunity for you. But there isn't anyone else who can work on the analysis phase of this project except Roger. He's the only one left who has a solid understanding of the mainframe legacy code. Unfortunately, those old programs were never documented well, and they've evolved over the years into programs on top of programs. Without Roger's knowledge of the existing system, we'd blow the budget and time estimates already established for this project. Since I need both of you on this project, here's what I propose. I will clearly outline the roles and responsibilities for all the key team members at the kickoff meeting. I'll also make it clear that negative team interactions won't be allowed. And if you have a problem with Roger that you can't resolve on your own, you should get me involved right away."

The time periods your project staff are available are documented in the resource availability output. This document comes in handy when you're creating the final schedule and assigning resources to activities.

The *staffing management plan* might require updates to document the project roles and responsibilities of the staff assigned to the project. This document might require updates throughout the project if you have staff members leave because of a promotion or, heaven forbid, if they leave for employment in another company (unless you want them to leave—that's another story).

Now that you have the team, what do you do with them? You'll look at topics such as motivation, rewards, and recognition in the next process, Develop Project Team.

Developing the Project Team

Projects exist to create a unique product, result, or service within a limited time frame. Projects are performed by people, and most projects require more than one person to perform all of the activities. If you've got more than one person working on your project, you've got a team. And if you've got a team, you've got a wide assortment of personalities, skills, needs, and issues in the mix. Couple this with part-time team members, teams based in functional organizations whose loyalty lies with the functional manager, or teams based in matrix organizations that report to you for project-related activities and another manager for their functional duties, and you could have some real challenges on your hands. Good luck—OK, I won't leave you hanging like that.

The *Develop Project Team* process is about creating an open, encouraging environment for your team and developing it into an effective, functioning, coordinated group. Projects are performed by individuals, and the better they work together, the smoother and the more efficient the execution of the project will be. I'm sure you all have had the experience of working with a team that pitched in and shared workloads when the work became unbalanced. I'm also sure you all have worked with teams that didn't do this—teams whose members took on a "me first" attitude and couldn't care less about the plight of their fellow team members. I'd much rather work with a team like the first example.

> The proper development of the team is critical to a successful project. Since teams are made up of individuals, individual development becomes a critical factor to project success. Individual team members need the proper development and training to perform the activities of the project or to enhance their existing knowledge and skills. The development needed will depend on the project. Perhaps you have a team member who's ready to make the jump into a lead role but they don't have any experience at lead work. Give them some exposure by assigning them a limited amount of activities in a lead capacity, provide them with some training if needed, and be available to coach and mentor where needed. The best option is to work with the management team to provide this person with the development they need prior to the start of the project (if you're lucky enough to know early on who your resources might be and what their existing skills are).

Develop Project Team inputs include project staff assignments, staffing management plan, and resource availability. Funny thing, these inputs are all outputs that I discussed in the Acquire Project Team process, so I'll move on.

Tools and Techniques of Develop Project Team

The tools and techniques of Develop Project Team are as follows:

- General management skills
- Training
- Team building activities
- Ground rules
- Co-location
- Recognition and rewards

I'll cover all these tools and techniques next.

General Management Skills

You learned about general management skills back in Chapter 1, "What Is a Project?" These include skills such as general business knowledge, budgeting, organizational skills, problem-solving skills, and so on. What's important to note here is that the general management skills of leadership, influence, negotiation, communications, empathy, and creativity are especially useful during this process and others in the Executing process group.

One other issue to consider regarding this tool and technique is that you'll have resources from other departments who have assignments on the project that you're responsible for overseeing. For example, the finance department and the marketing department might have assigned project activities, and as the project manager, you'll manage their progress. This implies that you'll need general knowledge management skills to understand what the assignments entail and strong leadership skills to influence the departments to stay on schedule.

Training

Training is a matter of assessing your team members' skills and abilities, assessing the project needs, and providing the training necessary for the team members to carry out their assigned activities. Training can sometimes be a reward as well. In the software industry, programmers seek out positions that offer training on the latest and greatest technologies, and they consider it a benefit or bonus to attend training on the company dollar and time. If you know early in the Planning processes that training is necessary, include the details of this in the staffing management plan. During the course of the project, you might observe team members who need training, or they might ask for training. Update the staffing management plan with this information.

Team-Building Activities

Many times, project teams consist of folks who don't know each other. They aren't necessarily aware of the project objectives and might not even want to be a part of the team. The project manager might not have worked with the people assigned to the project team before either. Sound like a recipe for disaster? It's not. Thousands of projects are started with team members and project managers who don't know each other and come to a successful completion. How is that done? It's a result of the project manager's team-building and communication skills.

The project manager's job is to bring the team together, get its members all headed in the right direction, and provide motivation, reward, and recognition to keep the team in tip-top shape. This is done using a variety of team-building techniques and exercises. *Team building* is simply getting a diverse group of people to work together in the most efficient and effective manner possible. This might involve events organized by the management team or individual actions designed to improve team performance. There are entire volumes on this subject, and it's beyond the scope of this book to go into all the team-building possibilities. The exam tends to focus more on the theories behind team building and the characteristics of effective teams, so that's what you'll spend your time exploring.

Dr. Bruce Tuckman developed a model that describes how teams develop and mature. According to Tuckman, all newly formed teams go through four stages of development:

1. Forming

2. Storming

3. Norming

4. Performing

You've probably seen this elsewhere, but since these stages might show up on the exam, you'll want to memorize them. Take a brief look at each of them:

Forming   This one is easy. Forming is the beginning stage of team formation, when all the members are brought together, introduced, and told the objectives of the project. This is where team members learn why they're working together. During this stage, team members tend to be formal and reserved and take on an "all-business" approach.

Storming   Storming is where the action begins. Team members become confrontational with each other as they're vying for position and control during this stage. They're working through who is going to be the top dog and jockeying for status.

Norming   Now things begin to calm down. Team members know each other fairly well by now. They're comfortable with their positions in the team, and they begin to deal with project problems instead of people problems. In the norming stage, they confront the project concerns and problems instead of each other. Decisions are made jointly at this stage, and team members exhibit mutual respect and familiarity with one another.

Performing   Ahh, perfection. Well, almost, anyway. This is where great teams end up. This stage is where the team is productive and effective. The level of trust among team members is high, and great things are achieved. This is the mature development stage.

Exam Spotlight

Different teams progress through the stages of development at different rates. When new team members are brought onto the team, the development stages start all over again. It doesn't matter where the team is in the development process—a new member will start the cycle all over again.

According to Tuckman, leaders adapt their leadership styles as the teams develop maturity and progress through the development stages. For example, early in the forming stage, leaders take on a direct style of leadership. As the team progresses, their leaders will employ a coaching, participating, and then delegating style of leadership to match the level of development the team has achieved.

You'll now take a closer look at focusing your team members throughout these stages of development, along with some of the characteristics of effective teams.

Team Focus

Have you ever watched any of those old pirate movies on late-night TV? Remember the scenes where the captain goes down into the bowels of the ship to check on the teams of rowers? He scrutinizes the crew and literally whips the rowers who aren't pulling their weight into shape. I don't recommend this as a team-building technique, but imagine for a minute that your project team members are like those rowing teams. If the members on the left are rowing one way and the members on the right are rowing another, you're creating a lot of energy and looking busy, but in the end you aren't making any progress.

It's paramount that the team members know and understand the goals and objectives of the project. They should all understand the direction you're headed and work toward that end. After all, that's the reason they've been brought together in the first place. Keep in mind that people see and hear things from their own perspective. A room full of people attending a speech will each come away with something a little different because what was said speaks to their particular situation in life at the time. In other words, their own perceptions filter what they hear. It's your job as project manager to make certain the team members understand the project goals and their own assignments correctly. The whip was effective for the captain in the old movies, but I suggest you use solid communication skills to get your point across. Ask your team members to tell you in their own words what they believe the project goals are. This is a great way to know whether you've got everyone on board and a great opportunity for you to clarify any misunderstandings regarding the project goals.

Effective Team Characteristics

Effective teams are typically very energetic teams. Their enthusiasm is contagious, and it feeds on itself. They generate a lot of creativity and become good problem solvers. Teams like this are every project manager's dream. Investing yourself in team building as well as relationship building—especially when you don't think you have the time to do so—will bring many benefits. Here's a sample of the benefits:

- Better conflict resolution
- Commitment to the project
- Commitment to the project team members and project manager
- High job satisfaction
- Enhanced communication
- A sense of belonging and purpose
- A successful project

Dysfunctional teams will typically produce the opposite results of the benefits just listed. Dysfunctional teams don't just happen by themselves any more than great teams do. Sure, sometimes you're lucky enough to get the right combination of folks together right off the bat. But usually, team building takes work and dedication on the part of the project manager. Even in the situations where you do get that dynamite combination of people, they will benefit from team-building exercises and feedback.

Unfortunately, sour attitudes are just as contagious as enthusiasm. Watch for these symptoms among your team members, and take action to correct the situation before the entire team is affected:

- Lack of motivation or "don't care" attitudes

- Project work that isn't satisfying

- Status meetings that turn into whining sessions

- Poor communication

- Lack of respect and lack of trust for the project manager

 No amount of team building will make up for poor project planning or ineffective project management techniques. Neglecting these things and fooling yourself into thinking that your project team is good enough to make up for the poor planning or poor techniques could spell doom for your project. And besides that, it's not fair to your project team to put them in that position.

Ground Rules

Ground rules are expectations set by the project manager and project team that describe acceptable team behavior. For example, one of my pet peeves is team members who interrupt each other. In this case, one of the ground rules is one person speaks at a time during a meeting. Another ground rule might be reporting potential issues as soon as the team member becomes aware of them. Outlining ground rules like this helps the team understand expectations regarding acceptable behavior and increases productivity.

Co-location

Team members are often in the same physical location—for example, the same office building or meeting space. This tool and technique is called co-location. *Co-location* enables teams to function more effectively than if they're spread out among different localities. Many times on large projects, the project manager will make provisions in the project budget to bring the team together at the same location. (It's difficult, but not impossible, to manage project team members who are not physically located together.) One way to achieve co-location might be to set aside a common meeting room, sometimes called a *war room*, for team members who are located in different buildings or across town to meet and exchange information.

Multiple locations can also be a big time waster for you as the project manager and for your team members. If some team members are located in one part of town and another set of team members are located across town, you'll find yourself in the car (or the bus) driving back and forth to make face-to-face contact and get status updates. Conducting team meetings also becomes a hassle as one set of team members or the other must drive to another location (or both to a central location) to have a meeting.

Our busy, conflicting schedules and differences in location don't always allow for face-to-face communication, so email is the next best thing. I'm a huge email fan—it's one of my favorite forms of communication. Email can keep the information flowing when you aren't able to meet in person, and it can even help take the heat out of conflicts that might escalate if you were meeting one on one. However, email cannot reveal tone of voice, facial expressions, or body language. Sometimes those nonverbal cues are more important than what's being said. If you don't know your team members or stakeholders well, I recommend meeting with them personally whenever you can. Once you've established good relationships with them, you should be able to balance the use of email and personal interactions and know when it's time to call a face-to-face meeting. In reality, it's often difficult to get your team together physically. A good solution in lieu of having people relocate is videoconferencing or conference calling. Team members scattered across the country all have access to the telephone, and it's relatively easy to find a time everyone can meet over the phone. Videoconferencing is the best option if it's available because it allows intonation and nonverbal behaviors to be part of the communication process.

Recognition and Rewards

I have quite a bit of ground to cover with recognition and rewards. As I said earlier, you could see several exam questions regarding team building, so dig out all your favorite memorization techniques and put them to use.

Team building starts with project planning and doesn't stop until the project is completed. It involves employing techniques to improve your team's performance and keeping team members motivated. Motivation helps people work more efficiently and produce better results. If clear expectations, clear procedures, and the right motivational tools are used, project teams will excel.

Motivation can be extrinsic or intrinsic. Extrinsic motivators are material rewards and might include bonuses, the use of a company car, stock options, gift certificates, training opportunities, extra time off, and so on.

Intrinsic motivators are specific to the individual. Some people are just naturally driven to achieve—it's part of their nature. (I suspect this is a motivator for you since you're reading this book.) Cultural and religious influences are forms of intrinsic motivators as well. Reward and recognition—a tool and technique of the Develop Project Team process—are examples of extrinsic motivators. You'll look at them next.

Recognition and rewards are an important part of team motivation. They are formal ways of recognizing and promoting desirable behavior and are most effective when carried out by the management team and the project manager. You should develop and document the criteria for rewards, especially monetary awards. Although rewards and recognition help build a team, they can also kill morale if you don't have an established method or criteria for handing them out. Track who is receiving awards throughout the project. For example, if you have consistent overachievers on the team, you could kill morale by consistently rewarding the same one or two people repeatedly. It could also be perceived that you're playing favorites. If team members believe the rewards are win-lose (also known as *zero-sum*) and that only certain team members will be rewarded, you might end up hurting morale more than helping. If you find yourself in this position, consider team awards. This is a win-win because all team members are recognized for their contributions. Recognition and rewards should be proportional to the achievement. In other words, appropriately link the reward to the performance. For example, a project manager who has responsibility for the project budget and the procurement process and keeps the costs substantially under budget without sacrificing the results of the project should be rewarded for this achievement. However, if these responsibilities are assigned to a functional manager in the organization, it wouldn't be appropriate to reward a project manager who was not the one responsible for keeping the costs in line.

Team members should be rewarded for going above and beyond the call of duty. Perhaps they put in a significant amount of overtime to meet a project goal or spent nights round-the-clock babysitting ill-performing equipment. These types of behaviors should be rewarded and formally recognized by the project manager and the management team. On the other hand, if the ill-performing equipment was a direct result of mistakes made or if it happened because of poor planning, rewards would not be appropriate, obviously.

Consider individual preferences and cultural differences when using rewards and recognitions. Some people don't like to be recognized in front of a group; others thrive on it. Some people appreciate an honest thank-you with minimal fanfare, and others just won't accept individual rewards as their culture doesn't allow it. Keep this in mind when devising your reward system.

There are many theories on motivation. As a project manager, it's important to understand them so that you can tailor your recognition and rewards programs to take into account the reasons people do what they do. You might encounter questions on these theories on the exam, so I'll discuss their primary points in the following sections.

 Real World Scenario

Baker's Gift Baskets

You're a contract project manager for Baker's Gift Baskets. This company assembles gift baskets of all styles and shapes with every edible treat imaginable. The company has recently experienced explosive growth, and you've been brought on board to manage its new project. The owners of the company want to offer "pick-your-own" baskets that allow customers to pick the individual items they want included in the basket. In addition, they're introducing a new line of containers to choose from, including items such as miniature golf bags, flowerpots, serving bowls, and the like. This means changes to the catalog and the website to accommodate the new offerings.

The deadline for this project is the driving constraint. The website changes won't cause any problems with the deadline. However, the catalog must go to press quickly to meet holiday mailing deadlines, which in turn are driving the project deadline.

Your team members put their heads together and came up with an ingenious plan to meet the catalog deadline. It required lots of overtime and some weekend work on their part to pull it off, but they met the date.

You decide this is a perfect opportunity to recognize and reward the team for their outstanding efforts. You've arranged a slot on the agenda at the next all-company meeting to bring your team up front and praise them for their cooperation and efforts to get the catalog to the printers on time. You'll also present each of them with two days of paid time off and a gift certificate for a dinner with their family at an exclusive restaurant in the city.

Motivational Theories

Motivational theories came about during the modern age. Prior to today's information- and service-type jobs and yesterday's factory work, the majority of people worked the land and barely kept enough food on the table to feed their family. No one was concerned about motivation at work. You worked because you wouldn't have anything to eat if you didn't. Fortunately, that isn't the only reason most people work today.

Today we have a new set of problems in the workplace. Workers in the service- and knowledge-based industries aren't concerned with starvation—that need has been replaced with other needs such as job satisfaction, a sense of belonging and commitment to the project, good working conditions, and so on. Motivational theories present ideas on why people act the way they do and how you can influence them to act in certain ways to get the results you want. Again, there are libraries full of books on this topic. I'll cover four of them here.

MASLOW'S HIERARCHY OF NEEDS

You have probably seen this classic example of motivational theory. Abraham Maslow theorized that humans have five basic needs arranged in hierarchical order. The first needs are physical needs, such as the need for food, clothing, and shelter. The idea is that these needs must be met before the person can move to the next level of needs in the hierarchy, which includes safety and security needs. Here, the concern is for the person's physical welfare and the security of their belongings. Once that need is met, they progress to the next level, and so on.

Maslow's hierarchy of needs theory suggests that once a lower-level need has been met, it no longer serves as a motivator and the next higher level becomes the driving motivator in a person's life. Maslow conjectures that humans are always in one state of need or another. Here is a recap of each of the needs, starting with the highest level and ending with the lowest:

Self-actualization   Performing at your peak potential

Self-esteem needs   Accomplishment, respect for self, capability

Social needs   A sense of belonging, love, acceptance, friendship

Safety and security needs   Your physical welfare and the security of your belongings

Basic physical needs   Food, clothing, shelter

The highest level of motivation in this theory is the state of self-actualization. The United States Army had a slogan a few years ago that I think encapsulates self-actualization very well: "Be all that you can be." When all the physical, safety, social, and self-esteem needs have been met, a person reaches a state of independence where they're able to express themselves and perform at their peak. They'll do good work just for the sake of doing good work. Recognition and self-esteem is the motivator at lower levels; now the need for being the best they can be is reached.

HYGIENE THEORY

Frederick Herzberg came up with the *Hygiene Theory*, also known as the *Motivation-Hygiene Theory*. He postulates that two factors contribute to motivation: hygiene factors and motivators. Hygiene factors deal with work environment issues. The thing to remember about hygiene factors is that they prevent dissatisfaction. Examples of hygiene factors are pay, benefits, the conditions of the work environment, and relationships with peers and managers. Pay is considered a hygiene factor because Herzberg believed that over the long term, pay is not a motivator. Being paid for the work prevents dissatisfaction but doesn't necessarily bring satisfaction in and of itself. He believed this to be true as long as the pay system is equitable. If two workers performing the same functions have large disparities in pay, then pay can become a motivator.

Motivators deal with the substance of the work itself and the satisfaction one derives from performing the functions of the job. Motivators lead to satisfaction. The ability to advance, the opportunity to learn new skills, and the challenges involved in the work are all motivators according to Herzberg.

Exam Spotlight

For the exam, remember that Herzberg was the inventor of the Hygiene Theory and that this theory claims that hygiene factors (pay, benefits, and working conditions) prevent dissatisfaction, while motivators (challenging work, opportunities to learn, and advancement) lead to satisfaction.

EXPECTANCY THEORY

The *Expectancy Theory* says that the expectation of a positive outcome drives motivation. People will behave in certain ways if they think there will be good rewards for doing so. Also note that this theory says the strength of the expectancy drives the behavior. This means the expectation or likelihood of the reward is linked to the behavior. For example, if you tell your two-year-old to put the toys back in the toy box and you'll give her a cookie to do so, chances are she'll put the toys away. This is a reasonable reward for a reasonable action. However, if you promise your project team members vacations in Hawaii if they get the project done early and they know there is no way you can deliver that reward, there is little motivation to work toward it.

This theory also says that people become what you expect of them. If you openly praise your project team members and treat them like valuable contributors, you'll likely have a high-performing team on your hands. Conversely, when you publicly criticize people or let them know that you have low expectations regarding their performance, they'll likely live up (or down as the case might be) to that expectation as well.

ACHIEVEMENT THEORY

Achievement Theory says that people are motivated by the need for three things: achievement, power, and affiliation. The achievement motivation is obviously the need to achieve or succeed. The power motivation involves a desire for influencing the behavior of others. And the need for affiliation is relationship oriented. Workers want to have friendships with their co-workers and a sense of camaraderie with their fellow team members. The strength of your team members' desire for each of these will drive their performance on various activities.

Exam Spotlight

Make certain you understand the theories of motivation and their premises for the exam. Here's a summary to help you memorize them.

> *Maslow*: Hierarchy of needs

> *Hygiene theory*: Work environment (pay, benefits, and working conditions) prevents dissatisfaction

> *Expectancy theory*: Expectation of positive outcomes drives motivation

> *Achievement theory*: People are motivated by achievement, power, and affiliation. I'll cover two more theories in the leadership section, which is next. These deal specifically with how leaders interact with their project team members.

Leadership versus Management

Chapter 1 introduced the differences between leaders and managers. I'll add a bit more information here regarding leadership theories and the types of power leaders possess, but first I'll recap leadership and management first before I talk about those theories.

Recall that leadership is about imparting vision and rallying people around that vision. Leaders motivate and inspire and are concerned with strategic vision. Leaders have a knack for getting others to do what needs done.

Two of the techniques they use to do this are power and politics. *Power* is the ability to get people to do what they wouldn't do ordinarily. It's also the ability to influence behavior. *Politics* imparts pressure to conform regardless of whether people agree with the decision. Leaders understand the difference between power and politics and when to employ each technique. I'll talk more about power shortly.

Good leaders have committed team members who believe in the vision of the leader. Leaders set direction and time frames and have the ability to attract good talent to work for them. Leaders inspire a vision and get things done through others by earning loyalty, respect, and cooperation from team members. They set the course and lead the way. Good leaders are directive in their approach but allow for plenty of feedback and input. Good leaders commonly have strong interpersonal skills and are well respected.

Managers are generally task oriented and concerned with issues such as plans, controls, budgets, policies, and procedures. They're generalists with a broad base of planning and organizational skills, and their primary goal is satisfying stakeholder needs. They also possess motivational skills and the ability to recognize and reward behavior.

Project managers need to use the traits of both leaders and managers at different times during a project. On large projects, a project manager will act more like a leader inspiring the subproject managers to get on board with the objectives. On small projects, project managers will act more like managers because they're responsible for all the planning and coordinating functions.

I'll discuss three theories regarding leadership and management. They are Douglas McGregor's Theory X and Theory Y and the Contingency Theory. Then I'll discuss the types of power leaders use and the outputs of Develop Project Team.

THEORY X AND THEORY Y

Douglas McGregor defined two models of worker behavior, Theory X and Theory Y, that attempt to explain how different managers deal with their team members. *Theory X* managers believe most people do not like work and will try to steer clear of it; they believe people have little to no ambition, need constant supervision, and won't actually perform the duties of their job unless threatened. As a result, Theory X managers are like dictators and impose very rigid controls over their people. They believe people are motivated only by punishment, money, or position. Unfortunately for the team members, Theory X managers unknowingly also subscribe to the Expectancy Theory. If they expect people to be lazy and unproductive and treat them as such, their team members probably will be lazy and unproductive.

Theory Y managers believe people are interested in performing their best given the right motivation and proper expectations. These managers provide support to their teams, are concerned about their team members, and are good listeners. Theory Y managers believe people are creative and committed to the project goals, that they like responsibility and seek it out, and that they are able to perform the functions of their positions with limited supervision.

CONTINGENCY THEORY

The Contingency Theory builds on a combination of Theory Y behaviors and the Hygiene Theory. The Contingency Theory, in a nutshell, says that people are motivated to achieve levels of competency and will continue to be motivated by this need even after competency is reached.

The Power of Leaders

As stated earlier, power is the ability to influence others to do what you want them to do. This can be used in a positive manner or a negative one. But that old saying of your grandmother's about attracting more flies with honey than vinegar still holds true today.

Leaders, managers, and project managers use power to convince others to do tasks a specific way. The kind of power they use to accomplish this depends on their personality, their personal values, and the company culture.

A project manager might use several forms of power. I've already talked about reward power, which is the ability to grant bonuses or incentive awards for a job well done. Here are a few more:

Punishment power   Punishment, also known as *coercive* or *penalty power*, is just the opposite of reward power. The employee is threatened with consequences if expectations are not met.

Expert power   Expert power occurs when the person being influenced believes the manager, or the person doing the influencing, is knowledgeable about the subject or has special abilities that make them an expert. The person goes along just because they think the influencer knows what they're doing and it's the best thing for the situation.

Legitimate power   Legitimate, or formal, power comes about as a result of the influencer's position. Because that person is the project manager, executive vice president, or CEO, they have the power to call the shots and make decisions.

Referent power   Referent power is inferred to the influencer by their subordinates. Project team members who have a great deal of respect and high regard for their project managers willingly go along with decisions made by the project manager because of referent power.

Punishment power should be used as a last resort and only after all other forms have been exhausted. Sometimes you'll have to use this method, but I hope much less often than the other three forms of power. Sometimes, you'll have team members who won't live up to expectations and their performance suffers as a result. This is a case where punishment power is enacted to get the employee to correct their behavior.

Exam Spotlight

Know the difference between leaders and managers, Theory X and Theory Y, the Contingency Theory, and the types of power for the PMP exam. Here's a summary to help you memorize them:

Leaders: Leaders motivate, inspire, and create buy-in for the organization's strategic vision. Leaders use power and politics to accomplish the vision.

Managers: Managers are task oriented and concerned with satisfying stakeholder needs.

Theory X: Most people don't like work.

Theory Y: People are motivated to perform their best given proper expectations and motivation.

Contingency Theory: People are motivated to achieve levels of competency and will continue to be motivated after competency is reached.

Reward power: You reward desirable behavior with incentives or bonuses.

Punishment power: You threaten team members with consequences if expectations are not met (also known as *penalty power*).

Expert power: The person doing the influencing has significant knowledge or skills regarding the subject.

Legitimate power: This is the power of the position held by the influencer (the president or vice president, for example).

Referent power: This is power that's inferred to the influencer.

Outputs of Develop Project Team

You're now ready to close out the Develop Project Team process. This process has only one output: team performance assessment. As a result of positive team-building experiences, you'll see individuals improving their skills, team behaviors and relationships improving, conflict resolutions going smoothly, and team members recommending ways to improve the work of the project. I talked about effective team characteristics an earlier in this chapter. Assessing these characteristics will help you determine where (or whether) the project team needs improvements.

Project managers wear a lot of hats. This is one of the issues that make this job so interesting. You need organization and planning skills to plan the project. You need motivation and sometimes disciplinary skills to execute the project plans. You need to exercise leadership and power where appropriate. And all the while, you have a host of relationships to manage, involving team members, stakeholders, managers, and customers. It's a great job and brings terrific satisfaction.

Distributing Project Information

The *Information Distribution* process is concerned with getting stakeholders information about the project in a timely manner. This can come about in several ways: status reports, project meetings, review meetings, and so on. Status reports are actually part of the work performance information you saw in the output of the Direct and Manage Project Execution process. Status reports inform stakeholders about where the project is today in regard to project schedule and budget, for example. They also describe what the project team has accomplished to date. This might include milestones completed to date, the percentage of schedule completion, and what remains to be completed. The Information Distribution process describes how this report is distributed and to whom.

In the Information Distribution process, the communications management plan that was defined during the Communications Planning process is put into action, and it's the only input to this process. Communication and Information Distribution work together to report the progress of the project team.

Information Distribution has several tools and techniques, which you'll look at next.

Tools and Techniques of Information Distribution

The tools and techniques of this process are as follows:

- Communication skills
- Information gathering and retrieval systems
- Information distribution methods
- Lessons learned process

Communication skills are probably the single most important skill in your project management toolbox. You'll start with this tool and technique.

Developing Great Communication Skills

Every aspect of your job as a project manager will involve communications. It has been estimated that project managers spend as much as 90 percent of their time communicating in one form or another. Therefore, communication skills are arguably one of the most important skills a project manager can have. They are even more important than technical skills. Good communication skills foster an open, trusting environment. The ability to communicate well is a project manager's best asset.

Exam Spotlight

According to the *PMBOK Guide*, communication skills are not the same as project management communication. They're related but not the same. Communication skills are a specific set of abilities used to create a message, transmit the message, and assure it is received and understood. Project management communication is the act of preparing and distributing information regarding the project (using communication skills).

Throughout this book I've emphasized how important good communication skills are. Now I'll discuss the act of communication, listening behaviors, and conflict resolution. You'll employ each of these techniques with your project team, stakeholders, customers, and management team.

Information Exchange

Communication is the process of exchanging information. All communication includes three elements:

Sender   The sender is the person responsible for putting the information together in a clear and concise manner. The information should be complete and presented in a way that the receiver will be able to correctly understand it. Make your messages relevant to the receiver. Junk mail is annoying, and information that doesn't pertain in any way whatsoever to the receiver is nothing more than that.

Message   The message is the information being sent and received. It might be written, verbal, nonverbal, formal, informal, internal, external, horizontal, or vertical. Horizontal communications are messages sent and received to peers. Vertical communications are messages sent and received down to subordinates and up to executive management.

Make your messages as simple as you can to get your point across. Don't complicate the message with unnecessary detail and technical jargon that others might not understand. A simple trick that helps clarify your messages, especially verbal messages, is to repeat the key information periodically. Public speakers are taught that the best way to organize a speech is to first tell the audience what you're going to tell them; second, tell them; and third, tell them what you just told them.

Receiver   The receiver is the person for whom the message is intended. They are responsible for understanding the information correctly and making sure they've received all the information.

Keep in mind that receivers filter the information they receive through their knowledge of the subject, culture influences, language, emotions, attitudes, and geographic locations. The sender should take these filters into consideration when sending messages so that the receiver will clearly understand the message that was sent.

This book is an example of the sender-message-receiver model. I'm the sender of the information. The message concerns topics you need to know to pass the PMP exam (and if I've done my job correctly, is written in a clear and easily understood format). You, the reader, are the receiver.

METHODS OF INFORMATION EXCHANGE

Senders, receivers, and messages are the elements of communication. The way the sender packages or encodes the information and transmits it and the way the receiver unpacks or decodes the message are the methods of communication exchange.

Senders encode messages. Encoding is a method of putting the information into a format the receiver will understand. Language, pictures, and symbols are used to encode messages. Encoding formats the message for transmitting.

Transmitting is the way the information gets from the sender to the receiver. Spoken words, written documentation, memos, email, voicemail, and so on, are all transmitting methods.

Decoding is what the receiver does with the information when they get it. They convert it into an understandable format. Usually, this means they read the memo, listen to the speaker, read the book, and so on.

FORMS OF COMMUNICATION

Communication occurs primarily in written or verbal form. Granted, you can point to something or indicate what you need with motions, but usually you use the spoken or written word to get your message across.

Verbal communication is easier and less complicated than written communication, and it's usually a fast method of communication. Written communication, on the other hand, is an excellent way to get across complex, detailed messages. Detailed instructions are better provided in written form because it gives the reader the ability to go back over information they're not quite sure about.

Both verbal and written communications might take a formal or an informal approach. Speeches and lectures are examples of formal verbal communications. Most project status meetings take more of a formal approach, as do most written project status reports. Generally speaking, the project manager should take an informal approach when communicating with stakeholders and project team members outside of the status meetings. This makes you appear more open and friendly and easier to approach with questions and issues.

Effective Listening Skills

What did you say? Often we think we're listening when we really aren't. In all fairness, we can take in only so much information at one time. But it's important to perform active listening when someone else is speaking. As a project manager, you will spend the majority of your time communicating with team members, stakeholders, customers, vendors, and others. This means you should be as good a listener as you are a communicator.

You can use several techniques to improve your listening skills. Many books are devoted to this topic, so I'll try to highlight some of the most common techniques here:

- Appear interested in what the speaker is saying. This will make the speaker feel at ease and will benefit you as well. By acting interested, you become interested and thereby retain more of the information being presented.

- Making eye contact with the speaker is another effective listening tool. This lets the speaker know you are paying attention to what they're saying and are interested.

- Put your speaker at ease by letting them know beforehand that you're interested in what they're going to talk about and that you're looking forward to hearing what they have to say. While they're speaking, nod your head, smile, or make comments when and if appropriate to let the speaker know you understand the message. If you don't understand something and are in the proper setting, ask clarifying questions.

- Another great trick that works well in lots of situations is to recap what the speaker said in your own words and tell it back to them. Start with something like this, "Let me make sure I understand you correctly, you're saying," and ask the speaker to confirm that you did understand them correctly.

- Just as your mother always said, it's impolite to interrupt. Interrupting is a way of telling the speaker that you aren't really listening and you're more interested in telling them what you have to say than listening to them. Interrupting gets the other person off track, they might forget their point, and it might even make them angry.

Not to disagree with Mom, but there probably are some occasions where interrupting is appropriate. For example, if you're in a project status meeting and someone wants to take the meeting off course, sometimes the only way to get the meeting back on track is to interrupt them. You can do this politely. Start first by saying the person's name to get their attention. Then let them know that you'd be happy to talk with them about their topic outside of the meeting or add it to the agenda for the next status meeting if it's something everyone needs to hear. Sorry, Mom.

Resolving Conflicts

I said earlier in this chapter that if you have more than one person working on your project, you have a team. Here's another fact: if you have more than one person working on your project, you'll have conflict. I put conflict resolution in the communication section because conflict resolution involves communication, as you'll see in a moment.

Everyone has desires, needs, and goals. Conflict comes into the picture when the desires, needs, or goals of one party are incompatible with the desires, needs, or goals of another party (or parties). *Conflict*, simply put, is the incompatibility of goals, which often leads to one party resisting or blocking the other party from attaining their goals. Wait—this doesn't sound like a party!

There are five ways of resolving conflict that might show up on the exam:

Forcing   *Forcing* is just as it sounds. One person forces a solution on the other parties. This is where the boss puts on the "Because I'm the boss and I said so" hat. Although this is a permanent solution, it isn't necessarily the best solution. People will go along with it because, well, they're forced to go along with it. It doesn't mean they agree with the solution. This isn't the best technique to use when you're trying to build a team. This is an example of a win-lose conflict resolution technique. The forcing party wins, and the losers are those who are forced to go along with the decision.

Smoothing   *Smoothing* does not lead to a permanent solution. It's a temporary way to resolve conflict where someone attempts to make the conflict appear less important than it is. Everyone looks at each other and scratches their head and wonders why they thought the conflict was such a big deal anyway. As a result, a compromise is reached, and everyone feels good about the solution until they get back to their desk and start thinking about the issue again. When they realize that the conflict was smoothed over and really is more important than they were led to believe, they'll be back at it, and the conflict will resurface. This is an example of a lose-lose conflict resolution technique because neither side wins.

Compromise *Compromise* is achieved when each of the parties involved in the conflict gives up something to reach a solution. Everyone involved decides what they will give on and what they won't give on, and eventually through all the give and take, a solution is reached. Neither side wins or loses in this situation. As a result, neither side is really gung ho about the decision that was reached. They will drag their feet and reluctantly trudge along. If, however, both parties make firm commitments to the resolution, then the solution becomes a permanent one.

Confrontation *Confrontation* is also called *problem solving* and is the best way to resolve conflict. One of the key actions you'll perform with this technique is a fact-finding mission. The thinking here is that one right solution to a problem exists, and the facts will bear out the solution. Once the facts are uncovered, they're presented to the parties, and the decision will be clear. Thus, the solution becomes a permanent one and the conflict expires. This is the conflict resolution approach project mangers use most often and is an example of a win-win conflict resolution technique.

Withdrawal *Withdrawal* never results in resolution. This occurs when one of the parties gets up and leaves and refuses to discuss the conflict. It is probably the worst of all the techniques because nothing gets resolved. This is an example of a lose-lose conflict resolution technique.

Exam Spotlight

Know each of the conflict resolution techniques for the exam. Also remember that these techniques will not necessarily yield long-term results. The smoothing and withdrawal techniques have temporary results and aren't always good techniques to use to resolve problems. Resolutions reached through forcing, compromise, and confrontation techniques might not always be satisfying for all parties, but they tend to produce longer-lasting results.

Keep in mind that group size makes a difference when you're trying to resolve conflict or make decisions. Remember the channels of communication you learned about in Chapter 4? The larger the group, the more lines of communication and the more difficult it will be to reach a decision. Groups of 5 to 11 people have been shown to make the most accurate decisions.

Use communication, listening, and conflict resolution skills wisely. As a project manager, you'll find that your day-to-day activities encompass these three areas the majority of the time. Project managers with excellent communication skills can work wonders. Communication won't take the place of proper planning and management techniques, but a project manager who communicates well with their team and the stakeholders can make up for a lack of technical skills any day, hands down. If your team and your stakeholders trust you and you can communicate the vision and the project goals and report on project status accurately and honestly, the world is your oyster.

Information Gathering and Retrieval Systems

The *information gathering and retrieval systems* tool and technique of the Information Distribution process includes ways that project information is stored and shared among project team members. You've probably used one or more of these gathering and retrieval systems such as project management software, manual filing systems, intranet project sites, and electronic databases.

Information Distribution Methods

Information distribution methods are ways of getting the project information to the project team or stakeholders. As the name implies, these are ways to distribute the information and might include email, hard copy, voicemail, videoconferencing, and so on.

Exam Spotlight

Don't confuse information gathering and retrieval systems with information distribution methods. Remember that retrieval systems are ways for the project team to get at project information, while distribution methods are ways of getting the information into the hands of the stakeholders or team members.

Lessons Learned Process

Lessons learned are information that you gather and document throughout the course of the project that can be used to benefit the current project, future projects, or other projects currently being performed by the organization. Lessons learned might include positive as well as negative lessons.

During the Information Distribution process, you'll begin conducting lessons learned meetings focusing on many different areas depending on the nature of your project. These areas might include project management processes, product development, technical processes, project team performance, stakeholder involvement, and so on.

Lessons learned meetings should always be conducted at the end of project phases and at the end of the project at minimum. Team members, stakeholders, vendors, and others involved on the project should participate in these meetings. It's important to understand, and to make your team members understand, that this is not a finger-pointing meeting. The purpose of lessons learned is to understand what went well and why—so you can repeat it on future projects—and what didn't go so well and why—so you can perform differently on future projects. These meetings can make good team-building sessions because you're creating an atmosphere of trust and sharing and you're building on each other's strengths to improve performance.

Some of the updates that might occur as a result of lessons learned meetings are updates to the lessons learned knowledge base; updates to policies, procedures, processes, and business skills; and updates to the risk management plan.

Exam Spotlight

According to the *PMBOK Guide*, it's a project manager's professional obligation to hold lessons learned meetings.

 I'll talk more about lessons learned in Chapter 11, "Controlling Work Results and Closing Out the Project."

Outputs of Information Distribution

The first output of the Information Distribution process is organizational process assets updates. The updates here consist of six elements:

Lessons learned documentation   You'll document the lessons learned I talked about earlier as this output. You should document the reasons or causes for the issues, the corrective action taken and why, and any other information that future projects might benefit from.

Project records   *Project records* include, as you might guess, memos, correspondence, and other documents concerning the project. The best place to keep information like this is in a project notebook or in a set of project notebooks, depending on the size of the project. The project notebooks are ordinary three-ring binders where project information gets filed. They are maintained by the project manager or project office and contain all information regarding the project. You could also keep the information on a project website, the company intranet, or CDs. If you're keeping the information electronically, make certain it's backed up regularly. Individual team members might keep their own project records as well in notebooks or electronically. These records serve as historical information once the project is closed.

Project reports   *Project reports* include the project status reports and minutes from project meetings. If you're keeping an issues log, the issues would be included with the project reports as well.

Project presentations   *Project presentations* involve presenting project information to the stakeholders and other appropriate parties when necessary. The presentations might be formal or informal and depend on the audience and the information being communicated.

Feedback from stakeholders   This one ties into lessons learned. Feedback you receive from the stakeholders that can improve future performance on this project or future projects should be captured and documented. If the information has an impact on the current project, distribute it to the appropriate team members so that future project performance can be modified to improve results.

Stakeholder notifications   Remember that the focus of this process is distributing information, so this element fits because you'll want to notify stakeholders when you have implemented solutions and approved changes. This also involves informing them of project status. I'll cover project status review meetings in Chapter 9, "Measuring and Controlling Project Performance."

The only other output of this process is requested changes, which I've talked about before.

In the next chapter, you'll examine the processes associated with finding and selecting vendors, administering contracts, managing stakeholders and team members, quality assurance, and reporting on performance.

Project Case Study: New Kitchen Heaven Retail Store

Dirk Perrier logs on and finds the following email addressed to all the stakeholders and project team members from you:

Project Progress Report

Project Name   Kitchen Heaven Retail Store

Project Number   081501-1910

Prepared By   Project manager

Date   September 20, 2006

Section 1: Action Items

- *Action Item 1*: Call cable vendor. Responsible party: Ricardo. Resolution date: 9/14

- *Action Item 2*: Check T1 connection status. Responsible party: Ricardo. Resolution date: Pending

- *Action Item 3*: Build-out begins. Responsible party: Jake. Resolution date: Pending

Section 2: Scheduled and Actual Completion Dates

- *Sign lease*: Scheduled: 8/21/06. Completed: 8/21/06

- *Gomez contract signed*: Scheduled: 9/12/06. Completed: 9/12/06

- *Ethernet cable run*: Scheduled: 9/18/06. Completed: 9/19/06

- *Build-out started*: Scheduled: 9/20/06. Completed: Open

Section 3: Activity That Occurred in the Project This Week

The Ethernet cable run was completed without a problem.

Gomez construction started the build-out process. This task was fast-tracked with the Ethernet cable run as planned.

Jill made initial calls regarding retail products order.

Section 4: Progress Expected This Reporting Period Not Completed

None. Project is on track to date.

Section 5: Progress Expected Next Reporting Period

Build-out will continue. Jake reports that Gomez expects to have electrical lines run and dry-wall started prior to the end of the next reporting period.

Ricardo should have a T1 update. There's a slim possibility that the T1 connection will have occurred by next reporting period.

Section 6: Issues

We had to start the build-out on the last day of the cable run (this is called *fast-tracking*) to keep the project on schedule. Jake and Ricardo reported only minor problems with this arrangement in that the contractors got into each other's way a time or two. This did not impact the completion of the cable run because most of day two this team was in the back room and Gomez's crew was in the storefront area.

A key member of the Gomez construction crew was out last week because of a family emergency. Gomez assures us that it will not impact the build-out schedule. They replaced the team member with someone from another project, so it appears so far that the build-out is on schedule.

Ricardo is somewhat concerned about the T1 connection because the phone company won't return his calls inquiring about status. We're still ahead of the curve on this one because hardware isn't scheduled to begin testing until January 21. Hardware testing depends on the T1 connection. This is a heads-up at this point, and we'll carry this as an issue in the status report going forward until it's resolved.

One of the gourmet food item suppliers Jill uses regularly went out of business. She is in the process of tracking down a new supplier to pick up the slack for the existing stores and supply the gourmet food products for the new store.

Sponsor Update

"Good job on the status," Dirk says as you pick up the phone. "I was beginning to wonder when we'd see some action on the project, but it looks like things are underway."

"A lot has happened in just the past two weeks, as you can see. I'll publish these project status updates twice a month in conjunction with the regular project status meetings. Starting in January, I'll publish them once a week until project completion."

"Keep me posted on that T1 line. That isn't going to be a showstopper, is it?"

"We have a contingency plan in place," you reply. "We talked about that last week."

"OK. I'll see you at the project meeting Friday."

"See you then," you say.

Project Case Study Checklist

Communication (reporting on work performance information)

- Sender makes it clear and concise.

- There's no unnecessary technical jargon.

- Formal written communication is provided.

- It's the receiver's responsibility to understand information.

- The status report is a vertical and horizontal communication method.

Direct and Manage Project Execution

- Deliverables

- Work results

- Work performance information

Develop Project Team

Information Distribution

- Project information is delivered to stakeholders in a timely manner.

- The information distribution method is status reports via email and project meetings.

- The status report is part of the project reports filed in the project notebook or filed for future reference as historical information.

Understanding How This Applies to Your Next Project

The topics in this chapter are some of my favorites because this is where project management shines—dynamic teams working under the direction of a capable, responsible leader who can effectively balance the needs of the team with the needs of the project (and ultimately the organization) and pull it all off successfully. There aren't many things better in an organization than a high-performing team working together to accomplish a well-understood goal. And it doesn't really matter whether the team members are all in the same company, department, or country. When they're working toward a common goal and functioning at the performing level, there's almost nothing they can't accomplish. The movies *Ocean's Eleven, Ocean's Twelve,* and *Ocean's 13* are good examples of strong leadership and dynamic teamwork at play. Although I'm certainly not advocating you turn to a life of crime, you can pick up a few pointers on how effective teams work from George Clooney and the gang.

So, how does this apply? As the project manager, it's your responsibility, and dare I say duty, to acquire the best team members possible for your project. In my experience, this doesn't always mean all my team members are highly qualified. To me, team fit and team dynamics are as important as the team members' skills. I know some will disagree with me on this next point, but I believe it's easier to train someone on a new skill (given they have the aptitude) than it is to take on a team member with an abrasive personality who is imminently qualified but can't get along with anyone else on the team. Sometimes you really don't have much choice when it comes to picking team members, as referenced in the "The Only Candidate" sidebar earlier in this chapter. When you find yourself in this situation, I recommend you lay down clear ground rules for communication, problem escalation, work assignments, and so on.

Make it a habit to read at least a couple of leadership books a month (or quarter or whatever you can fit into your schedule). You may already be familiar with the topic and think there isn't anything new to learn. However, staying current on the topic will reinforce concepts that you already know and will remind you of other points that you forgot about and haven't yet developed but know you should. And occasionally, you will pick up a gold nugget of information that is new and immediately applicable to your situation.

Leadership skills are invaluable, but communication skills are just as important. In my opinion, it's difficult to be an effective leader without also being an effective communicator. My guess is that if you take a close look at the leaders you respect and admire, you'll discover they are also good communicators. And communication is mostly listening—not talking. I make it a habit to practice active listening. It's amazing what people will tell you when you smile politely and ask an open-ended question or two.

Summary

This chapter described four processes from the Executing process group: Direct and Manage Project Execution, Acquire Project Team, Develop Project Team, and Information Distribution.

In Direct and Manage Project Execution, the project plans come to life. Activities are authorized to begin and the product, result, or service of the project is produced. Status review meetings are held to inform stakeholders of project progress and updates.

Acquire Project Team involves negotiation with other functional managers, project managers, and organizational personnel to obtain human resources to complete the work of the project. The project manager might not have control over who will be a part of the team. Availability, ability, experience, interests, and costs are all enterprise environmental factors that should be considered when you are able to choose team members.

Develop Project Team involves creating an open, inviting atmosphere where project team members will become efficient and cooperative, increasing productivity during the course of the project. It's the project manager's job to bring the team together into a functioning, productive group.

Team development has four stages, according to Bruce Tuckman's model: forming, storming, norming, and performing. All groups proceed through these stages, and the introduction of a new team member will always start the process over again.

Co-location is physically placing team members together in the same location. This might also include a common meeting room or gathering area where team members can meet and collaborate on the project.

Several motivational theories exist, including reward and recognition, Maslow's hierarchy of needs, the Hygiene Theory, the Expectancy Theory, and the Achievement Theory. These theories conjecture that motivation is driven by several desires, including needs, anticipation of expected outcomes, or needs for achievement, power, or affiliation. The Hygiene Theory proposes that hygiene factors prevent dissatisfaction.

Leaders inspire vision and rally people around common goals. Theory X leaders think most people are motivated only through punishment, money, or position. Theory Y leaders think most people want to perform the best job they can. The Contingency Theory says that people naturally want to achieve levels of competency and will continue to be motivated by the desire for competency even after competency is reached.

Leaders exhibit five types of power: reward, punishment, expert, legitimate, and referent power.

Communication skills are the most important skills a project manager exercises. People who send messages are responsible for making sure the messages are clear, concise, and complete. Receivers are responsible for understanding the messages correctly and making sure they've received all the information.

Listening skills put speakers at ease. Several techniques tell your speaker you're listening attentively, including making eye contact, nodding, asking clarifying questions, and limiting interruptions.

Information Distribution is a matter of getting project information out to the stakeholders. Information retrieval systems generally store project information and include project management software, filing cabinets, and electronic databases. Information distribution methods are ways to get the information to the stakeholders and include email, paper, voicemail, or videoconferencing.

Exam Essentials

Be able to identify the distinguishing characteristics of Direct and Manage Project Execution. Direct and Manage Project Execution is where the work of the project is performed, and the majority of the project budget is spent during this process.

Be able to name the four stages of group formation.   The four stages of group formation are forming, storming, norming, and performing.

Be able to define Maslow's highest level of motivation.   Self-actualization occurs when a person performs at their peak and all lower-level needs have been met.

Be able to name the five types of power.   The five levels of power are reward, punishment, expert, legitimate, and referent.

Be able to differentiate between senders and receivers of information.   Senders are responsible for clear, concise, complete messages, while receivers are responsible for understanding the message correctly.

Be able to identify the five styles of conflict resolution.   The five styles of conflict resolution are forcing, smoothing, compromise, confrontation, and withdrawal.

Key Terms

I've discussed in detail the processes you'll use while developing your project team. You need to understand each of these processes to effectively build your team and know them by the names used in the *PMBOK* to be successful on the exam:

Acquire Project Team

Develop Project Team

Direct and Manage Project Execution

Information Distribution

You learned a lot of new key words in this chapter. PMI has worked hard to develop and define standard project management terms that apply across industries. Here is a list of some of the terms you came across in this chapter:

Achievement Theory	Motivation-Hygiene Theory
administrative closure procedure	politics
co-location	power
communication	preassignment
conflict	project presentations
confrontation	project records
corrective actions	project reports
Expectancy Theory	recognition and rewards
Hygiene Theory	team building
information distribution methods	Theory X
information gathering and retrieval systems	Theory Y
lessons learned	virtual teams
Maslow's hierarchy of needs	

Review Questions

1. You are a project manager for an international marketing firm. You are ready to assign resources to your new project using a work authorization system. Which of the following statements is not true?

    A. Work authorization systems clarify and initiate the work for each work package.

    B. Work authorization systems are written procedures defined by the organization.

    C. Work authorization systems are used throughout the project Execution processes.

    D. Work authorization systems are used throughout the Execution processes and are a tool and technique of the Direct and Manage Project Execution process.

2. You are a project manager for a growing dairy farm. It offers its organic dairy products region-ally and is expanding its operations to the West Coast. It is in the process of purchasing and leasing dairy farms to get operations underway. You are in charge of the network operations part of this project. An important deadline is approaching that depends on the successful com-pletion of the testing phase. You've detected some problems with your hardware in the testing phase and discover that the hardware is not compatible with other network equipment. You take corrective action and exchange the hardware for more compatible equipment. Which of the following statements is true?

    A. This is not a corrective action because corrective action involves human resources, not project resources.

    B. Corrective action is taken here to make sure the future project outcomes are aligned with the project management plan.

    C. Corrective action is not necessary in this case because the future project outcomes aren't affected.

    D. Corrective action serves as the change request to authorize exchanging the equipment.

3. You are a project manager for a growing dairy farm. It offers its organic dairy products region-ally and is expanding its operations to the West Coast. It's in the process of purchasing and leasing dairy farms to get operations underway. The subproject manager in charge of network operations has reported some hardware problems to you. You're also having some other prob-lems coordinating and integrating other elements of the project. Which of the following state-ments is true?

    A. You are in the Direct and Manage Project Execution process.

    B. Your project team doesn't appear to have the right skills and knowledge needed to perform this project.

    C. You are in the Information Distribution process.

    D. Your project team could benefit from some team-building exercises.

4. Which of the following processes serve as inputs to each other?

   A. Executing, and Monitoring and Controlling

   B. Executing and Closing

   C. Planning, and Monitoring and Controlling

   D. Executing and Initiation

5. Your team members have just completed training on specialized equipment. This is one of the work results you've gathered and recorded. Which of the following outputs of the Direct and Manage Project Execution process does this describe?

   A. Corrective action

   B. Deliverable

   C. Preventive action

   D. Work performance information

6. You are reporting on project elements such as schedule status, deliverables completion, lessons learned, and resource utilization. Which of the following outputs of the Direct and Manage Project Execution does this describe?

   A. Corrective action

   B. Deliverable

   C. Preventive action

   D. Work performance information

7. You are in the process of making project staff assignments. You have several candidates for a position on the project team that requires specific qualifications. All the candidates seem to meet the qualifications. You also consider personal interests, characteristics, and availability of these potential candidates. Which of the following is true?

   A. You are considering the organizational process assets input of the Develop Project Team process.

   B. You are considering the staffing management plan input of the Develop Project Team process.

   C. You are considering the enterprise environmental factors input of the Acquire Project Team process.

   D. You are considering the roles and responsibilities input of the Acquire Project Team process.

8. Your project team consists of 12 people in the same building you're located in, 4 people from the West Coast office, 2 people from the Kansas City office, and 6 people from the London office. Your office works different hours than all the other offices. Additionally, not all of the resources in your building are available at the same times during the day. Three of the 12 team members work swing shift hours. You use tools like web conferencing and email to distribute information to the team. Which of the following is true?

A. This question describes the staffing management plan from the Acquire Project Team process and communication skills from the Information Distribution process.

B. This question describes resource availability from the Develop Project Team process and information distribution methods from the Information Distribution process.

C. This question describes virtual teams from the Acquire Project Team process and information distribution methods from the Information Distribution process.

D. This question describes project staff assignments from the Develop Project Team process and communication skills from the Information Distribution process.

9. You are the project manager for a cable service provider. Your team members are amiable with each other and are careful to make project decisions jointly. Which of the following statements is true?

A. They are in the smoothing stage of Develop Project Team.

B. They are in the norming stage of Develop Project Team.

C. They are in the forming stage of Develop Project Team.

D. They are in the forcing stage of Develop Project Team.

10. You are the project manager for a cable service provider. Your project team is researching a new service offering. They have been working together for quite some time and are in the performing stage of team development. A new member has been introduced to the team. Which of the following statements is true?

A. The team will start all over again with the storming stage.

B. The team will continue in the performing stage.

C. The team will start all over again with the forming stage.

D. The team will start all over again at the storming stage but quickly progress to the performing stage.

11. You are the project manager for a cable service provider. Your project team is researching a new service offering. They have been working together for quite some time and are in the performing stage of Develop Project Team. This stage of Develop Project Team is similar to which of the following?

A. Smoothing

B. Achievement Theory

C. Hygiene Theory

D. Self-actualization

12. Receivers in the communication model filter their information through all of the following except _____.

    A. culture

    B. knowledge of subject

    C. habits

    D. language

13. You've promised your team two days of paid time off plus a week's training in the latest technology of their choice if they complete their project ahead of schedule. This is an example of which of the following?

    A. Achievement Theory

    B. Expectancy Theory

    C. Maslow's theory

    D. Contingency Theory

14. Your team is split between two buildings on either side of town. As a result, the team isn't very cohesive because the members don't know each other very well. The team is still in the storming stage because of the separation issues. Which of the following should you consider?

    A. Corrective action

    B. Co-location

    C. Training

    D. Conflict resolution

15. Which conflict resolution technique do project managers use most often?

    A. Smoothing

    B. Norming

    C. Confronting

    D. Forcing

16. You are a fabulous project manager, and your team thinks highly of you. You are well respected by the stakeholders, management team, and project team. When you make decisions, others follow your lead as a result of which of the following?

    A. Referent power

    B. Expert power

    C. Legitimate power

    D. Punishment power

17. Theory Y managers believe which of the following?

   A. People are motivated only by money, power, or position.

   B. People will perform their best if they're given proper motivation and expectations.

   C. People are motivated to achieve a high level of competency.

   D. People are motivated by expectation of good outcomes.

18. You have accumulated project information throughout the project and need to distribute some important information you just received. Which of the following is not an information distribution method?

   A. Electronic databases

   B. Videoconferencing

   C. Electronic mail

   D. Voicemail

19. You know that the next status meeting will require some discussion and a decision for a problem that has surfaced on the project. To make the most accurate decision, you know that the number of participants in the meeting should be limited to _____.

   A. 1 to 5

   B. 5 to 11

   C. 7 to 16

   D. 10 to 18

20. You are holding end-of-phase meetings with your team members and key stakeholders to learn what has hindered and helped the project team's performance of the work. All of the following are true regarding this situation except for which one?

   A. The information learned from these meetings concerns processes and activities that have already occurred, so it should be documented because the information is only useful for future projects.

   B. These meetings are called lessons learned meetings and they're a tool and technique of the Information Distribution process. They're also a good team-building activity.

   C. Project reports, part of the organizational process output of the Information Distribution process, include status meetings and lessons learned (which this question describes).

   D. These meetings should be documented as part of the lessons learned documentation, which is an element of the organizational process assets updates output of the Information Distribution process.

Answers to Review Questions

1. D. Work authorization systems are a tool used during Project Execution processes but are not a specific tool and technique listed in the Direct and Manage Project Execution process. They formally initiate the work of each work package and clarify the assignments.

2. B. Corrective action brings anticipated future project outcomes back into alignment with the project management plan. Since there is an important deadline looming that depends on a positive outcome of this test, the equipment is exchanged so that the project plan and project schedule are not impacted.

3. A. The most difficult aspect of the Direct and Manage Project Execution process is coordinating and integrating all the project elements. The clue to this question is in the next-to-last sentence.

4. A. The Executing process group and Monitoring and Controlling process group serve as inputs to each other.

5. B. This question describes the deliverable output. Deliverables can be intangibles, such as the completion of training.

6. D. Work performance information includes elements such as schedule status, the status of deliverables completion, lessons learned, and resource utilization.

7. C. The enterprise environmental factors input of the Acquire Project Team process considers elements such as personal interests, characteristics, and availability of potential team members.

8. C. Virtual teams are teams that don't necessarily work in the same location or have the same hours but all share the goals of the project and have a role on the project. The web conferencing and email references describe the information distribution methods tool and technique of the Information Distribution process.

9. B. Teams in the norming stage of Develop Project Team exhibit affection and familiarity with one another and make joint decisions. Smoothing and forcing are conflict resolution techniques, not Develop Project Team stages.

10. C. The introduction of a new team member will start the formation and development of the team all over again with the forming stage.

11. D. The performing stage is similar to Maslow's self-actualization. Both involve team members at the peak of performance, concerned with doing good and being the best.

12. C. Receivers filter information through cultural considerations, knowledge of the subject matter, language abilities, geographic location, emotions, and attitudes.

13. B. The Expectancy Theory says that people are motivated by the expectation of good outcomes. The outcome must be reasonable and attainable.

14. B. Co-location would bring your team members together in the same location and allow them to function more efficiently as a team. At a minimum, team members meeting in a common room, such as a war room, for all team meetings would bring the team closer together.

15. C. Confronting is a problem-solving technique that seeks to determine the facts and find solutions based on the facts. That results in a win-win resolution for all parties.

16. A. Referent power is power that is inferred on a leader by their subordinates as a result of the high level of respect for the leader.

17. B. Theory Y managers believe that people will perform their best if they're provided with the proper motivation and the right expectations.

18. A. Electronic databases are a type of information gathering and retrieval system, not a distribution method.

19. B. Group sizes of 5 to 11 participants make the most accurate decisions.

20. B. Lessons learned (which is what this question describes) are useful for future processes and activities for the current project as well as future projects.

Chapter

9

Measuring and Controlling Project Performance

THE PMP EXAM CONTENT FROM THE EXECUTING THE PROJECT PERFORMANCE DOMAIN COVERED IN THIS CHAPTER INCLUDES THE FOLLOWING:

- ✓ Ensure Common Understanding and Set Expectations
- ✓ Implement Quality Management Plan
- ✓ Implement Approved Changes
- ✓ Implement Approved Actions and Workarounds

This chapter wraps up the Executing process group and introduces the Monitoring and Controlling process group. The Executing processes covered in this chapter are Request Seller Responses, Select Sellers, and Perform Quality Assurance. Then you'll move into the Monitoring and Controlling process group and examine several processes, including Monitor and Control Project Work, Contract Administration, Manage Project Team, Manage Stakeholders, and Performance Reporting.

Request Seller Responses and Select Sellers are both Executing processes. They are usually performed in conjunction with the Contract Administration process, which belongs to the Monitoring and Controlling process group. To keep the dividing line even, I'll talk about Request Seller Responses and Select Sellers together and then finish up the Executing process group with Perform Quality Assurance. Then I'll introduce the Monitor and Control Project Work process because it provides the framework for the Monitoring and Controlling process. *Then* I'll cover the Contract Administration process.

The Monitoring and Controlling process group involves taking measurements and performing inspections to find out whether there are variances in the plan. If you discover variances, you need to take corrective action to get the project back on track and repeat the affected project Planning processes to make adjustments to the plan as a result of resolving the variances.

During the Manage Team Project process, you'll monitor the performance of the team, provide feedback to team members, resolve issues, and take actions (when needed) to realign the project team's performance with the goals of the project. The Manage Stakeholders process involves communicating project status and issues and resolving stakeholder issues and concerns. Performance Reporting also concerns communicating information about the project's progress to the stakeholders.

Once again, you have a lot of ground to cover. Grab your favorite beverage and dig in.

Requesting Seller Responses

Many times project managers must purchase goods or services to complete some or all of the work of the project. Sometimes the entire project is completed on contract. The *Request Seller Responses* process is concerned with obtaining responses to bids and proposals from potential vendors.

This process has three inputs:

- Organizational process assets
- Procurement management plan
- Procurement documents

I've talked about these in previous chapters. In addition, I've discussed organizational process assets in several of the Planning processes covered in previous chapters. You prepared the procurement documents and procurement management plan during the Plan Contracting process. I talked about them in Chapter 6, "Resource Planning." Procurement documents include requests for proposals (RFPs), requests for information (RFIs), requests for quotations (RFQs), and so on. The vendors—or potential sellers—bear the majority of work in the Request Seller Responses process by preparing responses to the RFPs. Depending on the RFP and the effort needed to respond, costs to the vendor can become quite substantial.

 The Request Seller Responses process is used only if you're obtaining goods or services from outside your own organization. If you have all the resources you need to perform the work of the project within the organization, you won't use this process.

In the following sections, you'll examine some new tools and techniques that will help vendors give you a better idea of their responses, and then you'll move on to the outputs of this process, one of which is the vendor proposal.

Requesting Seller Responses Tools and Techniques

Remember that the purpose of the Request Seller Responses process is to obtain responses to your RFP (or similar procurement document). The three tools and techniques of this process are actually designed to assist the vendors in getting their proposals to you:

Bidder conferences *Bidder conferences* are meetings with prospective vendors or sellers that occur prior to the completion of their response proposal. You or someone from your procurement department arranges the bidder conference. The purpose is to allow all prospective vendors to meet with the buyers to ask questions and clarify issues they have regarding the project and the RFP. The meeting is held once, and all vendors attend at the same time. The bidder conference is held before the vendor prepares their responses so that they are sure their RFP response will address the project requirements.

Advertising *Advertising* is letting potential vendors know that an RFP is available. The company's Internet site, professional journals, or newspapers are examples of where advertising might appear.

Develop qualified sellers lists *Develop qualified sellers lists* is part of the organizational process asset input if they already exist in the organization. If the lists don't exist, you'll have to create them. They are lists of prospective sellers who have been preapproved or prequalified to provide contract services (or provide supplies and materials) for the organization. For example, your organization might require vendors to register and maintain information regarding their experience, offerings, and current prices on a qualified seller list. Vendors must usually go through the procurement department to get placed on the list. Project managers are then required to choose their vendors from the qualified seller list published by the procurement department. However, not all organizations have qualified seller lists. If a list isn't available, you'll have to work with the project team to come up with your own requirements for selecting vendors.

Request Seller Responses Outputs

The Request Seller Responses process has three outputs: qualified sellers list, procurement document package, and proposals. I talked about developing qualifying seller lists in the previous section. The output here can be the qualified seller lists you used as inputs (as part of the organizational process asset input) if they exist. If they don't exist, you'll need to develop them as an input and use them as an output.

The buyer prepares the procurement document package. This is the formal request that's posted, advertised, or otherwise sent to each of the sellers and is the basis for the seller's bid. These might be an RFP, RFQ, IFB, and so on.

Proposals are the seller-prepared documents that describe how the vendor intends to meet the needs of your project. And if they've done their job correctly, the proposal should detail responses to each of the items as they were outlined in your RFP. These proposals become the input to the next process, Select Sellers. After proposals are prepared and submitted, often vendors are invited to an oral presentation where they provide additional information about their product or service and where buyers can ask questions about the seller's proposal.

Exam Spotlight

The *Guide to the PMBOK* makes a distinction between the Request Seller Responses process and the Select Sellers process that you should know for the exam: Request Seller Responses *obtains* bids and proposals; Select Sellers is the *receipt* of bids and proposals and evaluating each in order to award a winner.

Selecting Sellers

In the *Select Sellers* process you evaluate the proposals you've received against your predefined evaluation criteria. I defined evaluation criteria in the Plan Contracting process.

Select Sellers has several inputs:

- Organizational process assets
- Procurement management plan
- Evaluation criteria
- Procurement document package
- Proposals
- Qualified sellers list
- Project management plan (risk register and risk-related contractual agreements)

I've covered all of these inputs previously, but you should be aware of a few points. Proposals, as mentioned, are obtained in the Request Seller Responses process and used as an input to the Select Sellers process. Proposals can be divided into sections, including a management section, technical approach section, and pricing section. Remember that although cost might be the primary driver behind your decision, the low-cost provider might not end up being low cost in the end if the provider is unable to deliver the products or services as described and on time. Take the time to evaluate the proposals on more than cost alone.

Evaluation criteria are what you'll use to compare proposals. You developed evaluation criteria as part of the Plan Contracting process in Chapter 6. However, you'll take a little closer look at this topic now since you'll actually be using the criteria during this process.

In practice, you will probably perform Plan Contracting, Request Seller Responses, and Select Sellers all as one process.

Evaluation Criteria

You can use *evaluation criteria* as one method of rating and scoring proposals. Keep in mind this is an input to the Select Sellers process, not a tool and technique, even though you'll be using it as you would a tool and technique.

The types of goods and services you're trying to procure will dictate how detailed your evaluation criteria are. (Of course, if your organization has policies in place for evaluating proposals, then you'll use the format or criteria already established.) The selection of some goods and services might be price driven only. In other words, the bidder with the lowest price will win the bid. This is typical when the items you're buying are widely available.

When you're purchasing goods, you might request a sample from each vendor in order to compare quality (or some other criteria) against your need. For example, perhaps you need a special kind of paper stock for a project you're working on at a bank. This stock must have a watermark, it must have security threads embedded through the paper, and when the paper is used for printing, the ink must not be erasable. You can request samples of stock from the vendors with these qualities and then test them to see whether they'll work for your project.

It's always appropriate to ask the vendor for references, especially when you're hiring contract services. It's difficult to assess the quality of services because it's not a tangible product. References can tell you whether the vendor delivered on time, whether the vendor had the technical capability to perform the work, and whether the vendor's management approach was appropriate when troubles surfaced. Create a list of questions to ask the references before you call.

You can request financial records to assure you—the buyer—that the vendor has the fiscal ability to perform the services they're proposing and that the vendor can purchase whatever equipment is needed to perform the services. If you examine the records of the company and find that it's two steps away from bankruptcy, that company might not be a likely candidate for your project. (Remember those general management skills? Here's another example where they come into play.)

One of the most important criteria is the evaluation of the response itself to determine whether the vendor has a clear understanding of what you're asking them to do or provide. If they missed the mark (remember, they had an opportunity at the bidder conferences to ask clarifying questions) and didn't understand what you were asking them to provide, you'll probably want to rank them very low.

Now you can compare each proposal against the criteria and rate or score each proposal for its ability to meet or fulfill these criteria. This can serve as your first step in eliminating vendors that don't match your criteria. Let's say you received 18 responses to an RFP. After evaluating each one, you discover that 6 of them don't match all the evaluation criteria. You eliminate those six vendors in this round. The next step is to apply the tools and techniques of this process to further evaluate the remaining 12 potential vendors.

Tools and Techniques of Select Sellers

You use the following tools and techniques of Select Sellers to further evaluate vendors:

- Weighting systems
- Independent estimates
- Screening systems
- Contract negotiation
- Seller rating systems
- Expert judgment
- Proposal evaluation techniques

You'll look at each one in the following sections.

Weighting Systems

Weighting systems assign numerical weights to evaluation criteria and then multiply them by the weights of each criteria factor to come up with total scores for each vendor. According to the *Guide to the PMBOK*, this tool and technique quantifies the qualitative data to keep personal biases to a minimum. Weighting systems are useful when you have multiple vendors to choose from because they allow you to rank the proposals to determine the sequence of negotiations.

You'll find an example of a weighted scoring system in Chapter 2, "Creating the Project Charter and Preliminary Scope Statement." These systems are commonly used to evaluate vendor proposals.

Independent Estimates

Your procurement department might conduct *independent estimates* (also known as *should cost estimates*) of the costs of the proposal and compare these to the vendor prices. If there are large differences between the independent estimate and the proposed vendor cost, one of two things is happening: the statement of work (SOW), or the terms of the contract, was not detailed enough to allow the vendor to come up with an accurate cost, or the vendor simply failed to respond to all the requirements laid out in the contract or SOW.

Screening Systems

Screening systems use predefined performance criteria or a set of defined minimum requirements to screen out unsuitable vendors. Perhaps your project requires board-certified engineers. One of the screening criteria would be that vendors propose project team members who have this qualification. If they don't, they're eliminated from the selection process.

Screening systems are used together with two other tools and techniques of this process, weighting systems and independent estimates, to rank vendor proposals.

Contract Negotiation

In *contract negotiation*, both parties come to an agreement regarding the contract terms. Negotiation skills are put into practice here as the details of the contract are ironed out between the parties. At a minimum, contract language should include price, responsibilities, regulations or laws that apply, and the overall approach to the project.

You might see the term *fait accompli* show up on the exam. Fait accompli tactics are used during contract negotiation when one party tries to convince the other party discussing a particular contract item that it is no longer an issue. It's a distraction technique, because the party practicing fait accompli tactics is purposely trying to keep from negotiating an issue and claims the issue cannot be changed. For example, during negotiations the vendor tells you that the key resource they're assigning to your project must start immediately or you'll lose that resource and they'll get assigned work elsewhere. However, you don't know—because the vendor didn't tell you—that the vendor can reserve this resource for your project and hold them until the start date. They used fait accompli tactics to push you into starting the project, or hiring this resource, sooner than you would have otherwise.

Seller Rating Systems

Seller rating systems use information about the sellers—such as past performance, delivery, contract compliance, and quality ratings—to determine seller performance. Your organization might have seller rating systems in place, and you should check with your procurement department to see whether they exist for the bidders on your project. Part of the Contract

Administration process (I'll talk about this one later in this chapter) concerns gathering and recording this type of information. Don't use seller rating systems as your sole criteria for evaluating vendors.

Expert Judgment

Expert judgment applies here as it has on many of the other processes I've discussed. Include experts from all areas of the organization when evaluating proposals and selecting vendors. Don't forget your legal and financial folks, marketing, sales, engineering, and so on.

Proposal Evaluation Techniques

Proposal evaluation techniques are a combination of all the techniques I've just discussed. All techniques use some form of expert judgment and evaluation criteria—whether it's objective or subjective criteria. The evaluation criteria are usually weighted, much like a weighted scoring system, and those participating as reviewers provide their ratings (usually to the project manager) to compile into a weighted proposal to determine an overall score. Scoring differences are also resolved using this technique.

After all the RFPs are examined and scored, you move to the outputs of this process, where sellers are selected and contracts awarded.

 Real World Scenario

Vendor Selection for Fitness Counts HR System

Amanda Jacobson is the project manager for Fitness Counts, a nationwide chain of gyms containing all the latest and greatest fitness equipment, aerobics classes, swimming pools, and such. Fitness Counts is converting its human resources data management system. The RFP addressed several requirements, including the following:

- The new system must run on a platform that's compatible with the company's current operating system.

- Hardware must be compatible with company standards.

- Data conversion of existing HR data must be included in the price of the bid.

- Fitness Counts wants to have the ability to add custom modules using internal programmers.

- Training of Fitness Counts programmers must be included in the bid.

The project team is in the Select Sellers process and has received bids based on the RFP published earlier this month. Fitness Counts is using a combination of selection criteria and weighted scoring model to choose a vendor.

One of the evaluation criteria said that the vendor must have prior experience with a project like this. Four vendors met that criteria and proceeded to the weighted scoring selection process.

Amanda is one of the members of the selection committee. She and four other members on the committee rated the four vendors who met the initial selection criteria. They read all of the proposals and rated the criteria using factors they had predetermined for each. For example, vendors who proposed a SQL database as part of the "Platform" criteria (along with the other predetermined factors) should receive a score of 5. Table 9.1 shows their results.

Vendor C is the clear winner of this bid. Based on the weighted scoring model, their responses to the RFP came out ahead of the other bidders. Amanda calls them with the good news and also calls the other vendors to thank them for participating in the bid. Vendor C is awarded the contract, and Amanda moves on to the Contract Administration process.

TABLE 9.1   Example Weighted Scoring Model

	Platform	Hardware	Data Conversion	Custom Modules/ Training	Totals
Weighting Factors*	5	4	5	4	
Vendor A					
Weighting	*3*	*3*	*3*	*4*	
Score	15	12	15	16	**58**
Vendor B					
Weighting	*2*	*3*	*4*	*3*	
Score	10	12	20	12	**54**
Vendor C					
Weighting	*4*	*4*	*4*	*3*	
Score	20	16	20	12	**68**
Vendor D					
Weighting	*3*	*3*	*2*	*4*	
Score	15	12	10	16	**53**

*1–5, with 5 being highest

Select Sellers Outputs

The Select Sellers process has six outputs:

- Selected sellers
- Contract
- Contract management plan
- Resource availability
- Project management plan updates
- Requested changes

The selected sellers output is obvious; you choose the seller (or sellers) to whom you'll award the project. I'll talk more about the contract and the contract management plan next. I've discussed the other outputs already.

Elements of a Contract

You might recall that a contract is a legally binding agreement between two or more parties, typically used to acquire goods or services. Contracts have several names, including agreements, memorandums of understanding (MOUs), subcontracts, and purchase orders.

The type of contract you'll award will depend on the product or services you're procuring and your organizational policies. I talked about the types of contracts—fixed price, cost reimbursable, and so on—in Chapter 6 if you need a refresher. If your project has multiple sellers, you'll award contracts for each of them.

The contract should clearly address the elements of the SOW, time period of performance, pricing and payment plan, acceptance criteria, warranty periods, dispute resolution procedures, and so on.

Since contracts are legally binding and obligate your organization to fulfill the terms, they'll likely be subject to some intensive review, often by several different people. Be certain you understand your organization's policies on contract review and approval before proceeding.

Contracts, like projects, have a life cycle of their own. You might encounter questions on the exam regarding the stages of the contract life cycles, so you'll look at this topic next.

Contract Life Cycles

The contract life cycle consists of four stages:

- Requirement
- Requisition
- Solicitation
- Award

These stages are closely related to the following Project Procurement Knowledge Areas processes from the *Guide to the PMBOK*:

- Plan Purchases and Acquisitions
- Plan Contracting
- Request Seller Responses
- Select Sellers

A description of each of the contract life cycles follows.

Requirement

The requirement stage is the equivalent of the *Guide to the PMBOK*'s Plan Purchases and Acquisitions process, I discussed in Chapter 6. You establish the project and contract needs in this cycle, and you define the requirements of the project. The SOW defines the work of the project, the objectives, and a high-level overview of the deliverables. You develop a work breakdown structure (WBS), a make-or-buy analysis takes place, and you determine cost estimates.

The buyer provides the SOW when the project is performed under contract to describe the requirements of the project. The product description can serve as the SOW.

Requisition

The requisition stage is similar to the *Guide to the PMBOK*'s Plan Contracting process, discussed in Chapter 6.

In the requisition stage, the project objectives are refined and confirmed. Solicitation materials such as the request for proposals (RFP), request for information (RFI), and request for quotations (RFQ) are prepared during this phase. Generally, the project manager is the one responsible for preparing the RFP, RFI, and RFQ. A review of the potential qualified vendors takes place, including checking references and reviewing other projects the vendor has worked on that are similar to your proposed project.

Solicitation

The solicitation stage is where vendors are asked to compete for the contract and respond to the RFP. You will use the tools and techniques of the *Guide to the PMBOK*'s Request Seller Responses process during this contract stage. The resulting output is the proposals.

Award

Vendors are chosen, and contracts are awarded and signed during the award stage. The equivalent to the award stage in the *Guide to the PMBOK* is the Select Sellers process.

The project manager—or the selection committee, depending on the organizational policy—receives the bids and proposals during the award phase and applies evaluation criteria to each in order to score or rank the responses. After ranking each of the proposals, an award is made to the winning vendor, and the contract is written.

Once you have a contract, someone has to administer it. In large organizations, this responsibility will fall to the procurement department. The project manager should still have a solid understanding of administering contracts because that person will work with the procurement department to determine the satisfactory fulfillment of the contract.

Contract Management Plan

The contract management plan describes the contract administrative activities of the project. The plan also outlines how the contract will be administered based on the SOW elements in the contract, delivery requirements, and performance requirements that both the buyer and the seller must meet. The contract management plan is a subsidiary of the project management plan.

Laying Out Quality Assurance Procedures

The Quality Planning process laid out the quality standards for the project and determined how those standards are satisfied. The *Perform Quality Assurance* process involves performing systematic quality activities and uses quality audits to determine which processes should be used to achieve the project requirements and to assure they are performed efficiently and effectively.

The project team members, the project manager, and the stakeholders are responsible for the quality assurance of the project. It could be that a quality assurance department or organization is assigned to the project to oversee these processes. In that case, quality assurance might be provided to (rather than by) the project team. The project manager will have the greatest impact on the quality of the project during this process.

You'll review the inputs to this process next and then spend some time exploring a few new tools and techniques for assuring a quality product and project.

Inputs to Perform Quality Assurance

The inputs to Perform Quality Assurance are what you use to measure the organizational project quality management processes against. The quality management processes were defined during Quality Planning. The inputs to the Perform Quality Assurance process are as follows:

- Quality management plan
- Quality metrics
- Process improvement plan
- Work performance information
- Approved change requests
- Quality control measurements
- Implemented change requests

- Implemented corrective actions
- Implemented defect repair
- Implemented preventive actions

You've heard about the inputs to Perform Quality Assurance before, so you'll move right into the tools and techniques of this section.

Exam Spotlight

The most important point to remember about Perform Quality Assurance is that quality management processes are what you use to make certain the project satisfies the quality standards laid out in the project management plan.

Perform Quality Assurance Tools and Techniques

The Perform Quality Assurance process has four tools and techniques: quality planning tools and techniques, quality audits, process analysis, and quality control tools and techniques.

I discussed quality planning tools and techniques along with the Quality Planning process in Chapter 6. You'll recall that the tools and techniques are cost benefit analysis, benchmarking, design of experiments, and cost of quality. You can use these tools during this process as well to measure project performance.

The quality control tools and techniques listed in this process are the same tools and techniques discussed in the Perform Quality Control process that I'll talk about in Chapter 11, "Controlling Work Results and Closing Out the Project." You'll look at the remaining tools and techniques in the following sections.

Quality Audits

Quality audits are independent reviews performed by trained auditors or third-party reviewers. The purpose of a quality audit is the same as the purpose of the Perform Quality Assurance process—to identify ineffective and inefficient processes used on the project. These audits might examine and uncover inefficient processes and procedures as well.

You can perform quality audits on a regular schedule or at random depending on the organizational policies. Quality audits performed correctly will provide the following benefits:

- The product of the project is fit for use and meets safety standards.
- Applicable laws and standards are adhered to.
- Corrective action is recommended and implemented where necessary.
- The quality plan for the project is adhered to.
- Quality improvements are identified.
- The implementation of approved change requests, corrective actions, preventive actions, and defect repairs are confirmed.

Quality improvements come about as a result of the quality audits. During the course of the audit, you might discover ways of improving the efficiency or effectiveness of the project, thereby increasing the value of the project and more than likely exceeding stakeholder expectations.

Quality improvements are implemented by submitting change requests or taking corrective action (two of the outputs of this process). Quality improvements interface with the Monitoring and Controlling processes because of the need to file change requests.

 You'll look at change requests and change request procedures in Chapter 10, "Monitoring and Controlling Change."

Experienced specialists generally perform quality audits. The specialist's job is to produce an independent evaluation of the quality process. Some organizations are large enough to have their own quality assurance departments or quality assurance teams; others might have to hire contract personnel to perform this function. Internal quality assurance teams report results to the project team and management team of the organization. External quality assurance teams report results to the customer.

Process Analysis

Process analysis looks at process improvement from an organizational and technical perspective. According to the *Guide to the PMBOK*, process analysis follows the steps in the process improvement plan and examines the following:

- Problems experienced while conducting the project

- Constraints of the project

- Inefficient and ineffective processes identified during process operation

One of the techniques of process analysis includes performing root cause analysis. (I talked about root cause analysis in the Risk Identification process in Chapter 5.) While you're examining problems and constraints, for example, you should look for what's causing the problem. The result of this exercise will allow you to develop preventive actions for problems that are similar to the problem you're examining or that have the similar root causes.

Perform Quality Assurance Outputs

The Perform Quality Assurance process has four outputs:

- Requested changes

- Recommended corrective actions

- Organizational process assets updates

- Project management plan updates

These aren't new, but there is one new idea embedded in the recommended corrective actions output. During this process, the recommended corrective actions, whether they are a result of a quality audit or process analysis, should be acted upon immediately. Let's say you're manufacturing parts for one of the deliverables of your project. Obviously, the moment you discover that the parts are not correct, you'd correct the process by calibrating the machine perhaps, or by using different raw materials, to make certain the parts are produced accurately.

Quality Improvements

Although it isn't stated as an output, one of the overarching goals of the Perform Quality Assurance process is to provide a foundation for continuous process improvements. As the name implies, continuous improvements are iterative. This process of continuous improvements sets the stage, so to speak, for improving the quality of all the project processes. This can mean project management processes, but it also means the processes involved in accomplishing the work of the project, or the organizational business processes.

I talked about continuous improvement in Chapter 4, "Creating the WBS and Communicating the Plan;" however, you need to know a little bit more about it. The advantage of continuous process improvement is that it reduces the time the project team spends on ineffective or inefficient processes. If the activities don't help you meet the goals of the project or, worse yet, hinder your progress, it's time to look at ways to improve them. The *Guide to the PMBOK* states that the organizational business processes are the objective for process improvement identification and review.

You've completed the Executing process group with the Perform Quality Assurance process. Remember that the Executing processes and Monitoring and Controlling processes serve as inputs to each other and that Executing and Monitoring and Controlling are both iterative process groups. As your project progresses and it becomes evident that you need to exercise controls to get the project back on track, you'll come back through the Executing process group and then proceed through the Monitoring and Controlling processes again. You'll move on to the Monitoring and Controlling process group now and find out what it's all about.

Monitoring and Controlling Project Work

The processes in the Monitoring and Controlling process group concentrate on monitoring and measuring project performance to identify variances from the project plan and get it back on track.

The *Monitor and Control Project Work* process is concerned with monitoring all the processes in the Initiating, Planning, Executing, and Closing process groups. Collecting data, measuring results, and reporting on performance information are some of the activities you'll perform during this process.

According to the *Guide to the PMBOK*, the Monitor and Control Project Work process involves the following:

- Reporting and comparing actual project results against the project management plan

- Analyzing performance data and determining whether corrective or preventive action should be recommended

- Monitoring the project for risks to make certain they're identified and reported, their status is documented, and the appropriate risk response plans have been put into action

- Documenting all appropriate product information throughout the life of the project

- Gathering, recording, and documenting project information that provides project status, measurements of progress, and forecasting to update cost and schedule information that is reported to stakeholders, project team members, management, and others

- Monitoring approved change requests

Monitor and Control Project Work Inputs

The inputs of this process include project management plan, work performance information, and rejected change requests. I've covered the inputs project management plan and work performance information in previous chapters. Rejected change requests should be documented so that if a request to perform the change comes up in the future, or there's a question about the disposition of the request, you have a record of what the change request was about and why it was rejected.

Tools and Techniques of Monitor and Control Project Work

You've seen most of the tools and techniques of the Monitor and Control Project Work process:

- Project management methodology

- Project management information system

- Earned value management

- Expert judgment

You'll look more closely at the earned value technique during the discussion of the Cost Control process, which I'll cover in Chapter 10.

Monitor and Control Project Work Outputs

The outputs of the Monitor and Control Project Work process will also look familiar. They are as follows:

- Recommended corrective actions

- Recommended preventive actions

- Forecasts
- Recommended defect repair
- Requested changes

The forecasts output includes information that has been gathered concerning project performance and has been used to predict future project outcomes. For example, you might use the amount of time it has taken to complete the project activities to date to help predict how much longer the project will take to complete.

 You'll examine several formulas that will help you do this in the next chapter.

Administering the Contract

You'll now shift your focus back to the procurement arena. I talked about Request Seller Responses and Select Sellers earlier in this chapter. Now that the contract has been awarded, you need to administer it.

The *Contract Administration* process concerns monitoring the vendor's performance and ensuring that all the requirements of the contract are met. When multiple vendors are providing goods and services to the project, Contract Administration entails coordinating the interfaces among all the vendors as well as administering each of the contracts. If vendor A has a due date that will impact whether vendor B can perform their service, the management and coordination of the two vendors become important. Vendor A's contract and due dates must be monitored closely because failure to perform could impact another vendor's ability to perform, not to mention the project schedule. You can see how this situation could multiply quickly when you have six or seven or more vendors involved.

 It's imperative that the project manager and project team are aware of any contract agreements that might impact the project so the team does not inadvertently take action that violates the terms of the contract.

Depending on the size of the organization, administering the contract might fall to someone in the procurement department. This doesn't mean you're off the hook as the project manager. It's still your responsibility to oversee the process and make sure the project objectives are being met, regardless of whether a vendor is performing the activities or your project team members are performing the activities. You'll be the one monitoring the performance of the vendor and informing them when and if performance is lacking. You'll also monitor the contract's financial conditions. For example, the seller should be paid in a timely manner when they've satisfactorily met the conditions of the contract, and it will be up to you to let the procurement department know it's OK to pay the vendor. If administering the contract is your responsibility, you might have to terminate the contract when the vendor violates the terms or doesn't meet the agreed-upon deliverables. If the procurement department has this responsibility, you'll have to document the situation and provide this to the procurement department so that they can enforce or terminate the contract.

Administering the contract is closely linked with project management processes. You'll monitor the progress of the contract, execute plans, track costs, measure outputs, approve changes, take corrective action, and report on status, just as you do for the project itself. According to the *Guide to the PMBOK*, you must integrate and coordinate the Direct and Manage Project Execution, Performance Reporting, Perform Quality Control, Integrated Change Control, and Risk Monitoring and Control processes during Contract Administration.

Exam Spotlight

You might find questions on the exam that involve the Request Seller Responses, Select Sellers, and Contract Administration processes. Request Seller Responses and Select Sellers are part of the Executing process group, while Contract Administration belongs to the Monitoring and Controlling group. Even though these processes belong to different process groups, they're usually performed in the order stated in the first sentence of this exam spotlight.

Contracting Inputs

Contract Administration has six inputs:

- Contract
- Contract management plan
- Selected sellers
- Performance reports
- Approved change requests
- Work performance information

The contract, contract management plan, and selected sellers are outputs from the Select Sellers process. I'll cover performance reports in more depth in Chapter 11. Performance reports for the Contract Administration process include information related to the seller (or vendor).

Approved Change Requests

Sometimes as you get into the work of the project, you'll discover changes need to be made. This could entail changes to the contract as well. Approved change requests are used to process the project or contract changes and might include things such as modifications to deliverables, changes to the product or service of the project, changes in contract terms, or termination for poor performance. Contracts can be amended at any time prior to contract completion provided the changes are agreed to by all parties and conform to the change control processes outlined in the contract.

Exam Spotlight

Work performance information is an output of the Direct and Manage Project Execution process. The results you gather in the Contract Administration process are actually collected as part of the Direct and Manage Project Execution work result output.

Work Performance Information

Work performance information concerns monitoring work results and examining the vendors' deliverables. This includes monitoring their work results against the project management plan and making certain activities are performed correctly and in sequence. You'll need to determine which deliverables are complete and which ones have not been completed to date. You'll also need to consider the quality of the deliverables and the costs that have been incurred to date.

Vendors request payment for the goods or services delivered in the form of *seller invoices*. Seller invoices should describe the work that was completed or the materials that were delivered and should include any supporting documentation necessary to describe what was delivered. The contract should state what type of supporting documentation is needed with the invoice.

Remember that seller invoices are an element of the work performance information input to the Contract Administration process, not an output. Also, don't confuse seller invoices with the payment system, which is a tool and technique of this process.

Administering Contracts Tools and Techniques

Administering the contract requires several tools and techniques:

- Contract change control system
- Buyer-conducted performance review
- Inspections and audits
- Performance reporting
- Payment system
- Claims administration

- Records management system
- Information technology

You will look at each of these in the following sections.

Contract Change Control System

Much like the management plans found in the Planning processes, the *contract change control system* describes the processes needed to make contract changes. Since the contract is a legal document, changes to it require the agreement of all parties. A formal process must be established to process and authorize (or deny) changes. (Authorization levels are defined in the organizational policies.)

The purpose of the contract change control system is to establish a formal process for submitting change requests. It documents how to submit changes, establishes the approval process, and outlines authority levels. It includes a tracking system to number the change requests and record their status. The procedures for dispute resolution are spelled out in the contract change control system as well.

The change control system, along with all the management plan outputs, becomes part of the Integrated Change Control process that I'll discuss later in this chapter.

Buyer-Conducted Performance Reviews

Buyer-conducted performance reviews examine the seller's performance on the contract to date. These reviews can be conducted at the end of the contract or at intervals during the contract period. Buyer reviews examine the contract terms and seller performance for elements such as these:

- Meeting project scope
- Meeting project quality
- Staying within project budgets
- Meeting the project schedule

The performance reviews themselves might take the form of quality audits or inspections of documents as well as the work of the product itself. The point of the review is to determine where the seller is succeeding at meeting scope, quality, cost, and schedule issues, for example, or where they're not measuring up. If the seller is not in compliance, action must be taken to either get them back into compliance or terminate the contract. The yardstick you're using to measure their performance against is the contract SOW and the terms of the contract. When the RFP is included as part of the contract (which it usually is), you might also use it to determine contract compliance.

Inspections and Audits

I talked about quality audits as part of the Perform Quality Assurance process. The idea is the same here. The buyer, or some designated third party, will physically inspect the work of the seller and perform audits to determine whether there are any deficiencies in the seller's product or service.

Performance Reporting

Performance reporting is a large part of project management. This tool and technique entails providing your managers and stakeholders with information about the vendor's progress in meeting the contract objectives. This information is also part of the Performance Reporting process that I'll discuss in depth later in this chapter.

Payment Systems

Vendors submit seller invoices as an input to this process, and the *payment system* is the tool and technique used to issue payment. The organization might have a dedicated department, such as accounts payable, that handles vendor payments, or it might fall to the project manager. In either case, follow the policies and procedures the organization has established regarding vendor payments.

Claims Administration

Claims administration involves documenting, monitoring, and managing contested changes to the contract. Changes that cannot be agreed upon are called *contested changes*. Contested changes usually involve a disagreement about the compensation to the vendor for implementing the change. You might believe the change is not significant enough to justify additional compensation, whereas the vendor believes they'll lose money by implementing the change free of charge. Contested changes are also known as *disputes*, *claims*, or *appeals*. These can be settled directly between the parties themselves, through the court system, or by a process called arbitration. *Arbitration* involves bringing all parties to the table with a third, disinterested party who is not a participant in the contract to try to reach an agreement. The purpose of arbitration is to reach an agreement without having to go to court.

Records Management System

It has been a while since I've talked about documentation, but discussing *records management systems* reminds me of the importance of having an organized system for contract documentation. A records management system involves not just documentation, but policies, control functions, and automated tools as part of the project management information system (which is both a part of the enterprise environmental factors and a tool and technique of several processes) used to manage project documents as well as contract documents. Records management systems typically index documents for easy filing and retrieval.

Information Technology

Information technology, in this process, refers to the automated ways you can put some of the tools and techniques, outputs, processes, and so on, to use. I don't know about you, but I've reached a point where I can't live without information technology. Having my email, contacts, project documents, to-do lists, policy documents, and so on, at my fingertips wherever I go is invaluable.

As mentioned earlier, using a project management software tool to help build the project schedule and allocate resources is much easier than developing all this by hand. Contract information and general project information and processes can be much more efficient when you use information technology to help you.

Managing Contract Outputs

The outputs to the Contract Administration process are as follows:

- Contract documentation
- Requested changes
- Recommended corrective actions
- Organizational process asset updates
- Project management plan updates

These outputs relate to the tools and techniques just talked about and, in practice, work hand in hand with them. I've talked about recommended corrective actions and project management plan updates before, and I don't have anything new to add here. The remaining outputs either are new or involve additional information you need to know.

Contract Documentation

Here's your favorite topic again. This output includes (but isn't limited to) all of the following:

- Contract
- Performance information
- Warranties
- Financial information (such as invoices and payment records)
- Inspection and audit results
- Supporting schedules
- Approved and unapproved changes

The records management system I talked about earlier is the perfect place to keep all these documents.

Requested Changes

Requested contract changes are coordinated with the Direct and Manage Project Execution and Integrated Change Control processes so that any changes impacting the project are communicated to the project team and appropriate actions are put into place to realign the objectives. This might also mean the project management plan will require changes. That requires you to jump back to the Planning process group to bring the project management plan up-to-date. Once the plan is up-to-date, the Direct and Manage Project Execution process might require changes as well to get the work of the project in line with the new plan. Remember that project management is an iterative process, and it's not unusual to revisit the Planning or Executing processes, particularly as changes are made or corrective actions are put into place.

Contract changes will not always impact the project management plan, however. For example, late delivery of key equipment probably would impact the project management plan, but changes in the vendor payment schedule probably would not. It's important that you are kept abreast of any changes to the contract so that you can evaluate whether the project management plan needs adjusting.

Organizational Process Asset Updates

Organizational process assets consist of organizational policies, procedures, and so on. Three elements of this output relate to contracts:

Correspondence   Correspondence is information that needs to be communicated in writing to either the seller or the buyer. Examples include changes to the contract, clarification of contract terms, results of buyer audits and inspections, and notification of performance issues. You would also use correspondence to notify a vendor that you're terminating the contract because performance is below expectations and is not satisfying the requirements of the contract.

Payment schedules and requests   Many times, contracts are written such that payment is made based on a predefined performance schedule. For example, perhaps the first payment is made after 25 percent of the product or service is completed. Or maybe the payment schedule is based on milestone completion. In any case, as the project manager, you will verify that the vendor's work (or delivery) meets expectations before the payment is authorized. It's almost always your responsibility as the project manager to verify that the terms of the contract to date have or have not been satisfied. Depending on your organizational policies, someone from the accounting or procurement department might request written notification from you that the vendor has completed a milestone or made a delivery. Monitoring the work of the vendor is as important as monitoring the work of your team members.

The *Guide to the PMBOK* states that the payment schedules and requests element pertains to payment systems that are external to the project. For example, if the procurement department is responsible for paying the contractor, then that department manages the payment schedule (which is one of the terms of the contract). The seller submits a payment request, an inspection or review of their performance is conducted to make certain the terms of the contract were fulfilled, and the payment is made. If the project team is managing the contract payments, this output is called *payments*.

Seller performance evaluation   Seller performance evaluation is a written record of the seller's performance on the contract. It should include information about whether the seller successfully met contract dates, fulfilled the requirements of the contract and/or contract statement of work, whether the work was satisfactory, and so on. Seller performance evaluations can be used as a basis for terminating the existing contract if performance is not satisfactory. They should also indicate whether this vendor should be allowed to bid on future work. Seller performance evaluations can also be included as part of the qualified sellers lists.

WARNING   Don't confuse payment systems (a tool and technique of Contract Administration) with payment schedules and requests (an output of Contract Administration). Payment systems include reviews and authorization to issue the check. The payment schedules and request output is where the check gets sent to the seller.

Exam Spotlight

I recommend remembering the inputs, tools and techniques, and outputs of the contracting processes, including Request Seller Responses, Select Sellers, and Contract Administration. Be certain you understand the purposes of these processes and don't simply memorize their components. Here's a brief recap:

> *Request Seller Responses*: Obtaining bids and proposals from potential vendors

> *Select Sellers*: Evaluating proposals against predetermined evaluation criteria to select vendors

> *Contract Administration*: Monitoring vendor performance to ensure contract requirements are met

---

Managing Project Teams

The *Manage Project Team* process is concerned with tracking and reporting on the performance of individual team members. During this process, performance appraisals are prepared and conducted, issues are identified and resolved, and feedback is given to the team members. Some team behavior is also observed during this process, but the main focus here is on individuals and their performance.

Exam Spotlight

Take note that the *Guide to the PMBOK* states that one of the outcomes or results of the Manage Project Team process is an update to the staffing management plan. However, staffing management plan updates are not listed as an output of this process.

You've seen all the inputs to this process before:

- Organizational process assets
- Project staff assignments
- Roles and responsibilities
- Project organization charts
- Staffing management plan
- Team performance assessment
- Work performance information
- Performance reports

Tools and Techniques for Managing Teams

Most of the tools and techniques for this process are new:

- Observation and conversation
- Project performance appraisals
- Conflict management
- Issue log

You'll take a closer look at each of these tools in the following sections.

Observation and Conversation

Observation and conversation is another one of those tools and techniques that is self-evident. To assess team member performance, you have to observe it. I hope you've also learned how important communication is to the success of the project. This includes communicating with your team members. I know project managers who are reticent to engage their teams in conversation unless it's official project business. I've even known project managers who instructed their administrative assistant to give a specific direction to another team member. It's difficult to understand a team member's attitude or viewpoint toward the project if you're communicating through someone else. Establish an open door policy with your team members and live up to it. The benefits are so great that it's worth a few minutes a day of chitchat to establish that feeling of trust and camaraderie. If your team perceives you as open, honest, and willing to listen, you'll be the first person they come to when issues arise.

 Real World Scenario

What Not to Do

Tina is a newly minted project manager. She has worked on many projects as the assistant project manager, but this is the first time she has led the charge. Tina is so shy she finds it difficult to give team members any kind of direction or to assign tasks, so she has her administrative assistant do it for her. Tina tells her administrative assistant what needs to be done and who needs to do it and leaves it to the assistant to inform the appropriate team members.

As the project progresses, schedule milestone dates are missed, and Tina discovers tasks that haven't started that were scheduled to start two weeks ago. Coming in from lunch one day she saw several project team members huddled around her administrative assistant's desk. From what she overheard, they were discussing a risk event that occurred on the project.

Fortunately for Tina, one of the project managers she has worked for in the past saw what was happening. Because the administrative assistant was the one who had established relationships with the team and was in effect giving the orders, the team began treating her as the project manager instead of Tina. Tina's friend had a one-on-one coaching session with Tina about her management style and the importance of conversation and observation. Together they were able to get the project back on track.

Project Performance Appraisal

Project performance appraisals are typically annual or semiannual affairs where managers let their employees know what they think of their performance over the past year and rate them accordingly. These are usually manager-to-employee exchanges but can incorporate a *360-degree review*, which takes in feedback from just about everyone the team member interacts with, including stakeholders, customers, project manager, peers, subordinates, and the delivery person if they have a significant amount of project interaction. I'm not a fan of 360-degree reviews because it makes most nonmanager types uncomfortable. "I don't want to rate my peer" is a typical response. I also find 360-degree reviews are biased. At best you'll get a response like this: "Oh, Ken is great, just great. No problems—a good guy." Or you'll get exactly the opposite if the person you're speaking with doesn't like the team member you're reviewing. Performance appraisal should be a bit more constructive than this. Nonetheless, understand the 360-degree concept for the exam.

No matter what type of appraisal is conducted, project managers should contribute to the performance appraisals of all project team members. You should be aware of potential loyalty issues when you're working in a matrix organizational structure. The team member in this structure reports to both you (as the project manager) and a functional manager. If the project manager does not have an equal say, or at least some say about the employee's performance, it will cause the team member to be loyal to the functional manager and show little loyalty to the project or project manager. Managing these dual reporting relationships is often a critical success factor for the project, and it is the project manager's responsibility to assure that these relationships are managed effectively.

Performance appraisal time is also a good time to explore training needs, to clarify roles and responsibilities, to set goals for the future, and so on.

Conflict Management

I talked about conflict management in the previous chapter. Here it's important to note that, as in any situation, you'll want to deal with conflict as soon as it arises. During the Manage Project Team process, most conflicts come about as a result of schedule issues, availability of resources (usually the lack of availability), or personal work habits. When project team members are having a conflict, address them first in private with the person who has the issue. Work in a direct and collaborative manner, but be prepared to escalate the issue into a more formalized procedure (potentially even disciplinary action) if needed.

If conflicts exist between two of the team members, encourage resolution between them without intervention on your part. The best conflict resolution will come about when they can work out the issues between them. When that isn't possible, you'll have to step in and help resolve the matter.

Remember that solid ground rules and established policies and procedures will help mitigate conflict before it arises.

Issue Log

The issue log is a place to document the issues that keep the project team from meeting project goals. These can range from differences of opinion to newly surfaced responsibilities that need to be assigned to a project team member. Each issue should be recorded in the log along with the person responsible for resolving it. You should also note the date the resolution is needed.

Managing Project Team Outputs

The outputs of the Manage Project Team process are the result of the conversations, performance appraisals, and conflict resolution I've talked about previously. This process has five outputs:

- Requested changes
- Recommended corrective actions
- Recommended preventive actions
- Organizational process assets updates
- Project management plan updates

Remember that the elements of these outputs pertain to human resources. For example, requested changes might come about as a result of a change in staffing, corrective actions might come about because of disciplinary actions or training needs, and preventive actions might be needed to reduce the impact of potential human resource issues. Any of these actions might cause changes to the staffing management plan, which means you should update the project management plan.

The organizational process asset updates output has two components: input to organizational performance appraisals and lessons learned documentation. Input to organizational performance appraisals comes from team members with significant interactions with the project and each other.

Lessons learned encompasses everything you've learned about the human resources aspect during this project, including documentation that can be used as templates on future projects (such as org charts, position descriptions, and the staffing management plan), techniques used to resolve conflict, the types of conflict that came up during the project, ground rules, when and how virtual teams were used on the project and the procedures associated with them, the staffing management plan, special skills needed during the project that weren't known about during the Planning processes, and the issue log.

Managing Stakeholders

In my experience, managing stakeholders is much more difficult than managing project team members. Stakeholders are often managers or directors in the organization who might be higher in the food chain than the project manager and aren't afraid to let you know it. Having said that, you *can* manage stakeholders, and you do this using communication.

 If you need a refresher on the definition and role of stakeholders, please see Chapter 1, "What Is a Project?"

The *Manage Stakeholders* process is about satisfying the needs of the stakeholders by managing communications with them, resolving issues, and improving project performance by implementing requested changes.

Stakeholders need lots of communication in every form you can provide. If you are actively engaged with your stakeholders and interacting with them, providing project status, and resolving issues, your chances of a successful project are much greater than if you don't do these things.

The inputs of this process are the communications management plan and organizational process assets. You've seen both of these before. The tools and techniques include communication methods and issue logs. Keep in mind that face-to-face communications are the most effective with stakeholders. The issue log in this process is more like an action item log where you record the actions needed to resolve stakeholder concerns and project issues they raise. As with the issue log in the Manage Project Team process, you'll assign a responsible party and a due date for resolution.

The outputs of the Manage Stakeholder process are resolved issues, approved change requests, approved corrective actions, organizational process assets updates, and project management plan updates. Resolved issues are logged in the issue log.

Establishing Performance Measurements

As mentioned, the Monitoring and Controlling process group concentrates on monitoring and measuring project performance to identify variances from the project plan. *Performance Reporting* is the process where the collection of baseline data occurs and is documented and reported. Performance Reporting is part of the Communications Management Knowledge Area, as is the Manage Stakeholders process. Thus, it involves collecting information regarding project progress and project accomplishments and reporting it to the stakeholders. This information might also be reported to project team members, the management team, and other interested parties. Reporting might include information concerning project quality, costs, scope, project schedules, procurement, and risk.

Performance Reporting Inputs

You've examined all the inputs to the Performance Reporting process. They are as follows:

- Work performance information
- Performance measurements
- Forecasted completion
- Quality control measurements
- Project management plan

- Approved change requests
- Deliverables

Note that the project management plan contains the project management baseline data (typically cost, schedule, and scope factors), which you'll use to monitor and compare results. Deviations from this data are reported to management. Performance measures are taken primarily during the Cost Control, Schedule Control, and Perform Quality Control processes, which you'll look at in the next chapter.

Performance Reporting Tools and Techniques

The tools and techniques of this process are as follows:

- Information presentation tools
- Performance information gathering and compilation
- Status review meetings
- Time reporting systems
- Cost reporting systems

Information Presentation Tools

Information presentation tools include automated tools such as spreadsheet and presentation software that help you create presentable reports and information regarding the progress and status of the project for stakeholder review.

Performance Information Gathering and Compilation

If you and your team members have been diligently documenting your project's performance, you need to gather all that information and keep it in one place. Performance information gathering and compilation can occur manually, as in everyone turns in hard copy reports to the project manager or other designated person, or you can gather information automatically from project management software systems, databases, or other systems. Performance data, as well as data used in progress reports, status reports, and forecasts, should be captured for future reference. The important part is that you should keep the documentation in one place and make it easily accessible to anyone who needs it.

Status Review Meetings

Status review meetings are important functions during the course of the project. (I introduced status review meetings with the Information Distribution Process in the previous chapter.) The purpose of the status meeting is to provide updated information regarding the progress of the project. These are not show-and-tell meetings. If you have a prototype to demo, set up a different time to do that. Status meetings are meant to exchange information and provide project updates. They are a way to formally exchange project information. I've worked on projects where it's not unusual to have three or four status meetings conducted for different audiences. They can occur between the project team and project manager, between the project manager and stakeholders, between the project manager and users or customers, between the project manager and the management team, and so on.

Notice that the project manager is always included in status review meetings. Take care that you don't overburden yourself with meetings that aren't necessary or meetings that could be combined with other meetings. Having any more than three or four status meetings per month is unwieldy.

> Regular, timely status meetings prevent surprises down the road because you are keeping stakeholders and customers informed of what's happening. Team status meetings alert the project manager to potential risk events and provide the opportunity to discover and manage problems before they get to the uncontrollable stage.

The project manager is usually the expediter of the status meeting. As such, it's your job to use status meetings wisely. Don't waste your team's time or the stakeholders' time either. Notify attendees in writing of the meeting time and place. Publish an agenda prior to the meeting, and stick to the agenda during the meeting. Every so often, summarize what has been discussed during the meeting. Don't let side discussions lead you down rabbit trails, and keep irrelevant conversations to a minimum. It's also good to publish status meeting notes at the conclusion of the meeting, especially if any action items resulted from the meeting. This will give you a document trail and serves as a reminder to the meeting participants of what actions need to be resolved and who is responsible for the action item.

It's important that project team members are honest with the project manager and that the project manager is in turn honest about what they report. A few years ago, a department in my agency took on a project of gargantuan proportions and unfortunately didn't employ good project management techniques. One of the biggest problems with this project was that the project manager did not listen to the highly skilled project team members. The team members warned of problems and setbacks, but the project manager didn't want to hear about it. The project manager took their reports to be of the "Chicken Little" ilk and refused to believe the sky was falling. Unfortunately, the sky *was* falling! Because the project manager didn't believe the reports, the project manager refused to report the true status of the project to the stakeholders and oversight committees. Millions of dollars were wasted on a project that was doomed for failure while the project manager continued to report that the project was on time and activities were completed when in fact they were not.

There are hundreds of project stories like this, and I'll bet you've got one or two from your experiences as well. Don't let your project become the next bad example. Above all, be honest in your reporting. No one likes bad news, but bad news delivered too late along with millions of dollars wasted is a guaranteed career showstopper.

Time and Cost Reporting Systems

Time and cost reporting systems are used to, obviously, record time and cost information about the project. Most specifically, these systems will report the time and cost that has been expended on the project to date.

Performance Reporting Outputs

The Performance Reporting process has several outputs:

- Performance reports
- Forecasts
- Requested changes
- Organizational process assets updates (lessons learned)

Performance reports are the primary output of this process. It's here that performance information is documented and reported to the stakeholders as outlined in the communication management plan. These reports might take many forms, including S curves (cost baselines are recorded this way), bar charts, tables, and histograms. Earned value information is often reported during this process as well. You'll examine this topic in the next chapter during the discussion of the Cost Control process.

In the next chapter, you'll explore the main change control processes and the measurement tools you'll use to provide the variance measurements that are gathered and reported to the stakeholder during the Performance Reporting process.

 Real World Scenario

Project Case Study: New Kitchen Heaven Retail Store

Your regularly scheduled status meeting is coming up. Let's see how it's progressing.

"Thank you all for coming," you begin. You note those stakeholders who are present and pass out the agendas. "First, we have a contract update. Jake, would you give us the update, please?"

"Gomez Construction has submitted a seller payment request for the work completed through November 30. Shelly in our contract management office manages the payment system and handles all payment requests. She'll get a check cut and out to Gomez by the end of this month. They are doing an outstanding job as always. As you know, I've also hired an independent inspector, aside from the city and county types, so that we make sure we're up to code before the city types get there. I don't want to get caught in that trap and end up delaying the project because we can't get the city inspector back out to reinspect quickly enough."

"Thank you, Jake. Any problems with those inspections so far?"

Jake clears his throat. "It turned out to be a good move because the contractor did find some things that we were able to correct before bringing out the official inspectors."

"Ricardo, do you have a contract update for us today?"

"Yes. The contract management office used a fixed-price contract on the hardware and IT supplies order. That contract is just now making its way through the sign-off processes. My group will manage the quality control and testing once all this equipment arrives."

"Jill, can you give us the update on the store?" you ask.

"I've ordered all the retail products, have ordered the cookware line, and have lined up the chef demos. The costs for the new gourmet supplier we're using are higher than our original vendor. This impacts ongoing operations, but the hit to the project budget is minimal. I should also mention that a change request was submitted."

You point everyone's attention to the issues list. "In the last meeting I reported that Gomez had an important crew member out on a family emergency. Gomez was able to replace the team member with no impact to the schedule. The next issue was the T1 connection—I reported that Ricardo was not receiving phone calls back. Good news—that issue has been cleared, the date has been set, and we can close this issue. Are there any new issues to be added this week?"

One of the stakeholders from the marketing department speaks up, "I need someone from the project team to work with me on the website announcement. I haven't heard anything, and I don't want to cut this so close that we put up something subpar on the website. The 50th anniversary deserves a little splash."

"OK," you reply. "I'll set up a meeting with you to get more information, and then we'll determine who is the best fit. I've noted we need to assign someone to this activity in the issue log. On another note, I have one more issue to report. Unfortunately, we lost a valuable team member last week. I don't want to go into all the details here, but this employee violated our Internet acceptable use policy. This person was placed on disciplinary action on this very issue once before. This will impact the project schedule because his activities were on the critical path. I've already interviewed two internal candidates who've expressed interest in working on the project. I believe either one would work out nicely. However, there is some ramp-up time needed."

"What's the forecast?" Dirk asks. "Are we on track for meeting the grand opening date given all these issues?

"I'll have performance figures for you at the next status meeting, and I have some ideas on how we can make up this time other ways so that we still meet the date."

You thank everyone for coming and remind them of the next meeting time.

Project Case Study Checklist

Contract Administration

- Contract documentation
- Seller invoices
- Payment systems
- Records management system

Perform Quality Assurance

- Quality audits

- Making certain the project will meet and satisfy the quality standards of the project

Manage Project Team

- Observation and conversation

- Recommended corrective actions

- Conflict management

- Issue log

Manage Stakeholders

- Communications methods

- Issue log

- Resolved issues

Performance Reporting

- Performance reports (status meetings)

- Forecasts

Understanding How This Applies to Your Next Project

This chapter is jammed with information you need to know for the exam as well as on the job. But depending on the size of your organization, many of the processes I discussed in the Executing process group might actually be handled by another department in your organization. I've worked in small companies (fewer than 100 people) and very large companies and have always had either a person or a department that was responsible for the vendor selection, contract negotiation, and contract administration. As the project manager, I have significant input to these processes, but the person or department responsible for procurement has the ultimate control. For example, we use only RFPs (and occasionally RFIs) to solicit vendors. We typically use a weighted scoring model in combination with a screening and rating system to choose a vendor. For small projects, we have a list of prequalified vendors from which to choose.

Someone who is skilled at writing contracts can best handle the contracts, which ideally should be reviewed by the legal team. The legal team should also review changes proposed by the vendor before signing on the dotted line. Clear, concise, and specific contracts, in my experience, are a critical success factor for any project. I've too often seen contract issues bring a project to a sudden halt. Another classic contract faux pas allows the vendor to think the work is complete while the buyer believes the vendor is weeks or months away from meeting the requirements. These types of disputes can almost always be traced back to an unclear, imprecise contract. It's important to be specific in your statement of work. Make sure that the project requirements are clear and broken down far enough to be measurable and that deliverables are defined with criteria that allow you to inspect for contract compliance prior to final acceptance.

Let me stress again that you cannot successfully manage a project team without communicating with them on a regular basis. The last thing you want is for a stakeholder to follow you into the elevator to inform you about a major problem with the project that you weren't aware of. That will happen if you haven't established a relationship with your team. If they don't believe you're trustworthy or they don't know you well enough to know whether you'll stand by them, you'll be one of the last people to find out what's happening. I know managers and project managers who subscribe to the "don't get too close to your team" theory. I subscribe to the "all things in moderation" theory. You do want to establish relationships and prove your loyalty to the team, but you also have to know where to draw the line. When it comes time to hold a team member accountable, it can be difficult to do if you have become very close on a personal basis. But I advocate erring on the side of developing a relationship with the team. My teams have to trust me to the point that they know they can come to me—at any time, with all types of news, good or bad—and I'll help them resolve the problem.

Managing your stakeholders is as important as managing the team. Stakeholders need proper doses of communication at the right time and in the right format. Remember the old adage that most people need to hear the same information six times before it registers with them. Stakeholders, understandably, are notorious for hearing what they want to hear. Here's an example: If I asked you to picture an elephant, you could likely picture an elephant in your mind. It might be live or stuffed and grey, brown, or pink, but you'd clearly understand the concept. *Elephant* is a word that's pretty hard to misinterpret. But what if I asked you to picture a three-bedroom house? There's lots of room for interpretation there. When I said *three-bedroom house*, I meant ranch style with the master on one end of the house and the other two bedrooms at the other end of the house. What did you picture? Make certain you're using language your stakeholders understand, and repeat it often until you're certain they get it.

Summary

This chapter finished up the Executing process group and looked at the first process in the Monitoring and Controlling process group. I discussed Request Seller Responses, Select Sellers, Contract Administration, and Perform Quality Assurance from the Executing process group. I also covered several processes in the Monitoring and Controlling process group including Monitor and Control Project Work, Contract Administration, Manage Project Team, Manage Stakeholders, and Performance Reporting. Request Seller Responses involves obtaining bids and responses from vendors. The tools and techniques of this process include bidder conferences, advertising, and develop qualified sellers list.

Select Sellers involves receiving bids or proposals. In this process, the selection committee will use evaluation criteria to prioritize the bids and proposals, and the outcome is that a seller (or sellers) is selected and contracts awarded.

During the Perform Quality Assurance process, quality audits are performed to ensure that the project will meet and satisfy the project's quality standards set out in the quality plan.

The Monitor and Control Project Work project concerns monitoring all the project process groups, collecting data, measuring results, reporting on performance information, and taking corrective action to keep the project in scope and on schedule.

Contract Administration is the process where you'll monitor the vendor's performance and ensure that all the requirements of the contract are met. If more than one vendor is working on the project, Contract Administration entails coordinating the interfaces among all the vendors as well as administering each of the contracts.

Contracts have cycles of their own, much like projects. Phases of the contracting life cycle include requirement, requisition, solicitation, and award. Changes to the contract are managed with change requests.

Changes that cannot be agreed upon are contested changes. These take the form of disputes, claims, or appeals. They might be settled among the parties directly, through a court of law, or through arbitration.

Request Seller Responses and Select Sellers belong to the Executing process group, and the Contract Administration belongs to the Monitoring and Controlling process group. In practice, you'll generally perform Request Seller Responses, Select Sellers, and Contract Administration in that order.

Manage Project Teams involves tracking and reporting on project team member performance. Performance appraisals are performed during this process and feedback is provided to the team members.

The Manage Stakeholders process concerns making certain communication needs of the stakeholders are met, managing any issues stakeholders might raise, and implementing change requests.

The last process covered in this chapter, Performance Reporting, is one of the ways stakeholders (and others) are kept informed of project progress. Performance Reporting includes tools and techniques such as information presentation tools and status reports to report performance, requested changes, forecast future project performance, and update organizational process assets.

Exam Essentials

Be able to describe the difference between the Request Seller Responses process and the Select Sellers process.   Request Seller Responses obtains bids and proposals from vendors. Select Sellers is the receipt of bids and proposals and the selection of a vendor.

Be able to name the tools and techniques of the Select Sellers process. The tools and techniques of the Select Sellers process are weighting systems, independent estimates, screening systems, contract negotiation, seller rating systems, expert judgment, and proposal evaluation techniques.

Be able to describe the purpose of the Perform Quality Assurance process. The Perform Quality Assurance process is concerned with making certain the project will meet and satisfy the quality standards of the project.

Be able to describe the purpose of the Monitor and Control Project Work process. The Monitor and Control Project Work process monitors the project process groups including Initiating, Planning, Executing, and Closing. This process reports and compares project results with the project management plan; monitors approved change requests; and analyzes, documents, and records project information.

Be able to name the contracting life cycle stages. Contracting life cycles include requirement, requisition, solicitation, and award.

Be able to name the tools and techniques of the Manage Project Team process. The tools and techniques of Manage Project Team are observation and conversation, project performance appraisal, conflict management, and issue log.

Be able to describe the purpose of the Manage Stakeholders process Manage Stakeholders concerns satisfying the needs of the stakeholders by managing communications with them.

Be able to define the purpose of the Performance Reporting process. The Performance Reporting process collects and reports information regarding project progress and project accomplishments. The technique used often to report on project performance is earned value analysis.

Key Terms

I've discussed in detail the processes you'll use while measuring and evaluating project performance. You need to understand each of these processes to effectively evaluate progress, recognize variances from the plan, and make adjustments to keep the project on track. Know them by the names used in the *PMBOK* so you'll recognize them on the exam.

Contract Administration	Perform Quality Assurance
Manage Project Team	Performance Reporting
Manage Stakeholders	Request Seller Responses
Monitor and Control Project Work	Select Sellers

You learned a lot of new key words in this chapter as well. PMI has worked hard to develop and define terms that apply across industries. Here is a list of some of the terms you came across in this chapter:

360-degree review	evaluation criteria
advertising	fait accompli
appeals	independent estimates
arbitration	payment system
bidder conferences	process analysis
claims	quality audits
claims administration	screening systems
contested changes	seller invoices
contract change control system	seller rating systems
contract negotiation	should cost estimates
develop qualified sellers lists	status review meetings
disputes	work performance information

Review Questions

1. You are a project manager for Dakota Software Consulting Services. You're working with a major retailer that offers its products through mail-order catalogs. The company is interested in knowing customer characteristics, the amounts of first-time orders, and similar information. As a potential bidder for this project, you worked on the RFP response and submitted the proposal. When the selection committee received the RFP responses from all the vendors bidding on this project, it used a weighted system to make a selection. Which process did this occur in?

   A. Select Sellers

   B. Request Seller Responses

   C. Plan Contracting and Purchases

   D. Contract Administration

2. You have been asked to submit a proposal for a project that has been put out for bid. First you attend the bidder conference to ask questions of the buyers and to hear the questions some of the other bidders will ask. Which of the following statements is true?

   A. Bidder conferences are a tool and technique of the Select Sellers process.

   B. Bidder conferences are an output of the Select Sellers process.

   C. Bidder conferences are an output of the Request Seller Responses process.

   D. Bidder conferences are a tool and technique of the Request Seller Responses process.

3. You have been asked to submit a proposal for a project that has been put out for bid. Prior to submitting the proposal, your company must register so that its firm is on the qualified seller list. Which of the following statements is true?

   A. The qualified seller list provides information about the sellers and is a tool and technique of the Request Seller Responses process.

   B. The qualified seller list provides information about the project and the company that wrote the RFP and is an output of the Select Sellers process.

   C. The qualified seller list provides information about the project and the company that wrote the RFP and is a tool and technique of the Select Sellers process.

   D. The qualified seller list provides information about the sellers and is an output to the Request Seller Responses.

4. Which of the following tools and techniques of the Select Sellers process is used to check proposed pricing?

   A. Screening systems

   B. Seller rating systems

   C. Independent estimates

   D. Proposal evaluation technique

5. During the opening rounds of contract negotiation, the other party uses a fait accompli tactic. Which of the following statements is true about fait accompli tactics?

    A. One party agrees to accept the offer of the other party but secretly knows they will bring the issue back up at a later time.

    B. One party claims the issue under discussion was documented and accepted as part of Scope Verification.

    C. One party claims the issue under discussion has already been decided and can't be changed.

    D. One party claims to accept the offer of the other party, provided a contract change request is submitted describing the offer in detail.

6. The tools and techniques of the Request Seller Responses process include all of the following except which one?

    A. Bidder conferences

    B. Information technology

    C. Advertising

    D. Develop qualified sellers list

7. All of the following are tools and techniques of the Contract Administration process except for which one?

    A. Contract change control system, buyer-conducted performance review, and inspections and audits

    B. Performance reporting, payment system, and claims administration

    C. Records management system and information technology

    D. Contract performance information gathering and contract reporting systems

8. You are a project manager for an engineering company. Your company won the bid to add ramp-metering lights to several on-ramps along a stretch of highway at the south end of the city. You subcontracted a portion of the project to another company. The subcontractor's work involves digging the holes and setting the lamp poles in concrete. The subcontractor's performance is not meeting the contract requirements. Which of the following is not a valid option?

    A. You document the poor performance in written form and send the correspondence to the subcontractor.

    B. You terminate the contract for poor performance and submit a change request through Contract Administration.

    C. You submit a change request through Contract Administration demanding that the subcontractor comply with the terms of the contract.

    D. You agree to meet with the subcontractor to see whether a satisfactory solution can be reached.

9. You are a project manager for an engineering company. Your company won the bid to add ramp-metering lights to several on-ramps along a stretch of highway at the south end of the city. You subcontracted a portion of the project to another company. The subcontractor's work involves digging the holes and setting the lamp poles in concrete. You discover, through an independent review, that the process the subcontractor uses to report its progress is inefficient. Which of the following is true?

   A. You are in the Perform Quality Assurance process and have performed a quality audit.

   B. You are in the Perform Quality Assurance process and have performed a process analysis.

   C. You are in the Contract Administration process and have completed a contract audit to ensure that the subcontractor's performance meets the contract requirements.

   D. You are in the Performance Reporting process and have completed a performance review of the contractor's work.

10. The purpose of a quality audit includes all of the following except which one?

   A. To determine which project processes are inefficient or ineffective

   B. To examine the work of the project and formally accept the work results

   C. To improve processes and reduce the cost of quality

   D. To improve processes and increase the percentage of product or service acceptance

11. You are a contract project manager for a wholesale flower distribution company. Your project involves developing a website for the company that allows retailers to place their flower orders online. You will also provide a separate link for individual purchases that are ordered, packaged, and mailed to the consumer directly from the grower's site. This project involves coordinating the parent company, growers, and distributors. You've discovered a problem with one of the technical processes needed to perform this project. You decide to perform root cause analysis to determine the cause of this problem and recommended preventive actions. Which of the following is true?

   A. You are using the process analysis technique.

   B. You are using the quality audit technique.

   C. You are using the root cause identification technique.

   D. You are using a Quality Control tool and technique.

12. The tools and techniques of the Perform Quality Assurance process include all of the following except which one?

   A. Quality audits

   B. Process analysis

   C. Continuous process improvements

   D. Quality Control tools and techniques

13. When working in a matrix environment, all of the following are true regarding the Manage Project Team process except for which one?

    A. Communication methods and issue logs are used to create performance appraisals, provide feedback, and track issues.

    B. Managing project teams in a matrix environment is often a critical success factor for the project.

    C. It's the project manager's responsibility to make certain this dual reporting relationship is managed effectively.

    D. Loyalty issues might arise when managing projects in a matrix environment.

14. You are preparing project performance appraisals and have decided you'd like each team member to get feedback regarding their performance from several sources, including peers, superiors, and subordinates. Which of the following is true?

    A. This is called *360-degree feedback* and is part of the input to the organizational project performance appraisals, which is part of the organizational process assets updates input of the Manage Project Team process.

    B. This is called *360-degree feedback* and is considered part of the team performance assessment input of the Manage Project Team process.

    C. This is called *360-degree feedback* and is considered part of the work performance information input of the Manage Project Team process.

    D. This is called *360-degree feedback* and is part of the project performance appraisals tool and technique of the Manage Project Team process.

15. You are performing actions such as reporting and comparing actual project results against the project management plan, analyzing performance data and determining whether corrective or preventive action should be recommended, documenting all appropriate product information throughout the life of the project, gathering and recording project information, and monitoring approved change requests. Which process are you performing?

    A. Performance Reporting

    B. Manage Stakeholders

    C. Monitor and Control Project Work

    D. Perform Quality Assurance

16. You are collecting information regarding project progress and project accomplishments and reporting it to the stakeholders. You will manage these communication needs and resolve issues using the communication management plan as your guideline. Which of the following is true?

    A. You are using the Performance Reporting process, which involves reporting project progress and accomplishments to the stakeholders. You are using the performance information gathering and compilation tool, which is used in conjunction with the communications management plan, to coordinate and report information.

B. You are using both the Performance Reporting and Manage Stakeholders processes, which are both part of the Project Communications Management Knowledge Area.

C. You are using the communications method (an input) and issue logs (a tool and technique) of the Manage Stakeholder process.

D. You are creating performance reports and recommended corrective actions, which are both outputs of the Performance Reporting process.

17. You are working on a project and discover that one of the business users responsible for testing the product never completed this activity. She has written an email requesting that one of your team members drop everything to assist her with a problem that could have been avoided if she would have performed the test. This employee reports to a stakeholder, not to the project team. All project team members and stakeholders are co-located. Since your team needs her to also participate in an upcoming test, you decide to do which of the following?

A. You decide to record the issue in the issue log and bring it up at the next status meeting. Everyone can benefit from understanding the importance of stakeholders fulfilling their roles and responsibilities on the project.

B. You decide to record the issue in the issue log and then phone the stakeholder to explain what happened. You know speaking with the stakeholder directly is the most effective means for resolving issues.

C. You decide to have a face-to-face meeting with the stakeholder because this is the most effective means for resolving issues with them.

D. You decide to email the stakeholder and explain what happened in a professional manner because this is the most effective means for resolving issues with them.

18. You are working on a project and discover that one of the business users responsible for testing the product never completed this activity. She has written an email requesting that one of your team members drop everything to assist her with a problem that could have been avoided if she would have performed the test. This employee reports to a stakeholder, not to the project team. You estimate that the project might not be completed on time as a result of this missed activity. All of the following are true except for which one?

A. You should recommend a corrective action to bring the expected future project performance back into line with the project management plan because of this employee's failure to perform this activity.

B. You should recommend a preventive action to reduce the possibility of future project performance veering off track because of this employee's failure to perform this activity.

C. You've created a forecast, an output of the Monitor and Control Project Work process, using past performance to predict what the project's future condition might look like.

D. You might have to request a change to the project schedule as a result of this missed activity.

19. All of the following are tools and techniques of the Performance Reporting process except which one?

   A. Performance measurements

   B. Cost reporting systems

   C. Information presentation tools

   D. Time reporting systems

20. Your project is progressing as planned. The project team has come up with a demo that the sales team will use when making presentations to prospective clients. You will do which of the following at your next stakeholder project status meeting?

   A. Preview the demo for stakeholders, and obtain their approval and sign-off.

   B. Report on the progress of the demo, and note that it's a completed task.

   C. Review the technical documentation of the demo, and obtain approval and sign-off.

   D. Report that the demo has been noted as a completed task in the information retrieval system.

Answers to Review Questions

1. A. Select Sellers involves the receipt of bids and proposals. Weighted systems are one of the tools and techniques of this process used to evaluate vendors based on selection criteria defined by the organization.

2. D. Bidder conferences are a tool and technique of the Request Seller Responses. Solicitation is where proposals are submitted by vendors and obtained by the organization.

3. D. Qualified seller lists are an output of the Request Seller Responses. Their purpose is to provide information about the sellers.

4. C. Independent estimates, also called *should cost estimates*, are a way to check proposed pricing.

5. C. Fait accompli is a tactic used during contract negotiations where one party convinces the other that the particular issue is no longer relevant or cannot be changed. Option B is not correct because Scope Verification does not generally occur during contract negotiations since the work of the project has not yet been performed.

6. B. Information technology is a tool and technique of the Contract Administration process.

7. D. The tools and techniques of the Contract Administration process are contract change control system, buyer-conducted performance review, inspections and audits, performance reporting, payment system, claims administration, records management system, and information technology.

8. C. The contract change control system describes the processes you'll use to make changes to the contract, not as a means of communication. The changes might include contract term changes, date changes, and termination of a contract.

9. A. You have performed a quality audit, which is a structured, independent review of the organizational processes or project processes, policies, or procedures. Process analysis examines the root causes and follows steps in the process improvement plan.

10. B. The acceptance of work results happens later during the Scope Verification process, not during Perform Quality Assurance.

11. A. The process analysis technique in the Perform Quality Assurance process includes root cause analysis to analyze a problem and solution and to create preventive actions.

12. C. Continuous process improvements are a result of the Perform Quality Assurance process but not a tool and technique.

13. A. Communication methods are not a tool and technique of the Manage Project Team process.

14. D. This technique is called *360-degree feedback*. It's part of the performance appraisals tool and technique of the Manage Project Team process.

15. C. The Monitor and Control Project Work process involves reporting and comparing project results, gathering and recording data, recommending actions, and monitoring approved change requests.

16. B. This question describes the Performance Reporting process (concerned with collecting and reporting information regarding project progress and project accomplishments to the stakeholders) and the Manage Stakeholders process (of which communications methods and issue logs are tools and techniques).

17. C. Face-to-face meetings are the most effective means for resolving stakeholder issues provided these meetings are practical.

18. B. You are in the Monitor and Control Project Work process. Preventive actions reduce the possibility of negative impacts from risk events and do not apply to this situation.

19. A. The tools and techniques of the Performance Reporting process are information presentation tools, performance information gathering and compilation, status review meetings, time reporting systems, and cost reporting systems.

20. B. Status meetings are to report on the progress of the project. They are not for demos or show-and-tell. Option C is not correct because stakeholders are not concerned about the content of the technical documentation; they need to know that a qualified technician has reviewed the technical documentation and that the documentation task is accurate and complete.

Chapter

10

Monitoring and Controlling Change

**THE PMP EXAM CONTENT FROM THE MON-
ITORING AND CONTROLLING THE PROJECT
PERFORMANCE DOMAIN COVERED IN THIS
CHAPTER INCLUDES THE FOLLOWING:**

- ✓ **Measure Project Performance**
- ✓ **Verify and Manage Changes to the Project**
- ✓ **Monitor All Risks**

You started examining the Monitoring and Controlling processes in the previous chapter. This chapter finishes the Monitoring and Controlling process group. I'll cover the Integrated Change Control, Cost Control, Schedule Control, and Risk Monitoring and Control processes.

Performance reports, which are an output of the Performance Reporting process, serve as an input to some of the Monitoring and Controlling processes I'll talk about in this chapter. Performance reports are used during the Monitoring and Controlling processes, along with tools and techniques, to measure project performance. These measurements and control tools allow the project manager to take corrective action during the Monitoring and Controlling processes to remedy wayward project results and realign future project results with the project management plan.

Integrated Change Control lays the foundation for all the change control processes. I'll take the time during this discussion to explain how change control works. The Cost Control and Schedule Control processes are similar to Integrated Change Control. Remember when you're reading these sections that the information from the Integrated Change Control process applies to these areas as well. Risk Monitoring and Control monitors the project for risks and monitors the risk response plans that have been put into action or might need to be put into action.

You've learned a lot about project management by this point and have just a few more topics to add to your study list. Keep up the good work. You're getting closer to exam day.

Managing Integrated Change Control

The *Integrated Change Control* process serves as an overseer, so to speak, of the Monitoring and Controlling processes. This is where you establish the project's change control process. Changes, updates, and corrective actions are common outputs across all the Monitoring and Controlling processes. (And don't forget that requested changes are also an output of the Direct and Manage Project Plan Execution process, which is an Executing process.) Both processes can generate the change requests that are managed through the Integrated Change Control process.

You've seen all the inputs, tools and techniques, and outputs of this process before. There isn't any new information to add to these. However, you're likely to see exam questions on several topics that involve change and the Integrated Change Control process. Configuration management, for example, isn't listed as a tool and technique of this process, but you really can't perform Integrated Change Control without it. I'll discuss this shortly. First, though, you'll look at change, what it is, and how it comes about.

Changes come about on projects for many reasons. It's the project manager's responsibility to manage these changes and see to it that organizational policies regarding changes are implemented. Changes don't necessarily mean negative consequences. Changes can produce positive results as well. It's important that you manage this process carefully, because too many changes—even one significant change—will impact cost, schedule, scope, and/or quality. Once a change request has been submitted, you have some decisions to make. Ask yourself questions such as these:

- Should the change be implemented?

- If so, what's the cost to the project in terms of project constraints: cost, time, scope, and quality?

- Will the benefits gained by making the change increase or decrease the chances of project completion?

Just because a change is requested doesn't mean you have to implement it. You'll always want to discover the reasons for the change to determine whether they're justifiable, and you'll want to know the cost of the change. Remember that cost can take the form of increased time. Let's say the change you're considering increases the schedule completion date. That means you'll need human resources longer than expected. If you've leased equipment or project resources for the team members to use during the course of the project, a later completion date means your team needs the leased equipment for a longer period of time. All this translates to increased costs. Time equals money, as the saying goes, so manage time changes wisely, and dig deep to find the impacts that time changes might make on the budget.

How Change Occurs

As the project progresses, the stakeholders or customers might request a change directly. Team members might also recommend changes as the project progresses. For example, once the project is underway, they might discover more efficient ways of performing tasks or producing the product of the project and recommend changes to accommodate the new efficiencies. Changes might also come about as a result of mistakes that were made earlier in the project in the Planning or Executing processes. (However, I hope you've applied all the great practices and techniques I've talked about to date and you didn't experience many of these.)

Changes to the project might occur indirectly as a result of contingency plans, other changes, or team members performing favors for the stakeholders by making that one little change without telling anyone about it. Many times, the project manager is the last to know about changes such as this one. There's a fine line here because you don't want to discourage good working relationships between team members and stakeholders, yet at the same time, you want to ensure that all changes come through the change control process. If a dozen little changes slip through like this, your project scope suddenly exits stage left.

Change Control Concerns

Integrated Change Control, according to the *PMBOK Guide*, is primarily concerned with the following:

- Influencing the factors that cause change and reaching agreement on their resulting change requests

- Determining that change is needed or has happened

- Managing approved changes

- Updating and maintaining the integrity of the requirements that impact scope, quality, schedule, and budgets based on approved changes

- Documenting requested changes and their impacts

Factors that might cause change include project constraints, stakeholder requests, team member recommendations, vendor issues, and many others. You'll want to understand the factors that are influencing or bringing about change and how a proposed change might impact the project if implemented. Performance measures and corrective actions might dictate that a project change is needed as well.

Modifications to the project are submitted in the form of change requests and managed through the change control process. Obviously, you'll want to implement those changes that are most beneficial to the project. I'll talk more about change requests later in this chapter.

Managing changes might involve making changes to the project scope, schedule, or cost baseline, also known as the *performance measurement baseline*. This baseline might also involve quality or technical elements. The performance measurement baseline is the approved project management plan that describes the work of the project. This is used through Executing and Monitoring and Controlling to measure project performance and determine deviations from the plan. It's your responsibility to maintain the reliability of the performance measurement baselines. Changes that impact an existing or completed project management process will require updates to those processes, which might mean additional passes through the appropriate Planning and Executing processes.

The management plans created during the Planning process group should reflect the changes as well, which might require updates to the project management plan or the project scope statement. This requires a close eye on coordination among all the processes that are impacted. For example, changes might require updates to risk response alternatives, schedule, cost, resource requirements, or other elements. Changes that impact product scope always require an update to the project scope.

I caution you to not change baselines at the drop of a hat. Examine the changes, their justification, and their impacts thoroughly before making changes to the baselines. Make certain your project sponsor approves baseline changes and that the project sponsor understands why the change occurred and how it will impact the project. And be sure to keep a copy of the original baseline for comparison purposes and for lessons learned.

Configuration Management

Configuration management is generally a subset of the project management information system. It describes the process for submitting change requests and includes processes for tracking the changes and their disposition, processes for defining the approval levels for approving and denying changes, and a process for authorizing the changes. I'll talk about each of these topics later.

The following items are what the *PMBOK Guide* notes as activities associated with configuration change management in the Integrated Change Control process:

Configuration identification   Configuration identification describes the characteristics of the product, service, or result of the project and makes sure the description is accurate and complete. This description is the basis that's used to verify when changes are made and how they're managed.

Configuration status accounting   This activity doesn't really have to do with financials as you might guess from its title. It's about accounting for the status of the changes by documenting and storing the configuration information needed to effectively manage the product information.

Configuration verification and auditing   Verification and audits are performed as part of configuration management to determine whether the performance and functional requirements have been met.

Change Control System

If you were to allow changes to occur to the project whenever requested, you would probably never complete the project. Stakeholders, the customer, and end users would continually change the project requirements if given the opportunity to do so. That's why careful planning and scope definition are important in the beginning of the project. It's your job as project manager to drive out all the compelling needs and requirements of the project during the Planning process so that important requirements aren't suddenly "remembered" halfway through the project. However, we're all human, and sometimes things are not known, weren't thought about, or simply weren't discovered until a certain point during the project. Stakeholders will probably start thinking in a direction they wasn't considering during the Planning process, and new requirements will come to light. This is where the *change control system* comes into play.

The Purpose of the Change Control System

Change control systems are documented procedures that describe how to submit change requests, how to manage change requests, and, according to the *PMBOK Guide*, how the management of the changes impacts the project performance. They are usually subsystems of the configuration management system. They can include preprinted change request forms that provide a place to record general project information such as the name and project number, the date, and the details regarding the change request.

The change control system also tracks the status of change requests, including their approval status. Not all change requests will receive approval. Those changes that are not approved are also tracked and filed in the change control log for future reference.

The change control system might define the level of authority needed to approve changes, if it wasn't previously defined in the configuration management system. Some change requests could receive approval based on the project manager's decision; others might need a review and formal approval by the project sponsor, executive management, and so on.

Procedures should be defined that detail how emergency changes are approved as well. For example, you and your team might be putting in some weekend hours and are close to the completion of a deliverable when you discover that thing 1 will not talk to thing 2 no matter what you do. The team brainstorms and comes up with a brilliant solution that requires a change request. Do you stop work right then and wait until the change control board or committee can meet sometime next week and make a decision, or do you—the project manager—make the decision to go forward with this solution and explain the change to the appropriate parties later? That answer depends on the change procedures you have in place to handle situations like this and depends on the authority you have to make emergency changes as outlined in the change control system.

Many organizations have formal change control or change request systems in place. If that's the case, you can easily adopt those procedures and use the existing system to manage project change. But if no procedures exist, you'll have to define them.

Exam Spotlight

The change control system and configuration management system together identify, document, and control the changes to the performance baseline.

🌐 **Real World Scenario**

But I Thought You Said

Marcus is working on a web redesign project for a division of the marketing department in his organization. The project started out as a simple redesign of the look and feel of the site. Marcus made the mistake of not defining change control procedures for the project from the beginning because he reasoned that the project was small, the design changes were well understood by all, and the project could be finished in a matter of weeks.

After the work of the project started, Marcus's team showed the initial design results to the business lead, Kendra. Kendra asked for a few modifications that seemed minor, and Marcus was happy to accommodate. When his team finished the work and turned the site over for initial testing, Kendra created a list of changes that extended beyond the initial scope of the project. Marcus thought everyone had agreed that the project involved only an update to the look and feel of the site, but Kendra was now requesting changes to the applications people used to order products from the website. Marcus knew that application changes need their own set of requirements and testing. Changing the look of the site is a lot different from changing the way an application works and the results it produces. Kendra and Marcus were in disagreement over what the changes entailed. Kendra thought she had carte blanche to make changes until she was satisfied with the project. Marcus knew that the projects waiting in the queue were going to suffer because of the never-ending stream of changes to Kendra's project. The additional time her project was taking already had pushed the deliverable of the next project on their list by two weeks.

To resolve the dilemma, Marcus had to negotiate with Kendra on the list of changes she had requested. He agreed to all changes that required less than four hours to complete, and the remaining changes were moved to a new project request. Marcus also vowed to implement change control procedures for all projects from this point forward, no matter what the size or complexity of the project.

Requirements for Change

You should require two things at the beginning of all projects regarding change. First, require that all change requests be submitted in writing. This is to clarify the change and make sure there's no confusion about what's requested. It also allows the project team to accurately estimate the time it will take to incorporate the change.

It's good practice to require all change requests in writing. This should be a documented procedure outlined in your change control system. Beware! Stakeholders are notorious for asking for changes verbally even when there is a detailed process in place. If they don't want to follow the process, someone on the project team should have the responsibility for documenting and logging the change requests for future reference.

Second, all change requests must come through the formal change control system. Make sure no one is allowed to go directly to team members and request changes without the project manager knowing about them. Also make certain your stakeholders understand that this can cause schedule delays, cost overruns, and sacrifices to quality and that it isn't good change management practice. Encourage them from the beginning of the project to use the formal procedures laid out in the change control system to request changes.

Configuration Control Board

In some organizations, a *configuration control board (CCB)* is established to review all change requests. The board is given the authority to approve or deny change requests as defined by the organization. It's important that its authority is clearly defined and that separate procedures exist for emergency changes. The CCB might meet only once a week, once every other week, or even once a month, depending on the project. When emergencies arise, the preestablished procedures allow the project manager to implement the change on the spot. This always requires follow-up with the CCB and completion of a formal change request, even though it's after the fact.

CCB members might include stakeholders, managers, project team members, and others who might not have any connection to the project at hand. Some organizations have permanent CCBs that are staffed by full-time employees dedicated to managing change for the entire organization, not just project change. You might want to consider establishing a CCB for your project if the organization does not have one.

Some organizations use other types of review boards that have the same responsibilities as the CCB. Some other names you might see are technical assessment board (TAB), technical review board (TRB), engineering review board (ERB), and change control board (CCB).

Integrated Change Control Inputs

The inputs to the Integrated Change Control process are similar to its outputs. The inputs are "requested" or "recommended," while the outputs are "approved." For example, requested changes are inputs, and approved or rejected change requests are outputs; recommended corrective actions are inputs and approved corrective actions are outputs. The inputs for the Integrated Change Control process are as follows:

- Project management plan
- Requested changes
- Work performance information
- Recommended corrective actions
- Recommended defect repair
- Deliverables

Remember that the project management plan includes all the documents together that make up that plan—the project schedule, budget, scope statement, and so on.

Integrated Change Control Tools and Techniques

You've seen all the tools and techniques for Integrated Change Control in previous processes:

- Project management methodology
- Project management information system
- Expert judgment

The project management methodology tool and technique really comes in handy with this process because part of this methodology defines how you'll perform change control. The project management information system is used to document and track change information, and expert judgment helps determine the disposition of change requests.

Integrated Change Control Outputs

The outputs of the Integrated Change Control process are as follows:

- Approved change requests
- Rejected change requests
- Project management plan updates
- Project scope statement updates
- Approved corrective actions
- Approved preventive actions
- Approved defect repair
- Validated defect repair
- Deliverables

Project management plan updates are typically required as a result of an approved change or corrective action. These changes are noted in the change control system or the configuration management system, and stakeholders are informed at the status meetings of the changes that have occurred, their impacts, and where the description of the changes can be found.

Exam Spotlight

"Recommended" corrective action is an output of several of the change control processes, including Scope Change Control, Schedule Control, Cost Control, Risk Monitoring and Control, and Perform Quality Control. "Approved" corrective action is an output of the Integrated Change Control process. Remember that Integrated Change Control is where all change requests are processed and either approved or denied. Also note that corrective action is an output of the Monitoring and Controlling processes and an input to the Executing processes.

You should document all the actions taken in the Integrated Change Control process (whether implemented or not). You should also record the reason for the variance. In other words, how did this particular change request come about? How did it change the original project management plan? Is this something you could or should have known about in the Planning processes? You should note the corrective action taken and the justification for choosing that particular corrective action as part of lessons learned also. You can use the information you capture here in your configuration management system as lessons learned for future projects. When you take on a new project, it's a good idea to review the lessons learned from similar projects so that you can plan appropriately and avoid, where possible, the variances that occurred in those projects.

Managing Cost Changes

The *Cost Control* process manages changes to project costs as outlined in the cost management plan. It's concerned with monitoring project costs to prevent unauthorized or incorrect costs from being included in the cost baseline. This means you're also using Cost Control to assure that the project budget isn't exceeded (resulting in cost overruns). You'll need to ensure that, if a change is implemented, the budget for the changed item stays within acceptable limits. All budget changes should be agreed to and approved by the project sponsor where applicable (the criteria for approvals should be outlined in the change control system documentation). Stakeholders should also be made aware of budget changes.

Cost Control Inputs

The Cost Control process includes the following inputs:

- Cost baseline
- Project funding requirements
- Performance reports
- Work performance information
- Approved change requests
- Project management plan

These inputs are examined using the tools and techniques of this process to determine whether revised cost estimates or budget updates are required. I've covered each of these inputs in previous chapters.

Cost Control Tools and Techniques

The tools and techniques of the Cost Control process are as follows:

- Cost change control system

- Performance measurement analysis
- Forecasting
- Project performance reviews
- Project management software
- Variance management

Cost Change Control System

The cost change control system describes how changes are submitted, approved, and tracked and is closely linked with the integrated change control system. Cost variances (both positive and negative) are calculated using a performance measurement analysis tool (specifically earned value techniques). You'll look at this next.

Performance Measurement Analysis

You can accomplish performance measurement analysis using a technique called *earned value technique (EVT)*. Simply stated, EVT compares what you've received or produced to what you've spent.

 Real World Scenario

Mustang Enterprises' New Accounting System

You are a stakeholder of the New Accounting System project for Mustang Enterprises. The existing accounting system resides on a mainframe, and some of the programs used to process data are more than 15 years old. Your company decided to hire a contract software services firm to write a thin-client, browser-based version of the accounting system so that the mainframe programs could be retired. You've also assigned a senior programmer to act as the project manager on behalf of your organization.

The project is in the Monitoring and Controlling process group, and the project manager keeps reporting that everything is OK and on schedule. When you asked him detailed questions and requested performance data, the project manager patted you on the back and said, "Don't worry, I've got everything under control."

You are a little worried because some of the key project team members have come to you confidentially to inform you of the progress of the project.

After further investigation, you discover that the project manager changed the database from SQL to Oracle midway through the project and didn't tell anyone except the project team. The project scope stated specifically that project development required a SQL database. The change in database products changed the project scope and product scope without letting the stakeholders know.

This change has caused schedule delays because the project team members have told you they need training in the new database development tools before they can proceed. Additionally, many of the programs have already been written to interface with SQL, not Oracle, and will have to be modified. To add insult to injury, the database switch will impact the project budget in two ways. First, purchasing the Oracle database involves substantially more money than the SQL database, and it requires the purchase of new development tools for the programming team. Second, several members of the programming staff will have to attend multiple training sessions on the new database product to fully integrate the programs and system. Training is currently running $2,200 per session per person.

Since you're a key stakeholder, you decide to bring this information out into the open at the next project status meeting. Additionally, you plan to meet with the project sponsor and the procurement department to determine what alternatives you have to request that the contracting firm realign the project to meet the original contractual requirements. However, you fear that since the project manager is the one who gave the orders to change the database, your organization might not have a lot of recourse. You will also make the project sponsor aware that the project manager doesn't have the skills needed to conduct this project and a new project manager should be hired as soon as possible. The project manager is invaluable to the organization as a programmer, but he doesn't have the project management experience needed to conduct a project of this size and complexity. This might cause further setback to the project, but the project management plan and project schedule will require updates anyway as a result of the existing project manager's decisions. You also determine to document all that has happened as a lesson learned and to set up a change control process to prevent this from happening in the future.

The EVT continuously monitors the planned value, earned value, and actual costs expended to produce the work of the project (I'll cover the definition of these terms shortly). When variances that result in cost changes are discovered (including schedule variances and cost variances), those changes are managed using the cost change control system. The primary function of this analysis technique is to determine and document the cause of the variance, to determine the impact of the variance (you'll do this with the EVT formulas shortly), and to determine whether a corrective action should be implemented as a result.

EVT looks at schedule, cost, and scope project measurements together and compares them to the actual work completed to date. It is the most often used performance measurement method. To perform the EVT calculations, you need to first gather the three measurements mentioned earlier: the planned value (PV), actual cost (AC), and earned value (EV).

If you do any research on your own regarding these values, you might come across acronyms that are different from what you see here. I've included their alternate names and acronyms at the end of each description. I recommend you memorize planned value (PV), actual cost (AC), and earned value (EV) and make certain you understand the meaning of each before progressing.

Refer to the following definitions before diving into the actual calculations:

Planned value   The *planned value (PV)* is the cost of work that has been budgeted for a schedule activity or WBS component to be completed during a given time period. These budgets are established during the Planning processes. PV is also called *budgeted cost of work scheduled* (BCWS).

Exam Spotlight

Remember to read exam questions carefully. PV might mean present value (like I talked about in Chapter 2) or planned value, as defined here.

Actual cost   *Actual cost (AC)* is the cost of completing the work (a schedule activity or WBS component) in a given time period. Actual costs might include direct and indirect costs but must correspond to what was budgeted for the activity. If the budgeted amount did not include indirect costs, do not include them here. Later you'll see how to compare this to PV to come up with variance calculation results. AC is also called *actual cost of work performed* (ACWP).

Earned value   *Earned value (EV)* is the value of the work (schedule activity or WBS component) completed to date as it compares to the budgeted amount assigned to the work component. EV is also called *budgeted cost of work performed* (BCWP).

Exam Spotlight

PV, AC, and EV are really easy to mix up. In their simplest forms, here's what each means:

PV: The approved budget assigned to work to be completed during a given time period

AC: Money that's actually been expended to date (or during a given time period) for completed work

EV: The value of the work completed to date compared to the budget

---

According to the earlier definition, EV is the sum of the cumulative budgeted costs for completed work for all activities that have been accomplished as of the measurement date. For example, if your total budget is $1,000 and 50 percent of the work has been completed as of the measurement date, your EV would equal $500. You can plot all the PV, AC, and EV measurements graphically to show the variances between them. If there are no variances in the measurements, all the lines on the graph remain the same, which means the project is progressing as planned. Figure 10.1 shows an example that plots these three measurements.

FIGURE 10.1   Earned value

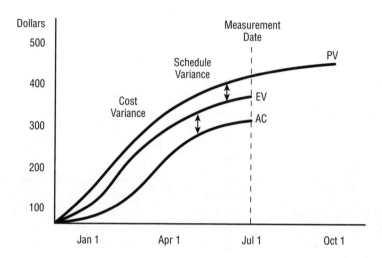

All of these measurements include a cost component. Costs are displayed in an S curve because spending is minimal in the beginning of the project, picks up steam toward the middle, and then tapers off at the end of the project. This means your earned value measurements will also take on the S curve shape.

Now you can calculate whether the project is progressing as planned using a variety of formulas discussed in the following sections. Use Figure 10.1 as your example for the formulas that follow. The Figure 10.1 totals are as follows: PV = 400, EV = 375, AC = 325.

Cost Variance

Cost variance is one of the most popular variances that project managers use, and it tells you whether your costs are higher than budgeted (with a resulting negative number) or lower than budgeted (with a resulting positive number).

The *cost variance (CV)* is calculated as follows:

CV = EV – AC

Let's calculate the CV using the numbers from Figure 10.1:

50 = 375 – 325

The CV is positive, which means you're spending less than what you planned as of July 1 (which Figure 10.1 shows because AC is less than EV).

If you come up with a negative number as the answer to this formula, it means that costs are higher than what you had planned as of July 1.

Schedule Variance

Schedule variance, also a popular variance, tells you whether the schedule is ahead or behind what was planned for this period in time. The *schedule variance (SV)* is calculated as follows:

SV = EV – PV

Let's plug in the numbers:

$$-25 = 375 - 400$$

The resulting schedule variance is negative, which means you are behind schedule, or behind where you planned to be as of July 1.

Together, the CV and SV are known as *efficiency indicators* for the project.

Performance Indexes

Cost and schedule performance indexes are primarily used to calculate performance efficiencies. They're often used in trend analysis to predict future performance. You'll need to know the calculations and what the results mean. If your result in either formula is greater than 1, you've got better than expected performance. If the result is less than 1, you've got poor performance. If it equals 1, you're right on target.

The *cost performance index (CPI)* is calculated this way:

$$CPI = EV \div AC$$

Let's plug in the numbers and see where you stand:

$$1.15 = 375 \div 325$$

This means cost performance is better than expected. You get an A+ on this assignment!

Cumulative CPI (CPI^C) is a commonly used calculation to predict project costs at the completion of the project. It also represents the cumulative CPI of the project at the point the measurement is taken. First you need to sum the earned value calculations taken to date (EV^C) and the actual costs to date (AC^C). The formula looks just like the CPI formula only it uses the sums as follows:

$$CPI^C = EV^C \div AC^C$$

The difference between this and the CPI formula earlier is that the CPI formula is used for a single work component whereas the CPI^C is calculated using the sum of all the costs of all the work components. Additionally, you might also use CPI to calculate the total cost of a work component such as a deliverable, for example. Let's say you have a deliverable with 75 schedule activities that need to be completed. You would total the EV and AC at the measurement date for all 75 schedule activities to determine the cost performance index for the deliverable.

The *schedule performance index (SPI)* is calculated this way:

$$SPI = EV \div PV$$

Again, let's see where you stand with this example:

$$.94 = 375 \div 400$$

Uh-oh, not so good. Schedule performance is not what you expected. Let's not grade this one.

Forecasting

Forecasting uses the information you've gathered to date and estimates the future conditions or performance of the project based on what you know when the calculation is performed. Forecasts are based on work performance information (an output from the Executing process group). There are two types of forecasting techniques: estimate to complete and estimate at completion. Each has three variations. Both of these formulas use a new parameter you haven't seen yet called *budget at completion (BAC)*. BAC is the sum of all the budget values established for all the work of the project.

You'll now look at each of the techniques.

Estimate to Complete

Estimate to complete (ETC) tells you how much it will cost to complete all the work remaining for a schedule activity or WBS component or the project. One variation of ETC that doesn't require a formula. It's called ETC based on a new estimate. This is simply a revised estimate based on the performance of the resources to date. By examining how quickly or how productively the resources have been utilized so far, the project team can determine a noncalculated ETC by looking at the remaining work and determining a new estimate based on the comparison to past work. This ETC, according to the *PMBOK Guide*, is the most accurate and comprehensive ETC calculation.

The two remaining ETC calculations use earned value data. These are quick to perform but not as accurate as the project team manually examining the remaining work and making a new estimate based on past performance.

When you believe that future cost variances will be similar to the types of variances you've seen to date, you'll use this formula to calculate ETC:

$$ETC = (BAC - EV^C) \div CPI^C$$

Assuming your EV^C value is 725, CPI^C value is 1.12, and BAC is 1000, plug in the numbers:

$$245.5 = (1000 - 725) \div 1.12$$

Therefore, at the measurement date (July 1), you need $245.50 to complete all the remaining work of this work component (or project if you're using project totals), assuming variances in the future will be the same as they have been to date.

When you believe that future cost variances will *not* be similar to the types of variances you've seen to date, you'll use this formula to calculate ETC:

$$ETC = (BAC - EV^C)$$

Now calculate your value:

$$275 = (1000 - 725)$$

In this case, you need $275 to complete all the remaining work of this work component assuming variances in the future are different than they have been to date.

Estimate at Completion

There are only a few calculations remaining that will help you finish up your analysis of project progress. *Estimate at completion (EAC)* estimates (or forecasts) the expected total cost of a work component, a schedule activity, or the project at its completion. This is the probable final value for the work component (or project).

You can calculate EAC in three ways. The first one is EAC using a new estimate. This assumes that the original assumptions used when estimating were flawed or that changes have occurred that have changed the original estimates. ETC in this calculation is provided by the performing organization (the ETC based on a new estimate figure). The formula looks like this:

$$EAC = AC^C + ETC$$

Assuming your AC^C is 650 and ETC is 275, you get this:

$$925 = 650 + 275$$

This means the expected total value of the project $925.

The last two methods for calculating EAC are the most common. The first EAC uses CPI^C, and the second calculates EAC using remaining budget. Let's look at EAC using CPI^C first.

EAC using CPI^C is the second way to perform an ETC calculation. This formula is the AC^C plus ETC (when variances are typical). It looks like this:

$$EAC = AC^C + ((BAC - EV) \div CPI^C)$$

So, your numbers look like this:

$$1096.43 = 650 + ((1000 - 500) \div 1.12)$$

When using the CPI^C efficiency indicator and ETC with typical variances, your expected final value for this work component (or project) is $1,096.43.

EAC using remaining budget is the AC^C plus the budget needed to finish the remaining work. This calculation is used when you expect variances to be atypical. The formula looks like this:

$$EAC = AC^C + BAC - EV$$

Your example project estimates look like this using an EV value of 500:

$$1150 = 650 + 1000 - 500$$

Based on your remaining budget, the expected final value for this work component assuming variances are atypical is $1,150.

For study purposes, the three EAC calculations are shown together here:

$EAC = AC^C + ETC$ (Use this when you have a new estimate or when original assumptions were flawed.)

$EAC = AC^C + ((BAC - EV) \div CPI^C)$ (Use this when variances are typical.)

$EAC = AC^C + BAC - EV$ (Use this when variances are atypical.)

Project Performance Reviews

Project performance reviews are similar to status reviews. They examine milestones due and those that have been met. They also look at the costs associated with performance and schedule activities that are over and under budget. Typically, performance reviews take place as meetings, and their purpose is to examine schedule activities, work packages, or cost account status and their progress to date. Three types of analyses are associated with performance reviews: variance analysis, trend analysis, and earned value technique. I've already covered the earned value technique, so you'll now look at the other two.

Variance at Completion

Variance at completion (VAC) calculates the difference between the budget at completion and the estimate at completion. It looks like this:

VAC = BAC – EAC

Use the most optimistic EAC number:

–171.43 = 925 – 1096.43

The negative number means you're not doing as well with costs as you anticipated and that variance exists. As the project progresses, variances will become smaller.

Remember that variance analysis is a tool and technique of both Schedule Control and Scope Control and this formula can be used in conjunction with the variance analysis tool and technique of these processes.

Trend Analysis

According to the *PMBOK Guide*, trend analysis determines whether project performance is improving or worsening over time by periodically analyzing project results. These results are measured with mathematical formulas that attempt to forecast project outcomes based on historical information and results. You can use several formulas to predict project trends, but it's outside the scope of this book to go into them. For the exam, you're expected to understand the concept behind trend analysis, not the formulas used to calculate it. You'll want to remember that you can use the results you've analyzed using trend analysis formulas to predict future project behavior or trends.

NOTE You'll be given some scratch paper when you go into the exam. I recommend that you write these formulas down on a piece of your scratch paper before you start the exam and keep it handy. That way, the formulas are off your mind and you've got them in front of you to reference when you get to the portion of the exam where these questions appear. You might want to use this tip for other items you've memorized as well. If you write them down before you begin, you don't have to jog your memory on every question. If you forget something, leave a blank space where it goes and as soon as you remember it or see a question that reminds you what it is, fill in the blank.

Project Management Software and Variance Management

I know you thought you were done, but you should know about the remaining tools and techniques of this process: project management software and variance management.

I've discussed project management software before. Obviously, you can perform and monitor many of these calculations using project management software.

Variance management includes the processes for managing cost variances and appropriate responses based on the impact and level of variance. The cost management plan should describe the variance management.

Cost Control Outputs

The Cost Control process has eight outputs:

- Cost estimate updates
- Cost baseline updates
- Performance measurements
- Forecasted completion
- Requested changes
- Recommended corrective actions
- Organizational process assets updates (lessons learned)
- Project management plan updates

I've discussed most of these before, or they are self-explanatory. However, I'll point out a few points you should be aware of for the exam.

Updated cost estimates include updating original cost estimates and other areas of the project management plan that these estimates might impact. As an example, perhaps the cost estimate for new hardware required for your project was recently revised. Suppose the cost estimate was needed because the equipment originally planned for in the project is no longer available and new equipment is ordered in its place. This might require revisions to other project activities, which will require you to revisit the project Planning and Executing processes.

Recap of Formulas

You have a lot of formulas to memorize. Keep in mind that you'll be given a calculator when you take the exam, so you don't have to do the math manually. Remember that EVT is used with both the performance analysis measurement tool and technique and the project performance reviews tool and technique. Variance and trend analysis are part of the project performance reviews tool and technique. Here are the formulas I've covered in this chapter:

Performance measurements

Cost variance: $CV = EV - AC$

Schedule variance: $SV = EV - PV$

Performance indexes

Cost performance index: $CPI = EV \div AC$

Cumulative cost performance index: $CPI^c = EV^c \div AC^c$

Schedule performance index: $SPI = EV \div PV$

Forecasting

Estimate to complete (cost to complete remaining work)

- Based on new estimate: manual calculation by project team

- ETC with typical variances: ETC = (BAC – EV^c) ÷ CPI^c

- ETC with atypical variances: ETC = (BAC – EV^c)

Estimate at completion (expected total cost at completion)

- Using new estimate when assumptions are flawed: EAC = AC^c + ETC

- EAC using CPI^c (typical variances): EAC = AC^c + ((BAC – EV) ÷ CPI^c)

- EAC using remaining budget (atypical variances): EAC = AC^c + BAC – EV

Variance analysis

Variance analysis: VAC = BAC – EAC

Remember that there are 12 formulas total (one is simply a manual calculation by the project team). You might want to devise an acronym or some other mnemonic to help you memorize them. For example, the earned value and performance index formulas are (based on the first letter of each formula): C-S-C-C-S. The forecasting formulas are ETC new; ETC typical, ETC atypical; EAC new, EAC atypical, EAC typical.

NOTE Cost Control problems come about for many reasons, including incorrect estimating techniques, predetermined or fixed budgets with no flexibility, schedule overruns, inadequate WBS development, and so on. Good project management planning techniques during the Planning processes might prevent cost problems later in the project. At a minimum, proper planning will reduce the impact of these problems if they do occur.

Always inform appropriate stakeholders of revised cost estimates and any changes of significant impact to the project. Keep them updated on changes, status, and risk conditions during regularly scheduled project meetings.

Monitoring and Controlling Schedule Changes

The *Schedule Control* process involves determining the status of the project schedule, determining whether changes have occurred or should occur, and influencing and managing schedule changes. In the following sections, you will look at this process's inputs, tools and techniques, and outputs.

Schedule Control Inputs

Schedule Control inputs include the following:

- Schedule management plan
- Schedule baseline
- Performance reports
- Approved change requests

I've covered each of these inputs previously. Keep in mind that the Schedule Control process works hand in hand with the Integrated Change Control process covered earlier (as all the change control processes do).

Schedule and Control Tools and Techniques

The tools and techniques of the Schedule Control process are as follows:

- Progress reporting
- Schedule change control system
- Performance measurement
- Variance analysis
- Project management software
- Schedule comparison bar charts

Progress Reporting

Progress reporting examines elements such as actual start and end dates for schedule activities and the remaining time to finish uncompleted activities. If you've taken earned value measurements, that information is included in the progress report. You should document all of this information.

Schedule Change Control System

As you've probably already guessed, the *schedule change control system* works just like the cost change control system, except that it defines how changes to the schedule are made and managed. It tracks and records change requests, describes the procedures to follow to implement schedule changes, and details the authorization levels needed to approve the schedule changes.

> Schedule changes might be potential hot buttons with certain stakeholders and can burn you if you don't handle them correctly. No one likes to hear that the project is going to take longer than originally planned. That doesn't mean you should withhold this information, however. Always report the truth. If you've been keeping your stakeholders abreast of project status, they should already know that the potential for schedule changes exists. Nevertheless, be prepared to justify the reason for the schedule change or start dusting off your résumé—maybe both, depending on the company.

Performance Measurement

Performance measurements for schedule control include the schedule variance and schedule performance index. Both of these should be used to determine whether corrective action is needed to get the schedule back on track.

Variance Analysis

Variance analysis is a key factor in monitoring and controlling project time because this technique helps determine variances in schedule start and end dates. Comparing the estimated dates to the actual or forecasted dates will show you where variances have occurred—or might occur—and will allow you to implement corrective actions to keep the schedule on track.

> Keeping the schedule on track means you're monitoring and controlling time—one of the triple constraints.

Make sure to examine the float variance of the critical path activities. Thinking back to the Schedule Development process, you'll recall that float is the amount of time you can delay starting an activity without increasing the amount of time it takes to complete the project. Because the activities with the least amount of float have the potential to cause the biggest schedule delay, examine float variance in ascending order of critical activities.

However, not all schedule variances will impact the schedule. For example, a delay to a noncritical path task will not delay the overall schedule and might not need corrective action. Use caution here, though—if a delay occurs on a noncritical path task or its duration is increased for some reason, that task can actually become part of the critical path. Delays to critical path tasks will *always* cause delays to the project completion date and require corrective action.

Careful watch of the variances in schedule start and end dates helps you control the total time element of the project.

Project Management Software

Project management software is used to track the actual schedule dates against planned schedule dates. One particular use for project management software in the Schedule Control process is to forecast the impacts of schedule changes (both potential changes and actual changes) to the schedule.

Schedule Comparison Bar Charts

The last tool and technique is the schedule comparison bar charts. This is a standard bar chart that depicts two bars for each schedule activity—one bar for the approved schedule baseline and one bar for the actual status.

Schedule Control Outputs

The Schedule Control process has the following outputs:

- Schedule model data updates
- Schedule baseline updates
- Performance measurements
- Requested changes
- Recommended corrective action
- Organizational process asset updates (lessons learned)
- Activity list updates
- Activity attributes updates
- Project management plan updates

Schedule data model updates involve adjusting activities and dates to coincide with approved changes and/or corrective actions and updating any schedule model data used to manage the project.

Often, project schedule network diagrams require updates as a result of schedule model data updates. Don't forget to document these changes and inform your stakeholders.

Changes to approved schedule start and end dates (in the schedule baseline) are called *revisions*. These generally occur as a result of a project scope change or changes to activity estimates and might result in a schedule baseline update. Schedule baseline updates occur when significant changes to the project schedule are made like the changes just mentioned. This means a new schedule baseline is established that reflects the changed project activity dates. Once the new baseline is established, it is used as the basis for future performance measurements. Never rebaseline a schedule without first having it approved by the project sponsor and archiving a copy of the original baseline and schedule.

Take care when rebaselining a project schedule. Don't lose the original baseline information. Why do you care? Because the original baseline serves as historical information to reference for future projects. Make a backup copy of the original schedule so that you have a record of the original baseline as a reference. Even though some project management software allows you to save several baselines plus the original, it's still good practice to make a backup copy of the original.

The performance measurements for Schedule Control are the schedule variance and schedule performance index. I know this sounds like a broken record, but make certain to document this information and communicate it to the stakeholders.

Changes to the project schedule might or might not require updates to other elements of the project plan. For example, extending a schedule activity involving a contractor might impact the costs associated with that activity.

Recommended corrective actions, as with other processes you've looked at, require root cause analysis. In the Schedule Control process, because you're dealing with time issues, it's imperative that you act as quickly as possible to implement corrective actions so that the schedule is brought back in line with the plan and the least amount of schedule delay as possible is experienced. I've already discussed the remaining Schedule Control outputs.

Monitoring and Controlling Risk

Now you'll shift your attention to risk. The *Risk Monitoring and Control* process primarily involves identifying and responding to new risks as they occur. The other functions of this process are as follows:

- Tracking and monitoring identified risks
- Evaluating risk response plans that are put into action as a result of risk events
- Monitoring the project for risk triggers
- Reexamining existing risks
- Monitoring residual risks
- Ensuring that policies and procedures are followed
- Ensuring that risk response plans and contingency plans are put into action appropriately and are effective
- Contingency reserves (for schedule and cost) are updated

Risk Monitoring and Control is a busy process. During the course of the project, risk responses (developed during the Planning process group) have been implemented and have reduced or averted the impact of risk events (or you hope they did).

Risk Monitoring and Control Inputs

This process has five inputs:

- Risk management plan
- Risk register
- Approved change requests
- Work performance information
- Performance reports

You'll recall that the risk management plan details how risk is managed and the risk response plan describes how you will implement plans and strategies in the event of an actual risk event. Keep in mind that some risk events identified in risk planning will happen and some will not. You will have to stay alert for risk event occurrences and be prepared to respond to them when they do occur. This means you should monitor the risk register regularly.

Approved change requests can introduce new risks to the project. It's good practice to review all approved change requests for the potential for new threats or opportunities or in light of previously identified risks and opportunities. They might also alter previously identified risks, which can mean action is needed during this process to bring response plans into alignment with the changes.

Work performance information gathered during the Performance Reporting process, cost changes, schedule changes, and/or scope changes might identify new risks.

Performance reports include information such as status reports, performance measurements, and forecasts. These should also be examined from the perspective of risks or risk response plans that might need close monitoring or changes to the response plans to coincide with the performance reports data.

Additional risk response planning might be needed to deal with the new risks or with expected risks whose impact was greater than expected. This might require repeating the Risk Response Planning process to create new contingency plans or alternative plans to deal with the risk, or it might require modification to existing plans.

Risk Monitoring and Control Tools and Techniques

The tools and techniques of Risk Monitoring and Control are used to monitor risks throughout the life of the project. You should perform periodic reviews, audits, and new earned value analyses to check the pulse of risk activity and to make certain risk management is enacted effectively.

The tools and techniques of this process are as follows:

- Risk reassessment
- Risk audits
- Variance and trend analysis
- Technical performance measurement

- Reserve analysis
- Status meetings

You'll look at risk reassessment, risk audits, and technical performance measurements next. You've examined all the other tools and techniques of this process in discussions of previous processes.

Risk Reassessment

Periodic, scheduled reviews of identified risks, risk responses, and risk priorities should occur during the project. The idea here is to monitor risks and their status and determine whether their consequences still have the same impact on the project objectives as when they were originally planned. Every status meeting (another output of this process) should have a time set aside to discuss and review risks and response plans.

Risk identification and monitoring is an ongoing process throughout the life of the project. Risks can change, and previously identified risks might have greater impacts than originally thought as more facts are discovered. Reassessment of risks should be a regular activity performed by everyone involved on the project. Monitor the risk register, including those risks that have low scores, and risk triggers. You should also monitor the risk responses that have been implemented for their effectiveness in dealing with risk. You might have to revisit the Qualitative and Quantitative Risk Analysis processes when new risk consequences are discovered or risk impacts are found to be greater than what was originally planned.

Risk Audits

Risk audits are carried out during the entire life of the project by risk auditors. Risk auditors are not typically project team members and are expertly trained in audit techniques and risk assessment. These audits are specifically interested in looking at the implementation and the effective use of risk strategies.

Technical Performance Measurements

This tool and technique compares the technical accomplishments of project milestones completed during the Executing processes to the technical milestones defined in the project Planning processes. Variances might indicate that a project risk is looming, and you'll want to analyze and prepare a response to it if appropriate. For example, a technical milestone for a new computer software project might require that the forms printed from a particular module include a bar code at the bottom of the page. If the bar code functionality does not work once the module is coded, a technical deviation exists, which means you should reexamine project risks. In this particular example, project scope is likely at risk.

Risk Monitoring and Control Outputs

Risk Monitoring and Control should occur throughout the life of the project. Identified risks are monitored and plans are reexamined to determine whether they will adequately resolve the risk as it approaches during this process. Several outputs might come about as a result of monitoring risks:

- Risk register updates
- Requested changes
- Recommended corrective action
- Recommended preventive action
- Organizational process updates (lessons learned, risk templates)
- Project management plan updates

I've discussed many of these outputs before, so I'll just bring to your attention the new points you need to know here.

The risk register should be updated under two conditions. The first condition is when a risk audit or risk reassessment concludes that some element of the original risk information has changed. For example, the impact or probability scores are updated to reflect new conditions, the priority of the risk has changed, or the response plan has been updated, and so on. The second condition for updating the risk register is when the risk needs to be closed. If a risk event occurs, you'll record that in the risk register along with the effectiveness of the response plan. This information becomes an input to the Close Project Process, which I'll cover in the next chapter.

Requested changes must be processed through the Integrated Change Control process. You might find a workaround is needed when implementing a requested change or recommended corrective action. A *workaround* is an unplanned response to a negative risk event. It attempts to deal with the risk in a productive, efficient manner. If no risk response plan exists (this might be the case when you accept a risk event during the Planning process) or an unplanned risk occurs, workarounds are implemented to deal with the consequences of the risk.

Project Case Study: New Kitchen Heaven Retail Store

Stakeholders have asked for an updated status on the project schedule as well as a remaining cost projection. You decide to provide several cost and schedule performance figures for the project on the status report.

"Build-out is behind schedule. They were scheduled to be completed by the 15th of January, but they aren't going to finish up until the 24th."

"What's that going to do to my schedule?" Jill asks. "I'm starting interviews for the store positions on the 16th. I hope to have that wrapped up by the 19th. As long as I have the majority of the staff hired by the 20th, we can have them stocking shelves starting the 22nd."

You tell Jill, "Let's finish up the status of the other items, and I'll come back to that."

You've calculated some performance measurements, including earned value measures, and you show them to Jill and Dirk (all figures are in millions of dollars):

BAC = 2; PV = 1.86; EV^c = 1.75; ACc = 1.70

CPI^c is 1.03. (1.75 ÷ 1.70)

SPI is .94 (1.75 ÷ 1.86)

EAC is 1.94 (1.70 + ((2 − 1.75) ÷ 1.03)))

ETC is .254 (2 − 1.75)

"What is all this telling us?" Dirk asks.

"The cost performance index tells us we're getting a good return for the money spent on the project so far. In other words, we've experienced a $1.03 value for every dollar spent to date," you respond.

"The schedule performance index isn't as cheery, but it's not dreadful news either. This performance indicator says that work is progressing at 94 percent of what we anticipated by this point.

"The estimate at completion tells us that based on what we know today, the total project will cost $1.90 million. That's coming in under the original $2 million we had budgeted for completion, so we're on track with the project budget.

"The last figure is the estimated cost of the remaining work."

"It looks like we're a little behind schedule based on what you have figured here," Dirk says.

"Yes, that's correct," you reply. "That brings us back to Jill's question. I have two alternatives to propose. One, we overlap the schedule and allow Gomez's crew to complete their work while Jill's staff starts stocking shelves."

Jill says, "I don't like this option. We'll be tripping over each other, and I don't want merchandise damaged by workers who are still dragging equipment around inside the store. What's your other option?"

"We could ask Gomez to increase the crew size so that they complete on time according to the contract. We have a provision in the contract that stipulates they add crew members if it looks as though they'll miss the scheduled completion date. I will instruct the contract management department to inform Gomez that we're requiring additional crew members."

"That will do the trick," Jill says. "We need the storefront to ourselves when stocking and preparing for opening. I'm glad you had that stipulation in the contract."

Your next agenda item is change requests. Ricardo submitted a change request regarding the hardware installation at the new store site. A new, much anticipated operating system was just released, and Ricardo has plans to upgrade the entire company to the new operating system. Since he must purchase new equipment for this store anyway, he contends that it makes sense to go ahead and purchase the hardware with the newest operating system already loaded. His staff won't have to upgrade this store as part of the upgrade project because the store will already have the new operating system.

Ricardo's change request was submitted in writing through the change control system. A CCB was set up during the Planning stages of this project to handle change requests. At the CCB meeting, the following questions come up regarding Ricardo's request: Has the new operating system been tested with the existing system? Are there compatibility problems? If so, what risks are associated with getting the problems resolved and the equipment installed by opening day? Is the vendor ready to ship with the new operating system?

The CCB defers their decision for this request until Ricardo gives them answers to these questions.

During the next CCB meeting, the board reviews a change request from Jill. The gourmet food supplier she used went out of business a month or so ago, and Jill contracted with a new vendor. She received a sample shipment from the new vendor and was very unhappy with the results. Upon inspecting the products, she found broken containers and damaged packaging. Meanwhile, Jill found another vendor, who has sent her a sample shipment. She is very pleased with the new vendor's products and service. However, this vendor's prices are even higher than the first replacement vendor she contracted with. Jill submitted a cost change request to the CCB because of the increased cost of the gourmet food product shipment. The change in cost does not have a significant impact on the budget because the new EAC with this change is $1.90 million. The original project budget estimate was $2 million, so the project is still coming in under budget.

You hold a seat on the CCB and are aware of the change requests and their impacts to the project. Ricardo satisfactorily answered all the questions the CCB had, so his request and Jill's request were both approved during the meeting.

Project Case Study Checklist

  Integrated change management

- Identify that a change has occurred

- Review and approve changes

  Configuration management systems

- Configuration identification

- Configuration status accounting

- Configuration verification and auditing

- Change control system

    Formal change request procedures

    Cost change

- Cost change control system

- Performance measurement analysis

- Forecasting

Understanding How This Applies to Your Next Project

I've learned from experience the value of having a change control process in place for all projects. I've never managed a project that didn't encounter change. And there are hundreds of reasons that bring about change. One of the ways to help reduce the amount of change you might experience is to make certain you've documented the requirements of the project accurately and have obtained sign-off from the stakeholders. Be aware—just because the stakeholders have agreed to the requirements doesn't mean they won't want change. As you elaborate the deliverables and requirements, the product or end result becomes clearer, and that means some elements not previously known or at least not known in their entirety early in the planning process will require change.

If you don't already have a change control process in place, I recommend setting one up before you begin your next project. Document the procedures for requesting, tracking, and approving or denying changes. Make them one of the agenda items for discussion at your project kickoff meeting. It's easier to enforce change procedures (and deny changes that are out of scope) if the process is discussed with the stakeholders early in the project. You will likely want to include important stakeholders on the change control board, and that gives you another great opportunity to discuss and reinforce the process.

The earned value technique is a tool you can't live without for measuring performance on your project, particularly the cost and schedule variance and the cost and schedule performance indexes. The size and complexity of the project will dictate how often you should run the performance measurements.

Monitoring and Controlling Risk is a process you'll perform once the work of the project begins throughout the remainder of the project. Just like change, risk is something that will occur on most every project you undertake. I've never managed a project (except for projects that were started and finished within a matter of days) that didn't encounter risk. And I'd say my experience has been that most risks are unknown, which makes contingency reserves (both time and money) essential on any project. For example, as I write this we're in the process of remodeling a bathroom. We are down to the very last task, which is tiling the floor. We ripped out the carpet and found the subfloor was almost rotted away from prior water damage. (The previous owners didn't tell us about this, hmm....) The subfloor has to be replaced and cement board has to be installed before tiling can commence. Wrecking out old subfloor and replacing it is not something I want to take on. So, I'll have to dip into the reserves to hire a pro to do the job. Taking on a project without knowing that risks will occur and without having some contingency set aside is a huge gamble because even the smallest projects have risks.

To successfully complete your projects, you just can't skip some processes. I don't recommend skipping or cutting corners with the Change Control or Monitoring and Controlling Risk processes.

Summary

This chapter examined several change control processes starting with Integrated Change Control. Change control is an important part of the project process. It's your responsibility as project manager to manage change and implement corrective action where needed to keep the project on track with the plan.

Integrated Change Control concerns influencing the things that cause change and managing the change once it has occurred. One or more of the triple constraints are generally affected when change occurs. Managing change might involve changes to the project plan, the project schedule, or the project budget. Changes that impact processes you've already completed require updates to those processes. Corrective action is often a result of change and ensures that the future performance of the project lines up with the project management plan.

Configuration management systems typically include change control systems that document the procedures to manage change and how change requests are implemented. Change requests might come in written or verbal forms, but ideally you should ask for all your change requests in writing. Change requests are processed through a formal change control system, and configuration control boards have the authority to approve or deny change requests.

Lessons learned become part of the historical information used on future projects. They also are used to document the causes of the variances that occur on the project. Lessons learned are updated as part of the organizational process asset outputs of the change control processes.

Schedule Control involves determining the status of the project schedule, determining whether changes have occurred or should, and influencing and managing schedule changes.

Cost Control involves managing changes to project costs. It's also concerned with monitoring project costs to prevent unauthorized or incorrect costs from getting included in the cost baseline. Cost Control uses tools and techniques such as performance measurement analysis (such as CV, SV, CPI, SPI), forecasting (ETC and EAC), and project performance reviews (variance analysis, trend analysis, and EVT) to monitor costs.

Risk Monitoring and Control responds to risks as they occur and implements workarounds for unplanned risk events. Some risks planned for during the Risk Response Planning process will occur, and some will not. Perhaps risks that were previously identified do occur, and their impacts are much greater than anticipated during the Risk Response Planning process. These will require updates to the risk management plan or workarounds.

Exam Essentials

Name the purpose of the Integrated Change Control process.   Integrated Change Control is performed throughout the life of the project and involves reviewing all the project change requests, establishing a configuration management and change control process, and approving or denying changes.

Be able to define the purpose of a configuration management system.   Configuration management systems are documented procedures that describe the process for submitting change requests, the processes for tracking changes and their disposition, and the processes for defining the approval levels for approving and denying changes, and it includes a process for authorizing the changes. Change control systems are generally a subset of the configuration management system. Configuration management also describes the characteristics of the product of the project and ensures accuracy and completeness of the description.

Be able to describe a CCB.   The configuration control board (CCB) has the authority to approve or deny change requests. Their authority is defined and outlined by the organization.

Name the purpose of the Cost Control process.   The Cost Control process is concerned with monitoring project costs to prevent unauthorized or incorrect costs from getting included in the cost baseline.

Be able to describe performance measurement techniques.   Performance measurement techniques use the earned value technique (EVT) to continuously monitor the planned value, earned value, and actual costs expended to produce the work of the project. There are performance measures, performance indexes, forecasting, and variance analysis techniques.

Describe the purpose of Risk Monitoring and Control   Risk Monitoring and Control involves identifying and responding to new risks as they occur. Risk monitoring and reassessment should occur throughout the life of the project.

Key Terms

The processes introduced in this chapter give you the tools and techniques you need to keep your projects on track. Without these control processes in place, even the best-planned projects can become mired or spin out of control. Know these processes by the PMI terms if you want to be successful in obtaining your PMP certification. Understand and use them in your day-to-day work if you intend to have your projects come in on time and on budget.

Cost Control

Integrated Change Control

Risk Monitoring and Control

Schedule Control

You've learned a lot of new key words in this chapter. PMI has worked hard to develop and define standard project management terms that apply across industries. Here is a list of some of the terms you came across in this chapter:

actual cost (AC)	estimate to complete (ETC)
budget at completion (BAC)	performance measurement baseline
change control system	planned value (PV)
configuration control board (CCB)	project performance review
configuration management	Revisions
cost performance index (CPI)	schedule change control system
cost variance (CV)	schedule performance index (SPI)
cumulative CPI (CPIc)	schedule variance (SV)
earned value (EV)	variance at completion (VAC)
earned value technique (EVT)	Workaround
estimate at completion	

Review Questions

1. You are a project manager for Bluebird Technologies. Bluebird writes custom billing applications for several industries. A schedule change has been requested. You know change is concerned with all of the following except which one?

   A. Managing change

   B. Verifying change

   C. Influencing causes of change

   D. Determining that a change occurred

2. You are a project manager for Bluebird Technologies. Bluebird writes custom billing applications for several industries. One of your users verbally requests changes to one of the screen displays. You explain to her that the change needs to go through the change control system, which is a subset of the configuration management system. You explain that a change control system does all of the following except for which one?

   A. Documents procedures for change requests

   B. Tracks the status of change requests

   C. Describes the management impacts of change

   D. Determines whether changes are approved or denied

3. You are a project manager for Star Light Strings. Star Light manufactures strings of lights for outdoor display. Its products range from simple light strings to elaborate lights with animal designs, bug designs, memorabilia, and so on. Your newest project requires a change. You have documented the characteristics of the product and its functionality using which of the following tools and techniques?

   A. Change control system

   B. Corrective action

   C. Configuration management

   D. Updates to the project management plan

4. You are a project manager for Star Light Strings. Star Light manufactures strings of lights for outdoor display. Its products range from simple light strings to elaborate lights with animal designs, bug designs, memorabilia, and so on. Your newest project requires a change. One of the business unit managers submitted a change through the change control system, which utilizes a CCB. Which of the following is true regarding the CCB?

   A. The CCB describes how change requests are managed.

   B. The CCB requires all change requests in writing.

   C. The CCB approves or denies change requests.

   D. The CCB requires updates to the appropriate management plan.

5. Which of the following statements is true regarding schedule variances?

    A. Schedule variances impact scope, which impacts the schedule.

    B. Schedule variances sometimes impact the schedule.

    C. Schedule variances always impact the schedule.

    D. Schedule variances never impact the schedule.

6. You are a project manager for Laurel's Theater Productions. Your new project is coming in over budget and requires a cost change through the cost change control system. You know all of the following statements are true regarding Cost Control except for which one?

    A. Performance is monitored to detect variances.

    B. Changes are reflected in the cost baseline.

    C. Changes are monitored and reflected in the project scope.

    D. Changes are monitored so that inappropriate changes do not get into the cost baseline.

7. Which of the following might require rebaselining of the cost baseline?

    A. Corrective action

    B. Revised cost estimates

    C. Updates to the cost management plan

    D. Budget updates

8. All of the following are activities of the configuration management system except for which one?

    A. Variance analysis

    B. Identification

    C. Status accounting

    D. Verification and auditing

9. Which of the following is not an activity of configuration management during the Integrated Change Control process?

    A. Verification

    B. Funding

    C. Status accounting

    D. Auditing

10. What are the performance measurements for the Schedule Control process?

    A. SV (EV − PV) and SPI (EV ÷ PV)

    B. SV (EV − AC) and SPI (EV ÷ AC)

    C. SV (EV − BAC) and SPI (EV ÷ BAC)

    D. SV (PV − EV) and SPI (PV ÷ EV)

11. This measurement is the value of the work that has been completed to date compared to the budget.

  A. PV

  B. AC

  C. EV

  D. EAC

12. You are a contract project manager for a wholesale flower distribution company. Your project is to develop a website for the company that allows retailers to place their flower orders online. You will also provide a separate link for individual purchases that are ordered, packaged, and mailed to the consumer directly from the grower's site. This project involves coordinating the parent company, growers, and distributors. You are preparing a performance review and have the following measurements at hand: PV = 300, AC = 200, and EV = 250. What do you know about this project?

  A. The EAC is a positive number, which means the project will finish under budget.

  B. You do not have enough information to calculate CPI.

  C. The CV is a negative number in this case, which means you've spent less than you planned to spend as of the measurement date.

  D. The CV is a positive number in this case, which means you're under budget as of the measurement date.

13. A negative result from an SV calculation means which of the following?

  A. PV is higher than EV.

  B. PV equals 1.

  C. EV is higher than PV.

  D. EV is higher than AC.

14. You are a contract project manager for a wholesale flower distribution company. Your project is to develop a website for the company that allows retailers to place their flower orders online. You will also provide a separate link for individual purchases that are ordered, packaged, and mailed to the consumer directly from the grower's site. This project involves coordinating the parent company, growers, and distributors. You are preparing a performance review and have the following measurements at hand: PV = 300, AC = 200, and EV = 250. What is the CPI of this project?

  A. 0.80

  B. 1.25

  C. 1.5

  D. 0.83

15. You do not expect the types of variances that have occurred on the project to date to continue. If BAC = 800, ETC = 275, PV = 300, AC^C = 200, EV = 250, and CPI^C = 1.25, what is the EAC?

    A. 640

    B. 750

    C. 600

    D. 550

16. You know that BAC = 375, PV = 300, AC = 200, and EV^C = 250. Variances that have occurred on the project to date are not expected to continue. What is the ETC?

    A. 75

    B. 50

    C. 125

    D. 150

17. You expect the types of variances that have occurred on the project to date to continue. If BAC = 800, ETC = 275, PV = 300, AC^C = 200, EV = 250, and CPI^C = 1.25, what is the EAC?

    A. 640

    B. 750

    C. 600

    D. 550

18. You know that BAC = 500, PV = 325, AC^C = 275, CPI = .9, and EV = 250 and that you are experiencing atypical variances. Variance at completion tells you which of the following?

    A. 25

    B. −52

    C. 52

    D. −25

19. You know that BAC = 500, PV = 325, AC^C = 275, and EV^C = 250 and that you are experiencing typical variances. What is ETC?

    A. 227.3

    B. 250

    C. 274.7

    D. 525

20. Your project progressed as planned up until yesterday. Suddenly, an unexpected risk event occurred. You quickly devised a response to deal with this negative risk event using which of the following outputs of Risk Monitoring and Control?

    A. Risk management plan updates

    B. Workarounds

    C. Corrective action

    D. Additional risk identification

Answers to Review Questions

1. B. Integrated Change Control, Schedule Control, and Cost Control are all concerned with three issues: influencing the things that cause change, determining that change is needed or has happened, and managing the change.

2. D. Change control systems are documented procedures that describe how to submit change requests. They track the status of the change requests, document the management impacts of change, track the change approval status, and define the level of authority needed to approve changes. Change control systems do not approve or deny the changes—that's the responsibility of the configuration control board (CCB).

3. C. The key to this question was that the characteristics of the product were documented with this tool. Configuration management documents the physical characteristics and the functionality of the product of the project.

4. C. Configuration control boards (CCBs) review change requests and have the authority to approve or deny them. Their authority is defined by the organization.

5. B. Schedule variances will sometimes—but not always—impact the schedule. Changes to non-critical path tasks will not likely impact the schedule, but changes to critical path tasks will always impact the schedule.

6. C. Cost Control tracks project performance to detect variances and reflect them in the cost baseline. It's also used to prevent inappropriate changes from getting into the cost baseline.

7. D. Budget updates might require cost rebaselining.

8. A. The three activities associated with configuration management are configuration identification, configuration status accounting, and configuration verification and auditing.

9. B. Configuration identification involves identifying the products of the project, determining the status of changes to the configuration, and verifying and auditing the configuration to determine whether the performance and functional requirements have been met.

10. A. Schedule variance is $(EV - PV)$ and schedule performance index is $(EV \div PV)$.

11. C. Earned value is referred to as the value of the work that's been completed to date compared to the budget.

12. D. The CV is a positive number and is calculated by subtracting AC from EV as follows: $250 - 200 = 50$. A positive CV means the project is coming in under budget, meaning you've spent less than you planned as of the measurement date.

13. A. The SV calculation is $EV - PV$. If PV is a higher number than EV, you'll get a negative number as a result.

14. B. CPI is calculated as follows: $EV \div AC$. In this case, $250 \div 200 = 1.25$.

15. B. When variances are not expected to continue, or are atypical in nature, EAC is calculated as follows: $AC^C + BAC - EV$. Therefore, the calculation for this question looks like this: $(200 + 800) - 250 = 750$.

16. C. The correct formula for ETC for this question is as follows: $BAC - EV^C$. Therefore, ETC is as follows: $375 - 250 = 125$.

17. A. When variances are expected to continue, EAC is calculated as follows: $AC^C + ((BAC - EV) \div CPI^C)$. Therefore, the calculation for this question looks like this: $200 + ((800 - 250) \div 1.25) = 640$.

18. D. You first have to calculate EAC in order to calculate VAC. EAC for variances that are atypical is $AC^C + BAC - EV$. So our numbers are $275 + 500 - 250 = 525$. VAC is calculated this way: $BAC - EAC$. Therefore, $500 - 525 = -25$. Our costs are not doing as well as anticipated.

19. C. You must first calculate CPI^C in order to calculate ETC. CPI^C is $EV^C \div AC^C$. We have $250 \div 275 = .91$. ETC with typical variances is $(BAC - EV^C) \div CPI^C$. Our numbers are $(500 - 250) \div .91 = 274.7$.

20. B. Workarounds are unplanned responses. Workarounds deal with negative risk events as they occur. As the name implies, workarounds were not previously known to the project team. The risk event was unplanned, so no contingency plan existed to deal with the risk event, and thus it required a workaround.

Chapter

11

Controlling Work Results and Closing Out the Project

THE PMP EXAM CONTENT FROM THE MON-ITORING AND CONTROLLING THE PROJECT PERFORMANCE DOMAIN COVERED IN THIS CHAPTER INCLUDES THE FOLLOWING:

✓ Ensure Project Deliverables Conform to Quality Standards

THE PMP EXAM CONTENT FROM THE CLOSING THE PROJECT PERFORMANCE DOMAIN COVERED IN THIS CHAPTER INCLUDES THE FOLLOWING:

✓ Obtain Final Acceptance for the Project

✓ Obtain Financial, Legal, and Administrative Closure

✓ Release Project Resources

✓ Identify, Document, and Communicate Lessons Learned

✓ Create and Distribute Final Project Report

✓ Archive and Retain Project Records

✓ Measure Customer Satisfaction

You've made it to the homestretch. This chapter covers the last group of project processes. I'll close out the Monitoring and Controlling process group and also discuss the Closing process group. Most of the hard part is over, but you aren't quite done yet.

In the Monitoring and Controlling group, I'll cover Perform Quality Control, Scope Verification, and Scope Control. The Perform Quality Control process involves several new tools and techniques that might show up on the exam. Take some time here to understand the tools and techniques in the Perform Quality Control process and to differentiate them from the tools and techniques associated with the Quality Planning and Perform Quality Control processes. Remember that Perform Quality Control tools and techniques are listed as tools and techniques for the Perform Quality Assurance process. Scope Verification involves verifying and accepting work results. Scope Control is like the change control processes I discussed in Chapter 10 and is concerned with controlling changes to project scope.

The Closing process group has two processes: Close Project and Contract Closure. The Close Project process is concerned with verifying that the work of the project was completed correctly and to the stakeholders' satisfaction. Contract Closure supports the Close Project process and also verifies that the work of the project was completed correctly and the deliverables accepted.

Project closeout is the most often neglected process of all the project processes. Once the project is over, it's easy to pack things up, throw some files in a drawer, and start moving right into planning the next project. However, don't be so quick to chuck your project just yet. You have a few things to take care of during this process that might make life easier for you on the next project.

One of the most important functions of this process is obtaining formal acceptance of the product of the project from stakeholders and customers. You'll want to get an official sign-off from the stakeholders acknowledging acceptance of the product and then file this with the project documents.

Utilizing Perform Quality Control Techniques

Quality Planning, Perform Quality Assurance, and Perform Quality Control are part of the project Quality Management Knowledge Area. These processes work together to define and monitor the work of the project and to make certain the results meet the quality requirements laid out in the plan.

Perform Quality Control is specifically concerned with monitoring work results to see whether they comply with the standards set out in the quality management plan. You should practice Perform Quality Control throughout the project to identify and remove the causes of unacceptable results. Remember that Perform Quality Control is concerned with project results both from a management perspective, such as schedule and cost performance, and from a product perspective. In other words, the end product should conform to the requirements and product description defined during the Planning processes.

Perform Quality Control Inputs

Perform Quality Control includes the following inputs:

- Quality management plan
- Quality metrics
- Quality checklists
- Organizational process assets
- Work performance information
- Approved change requests
- Deliverables

I've discussed each of these inputs previously, so I'll move on to tools and techniques.

Perform Quality Control Tools and Techniques

This list of tools and techniques in the Perform Quality Control process includes several that I haven't discussed before:

- Cause-and-effect diagram
- Control chart
- Flowchart
- Histogram
- Pareto chart
- Run chart
- Scatter diagram
- Statistical sampling
- Inspection
- Defect repair review

The primary purpose of each of these tools is to examine the product, service, or result as well as the project processes for conformity to standards. If the results fall within the tolerance range specified, the results are acceptable. Alternatively, if the results fall within the control limits set for the product (as defined by the various tools and techniques I'll discuss in the following sections), the process you are examining is said to be *in control*. Spend time understanding these tools and techniques and their individual uses because you might see exam questions about each of them.

I talked about cause-and-effect diagrams as a diagramming technique in the Risk Identification process in Chapter 5, "Risk Planning." If you need a refresher, refer to Figure 5.2 in that chapter.

I also discussed flowcharts in the same section of Chapter 5. Flowcharts are diagrams that show the logical steps that must be performed in order to accomplish an objective. They can also show how the individual elements of a system interrelate. Flowcharting can help identify where quality problems might occur on the project and how problems happen. This is important because it gives the project team the opportunity to develop alternative approaches for dealing with anticipated quality problems identified with this tool and technique.

Histograms are typically bar charts that depict the distribution of variables over time. Chapter 6, "Resource Planning," contains an example histogram. In Perform Quality Control, the histogram usually depicts the attributes of the problem or situation. (I'll discuss attributes shortly.)

You will look at the other tools and techniques in more detail in the following sections.

Control Charts

Control charts measure the results of processes over time and display the results in graph form. Control charts are a way to measure variances to determine whether process variances are in control or out of control.

A control chart is based on sample variance measurements. From the samples chosen and measured, the mean and standard deviation are determined. Perform Quality Control is usually maintained—or said to be in control—within plus or minus three standard deviations. In other words, Perform Quality Control says that if the process is in control (that is, the measurements fall within the control limits), you know that 99.73 percent of the parts going through the process will fall within an acceptable range of the mean. If you discover a part outside of this range, you should investigate and determine whether corrective action is needed.

Figure 11.1 illustrates an example control chart.

You've determined from your sample measurements that 5 mm is the mean in the example control chart. One standard deviation equals 0.02. Three standard deviations on either side of the mean become your upper and lower control points on this chart. Therefore, if all control points fall within plus or minus three standard deviations on either side of the mean, the process is in control. If points fall outside the acceptable limits, the process is not in control, and corrective action is needed.

Control charts are used most often in manufacturing settings where repetitive activities are easily monitored. For example, the process that produces widgets by the case lot must meet certain specifications and fall within certain variances to be considered in control. However, you aren't limited to using control charts only in the manufacturing industry. You can use them to monitor any output. You might consider using control charts to track and monitor project management processes. You could plot cost variances, schedule variances, frequency or number of scope changes, and so on, to help monitor variances in the project management process.

FIGURE 11.1   Control chart

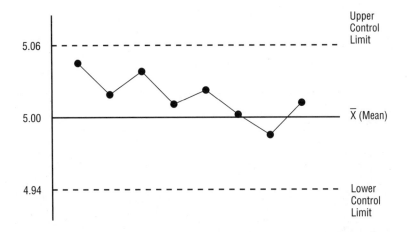

Pareto Chart

You have probably heard of the 80/20 rule. Vilfredo Pareto is the person credited with discovering this rule. He observed that 80 percent of the wealth and land ownership in Italy was held by 20 percent of the population. Over the years, others have shown that the 80/20 rule applies across many disciplines and areas. As an example, generally speaking, 80 percent of the deposits of any given financial institution are held by 20 percent of its customer base. Let's hope that rule doesn't apply to project managers, though, with 20 percent of the project managers out there doing 80 percent of the work!

The 80/20 rule as it applies to quality says that a small number of causes (20 percent) create the majority of the problems (80 percent). Have you ever noticed this with your project or department staff? It always seems that just a few people cause the biggest headaches. But I'm getting off track.

Pareto charts are displayed as histograms that rank-order the most important factors such as delays, costs, defects, or other factors by their frequency over time. His theory is that you get the most benefit if you spend the majority of your time fixing the most important problems. The information shown in Table 11.1 is plotted on an example Pareto chart shown in Figure 11.2.

TABLE 11.1   Frequency of Failures

Item	Defect Frequency	Percent of Defects	Cumulative Percent
A	800	.33	.33
B	700	.29	.62

TABLE 11.1 Frequency of Failures *(continued)*

Item	Defect Frequency	Percent of Defects	Cumulative Percent
C	400	.17	.79
D	300	.13	.92
E	200	.08	1.0

FIGURE 11.2 Pareto chart

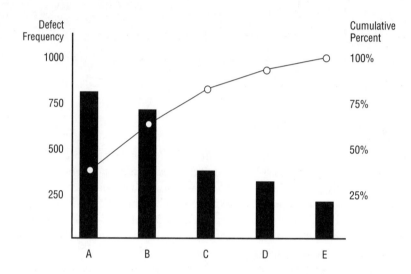

The problems are rank-ordered according to their frequency and percentage of defects. The defect frequencies in this figure appear as black bars, and the cumulative percentages of defects are plotted as circles. The rank-ordering of these problems shows you where corrective action should be taken first. You can see in Figure 11.2 that problem A should receive priority attention because the most benefit will come from fixing this problem.

Run Charts

Run charts are used to show variations in the process over time or to show trends (such as improvements or lack of improvements) in the process. Differences in results will occur in processes because there is no such thing as a perfect process. When processes are considered in control, differences in results might occur because of common causes of variances or special-cause variances.

Common causes of variances come about as a result of circumstances or situations that are relatively unique to the process you're using and are easily controlled at the operational level.

Perhaps a machine needs calibration or procedures for the process need refinement. Perhaps your process is very detailed, with specific procedures that are carried out to produce the output. Not following these detailed procedures could result in variances known as *special-cause variances*.

For the exam, you should understand the three types of variances that make up common causes of variances:

Random variances   Random variations might be normal, depending on the processes you're using to produce the product or service of the project, but they occur as the name implies, at random.

Known or predictable variances   Known or predictable variances are variances that you know exist in the process because of particular characteristics of the product, service, or result you are processing. These are generally unique to a particular application.

Variances that are always present in the process   The process itself will have inherent variability that is perhaps caused by human mistakes, machine variations or malfunctions, the environment, and so on, which are known as variances always present in the process. These variances generally exist across all applications of the process.

Common cause variances that do not fall within the acceptable range are difficult to correct and usually require a reorganization of the process. This has the potential for significant impact, and decisions to change the process always require management approval.

Exam Spotlight

According to the *PMBOK Guide*, when a process is in control, it should not be adjusted. When a process falls outside the acceptable limits, it should be adjusted.

Trend analysis is another technique that's carried out using run charts. Trend analysis in the Perform Quality Control process is a mathematical technique that uses historical results to predict future outcomes. Trend analysis often tracks variances in cost and schedule performance by monitoring the number of activities completed with significant variances within a certain time period. This information can then be used to forecast future performance. Trend analysis also tracks technical performance by determining the number of defects observed and the number of defects not corrected. *Technical performance measurements* compare the technical accomplishments of project milestones completed to the technical milestones defined in the project Planning process group.

Scatter Diagrams

Scatter diagrams use two variables, one called an *independent* variable, which is an input, and one called a *dependent* variable, which is an output. Scatter diagrams display the relationship between these two elements as points on a graph. This relationship is typically analyzed to prove or disprove cause-and-effect relationships. As an example, maybe your scatter diagram plots the ability of your employees to perform a certain task. Their experience performing this task in months is plotted as the independent variable on the X axis, and the accuracy they achieve in performing this task expressed as a score—the dependent variable—is plotted on the Y axis. The scatter diagram can then help you determine whether cause-and-effect (in this case, increased experience over time versus accuracy) can be proved. Scatter diagrams can also help you look for and analyze root causes of problems.

The important point to remember about scatter diagrams is that they plot the dependent and independent variables, and the closer the points resemble a diagonal line, the closer these variables are related. Figure 11.3 shows a sample scatter diagram.

FIGURE 11.3   Scatter diagram

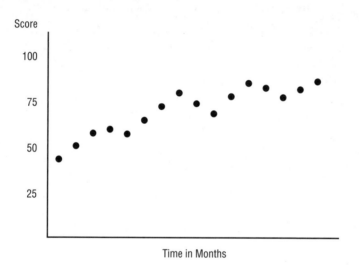

Statistical Sampling

Statistical sampling involves taking a sample number of parts from the whole population and examining them to determine whether they fall within acceptable variances. The formula to calculate the correct sample size is beyond the scope of this book. However, Creative Research Systems has an online calculator and an explanation of statistical sampling that you might find useful. You can find them at `http://www.surveysystem.com/sscalc.htm`.

Perhaps you determine to statistically sample 25 parts out of a lot or run. The quality plan outlines that the lot will pass if four parts or fewer fall outside the allowable variance.

Statistical sampling might also involve determining the standard deviation for a process, as discussed in the control chart tool and technique. The quality plan determines whether plus or minus two standard deviations—95.44 percent of the population—is adequate or whether plus or minus three standard deviations—99.73 percent—is adequate.

Inspection

Inspection involves physically looking at, measuring, or testing results to determine whether they conform to the requirements or quality standards. It's a tool used to gather information and improve results. Inspections might occur after the final product is produced or at intervals during the development of the product to examine individual components. Acceptance decisions are made when the work is inspected and the work is either accepted or rejected. When work is rejected, it might have to go back through the process for rework. Inspection is also known as *reviews* or *peer reviews*.

Exam Spotlight

Don't confuse inspection with prevention; they're two different tools. Inspection keeps errors in the product from reaching the customer. *Prevention* keeps errors from occurring in the process. It always costs less to prevent problems in the first place than it does to fix problems built into the product after the fact. Rework, labor costs, material costs, and potential loss of customers are all factors to consider when weighing prevention costs versus the cost of rework. Philip Crosby developed the theory of Zero Defects, which deals with prevention costs. Loosely translated, Zero Defects means doing it right the first time.

Inspection might take actual measurements of components to determine whether they meet requirements. Maybe a component part for your product must be exactly 5 mm in length. To pass inspection, the parts are measured and must meet the 5 mm length requirement. If they measure 5 mm, they pass; if they do not, they fail.

Measurements can vary even if the variances are not noticeable. Machines wear down, people make mistakes, the environment might cause variances, and so on. Measurements that fall within a specified range are called *tolerable results*. So, instead of 5 mm exactly, maybe a range between 4.98 mm and 5.02 mm is an acceptable or tolerable measurement for the component. If the samples that are measured fall within the tolerable range, they pass; otherwise, they fail inspection.

One inspection technique uses measurements called *attributes*. The measurements taken during attribute sampling determine whether they meet one of two options, conforming or nonconforming. In other words, the measurements conform or meet the requirement, or they do not conform. This can also be considered a pass/fail or go/no-go decision.

Attribute conformity and inspections are not necessarily performed on every component part or every end product that's produced. That's time-consuming and inefficient when you're producing numerous components. Inspection in cases like this is usually performed on a sampling of parts or products where every *x* number of parts is tested for conformity or measurement specifics.

Inspection will tell you where problems exist and give you the opportunity to correct them, thus leading to quality improvements. The other tools and techniques I'll talk about in these sections also lead to quality improvements in the product or process, or both. Quality improvements are an output of the Perform Quality Control process.

Defect Repair Review

In this tool and technique, the quality control department reviews the repairs that were made (as a result of quality audits) to make certain the repairs were made correctly and that the deliverable, or product of the project, is in compliance. You'll remember that approved defect repairs are a result of a quality audit performed during the Perform Quality Assurance process or an inspection as part of the Perform Quality Control process. (Approved defect repairs are an input to the Direct and Manage Project Execution process.) Defect repairs correct problems you find with the product of the project. Now you'll examine those repairs (using inspection) to make certain they corrected the problem.

Perform Quality Control Outputs

Quality improvements, as mentioned in the Perform Quality Assurance process discussed in Chapter 9, "Measuring and Controlling Project Performance," are a primary goal of the quality processes. Failure to meet quality requirements can have a significant impact on the project and the project team and might result in rework. *Rework* causes a project to take longer and cost more than originally planned because the project team has to repeat processes to correct the work. You should try to keep rework to a minimum so as not to impact the project schedule and budget. Rework has the potential to cause morale issues as well, especially if the team members thought they were doing a good job all along. Rework might require the project team to put in extra long hours, which in turn might cause more errors or other negative consequences. Monitor quality periodically so that rework is kept to a minimum.

Perform Quality Assurance is concerned with assuring that the project is using the correct and most efficient processes to meet the project requirements; Perform Quality Control is concerned with the accuracy of the project results.

 Real World Scenario

An Ounce of Prevention

One of the main thoroughfares into your city requires a bridge replacement. You were appointed the project manager for the city and have managed this project since its initiation 15 months ago.

The project entailed hiring a contractor to build the new bridge and manage the contract and the work of the contracting agency to bring the project to a successful completion.

Approximately 28,000 vehicles travel across this bridge on a daily basis, carrying commuters and college students back and forth to the downtown area. One of the requirements was the closure of no more than three of the six lanes of traffic at one time during construction. Each piece of steel was required to be painted (two coats) before bringing it on-site. A third coat of paint was to be applied at the site after construction. The paint was to be guaranteed to last 25 to 30 years.

An on-site quality control inspection revealed that some of the paint was peeling. After further investigation, you discovered that the contractor did not allow the first coat of paint to cure properly, so when the second coat was applied, it peeled and flaked.

You've instructed the contractor that, according to the terms of the contract and the SOW specifications, they're required to apply three coats of paint to the bridge, and the paint is required to last 25 to 30 years. Paint that peels before construction is completed does not comply with specifications. Corrective action is needed. As a result, the contract company decides to subcontract out the painting work to another company while they finish up their remaining tasks on the project.

Unfortunately, the subcontractor who was hired found they were in way over their heads and were not able to complete the paint job. Several months have passed, and the original project completion date was missed long ago. Obviously, revisions to the project schedule were required when it became clear that the subcontractor wasn't going to make the date. Now another revision to the project schedule is necessary because of the subcontractor's failure to complete the painting task.

The original contractor did some searching and found another subcontractor capable of completing the painting job. It's now the middle of winter. Because the temperatures are cold, the painting crew must hang insulated tarps between the bays on the bridge and use heaters to warm up small areas of steel to the proper temperature to apply the paint. This process extended the completion date by more than three times its original estimate and ultimately delayed the completion of the project by two years. Additional costs were incurred to hire the subcontractor and rent the heaters.

Corrective action was taken as a result of the inspection, and eventually the project was completed, but not without schedule delays, schedule changes, scope changes, and rework—not to mention the increased cost to the original contractor. Since the contract was a fixed-price contract, the contractor's profit was eaten away paying for the painting job. The cost to correct the quality issue did not impact the city, but it did impact the contractor. This is a case where an ounce of prevention would have been worth several gallons of cure, as the old saying goes.

Perform Quality Control has several outputs:

- Quality control measurements
- Validated defect repair
- Quality baseline updates
- Recommended corrective actions
- Recommended preventive actions
- Requested changes
- Recommended defect repair

- Organizational process asset updates (checklists, lessons learned)
- Validated deliverables
- Project management plan updates

I've already discussed many of these outputs, but I'll add a few quick notes here.

Validated defect repairs are the results of defects that have been corrected and examined. Recommended corrective and preventive actions might result in quality improvements. Remember that processes that are in control should not be adjusted. Processes out of control might require adjusting, but this should occur only as a result of a management decision.

Recommended defect repairs might also result from this process. The quality control department or team identifies the defects using the tools and techniques of this process, and the defects should be logged in a database or some other tracking tool to keep track of status and resolution.

Completed checklists become part of the project's documentation and are included as part of the organizational process asset updates. Lessons learned should include the causes of variances found during this process and why the corrective actions were recommended.

Validated deliverables are the result of the work of the project. This output assures that the deliverables meet the quality standards outlined in the quality management plan.

Verifying Project Scope

Managing and reporting on project progress are the primary focus of the Monitoring and Controlling processes. One of the Monitoring and Controlling processes that helps manage and control project progress is the *Scope Verification* process.

Exam Spotlight

The most important fact you should know about the Scope Verification process is that Scope Verification formalizes the acceptance of the project scope and is primarily concerned with the acceptance of work results. Don't confuse this process with the Perform Quality Control process I just discussed.

You can remember the difference between Scope Verification and Perform Quality Control this way:

- Scope Verification = *accepting* work results

- Perform Quality Control = *checking* for correct work results (assuring that the quality requirements are met)

The inputs of the Scope Verification are the project scope statement, WBS dictionary, project scope management plan, and deliverables. This process involves evaluating these inputs to determine whether the work is complete and whether it satisfies the project objectives. Evaluation is performed using inspection, which is the only tool and technique of this process. You should perform Scope Verification—even if the project is canceled—to document the degree to which the project was completed. This serves as historical information, and if the project is ever started up again, you've got documentation that tells you what was completed and how far the project progressed.

The outputs of Scope Verification are accepted deliverables, requested changes, and recommended corrective actions. Accepted deliverables concern the formal acceptance of the work by the stakeholders. Remember that stakeholders include customers, the project sponsor, the project team, the management team, and so on. Document their acceptance with formal sign-off, and file it in your project notebook.

Controlling Scope Changes

The Scope Management Knowledge Area includes Scope Planning, Scope Definition, Create WBS, Scope Verification, and Scope Control. You'll recall that project scope describes the work required to produce the product, service, or result of the project. This broad statement usually includes the product scope statement and the product description, which describes the characteristics, features, and functionality of the product, service, or result. You can conclude from this that the *Scope Control* process involves changes to the project scope. Any modification to the agreed-upon WBS is considered a scope change. (It has been eons ago that you looked at this, so remember that the work breakdown structure [WBS] is a deliverables-oriented hierarchy that defines the total work of the project.) This means the addition or deletion of activities or modifications to the existing activities on the WBS constitute a project scope change.

Changes in product scope require changes to the project scope as well. Let's say one of your project deliverables is the design of a piece of specialized equipment that's integrated into your final product. Now let's say that because of engineering setbacks and some miscalculations, the specialized equipment requires design modifications. The redesign of this equipment impacts the end product or product scope. Since changes to the product scope impact the project requirements, which are detailed in the scope document, changes to project scope are also required. This change, along with recommended corrective actions, should be processed through the Integrated Change Control process.

Scope Control Inputs

The Scope Control process has seven inputs, all of which you've seen before:

- Project scope statement
- WBS
- WBS dictionary
- Project scope management plan
- Performance reports
- Approved change requests
- Work performance information

I covered the first four inputs in the Planning process group and the last three in the Monitoring and Controlling process group.

Scope Control Tools and Techniques

The Scope Control process has four tools and techniques:

- Change control system
- Variance analysis
- Replanning
- Configuration management system

The change control system here is just like the one described in the discussion of the Integrated Change Control process. It tracks and records change requests, describes the procedures to follow to implement scope change, and details the authorization levels needed to approve or reject the changes. When your project is performed under contract, scope changes also require conformance to the provisions of the contract and the contract change system.

Variance analysis includes reviewing project performance measurements to determine whether there are variances in project scope. It's also important to determine and document the cause of variances and examine those against the scope baseline so that you can implement corrective actions if needed.

Replanning involves updating the WBS, WBS dictionary, project scope statement, and project management plan when a change in scope has occurred.

If you are using a configuration management system to control product scope, the change control system must also integrate with it. The configuration management system manages changes to product and project scope and ensures that these changes are reasonable and make sense before they're processed through the Integrated Change Control process.

Scope Control Outputs

The outputs of the Scope Control process are as follows:

- Project scope statement updates
- WBS updates
- WBS dictionary updates
- Scope baseline updates
- Requested changes
- Recommended corrective action
- Organizational process assets update
- Project management plan updates

I'll now cover the project scope statement changes and scope baseline updates. I've discussed all the remaining outputs already.

Changes to scope will likely require that you run back through the project Planning processes and make any needed adjustments. This also means you'll need to update the project scope statement so it accurately reflects the project work after the change.

Scope changes include any changes to the project scope as defined by the agreed-upon WBS. This in turn might require changes or updates to project objectives, costs, quality measures or controls, or time in the form of schedule revisions. Scope changes almost always affect project costs and/or require schedule revisions.

> Schedule revisions are almost always needed as a result of scope changes. But not all scope changes lengthen the project schedule. Some scope changes (a reduction in overall project requirements, for example) might reduce the number of hours needed to complete the project, which in turn might reduce the project budget. This most often occurs when the schedule is the primary constraint on the project and the start or end dates cannot be changed.

When scope changes are requested, all areas of the project should be investigated to determine what the changes will impact. The project team should perform estimates of the impact and of the amount of time needed to make the change. Sometimes, however, the change request is so extensive that even the time to perform an estimate should be evaluated before proceeding. In other words, if the project team is busy working on estimates, they aren't working on the project. That means extensive change requests could impact the existing schedule because of the time and effort needed just to evaluate the change. Cases like these require you to make a determination or ask the change control board (CCB) to decide whether the change is important enough to allow the project team time to work on the estimates.

Changes in scope require an update to the project scope baseline. They might also require updates to the schedule, cost, or performance measurement baselines established during the Planning processes. When change is necessary, adjustments to the performance measurement baselines are made, documented, and distributed to the stakeholders as needed.

Always remember to update your stakeholders regarding the changes you're implementing and their impacts. They'll want to know how the changes impact the performance baselines, including the project costs, project schedule, project scope, and quality.

This process concludes the Monitoring and Controlling process groups. You'll look at the Closing processes in the next section.

Formulating Project Closeout

All good projects must come to an end, as the saying goes. Ideally, you've practiced all the topics I've talked about that have led up to this point, and you've delivered a successful project to the stakeholders and customers. You've also put some of the vital tools of project management into play—planning, executing, controlling, and communicating—to help you reach that goal.

But how do you know when a project has ended successfully? Delivering the product or service of the project doesn't mean it has been completed satisfactorily. Remember back in the opening chapters that I said a project is completed successfully when it meets or exceeds stakeholders' expectations and satisfies the goals of the project. During the Closing processes—Close Project and Contract Closure—you'll document the acceptance of the product of the project with a formal sign-off and file it with the project records for future reference. The formal sign-off is the way stakeholders indicate that the goals have been met and that the project meets or exceeds their expectations so that the project ends.

Characteristics of Closing

A few characteristics are common to all projects during the Closing processes. One is that the probability of completing the project is highest during this process and risk is lowest. You've already completed the majority of the work of the project—if not all of the work—so the probability of not finishing the project is very low.

Stakeholders have the least amount of influence during the Closing processes, while project managers have the greatest amount of influence. Costs are significantly lower during this process because the majority of the project work and spending has already occurred. Remember those cost S curves we talked about in the Cost Budgeting process? This is where they taper off as project spending comes to an end.

One last common characteristic of projects during closing is that weak matrix organizations tend to experience the least amount of stress during the Closing processes. This is because, in a weak matrix organization, the functional manager assigns all tasks (project related tasks, as well) so the team members have a job to return to once the project is completed and there's no change in reporting structure.

All projects do eventually come to an end. You'll now examine a few of the reasons for project endings before getting into the Close Project and Contract Closure processes.

Project Endings

Projects come to an end for several reasons:

- They're completed successfully.
- They're canceled or killed prior to completion.
- They evolve into ongoing operations and no longer exist as projects.

Four formal types of project endings exist that you might need to know for the exam:

- Addition
- Starvation
- Integration
- Extinction

You'll look at each of these ending types in detail in the following sections.

Addition

Projects that evolve into ongoing operations are considered projects that end because of *addition*; in other words, they become their own ongoing business unit. An example of this is the installation of an enterprise resource planning system. These systems are business management systems that integrate all areas of a business, including marketing, planning, manufacturing, sales, financials, and human resources. After the installation of the software, these systems can develop into their own business unit because ongoing operations, maintenance, and monitoring of the software require full-time staff. These systems usually evolve into an arm of the business reporting system that no one can live without once it's installed.

A project is considered a project when it meets these criteria: it is unique, has a definite beginning and ending date, and is temporary in nature. When a project becomes an ongoing operation, it is no longer a project.

Starvation

When resources are cut off from the project or are no longer provided to the project, it's starved prior to completing all the requirements, and you're left with an unfinished project on your hands. *Starvation* can happen for any number of reasons:

- Other projects come about and take precedence over the current project, thereby cutting the funding or resources for your project.
- The customer curtails an order.
- The project budget is reduced.
- A key resource quits.

Resource starving can include cutting back or withholding human resources, equipment and supplies, or money. In any case, if you're not getting the people, equipment, or money you need to complete the project, it's going to starve and probably end abruptly.

This is one of those cases where documentation becomes your best friend. Organizations tend to have short memories. As you move on to bigger and better projects, your memory regarding the specifics of the project will fade. Six months from now when someone important wonders why that project was never completed and begins the finger-pointing routine, the project documents will clearly outline the reasons why the project ended early. That's one of the reasons why project documentation is such an important function. I'll talk more about documenting project details shortly.

Integration

Integration occurs when the resources of the project—people, equipment, property, and supplies—are distributed to other areas in the organization or are assigned to other projects. Perhaps your organization begins to focus on other areas or other projects, and the next thing you know, functional managers come calling to retrieve their resources for other, more important things. Again, your project will come to an end due to lack of resources because they have been reassigned to other areas of the business or have been pulled from your project and assigned to another project.

The difference between starvation and integration is that starvation is the result of staffing, funding, or other resource cuts, while integration is the result of reassignment or redeployment of the resources.

Again, good documentation describing the circumstances that brought about the ending of a project because of integration should be archived with the project records for future reference.

Extinction

This is the best kind of project end because *extinction* means the project has been completed and accepted by the stakeholders. As such, it no longer exists because it had a definite ending date, the goals of the project were achieved, and the project was closed out.

 Real World Scenario

Pied Piper

Jerome Reed is the project manager for Pied Piper's newest software project. His team is working on a program that will integrate the organization's human resource information, including payroll records, leave-time accruals, contact information, and so on. His top two programmers, Brett and Kathy, are heading up the coding team and are in charge of the programming and testing activities.

Pied Piper recently hired a new CIO who started working with the company just a few weeks ago. Jerome is concerned about his human resources project. It was the former CIO's pet project, but he's not sure where it falls on the new CIO's radar screen.

Jerome is in the computer room checking out the new hardware that just arrived for his project. Liz Horowitz, the director of network operations, approaches Jerome.

"That's a nice piece of hardware," Liz comments.

"It sure is. This baby is loaded. It's going to process and serve up data to the users so fast they'll be asking us to upgrade all the servers."

Liz replies, "You're right about that. I've asked Richard to burn it in and load the software."

"What software?" Jerome asks.

"You know, the new customer relationship management software. The CIO hired some vendor she has worked with before to come in and install their CRM system here. She said it was our top priority. I knew this new server was already on order, and it happens to be sized correctly for the new CRM system."

"I purchased this server for the human resources project. What am I supposed to use for that?"

Liz answers, "I've got a server over there on the bottom of the third rack that might work, or maybe you can order another one. But you should take this up with the CIO. All I know is she authorized me to use this server. She understood I was taking it from your project, so maybe she's thinking about going another direction with the human resources project.

"You probably should know I also asked to have Brett and Kathy assigned to the CRM project. Even though it's a vendor project, it still requires some of our coders. The CIO wanted the best, and they're the best we've got. It shouldn't take them long to make the changes I need, and then you can have them back for your project. In the meantime, they can give directions to your other programmers so they can keep working."

"I'm going to go see whether the CIO is in," Jerome replies.

This is a case where Jerome's project ends by integration because of the reassignment of resources. The new CIO came on board and changed the direction and focus of the project priorities, making her new project a higher priority than the previous project. As a result, Jerome's hardware and his top two resources were reassigned to the new project. Had the CIO cut the resources and equipment on the original project altogether, it would have ended because of starvation.

Closing Out the Project

The key activity of the *Close Project* process is concerned with gathering project records and disseminating information to formalize the acceptance of the product, service, or project as well as to perform project closure. You'll want to review the project documents to make certain they are up-to-date. For example, perhaps some scope change requests were implemented that changed some of the characteristics of the final product. The project information you're collecting during this process should reflect the characteristics and specifications of the final product. Don't forget to update your resource assignments as well. Some team members will have come and gone over the course of the project; you need to double-check that all the resources and their roles and responsibilities are noted.

Once the project outcomes are documented, you'll request formal acceptance from the stakeholders or the customer. (I'll cover formal acceptance later when I talk about the outputs.) They're also interested in knowing whether the product or service of the project meets the goals the project set out to accomplish. If your documentation is up-to-date, you'll have the project results at hand to share with them.

The Close Project process is also concerned with analyzing the project management processes to determine their effectiveness and to document lessons learned concerning the project processes. And one of the other key functions of the Close Project process is to archive all project documents for historical reference. You can probably guess that Close Project belongs to the Project Integration Management Knowledge Area since this process touches so many areas of the project.

Every project requires closure. According to the *PMBOK Guide*, the completion of each project phase requires project closure as well.

Exam Spotlight

Project closure occurs at the end of each phase of the project in order to properly document project information and keep it safe for future reference. You shouldn't wait until project completion to perform the Close Project process but rather perform it at the end of every phase, no matter whether the project phase was completed successfully or ended for some other reason.

Close Project Inputs

The Close Project process gathers all the project records and verifies that they are up-to-date and accurate. The project records must correctly identify the final specifications of the product or service the project set out to produce. Close Project is the place to ensure that this information accurately reflects the true results of the project.

The six inputs to the Close Project process are as follows:

- Project management plan
- Contract documentation
- Enterprise environmental factors
- Organizational process assets
- Work performance information
- Deliverables

I've talked about all of these inputs with the exception of contract documentation. Contract documentation includes the contract and any other information, such as contract changes, product descriptions, technical specifications, and so on.

Close Project Tools and Techniques

You've seen all of the tools and techniques of Close Project in other processes:

- Project management methodology
- Project management information system (PMIS)
- Expert judgment

The project management methodology should outline processes for both project and administrative closeout. The PMIS and expert judgment are used to perform these processes.

Close Project Outputs

Sometimes you'll work on projects where everything just clicks. Your project team functions at the performing stage, the customers and stakeholders are happy, and things just fall into place according to plan. I often find it difficult to close projects that have progressed particularly well, just because I don't want them to end. Believe it or not, the majority of your projects can fall into this category if you practice good project management techniques and exercise those great communication skills.

The Close Project process has the following outputs:

- Administrative closure procedure
- Contract closure procedure
- Final product, service, or result
- Organizational process assets updates

You'll take a brief look at each in the following sections.

Administrative Closure Procedure

Administrative closure procedures involve collecting all the records associated with the project, analyzing the project success (or failure), documenting and gathering lessons learned, and archiving project records. Keep in mind that when projects are performed under contract, the archiving of financial records is especially important. These records might need to be accessed if there are payment disputes, so you need to know where they are and how they were filed. Projects with large financial expenditures also require particular attention to the archiving of financial records for the same reasons. Financial information is especially useful when estimating future projects, so again, make sure to archive the information so it's easily accessible.

All of these documents should be indexed for reference and filed in a safe place. Don't forget to include electronic databases and electronic documents as part of your project archives as well. These records can be stored on a network drive or copied onto a CD that's kept with the project binder.

Administrative closure procedures also document the project team members' and stakeholders' roles and responsibilities in performing this process. According to the *PMBOK Guide*, this should include the processes and methodologies for defining the following:

- Approval requirements of the stakeholders for project deliverables and changes to deliverables.
- Assuring and confirming that the project meets the requirements of the stakeholders, customers, and sponsor. Documenting necessary actions to verify that the deliverables have been accepted and exit criteria have been met.
- Assuring and confirming that the exit criteria for the project are satisfied.

Contract Closure Procedure

Contract closure procedures, like the administrative closure procedures, document the roles and responsibilities of the project team members and stakeholders in closing out the contract. This procedure details the methodology you use to assure that contract exit criteria and contract conditions have been satisfied. I'll talk more about contract closure in the section "Contract Closure."

Final Product, Service, or Result

The name of this output is somewhat misleading. This actually refers to the acceptance of the final product, service, or result and the turnover of the product to the organization. This usually requires a formal sign-off (I'll talk about that next) and, in the case of a project performed on contract, definitely requires a formal sign-off or receipt indicating acceptance of the project.

Formal acceptance includes distributing notice of the acceptance of the product or service of the project by the stakeholders, customer, or project sponsor to stakeholders and customers. You should require formal sign-off indicating that those signing accept the product of the project.

The final product, service, or result is concerned with obtaining formal acceptance; organizational process assets involves documenting and archiving formal acceptance.

Organizational Process Assets Updates

The organizational process assets output is where the formal sign-off of the acceptance of the product is documented, collected, and archived for future reference. Documenting formal acceptance is important because it signals the official closure of the project, and it is your proof that the project was completed satisfactorily.

Another function of sign-off is that it kicks off the beginning of the warranty period. Sometimes project managers or vendors will warranty their work for a certain time period after completing the project. Projects that produce software programs, for example, might be warranted from bugs for a 60- or 90-day time frame from the date of implementation or acceptance. Typically in the case of software projects, bugs are fixed for free during the warranty period. Watch out, because users will try to squeeze new requirements into the "bug" category mold. If you offer a warranty, it's critical that the warranty spells out exactly what is covered and what is not.

This is also where the other project records and files are collected and archived. This includes the project planning documents (project scope statement, budget, schedule, risk responses, quality plan and baselines, and so on), change records and logs, issue logs, and so on.

Project closure documents are included in this output. These include documentation showing the transfer of the product of the project to the organization (or department responsible for ongoing maintenance and support). If your project is canceled or ends prematurely, you should document the reasons for its premature end as well as the procedures for transferring the completed and uncompleted deliverables.

Lessons learned are used to document the successes and failures of the project. As an example, lessons learned document the reasons why specific corrective actions were taken, their outcomes, the causes of performance variances, unplanned risks that occurred, mistakes that were made and could have been avoided, and so on.

Unfortunately, sometimes projects do fail. You can learn lessons from failed projects as well as from successful projects, and you should document this information for future reference. Most project managers, however, do not document lessons learned. The reason for this is that employees don't want to admit to making mistakes or learning from mistakes made during the project. And they do not want their name associated with failed projects or even with mishaps on successful projects.

Lessons learned can be some of the most valuable information you'll take away from a project. We can all learn from our experiences, and what better way to have even more success on your next project than to review a similar past project's lessons learned document? But lessons learned will be there only if you document them now. I strongly recommend you not skip this step.

You and your management team will have to work to create an atmosphere of trust and assurance that lessons learned are not reasons for dismissing employees but are learning opportunities that benefit all those associated with the project. Lessons learned allow you to carry knowledge gained on this project to other projects you'll work on going forward. They'll also prevent repeat mistakes in the future if you take the time to review the project documents and lessons learned prior to undertaking your new project.

Post-implementation audits aren't an official output, but they are a good idea. These go hand in hand with lessons learned because they examine the project from beginning to end and look at what went right and what went wrong. They evaluate the project goals and determine whether the product or service of the project satisfies the objectives. Post-implementation audits also examine the activities and project processes to determine whether improvements are possible on future projects.

Organizations might conduct post-implementation audits instead of lessons learned sessions. Documenting and gathering information during this procedure can serve the same function as lessons learned if you're honest and include all the good, the bad, and the ugly. Let's hope there's very little ugly.

 Real World Scenario

Cimarron Research Group

The Cimarron Research Group researches and develops organic pesticides for use on food crops. It is a medium-sized company and has established a project management office (PMO) to manage all aspects of project work. The PMO consists of project managers and administrative staff who assist with information handling, filing, and disbursement.

Terri Roberts is the project manager for a project that has just closed. Terri diligently filed all the pertinent project documents as the project progressed and has requested the research files and engineering notes from the director of engineering to include them with the project archives as well. All information regarding the research on this project is included with the project archives. The engineering department chooses to keep its own set of research records as well, but it's important to keep a copy of these notes with the project archives so that all the information about the project is in one place.

Terri's assistant has indexed all the project documents and recently sent notice of formal acceptance and approval of this project to the stakeholders, project sponsor, and management team. This notice officially closes the project. The next step is to archive the files onto CDs and store them.

Closing Out the Contract

Contracts have life cycles of their own—just like projects. I talked about the contract life cycles in Chapter 9. As such, contracts come to a close just as projects come to a close. As you might guess, there is a process that deals with contract closings; it's called Contract Closure.

The *Contract Closure* process is concerned with completing and settling the terms of the contract. It supports the Close Project process because the Contract Closure process determines whether the work described in the contract was completed accurately and satisfactorily. This is called *product verification*. Projects that have multiple deliverables might have contracts for some of the deliverables but not all. Obviously, this process applies only to those phases, deliverables, or portions of the project that were performed under contract.

Contract Closure updates records and archives the information for future reference. These records detail the final results of the work of the project. I'll talk about the specifics of this when I cover the Contract Closure outputs.

Contracts might have specific terms or conditions for completion and closeout. You should be aware of these terms or conditions so that project closure isn't held up because you missed an important detail. If you are not administering the contract yourself, be certain to ask your procurement department whether there are any special conditions that you should know about so that your project team doesn't inadvertently delay contract or project closure.

Close Project verifies and documents the project outcomes just like the Contract Closure process. Keep in mind that not all projects are performed under contract, so not all projects require Contract Closure. However, all projects do require the Close Project process. Since verification and documentation of the project outcomes occur in both of these processes, projects that are performed under contract need to have project results verified only one time.

Exam Spotlight

For the exam, remember that product verification performed during the Closing processes determines whether all of the work of the project was completed correctly according to the contract terms and satisfactorily according to stakeholder expectations, whereas product documentation is verified and accepted during the Scope Verification process. One more note: when projects end prematurely, the Scope Verification process is where the level of detail concerning the amount of work completed gets documented.

Contract Closure Inputs

The Contract Closure process has four inputs:

- Procurement management plan
- Contract management plan
- Contract documentation
- Contract Closure procedure

I've discussed all these inputs before, but you should know a few more things about contract documentation for this process. Contract documentation includes the contract itself and all the supporting documents that go along with it. These might include things such as the WBS, the project schedule, change control documents, technical documents, financial and payment records, quality control inspection results, and so on. This information—along with all the other information gathered during the project—is filed once the project is closed out so that anyone considering a future project of similar scope can reference what was done.

 Contract documentation is an input to both the Close Project and Contract Closure processes.

Contract Closure Tools and Techniques

The Contract Closure process has two tools and techniques: procurement audits and records management system. The records management system here serves the same function as the records management system I talked about in the discussion of the Contract Administration process in Chapter 9. *Procurement audits* are reviews of procurement processes to determine whether they are meeting the right needs and are being performed correctly and according to standards. The *PMBOK Guide* says procurement audits are concerned with reviewing the procurement process, starting with the Plan Purchases and Acquisitions process all the way through Contract Administration.

The primary purpose of the procurement audit is to identify lessons learned during the procurement process. Procurement audits examine the procurement process to determine areas of improvement and to identify flawed processes or procedures. This allows you to reuse the successful processes on other procurement items for this project, on future projects, or elsewhere in the organization. It also alerts you to problems in the process so that you don't repeat them.

Procurement audits might be used by either the buyer or the vendor, or by both, as an opportunity for improvement. Documenting the lessons learned—including the successes and failures that occurred—allows you to improve other procurement processes currently underway on this project or other projects. It also gives you the opportunity to improve the process for future projects.

Contract Closure Outputs

One of the purposes of the Contract Closure process is to provide formal notice to the seller—usually in written form—that the contract is complete. The output of Contract Closure that deals with this is called *closed contracts*. This is *formal acceptance and closure* of the contract. It's your responsibility as project manager to document the formal acceptance of the contract. Many times the provisions for formalizing acceptance and closing the contract are spelled out in the contract.

If you have a procurement department that handles contract administration, they will expect you to inform them when the contract is completed and will in turn follow the formal procedures to let the seller know the contract is complete. However, you'll still note the contract completion in your copy of the project records.

Depending on the terms of the contract, early termination (whether by agreement, via default, or for cause) might result in additional charges to the buyer. Be certain to note the reasons for early termination in your contract documentation.

The other output of Contract Closure is organizational process updates. This includes updating the contract file, deliverables acceptance, and lessons learned. The *contract file* is simply a file of all the contract records and supporting documents. These records should be indexed for easy reference and included as part of the project files in the Close Project process.

Exam Spotlight

The *PMBOK Guide* shows the Close Project process being performed before the Contract Closure process. In practice, you will likely close out the contract before closing the project and archiving the project documents. Note that the contract file (part of the organizational process assets update) output of the Contract Closure process is an input to the Close Project process (called *contract documentation*).

This process is your organization's way of formally accepting the product of the project from the vendor and closing out the contract. The deliverable acceptance portion of the organizational process updates includes the formal written notice from the buyer that the deliverables are acceptable and satisfactory or have been rejected. If the product or service does not meet expectations, the vendor will need to correct the problems before you issue a formal acceptance notice. Ideally, quality audits have been performed during the course of the project, and the vendor was given the opportunity to make corrections earlier in the process than the Closing stage. It's not a good idea to wait until the very end of the project and then spring all the problems and issues on the vendor at once. It's much more efficient to discuss problems with your vendor as the project progresses because it provides the opportunity for correction when the problems occur.

Lessons learned include information and documentation about what worked well and what didn't work well regarding the procurement processes. You can use this information on future projects to improve performance and prevent inefficiencies.

Releasing Project Team Members

Releasing project team members is not an official process. However, it should be noted that at the conclusion of the project, you will release your project team members, and they will go back to their functional managers or be assigned to a new project if you're working in a matrix type organization.

You will want to keep the functional managers or other project managers informed as you get closer to project completion so that they have time to adequately plan for the return of their employees. Start letting them know a few months ahead of time what the schedule looks like and how soon they can plan on using their employees on new projects. This gives the other managers the ability to start planning activities and scheduling activity dates.

Project Case Study: New Kitchen Heaven Retail Store

Dirk strolls into your office maintaining his formal and dignified manners as always and then sits down in the chair beside your desk.

"I just want to congratulate you on a job well done," he says. "The grand opening was a success, and the store had a better-than-expected week the first week. I'm impressed you were able to pull this off and get the store opened prior to the Garden and Home Show. That was the key to the great opening week."

"Thank you, Dirk. Lots of people put in a lot of hard work and extra hours to get this job done. I'm glad you're happy with the results."

"I thought the banner with our logo, 'Great Gadgets for People Interested in Great Food,' was a wonderful touch."

"That was Jill's idea. She had some great ideas that made the festivities successful. As you know, though," you continue, "we did have some problems on this project. Fortunately, they weren't insurmountable, but I think we learned a thing or two during this project that we can carry forward to other projects."

"Like what?" Dirk asks.

"We should have contracted with Gomez Construction sooner so that we didn't have to pay overtime. We had a very generous budget, so the overtime expense didn't impact this project, but it might impact the next one.

"And we came fairly close to having a hardware disaster on our hands. Next time, we should order the equipment sooner, test it here at headquarters first, and then ship it out to the site after we know everything is working correctly."

"Good ideas. But that's old news. Now that this project is over, I'd like to get you started on the next project. We're going to introduce cooking classes in all of our retail stores. The focus is the home chef, and we might just call the classes the Home Chef Pro series. We'll offer basic classes all the way to professional series classes if the project is a hit. We'll bring in guest chefs from the local areas to give demos and teach some of the classes as well."

"I'm very interested in taking on this project and can't wait to get started. I'm thrilled that you want me to head this up. But I do have a few things here to wrap up before I start work on the new project," you reply.

Dirk says, "The project is over. The grand opening was a success. It's time to move on. Let Jill take over now; the retail stores are her responsibility."

"Jill has taken over the day-to-day operations. However, I've got to finish collecting the project information, close out the contract with Gomez, and make the final payment. Jake verified that all the work was completed correctly and to his satisfaction. Then I need to publish the formal acceptance notice to all of the stakeholders via email. I will also create a document that outlines those things I told you earlier about that we should remember and reference during the next project; that document is called *lessons learned*. Then after all those things are completed, all of the project records need to be indexed and archived. I can have all that done by the end of the week and will be free starting Monday to work on requirements gathering and the charter document for the new project."

"This is just like the planning process discussion we got into with the tree, the breakdown structure thing, and all the planning, I suspect. I do have to admit all the planning paid off. I'll give you until the end of the week to close out this project. Come see me Monday to get started on Home Chef Pro."

Project Case Study Checklist

Scope Verification

- Verified work results

Perform Quality Control

- Assured quality requirements were met

Close Project

- Product verification (work was correct and satisfactory)

- Collecting project documents

- Disseminating final acceptance notice

- Documenting lessons learned

- Archiving project records

Contract Closure

- Product verification (work was correct and satisfactory)

- Formal acceptance and closure

Celebrate!

I think it's a good idea to hold a celebration at the conclusion of a successfully completed project. The project team should celebrate their accomplishment, and you should officially recognize their efforts and thank them for their participation. Any number of ideas come to mind here—a party, a trip to a ball game, pizza and sodas at lunchtime, and so on. This shouldn't be the only time you've recognized your team, as discussed during the Team Development process, but now is the time to officially close the project and thank your team members. Even if no funds are available for a formal celebration, your heartfelt "thank you" can go a long way with the members of your team. It's tough for team members to remain disgruntled, and it's easier to revive them when they know their efforts are appreciated.

A celebration helps team members formally recognize the project end and brings closure to the work they've done. It also encourages them to remember what they've learned and to start thinking about how their experiences will benefit them and the organization during the next project.

Understanding How This Applies to Your Next Project

The focus of this chapter was twofold: verifying and accepting the work (or results) of the project and closing out the project. Verifying and accepting the work of the project shouldn't be a mind-boggling task at this point if you've been following the project management processes all along. For example, you should monitor and inspect deliverables as they're completed. At project's end, there might additional testing or inspection needed to be certain all the deliverables work together (if they're required to do so), but many issues or problems you've discovered regarding the deliverables should have been discovered by now. However, before you begin to barrage me with emails, let me say that exceptions do exist. It isn't always possible to inspect the work of the project as it progresses because some projects aren't complete until the last piece of the puzzle is put into place. In that case, inspection, testing, and deliverables acceptance won't occur until the end of the project. But again, if you've used sound Monitoring and Controlling tools and techniques to monitor the processes, ideally you won't encounter any big surprises at this stage.

Scope Change Control is absolutely essential for all projects. Time and again I've seen changes to scope end up pitting stakeholders against the project team because the requirements weren't defined adequately in the first place and because neither party clearly understand what was being requested. Scope changes can kill a project by significantly delaying the finish date or by so drastically modifying the original objective of the project that it no longer resembles what it set out to accomplish. I try to keep the questions regarding scope change simple, as in "Do you absolutely have to have this to meet the objective of this project?" That isn't always easy for people to understand because we often confuse wants with needs. So, I might come up with an analogy they can relate to—something like this: "Let's say your one and only culinary skill is boiling water. Do you really need a designer stove with dual fuel options and a built-in warming oven to boil water? Wouldn't a simple store-brand stove work?"

Closing out the project should always include a formal sign-off (from the project sponsor and key stakeholders at a minimum) that the work of the project is acceptable and complete. Also, you've probably experienced, as I have, stakeholders with short-term memory lapses. I'll get to the end of the project and find the stakeholder has a list of additional requirements longer than their arm. Again, some of this goes back to assuring requirements are accurately defined during the Planning processes and that ongoing communication regarding project status, along with feedback from the stakeholders, is occurring on a regular basis. Another key here is making certain you are managing stakeholder expectations throughout the project. You might indeed have identified all the requirements and accurately documented the objective of the project. But if the stakeholder had expectations that weren't captured or that begin to take shape after the work of the project begins, you could end up with a very unhappy stakeholder on your hands and, potentially, a failed project. In my experience, stakeholder expectations tend to stray midway through the project because they are beginning to see some completed or nearly completed deliverables at this point, and new possibilities for the product of the project begin to develop that they hadn't thought of during the Planning stage. It's similar to buying a new house based on blueprints and then going on that first walk-through when the framing is finished. It's during walk-through that you think, "Gee, I thought that closet was bigger than this." Tune in to what your stakeholders are saying and get at the basis of their questions (dig deep) so that there are no hidden expectations and you're able to manage any new expectations that pop up.

Summary

I closed out the Monitoring and Controlling process group with this chapter by covering the Perform Quality Control, Scope Verification, and Scope Control processes.

Perform Quality Control monitors work results to see whether they fulfill the quality standards outlined in the quality management plan. Perform Quality Control should occur throughout the life of the project. It uses many tools and techniques. Inspection measures results to determine whether the results conform to the quality standards. Attributes are measurements that either conform or do not conform. Control charts measure the results of processes over time, and Pareto charts are histograms that rank-order the most important quality factors by their frequency over time. You should not adjust processes that are in control; however, you can change these processes to realize improvements.

Scope Verification involves verifying and accepting work results, while Scope Control is concerned with controlling changes to project scope.

Project closure is the most often neglected process of all the project management processes. The two processes in the Closing process group are Close Project and Contract Closure. The four most important tasks of closure are as follows:

- Checking the work for completeness and accuracy

- Documenting formal acceptance

- Disseminating project closure information

- Archiving records and lessons learned

Close Project involves checking that the work of the project was completed correctly and to the satisfaction of the stakeholders. Documenting formal acceptance of the product of the project is an important aspect of project closure as well. This assures that the stakeholder or customer is satisfied with the work and that it meets their needs.

Projects come to an end in one of four ways: addition, starvation, integration, or extinction. Addition is when projects evolve into their own business unit. Starvation happens because the project is starved of its resources. Integration occurs when resources are taken from the existing project and dispersed back into the organization or assigned to other projects. And extinction is the best end because the project was completed, accepted, and closed.

Close Project is performed at the end of each phase of the project as well as at the end of the project. Close Project involves documenting formal acceptance and disseminating notice of acceptance to the stakeholders, customer, and others. All documentation gathered during the project and collected during this process is archived and saved for reference purposes on future projects.

Contract Closure is performed after Close Project and is concerned with settling the contract and completing the contract according to its terms. Its primary outputs include the contract file and formal acceptance and closure (both are components of the organizational process assets update).

Lessons learned document the successes and failures of the project and of the procurement processes. Many times lessons learned are not documented because staff members do not want to assign their names to project errors or failures. You and your management team need to work together to assure employees that lessons learned are not exercises used for disciplinary purposes but benefit both the employee and the organization. Documenting what you've learned from past experiences lets you carry this forward to new projects so that the same errors are not repeated. It also allows you to incorporate new methods of performing activities that you learned on past projects.

Exam Essentials

Be able to name the tools and techniques of Perform Quality Control.   The tools and techniques of the of Perform Quality Control process are cause-and-effect diagram, control charts, flowcharting, histogram, Pareto chart, run chart, scatter diagram, statistical sampling, inspection, and defect repair review.

Name the purpose of the Scope Verification process.   The purpose of Scope Verification is to determine whether the work is complete and whether it satisfies the project objectives.

Be able to name the purpose of the Closing processes.   The purpose of the Closing processes is to verify that the work was satisfactorily completed, to disseminate information, to document formal acceptance, to archive records, to close out the contract, and to document lessons learned.

Be able to describe product verification.   Product verification confirms that all the work of the project performed on contract was completed accurately and to the satisfaction of the stakeholder.

Be able to name the primary activity of the Closing processes.   The primary activity of the Closing processes is to distribute information that formalizes project completion.

Be able to describe when the Close Project process is performed.   Close Project is performed at the close of each project phase and at the close of the project.

Be able to define the purpose for lessons learned.   The purpose of lessons learned is to describe the project successes and failures and to use the information learned on future projects.

Key Terms

I've discussed in detail the processes you'll use while closing out your project. You need to understand and use each of these processes to be an effective project manager. You'll need to know them by the names used in the PMBOK to be successful on the exam.

Close Project	Scope Control
Contract Closure	Scope Verification
Perform Quality Control	

You've learned a lot of new key words in this chapter. PMI has worked hard to develop and define standard project management terms that apply across industries. Here is a list of some of the terms you came across in this chapter:

addition	prevention
attributes	procurement audits
common causes of variances	product verification
contract file	rework
control charts	run charts
extinction	scatter diagrams
formal acceptance and closure	starvation
inspection	statistical sampling
integration	technical performance measurements
Pareto charts	tolerable results

Review Questions

1.   You are working on a project that was proceeding well until a manufacturing glitch occurred that requires corrective action. It turns out the glitch was an unintentional enhancement to the product, and the marketing people are absolutely crazy about its potential. The corrective action is canceled, and you continue to produce the product with the newly discovered enhancement. As the project manager, you know that a change has occurred to the product scope because the glitch changed the characteristics of the product. Which of the following statements is true?

   A.   Changes to product scope are reflected in the project scope.

   B.   Changes to product scope are reflected in the integrated change control plan.

   C.   Changes to product scope are a result of changes to the product description.

   D.   Changes to product scope are a result of corrective action.

2.   You are working on a project that was proceeding well until a manufacturing glitch occurred that requires corrective action. It turns out the glitch was an unintentional enhancement to the product, and the marketing people are absolutely crazy about its potential. The corrective action is canceled, and you continue to produce the product with the newly discovered enhancement. As the project manager, you know that a change has occurred to the project scope. Which of the following statements is true?

   A.   Project scope changes do not require CCB approval.

   B.   Performance measurement baselines might be affected by scope changes.

   C.   Project scope change uses inspection to determine whether change has occurred.

   D.   Project scope change uses workarounds to correct unexpected problems with scope change.

3.   Your project has experienced some changes to the agreed-upon WBS elements. The changes were approved through the proper change control process. The WBS changes might in turn require which of the following?

   A.   Scope changes

   B.   Cost changes

   C.   Schedule revisions

   D.   Risk response changes

4.   You are a project manager for Dakota Software Consulting Services. You're working with a major retailer that offers its products through mail-order catalogs. It is interested in knowing customer characteristics, the amounts of first-time orders, and similar information. The stakeholders have accepted the project scope. Work has begun on the project, and you're confirming some of the initial work results with the stakeholders. You've asked for acceptance of the work results. Which process are you in?

   A.   Quality Assurance

   B.   Quality Control

   C.   Scope Verification

   D.   Close Project

5. You are the project manager for a top-secret software project for an agency of the United States government. Your mission—should you choose to accept it—is to complete the project using internal resources. The reason is that finding contractors with top-secret clearances takes quite a bit of time, and waiting for clearances would jeopardize the implementation date. Your programmers are 80 percent of the way through the programming and testing work when your agency appoints a new executive director. Slowly but surely your programmers are taken off this project and reassigned to the executive director's hot new project. Which of the following type of project ending is this?

    A. Starvation

    B. Extinction

    C. Addition

    D. Integration

6. You are the project manager for a top-secret software project for an agency of the United States government. Your mission—should you choose to accept it—is to complete the project using internal resources. The reason is that getting top-secret clearances for contractors takes quite a bit of time, and waiting for clearances would jeopardize the implementation date. Your programmers are 80 percent of the way through the programming and testing work when your agency appoints a new executive director. Your programmers are siphoned off this project to work on the executive director's hot new project. Which of the following addresses the purpose of Scope Verification in this case?

    A. Scope Verification determines the correctness and completion of all the work.

    B. Scope Verification documents the level and degree of completion.

    C. Scope Verification determines whether the project results comply with quality standards.

    D. Scope Verification documents the correctness of the work according to stakeholders' expectations.

7. You are a project manager for Cinema Snicker Productions. Your company specializes in producing comedy films for the big screen. Your latest project has just been canceled because of budget cuts. Which of the following statements is true?

    A. This project ended due to starvation because the funding was cut off.

    B. This project ended due to integration because the resources were distributed elsewhere.

    C. This project ended due to starvation because the resources were distributed elsewhere.

    D. This project ended due to integration because the funding was cut off.

8. You are a project manager for Cinema Snicker Productions. Your company specializes in producing comedy films for the big screen. Your latest project has just been completed and accepted. You've been given your next project, which starts right away. Which of the following statements is true?

    A. This project ended due to extinction because it was completed and accepted.

    B. This project ended due to integration because it was completed and accepted and the project manager moved on to a new project.

    C. This project ended due to addition because it was completed and accepted and archived into the company's catalog of available films.

    D. This project ended due to integration because it was completed and accepted.

9. Which of the following processes are performed in the Closing process group and in what order?

    A. Contract Closure and then Close Project

    B. Scope Verification and then Close Project

    C. Contract Closure and then Scope Verification

    D. Close Project and then Contract Closure

10. You are a project manager for Dutch Harbor Consulting. Your latest project involves the upgrade of an organization's operating system on 236 servers. You performed this project under contract. You are in the Contract Closure process and know that you should document which of the following? (Choose the best response.)

    A. Administrative closure procedures

    B. Contract closure procedures

    C. Formal acceptance

    D. Product verification

11. You are a project manager for Dutch Harbor Consulting. Your latest project involves the upgrade of an organization's operating system on 236 servers. You performed this project under contract. You are in the Closing process and know that product verification is for what purpose?

    A. To verify the goals of the project and ensure that the product of the project is complete

    B. To evaluate all the work of the project and compare the results to project scope

    C. To verify that all the work was completed correctly and satisfactorily

    D. To evaluate project goals and ensure that the product of the project meets the requirements

12. You are a project manager for Dutch Harbor Consulting. Your latest project involves the upgrade of an organization's operating system on 236 servers. You performed this project under contract. You are in the Contract Closure process and have reviewed the contracting process to identify lessons learned. What is the name of the tool and technique you used to perform this function?

    A. Procurement audits

    B. Performance reviews

    C. Performance audits

    D. Procurement reviews

13. You are a project manager for Penguin Software. Your company creates custom software programs for hospitals and large dental offices. You have just completed a project and are gathering the documentation of the product of the project. This might include all of the following except _____.

    A. technical specifications

    B. electronic files

    C. organizational process assets

    D. enterprise environmental factors

14. The outputs of the Close Project process include all of the following except for which one?

   A. Administrative closure procedure

   B. Formal acceptance

   C. Lessons learned

   D. Closed contracts

15. You have collected the work performance information for your project to be included in the project archives. What is the purpose of the work performance information?

   A. The work performance information is used as part of the formal acceptance process to verify contract expenditures.

   B. The work performance information is used to determine the status of project activities and make certain the project goals and objectives are met.

   C. The work performance information is included in the project archive documentation after its accuracy is confirmed.

   D. The work performance information is used as historical information for future projects that are similar in scope to this project.

16. Your project was just completed. Because of some unfortunate circumstances, the project was delayed, causing cost overruns at the end of the project. Which of the following statements is true?

   A. You should document the circumstances as lessons learned.

   B. You should pay particular attention to archiving the financial records for this project.

   C. Your project ended because of starvation because of the cost overruns.

   D. You should document the circumstances surrounding the project completion during the Scope Verification process.

17. Your project was just completed. Because of some unfortunate circumstances, the project was delayed, causing cost overruns at the end of the project. This information might be useful on future projects in all of the following activities except for which one?

   A. Cost estimating

   B. Allocating resources

   C. Product verification

   D. Activity estimating

18. Your project was just completed, accepted, and closed. As is customary for your organization, you conduct a post-implementation audit. The purpose of this audit includes all of the following except for which one?

   A. Evaluating project goals and comparing them to the project's product

   B. Reviewing successes and failures

   C. Documenting the acceptance of the work results

   D. Documenting possible improvements for future projects

19. Contract documentation is an input to both the Close Project and Contract Closure processes. Contract documentation might include all of the following except for which one?

    A. Supporting documents

    B. Contract changes

    C. Financial documents

    D. Procurement audit documents

20. Procurement audits review which of the following?

    A. The procurement process from Procurement Planning through Contract Administration

    B. The contract administration process from Solicitation Planning through Contract Administration

    C. The procurement process from Procurement Planning through Contract Closure

    D. The contract administration process from Solicitation Planning through Contract Closure

Answers to Review Questions

1. A. Changes to product scope should be reflected in the project scope.

2. B. A project scope change affects the performance measurement baselines, which might include schedule baselines and cost baselines.

3. C. WBS element changes are scope changes. Schedule revisions are often required as a result of scope changes.

4. C. The Scope Verification process is concerned with the acceptance of work results. It also formalizes the acceptance of the project scope.

5. D. Integration occurs when resources, equipment, or property are reassigned or redeployed back to the organization or to another project.

6. B. Scope Verification should document the level and degree of completion of the project. If you come back at a later date and restart this project, Scope Verification will describe how far the project progressed and give you an idea of where to start.

7. A. Starvation occurs because the project no longer receives the resources needed to continue. Resources could include people, equipment, money, and the like.

8. A. Extinction is the best type of project end because it means the project was completed successfully and accepted by the sponsor or customer.

9. D. Close Project and Contract Closure are the processes in the Closing process group and are performed in that order.

10. C. The project manager is responsible for documenting the formal acceptance of the work of the contract. This should be done during Contract Closure when projects are performed under contract or during Close Project if no work was performed under contract. In cases where part of the work was performed under contract and part with in-house staff, formal acceptance should occur in both of these processes.

11. C. Product verification is performed by the buyer and examines all the work of the project and verifies that the work was completed correctly and satisfactorily.

12. A. Procurement audits are used to review the procurement process and identify and document any lessons learned during the procurement process for future reference.

13. D. Enterprise environmental factors is an input to the Close Project process and wouldn't be included in the documentation of the product of the project.

14. D. Closed contracts are an output of the Contract Closure process. Formal acceptance is part of the final product, service, or result output. Lessons learned are part of organizational process assets updates.

15. B. The work performance information is reviewed to determine the status of project activities and make certain the project goals and objectives are met. This is an input to the Close Project process.

16. A. Lessons learned document the experiences, successes, and failures that occurred during this project for future reference. There isn't enough information in the question to determine whether B or D is correct. C is not correct because the project was completed.

17. C. Product verification involves examining the work of the project for completeness and correctness. This process occurs on the existing project and isn't of much benefit to future projects because you'll perform product verification on future project work at the close of the project. By definition, a project is unique and creates a unique product or service.

18. C. Post-implementation audits are similar to lessons learned in that they review and document the project successes and failures, look for possible improvements for future projects, and evaluate the project goals and compare these to the end product.

19. D. Procurement audits are a tool and technique of Contract Closure and not an input. Contract documentation might include all of the other options shown as well as the contract itself, technical documentation, quality inspection reports related to the contract, and so on.

20. A. According to the *PMBOK Guide*, the procurement audit examines the procurement process from Procurement Planning through Contract Administration.

Chapter

12

Applying Professional Responsibility

THE PMP EXAM CONTENT FROM THE PRO-FESSIONAL AND SOCIAL RESPONSIBILITY PERFORMANCE DOMAIN COVERED IN THIS CHAPTER INCLUDES THE FOLLOWING:

- ✓ Ensure Individual Integrity
- ✓ Contribute to the Project Management Knowledge Base
- ✓ Enhance Personal Professional Competence
- ✓ Promote Interaction Among Stakeholders

Congratulations! You've made terrific progress and are well equipped to take the Project Management Professional (PMP) exam. I've covered all of the *PMBOK Guide* process groups, so the good news is you don't have any more inputs, tools and techniques, outputs, or formulas to memorize. However, the PMP exam will include one final area: professional responsibility.

Once you've obtained the PMP designation, you have an obligation to maintain integrity, apply your subject matter knowledge and project management knowledge, and maintain the code of conduct published by the PMI. You'll also be required to balance the interests and needs of stakeholders with the organization's needs. The exam might include questions on any of these topics.

As a project manager, you'll find yourself in many unique situations, different organizations, and possibly even different countries. Even if you never get involved in international project management, you will still come in contact with people from different cultures and backgrounds than yours. If you work as a contract project manager, you'll be exposed to many different organizations that each has its own cultures and ways of doing things. You should always strive to act in a professional, courteous manner in these situations.

I'll talk about each of these topics in this chapter.

Ensuring Integrity

As a project manager, one of your professional responsibilities is to ensure integrity of the project management process, the product, and your own personal conduct. I've spent the majority of this book discussing how to achieve project management integrity by following the project management processes. Now you'll focus on accurately ensuring the integrity of the product.

A product that has integrity is one that is complete and sound or fit for use.

Correctly applying the project management processes you've learned will ensure the integrity of the product. The effective execution of the Planning, Executing, and Monitoring and Controlling processes, including documenting scope, performing quality inspections, measuring performance, and taking corrective actions, will ensure that a quality product is produced that satisfies the requirements of the stakeholders (and the project plan). And as you learned in Chapter 11, "Controlling Work Results and Closing Out the Project," you will seek acceptance of the product from the stakeholders and customer during the Closing process group.

There are several facets of integrity including personal integrity, avoiding conflict of interest situations, and professionalism. You'll look at each of these next.

Personal Integrity

Personal integrity means sticking to an ethical code. As a certified Project Management Professional, you are required to adhere to the PMI's *Project Management Professional Code of Professional Conduct*. You can find a copy of this code at the PMI website at www.pmi.org.

You should read and understand this code because you will be agreeing to adhere to its terms as part of the certification process. One of the aspects of personal integrity includes your truthfulness about your PMP application and certification, your qualifications, and the continuing reports you provide to PMI to maintain your certification.

Exam Spotlight

I recommend reading the *PMP Code of Professional Conduct* as part of your project management studies.

Truthfulness and integrity involve not only information regarding your own background and experience, but information regarding the project circumstances as well. For example, let's say you're a project manager working on contract. Part of your compensation consists of a bonus based on total project billing. Now let's suppose your project is finishing sooner than anticipated, and this means your personal profit will decrease by $1,500. Should you stretch the work to meet the original contracted amount so that your personal bonus comes in at the full amount even though your project team is finished? I think you know the answer is of course not.

Your personal gain should never be a consideration when billing a customer or completing a project. Personal gain should never be a factor in any project decision. If the project finishes sooner than planned, you should bill the customer for the work completed, not for the full contracted amount. Compromising the project for the sake of your personal gain shows a lack of integrity, which could ultimately cost you your PMP status and even your job.

Conflict of Interest

Another area the *PMP Code of Professional Conduct* discusses is your responsibility to report to the stakeholders, customers, or others any actions or circumstances that could be construed as a *conflict of interest*.

A conflict of interest is when you put your personal interests above the interests of the project or when you use your influence to cause others to make decisions in your favor without regard for the project outcome. In other words, your personal interests take precedence over your professional obligations, and you make decisions that allow you to personally benefit regardless of the outcome of the project. You'll now see a few examples.

Associations and Affiliations

Conflicts of interest might include your associations or affiliations. For example, perhaps your brother-in-law owns his own construction company and you are the project manager for a construction project that has just published an RFP. Your brother-in-law bids on the project and ends up winning the bid.

If you sit on the decision committee and don't tell anyone about your association with the winning bidder, that is clearly a conflict of interest. If you influence the bid decision so that it goes to your brother-in-law, he benefits from your position—again, a conflict of interest. You put your personal interests, or in this case the interests of your associations, above the project outcome. Even if you did not influence the decision in any way, when others on the project discover the winning bidder is your brother-in-law, they will assume a conflict of interest occurred. This could jeopardize the awarding of the bid and your own position as well.

The correct thing to do in this case would be to, first, inform the project sponsor and the decision committee that your brother-in-law intends to bid on the project. Second, refrain from participating on the award decision committee so as not to unduly influence others in favor of your brother-in-law. And last, if you've done all these things and your brother-in-law still wins the bid, appoint someone else in your organization to administer the contract and make the payments for the work performed by him. Also, make certain you document the decisions you make regarding the activities performed by him and keep them with the project files. The more documentation you have, the less likely someone can make a conflict of interest accusation stick.

Vendor Gifts

Many professionals work in situations in which they are not allowed to accept gifts in excess of certain dollar amounts. This might be driven by company policy, the department manager's policy, and so on. In my organization, it's considered a conflict of interest to accept anything from a vendor, including gifts (no matter how small), meals, or even a cup of coffee. Vendors and suppliers often provide their customers and potential customers with lunches, gifts, ballgame tickets, and the like. It's your responsibility to know whether a policy exists that forbids you from accepting these gifts. It's also your responsibility to inform the vendor if they've gone over the limit and you are unable to accept the gift.

The same situation can occur here as with the brother-in-law example earlier. If you accept an expensive gift from a vendor and later award that vendor a contract or a piece of the project work, it looks like and probably is a conflict of interest. This violates PMI guidelines and doesn't look good for you personally either.

NOTE   Using the "I didn't know there was a policy" reasoning probably won't save you when there's a question of conflict of interest. Make it your business to find out whether the organization has a conflict of interest policy and understand exactly what it says. Get a copy, and keep it with your files. Review it periodically. Put a note on your calendar every six months to reread the policy to keep it fresh in your mind. This is a case where not knowing what you don't know can hurt you.

Don't accept gifts that might be construed as a conflict of interest. If your organization does not have a policy regarding vendor gifts, set limits for yourself depending on the situation, the history of gift acceptance by the organization in the past, and the complexity of the project. It's always better to decline a gift you're unsure about than to accept it and later lose your credibility, your reputation, or your PMP status because of bad judgment.

Stakeholder Influence

Another potential area for conflict of interest comes from stakeholders. Stakeholders are usually folks with a good deal of authority and an important position in the company. Make certain you are not putting your own personal interests above the interests of the project when you're dealing with powerful stakeholders. They might have the ability to promote you or reward you in other ways. That's not a bad thing, but if you let that get in the way of the project or let a stakeholder twist your arm with promises like this, you're getting mighty close to a conflict of interest. Always weigh your decisions with the objectives of the project and the organization in mind—not your own personal gain.

Keep in mind that you might not always be on the receiving end of the spectrum. You should not offer inappropriate gifts or services or use confidential information you have at your disposal to assist others, because this can also be considered a conflict of interest.

Professional Demeanor

Acting in a professional manner is required of most everyone who works in the business world. Although you are not responsible for the actions of others, you are responsible for your own actions and reactions. Part of acting professionally involves controlling yourself and your reactions in questionable situations. For example, a stakeholder or customer might lash out at you but have no basis for their outburst. You can't control what they said or did, but you can control how you respond. As a professional, your concern for the project and the organization should take precedence over your concern for your own feelings. Therefore, lashing out in return would be unprofessional. Maintain your professional demeanor, and don't succumb to shouting matches or ego competitions with others.

As project manager, you have a good deal of influence over your project team members. One of the items on the agenda at the project team kickoff meeting should be a discussion of where the team members can find a copy of organizational policies regarding conflict of interest, cultural diversity, standards and regulations, and customer service and standards of performance. Better yet, have copies with you that you can hand out at the meeting or have available the addresses of website where they can find these documents.

When you see project team members acting out of turn or with less-than-desirable customer service attitudes, coach and influence those team members to conform to the standards of conduct expected by you and your organization. Your team members represent you and the project. As such, they should act professionally. It's your job as the project leader to ensure that they do.

🌐 Real World Scenario

The Golf Trip

Amanda Lewis is a project manager for a network upgrade project for her organization. This project will be outsourced to a vendor. Amanda will manage the vendor's work. She also wrote the RFP and is a member of the selection committee.

The project consists of converting the organization's network from 100MB Ethernet to Gigabit Ethernet. This requires replacing all of the routers and switches. Some of the cabling in the buildings will need to be replaced as well. The RFP requires that the vendor who wins the bid install all the new equipment and replace the network interface cards in each of the servers with Gigabit Ethernet cards. The grand total for this project is estimated at $1.2 million.

Don James is a vendor with whom Amanda has worked in the past. Don is very interested in winning this bid. He drops in on Amanda one day shortly after the RFP is posted.

"Amanda, it's good to see you," Don says. "I was in the neighborhood and thought I'd stop in to see how things are going."

"Just great, Don," Amanda replies. "I'll bet you're here to talk to me about that RFP. You know I can't say anything until the whole process closes."

"You bet we bid on the project. I know you can't talk about the RFP, so I won't bring it up. I wanted to chat with you about something else. My company is sending 15 lucky contestants and one friend each to Scottsdale, Arizona, for a 'conference.' The conference includes the use of the Scottsdale Golf Club (green fees paid, of course), and all the hotel and meal expenses are on us for the length of the trip. I know Scottsdale is one of your favorite places to golf, so I thought of you. What do you say?"

Amanda sits forward in her chair and looks at Don for a minute. "That sounds fabulous, and I do love Scottsdale. But you and I both know this isn't a conference. I wouldn't feel right about accepting it."

"Come on, Amanda. Don't look a gift horse in the mouth. It is a conference. I'll be there and so will the top brass from the company. We have some presentations and demonstrations we'd like to show you while you're there, no obligation of course, and then you're free to spend the rest of the time however you'd like."

"I appreciate the offer. Thanks for thinking of me, but no thanks. I'm on the selection committee for the RFP, and it would be a conflict of interest if I attended this conference. Besides, the value of the conference is over the $100 limit our company sets for vendor gifts and meals," Amanda says.

"OK, we'll miss you. Maybe next time."

You probably remember something your mother always told you: actions speak louder than words. Always remember that you lead by example. Your team members are watching. If you are driven by high personal ethics and a strong desire to produce excellent customer service, those who work for you will likely follow your lead.

Applying Professional Knowledge

Professional knowledge involves the knowledge of project management practices as well as specific industry or technical knowledge required to complete an assignment.

As a PMP, you should apply project management knowledge to all your projects. Take the opportunity to educate others regarding project management practices by keeping others up-to-date on project management practices, training your team members to use the correct techniques, informing stakeholders of the correct processes, and then sticking to those processes throughout the course of the project. This isn't always easy, especially when the organization doesn't have any formal processes in place. But once the stakeholders see the benefits of good project management practices, they'll never go back to the "old" way of performing their projects.

One way to apply professional knowledge is to become and remain knowledgeable in project management best practices techniques. I'll cover this topic next along with discussing the *PMP Code of Professional Conduct*, how to become a PMI education provider, and the importance of having industry knowledge.

Project Management Knowledge

Project management is a growing field. Part of your responsibility as a PMP is to stay abreast of project management practices, theories, and techniques. You can do this in many ways, one of which includes joining a local PMI chapter. There are hundreds of local chapters in every state and in other countries as well. You can check the PMI website (www.pmi.org) to find a chapter near you.

Chapter meetings give you the opportunity to meet other project managers, find out what techniques they're using, and seek advice regarding your project. Usually guest speakers appear at each chapter meeting and share their experiences and tips. Their stories are always interesting, and they give you the opportunity to learn from someone else's experiences and avoid making wrong turns on your next project. You might have a few stories of your own worth sharing with your local chapter. Volunteer to be a speaker at an upcoming meeting, and let others learn from your experiences.

One of the things you'll get when you join the PMI organization and pay your yearly dues is its monthly magazine. This publication details real-life projects and the techniques and issues project managers have to deal with on those projects. Reading the magazine is a great way to learn new project management techniques or reinforce the information you already know. You might discover how to apply some of the knowledge you've already learned in more efficient ways as well.

PMI offers educational courses through their local chapters and at the national level as well. These are yet another way for you to learn about project management and meet others in your field.

Next you'll look at your responsibility in accurately and honestly reporting the level of knowledge and qualifications you possess, what an education provider is, and why industry knowledge is important.

Professional Conduct

I talked about honesty earlier in this chapter, but it's worth repeating: don't mislead others regarding your experience in the project management field. The *PMP Code of Professional Conduct* requires that you honestly report your qualifications, your experience, and your past performance of services to potential employers, customers, PMI, and others.

Be honest about what you know and what you don't know. For example, the Quality Control processes as described in the *PMBOK Guide* are used extensively in the manufacturing industry. However, the information technology field looks at quality issues in different ways. If you're a project manager in the information technology field, you've probably never used control charts and cause-and-effect diagramming techniques. Don't lead others to believe that you have used techniques you haven't used or that you have experience you don't have.

Emphasize the knowledge you do have and how you've used it in your specific industry, and don't try to fudge it with processes and techniques you've never used. Potential clients and employers would much rather work with you and provide training where you might need it than think they've got someone fully experienced with the project or industry techniques needed for a project when they don't.

If you're working on contract or you're self-employed, you have a responsibility to ensure that the estimates you provide potential customers are accurate and truthful. Make certain you clearly spell out what services you're providing and let the customer know the results they can expect at the end of the project. Accurately represent yourself, your qualifications, and your estimates in your advertising and in person.

Education Providers

The PMI has a program that allows you or your organization to become a Registered Education Provider (REP). This allows you—once you're certified—to conduct PMI-sanctioned project management training, seminars, and conferences. The best part is that your attendees are awarded professional development units (PDUs) for attending the training or seminar. As a PMP, and especially as an REP, you have a responsibility to the profession and to the PMI to provide truthful information regarding the PMI certification process, the exam applications, the PDU requirements, and so on. Keep up-to-date on the PMI's certification process by periodically checking the website.

Industry Knowledge

Contributing and applying professional knowledge goes beyond project management experience. You likely have specific industry or technical experience as well. Part of applying your professional knowledge includes gaining knowledge of your particular industry and keeping others informed of advances in these areas.

Information technology has grown exponentially over the past several years. It used to be that if you specialized in network operations, for example, it was possible to learn and become proficient in all things related to networks. Today that is no longer the case. Each specialized area within information technology has grown to become a knowledge area in and of itself. Many other fields have either always had individual specialties or just recently experienced this phenomenon, including the medical field, bioengineering, manufacturing, pharmaceuticals, and so on. You need to stay up-to-date regarding your industry so that you can apply that knowledge effectively. Today's fast-paced advances can leave you behind fairly quickly if you don't stay on top of things.

I mentioned in the beginning of the book that as a project manager you are not required to be a technical expert, and that still holds true. But it doesn't hurt to stay abreast of industry trends and knowledge in your field and have a general understanding of the specifics of your business. Again, you can join industry associations and take educational classes to stay on top of breaking trends and technology in your industry.

Truthful Reporting

As a project manager, you are responsible for truthfully reporting all information in your possession to stakeholders, customers, the project sponsor, and the public. Always be up front regarding the project's progress.

Nothing good will come of telling stakeholders or customers that the project is on track and everything looks great when in fact the project is behind schedule or several unplanned risks have occurred that have thrown the project team a curveball. I've personally witnessed the demise of the careers of project managers who chose this route.

Tell the truth regarding project status, even when things don't look good. Stakeholders will likely go to great lengths to help you solve problems or brainstorm solutions. Sometimes, though, the call needs to be made to kill the project. This decision is usually made by the project sponsor and/or the stakeholders based on your recommendation and predictions of future project activities. Don't skew the reporting to prevent stakeholders from making this decision when it is the best solution based on the circumstances.

Truthful reporting is required when working with the public as well. When working in situations where the public is at risk, truthfully report the facts of the situation and what steps you're taking to counteract or reduce the threats. I recommend you get approval from the organization regarding public announcements prior to reporting the facts. Many organizations have public relations departments that will handle this situation for you.

Laws and Regulations Compliance

This might seem obvious, but since it's part of the *PMP Code of Professional Conduct*, I'll mention it here. As a professional, you're required to follow all applicable laws and rules and regulations that apply to your industry, organization, or project. This includes PMI organizational rules and policies as well. You should also follow any ethical standards and principles that might govern your industry or the state or country in which you're working. Remember that rules or regulations you're used to in the United States might or might not apply to other countries, and vice versa.

As a PMP, one of the responsibilities that falls into this category is the responsibility to report violations of the PMP code of conduct. To maintain integrity of the profession, PMPs must adhere to the code of conduct that makes all of us accountable to each other.

When you know a violation has occurred and you've verified the facts, notify the PMI. Part of this process—and a requirement of the code of conduct—is that you'll comply with ethics violations and will assist the PMI in the investigation by supplying information, confirming facts and dates, and so on. Violations include anything listed in the *PMP Code of Professional Conduct*, such as conflicts of interest, untruthful advertising and reporting of PMP experience and credentials, and so on, as well as appearances of impropriety. This one calls for some judgment on your part, but it's mostly based on common sense. For example, a PMP in most situations should not have a family member working on the project team reporting to them (unless they own and run a family business).

Confidential Information

Many project managers work for consulting firms where their services are contracted out to organizations that need their expertise for particular projects. If you work in a situation like this, you will likely come across information that is sensitive or confidential. Again, this might seem obvious, but as part of the *PMP Code of Professional Conduct*, you agree not to disclose sensitive or confidential information or use it in any way for personal gain.

Often when you work under contract, you'll be required to sign a nondisclosure agreement. This agreement simply says that you will not share information regarding the project or the organization with anyone—including the organization's competitors—or use the information for your personal gain.

However, you don't have to work on contract to come into contact with sensitive or private information. You might work full-time for an organization or a government agency that deals with information regarding its customer base or citizens. For example, if you work for a bank, you might have access to personal account information. If you work for a government agency, you might have access to personal tax records or other sensitive material. It would be highly unethical and maybe even illegal to look up the account information of individuals not associated with the project at hand just to satisfy your own curiosity. In my organization, that is grounds for dismissal.

Don't compromise your ethics or your organization's reputation by sharing information that is confidential to the organization or would jeopardize an individual's privacy.

Company Data

Although it might seem obvious that you should not use personal information or an organization's trade secrets for personal gain, sometimes the organization has a legitimate need to share information with vendors, governmental agencies, or others. You need to determine which vendors or organizations are allowed to see sensitive company data. In some cases, you might even need to determine which individuals can have access to the data. When in doubt, ask.

Here are some examples. Maybe the company you're working with has periodic mailings it sends to its customer base. If one of your project activities includes finding a new vendor to print the mailing labels, your organization might require the vendor to sign a nondisclosure agreement to guard the contents of the customer lists. Discovering just who should have access to this information might be tricky.

Another example involves data on citizens that is maintained by the government. You might think that because the data belongs to one agency of the government—say the Internal Revenue Service—any other agency of the government can have access to it. This isn't the case. Some agencies are refused access to the data even though they might have good reason to use it. Others might have restricted access, depending on the data and the agency policy regarding it. Don't assume that others should have access to data because it seems logical.

Most organizations require vendors or other organizations to sign nondisclosure agreements when the vendors or others will have access to sensitive company data. It's your responsibility to ensure that the proper nondisclosure agreements are signed prior to releasing the data. The procurement department often handles this function.

Intellectual Property

You are likely to come into contact with intellectual property during the course of your project management career. Intellectual property includes items developed by an organization that have commercial value but are not tangible and copyrighted material such as books, software, and artistic works. It might also include ideas or processes that are patented. Or it might involve an industrial process, business process, or manufacturing process that was developed by the organization for a specific purpose.

Intellectual property is owned by the business or person who created it. You might have to pay royalties or ask for written permission to use the property. Intellectual property should be treated just like sensitive or confidential data. It should not be used for personal gain or shared with others who should not have access to it.

Balancing Stakeholders' Interests

Projects are undertaken at the request of customers, project sponsors, executive managers, and others. Stakeholders are those who have something to gain or lose by implementing the project. As such, stakeholders have different interests and needs, and one of your jobs is to balance the needs of the stakeholders.

Customer satisfaction is probably the primary goal you're striving for in any project. If your customer is satisfied, it means you've met or exceeded their expectations and delivered the product or service they were expecting. You've got a winning combination when the customer is satisfied with the product, and you've also provided excellent customer service along the way. Satisfied customers tell others about your success and will most likely use your services in the future.

One of the key ways to assure that customer satisfaction is achieved is to apply appropriate project management techniques to your project. This includes taking the time to discover all the requirements of the project and documenting them in the scope statement. You will find that stakeholders who have a clear understanding of the requirements and have signed off on them won't suffer from faulty memory and pull the ever-famous "I thought that *was* included" technique. Take the time to define your requirements and get stakeholder sign-off. You can't forget or fudge what's written down.

In the following sections, I'll discuss how to juggle the competing needs of stakeholders, how to handle the issues and problems with stakeholders, and finally how to balance project constraints against stakeholder needs.

Competing Needs

Stakeholders come from all areas of the organization and include your customer as well. Because stakeholders do not all work in the same areas, they have competing needs and interests. One stakeholder's concern on a typical IT project might take the form of system security issues, while another stakeholder is concerned about ease of use. As the project manager, you will have situations in which stakeholder needs compete with each other, and you'll have to decide between them and set priorities. Sometimes you'll be able to accommodate their needs, and sometimes you'll have to choose. You need to examine the needs against the project objectives and then use your negotiation and communication skills to convince the stakeholders of priorities.

Individual stakeholders might or might not have good working relationships with other stakeholders. Because of this, office politics come into play. I advise you to stay away from the politics game but get to know your stakeholders. You'll need to understand their business processes and needs in order to make decisions about stakeholder requirements.

Dealing with Issues and Problems

Problems will occur on your project—it's part of the process. I've talked throughout this book about how to deal with problems and risks and how to use conflict resolution techniques in handling problems. Balancing stakeholder needs comes into play here also.

You'll have to determine alternatives that will meet the key requirements of the project without jeopardizing the competing needs of stakeholders. Once you're into the Executing processes of the project and beyond, redefining scope becomes less and less of an option. So your responsibility is to resolve issues and determine alternative solutions to problems as they occur without changing the original objectives of the project. Enlist the help of your project team members and stakeholders during these times. Use some of the techniques I talked about in Chapter 5, "Risk Planning," such as brainstorming and the Delphi technique, to find solutions.

You might also have difficulty trying to make stakeholders understand your decision or the technical nature of a problem. Again, this is where communication skills help you immensely. Take the case of a technical problem that's cropped up on your project. You should not expect your stakeholder to understand the technical aspects of rocket science if they work in the finance department, for example. It's up to you to keep the explanation at a level they can understand without loading them down with technical jargon and specifications. Keep your explanations simple, yet don't skip important details they'll need to make decisions.

Balancing Constraints

Your toughest issues will almost always center on the triple constraints: time, cost, and scope. Because of the nature of the constraints, one of these is the primary driver, and one is the least important. Keep a close eye on stakeholders who want to switch the priority of the constraints for their own purposes. Let's say the project sponsor already told you that time is the primary constraint. Another stakeholder tells you that a requirement of the project is being overlooked and quality is suffering. Be careful that the stakeholder isn't trying to divert the primary constraint from time to quality to suit their own objectives.

 Real World Scenario

The Geographic Information System

Ryan Loveland is a project manager for a multinational company. He's working on a complex software project that involves rewriting the organization's mainframe accounting system to become a browser-based system running on thin-client architecture. A major problem with the existing system occurs when new accounts are entered into the system or account information changes. The accounts are tied to geographic areas, which are assigned to individual sales associates. Sales commissions are paid based on where the account resides. To date, the process of determining which territory an account belongs to has been done manually by looking at a map.

The project sponsor, Victor, requested a geographic information system (GIS) as part of the requirements of this project. The hope is that errors will be eliminated and commissions will be processed correctly. The sponsor is hoping that Ryan's internal team can write the GIS that will tie to the accounting system. Let's drop in on Ryan and Victor's conversation.

"I just don't understand," Victor says. "I can go onto that Internet site and plug in an address and get directions and a map detailing those directions from my house to anywhere in the country. It seems easy enough to me. Why can't your team write code like that?"

"It isn't that we can't write a program to do that. But there are several issues surrounding this request that I'd like to explain to you. I'd like you to understand why I'm asking to purchase a software product from an external vendor that will take care of these functions for us."

"Let's hear it," Victor says.

"One of the first problems is that our sales force is multinational. It would take us months just to obtain address information to populate the program. The second issue is that our sales districts are not divided by any known boundaries. Most GIS systems work off of latitude and longitude or geographic boundaries such as county borders or ZIP code boundaries."

Victor interrupts, "Well, here's what we do. You give me a set of maps, I'll hand-draw in the sales districts, and then you can scan it into the system."

"Unfortunately, it's not that easy. Our sales district boundaries are not consistent with known boundaries, and our existing address database is not standardized. For example, some addresses use the word *Street* spelled out; some use the abbreviation *St.* All of the addresses need to be standardized, and then we have to figure out which addresses belong to which territory.

"This process could take a great deal of time. There are vendors that specialize in GIS that could have us operational in a matter of weeks. I've already checked on a couple of the top vendors, and there aren't any problems interfacing with our new system. The time we'd save in the long run far outweighs the cost associated with purchasing this system from a vendor. And one last point: if I were to build this system internally, I'd have to take our top programming team off of existing project priorities to put them on this. GIS is extremely complicated. We're talking several months—if not a year or more delay—to get our programmers up to speed on GIS techniques and then write the programs."

Victor says, "If we're talking about a major delay in the schedule as you say, we can at least look at what these vendors have to offer. It's important that this system is accurate as well, and I think I hear you saying, 'Why reinvent the wheel?' Let's have a look at the costs."

Respecting Differences in Diverse Cultures

You have probably taken diversity or cultural differences training classes sometime during your career. Most organizations today require diversity training for all employees and contractors. Project managers who work on contract might find themselves taking these classes multiple times, because companies want to ensure that every employee and contractor has taken their own version of the class.

I won't attempt to repeat diversity training here, but I will point out some of the things you should know about working in other countries and about working with people who have backgrounds and belief systems different from yours. I'll also touch on training as a diversity awareness tool and discuss how people's perceptions influence their reactions.

Global Competition

More and more companies compete in the global marketplace. As a result, project managers with multinational experience are increasingly in demand. This requires a heightened awareness of cultural influences and customary practices of the country where you're temporarily residing.

If you are used to working in the United States, for example, you know that the culture tends to value accomplishments and individualism. U.S. citizens tend to be informal and call each other by their first names, even if they've just met. In some European countries, people tend to be more formal, using surnames instead of first names in a business setting, even when they know each other well. Their communication style is more formal than in the United States, and although they tend to value individualism, they also value history, hierarchy, and loyalty. The Japanese, on the other hand, tend to communicate indirectly and consider themselves part of a group, not as individuals. The Japanese value hard work and success, as most of us do.

One thing I've witnessed when working in foreign countries is U.S. citizens who try to force their own culture or customs on those with whom they're visiting or working. That isn't recommended, and it generally offends those you're trying to impress. Don't expect others to conform to your way of doing things, especially when you're in their country. You know the saying "When in Rome, do as the Romans do"? Although you might not want to take that literally, the intent is good. For example, a quick kiss on both cheeks is a customary greeting in many countries. If that is the case and it's how you're greeted, respond with the same.

Culture Shock

Working in a foreign country can bring about an experience called *culture shock*. When you've spent years acting certain ways and expecting normal, everyday events to follow a specific course of action, you might find yourself disoriented when things don't go as you expected.

One of the ways you can avoid this culture shock is to read about the country you're going to work in before getting there. The Internet is a great resource for information such as this. Your local library is another place to research customs and acceptable practices in foreign countries.

When in doubt about a custom or what you should do in a given situation, ask your hosts or a trusted contact from the company you'll be working with to help you. People are people all over the world, and they love to talk about themselves and their culture. They're also generally helpful, and they will respect you more for asking what's expected rather than acting as though you know what to do when you clearly do not.

Respecting Your Neighbors

Americans tend to run their lives at high speed and get right down to business when working with vendors or customers. It isn't unusual for a businessperson to board a plane in the morning, show up at the client site and take care of business, and hop another flight to the next client site that night.

You'll find that this is not that common in many other countries. People in other countries will expect you to take time to get to know them first, building an atmosphere of trust and respect. Some cultures build relationships first and then proceed to business. And don't expect to do that relationship building in a few hours. It could take several days, depending on the culture. They might even want you to meet their family and spend time getting to know them. Resist the urge to get right down to business if that's not customary in the culture because you'll likely spoil the deal or damage relationships past the point of repair.

> Spend time building relationships with others. Once an atmosphere of mutual trust and cooperation is established, all aspects of project planning and management—including negotiating and problem solving—are much easier to navigate.

Training

Sometimes you might find yourself working with teams of people from different countries or cultures. Some team members might be from one country and some from another. The best way to ensure that cultural or ethical differences do not hinder your project is to provide training for all team members.

Team-building activities are ways to build mutual trust and respect and bond team members with differing backgrounds. Choose activities that are inoffensive and ones in which everyone can participate.

Diversity training makes people aware of differences between cultures and ethnic groups, and it helps them to gain respect and trust for those on their team. Provide training regarding the project objectives and the company culture as well.

> Project objectives are why you are all together in the first place. Project objectives cut across cultural boundaries and keep everyone focused on the project and tasks at hand.

Perceiving Experiences

All of us see the world through our own experiences. Your experiences are not someone else's experiences, and therefore what you perceive about a situation might be very different from what others believe. Keep this in mind when it appears that a misunderstanding has occurred or that someone you're working with didn't respond as you expected. This is especially true when you're working with someone from another country. Always give others the benefit of the doubt and ask for clarification if you think there is a problem. Put your feelings in check temporarily, and remember that what you think the other person means is not necessarily as it appears.

Project Case Study: New Kitchen Heaven Retail Store

Jill Overstreet thought you did such a great job of managing this project that she has offered to buy you lunch at one of those upscale, white tablecloth–type French restaurants. The iced teas have just been delivered, and you and Jill are chatting about business.

"I'm impressed with your project management skills. This store opening was the best on record. And you really kept Dirk in line—I admire that. He can be headstrong, but you had a way of convincing him what needed doing and then sticking to it."

"Thanks," you reply. "I've got a few years of project management experience, so many of those lessons learned on previous projects helped me out with this project. I enjoy project management and read books and articles on the subject whenever I get the chance. It's nice when you can learn from others' mistakes and avoid making them yourself."

Jill takes a long drink of tea. She glances at you over the top of her glass and pauses before setting it down. The look on her face implies she's sizing you up and deciding whether to tell you what's on her mind.

"You know," Jill starts, "we almost didn't hire anyone for your position. Dirk wanted to do away with the project management role altogether. He had a real distaste for project management after our last project."

"Why is that?"

Jill explains, "The last project manager got involved in a conflict of interest situation. She was working on a project that involved updating and remodeling all the existing stores. Things like new fixtures, signs, shelving, display cases, and such were up for bid. And it was a very sizable bid. Not only did she accept an all-expenses-paid weekend visit to a resort town from one of the vendors bidding on the contract, she also revealed company secrets to them, some of which leaked to our competitors."

Your mouth drops open. "I can't believe she would accept gifts like that from a vendor. And revealing company secrets is almost worse. Conflict of interest situations and not protecting intellectual property violate the code of professional conduct to which certified PMPs agree to adhere. I can understand why Dirk didn't want to hire another project manager. Behavior like that makes all project managers look bad."

"I'm glad you kept things above board and won Dirk back over. The project management role is important to Kitchen Heaven, and I know your skills in this discipline are what made this project such a success."

"Jill, not only would I never compromise my own integrity through a conflict of interest situation, I would report the situation and the vendor to the project sponsor and to the PMI as an ethics violation. It's better to be honest and let the project sponsor or key stakeholders know what's happening than to hide the situation or, even worse, compromise your own integrity by getting involved in it in the first place. You have my word that I'll keep business interests above my own personal interests. I'll report anything that even looks like it would call my actions into question just to keep things honest and out in the open."

"That's good to hear," Jill replies. "Congratulations on your new assignment. Dirk and I were discussing the new Home Chef Pro project yesterday. We're venturing into new territory with this project, and I'm confident you'll do an excellent job heading it up. Dirk made a good choice."

Project Case Study Checklist

- Ensuring personal and professional integrity

- Adhering to the *PMP Code of Professional Conduct*

- Not placing personal gain above business needs

- Avoiding conflict of interest situations

- Truthfully reporting questionable situations and maintaining honesty

- Protecting intellectual property

Understanding How This Applies to Your Next Project

I think this chapter can easily be boiled down to the golden rule, "Do unto others as you would have them do unto you." I wish I could tell you that everything I talked about here is practiced by all project managers everywhere. But you've likely read, as I have, the endless stories in the news lately of this corporate exec or the other acting in their own best interest rather than that of the organization. Project managers make the news as well, especially when they're working on projects that involve public funds or charitable organizations. In my humble opinion, ignoring the practices and advice in this chapter isn't worth the damage it might cause to my organization, to the project, or to my career.

I'd also add that if your first thought on a new project is what a great résumé builder it's going to be for you and how you'll likely score that next big promotion after the project is complete, you've started off on the wrong foot. Although I'm the first to admit big projects (when executed well and delivered on time and on budget) *are* résumé builders, it's the wrong reason to take on a project. Consider your experience level and how and what you'll be able to contribute to the project to make it a success. It's OK if the project is a stretch for you—you can't grow your experience without taking on more complex projects as your career progresses. But also be wise enough to know when you might be in over your head.

There's no substitute for integrity and honesty when conducting your projects. Once you've tarnished your integrity, whether intentional or not, it's almost impossible to regain the trust of your stakeholders and management staff. Because of this, I'm never afraid of telling anyone, "I don't know," but I always follow it up with, "But I'll find out." You're a project manager, not a miracle worker. No one expects you to have all the answers anymore than they expect you to perform every single task on the project.

I've had the unfortunate experience of being told to lie about project status and to purposely withhold project information from oversight boards. I spent a few sleepless nights worrying about where I'd find my next job because I immediately disobeyed those orders and reported the truth. I knew it would cost me my job. But I also knew it was better for me to lose the job than to compromise my integrity. As it turned out, I found a new job quickly. And in retrospect, if I had not left the position when I did, my reputation would have taken a hit—not because of anything I had done but through association with the people on the project who had compromised when they shouldn't have.

I hope you've found this study guide helpful both for your studies for the PMP exam and for your next project. Thank you for spending some time with me in the pages of this book. I wish you the best of luck in your project management endeavors.

Summary

Project management professionals are responsible for reporting truthful information about their PMP status and project management experience to prospective customers, clients, and employers and to the PMI. As a project manager, you're responsible for the integrity of the project management process and the product. In all situations, you are responsible for your own personal integrity.

Personal integrity means adhering to an ethical standard. As a PMP, you'll be required to adhere to the *PMP Code of Professional Conduct* established by the PMI. Part of this code involves avoiding putting your own personal gain above the project objectives.

As a professional, you should strive to maintain honesty in project reporting. You're required to abide by laws, rules, and regulations regarding your industry and project management practices. You should also report any instances that might appear to be a conflict of interest. It's always better to inform others of an apparent conflict than to have it discovered by others and have your methods called into question after the fact.

You will likely come across confidential information or intellectual property during your project management experiences. Respect the use of this information and always verify who might have permission to access the information and when disclosures are required.

Stakeholders have competing needs and business issues and as such will sometimes cause conflict on your project. You will be required to balance the needs and interests of the stakeholders with the project objectives.

Many project managers today are working in a global environment. It's important to respect and understand the cultural differences that exist and not try to impose your cultural beliefs on others. Culture shock is an experience that occurs when you find yourself in a different cultural environment than you're familiar with. Training is a good way to provide project team members with relationship management techniques regarding cultural and ethnic differences.

Exam Essentials

Be able to define integrity.   Integrity means adhering to an ethical standard.

Be able to name the ethical standard to which PMPs are required to adhere.   The ethical standard PMPs are required to adhere to is described in the *PMP Code of Professional Conduct*.

Describe the areas in which PMPs must apply professional knowledge.   PMPs must apply professional knowledge in the areas of project management practices, industry practices, and technical areas.

Know the key activity that ensures customer satisfaction.   The key activity that ensures customer satisfaction is documenting project requirements and meeting them.

Define how multinational project managers must manage relationships.   Multinational project managers manage relationships by building relationships based on mutual trust and acceptance and recognizing and respecting diverse cultures and ethnic beliefs.

Key Terms

Once again, you've learned some new key words in this chapter. PMI has worked hard to develop and define standard project management terms that apply across industries. Here are the terms you came across in this chapter:

conflict of interest

culture shock

Project Management Professional Code of Professional Conduct

Review Questions

1. As a project manager, you're responsible for maintaining and ensuring integrity for all of the following except which one?

    A. Personal integrity of others

    B. Project management process

    C. Personal integrity

    D. Product integrity

2. You are a project manager working on contract. You've performed earned value analysis and discovered that the project will be completed on time and under the original estimated amount. This means the profit to your company will decrease as will your personal bonus. Which of the following should you do?

    A. Add activities to the project to increase the cost enough to meet the original estimated amount.

    B. Tell the customer you're adding requirements to the project that were originally cut because of cost constraints.

    C. Upon completion, inform the customer the project has come in under budget.

    D. Bill the customer for the full amount of the contract because this was the original agreed-upon price.

3. Integrity in the project management field is accomplished through all of the following except which one?

    A. Training to learn how to manage relationships with others from different cultures

    B. Adhering to an ethical code

    C. Applying established project management processes

    D. Following the *PMP Code of Professional Conduct*

4. You are a project manager for a manufacturing firm that produces Civil War–era replicas and memorabilia. You discover a design error during a test production run on your latest project. Which of the following is the most likely response to this problem?

    A. Reduce the technical requirements so that the error is no longer valid.

    B. Go forward with production, and ignore the error.

    C. Go forward with production, but inform the customer of the problem.

    D. Develop alternative solutions to address the error.

5. You are a project manager for a telecommunications firm. You're working on a project that entails upgrading technical hardware and equipment. The estimated cost of the hardware and equipment is $1,725,000. You are reviewing products from three different vendors. One of the vendors invites you to lunch. What is the most appropriate response?

   A. Thank them, but let them know this could be a conflict of interest since you haven't made a decision about which vendor you're going to choose.

   B. Thank them, and decline. You know this could be considered personal gain, which could call your integrity into question.

   C. Thank them, and accept. You don't believe there is a conflict of interest or a personal integrity issue.

   D. Thank them, and decline. You believe this could be a conflict of interest on the part of the vendor, and you don't want to encourage that behavior.

6. You are a project manager for a telecommunications firm. You're working on a project that entails upgrading technical hardware and equipment. The estimated cost of the hardware and equipment is $1,725,000. You are reviewing products from three vendors. One of the vendors offers you and your family the use of the company yacht for the upcoming three-day weekend. What is the most appropriate response?

   A. Thank them, and accept. You don't believe there is a conflict of interest or an integrity issue at stake.

   B. Thank them, and decline. You know this could be considered personal gain, which could call your integrity into question.

   C. Thank them, and accept. Immediately report your actions to the project sponsor so that your motives are not called into question after the fact.

   D. Thank them, and decline. You know this could be considered an integrity issue on the part of the vendor.

7. You are a project manager working on contract with a company in a foreign country. At the project kickoff meeting, you are given an expensive-looking gift. The person who presented this to you said that it is customary in their country to give their business partners gifts. What is the most appropriate response?

   A. Thank them, and decline. Explain that this is considered personal gain, which is unacceptable in your country.

   B. Thank them, and accept. You don't believe there is a conflict of interest or an integrity issue at stake.

   C. Thank them, and decline. Explain that this is considered a conflict of interest, which is unacceptable in your country.

   D. Thank them, and accept since you know that it would be considered offensive to decline the gift in their culture. Immediately report the acceptance of the gift to the appropriate parties at your company so that your actions are not called into question later.

8. Life seems to be going very well for your close friend, a fellow PMP. She has taken a trip to France, bought a new car, and stocked her wine cellar with a half dozen expensive bottles of wine, all within the last six months. After a few cocktails one evening, she tells you her secret. The vendor she's working with on the $4 billion project she's managing has given her all of these items as gifts. Which of the following should you do? (Choose the best answer.)

A. You tell your friend these gifts probably aren't appropriate and leave it at that.

B. You and your friend have a long conversation about the gifts, and she decides to return them (with the exception of the trip) and not accept any more gifts in the future.

C. You're happy for your friend and say nothing.

D. Your friend doesn't see a problem with accepting these gifts at all. You know this is a conflict of interest situation and should be reported as a *PMP Code of Professional Conduct* violation.

9. As a project manager, you know that the most important activity to ensure customer and stakeholder satisfaction is which of the following?

A. Documenting and meeting the requirements

B. Documenting and meeting the performance measurements

C. Reporting changes and updating the project plan and other project documents where appropriate

D. Reporting project status regularly and in a timely manner

10. As a PMP, you will be required to comply with the *PMP Code of Professional Conduct*. This code refers to all of the following except which one?

A. Reporting conflicts of interest

B. Reporting experience and PMP status truthfully

C. Complying with the stakeholder requirements

D. Complying with the rules and standards of foreign countries

11. You are a contract project manager working with the State of Bliss. Your latest project involves rewriting the Department of Revenue's income tax system. One of the key stakeholders is a huge movie buff, and she has the power to promote you into a better position at the conclusion of this project. She has discovered that one of her favorite superstars lives in the State of Bliss and therefore must file income tax returns in that state. She asks you to look up the account of this movie star. What is the most appropriate response?

A. Report her to the management team.

B. Refuse to comply with the request, citing conflict of interest and violation of confidential company data.

C. Look up the information she has requested. Since the data is considered part of the project, there is no conflict of interest.

D. You believe that tax records are public information, so you comply with the request.

12. You are a contract project manager working with the State of Bliss. Your latest project involves rewriting the Department of Revenue's income tax system. As project manager, you have taken all the appropriate actions regarding confidentiality of data. One of the key stakeholders is a huge movie buff, and she has the power to promote you into a better position at the conclusion of this project. She's reviewing some report data that just happens to include confidential information regarding one of her favorite movie superstars. What is the most appropriate response?

A. Report her to the management team.

B. Request that she immediately return the information, citing conflict of interest and violation of confidential company data.

C. Do nothing, because she has the proper level of access rights to the data and this information showed up unintentionally.

D. Request that she immediately return the information until you can confirm that she has the proper level of access rights to the data.

13. As a PMP, you are required to comply with the *PMP Code of Professional Conduct*. Part of your responsibility concerns applying professional knowledge. All of the following are part of applying professional knowledge except for which one?

A. Developing relationships based on mutual respect

B. Staying abreast of project management practices

C. Keeping up with industry trends and new technology

D. Honestly reporting your project management experience

14. You are a project manager with several years of experience in project management. You've just accepted your first project in a foreign country. You've been in the country a week or two and are experiencing some disorientation. This is known as which of the following?

A. Collocation

B. Diversity shock

C. Global culturing

D. Culture shock

15. You are a project manager for a software manufacturing firm. The project you've just finished created a new software product that is expected to become a number-one seller. All prerelease of software is handled through the marketing department. A friend of yours is a certified software instructor. They have asked you for a copy of the software prior to the beta release so they can get familiar with it. What is the most appropriate response?

A. Since your friend is certified to teach your company's brand of software, provide them with a copy of the software.

B. Ask them to sign a nondisclosure agreement before releasing a copy of the software.

C. Decline the request since you stand to gain from this transaction by receiving free training.

D. Decline the request because the software is the intellectual property of the company.

16. Your upcoming project includes project team members from a foreign country. To make certain that cultural differences don't interfere with team performance, thereby affecting the success of the project, your first course of action is to do which of the following?

    A. Provide diversity training to all the team members.

    B. Collocate the project team.

    C. Perform team-building exercises.

    D. Inform the team members of the organization's rules and standards.

17. You are a project manager for Pizza Direct, which is a retail pizza delivery store. Your company is competing with another retail store for the option of opening two new stores in a foreign country. You have been invited to dinner with the prospective foreign business partners and their spouses upon your arrival. You know that all of the following statements are generally true except for which one?

    A. You should spend time building relationships with your prospective foreign business partners before getting down to business.

    B. You should explain your company's rules, standards, and operating policies at your first meeting with the prospective foreign business partners.

    C. You should build an atmosphere of mutual trust and cooperation.

    D. You should respect the cultural differences you'll encounter when working with your prospective foreign business partners.

18. You are a project manager for Pizza Direct, which is a retail pizza delivery store. Your company is competing with another retail store for the option of opening two new stores in a foreign country. You've been told that it is culturally unacceptable to eat certain foods in this country. You know that one of these foods happens to be a secret ingredient in the pizza sauce. What is the most appropriate response?

    A. Inform the potential partners that your sauce recipe is secret, but you're certain there are no forbidden ingredients in it.

    B. Inform the potential partners that you suspect there might be a forbidden ingredient in the sauce, and you'll request an investigation to determine whether it exists in the sauce.

    C. Inform the potential partners that a forbidden ingredient exists in the sauce and work with them to come up with another ingredient to replace that one.

    D. Don't tell the potential partners about the ingredient because the sauce they'll be using in the stores is shipped to them already prepared in cans. They won't know the ingredient is in the sauce.

19. You are a project manager for Pizza Direct, which is a retail pizza delivery store. Your company is competing with another retail store for the option of opening two new stores in a foreign country. You know, but have not yet informed your company, that you are going to go to work for the competitor, which happens to be bidding for this same opportunity. What is the most appropriate response?

A. You decline to participate in the initial meetings with the foreign business partners because of a conflict of interest.

B. You've not yet received an official offer from the competing company for your new job opportunity, so you choose to participate in the initial meetings with the foreign business partners.

C. You decide to participate in the initial meetings with the foreign business partners because any information you gain now will help you when you make the move to the new company.

D. You inform the foreign business partners that you're going to be working with a new company and that you know the deal they'll receive from the competing company is better than the one this company is proposing.

20. You are the project manager for a new construction project in your city. Your longtime personal friend is bidding on the project. Your friend has asked you to give them an indication of the budget for this project so that they do not overbid and lose the deal. What is the most appropriate response?

A. Give the information to your friend. You know their character and can trust that they won't tell anyone.

B. Tell your friend that after all this time, they should know you better than to think you'd put your personal integrity on the line or compromise your job because of a conflict of interest. Decline to give them the information.

C. Tell your friend you'll give them the information if they'll promise not to tell anyone and if they'll agree to help you with some materials on your basement-refinishing project.

D. Give the information to your friend and inform the project sponsor so that the information can be shared with the other bidders as well.

Answers to Review Questions

1. A. You are not responsible for the personal integrity of others, but as project manager you do have influence over others, such as your project team members.

2. C. Integrity means you'll honestly report project outcomes and status. Your personal gain should not be placed above the satisfaction of the customer.

3. A. Diversity training is used to help you manage project teams that consist of people from other countries or cultures. Integrity is accomplished by following an ethical code and applying project management practices.

4. D. The best answer to this problem is to develop alternative solutions to address the design error. Reducing technical requirements might be an alternative solution, but it's not one you'd implement without looking at all the alternatives. Ignoring the error and going forward with production will result in an unsatisfactory product for the customer.

5. A. A luncheon date could be considered a conflict of interest prior to awarding a contract to a vendor. Consider what a competitor of this vendor would think if they spotted you having lunch together.

6. B. The best response to this situation is to thank the vendor and decline based on the fact that this could be considered personal gain on your part. Answer D might seem correct, but remember, you're not responsible for the integrity of others. And it's often common business practice for vendors to offer gifts to potential customers.

7. D. The best response in this case is to accept the gift because it would cause great offense to the other party if you were to decline. Report the gift and the circumstances as soon as possible to the appropriate parties at your company.

8. D. This is a conflict of interest situation, and you should report it as a violation of the *PMP Code of Professional Conduct*.

9. A. Documenting the requirements and meeting them is one of the key things you can do to ensure customer satisfaction. The requirements describe what the customer is looking for, and the final product is compared against them to determine whether all of the requirements were met.

10. C. Stakeholder requirements are needed to determine whether the project is successful and are not a part of the professional code.

11. B. The situation presented here requires you to put the interest of the company and the confidentiality of the data above your own personal interests or those of your stakeholders. D is not the most correct response because it says you believe the information is public. This implies you haven't verified whether the data is private or public. Until you know, treat the data as confidential. In this case, the information is confidential and should be shared only with those who have a valid reason for using it.

12. C. As project manager, it's your responsibility to make sure the people you will be sharing data with have the proper permissions to see the data; this question indicated that you did that. In this case, D is not correct because it implies that you did not verify ahead of time that the stakeholder had the proper level of approvals to use the data.

13. A. Applying professional knowledge involves staying abreast of project management practices, industry trends, and new technology and honestly reporting your experiences.

14. D. Culture shock is the disoriented feeling that people might experience when working in a foreign country.

15. D. The most appropriate response is to deny the request. Software is considered intellectual property and should not be used for personal gain or given to others without prior consent from the organization. This question states that the release of the beta software is handled through the marketing department, so you should not give your friend a copy of the software outside of this process.

16. A. The most correct response is to first provide training to your team members to teach them how to respect and work with others from different cultures. Collocation might not be possible when you're working with team members from two different countries. Team-building exercises are a good idea as well but are not your first course of action.

17. B. Your first meeting with foreign partners should be spent getting to know them on a personal basis. Many cultures like to spend time building relationships first and then talking business. Since you've been invited to dinner upon your arrival and the dinner includes the spouses of your prospective partners, chances are they want to spend some time getting to know you personally first. The discussion of the company's rules, standards, and operating policies should occur at the second or third meeting.

18. C. The most appropriate response is to inform the potential partners that an ingredient exists in the sauce that is not acceptable and decide to come up with a solution to the problem. As a professional, you're required to be honest in your reporting. Not telling them, or stalling by promising an investigation, is not an honest response.

19. A. The most appropriate response is to decline to participate because of a conflict of interest.

20. B. This situation is clearly a conflict of interest and should be avoided. Decline to provide your friend this information.

Appendix

Process Inputs and Outputs

Throughout this book, *PMP: Project Management Professional Study Guide*, I've discussed the inputs and outputs to the PMI processes. In this appendix, you'll find the inputs, tools and techniques, outputs, and Knowledge Areas of the project management processes listed by process. I think you'll appreciate the convenience of having all this information in one location. Enjoy!

Initiating Processes

Table A.1 lists the inputs, tools and techniques, outputs, and Knowledge Areas for the Initiating process group.

TABLE A.1   Initiating Processes

Process Name	Inputs	Tools and Techniques	Outputs	Knowledge Area
Develop Project Charter	Contract (when applicable)	Project selection methods	Project charter	Integration
	Project statement of work	Project management methodology		
	Enterprise environmental factors	Project management information system		
	Organizational process assets	Expert judgment		
Develop Preliminary Project Scope Statement	Project charter	Project management methodology	Preliminary project scope statement	Integration

TABLE A.1   Initiating Processes *(continued)*

Process Name	Inputs	Tools and Techniques	Outputs	Knowledge Area
	Project statement of work	Project management information system		
	Enterprise environmental factors	Expert judgment		
	Organizational process assets			

Planning Processes

Table A.2 lists the inputs, tools and techniques, outputs, and Knowledge Areas for the processes in the Planning process group.

TABLE A.2   Planning Processes

Process Name	Inputs	Tools and Techniques	Outputs	Knowledge Area
Develop Project Management Plan	Preliminary project scope statement	Project management methodology	Project management plan	Integration
	Project management processes	Project management information system		
	Enterprise environmental factors	Expert judgment		
	Organizational process assets			

TABLE A.2 Planning Processes *(continued)*

Process Name	Inputs	Tools and Techniques	Outputs	Knowledge Area
Scope Planning	Enterprise environmental factors	Expert judgment	Project scope management plan	Scope
	Organizational process assets	Templates, forms, standards		
	Project charter			
	Preliminary project scope statement			
	Project manage-ment plan			
Scope Definition	Organizational process assets	Product analysis	Project scope statement	Scope
	Project charter	Alternatives identification	Requested changes	
	Preliminary project scope statement	Expert judgment	Project scope management plan (updates)	
	Project scope management plan	Stakeholder analysis		
	Approved change requests			
Create WBS	Organizational process assets	Work break-down structure templates	Project scope statement (updates)	Scope
			Work break-down structure	
	Project scope statement	Decomposition	WBS dictionary	

TABLE A.2   Planning Processes *(continued)*

Process Name	Inputs	Tools and Techniques	Outputs	Knowledge Area
	Project scope management plan		Scope baseline	
	Approved change requests		Project scope management plan (updates)	
			Requested changes	
Communications Planning	Enterprise environmental factors	Communications requirements analysis	Communications management plan	Communications
	Organizational process assets	Communications technology		
	Project scope statement			
	Project management plan (constraints and assumptions)			
Quality Planning	Enterprise environmental factors	Cost-benefit analysis	Quality management plan	Quality
	Organizational process assets	Benchmarking	Quality metrics	
	Project scope statement	Design of experiments	Quality checklists	
	Project management plan		Process improvement plan	
		Cost of quality (COQ)	Quality baseline	

TABLE A.2 Planning Processes *(continued)*

Process Name	Inputs	Tools and Techniques	Outputs	Knowledge Area
		Additional quality planning tools	Project management plan (updates)	
Risk Management Planning	Enterprise environmental factors	Planning meetings and analysis	Risk management plan	Risk
	Organizational process assets			
	Project scope statement			
	Project management plan			
Risk Identification	Enterprise environmental factors	Documentation reviews	Risk register	Risk
	Organizational process assets	Information gathering techniques		
	Project scope statement	Checklist analysis		
	Risk management plan	Assumptions analysis		
	Project management plan	Diagramming techniques		
Qualitative Risk Analysis	Organizational process assets	Risk probability and impact assessment	Risk register (updates)	Risk
	Project scope statement	Probability and impact matrix		
	Risk management plan	Risk data quality assessment		

TABLE A.2   Planning Processes *(continued)*

Process Name	Inputs	Tools and Techniques	Outputs	Knowledge Area
	Risk register	Risk categorization		
		Risk urgency assessment		
Quantitative Risk Analysis	Organizational process assets	Data gathering and representation techniques	Risk register (updates)	Risk
	Project scope statement	Quantitative risk analysis and modeling techniques		
	Risk management plan			
	Risk register			
	Project management plan (project schedule management plan, project cost management plan)			
Risk Response Planning	Risk management plan	Strategies for negative risk or threats	Risk register (updates)	Risk
	Risk register	Strategies for positive risk or opportunities	Project management plan (updates)	
		Strategy for both threats and opportunities	Risk-related contractual agreements	
		Contingent response strategy		

TABLE A.2   Planning Processes *(continued)*

Process Name	Inputs	Tools and Techniques	Outputs	Knowledge Area
Plan Purchases and Acquisitions	Enterprise environmental factors	Make-or-buy analysis	Procurement management plan	Procurement
	Organizational process assets	Expert judgment	Contract statement of work	
	Project scope statement	Contract types	Make-or-buy decisions	
	Work breakdown structure		Requested changes	
	WBS dictionary			
	Project management plan (risk register, risk-related contractual agreements, resource requirements, project schedule, activity cost estimates, cost baseline)			
Plan Contracting	Procurement management plan	Standard forms	Procurement documents	Procurement
	Contract statement of work	Expert judgment	Evaluation criteria	
	Make-or-buy decision		Contract statement of work (updates)	

TABLE A.2   Planning Processes *(continued)*

Process Name	Inputs	Tools and Techniques	Outputs	Knowledge Area
	Project management plan (risk register, risk-related contractual agreements, resource requirements, project schedule, activity cost estimates, cost baseline)			
Human Resource Planning	Enterprise environmental factors	Organization charts and position descriptions	Roles and responsibilities	Human Resource
	Organizational process assets	Networking	Project organization charts	
	Project management plan (activity resource requirements)	Organizational theory	Staffing management plan	
Activity Definition	Enterprise environmental factors	Decomposition	Activity list	Time
	Organizational process assets	Templates	Activity attributes	
	Project scope statement	Rolling wave analysis	Milestone list	
	Work breakdown structure	Expert judgment	Requested changes	
	WBS dictionary	Planning component		

TABLE A.2   Planning Processes *(continued)*

Process Name	Inputs	Tools and Techniques	Outputs	Knowledge Area
	Project management plan			
Activity Sequencing	Project scope statement	Precedence diagramming method (PDM)	Project schedule network diagrams	Time
	Activity list	Arrow diagramming method (ADM)	Activity list (updates)	
	Activity attributes	Schedule network templates	Activity attributes (updates)	
	Milestone list	Dependency determination	Requested changes	
	Approved change requests	Applying leads and lags		
Activity Resource Estimating	Enterprise environmental factors	Expert judgment	Activity resource requirements	Time
	Organizational process assets	Alternatives analysis	Activity attributes (updates)	
	Activity list	Published estimating data	Resource breakdown structure	
	Activity attributes	Project management software	Resource calendars (updates)	
	Resource availability	Bottom-up estimating	Requested changes	
	Project management plan			

TABLE A.2   Planning Processes *(continued)*

Process Name	Inputs	Tools and Techniques	Outputs	Knowledge Area
Activity Duration Estimating	Enterprise environmental factors	Expert judgment	Activity duration estimates	Time
	Organizational process assets	Analogous estimating	Activity attributes (updates)	
	Project scope statement	Parametric estimating		
	Activity list	Three-point estimates		
	Activity attributes	Reserve analysis		
	Activity resource requirements			
	Resource calendars			
	Project management plan (risk register, activity cost estimate)			
Schedule Development	Organizational process assets	Schedule network analysis	Project schedule	Time
	Project scope statement	Critical path method	Schedule model data	
	Activity list	Schedule compression	Schedule baseline	
	Activity attributes	What-if scenario analysis	Resource requirements (updates)	

TABLE A.2 Planning Processes *(continued)*

Process Name	Inputs	Tools and Techniques	Outputs	Knowledge Area
	Project schedule network diagrams	Resource leveling	Activity attributes (updates)	
	Activity resource requirements	Critical chain method	Project calendar (updates)	
	Resource calendars	Project management software	Requested changes	
	Activity duration estimates	Applying calendars	Project management plan (updates, schedule management plan updates)	
	Project management plan (Risk register)	Adjusting leads and lags		
		Schedule model		
Cost Estimating	Enterprise environmental factors	Analogous estimating	Activity cost estimates	Cost
	Organizational process assets	Determine resource cost rates	Activity cost estimate supporting details	
	Project scope statement	Bottom-up estimating	Requested changes	
	Work breakdown structure	Parametric estimating	Cost management plan (updates)	
	WBS dictionary	Project management software		

TABLE A.2   Planning Processes *(continued)*

Process Name	Inputs	Tools and Techniques	Outputs	Knowledge Area
	Project management plan (schedule management plan, staffing management plan, risk register)	Vendor bid analysis		
		Reserve analysis		
		Cost of quality		
Cost Budgeting	Project scope statement	Cost aggregation	Cost baseline	Cost
	Work breakdown structure	Reserve analysis	Project funding requirements	
	WBS dictionary	Parametric estimating	Cost management plan (updates)	
	Activity cost estimates	Funding limit reconciliation	Requested changes	
	Activity cost estimate supporting detail			
	Project schedule			
	Resource calendars			
	Contract			
	Cost management plan			

Executing Processes

Table A.3 lists the inputs, tools and techniques, outputs, and Knowledge Areas for the processes in the Executing process group.

TABLE A.3 Executing Processes

Process Name	Inputs	Tools and Techniques	Outputs	Knowledge Area
Direct and Manage Project Execution	Project management plan	Project management methodology	Deliverables	Integration
	Approved corrective actions	Project management information system	Requested changes	
	Approved preventive actions		Implemented change requests	
	Approved change requests		Implemented corrective actions	
	Approved defect repair		Implemented preventive actions	
	Validated defect repair		Implemented defect repair	
	Administrative closure procedure		Work performance information	
Acquire Project Team	Enterprise environmental factors	Preassignment	Project staff assignments	Human Resource
	Organizational process assets	Negotiation	Resource availability	
	Roles and responsibilities	Acquisition	Staffing management plan (updates)	

TABLE A.3   Executing Processes *(continued)*

Process Name	Inputs	Tools and Techniques	Outputs	Knowledge Area
	Project organization charts	Virtual teams		
	Staffing management plan			
Develop Project Team	Project staff assignments	General management skills	Team performance assessment	Human Resource
	Staffing management plan	Training		
	Resource availability	Team-building activities		
		Ground rules		
		Collocation		
		Recognition and rewards		
Information Distribution	Communications management plan	Communications skills	Organizational process assets (updates)	Communications
		Information gathering and retrieval systems	Requested changes	
		Information distribution methods		
		Lessons learned process		
Request Seller Responses	Organizational process assets	Bidder conferences	Qualified sellers list	Procurement
	Procurement management plan	Advertising	Procurement document package	

TABLE A.3 Executing Processes *(continued)*

Process Name	Inputs	Tools and Techniques	Outputs	Knowledge Area
	Procurement documents	Develop qualified sellers list	Proposals	
Select Sellers	Organizational process assets	Weighting system	Selected sellers	Procurement
	Procurement management plan	Independent estimates	Contract	
	Evaluation criteria	Screening system	Contract management plan	
	Procurement document package	Contract negotiation	Resource availability	
	Proposals	Seller rating system	Procurement management plan (updates)	
	Qualified sellers list	Expert judgment	Requested changes	
	Project management plan (risk register, risk-related contractual agreements)	Proposal evaluation techniques		
Perform Quality Assurance	Quality management plan	Quality planning tools and techniques	Requested changes	Quality
	Quality metrics	Quality audits	Recommended corrective actions	
	Process improvement plan	Process analysis	Organizational process assets (updates)	

TABLE A.3   Executing Processes *(continued)*

Process Name	Inputs	Tools and Techniques	Outputs	Knowledge Area
	Work performance information	Quality control tools and techniques	Project management plan (updates)	
	Approved change requests			
	Quality control measurements			
	Implemented change requests			
	Implemented defect repair			
	Implemented preventive actions			

Monitoring and Controlling Processes

Table A.4 lists the inputs, tools and techniques, outputs, and Knowledge Areas for the Monitoring and Controlling group processes.

TABLE A.4   Monitoring and Controlling Processes

Process Name	Inputs	Tools and Techniques	Outputs	Knowledge Area
Monitor and Control Project Work	Project management plan	Project management methodology	Recommended corrective actions	Integration
	Work performance information	Project management information system	Recommended preventive actions	

TABLE A.4   Monitoring and Controlling Processes *(continued)*

Process Name	Inputs	Tools and Techniques	Outputs	Knowledge Area
	Rejected change requests	Earned value technique	Forecasts	
		Expert judgment	Recommended defect repair	
			Requested changes	
Contract Administration	Contract	Contract change control system	Contract documentation	Procurement
	Contract management plan	Buyer conducted performance review	Requested changes	
	Selected sellers	Inspection and audits	Recommended corrective actions	
	Performance reports	Performance reporting	Organizational process assets (updates), including the procurement management plan and contract management plan	
	Approved change requests	Payment system		
	Work performance information	Claims administration		
		Records management system		
		Information technology		

TABLE A.4   Monitoring and Controlling Processes *(continued)*

Process Name	Inputs	Tools and Techniques	Outputs	Knowledge Area
Manage Project Team	Organizational process assets	Observation and conversation	Requested changes	Human Resource
	Project staff assignments	Project performance appraisals	Recommended corrective actions	
	Roles and responsibilities	Conflict management	Recommended preventive actions	
	Project organization charts	Issue log	Organizational process assets (updates)	
	Staffing management plan		Project management plan (updates)	
	Team performance assessment			
	Work performance assessment			
	Performance reports			
Manage Stakeholders	Communications management plan	Communications methods	Resolved issues	Communications
	Organizational process assets	Issue logs	Approved change requests	
			Approved corrective actions	
			Organizational process assets (updates)	

TABLE A.4 Monitoring and Controlling Processes *(continued)*

Process Name	Inputs	Tools and Techniques	Outputs	Knowledge Area
			Project management plan (updates)	
Performance Reporting	Work performance information	Information presentation tools	Performance reports	Communications
	Performance measurements	Performance information and gathering and compilation	Forecasts	
	Forecasted completion	Status review meetings	Requested changes	
	Quality control measurements	Time reporting systems	Recommended corrective actions	
	Project management plan (performance measurement baseline)	Cost reporting systems	Organizational assets (updates)	
	Approved change requests			
	Deliverables			
Integrated Change Control	Project management plan	Project management methodology	Approved change requests	Integration
	Requested changes	Project management information system	Rejected change requests	
	Work performance information	Expert judgment	Project management plan (updates)	

TABLE A.4   Monitoring and Controlling Processes *(continued)*

Process Name	Inputs	Tools and Techniques	Outputs	Knowledge Area
	Recommended preventive actions		Project scope statement (updates)	
	Recommended corrective actions		Approved corrective actions	
	Recommended defect repair		Approved preventive actions	
	Deliverables		Approved defect repair	
			Validated defect repair	
			Deliverables	
Cost Control	Cost baseline	Cost change control system	Cost estimate (updates)	
	Project funding requirements	Performance measurement analysis	Cost baseline (updates)	
	Performance reports	Forecasting	Performance measurements	
	Work performance information	Project performance reviews	Forecasted completion	
	Approved change requests	Project management software	Requested changes	
	Project management plan	Variance management	Recommended corrective actions	
			Organizational process assets (updates)	

TABLE A.4   Monitoring and Controlling Processes *(continued)*

Process Name	Inputs	Tools and Techniques	Outputs	Knowledge Area
			Project management plan (updates)	
Schedule Control	Schedule management plan	Progress reporting	Schedule model data (updates)	Time
	Schedule baseline	Schedule change control system	Schedule baseline (updates)	
	Performance reports	Performance measurement	Performance measurements	
	Approved change requests	Project management software	Requested changes	
		Variance analysis	Recommended corrective actions	
		Schedule comparison bar charts	Organizational process assets (updates)	
			Activity list (updates)	
			Activity attributes (updates)	
			Project management plan (updates)	
Risk Monitoring and Control	Risk management plan	Risk reassessment	Risk register (updates)	Risk
	Risk register	Risk audits	Requested changes	

TABLE A.4   Monitoring and Controlling Processes *(continued)*

Process Name	Inputs	Tools and Techniques	Outputs	Knowledge Area
	Approved change requests	Variance and trend analysis	Recommended corrective actions	
	Work performance information	Technical performance measurement	Recommended preventive actions	
	Performance reports	Reserve analysis	Organizational process assets (updates)	
		Status meetings	Project management plan (updates)	
Perform Quality Control	Quality management plan	Cause-and-effect diagram	Quality control measurements	Quality
	Quality metrics	Control charts	Validated defect repair	
	Quality checklists	Flowcharting	Quality baseline (updates)	
	Organizational process assets	Histogram	Recommended corrective actions	
	Work performance information	Pareto chart	Recommended preventive actions	
	Approved change requests	Run chart	Requested changes	
	Deliverables	Scatter diagram	Recommended defect repair	
		Statistical sampling	Organization process assets (updates)	

TABLE A.4   Monitoring and Controlling Processes *(continued)*

Process Name	Inputs	Tools and Techniques	Outputs	Knowledge Area
		Inspection	Validated deliverables	
		Defect repair review	Project management plan (updates)	
Scope Verification	Project scope statement	Inspection	Accepted deliverables	Scope
	WBS dictionary		Requested changes	
	Project scope management plan		Recommended corrective actions	
	Deliverables			
Scope Control	Project scope statement	Change control system	Project scope statement (updates)	Scope
	Work breakdown structure	Variance analysis	Work breakdown structure (updates)	
	WBS dictionary	Replanning	WBS dictionary (updates)	
	Project scope management plan	Configuration management system	Scope baseline (updates)	
	Performance reports		Requested changes	
	Approved change requests		Recommended corrective action	

TABLE A.4   Monitoring and Controlling Processes *(continued)*

Process Name	Inputs	Tools and Techniques	Outputs	Knowledge Area
	Work performance information		Organizational process assets (updates)	
			Project management plan (updates)	

Closing Processes

Table A.5 lists the inputs, tools and techniques, outputs, and Knowledge Areas for the processes in the Closing process group.

TABLE A.5   Closing Processes

Process Name	Inputs	Tools and Techniques	Outputs	Knowledge Area
Close Project	Project management plan	Project management methodology	Administrative closure procedure	Integration
	Contract documentation	Project management information system	Contract closure procedure	
	Enterprise environmental factors	Expert judgment	Final product, service, or result	
	Organizational process assets		Organizational process assets (updates)	
	Work performance information			

TABLE A.5   Closing Processes *(continued)*

Process Name	Inputs	Tools and Techniques	Outputs	Knowledge Area
	Deliverables			
Contract Closure	Procurement management plan	Procurement audits	Closed contracts	Procurement
	Contract management plan	Records management system	Organizational process asset (updates)	
	Contract documentation			
	Contract closure procedure			

Glossary

Numbers

360-degree review   This is a form of project performance appraisal (a tool and technique of the Manage Project process) that solicits feedback from everyone the team member interacts with, including the stakeholders, customers, project manager, peers, subordinates, and others.

A

acceptance   Acceptance is a strategy for threats or opportunities and is a tool and technique of the Risk Response Planning process. This strategy implies that the organization is willing to accept the consequences of the risk should it occur.

acceptance criteria   Acceptance criteria refers to the product of the project and includes the process and the criteria that will be used to determine whether the deliverables and the final product or service of the project are acceptable and satisfactory.

Achievement Theory   This motivational theory says people are motivated by the need for three things: achievement, power, and affiliation.

Acquire Project Team   This process involves attaining human resources and assigning them to the project. Human resources may come from inside or outside the organization. Acquire the Project Team belongs to the Executing process group.

activity attributes   Activity attributes describe the characteristics of the activities such as the activity identifier or code, descriptions, constraints and assumptions associated with the activity, predecessor activities, successor activities, resource requirements, the individual responsible for completing the work, and so on. The activity attributes are an extension of the activity list and are used in the schedule model tool and technique of the Schedule Development process.

Activity Definition   This process identifies the activities of the project that need to be performed to produce the product or service of the project.

activity duration estimates   Activity duration estimates are quantifiable estimates of the number of work periods needed to complete the schedule activities listed. They are an output of the Activity Duration Estimating process.

Activity Duration Estimating   This process assesses the number of work periods needed to complete the project activities. Work periods are usually expressed in hours or days. Large projects might express duration in weeks or months.

activity list   This is an extension of the WBS that contains all the activities of the project and a description of each activity. The activity list is an output of the Activity Definition process.

activity on arrow (AOA)   This is a diagramming method that places activities on arrows, which connect to dependent activities using nodes. This is also known as the *arrow diagramming method*.

activity on node (AON)   This is a diagramming method that places activities on nodes, which connect to dependent activities using arrows. This is also known as the *precedence diagramming method.*

Activity Resource Estimating   This process determines the types of resources needed (both human and materials) and in what quantities for each schedule activity within a work package.

Activity Sequencing   This process sequences activities in logical order and determines whether dependencies exist among the activities.

actual cost (AC)   This is the actual cost of work to date or during a given time period, including direct and indirect costs.

addition   This is a type of project ending where the project evolves into an ongoing operation.

administrative closure procedures   Administrative closure procedures is a document that outlines how administrative closure will occur on the project, the activities needed to perform this procedure, and the essential roles and responsibilities. This is an output of the Direct and Manage Project Execution process.

advertising   This is the act of informing potential vendors that an RFP, RFQ, and so on, is available. This is a tool and technique of the Request Seller Responses process.

alternatives identification   This is a technique used to discover different methods or ways of accomplishing the project. Alternatives identification is a tool and technique of the Scope Definition process.

analogous estimating   This technique uses the actual duration of a similar, completed activity to determine the duration of the current activity. This is also called *top-down estimating* and uses both expert judgment and historical information.

appeals   See *contested changes.*

approval requirements   Approval requirements refer to how the objectives, deliverables, project management documents, and other outcomes and results of the project will be approved.

arbitration   This is a negotiation technique used to settle contract disputes. All parties come to the table with a third, disinterested party who is not a participant in the contract to try to reach an agreement. The purpose of arbitration is to reach an agreement without having to go to court.

arrow diagramming method (ADM)   This is a diagramming method that places activities on arrows, which connect to dependent activities using nodes. This is also known as *activity on arrow.*

assumption   This is an event or action believed to be true. Project assumptions should always be documented.

attributes   These are measurements of deliverables (or certain characteristics of the deliverable) that meet one of two options: conforming or nonconforming. Conforming meets the requirement; nonconforming does not. This is an inspection technique (which is a tool and technique) of the Perform Quality Control process.

avoid   The avoid strategy is used for risks that pose threats to the project or have negative impacts. It's a tool and technique of the Risk Response Planning process. This strategy requires changes to the project plan in order to avoid or eliminate risk events and their impacts to the project objectives.

B

backward pass   This is a calculation used in CPM to determine late start and late finish dates for activities.

balanced matrix   This is a type of organizational structure where power is balanced between project managers and functional managers.

bar charts   This is a method of displaying schedule activities. See also *Gantt charts*.

benefit measurement methods   This is a category of project selection methods, which are a tool and technique of the Develop Project Charter process. They employ various forms of analysis and comparative approaches to make project decisions and include cost-benefit analysis, scoring models, benefit contribution methods, and economic models.

bidder conferences   Meetings with prospective vendors or sellers are held prior to the completion of their response proposal to clarify project objectives and answer questions. Bidder conferences are a tool and technique of the Select Seller process.

brainstorming   This is an information-gathering technique that is a tool and technique of the Risk Identification process. It involves assembling in one place subject matter experts, team members, risk management team members, and anyone else who might benefit the process and querying them on possible risk events.

budget at completion (BAC)   This is the remaining budget less the work that has been done to date. This figure is used in earned value analysis calculations.

buffer   See *reserve time*.

C

calculation methods   This is a category of selection methods outlined in the project selection methods tool and technique of the Initiation process. Calculation methods provide a way to calculate the value of the project. This value is used in the project selection decision-making process.

cardinal scale   This is a scale of values that are linear or nonlinear and referenced in the Qualitative Risk Analysis process.

cause-and-effect diagram   This diagram shows the relationship between the effects of problems and their causes. It depicts every potential cause and subcause of a problem and the effect that each proposed solution will have on the problem. This diagram is also called a *fishbone diagram* or an *Ishikawa diagram*.

change control system   This includes documented procedures that describe how to submit change requests and how to manage change requests. The change control system tracks the status of change requests and defines the level of authority needed to approve changes. It describes the management impacts of the changes as they pertain to project performance. Change control systems are a subset of the configuration management system.

claims   See *contested changes*.

claims administration   Claims administration involves documenting, monitoring, and managing changes to the contract.

Close Project   This process is concerned with gathering and disseminating information to formalize project closure. The completion of each project phase requires administrative closure also.

Closing   This is the last of the five project management process groups. Closing brings a formal, orderly end to the activities of a project phase or to the project itself. All the project information is gathered and archived for future reference. Contract closeout occurs here, and formal acceptance and approval are obtained from project stakeholders.

collocated   This is when team members are physically working at the same location or holding project meetings in a common area such as a war room.

collocation   Team members physically working at the same location or holding project meetings in a common area such as a war room.

common causes of variances   These are process variances seen in run charts (a tool and technique of the Perform Quality Control process) that are a result of random variances, known or predictable variances, or variances that are always present in the process.

communication   This is the process of exchanging information. There are three elements to all communication: the sender, the message, and the receiver. Communication can be written or verbal and formal or informal. A project manager spends 90 percent of their time communicating.

compromise   Compromise is a conflict resolution technique. Compromise is achieved when each of the parties involved in the conflict gives up something to reach a solution.

configuration control board (CCB)   This is a team that is established by the organization and given the authority to review all change requests and approve them or deny them. This is also known as a *change control board*.

configuration management   This consists of documented procedures that describe how to submit change requests and how to manage change requests. Configuration management tracks the status of change requests and defines the level of authority needed to approve changes. It describes the characteristics of the product of the project and ensures that the description is accurate and complete. Configuration management controls changes to the characteristics of an item and tracks the changes made or requested and their status.

conflict   This is the incompatibility of goals, which often leads to one party resisting or blocking the other party from attaining their goals.

conflict of interest   Conflict of interest occurs when personal interests are put above the interests of the project. It also occurs when personal influence is used to cause others to make decisions in favor of the influencer without regard for the project outcome.

confrontation   Confrontation is a conflict resolution technique also known as *problem solving*. This technique involves discovering all the facts related to the conflict. Once all the facts are known, a solution will become clear. This is the preferred method of conflict resolution.

constrained optimization methods   See *mathematical models*.

constraint   This is anything that either restricts the actions of the project team or dictates the actions of the project team.

contested changes   These are contract changes that cannot be agreed upon. They usually involve a disagreement about the compensation to the vendor for implementing the change.

contingency planning   This is a risk response strategy that involves planning alternatives to deal with the risks should they occur. Contingency planning is a tool and technique of the Risk Response Planning process.

contingency reserves   Contingency reserves hold project funds, time, or resources in reserve to offset any unavoidable threats that might occur to project scope, schedule, cost overruns, or quality. This is a tool and technique of the Risk Response Planning process.

contingency time   See *reserve time*.

contract   This is a legally binding agreement between two or more parties used to acquire products or services. Contracts can be made between two or more parties, and money is typically exchanged for goods or services. They are enforceable by law and require an offer and an acceptance.

Contract Administration   This process involves monitoring vendor performance and ensuring that all the requirements of the contract are met.

contract change control system   This describes the processes needed to make contract changes and is a tool and technique of the Contract Administration process.

Contract Closure   This process is concerned with completing and settling the terms of the contract and determines whether the work described in the contract was completed accurately and satisfactorily. This process is performed after Close Project, but its output (contract file) becomes an input to the Close Project process (contract documentation).

contract file   This is a file of all the contract records and supporting documents. This is part of the organizational process asset output of the Contract Closure process.

contract negotiation   Contract negotiation occurs when all parties discuss the terms of the contract and reach an agreement.

contract statement of work (SOW)   This is a detailed, concise description of the work of the project included with the contract. Either the buyer or the seller can write this. See also *statement of work*.

control chart   This is a tool and technique of the Quality Control process that measures the results of processes over time and displays them in graph form. Control charts measure variances to determine whether process variances are in control or out of control.

corrective actions   This is when you take action to align the anticipated future project outcomes with the project plan.

cost baseline   This is the expected cost for the project. Cost baselines are produced during the Cost Budgeting process and are represented as S curves.

Cost Budgeting   This process assigns cost estimates to activities and is used to create the cost baseline, which measures the variance and performance of the project throughout the project's life.

Cost Control   This process manages the changes to project costs using the cost change control system.

Cost Estimating   This process develops an approximation of the cost of resources needed for each project activity.

cost performance index (CPI)   This is an earned value analysis technique that is used to calculate cost performance efficiencies: $CPI = EV \div AC$.

cost plus fee (CPF)   Cost plus fee contracts reimburse the seller for all allowable costs and include a fee that's calculated as a percentage of total costs. This is also called a *cost plus percentage of cost contract*.

cost plus fixed fee (CPFF)   Cost plus fixed fee contracts charge back all allowable project costs to the seller and include a fixed fee upon completion of the contract.

cost plus incentive fee (CPIF)   This type of contract charges the allowable costs associated with producing the goods or services of the project to the buyer and includes an incentive for exceeding the performance criteria laid out in the contract.

cost plus percentage of cost (CPCC)   See *cost plus fee (CPF)*.

cost reimbursable contract   This type of contract charges the allowable costs associated with producing the goods or services of the project to the buyer.

cost variance (CV)   This is an earned value analysis technique that determines whether costs are higher or lower than budgeted during a given period of time: $CV = EV - AC$.

cost-benefit analysis   This compares the financial benefits to the company of performing the project to the costs of implementing the project.

crashing   Crashing is a compression technique that looks at cost and schedule trade-offs. One of the things you might do to crash the schedule is add resources, from either inside or outside the organization, to the critical path tasks.

critical chain method   This is a tool and technique from the Schedule Development process that allows for modifying the project schedule because of limited or restricted resources. This is a technique that's designed to help manage the uncertainties of a project. It combines deterministic and probabilistic approaches.

critical path (CP)   This is the longest path through the project. It's made up of activities with zero float.

Critical Path Method (CPM)   This determines a single early and late start date and early and late finish date for each activity on the project to determine both the longest path of the project schedule network diagram and the finish date of the project.

critical success factors   These are the elements that must be completed in order for the project to be considered complete.

culture shock   This is a disorienting experience that occurs when working in foreign surroundings or cultures that you are not familiar with.

cumulative cost performance index (CPI^c)   This is an earned value analysis technique that is used to calculate cost performance efficiencies: $CPI^c = EV^c \div AC^c$.

D

decision models   This is a category of selection methods outlined in the project selection methods tool and technique of the Develop Project Charter process. Decision models are used to examine different criteria to help make a decision regarding project selection. (See also *calculation methods*.)

decision trees   These are diagrams that show the sequence of interrelated decisions and the expected results of choosing one alternative over the other. This is a Quantitative Risk Analysis modeling technique, which is a tool and technique of this process.

deliverable   This is a measurable outcome, measurable result, or specific item that must be produced to consider the project or project phase completed. Deliverables are tangible and can be measured and easily proved.

Delphi technique   This is a Risk Identification technique used to gather information. Similar to brainstorming, except participants don't usually know each other, and they don't have to be present at the same location.

dependencies   See *logical relationships*.

Develop Project Management Plan   This is the first process in the Planning process group. The purpose of this process is to define, coordinate, and integrate all subsidiary project plans. The subsidiary plans might include the following: project scope management plan, schedule management plan, cost management plan, quality management plan, process improvement plan, staffing management plan, communication management plan, risk management plan, procurement management plan, milestone list, resource calendar, schedule baseline, cost baseline, quality baseline, and risk register.

Develop Project Team   This process concerns creating an open, encouraging environment for team members as well as developing them into an effective, functioning, coordinated group.

develop qualified sellers lists   These are lists of prospective sellers who have been preapproved or prequalified to provide contract services (or provide supplies and materials) for the organization. Qualified seller lists are an output of the Request Seller Responses process.

Direct and Manage Project Execution   This process involves carrying out the project plan. Activities are clarified, the work is authorized to begin, resources are committed and assigned to activities, and the product or service of the project is created. The largest portion of the project budget will be spent during this process.

discounted cash flow   This compares the value of the future cash flows of the project to today's dollars using time value of money techniques.

discretionary dependencies   These are dependencies defined by the project management team. Discretionary dependencies are usually process or procedure driven. They are also known as *preferred logic*, *soft logic*, and *preferential logic*. See also *logical relationships*.

disputes   See *contested changes*.

E

earned value (EV)   This is a measurement of the project's progress to date or the value of the work completed to date.

earned value technique (EVT)   This is the most commonly used performance measurement method. It looks at schedule, cost, and scope project measurements and compares their progress as of the measurement date against what was expected. The three measurements needed to perform earned value analysis are *planned value (PV)*, *actual cost (AC)*, and *earned value (EV)*.

enhance   Enhance is a Risk Response Planning strategy used for risks that pose an opportunity to the project.

estimate at completion (EAC)   This is an earned value analysis technique that forecasts the expected total cost of a work component, the schedule activity, or the project at its completion.

estimate to complete (ETC)   This is an earned value analysis technique that determines the additional expected costs to complete the schedule activity, WBS component, or control account (or project).

evaluation criteria   This is a method of rating and scoring vendor proposals. Evaluation criteria are an output of the Select Sellers process.

Executing   This is the third of the project management process groups. The Executing process group involves putting the project management plan into action, including coordinating and directing project resources to meet the objectives of the project plan. The Executing processes ensure the project plan stays on track and that future execution of project plans stays in line with project objectives.

Expectancy Theory   This is a motivational theory that states that the expectation of a positive outcome drives motivation and that people will behave in certain ways if they think there will be good rewards for doing so. The strength of the expectancy drives the behavior.

expected monetary value (EMV)   EMV is a statistical technique that calculates the average, anticipated impact of the decision. This is a Quantitative Risk Analysis modeling technique, which is a tool and technique of this process.

expected value   This is the value calculated by using the three-point estimates for activity duration (most likely, pessimistic and optimistic) and then finding the weighted average of those estimates.

expert judgment   Expert judgment is a tool and technique of several processes. Expert judgment relies on individuals or groups of people who have training, specialized knowledge, or skills about the inputs you're assessing.

exploit   Exploit is a Risk Response Planning strategy used for risks that pose an opportunity to the project.

external dependencies   These are the dependencies that are external to the project. See also *logical relationships*.

extinction   This is a type of project ending where the work of the project is completed and accepted by the stakeholders.

F

fait accompli   Fait accompli happens during contract negotiation when one party tries to convince the other party discussing a particular contract term that it is no longer an issue. It's a distraction technique because the party practicing fait accompli tactics is purposely trying to keep from negotiating an issue and claims the issue cannot be changed.

fast tracking   This is a schedule compression technique where two activities that were previously scheduled to start sequentially start at the same time. Fast tracking reduces schedule duration if applied to the critical path.

feasibility study   Feasibility studies are undertaken to determine whether the project is a viable project, the probability of project success, and the viability of the product of the project.

fixed-price contract   This type of contract sets a specific, firm price for the goods or services rendered based on a well-defined deliverable agreed upon by the buyer and seller. The biggest risk is borne by the seller with a fixed-price contract.

fixed-price plus incentive contract   This type of contract sets a specific, firm price for the goods or services rendered (like the fixed price contract) and includes an extra incentive for exceeding agreed-upon performance criteria.

float   The amount of time you can delay the early start of a task without delaying the finish date of the project. This is also known as *slack time*.

float time   See *float*.

force majeure   Catastrophic risks that are outside the scope of risk management planning such as earthquakes, meteorites, volcanoes, floods, civil unrest, and terrorism. This is referenced in the risk categories section of the Risk Identification process.

forcing   This is a conflict resolution technique where one person forces a solution on the other parties.

formal acceptance and closure   Formal acceptance and closure involves providing formal notice to the seller—usually in written form—that the contract is complete. It's the organization's way of formally accepting the product of the project from the vendor and closing out the contract. This is an element of both the Close Project and Contract Closure processes.

forward pass   A calculation used in CPM to determine early start and early finish dates for activities.

free float   This is the amount of time the start of a task can be delayed without delaying the early start of a successor task.

functional organization   This is a form of organizational structure. Functional organizations are traditional organizations with hierarchical reporting structures. The functional manager traditionally has more authority in this type of organization than the project manager has.

G

Gantt charts   This is a method of displaying schedule activities. Gantt charts might also show activity sequences, activity start and end dates, resource assignments, activity dependencies, and the critical path.

H

hammocks   These are summary-level activities or aggregate activities shown as a summary activity on a project schedule network diagram.

handoffs   This is the process of ending one project life cycle phase and beginning the next.

hard dependencies   See *mandatory dependencies*.

hard logic   See *mandatory dependencies*.

historical information   This is an input to several Planning processes that refers to information or records regarding past projects and their performance. Records are available for reference on the existing project.

Human Resource Planning   This process documents the roles and responsibilities of individuals or groups for various project elements and then documents the reporting relationships for each.

Hygiene Theory   Fredrick Herzberg developed this theory. It's also known as the Motivation-Hygiene Theory. Hygiene factors and motivators contribute to motivation. Hygiene factors prevent dissatisfaction and deal with work environment issues.

I

impact   This is the amount of damage or opportunity a risk event poses to a project.

impact scale   This is a scale in which a value is assigned to depict the severity of a potential risk impact using a cardinal value or actual numeric value.

independent estimates   This is the process of comparing the costs of a vendor proposal with outside sources or other vendor prices to determine whether estimates are reasonable. This is a tool and technique of the Select Sellers process.

influence diagrams   This is a diagramming technique referenced in the Risk Identification process that shows the causal influences among project variables, the timing or time order of events, and the relationships among other project variables and their outcomes.

Information Distribution   This process is concerned with providing stakeholders with information regarding the project in a timely manner via status reports, project meetings, review meetings, email, and so on. The communications management plan is put into action during this process.

information distribution methods   This tool and technique of the Information Distribution process involves getting the project information to the project team or stakeholders.

information gathering and retrieval systems   This tool and technique of the Information Distribution process describes ways that project information is stored and shared among project team members.

Initiating   This is the first project management process group and generally the first phase of a project life cycle. It acknowledges that the project, or the next phase in an active project, should begin.

inspection   This tool and technique of the Scope Verification, Perform Quality Control, and Contract Administration processes involves physically looking at, measuring, or testing results to determine whether they conform to the requirements or quality standards.

Integrated Change Control   This process is concerned with influencing the things that cause change, determining that change is needed or has happened, and managing change. All other change control processes are integrated with this process.

integration   This is a type of project ending where the financial or human resources assigned to the project are diverted or reassigned elsewhere in the organization.

internal rate of return (IRR)   This is the discount rate when the present value of the cash inflows equals the original investment. Projects with higher IRR values are generally considered better than projects with lower IRR values. IRR assumes that cash inflows are reinvested at the IRR value.

interviews   Interviews are question-and-answer sessions held with other project managers, subject matter experts, stakeholders, customers, the management team, project team members, and users. Typically these folks have previous experience on projects similar to the current project, or they have specialized knowledge or industry expertise.

iterative   This means to repeat processes more than once. The five process groups are repeated throughout the project's life because of change requests, responses to change, corrective action, and so on.

L

lags   Lags delay successor activities and require the dependent activity to have time added either to the start date or to the finish date of the activity.

leaders   Leaders impart vision, gain consensus for strategic goals, establish direction, and inspire and motivate others.

leads   Leads speed up successor activities and require time to be subtracted from the start date or the finish date of the dependent activity.

lessons learned   These consist of information gained throughout the course of the project that can be used to benefit the current project, future projects, or other projects currently being performed by the organization. Lessons learned should be documented and might include positive as well as negative lessons.

logical relationships   These are dependencies between two project activities whereby one activity must do something (finish or start) before another activity can do something (start or finish). Logical relationships can also exist between an activity and a milestone. These are also known as *precedence relationships*. The four types of logical relationships are finish-to-start, finish-to-finish, start-to-start, and start-to-finish.

lump-sum contracts   See *fixed-price contracts*.

M

make-or-buy analysis   This tool and technique of the Plan Purchases and Acquisitions process determines whether it's more cost effective for the organization to purchase goods and services or to produce the goods and services itself. Make-or-buy analysis can also include capacity issues, skills, availability, trade secrets, and so on.

Manage Project Team   Manage Project Team is concerned with tracking and reporting on the performance of individual team members and preparing performance appraisals.

Manage Stakeholders   Manage Stakeholders is concerned with satisfying the needs of the stakeholders by managing communications with them, resolving issues, and improving project performance by implementing requested changes.

managers   Managers focus on results and are concerned with getting the job done according to the requirements.

mandatory dependencies   These are dependencies that are directly related to the nature of the work being performed. This is also known as *hard dependencies* or *hard logic*. See also *logical relationships*.

Maslow's hierarchy of needs   A motivational theory that hypothesizes that people have five basic needs, and they fall in hierarchical order: basic physical needs, safety and security needs, social needs, self-esteem needs, and self-actualization.

mathematical models   Mathematical models, also called *constrained optimization methods*, are a category of project selection methods, which are a tool and technique of the Develop Project Charter process. They are complex mathematical models that use linear, dynamic, integer, nonlinear, and/or multiobjective programming in the form of algorithms, or in other words, a specific set of steps to solve a particular problem.

matrix organization   This is a form of organizational structure. Employees in a matrix organization report to one functional manager and at least one project manager. Functional managers assign employees to projects and carry out administrative duties, while project managers assign tasks associated with the project to team members and execute the project.

milestone   This is a major deliverable or key event in a project used to measure project progress.

milestone chart   This is a method to display project schedule information that shows the start and/or finish date of milestones.

mitigate   This is a strategy for negative risks or threats, which is a tool and technique of the Risk Response Planning process. Mitigation reduces the probability of a risk event and its impacts to an acceptable level.

Monitor and Control Project Work   Monitor and Control Project Work is concerned with monitoring all the processes in the Initiating, Planning, Executing, and Closing process groups. Collecting data, measuring results, and reporting on performance information are some of the activities performed during this process.

Monitoring and Controlling   This is the fourth project management process group. The Monitoring and Controlling process group involves taking performance measurements and analyzing them to determine whether the project is staying true to the project plan. Corrective action is applied where necessary to get the project activities realigned with the project plan.

Monte Carlo analysis   This is a simulation technique that is discussed in the modeling and simulation tool and technique of the Quantitative Risk Analysis and Schedule Development processes. Monte Carlo typically simulates schedule and cost variables many times to calculate a distribution of probable duration results.

motivational theories   Motivational theories present ideas on why people act the way they do and how they can be influenced to act in certain ways to get the results desired.

Motivation-Hygiene Theory   See *Hygiene Theory*.

N

net present value (NPV)   Net present value evaluates the cash inflows using the discounted cash flow technique, which is applied to each period the inflows are expected. The total present value of the cash flows is deducted from the initial investment to determine NPV. NPV assumes that cash inflows are reinvested at the cost of capital. This is similar to *discounted cash flow*.

nominal group technique   This is an information-gathering technique similar to the Delphi technique that can be used during the Risk Identification process.

O

objectives   These describe the purpose of the project. They are the quantifiable criteria used to measure project success. All project work is directed at completing the objective of the project. Describe the results and/or the product or service the project intends to produce. Objectives should be stated in tangible terms that are specific, measurable, accurate, realistic, and time bound.

operations   These are an ongoing endeavor typically involving repetitive processes that produce the same results.

ordinal scale   These are values that are rank-ordered such as high, medium, or low. They are referenced in the Qualitative Risk Analysis process.

organization breakdown structure (OBS)   This relates the WBS elements to the organizational unit responsible for completing the work.

P

parametric estimating   Parametric estimating is a quantitatively based estimating method that multiplies the quantity of work by the rate.

Pareto charts   Pareto charts are a tool and technique of the Perform Quality Control process. They rank-order the most important factors such as delays, costs, or defects by their frequency over time and are displayed as histograms.

passive acceptance   Passive acceptance means that no plans will be made to avoid or mitigate the risk. The consequences of the risk event are accepted should the risk event occur.

payback period   This is the length of time it takes a company to recover the initial cost of producing a product or service of a project.

payment system   A payment system is the tool and technique of Contract Administration that is used to issue payment based on the input of seller invoices.

Perform Quality Assurance   This process involves performing systematic quality activities and uses quality audits to determine which processes should be used to achieve the project requirements and to assure that they are performed efficiently and effectively.

Perform Quality Control   This process is concerned with monitoring work results to see whether they fulfill the quality standards set out in the quality management plan. The Perform Quality Control process determines whether the end product conforms to the requirements and product description defined during the Planning processes.

performance measurement baselines   The project plan baseline, schedule baseline, and cost baseline are collectively known as the performance measurement baselines.

Performance Reporting   This process concerns collecting information regarding project progress and project accomplishments and reporting it to the stakeholders, project team members, management team, and other interested parties. It also makes predictions regarding future project performance.

Plan Contracting   This process prepares the documents used in the Request Seller Responses and Select Sellers processes.

Plan Purchases and Acquisitions   This process involves identifying the goods or services that will be purchased from outside of the organization, the quantity needed, and when they need to be purchased. It also involves identifying the project needs that can be met by the project team.

planned value (PV)   This is the cost of work that has been budgeted for an activity during a certain time period. (Note: *PV* also stands for *present value.*)

Planning   This is the second project management process group. The Planning process group consists of processes that involve formulating and revising project goals and objectives and creating the project management plan that will be used to achieve the goals the project was undertaken to address. Planning involves determining alternative courses of action and selecting from among the best of those to produce the project's goals. The Planning process group is where the project requirements are determined and stakeholders are identified.

politics   This is a technique used to influence people to perform. It involves getting groups of people with different interests to cooperate creatively even in the midst of conflict and disorder.

portfolio   This is a collection of projects or programs that meet a specific business goal or objective.

portfolio management   This is the management of collections of programs and projects to meet and maximize the strategic objectives of the business. It involves monitoring active projects, balancing the portfolio among other investments, assuring efficient use of resources, and assessing the value of projects and potential projects against the portfolio's strategic objectives.

power   This is a technique used to influence people to perform. It's the ability to get people to do things they wouldn't do otherwise, to change minds and the course of events, and to influence outcomes.

preassignment   This is a tool and technique of the Acquire Project Team process. This occurs when a project is put out for bid and specific team members are promised as part of the proposal or when internal project team members are promised and assigned as a condition of the project.

precedence diagramming method (PDM)   This is a diagramming method that places activities on nodes, which connect to dependent activities using arrows. This is also known as *activity on node*.

precedence relationships   See *logical relationships*.

preferential logic   See *discretionary dependencies*.

preferred logic   See *discretionary dependencies*.

preliminary scope statement   This is a definition of what the project entails, including a high-level look at the project objectives and deliverables. It provides a brief background of the project and describes the business opportunity the company is attempting to benefit from. It also describes the business objectives the project should meet.

prevention   This keeps errors from occurring in the process. Prevention is a quality concern.

preventive action   Preventive action involves anything that will reduce the potential impacts of risk events should they occur. Contingency plans and risk responses are examples of preventive action. These are inputs to the Direct and Manage Project Execution process.

probability   This is the likelihood that an event will occur.

probability and impact matrix   The probability and impact matrix defines the combination of probability and impact that helps determine which risks need detailed risk response plans. It's defined during the Risk Management Planning process and included in the risk management plan. The matrix is used in the Qualitative Risk Analysis process to assign an overall risk rating to each of the project's identified risks. The combination of probability and impact results in a classification usually expressed as high, medium, or low. High risks are considered a red condition, medium risks are considered a yellow condition, and low risks are considered a green condition.

process analysis   Process analysis is a tool and technique of the Perform Quality Assurance process. It looks at process improvement from an organizational and technical perspective. Process analysis steps are documented in the process improvement plan and examine problems experienced while conducting the project, the constraints of the project, and inefficient and ineffective processes identified during process operation.

procurement audits   This tool and technique of the Contract Closure process examines the procurement processes to determine the effectiveness of the processes. Procurement audits are performed on all the Project Procurement Management Knowledge Area processes except the Contract Closure process.

procurement documents   Procurement documents are prepared in the Plan Contracting process and are used to solicit vendors and suppliers to bid on project procurement needs. A procurement document might be called *request for proposal* (RFP), *request for information* (RFI), *invitation for bid* (IFB), or *request for quotation* (RFQ).

procurement management plan   This details how the procurement process will be managed throughout the project and includes elements such as the types of contracts used, the authority of the project team, and where to find standard procurement documents.

product analysis   This is a description of the product of the project that might include performing value analysis, function analysis, quality function deployment, product breakdown analysis, systems engineering techniques, value engineering, and function deployment techniques to further define and better understand the product or service of the project. This is a tool and technique of the Scope Definition process.

product description   See *product scope description.*

product scope   See *product scope description.*

product scope description   This is a description of the product features typically documented in the product description.

product verification   This determines whether the work described in the contract was completed accurately and satisfactorily. It's one of the purposes of the Contract Closure process.

Program Evaluation and Review Technique (PERT)   PERT uses expected value—or weighted average—of critical path tasks to determine project duration by establishing three estimates: most likely, pessimistic, and optimistic. PERT is used when activity duration estimates are highly uncertain.

program   This is a grouping of projects that are managed together. The individual projects are usually part of one bigger project and are therefore related.

program management   The central management and coordination of groups of related projects and operations work to obtain benefits and administer controls that aren't possible when the projects and operations are managed individually to achieve the program's strategic objectives.

progressive elaboration   This is the process of taking incremental steps to examine and refine the characteristics of the product of the project. Processes may be progressively elaborated as well.

project   Projects are temporary in nature; have definite start and end dates; create a unique product, service, or result; and are completed when the goals and objectives of the project have been met and signed off on by the stakeholders.

project boundaries   These define what is and what is not included in the work of the project. These should specifically state what is excluded from the work of the project. This is an element of the project scope statement.

project calendars   Project calendars are an input to the Schedule Development process. They concern all the resources involved in the project and specify the working periods for all resources.

project charter   This is an official, written acknowledgment and recognition that a project exists. The project charter is issued by senior management and gives the project manager the authority to assign organizational resources to the work of the project.

Project Communications Management   This is one of the nine Knowledge Areas of project management. Project Communications Management ensures proper and timely communications and includes these processes: Communications Planning, Information Distribution, Performance Reporting, and Manage Stakeholders.

Project Cost Management   This is one of the nine Knowledge Areas of project management. Project Cost Management ensures proper cost planning, budgets, and controls and includes these processes: Cost Estimating, Cost Budgeting, and Cost Control.

Project Human Resource Management   This is one of the nine Knowledge Areas of project management. Project Human Resource Management ensures effective use of human resources and includes these processes: Human Resource Planning, Acquire Project Team, Develop Project Team, and Manage Project Team.

Project Integration Management   This is one of the nine Knowledge Areas of project management. Project Integration Management involves coordinating all aspects of the project and includes these processes: Develop Project Charter, Preliminary Project Scope Statement, Develop Project Management Plan, Direct and Manage Project Execution, Monitor and Control Project Work, Integrated Change Control, and Close Project.

project life cycle   This is the grouping of project phases in a sequential order from the beginning of the project to the close.

project management Knowledge Areas   These nine project management groupings—known as *Knowledge Areas*—bring together common or related processes.

project management office (PMO) This is the office established by organizations to create and maintain procedures and standards for project management methodologies to be used throughout the organization.

project management plan This plan defines how the project is executed, how it's monitored and controlled, and how it's closed and also documents the outputs of the Planning group processes. The size and complexity of the project will determine the level of detail contained in this plan.

Project Management Professional Code of Professional Conduct This is an ethical code established by PMI to ensure personal and professional conduct on the part of PMPs.

project management This is the process that's used to initiate, plan, execute, monitor, control, and close out projects by applying skills, knowledge, and project management tools and techniques to fulfill the project requirements.

project manager This is the person responsible for applying the skills, knowledge, and project management tools and techniques to the project activities in order to successfully complete the project objectives.

project performance review Project performance reviews are similar to status reviews. Their purpose is to examine schedule activities, work packages, or cost account status and their progress to date. The three types of analyses associated with performance reviews are variance analysis, trend analysis, and earned value technique.

project plan This is an assortment of documents (outputs from the Planning process group) that constitutes what the project is, what the project will deliver, and how all the processes will be managed. The project plan is used as the guideline throughout the project Executing and Controlling process groups to track and measure project performance and to make future project decisions. It's also used as a communication and information tool for stakeholders, team members, and the management team.

project presentations Project presentations are part of the organizational process assets updates, which is an output of the Information Distribution process. These concern presenting project information to the stakeholders and other appropriate parties.

Project Procurement Management This is one of the nine Knowledge Areas of project management. Project Procurement Management concerns procurement and contract oversight. The processes included in this Knowledge Area are Plan Purchases and Acquisitions, Plan Contracting, Request Seller Responses, Select Sellers, Contract Administration, and Contract Closure.

Project Quality Management This is one of the nine Knowledge Areas of project management. Project Quality Management ensures that the quality requirements of the project are satisfied. The processes included in this Knowledge Area are Quality Planning, Perform Quality Assurance, and Perform Quality Control.

project records   Project records are all information regarding the project, including project reports, memos, project schedules, project plans, and other documents.

project reports   This is an element of the organizational process assets update output of the Information Distribution process that includes project information such as the project status reports and minutes from project meetings.

Project Risk Management   This is one of the nine Knowledge Areas of project management. Project Risk Management is concerned with identifying and planning for potential risks that may impact the project. Its processes include Risk Management Planning, Risk Identification, Qualitative Risk Analysis, Quantitative Risk Analysis, Risk Response Planning, and Risk Monitoring and Control.

project schedule   The project schedule determines the start and finish dates for project activities and assigns resources to the activities.

project scope   The project scope describes the work required to produce the product or the service of the project. This includes the requirements of the product, which describe the features and functionality of the product or service.

Project Scope Management   This is one of the nine Knowledge Areas of project management. Project Scope Management is concerned with the work of the project and only the work that is required to complete the project. Its processes include Scope Planning, Scope Definition, Create WBS, Scope Verification, and Scope Control.

project scope management plan   The project scope management plan has a direct influence on the project's success and describes the process for defining project scope and verifying the work of the project. It facilitates the creations of the WBS, describes how the product or service of the project is verified and accepted, and documents how changes to scope will be handled. It is an output of the Scope Planning process.

project scope statement   The project scope statement documents the project objectives, deliverables, and requirements, which are used as a basis for future project decisions. It also includes other elements, such product scope description, project boundaries, product acceptance criteria, constraints, assumptions, project organization, risks, milestones, fund limitations, cost estimate, configuration management requirements, project specifications, and approval requirements.

project sponsor   This is usually an executive in the organization. The project sponsor has the authority to assign resources and enforce decisions regarding the project.

project statement of work (SOW)   This describes the product or service the project was undertaken to complete. It is an input to several processes. (See also *contract statement of work*.)

Project Time Management   This is one of the nine Knowledge Areas of project management. Project Time Management is concerned with estimating the duration of the project plan activities, devising a project schedule, and monitoring and controlling deviations from the schedule. Its processes include Activity Definition, Activity Sequencing, Activity Resource Estimating, Activity Duration Estimating, Schedule Development, and Schedule Control.

projectized organization   This is a type of organizational structure focused on projects. Project managers generally have ultimate authority over the project. Sometimes, supporting departments such as human resources and accounting might report to the project manager. Project managers are responsible for making project decisions and acquiring and assigning resources.

Q

qualified seller lists   See *develop qualified seller lists*.

Qualitative Risk Analysis   This process determines what impact the identified risks will have on the project and the probability that they'll occur, and it puts the risks in priority order according to their effect on the project objectives.

quality audits   Quality audits are independent reviews performed by trained auditors or third-party reviewers. The purpose of a quality audit is to identify ineffective and inefficient processes used on the project. Audits may also examine and uncover inefficient processes and procedures.

Quantitative Risk Analysis   This process assigns numeric probabilities to each identified risk and examines their potential impact to the project objectives.

R

RACI chart   This is a matrix-based chart that shows the type of resource and their responsibility on the project. RACI stands for *responsible*, *accountable*, *consult*, and *inform*. This is a tool and technique of the Human Resource Planning process.

recognition and rewards   This is a tool and technique of the Develop Project Team process; recognition and rewards systems are formal ways for the management team and the project manager to recognize and promote desirable behavior.

records management system   A records management system is a tool and technique of the Contract Administration process and involves documenting policies, control functions, and automated tools used to manage project documents and contract documents. A records management system is part of the project management information system.

Request Seller Responses   This process involves obtaining bids and proposals from vendors in response to RFPs and similar documents prepared during the Plan Contracting process.

requirements   These are the specifications of the objective or deliverable that must be met in order to satisfy the needs of the project. Requirements might also describe results or outcomes that must be produced in order to satisfy a contract, specification, standard, or other project document (typically the scope statement). Requirements quantify and prioritize the wants, needs, and expectations of the project sponsor and stakeholders.

reserve time   This is the practice of adding a portion of time (percentage of total time or number of work periods) to an activity to account for schedule risk.

residual risk   This is a risk that remains after implementing a risk response strategy.

resource breakdown structure (RBS)   This is a hierarchical chart of resources that breaks down the work of the project according to the types of resources needed.

resource calendars   Calendars are an input to the Schedule Development process. Resource calendars refer to specific resources—or categories of resources—and their individual (or group) availability.

resource leveling   Resource leveling attempts to smooth out the resource assignments so that tasks are completed without overloading the individual and without negatively affecting the project schedule. Some ways to perform resource leveling include delaying the start of a task to match the availability of a key team member or giving more tasks to underallocated team members. Resource leveling is also known as the *resource-based method*.

resource-based method   See *resource leveling*.

resources   Resources include the people, equipment, and materials needed to complete the work of the project.

Responsibility Assignment Matrix (RAM)   The RAM ties roles and responsibilities with the WBS elements to ensure that each element has a resource assigned.

reverse resource allocation scheduling   This is a resource-leveling technique used when key resources are required at a specific point in the project and they are the only resources available to perform these activities. Reverse resource allocation scheduling requires that the resources be scheduled in reverse order, that is, from the end date of the project rather than from the beginning, in order to assign key resources at the correct time.

revisions   These are adjustments to approved schedule start and end dates for activities to coincide with approved changes and/or corrective actions. This is another term for *schedule updates*.

rework   Failing to meet quality requirements or standards might result in rework (performing the work again to make it conform). Rework might increase the project schedule.

risk breakdown structure (RBS)   An RBS is a graphical way to display risk categories and their subcategories. The RBS is an element of the risk management plan.

risk categories   Risk categories systematically identify risks and provide a foundation for understanding. The use of risk categories helps improve the Risk Identification process by giving everyone involved a common language or basis for describing risk. Risk categories are an element of the risk management plan.

risk identification   This process identifies the potential project risks and documents their characteristics.

risk management plan   Describes how risks are defined, monitored, and controlled throughout the project. The risk management plan is a subsidiary of the project management plan, and it's the only output of the Risk Management Planning process.

Risk Management Planning   This process determines how risks will be managed for a project.

Risk Monitoring and Control   This process involves responding to risks as they occur. The risk management plan details how risk is managed, and the risk response plan details how risk response strategies are implemented in the event of an actual risk event. This process implements risk response according to the plan.

risk register   This is the output of the Risk Identification process that contains the list of identified risks. The risk register is updated, and its update becomes an output of every remaining Risk process. At the end of the Risk Response Planning process, the risk register contains these elements: list of identified and prioritized risks, risk owners and their responsibilities, risk triggers, response plans and strategies, cost and schedule activities needed to implement risk responses, contingency reserves for cost and time, contingency plans, fallback plans, residual and secondary risks, probabilistic analysis of the project, and other outputs of the Qualitative and Quantitative Risk Analysis processes.

Risk Response Planning   This process defines what steps to take to reduce threats and take advantage of opportunities and assigns departments or individual staff members the responsibility of carrying out the risk response plans developed in this process.

risk tolerance   Risk tolerance is the level at which stakeholders are comfortable taking a risk because the benefits to be gained outweigh what could be lost or at which risks are avoided because the cost is too great.

run chart   A run chart is a tool and technique of the Perform Quality Control process that are used to show variations in the process over time. A run chart might also show trends in the process.

S

Scatter diagrams   Scatter diagrams are a tool and technique of the Perform Quality Control process. They use two variables: an independent variable, which is an input, and a dependent variable, which is an output, to display the relationship between these two elements as points on a graph.

schedule baseline   The approved project schedule serves as the schedule baseline that will be used in the Executing and Monitoring and Controlling processes to measure schedule process.

schedule change control system This defines how changes to the schedule are made and managed. This tracks and records change requests, describes the procedures to follow to implement schedule changes, and details the authorization levels needed to approve the schedule changes.

schedule compression This is a form of mathematical analysis that's used to shorten the project schedule without changing the project scope. Compression is simply shortening the project schedule to accomplish all the activities sooner than estimated. Crashing and fast tracking are two examples of schedule compressions.

Schedule Control This process involves documenting and managing changes to the project schedule.

Schedule Development This process calculates and prepares the schedule of project activities, which becomes the schedule baseline. It determines activity start and finish dates, finalizes activity sequences and durations, and assigns resources to activities.

schedule network analysis This technique of Schedule Development creates the project schedule. It uses a schedule model and other analytical techniques such as critical path and critical chain method, what-if analysis, and resource leveling (all of which are other tools and techniques in this process) to help calculate these dates and the project schedule.

schedule performance index (SPI) This is a performance index that calculates schedule performance efficiencies: $SPI = EV \div PV$.

schedule updates Schedule updates are an output of the Schedule Control process and involve adjusting activities and dates to coincide with approved changes and/or corrective actions.

schedule variance (SV) This is an earned value analysis technique that determines whether the project schedule is ahead or behind what was planned for a given period of time: $SV = EV - PV$.

scope Scope includes all of the components that make up the product or service of the project and the results the project intends to produce.

Scope Control This process involves documenting and managing changes to project scope. Any modification to the agreed-upon WBS is considered a scope change. Changes in product scope will require changes to the project scope. (See also *product scope* and *project scope*.)

Scope Definition This Planning process further elaborates the objectives and deliverables of the project into a project scope statement that's used as a basis for future project decisions.

scope management plan See *project scope management plan*.

Scope Planning The primary purpose of the Scope Planning process is to document the scope management plan. This is a planning tool that documents how the project team will go about defining project scope, how the work breakdown structure will be developed, how changes to scope will be controlled, and how project scope will be verified.

scope statement   See *project scope statement*.

Scope Verification   This process formalizes the acceptance of the project scope and is primarily concerned with the acceptance of work results.

scoring model   This is a project selection method used to score and rank project proposals. Project selection methods are a tool and technique of the Develop Project Charter process. Scoring models might also be used in the Select Seller process.

screening systems   This is a set of predetermined performance criteria used to screen vendors. Screening systems are a tool and technique of the Select Sellers process.

secondary risks   These are risks that come about as a result of implementing a risk response.

Select Sellers   This process involves the receipt of bids or proposals and choosing a vendor to perform the work or supply the goods or services.

seller invoices   These are requests for the payment of goods or services that should describe the work that was completed or the materials that were delivered. Seller invoices are part of the Contract Administration process.

seller rating systems   Seller rating systems are a tool and technique of the Select Sellers process. These systems use information about the sellers—such as past performance, delivery, contract compliance, and quality ratings—to determine seller performance.

sensitivity analysis   This is a quantitative method of analyzing the potential impact of risk events on the project and determining which risk events have the greatest potential for impact by examining all the uncertain elements at their baseline values. This is a Quantitative Risk Analysis modeling technique.

share   Share is a Risk Response Planning strategy for risks that pose an opportunity to the project.

should cost estimates   See *independent estimates*.

slack time   This is the amount of time you can delay the early start of a task without delaying the finish date of the project. This is also known as *float time*.

smoothing   Smoothing is a conflict resolution technique that is a temporary way to resolve conflict where someone attempts to make the conflict appear less important than it is. This is a temporary solution.

soft logic   See *discretionary dependencies*.

stakeholder   This is an organization or person who has a vested interest in the project and stands to gain or lose something as a result of the project.

starvation   This is a type of project ending where financial or human resources are cut off from the project.

statistical sampling   This means making a sample number of parts from the whole population and examining them to determine whether they fall within the variances outlined by the quality control plan. Statistical sampling is a tool and technique of the Perform Quality Control process.

status review meetings   Status meetings are a tool and technique of the Project Plan Execution process. The purpose of status meetings is to provide updated information regarding the progress of the project. They are not show-and-tell meetings.

steering committee   This is a group of high-level managers or executives in the organization who manage project prioritization and various project decisions. The steering committee typically represents functional areas or departments within the organization.

successor activities   These are activities that follow predecessor activities.

T

tailoring   This means determining which processes and process groups should be performed for the project. The project manager and project team should take into consideration the size and complexity of the project and the various inputs and outputs of each of the processes when determining which ones to perform. It's generally accepted that performing all five process groups is good practice for any project.

team building   Team building activities are a tool and technique of the Develop Project Team process. They involve getting a diverse group of people to work together in the most efficient and effective manner possible.

technical performance measurements   These measurements are usually determined during trend analysis (which is used with the run chart tool and technique of the Perform Quality Control process) to compare the technical accomplishments of project milestones completed to the technical milestones defined in the project Planning processes.

Theory X   This is a motivational management theory that proposes that most people do not like work and will try to steer clear of it. It postulates that people have little to no ambition, need constant supervision, and won't actually perform the duties of their job unless threatened.

Theory Y   This is a motivational management theory that proposes that people are interested in performing their best given the right motivation and proper expectations.

three-point estimates   Three-point estimates are a tool and technique of the Activity Duration Estimating process used to determine activity estimates. The three estimates are the most likely estimate, an optimistic estimate, and a pessimistic estimate.

time and materials (T&M) contract   This is a type of contract that is a cross between the fixed-price contract and the cost-reimbursable contract. Preset unit rates are agreed to at contract signing, but costs are charged to the buyer as they're incurred.

tolerable results   These are quality measurements that fall within a specified range. Tolerable results are a concern of the Perform Quality Control process. These are also known as *tolerances*.

top-down estimating   See *analogous estimating*.

tornado diagram   This is a diagramming method for sensitivity analysis data. The variables with the greatest effect on the project are displayed as horizontal bars at the top of the graph and decrease in impact as they progress down through the graph. This gives a quick overview of how much the project can be affected by uncertainty in the various elements and which risks have the greatest impact on the project.

total float   This is the amount of time the earliest start of a task can be delayed without delaying the ending of the project.

training   This tool and technique of the Develop Project Team process improves the competencies of the project team members.

transference   Transference is a strategy for negative risks or threats, which is a tool and technique of the Risk Response Planning process. This strategy transfers the consequences of a risk to a third party. Insurance is an example of transference.

triggers   These are risk symptoms that imply a risk event is about to occur.

V

variance at completion (VAC)   This is an earned value analysis technique that calculates the difference between the budget at completion (BAC) and the estimate at completion (EAC): VAC = BAC − EAC.

virtual teams   Virtual teams are teams that don't necessarily work in the same location but all share the goals of the project and have a role on the project. This type of team allows the inclusion of resources from different geographic locations, those who work different hours or shifts from the other team members, those with mobility limitations, and so on.

W

weighted scoring model   See *weighting system*.

weighting system   This is a way to rank and score vendor proposals or project proposals. Weighting systems assign numerical weights to evaluation criteria and then multiply this by the weight of each criteria factor to come up with total scores for each project or vendor. These systems keep personal biases to a minimum. Weighting systems are a tool and technique of the Selecting Sellers process and a project selection method, which is a tool and technique of the Develop Project Charter process.

withdrawal   This conflict resolution technique occurs when one of the parties gets up and leaves and refuses to discuss the conflict. This never results in resolution.

work authorization systems   Work authorization systems clarify and initiate the work of each work package or activity. This is a formal procedure that authorizes work to begin in the correct sequence and at the right time. Work authorization systems are usually written procedures defined by the organization. These are used in the Executing processes of the project.

work performance information   Work performance information is an input to the Contract Administration process. Work performance information is used to monitor work results and examine the vendor's deliverables and compares their work results against the project management plan. It also makes certain activities are performed correctly and in sequence.

workaround   This is an unplanned response to a risk event that was unknown and unidentified or an unplanned response to a risk that was previously accepted. Workaround plans are an element of the Risk Monitoring and Control process.

Index

Note to the Reader: Throughout this index **boldfaced** page numbers indicate primary discussions of a topic. *Italicized* page numbers indicate illustrations.

A

AC (actual cost), 428–429, 553
acceptance
    Contract Closure process, 482
    defined, 552
    project scope statements, **111**
    Risk Response Planning process,
        211–212
accounting
    in configuration management, 421
    skills requirements, 11
accuracy in SMART rule, 107
Achievement Theory, 346, 552
Acquire Project Team process, 36,
        333–334
    defined, 552
    inputs, 538–539
    outputs, 335–336, 538–539
    tools and techniques, 334–335
acquisitions. *See* Plan Purchases and
        Acquisitions process
active risk acceptance, 212
activity attributes, 552
Activity Definition process, 34,
        248–249
    defined, 552
    inputs, **249**, 533–534
    outputs, **250–251**, 533–534
    tools and techniques, **249–250**
activity duration estimates, 552
Activity Duration Estimating process,
        34, 275
    defined, 552
    inputs, **276**, *535*
    outputs, **279**, *535*
    tools and techniques, 276–278
activity lists, 250, 552
activity on arrow (AOA) method, 254,
        552
activity on node (AON) method, 253,
        553
Activity Resource Estimating process,
        34, **272–273**
    defined, 553
    inputs, **273**, 534
    outputs, 274–275, 534
    tools and techniques, 273–274
Activity Sequencing process, 34, **251**
    arrow diagramming method, 254,
        254

defined, 553
dependencies, 252–253
inputs, 534
lags and leads, 254
outputs, 255–256, 534
precedence diagramming method,
        253, *253*
schedule network templates, 254
actual cost (AC), 428–429, 553
actual cost of work performed
        (ACWP), 429
addition ending type, 473, 553
ADM (arrow diagramming method),
        254, *254*, 553
administrative closure procedures
    defined, 553
    Direct and Manage Project
        Execution process, **329**
    overview, **477**
advertising, 373, 553
affiliations, conflicts of interest with,
        500
aggregation, 303
alternative analysis in Activity
        Resource Estimating process,
        274
alternatives identification in Scope
        Definition process, **102**, 553
analogous estimating
    Activity Duration Estimating
        process, 276–277
    Cost Estimating process, 300
    defined, 553
AOA (activity on arrow) method, 254,
        552
AON (activity on node) method, 253,
        553
appraisal costs in Quality Planning
        process, 155
appraisals in Manage Project Team
        process, **396**
approval requirements
    defined, 553
    project scope statements, 116
approving project scope statements,
        116
arbitration, 553
arrow diagramming method (ADM),
        254, *254*, 553
associations, conflicts of interest with,
        500

assumptions
    defined, 553
    project scope statements, **113–114**
    Risk Identification process, **190**
attributes
    activity, **250–251**
    defined, 553
    in inspection, 465
audits
    in configuration management, 421
    Contract Administration process,
        390
    Perform Quality Assurance
        process, **383–384**
    procurement, 481–482, 568
    risk, 442
authority in Human Resource Planning
        process, 247
authorization systems
    Direct and Manage Project
        Execution process, **326–327**
    enterprise environment, 58
availability, team member, 334
avoidance in Risk Response Planning
        process, **209**, 554
award stage in contracts, 381

B

BAC (budget at completion), 432, 554
backward passes, **283**, 554
balance of power in matrix
        organizations, **19–20**
balanced matrix organization, 21, *21*,
        554
bar charts
    defined, 554
    Schedule Control process, **439**
    Schedule Development process,
        296, *296*
baselines
    Cost Budget, **302–305**, *304–305*
    Integrated Change Control
        process, 420
    quality, **162**
    schedule, 279, **297**
    work breakdown structure,
        145–146
basic physical needs in needs hierarchy,
        344

BCWP (budgeted cost of work performed), 429
BCWS (budgeted cost of work scheduled), 429
behavior models, **347**
benchmarking, **154**
benefit/cost analyses
    defined, **558**
    project selection, **62–63**
    Quality Planning process, **154**
benefit measurement methods
    defined, **554**
    project selection, **62–67**
bidder conferences
    defined, **554**
    Request Seller Responses process, 373
bids in Plan Contracting, 239
bill of materials (BOM), 144
bottom-up estimating
    Activity Resource Estimating process, 274
    Cost Estimating process, **300**
boundaries, project, **111**, 569
brainstorming in Risk Identification process, 188, 554
budget at completion (BAC), 432, 554
budget constraints, 112
budgeted cost of work performed (BCWP), 429
budgeted cost of work scheduled (BCWS), 429
budgets
    Cost Budget Baseline process, 302–305, *304–305*
    cost estimates for. *See* Cost Estimating process
    in risk management plans, 183
    skills for, **11**
buffer time, **278**
business needs
    projects from, 54
    in statements of work, 57
buyer-conducted performance reviews, 390

C

calculation methods, **61–62**, **64–67**, 554
calendars
    resource, 275
    Schedule Development process, 293–294
cardinal scales
    defined, **554**
    in impact analysis, **196**

cash flow analysis techniques, **64–67**
categories, risk, **183–184**, 194, 201, 574
cause-and-effect diagrams, 190, *191*, 554–555
CCBs (configuration control boards), 424, *555*
celebrations, 485
champions for charters, **71–72**
change control
    Contract Administration process, 388–389
    costs. *See* Cost Control process
    exam essentials, 448
    integrated. *See* Integrated Change Control process
    key terms, 449
    Kitchen Heaven project, 443–446
    quality control. *See* Perform Quality Control process
    review questions, 450–455
    Risk Monitoring and Control process, 440–443
    schedules, 437–440
    summary, 447–448
change control systems, **421**
    contract, 390
    defined, *555*
    purpose, **422**
    requirements, 423–424
change requests
    Contract Administration process, 392–393
    Direct and Manage Project Execution process, 329, 331
charters, **56–57**
    defined, **570**
    elements, **72–73**
    enterprise environment factors, 58–59
    exam essentials, **82**
    expert judgment in, **69–70**
    key terms, **83**
    organizational process assets, 59
    project managers for, 70–71
    project selection methodologies. *See* project selection methodologies
    review questions, **84–90**
    sign-off, **73–74**
    stakeholders for, **70–72**
    statements of work, **57–58**
    summary, **81–82**
charts
    matrix-based, 245–246
    milestone, 296
    Perform Quality Control process, 460–463, *461*

checklists
    Human Resource Planning process, 243
    Quality Planning process, **160**
    Risk Identification process, **190**
claims administration, 555
Close Project process, 32, 475–476
    defined, *555*
    inputs, 476, 549–550
    outputs, 477–479, 549–550
    tools and techniques, 476
closeout processes, **471–472**
    celebrations, 485
    characteristics, 472
    Close Project, 475–479
    Contract Closure, 480–483
    exam essentials, 488
    key terms, 489
    Kitchen Heaven project, 483–485
    project endings, 472–474
    releasing team members, 483
    review questions, 490–496
    summary, 487–488
Closing process groups, 26, 555
co-located teams, 17, 341–342, 555
codes of accounts for WBS, 141
coercive power, 348
collective bargaining agreements, 243
combination approach in WBS, 137
commercial databases in enterprise environment, 58
common causes of variances, 462, 555
communication
    defined, *555*
    stakeholders, **104–105**
communication skills, **350**
    conflict resolution, 353–354
    forms of communication, 352
    information exchange, 351–352
    listening, 352–353
    project managers, **10**
communications management, **37**
communications management plans, 151–152
Communications Planning process, 37, 146
    inputs, 147, 529
    outputs, 529
    requirements analysis, 147–150, *148*
    technology, 150
company data, protecting, 507
competency
    Human Resource Planning process, 247
    team member, 334
compliance in staffing, 248
compression, duration, 289

compromise in conflict resolution, 354, 555

confidential information, **506–507**

configuration control boards (CCBs), **424**, 555

configuration management
defined, 555
Integrated Change Control
process, 421

configuration requirements in project
scope statements, 115

conflict management skills, **11**

conflict resolution, 353–354, 396

conflicts, 556

conflicts of interest, **499–501**, 556

conformity in inspection, 465

confrontation in conflict resolution, 354, 556

conservation in Manage Project Team
process, **395**

constrained optimization methods
defined, 556
project selection, 62, 68

constraints
defined, 556
project scope statements, **111–113**
with stakeholders, 509

contested changes, 391, 556

contingency planning, **212**, 556

contingency reserves, 212, 556

Contingency Theory, 347

contingency time, **278**

continuous probability distributions, 204

Contract Administration process, 39, **387–388**
defined, 556
inputs, 388–389, 542
outputs, 392–393, 542
tools and techniques, 390–392

contract change control systems, 390, 556

contract closure procedure, **478**

Contract Closure process, 39
defined, 556–557
inputs, 481, 550
outputs, 550
tools and techniques, 481–482

contract files, 482, 556

contract management plans, 382

contract negotiation in vendor
selection, 377, 556

contract statements of work, 57–58, **237–238**, 241, 557

contracting transfers, 210

contracts
administration process. See
Contract Administration
process

closeout process. See Contract
Closure process
defined, 556
elements, **380**
life cycles, **380–381**
Plan Purchases and Acquisitions
process, 233–234
cost reimbursable, **235–236**
fixed process and lump sum,
234
time and materials, **236**

contractual agreements, risk-related,
214

control charts, 460, *461*, 557

corrective actions
defined, 557
Direct and Manage Project
Execution process, **328**
Integrated Change Control
process, 424

correspondence in Contract
Administration process, 393

cost baselines
Cost Budgeting process, 302–305, *304–305*
defined, 557
Integrated Change Control, 420

cost-benefit analysis
defined, 557
project selection, **62–63**
Quality Planning process, **154**

Cost Budgeting process, 35, **302**
defined, 557
exam essentials, 314–315
inputs, 302, 537
key terms, 315–316
Kitchen Heaven project, 307–312, *309, 311*
outputs, 304–305, *304–305*, 537
review questions, 317–323
summary, 313–314
tools and techniques, 303

Cost Control process, 35, **426**
cost change control systems, **427**
defined, 557
forecasting, **431–433**
inputs, 426, 545–546
outputs, 435–436, 545–546
performance measurement
analysis, 427–431, *430*
projection performance reviews,
433–434
software and variance
management, **434**

cost estimates in project scope
statements, 115

Cost Estimating process, 35, **298–299**
defined, 557
inputs, 299, 536–537

outputs, 300–302, 536–537
tools, **299–300**

cost management, **35**

cost performance index (CPI), 431, 557

cost plus fee (CPF) contracts, 235, 557

cost plus fixed fee (CPFF) contracts,
235, 557

cost plus incentive fee (CPIF) contracts,
235, 557

cost plus percentage of cost (CPPC)
contracts, 235, 557

cost reimbursable contracts, 235–236,
557

cost variance (CV), **430**, 557

costs
in impact analysis, 197
in process groups, 27
of quality, **155–158**
reporting systems, 400

CP (critical path), 558

CPF (cost plus fee) contracts, 235, 557

CPFF (cost plus fixed fee) contracts,
235, 557

CPI (cost performance index), 431, 557

CPIC (cumulative cost performance
index), 431, 558

CPIF (cost plus incentive fee) contracts,
235, 557

CPM (Critical Path Method), **282**
critical path calculations,
283–284, *285*
defined, 558
forward passes and backward
passes, 283
gathering activity, 282–283

CPPC (cost plus percentage of cost)
contracts, 235, 557

crashing in duration compression, **289**,
558

Create WBS process, 33, 528–529

criteria
defined, 560
Plan Contracting, **240**
project scope statements, 111
scoring models, 63–64
Select Sellers process, 375–376

critical chain method, **291**, 558

Critical Path Method (CPM), **282**
critical path calculations,
283–284, *285*
defined, 558
forward passes and backward
passes, 283
gathering activity, 282–283

critical success factors, 109, 558

Crosby, Philip B., **156**

cultural issues, 511–512, 558

culture in enterprise environment, 58

cumulative cost performance index (CPIC), 431, 558
customer requests, 53–54
CV (cost variance), 430, 557

D

data quality assessment, 201
databases in enterprise environment, 58
dates
    CPM, 283
    imposed, 281
    project duration, 287–288
    Schedule Development process, 293–294
decision models, 61–62, 68, 558
decision tree analysis, 205–206, 206, 558
decomposition, 135–137
defect repairs
    Direct and Manage Project Execution process, 329
    Perform Quality Control process, 466
defined risks, 115
deliverables
    decomposing, 135–137
    defined, 558–559
    Direct and Manage Project Execution process, 331
    documenting, 110
    in phases, 23–24
    in scope statements, 108
Delphi technique, 189, 558
Deming, W. Edwards, 29, 156–157
dependencies
    Activity Sequencing process, 252–253
    CPM, 282–283
dependent variables in scatter diagrams, 464
descriptions
    project scope statements, 108
    statements of work, 57–58
design of experiments, 154
Develop Preliminary Project Scope Statement process, 32, 526–527
Develop Project Charter process, 32, 57, 526
Develop Project Management Plan process, 32, 92–93
    defined, 558–559
    documenting, 94–97
    inputs, 93–94, 527
    outputs, 527
Develop Project Team process, 36, 336–337
    co-location, 341–342

defined, 559
effective teams, 340–341
exam essentials, 362
focus, 340
general management skills, 338
ground rules, 341
inputs, 539
key terms, 362
motivation, 342–348
outputs, 349, 539
review questions, 363–369
summary, 360–361
team-building activities, 338–339
training, 338
develop qualified sellers lists technique, 373, 559
diagrams
    Activity Sequencing process, 253–254, 253–254
    Perform Quality Control process, 461–464, 461–462
    Risk Identification process, 190–191, 191–193
dictionaries, WBS, 145
Direct and Manage Project Execution process, 32, 326–327
    defined, 559
    inputs, 328–329, 548
    outputs, 330–333, 538
    tools and techniques, 329–330
directive constraints, 113
discounted cash flows, 65–66, 559
discretionary dependencies, 252, 559
distributing project information. See Information Distribution process
diversity issues, 510–512
DMADV method, 157
DMAIC method, 157
documenting
    Contract Administration process, 392
    cost baselines, 303–304
    deliverables, 110
    project management plans, 94–97
    project scope management plans, 100
    Risk Identification process, 188
duration
    compressing, 289
    estimating, 275–279
    in PERT, 287–288
dysfunctional teams, 340–341

E

EAC (estimate at completion), 432–433, 559

earned value (EV), 428–429, 430, 559
earned value management (EVM), 33
earned value technique (EVT), 427–430, 430, 559–560
economic conditions in Human Resource Planning process, 243
effective teams, 340–341
efficiency indicators, 431
80/20 rule, 461
EMV (expected monetary value), 560
encoding in information exchange, 351–352
endings, project, 472–474
engineering review boards (ERBs), 424
enhance risk strategy, 211, 559
enterprise environment factors, 58–59, 94
environment factors
    charters, 58–59, 94
    Human Resource Planning process, 242–243
ERBs (engineering review boards), 424
estimate at completion (EAC), 432–433, 559
estimate to complete (ETC), 432, 559
ethical codes, 499
EV (earned value), 428–429, 430, 559
EV (expected value)
    defined, 560
    PERT, 285–286
    Quantitative Risk Analysis, 205
evaluation criteria
    defined, 560
    Plan Contracting, 240
    Select Sellers process, 375–376
evaluation techniques, 378–379
EVM (earned value management), 33
EVT (earned value technique), 427–430, 430, 559–560
exam essentials
    change control, 448
    Develop Project Team process, 361–362
    performance control, 405–406
    professional responsibilities, 516
    project scope statements, 122
    projects, 41–42
    quality control and closeouts, 488
    resource planning, 260
    risk planning, 218–219
    Schedule Development and Cost Budgeting processes, 314–315
    work breakdown structure, 166–167
Executing process group, 26, 560
Expectancy Theory, 345–346, 560
expected monetary value (EMV), 560

expected value (EV)
   defined, *560*
   PERT, **285–286**
   Quantitative Risk Analysis, **205**
expert judgment
   Activity Duration Estimating
      process, **276**
   defined, *560*
   project selection, **69–70**
   Quantitative Risk Analysis
      process, **204**
   Scope Planning process,
      99–100
   Select Sellers process, **378**
expert power, 348
exploiting risk, **211**, *560*
external dependencies, 252, *560*
external failure costs, 155
external risks, 185
extinction ending type, **474**, *560*
extrinsic motivators, 342
eye contact, 352

F

failure costs, **155–156**
failure frequency diagrams, 461–462
fait accompli, 377, *560*
fast tracking, 24
   defined, *560*
   in duration compression, **289**
feasibility studies, **55–56**, *560*
FF (finish-to-finish) relationships, 253
FF (free float) time, 282, *562*
final product, **478**
financial records in vendor selection,
   375–376
financial skills, 11
finish-to-finish (FF) relationships, 253
finish-to-start (FS) relationships, 253
fishbone diagrams, 191
fitness for use premise, **156**
fixed price contracts, 234, *561*
fixed price plus incentive contracts,
   234, *561*
float time in CPM, 282, *561*
flowcharts, 191, *192*
focus in Develop Project Team process,
   340
force majeure, 185, *561*
forcing in conflict resolution, 353, *561*
forecasting, **431–432**
formal acceptance and closure, **482**,
   561
formal power, 348
Forming stage in team development,
   339
forms in Scope Planning process, 100

forward passes, **283**, *561*
free float (FF) time, 282, *562*
frequency of failures diagrams,
   461–462
FS (finish-to-start) relationships, 253
functional managers, **72**
functional organizations, **14–16**, *14*,
   562
fund limitations
   Cost Budgeting process, 303
   in project scope statements, 115
funding requirements, 305, *305*
future value (FV) calculations, 65

G

gain, personal, 499
Gantt charts, 296, *296*, *561*
general management skills, **338**
gifts from vendors, **500–501**
global competition, **511**
goals
   Develop Project Team process, 340
   project scope statements, **107**
governmental standards in enterprise
   environment, 58
grade vs. quality, 156
ground rules in Develop Project Team
   process, **341**

H

hammocks, 255, *561*
handoffs, **23**, *562*
hard dependencies, 252
Herzberg, Frederick, **345**
hierarchical charts, **244**
hierarchy of needs, **344–345**
histograms, 461–462
historical information
   in charters, 59
   Communications Planning, 147
   defined, *562*
   Project Communications
      Management, 37
honesty, **505**
human resource management, **36–37**
Human Resource Planning process, 36,
   241
   defined, *562*
   inputs, **242–244**, 533
   networking in, **246**
   organization charts and positional
      descriptions, **244–246**
   outputs, **246–248**, *247*, 533
human resources
   enterprise environment, 58

functional organizations, **15**
   skills for, **12–13**
Hygiene Theory, **345**, *562*

I

identified risks list, **193**
identifiers for WBS, **141–142**
identifying risk. *See* Risk Identification
   process
IFBs (invitations for bid), **239**
impact and impact scales
   defined, *562*
   impact matrices, **198–201**
   Qualitative Risk Analysis process,
      196–197
imposed dates, 281
independent estimates, **377**, *562*
independent variables in scatter
   diagrams, 464
industry knowledge requirements, **505**
industry standards, 58
influence diagrams, 191, *193*, *562*
influencing skills, **11–12**
information distribution methods, *562*
Information Distribution process, 37,
   349–350
   communication skills, **350–354**
   defined, *562*
   information gathering and
      retrieval systems, 355
   inputs, 539
   Kitchen Heaven project, **357–359**
   lessons learned, 355
   methods, 355
   outputs, **356–357**, 539
information exchange, **351–352**
information gathering
   Information Distribution process,
      355, *562*
   Performance Reporting process,
      399
   Risk Identification process,
      188–189
information presentation tools, 399
information technology in Contract
   Administration process, 391
initial defined risks, 115
initial project organization, 114
Initiating process group, 25, **52–53**,
   562
inputs in processes, 28
   Acquire Project Team, **538–539**
   Activity Definition, **249**, 533–534
   Activity Duration Estimating, **276**,
      535
   Activity Resource Estimating, **273**,
      534

Activity Sequencing, 534
Close Project, 476, 549–550
Communications Planning, 147, 529
Contract Administration, 388–389, 542
Contract Closure, 481, 550
Cost Budgeting, 302, 537
Cost Control, 426, 545–546
Cost Estimating, 299, 536–537
Create WBS, 528–529
Develop Preliminary Project Scope Statement, 526–527
Develop Project Charter, 526
Develop Project Management Plan, 93–94, 527
Develop Project Team, 539
Direct and Manage Project Execution, 328–329, 538
Human Resource Planning, 242–244, 533
Information Distribution, 539
Integrated Change Control, 424, 544–545
Manage Project Team, 394, 543
Manage Stakeholders, 543–544
Monitor and Control Project Work, 386, 541–542
Perform Quality Assurance, 382–383, 540–541
Perform Quality Control, 459, 547–548
Performance Reporting, 398–399, 544
Plan Contracting, 532–533
Plan Purchases and Acquisitions, 231–233, 532
Qualitative Risk Analysis, 195, 530–531
Quality Planning, 152–153, 529–530
Quantitative Risk Analysis, 531
Request Seller Responses, 372–373, 539–540
Risk Identification, 187–188, 530
Risk Management Planning, 179–180, 530
Risk Monitoring and Control, 441, 546–547
Risk Response Planning, 531
Schedule Control, 437, 546
Schedule Development, 280–281, 535–536
Scope Control, 469–470, 548–549
Scope Definition, 528
Scope Planning, 98–99, 528
Scope Verification, 548

Select Sellers, 540
work breakdown structure, 135
inspections
Contract Administration process, 390
defined, 563
Perform Quality Control process, 465
Integrated Change Control process, 32, 238, 418–419
change control systems, 421–424
concerns, 420
configuration management, 421
defined, 563
inputs, 424, 544–545
outputs, 425–426, 544–545
tools and techniques, 425
integration ending type, 473–474, 563
integration management, 32–33
integrity, 498–499
conflicts of interest, 499–501
personal, 499
professional actions, 501
intellectual property, 507
internal failure costs, 155
internal rate of return (IRR), 67, 563
interpersonal factors, 242
interruptions in listening, 353
interviews
defined, 563
Quantitative Risk Analysis process, 203–204
Risk Identification process, 189
intrinsic motivators, 342
invitations for bid (IFBs), 239
invoices in Contract Administration process, 389
IRR (internal rate of return), 67, 563
Ishikawa diagrams, 191
issue logs, 396–397
iterative processes, 28, 563

J

Juran, Joseph M., 156

K

Kaizen theory, 157
key events, 281
key terms
change control, 449
Develop Project Team process, 361–362

performance control, 406–407
professional responsibilities, 516
project scope statements, 123
project selection and charters, 83
projects, 42–43
quality control and closeouts, 489
resource planning, 261–262
risk planning, 219–220
Schedule Development and Cost Budgeting processes, 315–316
work breakdown structure, 167–168
kill points, 24
Kitchen Heaven project case study
change control, 443–446
closeouts, 483–485
Information Distribution process, 357–359
performance, 401–403
professional responsibilities, 513–514
project scope statement, 117–120
project selection, 76–79
resource planning, 256–257
risk planning, 214–216
schedule and budget, 307–312, 309, 311
WBS, 162–164, 163
knowledge application, 503
confidential information, 506–507
industry knowledge, 505
laws and regulations, 506
project management, 503–505
truthful reporting, 505
knowledge areas. See project management knowledge areas
known variance, 463

L

lags
Activity Sequencing process, 254
defined, 563
Schedule Development process, 294
laws, 506
leaders, 563
leadership
in motivation, 346–348
in project managers, 12
leads
Activity Sequencing process, 254
defined, 563
Schedule Development process, 294
legal requirements, 54

legitimate power, 348
lessons learned
　　Close Project, 479
　　defined, 563
　　Information Distribution process,
　　　355
　　Integrated Change Control
　　　process, 426
levels in WBS, 138–141, *139–140*
life-cycle costing, 35
life cycles
　　contracts, 380–381
　　projects, 23–24
lines of communications, 148–149,
　　148
listening skills, 352–353
location factors in Human Resource
　　Planning process, 242
logical relationships, 253, 563
logistics factors in Human Resource
　　Planning process, 242
logs, 396–397
lump sum procurement contracts, 234

M

make or buy analysis, 233, 238, 564
Manage Project Team process, 36
　　appraisals, 396
　　conflict resolution, 396
　　defined, 564
　　inputs, 394, 543
　　issue logs, 396–397
　　observation and conservation, 395
　　outputs, 397, 543
Manage Stakeholders process, 37
　　defined, 564
　　input and output summary,
　　　543–544
　　overview, 397–398
management information systems, 58
management software in Activity
　　Resource Estimating process, 274
managers
　　defined, 564
　　vs. leaders, 346–348
mandatory dependencies, 252, 564
market demand as project need, 53
marketplace conditions in enterprise
　　environment, 58
Maslow, Abraham, 344–345, 564
mathematical models, 61–67, 564
matrix-based charts, 245–246
matrix organizations, 19–22, *20–21*,
　　564
McGregor, Douglas, 347

measurability in SMART rule, 107
measurements in inspection, 465
meetings, status review, 399–400
messages in information exchange, 351
methodology in risk management
　　plans, 183
metrics in Quality Planning process,
　　160
milestone charts, 296, 564
milestones
　　Activity Definition process, **251**
　　defined, 565
　　project scope statements, 115
　　Schedule Development process,
　　　281
mitigation in Risk Response Planning
　　process, **210**, 564
models
　　behavior, 347
　　mathematical, 61–67, 565
　　Quantitative Risk Analysis
　　　process, 206
　　schedule, 294, **297**
　　scoring, 63–64, 576
money as constraint, 112
Monitor and Control Project Work
　　process, 32, 385–386
　　defined, 564
　　inputs, 386, 541–542
　　outputs, 386–387, 541–542
　　tools and techniques, 386
Monitoring and Controlling process
　　group, 26, 565
Monte Carlo Analysis
　　defined, 565
　　Quantitative Risk Analysis
　　　process, 206
　　Schedule Development process,
　　　289–290
motivation
　　leadership in, 346–348
　　reward and recognition systems,
　　　342–343
　　skills, 12–13
Motivation-Hygiene Theory, 345
motivational theories, 344
　　Achievement theory, 346
　　defined, 565
　　Expectancy theory, 345–346
　　Hygiene theory, 345
　　needs hierarchy, 344–345

N

needs and demands in projects,
　　53–54

needs hierarchy, 344–345
negotiation skills, 11–12
net present value (NPV), 66–67, 565
network analysis, schedule, 281–282
networking in Human Resource
　　Planning process, **246**
nodes in precedence diagrams, 253
Nominal Group Technique, **189**, 566
Norming stage in team development,
　　339
notes for status review meetings, 400
NPV (net present value), 66–67, 566

O

objectives
　　defined, 566
　　Develop Project Team process, 340
　　project scope statements,
　　　107–108
OBS (organizational breakdown
　　structure), 144, 244, 565
observation in Manage Project Team
　　process, 395
operational definitions, 160
operations
　　defined, 565
　　vs. projects, 3
opportunities from risk, 211–212
optimization methods in project
　　selection, 62, 68
ordinal scales, 198–201, 565
org charts
　　functional organizations, 14, *14*
　　Human Resource Planning
　　　process, 244
　　matrix organizations, 20–21,
　　　20–21
　　projectized organizations, 17–18,
　　　17
organization in project scope
　　statements, 114
organizational breakdown structure
　　(OBS), 144, 244, 565
organizational factors in Human
　　Resource Planning process, 242
organizational process assets
　　charters, 59
　　Contract Administration process,
　　　393
　　Human Resource Planning
　　　process, 243
　　updating, 478–479
organizational risks, 185
organizational skills, 10
organizational structures, 13

functional organizations, 14–16, *14*

matrix organizations, 19–22, *20–21*

projectized organizations, 17–18, *17*

organizational theory, 246

outputs in processes, 28

Acquire Project Team, 335–336, *538–539*

Activity Definition, 250–251, *533–534*

Activity Duration Estimating, 279, *535*

Activity Resource Estimating, 274–275, *534*

Activity Sequencing, 255–256, 534

Close Project, 477–479, 549–550

Communications Planning, 529

Contract Administration, 392–393, 542

Contract Closure, 550

Cost Budgeting, 304–305, *304–305, 537*

Cost Control, 435–436, 545–546

Cost Estimating, 300–302, *536–537*

Create WBS, 528–529

Develop Preliminary Project Scope Statement, 526–527

Develop Project Charter, 526

Develop Project Management Plan, 527

Develop Project Team, 349, 539

Direct and Manage Project Execution, 330–333, 538

Human Resource Planning, 246–248, *247, 533*

Information Distribution, 356–357, 539

Integrated Change Control, 425–426, 544–545

Manage Project Team, 397, 543

Manage Stakeholders, 543–544

Monitor and Control Project Work, 386–387, 541–542

Perform Quality Assurance, 384–385, 540–541

Perform Quality Control, 466–468, 547–548

Performance Reporting, 400, 544

Plan Contracting, 239–241, 532–533

Plan Purchases and Acquisitions, 236–238, 532

Qualitative Risk Analysis, 530–531

Quality Planning, 159–160, 529–530

Quantitative Risk Analysis, 207, 531

Request Seller Responses, 374, 539–540

Risk Identification, 193–194, 530

Risk Management Planning, 530

Risk Monitoring and Control, 442–443, 546–547

Risk Response Planning, 212–214, 531

Schedule Control, 439–440, 546

Schedule Development, 294–297, *295–296, 535–536*

Scope Control, 470–471, 548–549

Scope Definition, 528

Scope Planning, 528

Scope Verification, 548

Select Sellers, 380–382, 540

work breakdown structure, 144–145

P

parametric estimating

Activity Duration Estimating process, 277

defined, 566

Pareto, Vilfredo, 461

Pareto diagrams, 461–462, *462*, 566

passive risk acceptance, 212

payback periods, 64, 566

payment requests, 393

payment systems, 391, 566

PDM (precedence diagramming method), 253, *253*, 567

PDUs (professional development units), 504

peer reviews, 465

penalty power, 348

perception differences, 512–513

Perform Quality Assurance process, 36, 382

defined, 566

inputs, 382–383, 540–541

outputs, 384–385, 540–541

tools and techniques, 383–384

Perform Quality Control process, 36, 458–459

control charts, 460, *461*

defect repair review, 466

defined, 566

inputs, 459, 547–548

inspection, 465

outputs, 466–468, 547–548

Pareto diagrams, 461–462, *462*

run charts, 462–463

scatter diagrams, 463–464, *464*

statistical sampling, 464

tools and techniques, 459–460

performance appraisals, 396

performance control

contract administration. *See* Contract Administration process

exam essentials, 405–406

key terms, 406–407

Kitchen Heaven project, 401–403

Manage Project Team process, 394–397

Manage Stakeholders process, 397–398

measurements in. *See* Performance Reporting process

Monitoring and Control Project Work process, 385–387

Performance Reporting process, 398–401

quality assurance, 382–385

review questions, 408–415

summary, 404–405

performance indexes, 431

performance measurement analysis, 427–431, *430*

performance measurement baselines, 420, 566

Performance Reporting process, 37, 398

defined, 566

inputs, 398–399, 544

outputs, 400, 544

tools and techniques, 399–400

performance reports in Contract Administration process, 391

performance reviews

in Contract Administration process, 390

project, 433–434

performance risks in risk management plans, 184

Performing stage in team development, 339

personal integrity, 499

personnel administration, 58

PERT (Program Evaluation and Review Technique), 285

defined, 568

expected value in, 285–286

project duration in, 287–288

phase exits, 24

phases

project, 23–24

WBS, 137

physical needs in needs hierarchy, 344

Plan Contracting process, 39, 238–239

defined, 566

inputs, 532–533
outputs, 239–241, 532–533
Plan-Do-Check-Act cycle, 29–30
Plan Purchases and Acquisitions
    process, 39, 230–231
    contract type selection, 233–236
    defined, 566–567
    inputs, 231–233, 532
    make or buy analysis, 233
    outputs, 236–238, 532
planned value (PV), 428–429, 566
planning controls
    Plan Contracting process,
        238–241
    quality. *See* Quality Planning
        process
    risk
        identifying. *See* Risk
            Identification process
        qualitative. *See* Qualitative
            Risk Analysis process
        quantitative. *See* Quantitative
            Risk Analysis process
        responding to. *See* Risk
            Response Planning
            process
        Risk Management Planning
            process, 178–179
Planning process group, 25–26, 566
planning skills, 10
PMI certification process, 504
PMIS (project management
    information system), 69, 94
PMOs (project management offices), 8,
    570
PMP Code of Professional Conduct,
    499, 503, 506, 570
policies, procurement, 232
politics, 12
    defined, 567
    Human Resource Planning
        process, 242
    in leadership, 346
portfolios, 7, 567
position descriptions, 246
positive risk strategies, 211
potential risk responses, 193
power, 12
    defined, 567
    forms of, 348
    in leadership, 346
preassignment to teams, 335, 567
precedence diagramming method
    (PDM), 253, 253, 567
precedence relationships in Activity
    Sequencing process, 253
predictable variance, 463
preferential logic in Activity
    Sequencing process, 252

preliminary scope statements, 74–76,
    93, 567
present value (PV), 66–67
presentations in Information
    Distribution process, 356
prevention
    costs, 155
    in Crosby theory, 156
    defined, 568
    Direct and Manage Project
        Execution process, 328
    vs. inspection, 465
preventive actions, 567
priorities
    project selection, 60–61
    Qualitative Risk Analysis process,
        202
    Quantitative Risk Analysis
        process, 207
    risk, 442
probability
    defined, 567
    Quantitative Risk Analysis
        process, 204, 207
    risk management plans, 185–186
    risk probability analysis, 196–201
probability and impact matrices,
    185–186, 198–201, 567–568
problem-solving skills, 11
process analysis in Perform Quality
    Assurance process, 384, 568
process flow, 28–29, 28
process groups, 24–25, 28
    Closing, 26
    Executing, 26
    Initiating, 25
    Monitoring and Controlling, 26
    Planning, 25–26
process improvement plans, 161
process interactions, 29–30, 31
process variances, 462–463
procurement audits, 481–482, 568
procurement documents in Plan
    Contracting process, 239, 568
procurement management, 39,
    236–237
procurement management plans,
    236–237, 568
product analysis, 101, 568
product descriptions, 57–58
product scope process, 33, 568
product verification, 480, 568
professional actions, 501
professional conduct, 504
professional development units
    (PDUs), 504
professional responsibilities, 498
    diversity issues, 510–512
    exam essentials, 516

integrity, 498–501
key terms, 516
Kitchen Heaven project, 513–514
knowledge, 503–507
review questions, 517–524
stakeholder interests, 508–509
summary, 515–516
Program Evaluation and Review
    Technique (PERT), 285
    defined, 568
    expected value in, 285–286
    project duration in, 287–288
program management, 569
programs, 7, 568
progressive elaboration, 3, 569
project calendars, 293–294, 569
project champions, 71–72
project charters. *See* charters
project closeout. *See* closeout processes
Project Communications Man-
    agement, 37, 569
Project Cost Management, 35, 569
project duration, 287–288
project focus in matrix organizations,
    19
Project Human Resource
    Management, 36–37, 569
Project Integration Management,
    32–33, 569
project life cycles, 23–24, 569
project management, 6–9
    defined, 569
    integrating, 32–33
    knowledge requirements,
        503–505. *See also* project
        management knowledge
        areas
    risks, 185
project management information
    system (PMIS), 69, 94
project management knowledge areas,
    31
    communications management, 37
    cost management, 35
    defined, 570
    human resource management,
        36–37
    integration, 32–33
    procurement management, 39
    quality management, 36
    risk management, 38–39
    scope management, 33–34
    time management, 34–35
project management offices (PMOs), 8,
    570
project management plans, 92–93
    defined, 570
    documenting, 94–97

Human Resource Planning
process, **244**
inputs, **93–94**
Project Management Professional
Code of Professional Conduct,
499, 503, 506, *570*
project management software,
291–292
project managers
for charters, **70–71**
defined, *570*
skills, **9–13**
project plans
defined, *570*
execution. *See* Direct and Manage
Project Execution process
Schedule Development process.
See Schedule Development
process
project presentations, 356, *570*
Project Procurement Management, 39,
570
Project Quality Management, 36, *570*
project records, 356, *571*
project reports, 356, *571*
Project Risk Management, 38–39, *571*
project schedules, **294–296**, *295–296*,
571
project scope, *571*
Project Scope Management, 33–34,
571
project scope management plans
defined, *571*
documenting, **100**
requirements, **99**
updating, **116**
project scope statements. *See* scope
statements
project selection methodologies
applying, **68**
exam essentials, **82**
key terms, **83**
Kitchen Heaven project, **76–79**
mathematical models, **61–67**
prioritizing projects, **60–61**
review questions, **84–90**
summary, **81–82**
project sponsors
for charters, **71**
defined, *571*
as stakeholders, 4
project statements of work, *571*
Project Time Management, 34–35,
571–572
projectized organizations, **17–18**, *17*,
572
projects, **2–3**
boundaries, **111**, *569*

characteristics, **5–6**
defined, *569*
exam essentials, **41–42**
in functional organizations, **15–16**
key terms, **42–43**
life cycles, **23–24**
vs. operations, 3
performance reviews, 433, *571*
review questions, **44–50**
stakeholders in, **3–4**, *5*
summary, **41**
published data in Activity Resource
Estimating process, 274
publishing project scope statements,
116
punishment power, 348
purchases and acquisitions. *See* Plan
Purchases and Acquisitions
process
PV (planned value), **428–429**, *566*
PV (present value), **66–67**

Q

qualified seller lists, 373
Qualitative Risk Analysis process, 38,
194
defined, *572*
inputs, **195**, *530–531*
outputs, *530–531*
risk probability analysis, **196–201**
risk ranking, **202**
quality
in impact analysis, 197
in risk management plans, 184
in risk probability analysis, 201
quality assurance. *See* Perform Quality
Assurance process
quality audits, **383–384**, *572*
quality constraints, 112
quality control. *See* Perform Quality
Control process
quality management, 36
quality management plans, 159
Quality Planning process, 36, **152**
baselines, **162**
benchmarking, **154**
benefit/cost analysis, **154**
checklists, **160**
cost of quality, **155–158**
design of experiments, **154**
inputs, **152–153**, *529–530*
metrics, **160**
outputs, **159–160**, *529–530*
process improvement plans, **161**
tools, **158–159**
quality policies, 153

Quantitative Risk Analysis process, 38,
202–203
decision tree analysis, **205–206**,
206
defined, *572*
expected value in, 205
expert judgment in, 204
inputs, *531*
interviews, **203–204**
modeling simulation, 206
outputs, **207**, *531*
probability distributions, 204
sensitivity analysis, **204–205**, *205*
quotations in Plan Contracting, 239

R

R.E.P. (Registered Education
Provider), 504
RACI charts, 245, *572*
RAMs (responsibility assignment
matrices), 245, *574*
random variance, 463
ranking risk, 202
rating systems, **377–378**
RBS (resource breakdown structure),
144, 244, *573*
RBS (risk breakdown structure), 144,
183, *184*, *573*
realism in SMART rule, 107
recaps in listening, 353
receivers in information exchange, 351
recognition and rewards, 248, *572*
records in Information Distribution
process, 356
records management systems in
Contract Administration
process, 391, *572*
referent power, 348
register, risk
contents, **193–194**
defined, *574–575*
rankings, 202
updating, **213**
Registered Education Provider
(R.E.P.), 504
regulations, **152–153**, 506
releasing team members
criteria, 248
planning, 483
repairs in Direct and Manage Project
Execution process, 329
reports
Contract Administration process,
391
Information Distribution process,
356

performance. *See* Performance
    Reporting process
risk management plans, 183
truthful, **505**
Request Seller Responses process, 39,
    372
    defined, *572*
    inputs, 372–373, *539–540*
    outputs, **374**, *539–540*
    tools and techniques, **373**
requested changes
    Contract Administration process,
        392–393
    Direct and Manage Project
        Execution process,
        329, 331
    Plan Purchases and Acquisitions
        process, **238**
requests for information (RFIs), 239
requests for proposal (RFPs), 239
requests for quotation (RFQs), 239
requirement stage in contracts, 381
requirements
    change, **423–424**
    Communications Planning
        process, 147–150, *148*
    defined, *572–573*
    in scope statements, **109–111**
requisition stage in contracts, 381
reserve time, 278, *573*
residual risks, 213, *573*
resolving conflicts, 353–354, 396
resource-based methods, 290
resource breakdown structure (RBS),
    144, 244, *573*
resource calendars, 275, 293–294, *573*
resource leveling, 290–291, *573*
resource planning, 230
    activities. *See* Activity
        Definition process; Activity
        Sequencing process
    exam essentials, **260**
    human resources. *See* Human
        Resource Planning process
    key terms, **261–262**
    Kitchen Heaven project, 256–257
    purchases and acquisitions. *See*
        Plan Purchases and
        Acquisitions process
    review questions, 263–268
    summary, **259**
resource rates, 300
resources
    activity. *See* Activity Resource
        Estimating process
    defined, *573*
    in functional organizations, **16**

responsibilities
    Human Resource Planning
        process, **246–247**
    risk management plans, 183
responsibility assignment matrices
    (RAMs), **245**, *573*
retail store case study. *See* Kitchen
    Heaven project case study
reverse resource allocation scheduling,
    291, *573*
review questions
    change control, 450–455
    Develop Project Team process,
        363–369
    performance control, 408–415
    professional responsibilities,
        517–524
    project scope statements, 124–131
    project selection and charters,
        84–90
    projects, **44–50**
    quality control and closeouts,
        490–496
    resource planning, 263–268
    risk planning, 221–227
    Schedule Development and Cost
        Budgeting processes,
        317–324
reviews
    Perform Quality Control process,
        465
    project performance, **433**
revisions
    defined, *573*
    Schedule Control process, **439**
reward and recognition systems,
    342–343
rework, 140, 466, *573*
RFIs (requests for information), 239
RFPs (requests for proposal), 239
RFQs (requests for quotation), 239
risk analysis
    categories, 183–185, 194, 201, *573*
    qualitative. *See* Qualitative Risk
        Analysis process
    quantitative. *See* Quantitative Risk
        Analysis process
risk avoidance, **209**
risk breakdown structure (RBS), 144,
    183, *184*, *573*
risk events, 178
Risk Identification process, 38,
    186–187
    assumptions analysis, **190**
    checklists, **190**
    data quality assessment, **201**
    defined, *574*

diagrams, 190–191, *191–193*
    information gathering, 188–189
    inputs, 187–188, *530*
    outputs, 193–194, *530*
    urgency assessment, **201**
risk management, 38–39
Risk Management Planning process,
    38, **178–179**
    defined, *574*
    inputs, 179–180, *530*
    need for, **181**
    outputs, *530*
    tools and techniques, 180–181
risk management plans, **182–183**
    categories, **183–184**
    defined, *574*
    risk probability analysis, 185–186
Risk Monitoring and Control process,
    38, **440**
    defined, *574*
    inputs, 441, *546–547*
    outputs, 442–443, *546–547*
    tools and techniques for, 441–442
risk priorities, **442**
risk probability analysis, **196**
    data quality assessment, **201**
    impact in, 196–197
    probability and impact matrices,
        198–201
risk register
    contents, 193–194
    defined, *574*
    rankings, **202**
    updating, **213**
Risk Response Planning process, 38,
    208
    acceptance, 211–212
    avoidance, **209**
    contingency planning, **212**
    defined, *574*
    exam essentials, **218–219**
    inputs, *531*
    key terms, **219–220**
    mitigation, **210**
    outputs, 212–214, *531*
    positive risk, **211**
    review questions, 221–227
    summary, **218**
    transfer, 209–210
risk tolerance, 58, 180, *574*
role-responsibility-authority forms,
    246
roles
    Human Resource Planning
        process, **246–247**
    in risk management plans, 183
    stakeholder, **104**

rolling wave planning, 141
root risk causes, **189**, **194**
run charts, **462–463**, *574*

S

safety and security needs
    in hierarchy of needs, 344
    policies for, 248
sample variance, **460**, *461*
sampling, **464**
scales of probability, **196–198**
scatter diagrams, **463–464**, *464*, *574*
schedule activities, 249
schedule baselines, 279, 297, *574*
schedule constraints, 112–113
Schedule Control process, 34, **437**
    defined, *575*
    inputs, **437**, *546*
    outputs, **439–440**, *546*
    tools and techniques, **437–439**
    variances, **438–439**
Schedule Development process, 34,
    279–280
    calendars, **293–294**
    critical chain method, **291**
    critical path method, **282–284**,
        285
    defined, *575*
    duration compression, **289**
    exam essentials, 314–315
    inputs, **280–281**, *535–536*
    key terms, 315–316
    Kitchen Heaven project, **307–312**,
        309, *311*
    lags and leads, **294**
    outputs, **294–297**, *295–296*,
        535–536
    PERT in, **285–288**
    project management software,
        291–292
    resource leveling, **290–291**
    review questions, 317–324
    schedule network analysis,
        281–282
    summary, 313–314
    what-if analysis, **289–290**
schedule network analysis, **281–282**,
    575
schedule network templates, **254**
schedule performance index (SPI), **431**,
    575
schedule risks simulation, 206
schedule updates, *575*
schedule variance (SV), **430–431**, *575*
scheduled milestones, 115

schedules
    activity resources. *See* Activity
        Resource Estimating process
    change control systems, *575*
    compression, *575*
    Schedule Development process.
        See Schedule Development
        process
scope
    baselines, **145–146**
    defined, *575*
    in statements of work, 57
Scope Control process, 33, **469**
    defined, *575*
    inputs, **469–470**, *548–549*
    outputs, **470–471**, *548–549*
    tools and techniques, **470**
scope creep, 209
Scope Definition process, 33, **100–101**
    alternatives identification, **102**
    defined, *575*
    input and output summary, *528*
    product analysis, **101**
    stakeholders, **102–105**
scope management, 33–34
scope management plans
    defined, *572*
    documenting, 100
    requirements, 99
    updating, 116
Scope Planning process, 33, **98**
    defined, *575*
    documenting, 100
    inputs, **98–99**, *528*
    outputs, *528*
    tools and techniques, **99–100**
scope statements, **105–106**
    acceptance criteria, **111**
    approval requirements, **116**
    approving and publishing, **116**
    assumptions, **113–114**
    boundaries, **111**
    components, **106–107**
    configuration requirements, 115
    constraints, **111–113**
    cost estimates, 115
    defined, *572*
    deliverables, **108**
    descriptions, **108**
    exam essentials, **122**
    fund limitations, 115
    initial defined risks, 115
    initial project organization, 114
    key terms, **123**
    Kitchen Heaven project, **117–120**
    objectives, **107–108**
    preliminary, 74–76, 93
    requirements, **109–111**

review questions, **124–131**,
    169–175
scheduled milestones, 115
specifications, 115
summary, **121–122**
updating, 116
Scope Verification process, 33,
    468–469
    defined, *576*
    input and output summary, *548*
scoring models, **63–64**, *576*
screening systems in vendor selection,
    377, *576*
secondary risks, 213, *576*
Select Sellers process, 39, **374–375**
    contract negotiation, 377
    defined, *576*
    evaluation criteria, **375–376**
    evaluation techniques, **378–379**
    expert judgment in, 378
    independent estimates, 377
    inputs, *540*
    outputs, **380–382**, *540*
    rating systems, **377–378**, *577*
    screening systems, 377
    weighting systems, 376
self-actualization, 344
self-esteem needs, 344
seller invoices, 389, *576*
seller performance evaluation, 393
senders in information exchange, 351
sensitivity analysis, **204–205**, *205*, *576*
SF (start-to-finish) relationships, 253
share risk strategy, **211**, *576*
Shewhart, Walter, 29, 157
should cost estimates, 377, *576*
sign-off for charters, 73–74
simulation
    Quantitative Risk Analysis
        process, **206**
    Schedule Development process,
        289–290
Six Sigma management approach, 157
skills
    communication. *See*
        communication skills
    project managers, **9–13**
slack time, 282, *576*
SMART rule, 107
smoothing in conflict resolution, 353,
    576
social needs
    in needs hierarchy, 344
    projects from, 54
soft logic in Activity Sequencing
    process, 252
solicitation stage in contracts, 381

SOWs (statements of work), **57–58,** **237–238, 241,** *557, 572*
special cause variances, 462–463
specifications, 115
specificity in SMART rule, 107
SPI (schedule performance index), 431, *575*
sponsors
  for charters, **71**
  as stakeholders, 4
SS (start-to-start) relationships, 253
staff acquisition, 247
staff requirement plans, 336
staffing levels in process groups, 27
staffing management plans, **247–248**
stakeholders, **3–4,** *5*, **508**
  for charters, **70–72**
  communicating with, **104–105**
  competing needs of, **508**
  conflicts of interest, **501**
  constraints with, **509**
  defined, 576
  identifying, **103–104**
  issues and problems, **508–509**
  managing, 397–398
  in process groups, 27
  in risk management plans, 183
  risk tolerance, 58
  roles, **104**
  Scope Definition process, **102–105**
standard deviation in project duration, 287–288
standards
  enterprise environment, 58
  Quality Planning process, **152–153**
  Scope Planning process, 100
start-to-finish (SF) relationships, 253
start-to-start (SS) relationships, 253
starvation ending type, **473,** *576*
statements of work (SOWs), **57–58,** **237–238, 241,** *557, 572*
statistical sampling, **464,** *577*
status review meetings, **399–400,** *577*
steering committees, 60, *577*
Storming stage in team development, 339
Strengths, Weaknesses, Opportunities, and Threats (SWOT) analysis, 190
strong matrix organization, 19–21, *20*
subprojects, 137
successor activities, 254, *577*
SV (schedule variance), **430–431,** *575*
SWOT (Strengths, Weaknesses, Opportunities, and Threats) analysis, 190

T

T&M (time and materials) contracts, **236,** *577*
TABs (technical assessment boards), 424
tailoring, *577*
tangibles in SMART rule, 107
team-building skills, **12–13,** *577*
team members, releasing, 248, **483**
teams
  acquiring. *See* Acquire Project Team process
  developing. *See* Develop Project Team process
  Manage Project Team process, **394–397**
technical assessment boards (TABs), 424
technical factors in Human Resource Planning process, 242
technical performance measurements, **442,** *577*
technical review boards (TRBs), 424
technical risks, 185
technical skills, 9
technological advance as project need, 54
technology
  Communications Planning process, **150**
  constraints, 113
templates
  Human Resource Planning process, 243
  schedule network, **254**
  Scope Planning process, 100
  WBS, **140**
text-oriented formats, **246**
TF (total float) time, 282
Theory X, **347,** *577*
Theory Y, **347,** *577*
360-degree reviews, 396, *552*
three-point estimates, **277,** *577*
time
  in impact analysis, 197
  in SMART rule, 107
time and materials (T&M) contracts, **236,** *577*
time constraints, 112
time frames in projects, 6
time management, **34–35**
time-phased budgets, 303
time reporting systems, 400
time value of money, 64
timetables in staffing, 247

timing
  in communications, 150
  in risk management plans, 183
tolerable results, **465,** *578*
top-down estimating, **276–277**
tornado diagrams, 204, *205, 578*
total float (TF) time, 282, *578*
Total Quality Management (TQM), 157
tracking in risk management plans, 183
training
  cultural issues, **512**
  defined, *578*
  Develop Project Team process, **338**
  staff, 248
transfer, risk, **209–210,** *578*
transmission in information exchange, 352
TRBs (technical review boards), 424
trend analysis, 434
  Quantitative Risk Analysis process, 207
  run charts for, 463
triangular probability distributions, 204
triggers in Risk Identification process, **194,** *578*
truthfulness, 499, 505
Tuckman, Bruce, 339

U

uniqueness of projects, 3, 5
updating
  organizational process assets, **478–479**
  project scope statements, 116
  risk categories, **194**
urgency assessment, risk, **201**

V

VAC (variance at completion), **434,** *578*
validated defect repairs, 329
value engineering, 35
variables in scatter diagrams, 464
variance at completion (VAC), **434,** *578*
variances
  Perform Quality Control process, **460,** *461*
  Performance Reporting process, **430–431**
  Schedule Control process, **438–439**

vendor-bid analysis, 300
vendors
    gifts from, 500–501
    selection. *See* Select Sellers process
verbal communication, 352
verification
    in configuration management, 421
    in deliverable decomposition, 136
    product, 480
    Scope Verification process,
      468–469
virtual teams, 335, 578

W

WBS. *See* work breakdown structure
    (WBS)
weak matrix organization, 20–21, *20*
weighting systems
    defined, 578

project selection, 63–64
vendor selection, 376
what-if analysis, 289–290
withdrawal in conflict resolution, 354,
    579
work authorization systems, *58*, 330,
    579
work breakdown structure (WBS), 34
    creating, 134–135
    deliverables, 135–137
    dictionary, 145
    exam essentials, 166–167
    identifiers for, 141–142
    inputs, 135
    key terms, 167–168
    Kitchen Heaven project, 162–164,
      163
    levels, 138–141, *139–140*
    outputs, 144–145
    review questions, 169–175
    scope baselines, 145–146

    summary, 165–166
    templates, 140
    work packages, 142
work packages, 142
work performance information
    Contract Administration process,
      389
    defined, *579*
    Direct and Manage Project
      Execution process,
      332–333
workarounds, 443, *579*
written communications, 352

Z

zero defects theory, 156
zero-sum awards, 342

Wiley Publishing, Inc.
End-User License Agreement

The Absolute Best PMP Study Preparation Book/CD Package on the Market!

Prepare yourself for PMP 2005 exam with hundreds of challenging sample test questions!

- Chapter-by-chapter review questions from the book.

- A total of four bonus exams available only on the CD. Two for the PMP exam, as well as two additional CAPM exams.

- Supports question formats found on actual exam.

Sybex Test Engine

Assessment Test

☐ Mark   Time: 0 hr   0 min(s)   Question: 1 of 65

What is one of the most important skills a project manager can have?

○ A. Negotiation skills

○ B. Influencing skills

◉ C. Communication skills

○ D. Problem-solving skills

Your Answer: C

> (Show Answer)   (Finish) 🏠 ?

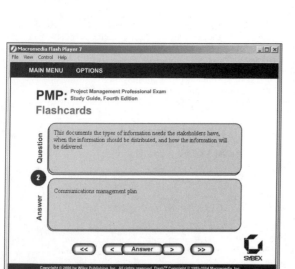

Reinforce understanding of key topics with flashcards for your PC, Pocket PC, or Palm handheld!

- Contains over 100 flashcard questions.

- Runs on multiple platforms for usability and portability.

- Quiz yourself anytime, anywhere!

Access the entire book in PDF!

- Full search capabilities let you quickly find the information you need.

- Complete with tables and illustrations.

- Adobe Acrobat Reader included.

Over two hours of audio review! Fine-tune your project management skills with audio instruction from author Kim Heldman.